KALLIS'

KEY *TO THE* SAT

SAT® is a registered trademark of the College Board. Unless indicated otherwise, the content in this text is created and designed exclusively by KALLIS. This publication is neither endorsed nor approved by the College Board.

KALLIS' Key to the SAT

KALLIS EDU, INC.
7490 Opportunity Road, Suite 203
San Diego, CA 92111
info@kallisedu.com
www.kallisedu.com
www.kallisprep.com

Copyright © 2019 KALLIS EDU, INC.

All rights reserved. Unless indicated otherwise, no part of this book may be reproduced, stored in a retrieval system, or transmitted in any form or by any means, electronic or mechanical, including photocopying, recording, or otherwise, without the prior written permission of KALLIS EDU.

ISBN-13: 978-0998482576
ISBN-10: 0998482579

Our **Key to the SAT** provides students with six full-length practice tests to help them develop strategies for the SAT. Detailed answer explanations and unique problem-solving strategies give students the opportunity to learn from their mistakes and see how the SAT tests each concept.

KALLIS

KALLIS'

KEY TO THE SAT

WITH 6 NEW PRACTICE TESTS

SAT® is a registered trademark of the College Board. Unless indicated otherwise, the content in this text is created and designed exclusively by KALLIS. This publication is neither endorsed nor approved by the College Board.

Table of Contents

GETTING STARTED 7
    Introducing the SAT 8

Ch. 1: SAT Reading Key Points 13

Ch. 2: SAT Writing & Language Key Points 27

Ch. 3: SAT Math Key Points 49

Ch. 4: SAT Key Strategies 61
    Section 1: **Reading Test** 65
    Section 2: **Writing & Language Test** 93
    Section 3: **Math Test (No-Calculator Section)** 119
    Section 4: **Math Test (Calculator Section)** 129

SAT Practice Test 1
    SAT Scoring Guides 151
    Answer Sheets 155
    Section 1: **Reading Test** 162
    Section 2: **Writing & Language Test** 172
    Section 3: **Math Test (No-Calculator Section)** 181
    Section 4: **Math Test (Calculator Section)** 187
    Section 5: **Essay Test** 198

SAT Practice Test 2
    Section 1: **Reading Test** 202
    Section 2: **Writing & Language Test** 212
    Section 3: **Math Test (No-Calculator Section)** 221
    Section 4: **Math Test (Calculator Section)** 227
    Section 5: **Essay Test** 238

SAT Practice Test 3
- Section 1: **Reading Test** — 242
- Section 2: **Writing & Language Test** — 252
- Section 3: **Math Test (No-Calculator Section)** — 261
- Section 4: **Math Test (Calculator Section)** — 267
- Section 5: **Essay Test** — 278

SAT Practice Test 4
- Section 1: **Reading Test** — 282
- Section 2: **Writing & Language Test** — 294
- Section 3: **Math Test (No-Calculator Section)** — 303
- Section 4: **Math Test (Calculator Section)** — 309
- Section 5: **Essay Test** — 320

SAT Practice Test 5
- Section 1: **Reading Test** — 324
- Section 2: **Writing & Language Test** — 334
- Section 3: **Math Test (No-Calculator Section)** — 343
- Section 4: **Math Test (Calculator Section)** — 349
- Section 5: **Essay Test** — 360

SAT Practice Test 6
- Section 1: **Reading Test** — 364
- Section 2: **Writing & Language Test** — 378
- Section 3: **Math Test (No-Calculator Section)** — 385
- Section 4: **Math Test (Calculator Section)** — 390
- Section 5: **Essay Test** — 400

SAT Practice Test #1 Answers & Explanations — 404

SAT Practice Test #2 Answers & Explanations — 420

SAT Practice Test #3 Answers & Explanations — 434

SAT Practice Test #4 Answers & Explanations — 449

SAT Practice Test #5 Answers & Explanations — 463

SAT Practice Test #6 Answers & Explanations — 477

References — 490

Getting Started

Introducing the SAT

What is the SAT?

Nearly a century ago, "SAT" stood for "Scholastic Aptitude Test." It was designed to measure which college applicants had an aptitude—a natural talent—for higher education. It borrowed methods from the Intelligence Quotient (IQ) tests of the time, which were used widely in schools and industry.

However, contemporary research into brain development suggests that brains are constantly changing, challenging the notion of innate scholastic aptitude. Most educators now agree that intelligence is fluid, that learning is a complex process, and that people are not born with a fixed level of intelligence. Many criticized the SAT for measuring a student's access to educational resources rather than equitably measuring academic ability.

In response to these criticisms, the College Board, the nonprofit organization that develops and administers the SAT, began distributing a redesigned version of the test in 2015 with the goal of making it more relevant. According to the College Board, the SAT now measures skills that are necessary for success in higher education, such as evaluating the evidence to support a claim. These are also recognized as skills that are honed through practice, including in typical high-school classrooms.

Why Take the SAT?

One obvious answer is that many colleges require SAT scores as part of the overall application package. College admissions officers know that some high schools are tougher than others; making decisions based only on grades would be unfair. Standardized tests such as the SAT attempt to provide a fair and objective measure of readiness. Most colleges try to balance their decisions by looking at students' grades and standardized test scores, as well as other factors.

Another reason to study for the SAT is that "studying for the SAT" should mean "practicing useful skills." At KALLIS, we offer only quizzes, tests, and explanations that we think will help develop critical thinking skills. And because we believe that learning comes from experience, we offer a lot of them. We fully expect that, through extensive practice review, you can acquire self-confidence as you approach the SAT. After all, preparation and confidence are the keys to success on the SAT—and so much more.

How do I register for the SAT?

The SAT is offered year-round in the United States and internationally. The vast majority of students take the SAT during their junior and senior years of high school. Most students take the SAT more than once and receive a better score the second time they take it.

To register for the SAT, visit the "Register" Page on the College Board's website, select a convenient test date and location, print your "Admission Ticket," and take it with you on the day of the test.

However, you must register for the SAT by mail if you:

- choose to pay for the test using a check or money order.
- are less than 13 years old.
- are unable to submit a digital photo during the online registration process.
- need to register for Sunday testing because of a religious observance.
- take the test in Nigeria, Ghana, or Cameroon.
- are requesting that a testing center be opened nearer to your home.

The Student Registration Guide for the SAT includes an SAT registration form and a return envelope. See your school's counselor for a registration guide and any additional information necessary for SAT mail registration.

If you are unable to pay the fee for the SAT, there are many resources available that may allow you to take the test at no cost and/or provide assistance throughout the college application process. More information is available on the College Board's website.

✓ An Overview of the SAT

The Redesigned SAT consists of a Reading Test, a Writing & Language Test, a Math Test, and an optional Essay Test. Below you will find an outline of the number of questions and time allotted for each test section of the SAT.

Test Name	Test Components	Number of Questions	Time Allotted (minutes)
Reading Test	• Four reading passages • One pair of reading passages • One to two visual components (such as graphs, tables, or diagrams)	52	65
Writing and Language Test	• Four reading passages containing grammatical and stylistic errors • One to two visual components (such as graphs, tables, or diagrams)	44	35

Math Test	• **No-Calculator portion**
	  - Multiple-choice section
	  - Student-produced response section
		20	25

Math Test	• **Calculator portion**
	  - Multiple-choice section
	  - Student-produced response section
		38	55

Essay Test (Optional)	• One reading passage with a corresponding writing prompt	1	50

Scoring the SAT

Scoring at a Glance

The Redesigned SAT employs a multi-level scoring system. The score report will contain an overall score, individual sub-scores for each of the three sections (Reading, Writing, and Math), a breakdown of your performance in each of the test's subtopics, and a score for the optional Essay Test.

The overall, or composite, score ranges from 400 – 1600. Thus, 400 points are awarded just for showing up and taking the test, and 1600 points are awarded for answering every question on the test correctly.

The composite score is broken into two sub-scores: a 200 – 800 point Reading and Writing Test score and a 200 – 800 point Math Test score. Each of these sub-scores are broken down further. The Reading, Writing & Language, and Math test scores will be reported individually and on a 10 – 40 point scale. Additionally, the Redesigned SAT score report will show test takers' skills in a number of Reading, Writing & Language, and Math test subtopics.

Optional student essays will be reviewed by two graders, each of whom will assign an essay a reading score, a writing score, and an analysis score ranging from 1 to 4 points. The graders' scores will then be added together, meaning each essay will receive three scores, with each score ranging from 2 to 8 points. These Essay scores are not calculated into a student's composite score, but they provide academic institues with a comprehensive overview of a student's writing abilites.

There is no penalty for wrong answers on the Redesigned SAT. Only correct answers will contribute toward a test taker's score; incorrect and unmarked answers will not negatively affect a test taker's score. This means that you should never leave a question blank, even if it means that you have to guess.

Scoring Flowchart

COMPOSITE SCORE
(400 - 1600)

Area Score
Reading and Writing Test (200 - 800)

Area Score
Math Test (200 - 800)

Test Score
Reading Test
(10 - 40)

Test Score
Writing and Language Test
(10 - 40)

Test Score
Math Test
(10 - 40)

CHAPTER 1

Key Points
SAT Reading

Literature is news that **stays news**.

— Ezra Pound

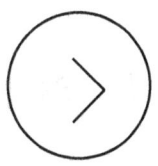

Breaking Down the Reading Passages

The SAT Reading test consists of four reading passages and one pair of passages. Each passage and passage pair is accompanied by ten to eleven multiple-choice questions. Usually, two of the four reading passages will include a chart, diagram, or table that contains information relevant to the passage's topic. Generally, passage pairs and literary excerpts will not be accompanied by a chart, diagram, or table.

The SAT Reading Tests will always contain passages on the following subjects:

- One literary excerpt (referred to in this study guide as a "humanities passage")
- One or two history/social science passages
- One or two science passages
- One passage pair (either history/social science or science)

Each multiple-choice question will have four answer choices, only one of which will be correct. As with all other sections of the SAT, there is no guessing penalty for incorrect answers.

Certain types of questions will appear in every set of questions. For example, many question sets include one or two words-in-context questions and two questions on supporting claims about the passage. Passages that are paired with a figure or another passage will always include several synthesis questions. By mastering the three types of questions just mentioned, you will be prepared for approximately half of the questions in the SAT Reading section.

General Words on SAT Reading

At its core, the SAT Reading section is a reading comprehension test. However, many of the questions it asks focus more on how the author constructs an argument than on the details of the argument itself. The job of the reader is not only to determine *what* the text says, but also *how* the text says it.

All the information needed to answer any question on the SAT Reading section is provided in the passage (or corresponding graph/diagram), but the specific words and phrases used in the answer choices will not likely appear in the passage. Part of testing reading comprehension is gauging a student's ability to paraphrase and summarize important pieces of information. In fact, answer choices that reuse exact words or phrases from the passage should be approached with caution; often, such choices look similar to the passage but contain inaccurate information.

Notes on Line Numbers

Most, if not all, questions on the SAT Reading section will require you to refer back to the passage. Some questions provide line numbers for reference while others do not. For questions that provide line numbers, be aware that the line numbers serve to refer the reader to a word, phrase, or sentence that is relevant to the question; they will not necessarily contain the answer to that question. If you cannot find an answer in the line numbers provided in the question, look to the surrounding information. Doing so will provide context and likely guide you to the correct answer.

Generally, questions are ordered based on what part of the text they reference: the first questions will usually ask about the beginning of the passage, and the last question will ask about the end of the passage. But this is not always true. Some questions that ask about the primary purpose or main argument of the passage will appear at the beginning or the end of the passage; questions regarding charts and diagrams are interspersed throughout the passage. When reading the passage, pay close attention to the order in which ideas are presented. Then, when you are answering questions that do not provide line numbers for reference, you will have less difficulty finding relevant information from the passage.

Many questions that ask about a passage's main argument or structure will not provide line numbers to reference. Thus, it is up to you to take note of these features; absorbing this information as you read will save you time.

Approaching Individual Passages

There is no "right" or "wrong" way to work through the SAT Reading section, and what works for one student may not work for another. You should develop your own test-taking strategies that work for you.

For fast readers, a popular approach is to read the entire passage before looking at the questions, and then to answer the questions while referencing and reviewing relevant portions of the passage. Although this strategy can be time-consuming, it allows students to get the gist of the passage and its structure before having to consider the specific features of the passage included in the questions.

Paraphrase and Summarize

Being able to rephrase information is one of the most important skills for mastering the SAT Reading section. Recognizing an accurate paraphrase or summary requires you to have processed the ideas and stored them in your brain, at least temporarily. As with all reading comprehension skills, the ability to summarize and paraphrase can be developed through practice. You can practice by reading academic articles and literature, or by simply taking plenty of practice tests. One way to build an advantage is to develop a large vocabulary, which allows you to more easily grasp and express ideas.

General Strategies for Answering Questions

1) The SAT Reading section questions fall into three difficulty categories: easy, medium, and hard. If possible, when answering straightforward easy or medium questions, **come up with your own answer before looking at the answer choices**. Then, read the choices and see if your assumption is a paraphrase or summary of one of the listed choices. This method may reduce the chance that you will be influenced by tricky wording in the incorrect choices.

2) One of your first steps when answering any question should be to **use the process of elimination** (POE). Eliminating the more obviously incorrect choices allows you to focus on the plausible choices, and it improves your chances of guessing correctly if you cannot narrow your options to one choice.

3) More often than not, **simple choices are good choices**. Wordy, convoluted, or very specific answer choices have higher probabilities of being incorrect because they contain more information that can be disproven. Simple answer choices may not always look as "academic" or as technical as more complex ones, but simple choices are often harder to disprove because they are more general and all-encompassing.

4) When interpreting passage information or answer choices, **be literal**. The less of your own interpretation you put into the text of the SAT Reading section, the better off you will be. Some questions ask for inferences or implications, but even these will be fully supported by the information presented in the passage.

5) **Avoid answer choices that include absolutes (but do not avoid them absolutely)**. Usually, answer choices that contain "only," "always," "never," "all," and "none" are incorrect because they tend to be limiting—they exclude *all* other possibilities. However, exceptions exist. If you are tempted to choose an answer choice that includes an absolute, make absolutely sure that you can support the choice with textual evidence that also deals in absolutes.

6) **Every word of an answer choice counts**. Even if a minor detail of an answer choice is unsupported by the passage, the entire answer choice is incorrect. For example, if the passage says, "*a researcher* claims that coffee is beneficial to health," and a corresponding answer choice claims, "*most researchers* conclude that coffee is healthy," then the answer choice is wrong. The passage only discusses *one* researcher, so we cannot conclude that *most researchers* have come to the same conclusion.

7) The SAT Reading section tests your comprehension of what an author states and implies, and how he or she states or implies it, so **refer to the passage frequently**. Ultimately, every correct answer is somewhere on the pages in front of you, and your task is to know where and how to find it. Moreover, your memory is fallible (especially during stressful situations like taking the SAT), so do not assume that you will remember every detail after one cursory reading.

✓ Spotting Mistakes

The majority of SAT Reading section questions contain two implausible answer choices, one plausible choice, and of course one correct choice. Most students can use the process of elimination to discard the implausible choices. The next step is to recognize the differences between an answer that is *almost* supported by the passage and one that *is* supported by the passage. Plausible choices make claims that seem intuitive, but that can be disproven based on some small element. The following excerpt and corresponding question illustrate this concept:

This passage is adapted from Herman Melville, Moby Dick, *published in 1851.*

line   Some years ago—never mind how long precisely—having little or no money in my purse, and nothing particular to interest me on shore, I thought I would sail about a little and see the watery part of the world. It is a way I have of driving off the spleen and regulating the circulation. Whenever I find myself growing grim about the mouth; whenever it is a damp, drizzly November
5 in my soul; whenever I find myself involuntarily pausing before coffin warehouses, and bringing up the rear of every funeral I meet; and especially whenever my hypos get such an upper hand of me, that it requires a strong moral principle to prevent me from deliberately stepping into the street, and methodically knocking people's hats off—then, I account it high time to get to sea as soon as I can.

In the passage, the narrator indicates that he

(A) has a life-threatening physical illness.

(B) spends his money frivolously.

(C) enjoys sailing more than he enjoys being on land.

(D) experiences bouts of melancholy.

The answer choices to the question above are fairly typical of what you can expect to encounter on the SAT Reading section. Each choice elaborates on some part of the passage above, but only one choice is completely verified by the text.

Choice (A) has the least amount of textual support. Although the narrator mentions his "spleen" and his "circulation," and he seems focused on death, nowhere does he indicate that he has a physical illness. Rather, he describes "November in my soul," a metaphor for sadness.

Choice (B) has slightly more textual support, but is still incorrect. The narrator claims that he had "little or no money" in his purse, but he does not clarify why *he is broke. Thus, we cannot assume that he is frivolous or irresponsible with his money.*

Choice (C) can almost be supported by the text. The narrator mentions his desire to "sail about" and "get to sea" at the beginning and end of the excerpt. Thus, we can conclude that he enjoys sailing. However, he never explicitly states that he prefers the sea to land. Thus, we cannot fully support (C), making it incorrect.

Choice (D) is correct because it is completely supported by the text. A person who feels "melancholy" feels sad and/or depressed, and the narrator implies several times in the excerpt that he experiences periods of sadness: his mouth becomes "grim" (unsmiling or forbidding), his soul becomes "damp" and "drizzly," and he becomes fixated on funerals.

Recognizing Wrong Choices

Many incorrect answer choices may seem correct at first glance, but on closer inspection, they can be proven inaccurate because they fall into one or more of the following categories:

- **Irrelevant**

    An *irrelevant* choice makes a claim that is entirely unsupported by the passage. Often, these choices will use words from the passage to state the exact opposite of what is true according to the text, or they will distort the text's intended meaning to the point of blatant inaccuracy. These choices are usually the easiest to eliminate.

- **Wrong perspective**

    A *wrong perspective* choice makes a claim that contains factual information, but does so from the wrong point of view. For example, a question might ask for the *author's* attitude, while a choice that gives the wrong perspective will convey one of the character's attitudes. These choices are especially common in attitude and inference questions.

- **Partially supported**

    A *partially supported* choice makes a claim for which there is only partial textual support. Often, these choices are tricky to recognize as incorrect because something as seemingly minor as a single word might be inaccurate. For example, if a passage describes a novel that influenced the development of a literary genre, a *partially supported* choice may claim that the novel "began" or "completely reshaped" the genre. These may seem like reasonable conclusions, but they do not summarize the passage information; rather, they extrapolate beyond the scope of the passage.

- **Overstated**

    An **overstated** choice lacks support; it makes a general assumption that cannot be supported by the passage information. For example, the text might state that someone oversleeps and ends up late for work as a result. A choice that lacks support might characterize the person in the text as "lazy." Although it seems reasonable, calling someone "lazy" based on an isolated incident is too presumptuous to be a correct SAT Reading section choice.

- **Does Not Fit the Context**

    A choice that *does not fit the context* may be factually true, but it does not apply to or answer the question. Incorrect choices in citation and words-in-context questions generally fall into this category, as do main idea questions that include a factual detail from the text instead of the main argument.

- **Too general**

    A choice that is *too general* makes a claim that is unsupportable because it is too all-encompassing. If the passage mentions "an American team of researchers," a choice that is too general might refer to "researchers," which is incorrect because the passage only refers to one team of *American* researchers.

Categorizing Question Types

SAT Reading section questions can be sorted into four general categories: **Words-in-Context**, **Textual Analysis**, **Author Analysis**, and **Synthesis**. These categories, plus the specific question types that comprise them, are elaborated on below.

Words-in-Context Questions

All reading questions will test your vocabulary to some extent. Whenever you encounter an unfamiliar word, use the *context* of the phrase, sentence, or paragraph in which the word appears to determine its meaning.

Understanding Words-in-Context Questions

The makers of the SAT maintain that being able to discern the meaning of a word through context is crucial to reading comprehension. In fact, up to twenty percent of the questions on the SAT Reading section will ask you to do just that. Often, the words and phrases used in words-in-context questions are relatively common, so the difficulty lies in determining *how* exactly the word is being used. After all, many words in the English language have multiple nuanced meanings.

Question formats vary from test to test, but the most common format for a words-in-context question is

- As used in line xx, "_____" most nearly means...

Textual Analysis Questions

Questions in this category ask you to make reasonable, supportable deductions based on the information presented in the passage. In other words, you must summarize or analyze *what* the author says or is trying to say. Textual-analysis question types include **inferences**, **summaries**, **analogies**, and **citations**.

 ## Understanding Inference Questions

The SAT Reading section will often ask you to make an inference, identify an implication, or find suggested information in a passage. The answers to theses types of questions will include information that is not explicitly stated in the passage, so you must interpret meaning.

At the same time, the correct answer will be entirely supportable based on the text; beware of answer choices that contain very specific or convoluted information. If an answer choice contains a detail or idea that seems logical and yet overreaches the implications in the passage, rule it out.

Common formats for inference questions are

- The author suggests that…
- The author indicates that…
- It can most reasonably be inferred that…
- The author most strongly implies which of the following about…
- Which choice most closely captures the meaning of _____?
- The references to _____ in the passage mainly have what effect?
- Which choice best reflects the narrator's view of _____?

 ## Understanding Summary Questions

When you recall something that you have read, you probably do not remember it word for word; most of the time you remember the main points and maybe a few details or examples. Thus, you tend to naturally summarize text whenever you recall it from memory.

Similarly, SAT summary questions require you to identify main topics, decide what pieces of information are relevant to these topics, and make appropriate connections between ideas. These may sound like difficult tasks, but you probably do all of these things automatically as you work to comprehend a text.

By the time you finish a Reading section passage, make sure you can answer the following questions:

- What is the main topic (or topics) of the passage?
- What evidence (details, examples, and/or opinions) supports the main topic or topics?

Common formats for summary questions are

- Which choice best summarizes the passage?
- The central claim in the passage is that…
- The central problem that the author describes in the passage is…
- In the passage, the author contends that…
- The author's main point about _____ is…
- The author uses _____ and _____ as examples of…
- The passage identifies which of the following as _____?

Understanding Analogy Questions

Analogy questions require you to relate a situation from the passage to a situation described in the answer choices. There are usually one or two analogy questions in each Reading section. Often, analogy questions require you to understand the implications of a relationship or situation in the passage, and then to recognize which choice contains similar implications, even though the situation itself may seem completely different.

Question formats vary from test to test, but the most common format for an analogy question is

- Which situation is most similar to the one described in lines xx – xx?

Understanding Citation Questions

Citation questions test your ability to recognize supporting evidence. These questions will ask you to select a quote that supports the answer to the preceding question.

When answering a citation question, mentally summarize the reason that you gave for your previous answer. Choose the sentence or phrase that offers the most substantial and direct reason.

Common formats for citation questions are

- Which choice provides the best evidence for the answer to the previous question?
- Which choice best supports the author's claim that _____?

Author Analysis Questions

Questions in this category ask you to explain *why* or *how* an author includes, organizes, or presents information. In other words, these questions ask you to analyze the structure and reasoning behind a written work. They require you to look at the "inner-workings" of a passage: instead of simply stating *what* an author says, you must explain *why* or *how* the author conveys it. Author analysis question types are **purpose**, **organization**, and **tone & attitude**.

Understanding Purpose Questions

Purpose questions ask you *why* the author included certain pieces of information. To answer these questions, you may have to analyze how one piece of information relates to another piece of information, or you may have to consider the overall purpose of the passage.

As you read a passage, try to infer the reasons that the author wrote it or included certain information. Authors often write to **describe**, **explain**, **persuade**, **analyze**, or **question**.

Common formats for purpose questions are

- The primary purpose of the passage is to…
- The main purpose of the (sentence, paragraph, etc.) is to…
- The discussion of _____ in lines xx – xx primarily serves to…
- The purpose of the (first, second, third, etc.) paragraph is…
- The author most likely includes the information in lines xx – xx to…

Understanding Organization Questions

Organization questions ask *how* the author structures and presents information in a passage. An organization question may ask you how one piece of information relates to another, or how that piece of information contributes to the passage's main idea(s). For example, an author might describe historical interpretations of a phenomenon, and then contrast these with its actual scientific cause.

Common formats for organization questions are

- Which choice best describes the structure of the paragraph/passage?
- What function does the (first, second, third, etc.) paragraph serve in the passage as a whole?
- Which choice best describes the overall sequence of events in the passage?
- During the course of paragraph (1, 2, 3, etc.), the narrator's focus shifts from…

Understanding Tone & Attitude Questions

Fundamentally, tone and attitude reflect emotion. The author's *attitude* toward a topic leads him or her to create a particular *tone* in the text through stylistic choices and diction.

For instance, consider the neutral statement "We ate dinner." Then think about how the statement can be embellished to imply a negative attitude toward the food: "We picked at our plates with as much politeness as we could muster." A positive embellishment, on the other hand, might be: "We sat and savored every bite of the meal."

Each of the statements contains the same basic information—the narrator ate a meal—but the embellishments create images of very different experiences.

Common formats for tone & attitude questions are

- The passage is written from the perspective of someone who is…
- The author's attitude is primarily characterized by…
- What main effect does _____ have on the tone of the passage?
- How do the words "_____" and "_____" in the (first, etc.) paragraph help establish the tone of the paragraph?

Synthesis Questions

Synthesis questions require you to understand the relationship between two passages, or between a passage and a graphical representation of data, such as a table, chart, or graph. Synthesis question types include **graphics and text synthesis** and **multiple-text synthesis**.

Understanding Graphics and Text Synthesis Questions

These questions ask you to make use of information that appears in a graphical representation of data that accompanies a reading passage. Ultimately, these questions are as much graphic analysis questions as they are reading questions. To answer them, you must be able to:

- recognize which pieces of information from the data are relevant to the passage.
- analyze how the data relates to the text. Does it support it, add new information, or contradict it?

Common formats for graphics and text synthesis questions are

- Which claim about _____ is supported by the graph?
- What information presented in lines xx – xx is represented by the graph?
- It can be reasonably inferred from the passage and the graph that...
- Which choice best summarizes the information presented in the graph?
- According to the graph, which statement is true about _____?
- Taken together, the two figures suggest that...

Understanding Multiple-Text Synthesis Questions

These questions ask you to recognize relationships between two related passages. To answer questions regarding multiple passages, you must be able to:

- recognize how the main topic(s) of a pair of passages relate to each other.
- summarize the tone and attitude of each author toward a topic.

Question formats vary from test to test, but common formats for multiple-text synthesis questions are

- How would the author of Passage 1 most likely respond to the claim about _____ made in Passage 2?
- Which choice best states the relationship between the two passages?
- Is the principle described in Passage 1 consistent with the situation described in Passage 2?
- One difference between the _____ in Passage 1 and the _____ in Passage 2 is...
- On which of the following would the authors of both passages most likely agree?
- Passage 2 expresses which of the following reservations about developments discussed in Passage 1?

Overview of the Redesigned SAT Reading

Question Type	Description	Specific Topics (SAT)	Question Format
Vocabulary (approx. 15 – 20% of score)	Use the context of a sentence, paragraph, or passage to determine the meaning of a word.	Words in context	• As used in line xx, "_____" most nearly means…
Textual Analysis (approx. 50% of score)	Make a reasonable, supportable deduction based on information presented in the text. In other words, summarize *what* the author says or is trying to say.	Inferences, Implications, and Suggestions	• The author suggests that… • The author indicates that…. • It can most reasonably be inferred that… • The author most strongly implies which of the following about _____?
		Summaries	• The author's main point about _____ is… • The author uses _____ and _____ as examples of…
		Analogies	• Which situation is most similar to the one described in lines xx – xx?
		Citations	• Which choice provides the best evidence for the answer to the previous question?
Author Analysis (approx. 20% of score)	Explain *why* or *how* the author says something.	Purpose	• The main purpose of the passage is to… • The discussion of _____ in lines xx – xx primarily serves to…
		Organization	• Which choice best describes the structure of the paragraph/passage?
		Attitude and Tone	• The passage is written from the perspective of someone who is… • The author's attitude is primarily characterized by… • What main effect does _____ have on the tone of the passage?
Synthesis (approx. 15% of score)	Explain a relationship between two passages or between a passage and a diagram.	Graphics and Test Synthesis	• Which claim about _____ is supported by the graph? • It can be reasonably inferred from the passage and the graph that… • According to the graph, which statement is true about _____?
		Multiple-Text Synthesis	• Which choice best states the relationship between the two passages? • On which of the following would the authors of both passages most likely agree? • How would the author of Passage 1 most likely respond to the claim (_____) made in Passage 2?

CHAPTER 2

Key Points
SAT Writing & Language

Either **write** something worth **reading** or do something worth writing.

— Benjamin Franklin

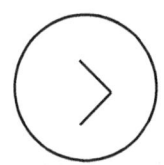

About SAT Writing & Language

The Redesigned SAT Writing & Language section assesses your ability to improve written information.

The test consists of four passages, each accompanied by 11 questions, for a total of 44 questions. You will have 35 minutes to complete the section.

The four passages fit loosely into the categories of careers, science, history/social science, and humanities. In addition, a graph or diagram accompanies one or two of the passages.

Writing & Language Questions

In the passages, the number "1" followed by underlined words or phrases in the text correlates with question 1, and so on. Some questions are expressed as sentences while other questions are implied by the answer choices.

Each multiple-choice question has four answer choices, and only one is correct. As with other sections of the SAT, you will not be penalized for incorrect answers.

For some questions, more than one answer may be technically correct, but just one is the "most effective" at conveying the information.

Certain types of questions will appear after nearly every passage. For instance, most passages include one or more questions that tests you understanding of precise vocabulary. Passages that are accompanied by graphs, charts, or tables will contain questions about how effectively and accurately the passage makes use of the data.

Expression of Ideas

A little more than half of the questions for each passage require you to make judgments about the content of a passage. You must evaluate whether the writer should support, lengthen, shorten, delete, reorganize, or change information. Sometimes you are asked why a writer has included or should include particular information.

Standard English Conventions

Nearly half of the questions in the Redesigned SAT Writing and Language section require you to identify language errors and choose the best option for improvement. You will not be tested on the names of grammatical structures. We have used grammar terms in these pages only for explanations. See pages 44-45 if you need a refresher.

Answer Strategy

- Read the whole passage quickly and carefully. That prepares you to answer questions about content.
- Read the first question and locate the underlined section in the passage.
- Look carefully at the four answer choices. Try to determine what is being tested in the question. What parts of the answers change from choice to choice?
- Select an answer and, before marking it on the answer sheet, check to make sure it would fit into the surrounding sentence or paragraph.

Expression of Ideas

🔑 Understanding Development Questions

Development questions are essentially about relevance. You will often evaluate whether the text focuses on and supports a claim. Or you might determine whether the text includes information that is not relevant to the main point. Development questions tend to ask whether a phrase or sentence should be added, deleted, or changed. They may also include questions about the relevance of accompanying graphs and diagrams.

Solving development questions may require you to:
- understand a passage's **main idea**.
- differentiate **relevant details** from superfluous or distracting information.

Passage Development Quick Look

Questions 1-2 are based on the following passage.

A vast walled complex in the heart of Beijing, the Forbidden City was once home to Chinese imperial rulers and their families. It also served as the policymaking and administrative hub, of which the emperor was at the center. The design and decoration of the city symbolized the emperor's primary role in society: to mediate the cosmic balance between heaven and earth.

1

At this point, the author is considering adding the following table.

Emperor Name (Anglicized)	Reign	Capital City
Hongxi Emperor	1424 – 1425	Beijing (Forbidden City)
Xuande Emperor	1425 – 1435	
Zhengtong Emperor	1434 – 1448 and 1457 – 1464	
Jingtai Emperor	1449 – 1457	
Chenghua Emperor	1464 – 1487	
Hongzhi Emperor	1487 – 1505	
Zhengde Emperor	1505 – 1521	

Should the author make this addition?

(A) Yes, because it clarifies who "Chinese imperial rulers" were.
(B) Yes, because it helps contextualize the passage.
(C) No, because it fails to clarify or relate to information in the passage.
(D) No, because it does not contain a wide enough range of dates to be useful.

2

At this point, the writer is considering adding the following sentence.

> It was called "forbidden" because commoners were forbidden from entering.

Should the writer make this addition here?

(A) Yes, because it supports the main idea that the Forbidden City was kept pristine.
(B) Yes, because it explains an important aspect of the Chinese empire.
(C) No, because it contradicts the description of the city as a "hub."
(D) No, because it interrupts a description of the Forbidden City's purposes.

1. Choice (C) is correct. Although the passage mentions the Chinese emperor, its main focus is the general purpose of the Forbidden City in ancient China, and specific emperors are not clearly relevant to the passage.
2. The answer is (D) because the surrounding sentences all describe functional and symbolic purposes of the city, while the added sentence addresses a different topic.

Understanding Organization Questions

When people talk about "organization" in a text, they are referring to a logical flow of information. To avoid confusing readers, writers often group similar ideas together and use transition words and phrases to indicate relationships among ideas.

Solving organization questions may require you to:

- recognize the **overall structure** of a passage. You must understand how each idea relates to previous information and to the main idea.
- use **transition words and phrases** to clarify relationships in or between paragraphs.

Passage Organization Quick Look

Questions 1-2 are based on the following passage.

[1] In young eyes, special muscles can easily squeeze an eye's crystalline lens, causing it to balloon out slightly. [2] In the eye, the curved lens bends incoming light rays in a special way: it focuses them. [3] They hit the sides of the convex lens and bend inward toward each other, and converge before they hit the retina farther back in the eye. In other words, they focus. [4] It is a bit like when you purse your lips, causing them to stick out. [5] But over 40 or 50 years, the eye's crystalline lens thickens, making it harder for the eye muscles to push the lens into a convex shape when the eye tries to focus on something close.

1

To make this paragraph most logical, sentence 4 should be placed

(A) before sentence 1.
(B) after sentence 1.
(C) after sentence 2.
(D) after sentence 3.

2

The author intends to add the following sentence to the passage.

> Most people have trouble focusing on near images as they reach middle age.

To make the paragraph most logical, the added sentence should be placed.

(A) before sentence 1.
(B) after sentence 1.
(C) after sentence 4.
(D) after sentence 5.

---

1. The answer is (B) because sentence 4 provides imagery of muscles contracting the lips and pushing them out, which is analogous to the phenomenon introduced in sentence 2.
2. The answer is (A) because the added sentence introduces the main phenomenon described in the paragraph. It also contrasts with the information in sentence 1, so it should be placed before it and introduce the sub-topic of "focusing on near images."

Understanding Effective Language Questions

Effective language questions focus on selecting the words that most effectively convey a particular style, tone, or meaning. You must recognize how to structure sentence to effectively express the writer's intended meaning.

Solving effective language questions may require you to:
- Use **precise diction**. That is, select the word that best fits the context in which its used.
- Select a word or phrase that best maintains a particular **style** or **tone**.
- Select the most **concise** choice. That is, one that is clearly stated and free of **redundancies**.
- Accurately **combine sentences** to clarify the relationship between them or achieve a stylistic goal.

Effective Language Quick Look

Questions 1-4 are based on the following passage.

Audiences embraced musical, non-verbal acrobatic shows in the 1990s, following the international **1** culmination of the Canadian-based Cirque du Soleil. Currently **2** the producer that is the largest theatrical entertainment one in the world, Cirque du Soleil refined the use of lyrical atmospheres for acrobatics. Meanwhile, the London-based touring group STOMP introduced sets that look like urban alleys. Audiences are immersed in a fantastical reality where seemingly disparate passers-by create **3** spontaneous rhythms with wild abandon. Taking the immersion a step further, the Argentine company De la Guarda created its sets overhead. Acrobats swooped on bungee cords over the audience, sometimes picking up an audience **4** member. Stage effects included "rain" that doused both performers and the audience.

1
(A) NO CHANGE
(B) attainment
(C) success
(D) magnanimity

2
(A) NO CHANGE
(B) the one producer that is the largest in theatrical entertainment
(C) larger than any other theatrical entertainment producers
(D) the largest producer of theatrical entertainment

3
Which choice most closely matches the stylistic pattern established earlier in the sentence?

(A) NO CHANGE
(B) rhythms with spontaneousness
(C) rhythm that is spontaneous
(D) rhythm, spontaneously,

4
Which choice most effectively combines the sentences at the underlined portion?

(A) member, but stage
(B) member; stage
(C) member so that stage
(D) member — stage

The answers are 1. (C) because "success" is the most precise meaning; 2. (D), because it is the most concise choice; 3. (A) because it matches the "adjective + noun" word pattern established earlier in the sentence; and 4. (B) because it uses a semicolon to effectively connect two complete, related thoughts.

Standard English Conventions Questions

Understanding Sentence-Formation Questions

Questions in this category require you to clarify sentence errors that may confuse or distract readers. For example, sentence-formation errors may leave a reader unsure of who did what or what was done.

Solving sentence formation questions may require you to:
- know how and when to use different types of **clauses** (independent, dependent, and relative).
- know how and when to use different types of **phrases** (participial, prepositional, and appositive).
- maintain **subject-verb agreement**.
- maintain **parallel structure**. That is, using consistent grammatical and word patterns.

Understanding Parts-of-Speech Questions

Questions in this category ask about grammatical mistakes at the individual-word level. Although these mistakes often look trivial, they can affect the meaning of the sentence as a whole.

Solving parts of speech question may require you to:
- Check that a verb's **tense** and **voice** is consistent with the information presented.
- Maintain **noun agreement**. Thus, you must consistently identify the same noun(s) as either singular or plural.
- Check that each **pronoun** matches its referent in terms of **person and number**.

Standard English Conventions Quick Look

Questions 1-7 are based on the following passage.

The development of river steamboats played a major role in the expansion of the United States, they could travel up and down the Mississippi and Ohio rivers and their tributaries in a matter of days. Connecting virtually every area claimed by the United States.

1

(A) NO CHANGE
(B) the United States. Steamboats
(C) the United States. Because they
(D) the United States, which they

2

(A) NO CHANGE
(B) They connected
(C) Connecting them to
(D) It was connecting

[Quick look continues on the next page.]

Western steam-powered river ferries were basically rafts with layers piled on top, like tiers on a wedding cake. On the main deck were the boilers. Keeping the boilers stoked with coal or wood, [3] it was where workers labored around the clock. Upper layers carried cargo and passengers. On the very top tier, the river pilot controlled the boat.

All steamboats were dangerous. Most were wooden, and their boilers contained highly pressurized steam. Explosions and fires were common. Another threat was [4] collisions; river pilots could not avoid all obstacles because [5] you could not see underwater. One submerged log could tear the hull open and sink the boat. Yet many people ignored the risks, including bored passengers who sometimes [6] have encouraged pilots to race other boats. Even people onshore gambled on the races. Although steamboats captured the [7] imagination they quickly became obsolete as railroads were built.

3

(A) NO CHANGE
(B) it was workers who
(C) workers there
(D) working and

4

(A) NO CHANGE
(B) collisions and
(C) collisions—although
(D) collisions,

5

(A) NO CHANGE
(B) your
(C) we
(D) they

6

(A) NO CHANGE
(B) had encouraged
(C) were encouraging
(D) encouraged

7

(A) NO CHANGE
(B) imagination, they quickly became obsolete as
(C) imagination, they quickly became obsolete, as
(D) imagination, they quickly became obsolete: as

The answers are 1. (B) because it is the only choice that corrects the run-on sentence without creating a sentence fragment or another run-on;
2. (B) because it is the only answer that creates a complete sentence with a pronoun subject that refers to the plural noun "steamboats";
3. (C) because the word that is being modified, "workers," should come immediately after the phrase that modifies it;
4. (A) because it is the only proper connection of two independent clauses;
5. (D) because it is the only pronoun that maintains consistency by correctly referring to "pilots";
6. (D) because it is the only verb that avoids an inappropriate shift in tense within the sentence; and
7. (B) because dependent clauses at the beginnings of sentences ("Although steamboats captured the imagination") are usually separated from main clauses by commas, while those ("as railroads were built") at the end are not.

Understanding Conventions of Usage Questions

Formal written English must follow certain rules to make meaning absolutely clear. Questions in this category ask you to identify the standard way of using the language.

Solving conventions-of-usage questions may require you to:
- differentiate **frequently confused words**, including homophones (like "their," "their," and "there") and words with phonetic similarity (like "affect" and "effect"). See the chart at the end of this section for some of the most common such words tested on the SAT.
- form **logical comparisons**.
- correct inappropriate uses of **pronouns**.
- correct **subject-verb and noun agreement** errors.
- correct errors in the use of **possessive determiners**.

Conventions of Usage Quick Look

Questions 1-7 are based on the following passage.

At the career fair, I picked up brochures about teaching preschool and about teaching adult school. I talked to my counselor about it, and she said it has some benefits and drawbacks. On the one hand, learning activities are fun, but on the other hand, 2 their still learning to manage their impulses. 3 Each young child wants what they want.

1

(A) NO CHANGE
(B) about it, and she said they have
(C) about them, and she said one has
(D) about teaching preschool, and she said it has

2

(A) NO CHANGE
(B) they're still learning to manage they're
(C) the children are still learning to manage their
(D) the children are still learning to manage the children's

3

(A) NO CHANGE
(B) A young child wants
(C) Young children want
(D) Everyone at that age wants

[Quick look continues on the next page.]

Taking turns in the form of lining up or waiting for a turn on a swing **4** is, one must admit, difficult to learn. For example, when two children **5** raise their hand at the same moment and enthusiastically shout their answer, the teacher must pause and re-inforce turn-taking. It takes tremendous **6** patients. Still, I may be more suited to working with this age group than I am to **7** adults.

4

(A) NO CHANGE
(B) were,
(C) will be,
(D) are,

5

(A) NO CHANGE
(B) raise their hands
(C) raises hands
(D) raises a hand of each

6

(A) NO CHANGE
(B) patient
(C) patiently
(D) patience

7

(A) NO CHANGE
(B) working with adults.
(C) those of adults.
(D) work with adults.

The answers are 1. (D), because it is the only choice that provides an antecedent for the pronoun.
2. (C), because the antecedent (children) is identified, and matched with the correct possessive determiner (their).
3. (C), because the plural noun and verb (children want) agree with the pronoun and verb that follows in the sentence (they want).
4. (A), because the subject of the verb is a gerund (taking turns). Gerunds are always singular, and thus the singular verb (is) agrees with the subject.
5. (B), because it is the only choice in which there is both subject-verb agreement (children raise) and noun agreement of the plural form (children, hands.)
6. (D), because "patience" refers to a personal quality, which should not be confused with the word "patients," which refers to people receiving medical treatment.
7. (B), because comparing "working with adults" to "working with this age group" is logical; the other choices do not quite make sense.

Understanding Conventions of Punctuation Questions

Questions in this category test both punctuation and sentence structure. After all, punctuation conveys information about how ideas are related and how the text should "sound."

Solving conventions-of-punctuation questions may require you to:
- determine when and how to **punctuate clauses** (independent, dependent, and relative).
- determine when and how to **punctuate phrases** (participial, prepositional, and appositive).
- determine when to use **colons** and **dashes**.
- determine how to use **apostrophes** to effectively **indicate possession**.
- recognize when and how to **combine similar concepts** and separate unrelated ones.

Conventions of Punctuation Quick Look

Questions 1-8 are based on the following passage.

Some sleep researchers theorize that modern lifestyles conflict with **1** humans natural sleep needs. They worry that biorhythms are **2** interrupted, when electric lighting provides illumination past sunset, and when our work or study indoors deprives us of midday sunlight.

However, University of California at Los Angeles (UCLA) **3** researcher, Jerome Siegel asked whether natural sleep patterns were indeed so different. He led a study of three societies that do not rely on **4** electricity: the Hadza in Tanzania, the San of Namibia, and the Tsimane in Bolivia. Some members of each society agreed to wear watch-like devices that kept track of sleeping times and light exposure.

1

(A) NO CHANGE
(B) human's natural sleep needs.
(C) humans' natural sleep needs.
(D) the need of humans' natural sleep.

2

(A) NO CHANGE
(B) interrupted—when
(C) interrupted. When
(D) interrupted when

3

(A) NO CHANGE
(B) researcher Jerome Siegel
(C) Jerome Siegel
(D) researcher, Jerome Siegel,

4

(A) NO CHANGE
(B) electricity; the Hadza
(C) electricity. The Hadza
(D) electricity, the Hadza

[Quick look continues on the next page.]

The data showed that [5] people (in all three societies) have sleep patterns similar to those of many people living in industrialized societies. They stayed up for several hours after [6] sunset; slept for about six-and-a-half hours, and got up just before sunrise. They tended to be out in the sun in the mornings, before retreating to shadier areas by [7] midday they rarely took naps.

As the study participants live fairly near the [8] equator they may represent a truly "natural" lifestyle for *homo sapiens*. Our species evolved at similar latitudes. Thus, for people now living in places at higher latitudes, which include the United States, there may be reassurance in the study. Its authors suggest that at latitudes with widely varying amounts of daylight in winter and summer, electric lighting, and indoor activities may restore—rather than interrupt—natural biorhythms.

[5]

(A) NO CHANGE
(B) (people in all three societies) have
(C) people in all (three) societies have
(D) people in all three societies have

[6]

(A) NO CHANGE
(B) sunset, slept
(C) sunset yet slept
(D) sunset slept

[7]

(A) NO CHANGE
(B) midday and they
(C) midday; they
(D) midday, so they

[8]

(A) NO CHANGE
(B) equator, and they
(C) equator, thus they
(D) equator, they

The answers are 1. (C), because it properly indicates the plural possessive "humans' needs";
2. (D), because when dependent clauses come after the main clause, they are not separated by commas;
3. (B), because the phrase preceding the name does not begin with "a" or "the," so it is a title, not an appositive;
4. (A), because the colon correctly introduces items in a series that elaborate upon the main idea and appears after an independent clause;
5. (D), because all of the underlined information is essential to the clause and should not be set off by parentheses or other punctuation;
6. (B), because the actions described in the sentence (stayed, slept, got up) are three items in a series, and thus should be separated by commas;
7. (C), because two coordinating clauses can be joined by a semicolon if the relationship between them is clear;
8. (D), because the dependent clause beginning with "as" comes before the main clause, so it should be separated by a comma.

Essay Test Basics

In the Redesigned SAT, the Essay Test is optional. Some colleges and universities do not require SAT Essay scores as part of the application process, but many do. That's why it is a great idea to tackle the Essay Test: it may give you more choices later. The good news is that the Redesigned SAT Essay has a standard prompt which includes very specific directions. Completing the following activities will help you practice, so when you face the Redesigned SAT essay prompt, you will know exactly what to do.

NOTE

All SAT Essay Tests follow the same procedure: within 50 minutes, you must read a passage and write an analysis of it.

1 First, you will be presented with the following instructions:

> As you read the passage below, consider how the author uses:
> - evidence, such as facts or examples, to support claims.
> - reasoning to develop ideas and to connect claims and evidence.
> - stylistic or persuasive elements, such as word choice or appeals to emotion, to add power to the ideas expressed.

2 After reading the instructions, you will be presented with a 650- to 750-word passage that argues a certain point. As you read the passage, take notes based on the considerations listed above. After the passage, a variation of the following prompt will appear:

> Write an essay in which you explain how the author builds an argument to persuade his/her audience about the author's claim. In your essay, analyze how the author uses one or more of the features listed above (or features of your own choice) to strengthen the logic and persuasiveness of his/her argument. Be sure that your analysis focuses on the most relevant features of the passage.
>
> Your essay should not explain whether you agree with the author's claims, but rather explain how the author builds an argument to persuade his/her audience.

🔑 Essay Test Skills

The SAT Essay Test is scored based on the following criteria: Reading, Analysis, and Writing.

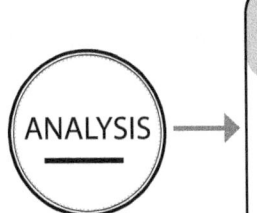

You are evaluated on your understanding of the passage, on the basis of:
- including accurate descriptions of central ideas, major details, and the relationships between ideas and details.
- accurately using quotes and/or paraphrases.

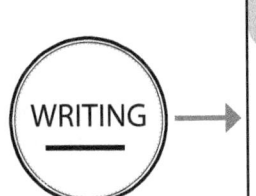

You are scored based on how well you explain the author's use of reasoning and stylistic elements in a passage. You can demonstrate analytical abilities by:
- showing that you understand what you are being asked to do by writing an analysis.
- commenting on several elements that the author uses to build the argument.
- supporting your points with references to the text.
- quoting and referencing the most relevant portions of the passage.

You are scored based on how clearly and concisely you present an analysis. You can demonstrate your writing abilities by:
- making and supporting a central claim regarding the passage.
- using varied sentence structures and a diverse vocabulary.
- connecting ideas in such a way that all information is relevant to the prompt.
- writing a well-organized essay that shows a logical progression.
- demonstrating proper grammar and use of punctuation.

NOTE

Essays are scored by two graders, each of whom assigns a score of 1 to 4 points (1 being the lowest) to each of the categories listed above. Thus, each category receives a score of 2 to 8 points.

Your Insight

While writing an analysis of an author's work might seem intimidating, you likely perform similar analyses every day without even realizing it. This can be easily illustrated with an example:

> *One afternoon, you hear your dog, Savannah, barking at the front door of your house. You open it to see a frightened-looking delivery person, whom you reassure by saying, "don't worry, my dog won't bite you. She's just making noise to let me know someone's at the door."*

In this scenario, you have identified barking as a strategy (*making noise*) and explained its purpose (*to let me know someone's at the door*). You could even comment on the effectiveness of this strategy by noting that, because the barking got your attention, it was employed successfully.

Analyzing rhetorical strategies in writing or speech is much the same: you must identify the strategy, explain why the strategy is being used, and comment on its effectiveness. Taken together, these form an insight into why and how the author composed his or her thoughts.

 **Key Points**
- Notice
- Label
- Deduce purpose

Your Basic Task

As you plan your central claim and paragraph topics, remember the prompt. Essentially, the essay prompt asks you to label and explain strategies.

Keep summary to a minimum. If you are talking to the delivery person, as in the example above, you do not need to tell the person that the dog is barking. That is obvious. You only need to mention the barking when you label it as a strategy (making noise) to achieve a goal (to let me know someone's at the door).

Also keep in mind that your job is to explain and evaluate the author's strategies rather than agreeing or disagreeing with the author on the topic. Your opinion only comes into the picture in the narrow sense of explaining what you think about how well the dog achieves her goals by barking. Make a reasoned judgment. Write about it at length; explain that barking is effective (or ineffective) because … etc.

One way to elaborate on the effectiveness is to talk about what the effect would have been if the author had *not* used the rhetorical strategy. Applying this to the example of a barking dog, if Savannah had *not* barked, you may never have noticed the delivery driver at your front door.

 **Key Points**
- State how
- Deduce why
- Judge its success
- Explain; use "because"

Example Text: Taking Notes

Read the passage entitled "The Perfect Ingredient for Public Education," by Tory Pines as well as the corresponding sample notes. Then follow along as we analyze the text and plan the essay.

Cooking is a laboratory science; it involves the combination of organic compounds, the application of heat, the manipulation of pH balance with lemon or sugar, the use of fermentation, the activation of rising agents such as yeast, and so on. The simple act of preparing a meal—or of just making a glass of iced tea—incorporates physics, chemistry, biology, and math. Thus, the benefits of public high schools offering elective classes on the science of cooking would be twofold: doing so would introduce students to the scientific processes that underlie everyday experiences, and it would foster the practical (and increasingly rare) skill of cooking.

> *Reasoning, comparison of cooking/applied science*

Nearly every basic recipe from any culture could form the basis of several science lessons. Consider a typical American summer picnic. Pickling cucumbers, making barbecue sauce, browning meat on a grill, packing ice with salt when chilling home-made ice cream—such lessons could memorably illustrate scientific principles. Being able to eat the day's learning product may help motivate even disaffected teens, of which there are many, as about 15 percent of them fail to graduate from high school on time with a regular diploma, according to the National Center for Education Statistics.

> *appeal to the senses: iced tea, pickled cucumber, barbecue, ice cream*

> *Appeal to emotions (create anxiety): disaffected teens, high school drop-out rate, suggestion that young people don't know how to cook*

A side benefit to cooking courses would be an improvement in Americans' "food literacy." It is so easy to drive thru, order out, or pull a packaged dinner from the freezer that someday, the public may not know how to toast bread. On average, Americans report spending less than 30 minutes a day preparing dinner, compared to about 60 minutes in 1965. Some food writers have begun to wring their hands with anxiety that younger generations do not know the simplest cooking techniques. Whether the latter is true or not, it is widely recognized that dining out and eating pre-packaged food do contribute to a diet lower in fiber and higher in fat and sodium. Given our rising rates of obesity in the U.S., we should offer our young people cooking classes as a matter of national health policy.

> *Evidence, expert opinion: food writers worry that young people may not know cooking techniques*

> *Evidence, facts: pre-packaged food, restaurant food often less healthy*

> *Appeal to emotions (call to action): "Given rising rates of obesity, we should offer our young people..."*

At one time, cooking was taught in most U.S. high schools as "Home Economics," and was, unfortunately, mainly taken by girls. Over the decades, such non-academic classes were phased out, and the former kitchen-classrooms re-figured for other purposes. It is like instead of re-routing the bus due to a road closure, schools just drove it to the junk yard. It is time to stop overlooking the academic and motivational potential of cooking.

> *Reasoning, simile: throwing out cooking classes instead of changing them was like throwing out buses instead of re-routing them*

CHAPTER 2 - Writing & Language Key Points | 41

Planning Your Essay

After reading the text, write down several strategies that seem like paragraph topics. Then consider them anew. Cross out any that seem redundant or less relevant. Then choose the most relevant rhetorical strategies considering the author's purpose.

Once you have determined three or four of the most relevant strategies, decide on a logical sequence for them. Group similar points together. Depending on the topic, it may be most effective to address counter-arguments first and place your strongest argument last. One possible order for an analysis of the text on the previous page is as follows:

Strategy 1: *Reasoning, comparison of cooking to applied science*

Strategy 2: *Appeal to emotions, anxiety about young people, call to action to help them*

Strategy 3: *Appeal to senses, evoking delicious food as solution*

3. Connect

Consider how you can connect your analyses of the strategies. Use transition words and phrases in your final essay response to express these connections and relationships:

Topic Sentence 1:	*The author uses reasoning to introduce his idea as an obvious, rational choice.*
Topic Sentence 2:	*Besides possible, the author presents the idea as humane.*
Topic Sentence 3:	*The most persuasive device is concrete examples of popular foods.*

 **Key Points**
- De-clutter
- Put in order
- Connect

42 | KALLIS' Key to the SAT

Developing Your Central Claim

Once you have planned what strategies you intend to discuss, and in what order you intend to discuss them, you are ready to create your precise central claim. You can improve your score by incorporating this claim into your essay's introduction. Doing so indicates that your essay will be focused, and it makes your central claim easier for the graders to locate.

Sometimes called a "thesis statement," the central claim must be specific and state your overall point. Claims can take many forms, but the following is one possible template.

1	2	3	4
In (article title),	(author's name) uses/employs	facts reasoning to diction etc.	claim that argue that persuade readers that explain that suggest that introduce etc.	(text's main idea)

Based on the essay plan created in the previous section, a precise central claim for an analysis of the essay could read:

> *In "The Perfect Ingredient for Public Education," Tory Pines appeals to her readers' sense of reasoning, their emotions, and their physical sensations to argue that public high schools should offer classes in cooking.*

 # Ready, Set, Write

Once you have identified the rhetorical strategies you want to analyze, determined in what order you intend to analyze them, and created a precise central claim that explains to the reader how you intend to do so, you are ready to compose your essay.

Incorporating short quotes from the passage to highlight your own analysis can strengthen your overall argument. But remember, too much summary will detract from your own analysis, so use quotes to support your claims, not the other way around.

Moreover, write clearly. Every student wants to sound intelligent and articulate when writing, which can translate to unnecessary wordiness and clumsy phrasing, especially on timed writing assignments such as the SAT Essay. Re-read your work as you go to make sure that you are making sense and sticking to your point.

Grammar Terms

Noun	a person (or people), place(s), thing(s), or idea(s).
Pronoun	a word that replaces and refers to a noun, noun phrase, or another pronoun.
Subject	the term or phrase that performs an action or is being described in a sentence.
Object	the term or phrase that is affected by the verb or that completes the preposition.

Article	a word that indicates whether the noun it precedes is specific or general. The three articles in English are "the," "a," and "an."
	• "*The*" indicates a specific noun or nouns.
	   The family next door met **the** other families that live on this street.
	• "*A*" and "*an*" refer to a single, general noun.
	   A new family is always interesting to neighbors.

Adjective	a word that describes or limits a noun.
	• An *adjective* is often placed in front of the noun(s) it describes.
	   A **cheerful** melody came from the **outdoor** cafe.
	• An *adjective* can also appear after a linking verb.
	   The cafe is **charming**.

Gerund	an action that acts as a noun. *Gerunds* are formed by adding "ing" to the end of a verb's base form. **Singing** releases stress.
Infinitive verb	the most basic form of a verb (i.e. *to see, to do, to play*). • *Infinitive verb* forms often act as nouns. **To befriend** a dog, throw a toy for it. Most dogs love **to play**.
Participle	a modifier (a word that describes or limits) that looks like a verb ending in "ing," "en," or "ed," as in "*living* organism," or "*decorated* cake." • A *participial phrase* is a group of words that begins with a participle and works together to modify a noun, noun phrase, or pronoun. The children walked by, **laughing among themselves**.

Main verb	a verb form that supplies a subject's action or describes its state-of-being.
	• An *action verb* describes a subject's activity.
	   I **went** to Hawaii. Please **call** me later.
	• A *linking verb* connects a noun, noun phrase, or pronoun to a "state of being" description. Common linking verbs include forms of *be, become, appear, stay, grow, seem, feel, look, taste,* and *smell*.
	   I **am** busy. The job **seems** endless.

Auxiliary verb	also called a "helping verb." It precedes a main verb in order to help express tense and meaning or to form questions and negative statements. • Common auxiliary verbs include forms of *be, do, have, can, must, might, should,* and *may*. I **am** working. **Can** you text me? We **did not** tell him the code.

Adverb	a modifier that describes or limits a verb, adjective, or another adverb. An adverb tells a reader *where, when, how,* or *how often* something occurs, and usually end in "-ly." • An adverb describing a verb: *The cat ate **delicately**.* • An adverb describing an adjective: *The sandwich was **immensely** filling.* • An adverb describing another adverb: *Simone felt as though she did **very** well on her geography midterm.*
Tense	a quality of verbs that expresses the time in which an action or state occurred, be it the past, present, or future.
Preposition	a word that shows direction, location, or time. Prepositions include "to," "from," "on," "under," "over," "about," "in," "out," and "of."

Conjunction	a word that joins ideas and expresses relationships between them. The most common conjunctions are "and" and "but."
	• "And" expresses agreement and addition.
	  *We shopped **and** cooked.*
	• "But" expresses contrast or opposition.
	  *We shopped, **but** we were too tired to cook.*

Sentence	a group of words that forms a complete thought. A sentence begins with a capital letter, contains at minimum a subject and a verb, and ends with a period, a question mark, or an exclamation point.
Clause	a group of words containing a subject and a verb.
Apostrophe (')	a punctuation mark that indicates that a noun shows possession, or that indicates omission of one or two letters from a word or a contraction. • Showing possession: *Adam has become good friends with **Sarah's** brother.* • Showing omission: *"I **don't** think **I'll** ever pass calculus!" the discouraged student moaned.*
Colon (:)	a punctuation mark that separates a term/phrase from a definition or description of, or an elaboration on, that term/phrase. • In formal written English, an independent clause must always precede a colon, but the information that follows a colon can be a single word, a phrase, or an entire clause. *Richard had set three goals for the day: avoid hitting the "snooze" button on his alarm clock, pack a lunch, and arrive at work on time.*

Comma (,)	a punctuation mark that, generally speaking, denotes a brief pause in a sentence. A comma can be used to separate a term, phrase, or an entire clause from the rest of a sentence. Common uses for commas include:
	• separating the items of a list.
	  *Jolene purchased sugar**,** flour**,** and milk from the grocery store.*
	• separating grammatically non-essential phrases from the rest of a sentence.
	  *Banksy**,** an enigmatic and reclusive street artist**,** directed the 2010 film* Exit Through the Gift Shop.
	• separating clauses from one another.
	  *Asia is the world's largest continent**,** and it has the highest population.*

Semicolon (;)	a punctuation mark that can effectively replace a period whenever a period separates sentences containing closely related information. Note that the first letter in the word following a semicolon should not be capitalized unless it is a proper noun.
Period (.)	a punctuation mark most commonly used to denote the end of a sentence.
Parentheses ( )	punctuation marks that are always used in pairs. They enclose additional, grammatically non-essential information that is added to a sentence.
Em dash (—)	a versatile punctuation mark that can effectively replace commas, parentheses, or colons. • Generally, em dashes are considered less formal, but more dramatic, than commas, parentheses, or colons.

Commonly Confused Words

In the English language, it is not uncommon for words with very different meanings to sound similar or the same. When speaking, the differences rarely matter. But in writing, using the correct word is crucial for expressing thoughts accurately. The chart below includes some of the most commonly confused words:

NOTE: The following definitions/synonyms only summarize the most common uses for each word.

Commonly Confused Words	Part of Speech	Definition/Synonyms
accept	verb	receive, gain; accept something as true, believe
except	preposition	not including, besides
affect	verb	influence, have an impact on
effect	noun	a change resulting from a cause, result, consequence
adverse	adjective	harmful, unlucky, unfavorable
averse	adjective	having a strong feeling of opposition
bare	verb, adjective	(verb) uncover, expose; (adjective) simple, unclothed
bear	verb, noun	(verb) transport, support; tolerate; (noun) a type of large mammal
capital	noun	money; a city or town with political and economic importance
capitol	noun	a building that houses the legislative branch of a government
complement	verb, noun	(verb) improve something by adding a part or component; (noun) an addition that completes something
compliment	verb, noun	(verb) mildly praise someone or something; (noun) an expression of mild praise
its	pronoun	gender-neutral third-person singular possessive pronoun
it's	contraction	the shortened form of the words "it is"
lose	verb	have something taken away, misplace
loose	adjective	unsecured, detached
passed	verb (past tense)	leave behind, progress, travel
past	adjective, noun	(adjective) no longer existing; (noun) the time before the present moment, former times
principal	adjective, noun	(adjective) main, primary; (noun) a person of authority, director
principle	noun	a concept that serves as the foundation of a behavior or system
their	pronoun	third-person plural possessive pronoun
there	demonstrative/ existential pronoun	(demonstrative) a pronoun that answers the question "where?"; (existential) a pronoun that indicates that something exists
they're	contraction	the shortened form of the words "they are"
to	preposition	indicating a particular direction, identifying something that is affected
too	adverb	extremely, excessively; additionally, also
two	number	2
whose	determiner/ pronoun	showing that something belongs to or is associated with a person
who's	contraction	the shortened form of the words "who is"

CHAPTER 3

Key Points
SAT Math

With me, **everything** turns into **mathematics**.

— René Descartes

SAT Math Test Basics

 ## Breaking Down the Math Test

The Math portion of the SAT consists of two tests:

- **One No-Calculator Math Test, 25 minutes**
  20 questions total: 15 multiple-choice questions, 5 student-produced response questions.

- **One Calculator Math Test, 55 minutes**
  38 questions total: 30 multiple-choice questions, 8 student-produced response questions including a pair of related questions (numbers 37 and 38) that are worth two points each.

Each correctly answered question is worth one point, with the exception of the pair at the end of the Calculator Test, which are worth two points per correctly answered question. Unanswered and incorrectly answered questions are worth zero points.

> **Note**
> There is no scoring penalty for wrong answers—this means you should always guess even if you are unsure of the answer to a question.

 ## Question Categories

The questions on the Math Tests can be classified according to four categories that correspond to the chapters of this book:

- **Mastering SAT Algebra:** Modeling and solving single equations and systems of equations; linear functions and their graphs

- **Mastering Advanced Topics in Math:** Polynomials and their graphs; factoring

- **Mastering SAT Geometry:** Geometry and trigonometry; complex numbers

- **Mastering SAT Data Analysis:** Graph and table analysis; probability and statistics

 ## Rate and Mark Questions

The questions on the SAT math test generally progress from easy to difficult. However, some topics may be more challenging to you, and hard problems may appear anywhere in the middle of the test. Because you have a limited amount of time, you should try to rate every question. When you encounter a difficult or time-consuming question, skip it and mark it for later. Since there is no penalty for guessing, you can even bubble in one of the answer choices in case you run out of time. However, if you do have time, you can return later to the difficult problems that you marked.

Use the Process of Elimination

Occasionally you'll encounter answer choices that fail to answer the question. Always eliminate these choices to help you narrow your options. In addition, when you come across a question that uses Roman numerals, eliminate any answer choices that contain a false Roman numeral. For most SAT math problems, you'll simply need to solve using arithmetic, so don't spend too much time eliminating each wrong answer choice.

 ## Check Your Work

You should always check your work on any math test, and the SAT is no different. We all make arithmetic errors from time to time, so be sure to double-check that your calculations make sense after solving a problem. If there are multiple methods of solving a problem, try using a different method when you check your answer. If both methods agree, then you've probably got it right. If you come up with a different solution, you may want to check your calculations.

 ## Read Carefully

On the SAT math test, many types of questions are also word problems. This means that you must read the question thoroughly to ensure you find the appropriate value. Often, the test makers will ask you to find a solution such as $x + 2$, but include x as an answer choice. Make sure you answer the question completely and understand exactly what value you are determining.

 ## Use the Formula Reference Chart

On the front page of each section of the SAT math test, there is an informational chart containing useful formulas. Many of you will already know these equations; however, referencing this chart during the test can ensure that you don't make a mistake with one of these formulas. In addition, the informational chart includes diagrams of special right triangles, which can make some triangle questions much easier.

 ## Study Accompanying Graphics

The SAT Math test includes several questions with charts, tables, and graphs. Make sure you read these graphics thoroughly. Look at the title, the x- and y-axes, and any captions or legends, and notice any obvious trends or relationships in the data. When reading graphs, it's important that you know what information is presented and where to find it. Then, when a question refers you to information in the graphic, you already know where to look.

Algebra Questions

The SAT Math test includes many problems that ask you to identify an unknown value or quantity. These questions often include variables (e.g. x and y) and require you to isolate unknown quantities to determine their values. Algebra questions include **systems of equations**, **factoring**, and **concentration and density** problems.

Understanding Systems of Equations

Systems of equations questions present you with two (or more) equations, each of which contains two (or more) variables. To answer these questions, you will have to eliminate one of these variables from one or both equations to isolate the remaining value. There are two useful strategies for solving systems of equations.

1. The Elimination Method

Many equations are easily manipulated so that one variable is eliminated when the two equations are added or subtracted. For example, if you add the equations below, the y term is eliminated, and you can easily find x by simplifying:

$$\begin{array}{r} x + y = 15 \\ +)\ 4x - y = 10 \\ \hline 5x = 25 \end{array} \rightarrow x = 5,\ y = 10$$

2. The Substitution Method

Another way to solve systems of equations is to solve for x in terms of y or vice versa. After you've isolated one variable, you substitute for that value in the second equation:

$x + y = 15 \rightarrow x = 15 - y$

substituting x into the second equation gives:

$4(15 - y) - y = 10$
$60 - 4y - y = 10$
$-5y = -50 \rightarrow y = 10,\ x = 5$

Understanding Factoring

Factoring questions will ask you to simplify algebraic expressions. To factor an algebraic expression, you need to extract similar terms using the distributive property. There are several tricks you can use to quickly factor expressions that fall into one of the following categories.

1. Factorization of Squares

A difference of squares can easily be factored using the following method: $a^2 - b^2 = (a + b)(a - b)$

2. Factorization of Cubes

A difference of cubes can easily be factored using the following formula: $a^3 - b^3 = (a - b)(a^2 + ab + b^2)$

A sum of cubes can be factored according to this formula: $a^3 + b^3 = (a + b)(a^2 - ab + b^2)$

3. Factoring Polynomials

Polynomials that don't fit one of the previous categories can also be factored by a process that resembles the **reverse** of multiplying binomials (FOIL: First, Outer, Inner, Last terms).

If $a^2 + bc + c = pqx^2 + (ps + qr)x + rs$,

where $a = pq$, $b = ps + qr$ and $c = rs$,

then the factored form is $(px + r)(qx + s)$.

> For example, in the equation $5x^2 + 25x + 20$, $pq = 5$, $ps + qr = 25$, and $rs = 20$. Thus, $p = 5$, $q = 1$, $s = 4$, and $r = 5$. Thus, the factored form of the equation is $(5x + 5)(1x + 4)$.

4. Factoring Quadratics

Any quadratic expression can always be solved by using the quadratic formula. This equation provides the roots (x-values of the points at which $y = 0$) for any polynomial of the form $ax^2 + bx + c$

$$x = \frac{-b \pm \sqrt{b^2 - 4ac}}{2a}$$

Understanding Concentration and Density

Concentration and density problems ask you to determine the concentration of a solution, or the amount of a substance within a solution. Alternatively, they may ask you about the density of a substance, or the volume of that substance. The following equations will help you solve concentration and density problems.

1. Concentration Formula

$$\text{Concentration of A} = \frac{\text{Amount of Substance A}}{\text{Amount of Mixture}}$$

2. Density Formula

$$\text{Density} = \frac{\text{Mass}}{\text{Volume}}$$

Geometry Questions

Geometry questions ask you about relationships between shapes and require you to recognize patterns. Many of these rely on important geometry theorems, and knowing these can help you solve most SAT geometry questions. Geometry questions include **triangles**, **circles**, and **radian conversions**.

Understanding Triangles

Triangle questions on the SAT will ask you about the angles or lengths of sides of a specific triangle. Sometimes, they will also ask you about congruency between two similar triangles. Most triangle questions can easily be solved by remembering a few basic theorems about shapes.

1. Pythagorean Theorem

This is the most common theorem used on questions about triangles. Most questions can be solved using *only* the Pythagorean Theorem if you forget other rules about triangles. However, remembering the other rules will make solving many triangle questions faster and easier.

If a, b, and c are the sides of a right triangle, and a and b are adjacent to the right angle, then $a^2 + b^2 = c^2$.

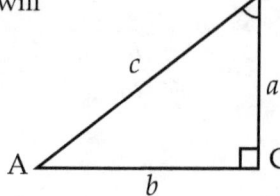

2. Triangle Side-Splitter Theorem

The side-splitter theorem states that if a line is parallel to a side of a triangle and intersects the other two sides, then this line divides those two sides proportionally. In the example below where the bases of the conjoined triangles are parallel, $\frac{AD}{DB} = \frac{CE}{EB}$.

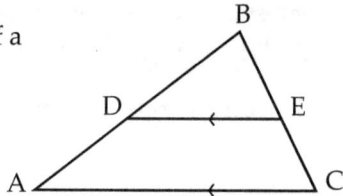

3. Isosceles Triangles

If two angles, b and c, of a triangle are the same, then the lengths of the two sides, $\overline{AB}$ and $\overline{AC}$, of the triangle are the same.

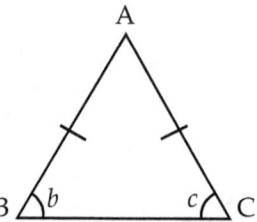

4. Triangle Theorem

The altitude of a right triangle drawn from the right angle creates three similar triangles. This is because each of the two resultant smaller triangles shares a common acute angle with the largest triangle.

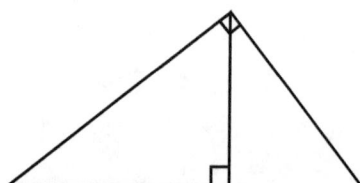

5. **Special Right Triangles**

There are "special" right triangles that always form a specific relationship between the angles or sides of the triangle. A "3-4-5-Right-Triangle," for example, has side lengths that are multiples of 3, 4, and 5. A "45-45-90-Triangle" is an isosceles right triangle whose two smaller sides and angles are equal.

Understanding Circles

Circle questions will ask you about features of a circle, such as its area or radius. They may also ask you about a circle in a coordinate plane, the length of an arc, or the area of a sector.

1. **Area and Circumference**

    The area of a circle, A, is found using the formula $A = \pi r^2$.
    The circle's circumference, C, is found using the formula $C = 2\pi r$
    Note: $\pi = 3.14$, and r is the radius of the circle.

2. **Arc Length and Sector Area**

    The length of an arc's sector, S, is found using the formula $S = \dfrac{\pi r \theta}{180}$.

    The area of a sector, A, is found using the formula $A = \dfrac{1}{2}rs = \dfrac{\pi r^2 \theta}{360}$.

    Note: $\pi = 3.14$, r is the radius of the circle, and θ is the measurement of the central angle of the arc, in degrees.

    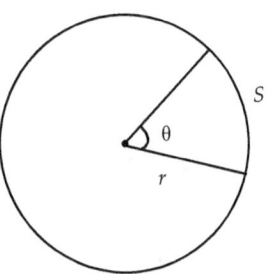

3. **Circle Equation and Coordinates**

    You find a circle's center point and radius using the equation of a circle:
    $(x - h)^2 + (y - k)^2 = r^2$, where (h, k) is the center and r is the radius of the circle.

Understanding Radian Conversions

Some geometry questions will directly ask you to convert an angle from radians to degrees or vice versa. Others will simply rely on your ability to convert between the two.

1. **Radians to Degrees**

    $(\text{angle in radians})\left(\dfrac{180}{\pi}\right) = \text{angle in degrees}$

2. **Degrees to Radians**

    $(\text{angle in degrees})\left(\dfrac{\pi}{180}\right) = \text{angle in radians}$

Problem-Solving Questions

Most SAT Math Test questions involve some element of problem solving. Word problems can be straightforward, or they can be complex. A few types of word problems that don't fall into any other category are **data analysis** and **unit conversions**.

Understanding Data Analysis

Data analysis questions require you to analyze a graph, table, or chart. You may be asked to compare two points on the graphic or you might have to solve an equation based on the information presented. There is extraneous information in most graphics, so be sure to read the data carefully.

1. Tables and Charts

Look at the headings and the values in the chart. Questions will likely ask you to compare two data points, so make sure to read carefully.

2. Graphs

Read the title and the x-axis and y-axis. Questions will likely ask you to extract a value from the graph, so make sure you know where to find appropriate information.

Understanding Unit Conversions

Unit conversion questions require you to convert from one unit to another. You will be given all the formulas you need to solve these problems, but they often require multiple steps. Be diligent to avoid arithmetic errors.

1. Unit Analysis

It's easy to ensure you've performed the correct conversion by writing the units out as you calculate. Whenever you multiply and divide by the same unit, that unit cancels. If you set up your equation correctly, all extraneous units will cancel, leaving you with only the desired unit.

Example: $770,000 \cancel{L} \times \dfrac{37.4 \cancel{MJ}}{\cancel{L}} \times \dfrac{1,000,000 \cancel{J}}{\cancel{MJ}} \times \dfrac{1 Kcal}{4185 \cancel{J}} = 6,880,000,000 Kcal$

Statistics Questions

The SAT Math Test has several questions that ask about simple statistical information. Statistics questions include **measures of center and spread** and **ratios and percentages**.

Understanding Measures of Center and Spread

Measures of center and spread will ask you about the mean, median, mode, or range of a dataset. These questions are easily solved by remembering the rules about computing each of these values.

1. **Mean**

    The mean is the arithmetic average of a set of numbers, calculated by summing every number in the set, then dividing by the number of values, as indicated by the formula below:

    $$\text{Mean} = \frac{1}{n}(a_1 + a_2 + \ldots a_n)$$

2. **Median**

    The median of a dataset is the middle value when the set is arranged in ascending order. If there are an even number of values in the set, the median is equal to the average of the two middle values.

3. **Mode**

    The mode is the value that appears most frequently within the dataset.

4. **Range**

    The range is the difference between the greatest and least values of a dataset.

Understanding Ratios and Percentages

Many SAT Math questions will ask about percentages or ratios. You must be comfortable converting between percentages and decimals and fractions.

1. **Percentage**

    A percentage is a way of representing parts of a whole in terms of hundredths. For example, 85% is equivalent to 0.85 or $\frac{85}{100}$.

2. **Percent Change**

    Some questions will ask you about a percent change, which is calculated as follows:

    $$\text{Percent change} = \frac{\text{change}}{\text{original}} \times 100\%$$

Properties-of-Numbers Questions

The SAT Math section asks many questions that test your knowledge of numbers, functions and their properties. Properties-of-numbers questions include **number rules**, and **functions and graphs**.

Understanding Number Rules

Number rules questions will test you on a variety of concepts, and are easily solved if you remember applicable rules.

1. Absolute Value

The absolute value of a number is defined as its distance from 0 on a number line. The absolute value of a number is always positive such that:

$$|x| = \begin{cases} x & \text{if } x \geq 0 \\ x & \text{if } x < 0 \end{cases}$$

2. Proportionality

When x and y are directly proportional, $\dfrac{x_1}{y_1} = \dfrac{x_2}{y_2}$.

When x and y are inversely proportional, $x_1 y_1 = x_2 y_2$.

3. Complex and Imaginary Numbers

The imaginary number i is defined as the square root of -1. A complex number is simply a combination of real and imaginary numbers and can be expressed as $a + bi$. Always simplify i when possible, and rationalize if it appears in the denominator of a fraction. To rationalize, multiply the complex number by its conjugate. The conjugate of $(a + bi)$ is $(a - bi)$:
$(a + bi)(a - bi) = a^2 - b^2(i)^2 = a^2 + b^2$

Understanding Functions and Graphs

Many questions will ask you about coordinates from a function or how to manipulate a graph. Several basic rules allow you to easily determine features of a function or graph.

1. Defining a Function

A function is a set of ordered pairs with a one-to-one relationship between the two values of each pair. Oftentimes, a function is denoted as $y = f(x)$, where each input, x, has a single output, y.

The domain of a function is the set of all the first coordinates of the ordered pairs. The domain of $y = f(x)$ is the set of x-coordinates on the graph of the function.

The range of a function is the set of all the second coordinates of the ordered pairs. The range of $y = f(x)$ is the set of y-coordinates on the graph of the function.

2. Graphing a Function

Any function can be graphed. You can graph functions using ordered pairs or with the exact equation for the function (if it has been provided). You can use the graph of a function to determine the values of specific ordered pairs or to create a formula for that function.

3. Quadratic Functions

A quadratic function includes a squared variable. Its graph is a parabola. The equation for a quadratic function takes one of two forms and gives us important information about the function.

Standard Form: $y = ax^2 + bx + c$

The vertex is $\left(-\dfrac{b}{2a}, f\left(-\dfrac{b}{2a}\right)\right)$.

The axis of symmetry is $x = -\dfrac{b}{2a}$

The y-intercept is $(0, c)$.

The x-intercepts are $\left(\dfrac{-b \pm \sqrt{b^2 - 4ac}}{2a}, 0\right)$.

Vertex Form: $y = a(x - h)^2 + k$

The vertex is (h, k).

If the x-intercepts are $(p, 0)$ and $(q, 0)$, then $h = \dfrac{p + q}{2}$.

Transforming Quadratic Functions

The graph of a quadratic function can easily be shifted and transformed by manipulating the equation of a parabola. Common transformations are shown below.

Original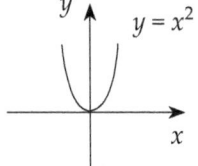

Upside-down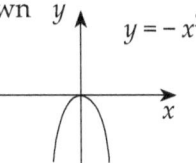

Narrower by a factor of a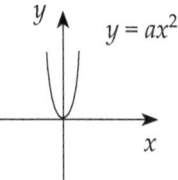

Wider by a factor of a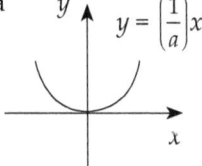

Move up by a units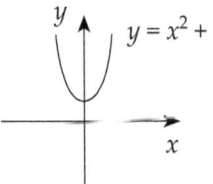

Move down by a units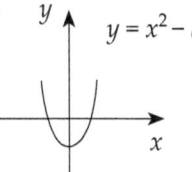

Move left a units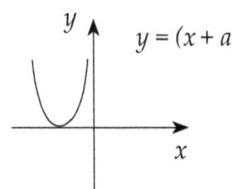

Move right a units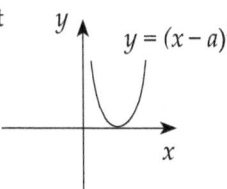

CHAPTER 4

Key Strategies

An ounce of **practice** is generally **worth more** than a ton of theory.

— Ernst M. Schumacher

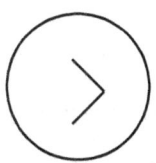

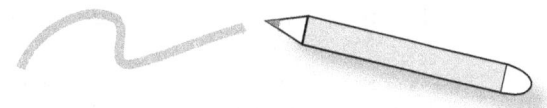

About Key Strategies

Now that you've had a chance to review the key points and concepts tested on the SAT, see how they are applied to individual test questions. KALLIS' Key Strategies consist of a "mini-SAT"—its only about half the length of a real test—with in-depth solutions to help you develop efficient and reliable answer strategies for the full-length test.

Careful review of this section will provide you with all the tools and strategies you need to approach any type of question encountered on the SAT.

Key Strategies: Content Overview

Key Strategies - SAT Reading 65

    Literary Excerpt 66
    Solving Main Purpose Questions
    Solving Attitude & Tone Questions
    Solving Inference Questions
    Solving Citation Questions
    Solving Words-in-Context Questions

    Social Science Passage 72
    Solving Main Purpose Questions
    Solving Summary Questions
    Solving Inference Questions
    Solving Citation Questions
    Solving Words-in-Context Questions
    Solving Graph Analysis Questions
    Solving Graph Synthesis Questions

    Natural Sciences Passage 80
    Solving Main Purpose Questions
    Solving Summary Questions
    Solving Inference Questions
    Solving Citation Questions
    Solving Words-in-Context Questions

    Social Science Passage Pair 86
    Solving Attitude & Tone Questions
    Solving Words-in-Context Questions
    Solving Text Synthesis Questions 1
    Solving Text Synthesis Questions 2
    Solving Citation Questions

Key Strategies - SAT Writing & Language 92

    Careers Passage 94
    Solving Passage Development Questions
    Solving Logical Comparison Questions
    Solving Pronoun/Referent Questions
    Solving Style & Tone Questions
    Solving Passage Organization Questions

    Science Passage 100
    Solving Concision Questions
    Solving Passage Development Questions
    Solving Text-Graphic Synthesis Questions
    Solving Combining Sentences Questions
    Solving Verb Questions

How to Use Key Strategies

There's no one "right" way to use this section. If you want to absorb each and every strategy, then we encourage going through this test as you would a real practice test; that is, by solving each question, checking your answers, and carefully reviewing incorrect responses. You can also use this section as a reference guide. Use the table of contents on the following page to quickly locate the concepts that you know you need to review and skip the information that's familiar.

And if any of the concepts tested in this Key Strategies section are unfamiliar, you can review them in the preceding Key Points section.

Social Science Passage ·· **106**
Solving Precise Diction Questions
Solving Passage Development Questions
Solving Conventional Expression Questions
Solving Phrase/Punctuation Questions
Solving Passage Organization Questions

Arts & Humanities Passage ·· **112**
Solving Development/Concision Questions
Solving Parallel Structure Questions
Solving Precise Diction Questions
Solving Passage Development Questions
Solving Pronoun/Referent Questions

Key Strategies - Math: No Calculator Section ································· **118**

Solving Algebra Questions
Solving Function & Graph Questions
Solving Algebra Questions
Solving Geometry Questions
Solving Ratio/Percentage/Rate Questions
Solving Geometry Questions
Solving Number Rules Questions
Solving Algebra Questions
Solving Ratio/Percentage/Rate Questions

Key Strategies - Math: Calculator Section ··· **129**

Solving Algebra Questions
Solving Function & Graph Questions
Solving System of Equality Word Problems
Solving Algebraic Word Problems
Solving System of Equality/Inequality Questions
Solving Concentration/Density Questions
Solving Geometry Questions
Solving Unit Conversion Questions
Solving Geometry Questions
Solving Geometry Questions
Solving Algebraic Word Problems
Solving Algebraic Word Problems
Solving Measures of Center & Spread Questions
Solving Data Analysis/Ratios Questions
Solving Data Analysis/Ratios Questions
Solving System of Equality/Inequality Questions
Solving Geometry Questions
Solving Algebraic Word Problems
Solving Algebraic Word Problems

SAT READING

 **Key Strategies**

DIRECTIONS

The following passages are shorter versions of the type of literature that you can expect to see on the official SAT. Each passage is followed by a number of common SAT question formats, as well as detailed strategies explaining how to solve various SAT question types.

SAT READING
Key Strategies - Literary Excerpt

Refer to the passage below to answer questions 1 – 5.

This passage is adapted from Ray Cummings, *Phantoms of Reality*, originally published in *Astounding Stories of Super-Science* in January 1930.

line   When I was some fifteen years old, I once made the remark, "Why, that's impossible."
      The man to whom I spoke was a scientist. He replied gently, "My boy, when you are grown older and wiser you will realize that nothing
5 is impossible."
      Somehow, that statement stayed with me. In our swift-moving wonderful world I have seen it proven many times. They once thought it impossible to tell what lay across the broad, unknown Atlantic Ocean. They thought the vault of the heavens revolved around the earth. It was
10 impossible for it to do anything else, because they could see it revolve. It was impossible, too, for anything to be alive and yet be so small that one might not see it. But the microscope proved the contrary. Or again, to talk beyond the normal range of the human voice was impossible, until the telephone came to show how simply and easily it might be
15 done.
      I never forgot that physician's remark. And it was repeated to me some ten years later by my friend, Captain Derek Mason, on that memorable June night of 1929.
      My name is Charles Wilson. I was twenty-five that June of 1929.
20 Although I had lived all of my adult life in New York City, I had no relatives there and few friends.

Solving Main Purpose Questions

01

The passage primarily serves to

(A) justify a doubt.
(B) establish a setting.
(C) explain an outlook.
(D) describe a process.

1. Determine the Question Type ← This question asks you to find the **primary purpose** of the excerpt; in other words, you must recognize *why* the author included it. Generally, an author will not explicitly state his or her purpose for writing, so it must be inferred from the passage.

2. Refer to the Passage ← Humanities passages usually serve some purpose within a larger narrative. The reader must infer the purpose of the excerpt in the overall story.

3. Come up with Your Own Answer ← Before looking at the answer choices, quickly come up with an answer to the question using your own words. The first two paragraphs describe the origin of the narrator's view that "nothing is impossible," followed by explanations of how "that statement stayed with me" (line 6). Based on this information, you can conclude that the passage serves *to describe the narrator's perspective*.

4. Use the Process of Elimination ← Once you have come up with your own answer, eliminate any choices that contradict your answer or stray from the passage's main focus:
- Eliminate choice (A) because it **lacks support**. While paragraph 1 does introduce a doubt ("that's impossible"), the rest of the passage is spent refuting, not justifying, this doubt.
- Eliminate choice (B) because it **lacks support**. The final paragraph briefly establishes the setting of New York City, but this is a minor point in the passage, not the *main focus* or *primary purpose* of the passage.
- Eliminate choice (D) because it is **irrelevant**. The passage focuses on why the narrator believes that "nothing is impossible," but does not focus on the process of his accepting that belief.

5. Confirm Your Choice ← Before selecting a response, make sure there is *nothing* about it that can be disproven by the passage:
- Choice (C) effectively summarizes the purpose of the passage. Paragraph 2 (lines 3 – 5) describes the *outlook* (that "nothing is impossible") and paragraph 3 (lines 6 – 15) *explains* how the narrator's outlook was confirmed.

Solving Attitude & Tone Questions

02

The narrator's attitude toward scientific progress is best described as one of
(A) stubbornness and determination.
(B) approval and admiration.
(C) envy and resentment.
(D) zeal and fervor.

1. Determine the Question Type

Attitude and **tone** questions ask you to identify *how the author*, the narrator, or another character in a passage feels about something. Generally, these questions are easily identifiable because they use the word "attitude" or "tone" in the question.

2. Read the Answer Choices & Review the Passage

Because the question does not provide line numbers for reference, you must consider the whole passage when answering. As you review, locate any information relating to the narrator's *attitude* toward scientific progress or his *tone* when discussing such progress. Review of the passage reveals that paragraph 3 (lines 6 – 15) describes many scientific advancements over the past several centuries, and throughout the paragraph, the narrator seems to be speaking *positively* of these advancements. (He implies that they contribute to "our swift-moving and wonderful world.") Thus, you can conclude that the correct choice will convey a positive attitude.

3. Use the Process of Elimination

Once you have reviewed the relevant portion(s) of the passage, eliminate any choices that do not coincide with the conclusions from step 2:
- Eliminate choice (A) because it is **irrelevant**. Based on the information in the passage, it is unclear what it would mean for someone to have a "stubborn" attitude towards scientific progress, making this an unsupportable choice.
- Eliminate choice (C) because it **lacks support**. "Resentment" is a negative attitude, so this choice is not supported by the passage.
- Eliminate choice (D) because it **lacks support**. Although "zeal and fervor" can be positive descriptions, they imply extreme excitement, which is not apparent in paragraph 3.

4. Confirm Your Choice

Before selecting a response, make sure there is *nothing* about it that can be disproven by the passage:
- Choice (B), "approval and admiration," accurately describes the narrator's attitude towards scientific progress because, in paragraph 3, he implies that such progress helps shape "our swift-moving wonderful world," which suggests that the narrator *approves* of such progress.

Solving Inference Questions

It can reasonably be inferred from the passage that the narrator

(A) is a well-known scientist.
(B) is not particularly social.
(C) has contributed to many scientific advancements.
(D) tells Captain Derek Mason that nothing is impossible.

1. Determine the Question Type

This question asks what "can reasonably be inferred" about the narrator, so the correct answer will not be directly stated in the passage. Because the question does not provide line numbers for reference, you must consider the entire passage when answering.

2. Read the Answer Choices & Review the Passage

As you review the passage, look over the answer choices and try to determine which portion(s) of the text make any reference to the answer choices:
- Both paragraph 2 (lines 3 – 5) and choice (A) mention "a scientist."
- Paragraph 5 (lines 19 – 21) appears to relate to choice (B), as it mentions that the narrator has "few friends."
- Paragraph 3 (lines 6 – 15) mentions a number of scientific advancements which may relate to choice (C).
- Both paragraph 4 (lines 16 – 18) and choice (D) mention "Captain Derek Mason."

3. Use the Process of Elimination

Once you have reviewed the relevant portion(s) of the passage, eliminate any choices that contradict the passage or fail to address the question:
- Eliminate choice (A) because it **lacks support**. Although paragraph 2 mentions "a scientist," the passage does not suggest that the narrator himself is a scientist.
- Eliminate choice (C) because it **lacks support**. The narrator lists many scientific achievements in paragraph 3, but he does not imply that he has made any contributions to science himself.
- Eliminate choice (D) because it is **irrelevant**. Paragraph 4 implies that Captain Mason told the narrator that "nothing is impossible," the opposite situation to what is stated in choice (D).

4. Confirm Your Choice

Before selecting a response, make sure there is *nothing* about it that can be disproven by the passage:
- Choice (B) provides the safest inference. You can assume that the narrator is not very social because he says that he had lived in New York for several years, yet he had "few friends" there.

Solving Citation Questions

04

Which choice provides the best evidence for the answer to the previous question?

(A) Lines 6 – 7 ("In our…times")
(B) Lines 13 – 15 ("to talk…done")
(C) Lines 16 – 18 ("I never…1929")
(D) Lines 20 – 21 ("Although…friends")

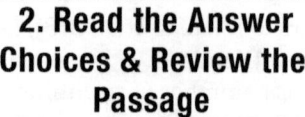

1. Determine the Question Type

This is a typical example of a **citation** question: it asks you to find textual evidence that supports the answer to the previous question. Citation questions are easily identifiable because the answer choices will always be passage excerpts. Before attempting to answer a citation question, review the answer to the previous question.

2. Read the Answer Choices & Review the Passage

When you refer to the line numbers provided in each answer choice, reread some of the information that comes before and after the referenced line numbers; doing so will help give each answer choice a bit of context.

3. Use the Process of Elimination

Once you have reviewed the relevant portion(s) of the passage, eliminate any choices that do not relate to the correct answer to choice (B) of number 3:
- Eliminate choices (A), (B), and (D) because they **do not fit the context** of the question. None of these choices support the answer to the previous question because they have nothing to do with the narrator's social life.

4. Confirm Your Choice

Before selecting a response, make sure there is *nothing* about it that can be disproven by the passage:
- The referenced text in choice (D) strongly suggests that the narrator "is not particularly social" because it mentions that he has "few friends" in New York City despite having "lived all of his adult life" there.

Solving Words-in-Context Questions

05

As used in line 13, "range" most nearly means

(A) spread.
(B) diversity.
(C) variety.
(D) limits.

1. Determine the Question Type ← This is a typical example of a **words-in-context** question: it asks you to find a synonym for a word in the passage. Words-in-context questions generally require you to select one of multiple meanings that are possible for the word.

2. Contextualize the Answer Choices ← Review the referenced line and its context, and use contextual clues to determine the word's meaning. In this case, you can determine that "range" relates to the extent "of the human voice" (line 13).

3. Use the Process of Elimination ← Once you have reviewed the relevant portion of the passage, eliminate any choices that do not reasonably relate to the *extent* of the human voice:
- Eliminate choices (A), (B), and (C) because they **do not fit the context** of the passage. Although these choices are accurate definitions for "range," they cannot effectively describe the *extent* or audibility of the human voice. "Spread" generally describes the area covered by a physical object, and "diversity" and "variety" commonly describe an assortment or mixture of something.

4. Confirm Your Choice ← Before selecting a response, make sure there is *nothing* about it that can be disproven by the passage:
- Based on the context in which the word appears, choice (D), "limits," is the best choice because "limits" is close in meaning to "extent," so it fits the context of the passage based on the information in step 2.

SAT READING
Key Strategies - Social Science

Refer to the passage below to answer questions 6 – 12.

This passage is adapted from Eric Jensen, "China Replaces Mexico as the Top Sending Country for Immigrants to the United States," published by the United States Census Bureau Blogs, May 1, 2015.

line
Based on my research, in 2013, China replaced Mexico as the top sending country for immigrants to the United States. This followed a decade where immigration from China and
5   India increased while immigration from Mexico decreased. Other top immigrant-sending countries in 2013 from Asia included Korea, the Philippines, and Japan. This new pattern in the national origins of recent immigrants is a notable
10 change from recent decades.
    The racial and ethnic composition of immigration flows to the United States has also been shifting. In 2000, nearly half of all foreign-born immigrants, 41.2 percent, were Hispanic,
15 compared with 23.6 percent for the non-Hispanic Asian alone population. Since 2009, a greater proportion of foreign-born immigrants have been non-Hispanic Asian alone (34.7 percent) than Hispanic (30.1 percent). By 2013, the percentage
20 of non-Hispanic Asian alone had increased to 40.2 percent of the total immigration flow, while the percentage Hispanic had dropped to 25.5 percent.
    The U.S. Census Bureau's Population Estimates Program measures net international
25 migration, including the foreign-born population whose residence one year ago was abroad. According to the 2013 American Community Survey, there were 1,201,000 immigrants. China was the top sending country with 147,000,
30 followed by India with 129,000, and Mexico with 125,000. The numbers of immigrants from India and Mexico were not statistically different from each other. In 2012, the American Community Survey showed that Mexico and China were
35 the top two sending countries with 125,000 and 124,000, respectively (which were not significantly different from each other).
    Change in the racial and ethnic composition of immigrant flows contributes to the overall
40 racial and ethnic makeup of the United States. While Hispanics are still the largest racial or ethnic minority group, a larger percentage of the Asian population was foreign-born (65.4) compared with the Hispanic population (35.2)
45 in 2013. Given the numbers above, it is likely that the contribution of immigration to overall population growth will be greater for Asians than for Hispanics.
    Historically, the national origins of immigrant
50 flows have changed dramatically. The earliest waves of immigrants originated in Northern and Western Europe. Immigrants from Southern and Eastern Europe later predominated. The most recent wave of immigrants has largely been
55 from Latin America, and to a lesser extent, Asia. Whether these recent trends signal a new and distinct wave of immigration is yet to be seen.

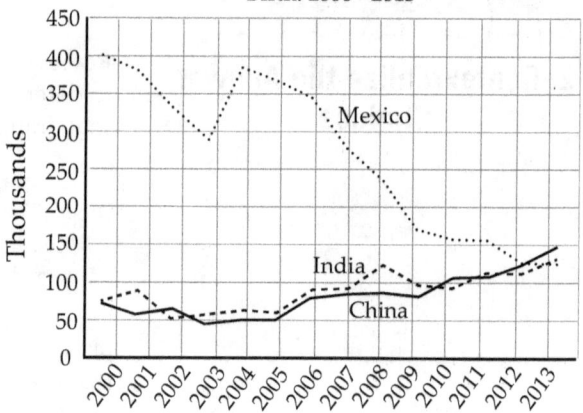

Foreign-Born Population Whose Residence One Year Ago Was Abroad by Selected Places of Birth: 2000 - 2013

Solving Main Purpose Questions

06

The primary purpose of the passage is to
(A) compare Chinese and Mexican immigration policies.
(B) describe immigration trends in the U.S.
(C) analyze the racial and ethnic composition of the U.S. by region.
(D) provide a chronological history of Asian immigration to the U.S.

1. Determine the Question Type

This question asks you to find the "**primary purpose**" of the passage; in other words, you must recognize *why* the author wrote the passage. Generally, an author will not state his or her purpose for writing directly, so it must be inferred from the passage.

2. Refer to the Passage

Often, an author will give the reader clues as to *why* he or she is writing something (the purpose) in the first paragraph, and will occasionally repeat this information in the conclusion. In this case, the first sentence of the first paragraph gives us a good idea of the author's intentions for writing.

3. Come up with Your Own Answer

Before looking at the answer choices, quickly come up with an answer to the question using your own words. The very first sentence allows you to infer that the passage's purpose is *to describe recent changes regarding where immigrants to the U.S. are coming from.*

4. Use the Process of Elimination

Once you have come up with your own answer, eliminate any choices that contradict your answer or stray from the passage's main focus:
- Eliminate choice (A) because it is **irrelevant**; the passage analyzes who is immigrating to the U.S., not immigration policies.
- Eliminate choice (C) because it is **irrelevant**; the passage does not mention the regional racial composition of the U.S. Instead, it discusses countries of origin for immigrants to the U.S..
- Eliminate choice (D) because it **distorts the focus** of the passage. With the exception of the final paragraph, the passage focuses on immigration from 2000 – 2013, so it does not focus on "history," but rather on recent immigration trends.

5. Confirm Your Choice

Before selecting a response, make sure there is nothing about it that can be disproven by the passage:
- The correct choice—(B)—is the simplest and most general choice, and it still provides an accurate summary of the passage's purpose. In this case, the safest assumption is the correct one, and the more specific and/or convoluted choices contain details that may appear correct, but are inaccurate based on the passage. This is a pattern that you may see in other SAT reading questions.

Solving Summary Questions

According to the passage, which of the following is true of Asian immigrants to the U.S.?

(A) Their recent surge in numbers has signaled a new wave of U.S. immigration.
(B) Over 1 million of them immigrated to the U.S. in 2013.
(C) They replaced Hispanic immigrants as the largest proportion of U.S. foreign-born immigrants in 2000.
(D) Since 2000, they have comprised an increasingly large proportion of foreign-born U.S. immigrants.

1. Determine the Question Type

This question asks "which of the following is true" of the passage. This tells you that the answer can be drawn directly from the passage, so the correct choice will **summarize** or **paraphrase** the relevant information.

2. Read the Answer Choices & Review the Passage

Because this question does not provide line numbers for reference, you must consider the entire passage. Look over the answer choices, and try to determine which portion(s) of the text make any reference to the answer choices:
- Information similar to choice (A) is located in the final sentence (lines 56 – 57), which mentions "waves of immigration."
- Paragraph 3 (lines 23 – 37) relates to choice (B), as both focus on U.S. immigration statistics.
- Paragraph 2 (lines 11 – 22) mentions the year 2000, so it likely focuses on the same information as choices (C) and (D).

3. Use the Process of Elimination

Once you have reviewed the relevant portion(s) of the passage, eliminate any choices that contradict the passage or fail to address the question:
- Eliminate choice (A) because it is only **partially supported**; the passage says that it has "yet to be seen" (line 57) whether the recent surge of Asian immigrants signals a new wave of immigration, so (A) makes an inference that cannot be supported by the passage.
- Eliminate choice (B) because it is **lacks support**; paragraph 3 states that the total number of immigrants to the U.S. in 2013 was over 1 million. The passage does not state the total number of Asian immigrants.
- Eliminate choice (C) because it is **irrelevant**; paragraph 3 states that, in 2000, the largest proportion of U.S. immigrants were Hispanic.

4. Confirm Your Choice

Before selecting a response, make sure there is *nothing* about it that can be disproven by the passage:
- In this case, choice (D) accurately summarizes the information in paragraph 2: from 2000 – 2013, the proportion of immigrants from Asia gradually increased while the proportion of Hispanic immigrants decreased.

Solving Inference Questions

It can reasonably be inferred from paragraph 3 (lines 23 – 37) that

(A) the majority of immigrants to the U.S. were from countries other than China, India, and Mexico.
(B) the U.S. Census Bureau predicts that the number of immigrants to the U.S. will increase drastically in coming years.
(C) the number of Hispanic immigrants to the U.S. decreased from 2012 to 2013.
(D) 2013 is the first year in which more Indians than Chinese immigrated to the U.S.

1. Determine the Question Type

The question asks what "can reasonably be **inferred**" from a particular portion of the text. The answer to a question that asks about an inference, implication, or suggestion will not be directly stated in the passage.

2. Read the Answer Choices & Review the Passage

As you review paragraph 3, look over the answer choices, and try to determine which portion(s) of the text make any reference to the answer choices:
- Lines 27 – 31 give immigration statistics relating to choice (A).
- Lines 27 – 37 provide statistics about the number of Hispanic immigrants to the U.S. in 2012 and 2013, relating to choice (C).
- Lines 27 – 31 provide statistics about the number of Chinese and Indian immigrants to the U.S. in 2013, which relates to choice (D).

3. Use the Process of Elimination

Once you have reviewed the relevant portion(s) of the passage, eliminate any choices that contradict the passage or fail to address the question:
- Eliminate choice (B) because it is **irrelevant**. Paragraph 3 does not speculate about future immigration trends; it only looks at immigration statistics from 2012 and 2013.
- Eliminate choice (C) because it is **irrelevant**. Paragraph 3 states that 125,000 Mexicans immigrated to the U.S. in 2012 *and* 2013, which disproves choice (C).
- Eliminate choice (D) because it is **irrelevant**. Paragraph 3 does not state that more people immigrated from India than from China.

4. Confirm Your Choice

Before selecting a response, make sure there is *nothing* about it that can be disproven by the passage:
- In this case, choice (A) makes an accurate inference based on the information in paragraph 3. The sum of the Chinese, Indian, and Mexican immigrants to the U.S. in 2013 totals just over 400,000, so it stands to reason that the remaining 800,000 (of the 1.2 million total U.S. immigrants) "were from countries other than China, India, and Mexico."

Solving Citation Questions

09

Which choice provides the best evidence for the answer to the previous question?

(A) Lines 23 – 26 ("The U.S. Census...abroad")
(B) Lines 27 – 31 ("According to...125,000")
(C) Lines 31 – 33 ("The numbers...other")
(D) Lines 33 – 36 ("In 2012...respectively")

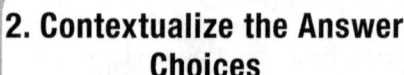

1. Determine the Question Type

This is a typical example of a **citation** question: it asks you to find textual evidence that supports the answer to the previous question. Citation questions are easily identifiable because the answer choices will always be passage excerpts.

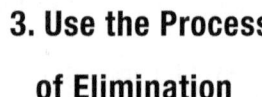

2. Contextualize the Answer Choices

When you refer to the line numbers provided in each answer choice, read some of the information that comes before and after the referenced line numbers. Also glance back at the previous question to make sure you remember what information you are supporting.

3. Use the Process of Elimination

Once you have reviewed the relevant portion(s) of the passage, eliminate any choices that do not relate to choice (A) of number 3:
- Eliminate choices (A), (C), and (D) because they **do not fit the context** of the question. Choice (A) fails to provide any information about where "the majority of immigrants to the U.S." come from. Choice (C) only mentions immigration statistics for Mexico and India, so we cannot use this quote to make an inference about "the majority of immigrants to the U.S." Similarly, choice (D) only references immigration statistics for Mexico and China.

4. Confirm Your Choice

Before selecting a response, make sure there is *nothing* about it that can be disproven by the passage:
- Choice (B) provides all the statistical information needed to infer that "the majority of immigrants to the U.S. were from countries other than China, India, and Mexico." Adding the total number of Chinese, Mexican, and Indian immigrants, and subtracting this sum from the total number of immigrants—all of which can be done using the information in (B)—gives you the correct answer to the previous question, making (B) the most appropriate choice.

Solving Words-in-Context Questions

10

As used in line 50, "dramatically" most nearly means

(A) spectacularly.
(B) sensationally.
(C) considerably.
(D) affectedly.

1. Determine the Question Type

This is a typical example of a **words-in-context** question: it asks you to find a synonym for a word in the passage. Words-in-context questions generally require you to select one of multiple meanings that are possible for the word.

2. Contextualize the Answer Choices

Review the referenced line and its context, and use contextual clues to determine the word's meaning. In this case, you can determine that "dramatically" describes the degree to which immigration trends in the U.S. have changed over time.

3. Use the Process of Elimination

Once you have reviewed the relevant portion of the passage, eliminate any choices that do not reasonably describe *how* or *to what extent* immigration trends have changed over time:

- Eliminate choices (A), (B), and (D) because they **do not fit the context** of the passage. Choices (A) and (B) are incorrect because both imply excitement or theatricality, which does not fit the academic tone of a passage about immigration statistics. Choice (D) is incorrect because "affectedly" most nearly means "artificially," which does not make sense when plugged into line 50.

4. Confirm Your Choice

Before selecting a response, make sure there is *nothing* about it that can be disproven by the passage:

- Based on the context in which the word appears, choice (C), "considerably," is the best choice because "considerable" reflects the "big" change in immigration shifts described in the passage.

Solving Graph Analysis Questions

11

According to the graph, between which two years did the number of Mexican immigrants to the U.S. undergo the greatest increase?

(A) 2001 – 2002
(B) 2003 – 2004
(C) 2006 – 2007
(D) 2008 – 2009

1. Determine the Question Type

This question asks you to interpret the graph, but it does not require you to reference the passage for any information, making it a **graph analysis** question. You will only see graph analysis questions on passages with corresponding graphs, charts, and/or diagrams. You will not generally see any graphic analysis questions in passage pairs or literary excerpts.

2. Refer to the Graph

When you refer to a graph (such as the one that corresponds with this passage), make sure you read the title of the graph and understand the relationship between the x- and y-axes before attempting to answer the question.

3. Use the Process of Elimination

At a glance, it appears that the greatest increase occurred from 2003 to 2004, when the number of Mexican immigrants increased by nearly 100,000, but check the other choices carefully, and eliminate any choice with an increase of less than 100,000:
- Eliminate choices (A), (C), and (D) because they all chart years where the number of Mexican immigrants *decreased*.

4. Confirm Your Choice

Before selecting a response, make sure there is *nothing* about it that can be disproven by the passage:
- Choice (B) is the correct answer because it completely addresses the question and is fully supported by the information in the graph.

Solving Graph Synthesis Questions

12

Data in the graph provide the most direct support for which idea from the passage?
(A) Overall immigration to the U.S. has decreased drastically since 2000.
(B) The number of Chinese and Indian immigrants to the U.S. has gradually been increasing for over a decade.
(C) India is expected to overtake China as the greatest contributor to U.S. immigration within a decade.
(D) The number of Indian immigrants to the U.S. peaked in 2008.

1. Determine the Question Type

Graph synthesis questions ask you to apply information from the passage to a corresponding graph, chart, or diagram. You will only see graph synthesis questions on passages with corresponding graphs, charts, and/or diagrams. You will not generally see any graphic synthesis questions in passage pairs or humanities passages.

2. Refer to the Graph and the Passage

Before you attempt to answer a graph synthesis question, make sure you fully understand the graph itself. Take note of the graph's title, the labels on its *x*- and *y*-axes, and any obvious trends or relationships in the graphed information. Then refer to the passage, and try to determine which portion(s) of the text make any references to the answer choices:
- Choice (B) summarizes the statistics about trends in Asian immigration to the U.S. in paragraph 2 (lines 11 – 22).

3. Use the Process of Elimination

Once you have reviewed the graph and any relevant portion(s) of the passage, eliminate any choices that contradict the passage or are unsupported by the graph:
- Eliminate choice (A) because it is only **partially supported**. The graph shows that Mexican immigration to the U.S. has decreased since 2000, but it does not provide any information regarding *overall* immigration trends. Moreover, the passage does not mention a decline in overall immigration.
- Eliminate choice (C) because it is **irrelevant**. Although the graph and passage indicate that India's immigration numbers have been increasing, there is nothing in the graph or passage that supports the claim that India will surpass China in terms of immigration to the U.S.
- Eliminate choice (D) because it is only **partially supported**. The graph shows a spike in Indian immigration, but the text makes no mention of it, so it does not fully address the question.

4. Confirm Your Choice

Before selecting a response, make sure there is *nothing* about it that can be disproven by the passage:
- Choice (B) is supported by *both* the passage and the graph. Paragraph 1 states that immigration from China and India increased over the last decade, and this information is supported by the graph, which shows a steady increase in Indian and Chinese immigrants since 2000.

SAT READING
Key Strategies - Science

Refer to the passage below to answer questions 13 – 17.

This passage is adapted from Mary Bates, "Oldest Fossil Evidence of Agriculture," originally published June 24, 2016.

An international team of researchers has discovered the oldest fossil evidence of agriculture, and it dates back millions of years before humans started farming. The team found
[5] evidence of fungus gardens within fossilized termite nests in 25-million-year-old sediments in Africa's Great Rift Valley.

Some termite species have developed a highly specialized, symbiotic relationship with fungi,
[10] which they cultivate in "gardens" within their subterranean nests or chambers. The termites consume woody material and excrete rounded pellets composed of concentrated, undigested plant fragments and fungal spores. The fungus
[15] germinates and colonizes the plant material, helping to convert it into a more easily digestible and nutritious food source.

Scientists had previously used DNA from modern termites to estimate that fungus-farming
[20] in termites began 25-30 million years ago. However, definitive fossil records of fungus-farming were elusive.

Now, Eric Roberts of James Cook University in Australia and colleagues have confirmed that
[25] date with the discovery of fossilized termite nests containing fungus gardens in southwestern Tanzania.

"This fossil discovery is special because it provides concrete evidence that we not only
[30] had termites in Africa 25 million years ago, but they had already formed this important symbiotic relationship with fungi," says Roberts. "This also supports the hypothesis that fungus-farming termites originated in central Africa and
[35] then radiated into other parts of Africa before dispersing into Asia."

Roberts says the fossilized termite nests and fungus gardens are remarkably similar to many modern termite nests and gardens: "They
[40] are hollow chambers that were constructed underground and are about the size of a baseball or softball," he says. "Within these hollow chambers are the fungus gardens. These are formed from termite excretions of partially
[45] digested wood (inoculated with fungal spores), which the termites mold into spheres and then pack together into a complex architectural construction that can look a bit like a mass of spaghetti noodles."

[50] The development of this symbiotic relationship increased the range of possible habitats for both the termites and their domesticated fungi. Although termite fungus-farming may have been born in the African
[55] rainforest, it allowed termites to disperse to less hospitable dry savannas and open landscapes, and eventually to migrate out of Africa and into Asia.

The origin of termite fungus-farming
[60] likely had a major effect on how nutrients were concentrated across the landscape. Understanding the development of this symbiotic relationship has implications for understanding the carbon cycle in deep time in this region.

[65] "The evolution of this symbiotic relationship had major implications for ecology and biogeography," says Roberts. "It likely links into really interesting patterns of landscape development in Africa associated with the
[70] initiation of the Rift Valleys."

"Oldest Fossil Evidence of Agriculture" is licensed under CC BY 4.0. For more information, see page 511.

Solving Main Purpose Questions

13

The primary purpose of the passage is to

(A) compare the agricultural methods of insects to those of humans.
(B) trace the spread of a species from Africa to Asia.
(C) describe a fossil discovery and its scientific implications.
(D) explain how fungi cultivation has shaped termite evolution.

1. Determine the Question Type ← This question asks you to find the **primary purpose** of the passage, so you must recognize why the author wrote the passage. Generally, an author will not explicitly state his or her purpose for writing, so it must be inferred from the passage.

2. Refer to the Passage ← As is the case in many passages, the first and last paragraphs of this passage explain or imply the author's purpose. Paragraph 1 focuses on researchers discovering "the oldest fossil evidence of agriculture," and the last paragraph discusses the "implications" of this discovery.

3. Come up with Your Own Answer ← Before looking at the answer choices, quickly come up with an answer to the question using your own words. Based on the first and last paragraphs, you can infer that the passage's purpose is to discuss "the oldest fossil evidence of agriculture" and its "implications."

4. Use the Process of Elimination ← Once you have come up with your own answer, eliminate any choices that contradict your answer or stray from the passage's main focus:
- Eliminate choice (A) because it **does not fit the context** of the question. Paragraph 1 briefly compares insect and human agriculture by claiming that termites had agriculture before humans, but this is not the *primary purpose* of the passage.
- Eliminate choice (B) because it **does not fit the context** of the question. The passage does discuss termites' "migration out of Africa and into Asia," but this discussion is presented in light of termite agriculture, and is not the passage's main purpose.
- Eliminate choice (D) because it is **partially supported** by the text. The passage discusses how fungi cultivation allowed termites to expand their geographic range, but we cannot infer that this "shaped termite evolution," so (D) is not fully supported by the information in the text.

5. Confirm Your Choice ← Before selecting a response, make sure there is *nothing* about it that can be disproven by the passage:
- The text fully supports the correct choice—(C). The majority of the passage describes the appearance and impact of "the oldest fossil evidence of agriculture" (a *fossil discovery*), and the conclusion discusses this agriculture's "implications for ecology and biogeography" (its *scientific implications*).

Solving Summary Questions

14

Which choice best summarizes paragraph 7 (lines 50 – 58)?
(A) Fungal "gardens" allowed termites to inhabit a greater variety of environments.
(B) Termites facilitated the spread of fungi from the forests of Africa to Asia.
(C) Termites cannot survive in dry, open environments without creating fungal "gardens."
(D) Termites and their domesticated fungi left Africa for the preferable climates of Asia.

1. Determine the Question Type

All the information necessary to answer **summary questions** is located in the passage. Although you will not have to make any major inferences or assumptions to answer summary questions, keep in mind that the correct answer likely will not use exact wording from the passage, so you will need to be able to paraphrase passage information.

2. Read the Answer Choices & Review the Passage

Refer to paragraph 7 and take note of its organization: the first sentence states the topic, and the rest of the paragraph provides a specific example of the topic. Then determine which answer choices provide partial or complete summaries of the paragraph:
- Choice (A) effectively paraphrases the topic of the paragraph and does not include any superfluous details.
- Choices (B) and (D) discuss termites' spread from Africa to Asia, which is discussed at the end of paragraph 7.
- Choice (C) summarizes the claim that fungus-farming "allowed termites to disperse to less hospitable dry savannas and open landscapes."

3. Use the Process of Elimination

Once you have reviewed the relevant portion(s) of the passage, eliminate any choices that contradict the passage or fail to address the question:
- Eliminate choice (B) because it is only **partially supported**. Although the text states that fungus-farming helped termites "migrate out of Africa and into Asia," the passage focuses on how fungus farming helped termites, not fungi, spread throughout Africa and Asia.
- Eliminate choice (C) because it **does not fit the context** of the question. While (C) accurately paraphrases a portion of paragraph 7, this information is not the main topic of the paragraph.
- Eliminate choice (D) because it **lacks support**. While paragraph 7 states that fungus-farming termites migrated from Africa to Asia, it neither states nor implies that Asia's climates are preferable.

4. Confirm Your Choice

Before selecting a response, make sure there is *nothing* about it that can be disproven by the passage:
- Because choice (A) paraphrases the paragraph's topic sentence, it provides the most thorough summary of the paragraph as a whole.

Solving Inference Questions

15

The passage suggests that termite agriculture
(A) is suspected of occurring, but has not yet been confirmed, in Asia.
(B) provides large quantities of food for termites at the expense of nutrition.
(C) likely inspired some human agricultural practices.
(D) has remained relatively unchanged for at least 25 million years.

1. Determine the Question Type

This question asks what "the passage **suggests**" about termite fungus-farming, so the correct answer will not be directly stated in the passage. Because the question does not provide line numbers for reference, you must consider the entire passage when answering.

2. Read the Answer Choices & Review the Passage

As you review the passage, look over the answer choices and try to determine which portion(s) of the text make any reference to the answer choices:
- Lines 14 – 17 relate to choice (B) because they provide information about the relationship between fungus-farming and termite nutrition.
- Paragraphs 1 and 5 explain that termites were fungus-farming at least 25 million years ago, and paragraph 6 states that termite "fungus gardens are remarkably similar to many modern termite…gardens," which supports choice (D).

3. Use the Process of Elimination

Once you have reviewed the relevant portion(s) of the passage, eliminate any choices that contradict the passage or fail to address the question:
- Eliminate choice (A) because it **lacks support.** The passage implies that termite fungus-gardens *have* been found in Asia, which suggests that (A) is untrue.
- Eliminate choice (B) because it **lacks support.** Paragraph 2 states that the fungi create an "easily digestible and nutritious food source," which disproves choice (B).
- Eliminate choice (C) because it **lacks support.** Paragraph 1 states that termite agriculture preceded human agriculture by millions of years, but this alone does not imply that termite agriculture influenced or inspired human practices.

4. Confirm Your Choice

Before selecting a response, make sure there is *nothing* about it that can be disproven by the passage:
- Choice (D) can be proven correct by synthesizing information from paragraphs 1, 5, and 6. Paragraphs 1 and 5 prove that termites have had fungus-based agriculture for at least 25 million years (lines 1 – 7 & 28 – 36), and paragraph 6 states that these ancient gardens are "remarkably similar to many modern termite…gardens" (lines 37 – 39).

Solving Citation Questions

16

Which choice provides the best evidence for the answer to the previous question?

(A) Lines 1 – 4 ("An international…farming")
(B) Lines 23 – 27 ("Eric Roberts…Tanzania")
(C) Lines 37 – 39 ("Roberts says…gardens")
(D) Lines 55 – 58 ("it allowed…Asia")

1. Determine the Question Type

This is a typical example of a **citation** question: it asks you to find textual evidence that supports the answer to the previous question. Citation questions are easy to identify because the answer choices will always be passage excerpts.

2. Contextualize the Answer Choices

When you refer to the line numbers provided in each answer choice, reread some of the information that comes before and after the referenced line numbers; doing so will help give each answer choice a bit of context. Also glance back at the previous question.

3. Use the Process of Elimination

Once you have reviewed the relevant portion(s) of the passage, eliminate any choices that do not relate to the correct answer to the previous question, which was number 3's choice (D).
- Eliminate choices (A), (B), and (D) because they **do not fit the context** of the question. None of these choices support the answer to the previous question because they state neither how long termites have had agriculture nor how little termite agriculture has changed over time.

4. Confirm Your Choice

Before selecting a response, make sure there is *nothing* about it that can be disproven by the passage:
- Although choice (C) does not state that termite agriculture has persisted for at least 25 million years, it provides the most substantial evidence to support the answer to the previous question because it clarifies that the 25-million-year-old "fossilized termite…fungus gardens are remarkably similar to many modern termite…gardens," meaning that—as the previous question stated—termite agriculture "has remained relatively unchanged."

Solving Words-in-Context Questions

17

As used in line 61, "concentrated" most nearly means

(A) focused.
(B) distributed.
(C) condensed.
(D) congregated.

1. Determine the Question Type ← This is a typical example of a **words-in-context** question: it asks you to find a synonym for a word from the passage. Words-in-context questions generally require you to select one of multiple meanings that are possible for the word.

2. Contextualize the Answer Choices ← Review the referenced line and its context, and use contextual clues to determine the word's meaning. In this case, you can determine that "concentrated" describes how food for termites occurred in specific spots over a wide region.

3. Use the Process of Elimination ← Once you have reviewed the relevant portion of the passage, eliminate any choices that do not reasonably describe *how* termite food sources were distributed:
- Eliminate choices (A), (C), and (D) because they **do not fit the context** of the passage. Although these choices are accurate definitions for "concentrated," they do not effectively describe how "nutrients" might be "concentrated across" an area. "Focused" implies an intentional action rather than a natural process. "Condensed" describes something that has been compressed or distilled. "Congregated" generally describes subjects assembling in a crowd like sheep flocking together; it does not make sense to claim that nutrients assemble themselves.

4. Confirm Your Choice ← Before selecting a response, make sure there is *nothing* about it that can be disproven by the passage:
- Based on the context in which the word appears, choice (B), "distributed," is correct because the sentence implies that nutrients were located throughout, or *distributed* across, an area. This particular words-in-context question highlights the fact that sometimes, the correct answer is the one whose meaning is furthest from the conventional meaning of the word in question: "to concentrate" usually means to gather or condense, but in this case it refers to resources being concentrated into countless termite mounds over a large area.

SAT READING
Key Strategies - Social Science Pair

Refer to the passage below to answer questions 18 – 22.

Passage 1 is adapted from a speech by English abolitionist William Wilberforce, which was delivered to the British Parliament on 12 May, 1789. Here, Wilberforce describes the conditions of African slaves as they are transported to the Americas and to Europe, as reported to him by an advocate of the slave trade. Passage 2 is adapted from ushistory.org, "The Middle Passage," accessed on September 16, 2016.

Passage 1

line
    One would think it had been determined to heap upon them all the varieties of bodily pain, for the purpose of blunting the feelings of the mind; and yet, in this very point (to show the
5 power of human prejudice) the situation of the slaves has been described by Mr. Norris, one of the Liverpool delegates, in a manner which, I am sure will convince the House how interest* can draw a film across the eyes, so thick, that
10 total blindness could do no more; and how it is our duty therefore to trust not to the reasonings of interested men, or to their way of coloring a transaction. "Their apartments," says Mr. Norris, "are fitted up as much for their
15 advantage as circumstances will admit. The right ankle of one, indeed is connected with the left ankle of another by a small iron fetter, and if they are turbulent, by another on their wrists. They have several meals a day; some of their
20 own country provisions, with the best sauces of African cookery; and by way of variety, another meal of pulse*, and so on, according to European taste. After breakfast they have water to wash themselves, while their apartments
25 are perfumed with frankincense and lime-juice. Before dinner, they are amused after the manner of their country. The song and dance are promoted," and, as if the whole was really a scene of pleasure and dissipation it is added,
30 that games of chance are furnished. "The men play and sing, while the women and girls make fanciful ornaments with beads, which they are plentifully supplied with." Such is the sort of strain in which the Liverpool delegates, and
35 particularly Mr. Norris, gave evidence before the privy council.

Passage 2

    Two by two the men and women were forced beneath deck into the bowels of the slave ship.
    The "packing" was done as efficiently as
40 possible. The captives lay down on unfinished planking with virtually no room to move or breathe. Elbows and wrists will be scraped to the bone by the motion of the rough seas.
    Some will die of disease, some of starvation,
45 and some simply of despair. This was the fate of millions of West Africans across three and a half centuries of the slave trade on the voyage known as the "Middle Passage."
    Two philosophies dominated the loading
50 of a slave ship. "Loose packing" provided for fewer slaves per ship in the hopes that a greater percentage of the cargo would arrive alive. With "tight packing," captains believed that transporting more slaves, despite higher
55 casualties, would yield a greater profit at the trading block.
    Doctors would inspect the slaves before purchase from the African trader to determine which individuals would most likely survive
60 the voyage. In return, the traders would receive guns, gunpowder, rum or other spirits, textiles or trinkets.
    The "Middle Passage," which brought the slaves from West Africa to the West Indies,
65 might take three weeks. Unfavorable weather conditions could make the trip much longer.
    Slaves were fed twice daily and some captains made vain attempts to clean the hold at this time. Air holes were cut into the deck to
70 allow the slaves breathing air, but these were closed in stormy conditions. The bodies of the dead were simply thrust overboard. And yes, there were uprisings.
    Upon reaching the West Indies, the slaves
75 were fed and cleaned in the hopes of bringing a high price on the block. Those that could not be sold were left for dead. The slaves were then transported to their final destination. It was in this unspeakable manner that between ten and
80 twenty million Africans were introduced to the New World.

* interest: in this case, meaning a financial investment

* pulse: dried, edible seeds that grow in a pod, such as lentils, chickpeas, and dried peas

Solving Attitude & Tone Questions

18

Wilberforce's attitude towards Mr. Norris in lines 4 – 13 is best described as one of

(A) appreciation.
(B) disinterest.
(C) censure.
(D) confusion.

1. Determine the Question Type

Attitude and tone questions ask you to identify *how* the narrator of or a character in a passage feels about something. Generally, these questions are easily identifiable because they use the word "attitude" or "tone" in the question.

2. Read the Answer Choices & Review the Passage

Review the lines referenced in the question, and look for key words or phrases that suggest how Wilberforce feels about Mr. Norris. In lines 11 – 12, Wilberforce claims that one should "trust not to the reasonings of interested men," and earlier, in lines 4 – 10, he implies that Mr. Norris has "interest" in slavery. Thus, based on the lines provided, Wilberforce suggests that Mr. Norris stands to profit from the slave trade and cannot be trusted in this matter.

3. Use the Process of Elimination

Once you have reviewed the relevant portion(s) of the passage, eliminate any choices that do not coincide with the conclusions from step 2:
- Eliminate choices (A), (B), and (D) because they **do not fit the context** of the passage. If, as determined in step 2, Wilberforce does not find Mr. Norris trustworthy, you can infer that Wilberforce has overall negative feelings towards Mr. Norris. Choice (A), "appreciation," is a positive attitude, so it can be eliminated. Choice (B), "disinterest," is neither negative nor positive, so it can be eliminated. Choice (D), "confusion," is possibly negative, but is not related to a lack of trust, so it can be eliminated.

4. Confirm Your Choice

Before selecting a response, make sure there is *nothing* about it that can be disproven by the passage:
- Even if you were not familiar with the word "censure," you could deduce that choice (C) is the correct choice using the process of elimination, as none of the other choices match the tone of the passage or the attitude of the speaker. Moreover, "censure" is an expression of disapproval or criticism, which matches the conclusions of step 2.

Solving Words-in-Context Questions

19

As used in line 13, "coloring" most nearly means

(A) painting.
(B) enlivening.
(C) tinting.
(D) distorting.

1. Determine the Question Type ← This is a typical example of a **words-in-context** question: it asks you to find a synonym for a word from the passage. Words-in-context questions generally require you to select one of multiple meanings that are possible for the word.

2. Contextualize the Answer Choices ← Review the referenced line and its context and use contextual clues to determine the word's meaning. In this case, you can determine that "coloring" describes the ways in which people with a financial interest in the business (i.e. investors) embellished details regarding the slave trade.

3. Use the Process of Elimination ← Once you have reviewed the relevant portion of the passage, eliminate any choices that do not describe embellishing speech:
- Eliminate choices (A), (B), and (C) because they do not fit the context of the passage. Although these choices are accurate definitions for "coloring," they do not effectively describe the methods used by proponents of the slave trade to conceal the harsh realities of their business model.

4. Confirm Your Choice ← Before selecting a response, make sure there is *nothing* about it that can be disproven by the passage:
- Based on the context in which the word appears, choice (D), "distorting," is the best choice because it implies that those who had a stake in the slave trade sought to cover up the truth about their business.

Solving Text Synthesis Questions 1

20

The primary purpose of both passages is to
(A) condemn those who attempted to justify or ignore the institution of slavery.
(B) describe the living conditions of enslaved Africans as they crossed the "Middle Passage."
(C) investigate the social and economic factors that allowed slavery to thrive.
(D) describe a journey across the "Middle Passage" from the perspective of a slave.

1. Determine the Question Type ← Any question that asks you to analyze the contents of both passages in a passage pair is a **textual analysis** question. Although the way these questions are worded varies considerably, most ask you to analyze the purpose of or relationship between the passages, or the attitudes of the authors.

2. Refer to the Passage ← To determine the "primary purpose" of both passages, review Passages 1 and 2 and look for the main topic of each. Here, Passage 1 mostly provides a romanticized description of the "Middle Passage," while Passage 2 provides a factual description of it.

3. Come up with Your Own Answer ← After reviewing the passage, answer the question using your own words. Keep your answer simple; first decide what the two passages have in common, and then determine, in your own words, each author's intention when writing. For instance, based on the information gathered in step 2, you can conclude that both passages primarily address the forced transport of Africans into slavery.

4. Use the Process of Elimination ← Once you have come up with your own answer, eliminate any choices that contradict the passage or fail to address the question:
- Eliminate choice (A) because it is only **partially supported**. Choice (A) does provide one of the implied purposes of Passage 1, as Wilberforce is criticizing the gross misrepresentation by slavery advocates such as Mr. Norris. However, (A) does not accurately describe Passage 2.
- Eliminate choice (C) because it **lacks support**. Lines 1 – 13 in Passage 1 discuss the social conditions under which slavery thrives, yet this is not the main purpose of Passage 1. And while Passage 2 briefly discusses the economics of slavery, this is not the main focus of the passage.
- Eliminate choice (D) because it is **irrelevant**. Neither passage provides a slave's perspective of the "Middle Passage", making this an unsupportable choice.

5. Confirm Your Choice ← Before selecting a response, make sure there is *nothing* about it that can be disproven by the passage:
- Choice (B) closely matches the self-produced answer from step 3. Passage 2 provides an unbiased description of the "Middle Passage," while Passage 1 provides a rosy description that the speaker ridicules. Yet both are focused on the living conditions of slaves during the "Middle Passage."

Solving Text Synthesis Questions 2

21

How would the author of Passage 2 likely respond to the description in lines 13 – 33 of Passage 1?
(A) With disbelief, because Mr. Norris' description denies the harsh reality of captured people's experiences.
(B) With criticism, because the conditions that Mr. Norris describes are economically unsupportable.
(C) With approval, because Mr. Norris' description is historically accurate.
(D) With interest, because such thorough descriptions of the journey across the "Middle Passage" are exceedingly rare.

1. Determine the Question Type	This question asks you to analyze the contents of two passages, so it is a **textual analysis** question. Although the way these questions are worded varies considerably, most ask you to analyze the relationship between the passages or the attitudes of the authors.
2. Refer to the Passage	Review the Passage 1 line numbers referenced in the question. If the reference is confusing or lacks context, read the surrounding lines. Next, determine if Passage 2 contains any similar or contrasting information. In this case, Passage 2 *contrasts* with lines 13 – 33 of Passage 1.
3. Come up with Your Own Answer	After reviewing the passage, decide whether the author of Passage 2 generally agrees or disagrees with the referenced text from Passage 1, then provide support. In this case, Passage 1's author would likely *disagree with or disregard the referenced text* because Passage 2 describes the journey across the "Middle Passage" as miserable and frequently fatal for captured people whereas Mr. Norris' account describes a pleasant journey.
4. Use the Process of Elimination	Once you have come up with your own answer, eliminate any choices that fail to address the question: • Eliminate choice (B) because it is only **partially supported**. Passage 2's author would likely criticize Mr. Norris' description, but not because the conditions that Mr. Norris describes are not "economically supportable". Rather, the author of Passage 2 would argue that Mr. Norris covers up the inhumane treatment of captives. • Eliminate choice (C) because it **lacks support**. In lines 5 – 13 Wilberforce says that Mr. Norris's investment in the business has given him "total blindness" to reality, and the author of Passage 2 would not likely approve of a dishonest account. • Eliminate choice (D) because it is **irrelevant**. There is no indication in either passage that descriptions such as Norris' are rare.
5. Confirm Your Choice	Before selecting a response, make sure there is *nothing* about it that can be disproven by the passage: • Because Mr. Norris' description of the journey known as the "Middle Passage" conflicts with the description in Passage 2, we can safely assume that the author of Passage 2 would react with *disbelief* to Mr. Norris' description, making choice (A) correct.

Solving Citation Questions

22

Which choice provides the best evidence for the answer to the previous question?

(A) Lines 44 – 48 ("Some will...Passage'")
(B) Lines 50 – 53 ("'Loose...alive")
(C) Lines 63 – 66 ("The 'Middle...longer")
(D) Lines 69 – 71 ("Air holes...conditions")

1. Determine the Question Type ← This is a typical example of a **citation** question: it asks you to find textual evidence that supports the answer to the previous question. Citation questions are easily identifiable because the answer choices will always be passage excerpts.

2. Contextualize the Answer Choices ← When you refer to the line number provided in each answer choice, read some of the information that comes before and after the referenced line numbers for a bit of context. Also glance back at the previous question.

3. Use the Process of Elimination ← Once you have reviewed the relevant portion(s) of the passage, eliminate any choices that do not relate to the correct answer to the previous question, which was number 4's choice (A):
- Eliminate choices (B), (C), and (D) because they **do not fit the context** of the passage. None of these choices provides a contradiction to Mr. Norris' description in lines 13 – 34; they do not provide evidence supporting the claim that Passage 2's author would react with disbelief to Mr. Norris' description.

4. Confirm Your Choice ← Before selecting a response, make sure there is *nothing* about it that can be disproven by the passage:
- The correct choice must provide evidence that Mr. Norris' description in lines 13 – 34 contradicts reality. Because choice (A) explains that many captured people died from mistreatment during the "Middle Passage," it refutes Mr. Norris' description and proves that the author of Passage 2 would react with disbelief to it.

END OF SECTION 1

SAT WRITING & LANGUAGE

 Key Strategies

> **DIRECTIONS**
>
> Each of the following passages is accompanied by approximately 11 questions. Some questions will require you to revise the passages in order to improve coherence and clarity. Other questions will require you to correct grammatical errors. Passages may be accompanied by graphs, charts, or tables that you must consider when making revisions. For most questions, you may select the "NO CHANGE" option if you believe that portion of the passage is clear, concise, and grammatically correct as is.
>
> Within the passages, highlighted numbers followed by underlined text indicate which part of the text corresponds with each question. Bracketed numbers such as [1] indicate sentence number. These bracketed numbers are only relevant to problems that require you to add or rearrange sentences in a paragraph.

SAT WRITING & LANGUAGE
Key Strategies - Careers Passage

Refer to the passage below to answer questions 1 – 5.

-- 1 --

Music can often help people get work done, according to research. A number of studies have looked at the effects of music on workers. One clear finding is that when a job is simple and repetitive, as in assembly-line work [1] music has a marked effect on productivity. In studies, people who listened to music while doing mundane work were happier and more productive [2] <u>then those who did not</u>. This was especially true if the music was in a major key.

-- 2 --

Music on headphones can also help to block out *external* noise. [3] <u>Not every sound may be blocked by it,</u> but it should dull any nearby conversations. Thus, music can help people focus on their work in a relatively distraction-free environment.

-- 3 --

Moreover, researchers suggest listening to familiar music when concentrating on a task. Doing so ensures that the brain does not focus on the novelty of unfamiliar lyrics or rhythms in the music.

-- 4 --

When it comes to cognitively taxing work, music can sometimes [4] <u>get more</u> concentration. For example, when workers use headphones, they are better able to manage *internal* emotional distractions: they can choose soothing rhythms when they are worried, upbeat music when they are tired, and so on.

Question [5] asks about the passage as a whole.

Solving Passage Development Questions

Music can often help people get work done, according to research. A number of studies have looked at the effects of music on workers. One clear finding is that when a job is simple and repetitive, as in assembly-line work  music has a marked effect on productivity. In studies, people who listened to music while doing mundane work were happier and more productive  then those who did not. This was especially true if the music was in a major key.

01

At this point, the writer wants to add a second example of a simple, repetitive job. Which choice would be most effective for this purpose?

(A) or data entry,
(B) or copyediting,
(C) or car sales,
(D) or party planning,

1. Determine the Question Type

This question is asking you to add an example to the passage, so it is a **passage development question**. Generally, development questions will have you add relevant details and/or remove irrelevant information from a passage.

2. Contextualize the Answer Choices

Always pay close attention to any instructions for SAT writing & language questions. Here, we are being instructed to select a "simple, repetitive job," and the passage provides "assembly-line work" as an example.

3. Use the Process of Elimination

Eliminate any answer choice that is not a "simple, repetitive job":
- Eliminate choice (B); copyediting may be repetitive (reading, marking text), but it is not considered "simple" since one must have a thorough knowledge of grammar and style.
- Eliminate choices (C) and (D) because car sales and party planning are associated with neither simplicity nor repetition.

4. Confirm Your Choice

Choice (A) is correct; "data entry" can be considered a "simple, repetitive job" because it involves inputting large amounts of information from one source to another. For example, someone working in data entry might input lab test results into a computer database.

Solving Logical Comparison Questions

Music can often help people get work done, according to research. A number of studies have looked at the effects of music on workers. One clear finding is that when a job is simple and repetitive, as in assembly-line work  music has a marked effect on productivity. In studies, people who listened to music while doing mundane work were happier and more productive **2** <u>then those who did not</u>. This was especially true if the music was in a major key.

02

(A) NO CHANGE
(B) then without music.
(C) than people who did not.
(D) than not listening to music.

1. Determine the Question Type

The sentence containing the underlined portion compares two quantities (*people who listened to music while doing mundane work* and the information in the underlined portion). The word "than" confirms that this is a **logical comparison question**. Note that the answer choices containing "then" are meant to mislead: "then" is NOT used in comparisons; it is used to indicate sequence.

2. Contextualize the Answer Choices

To solve logical comparison questions, determine what two quantities are being compared, and then ensure that they can reasonably be compared. Here, a group of "people who listened to music while doing mundane work" is being compared to a group of people who did not listen to music while doing the same work. Thus, the correct choice will express this idea as concisely as possible.

3. Use the Process of Elimination

Eliminate any answer choice that does not indicate that "people who listened to music" is being compared to people who did not listen to music:
- Eliminate choices (A) and (B) because "then" cannot be used to indicate a comparison.
- Eliminate choice (D) because the comparison should be between two groups of people, and (D) implies that "people who listened to music" is being compared to the act of "not listening to music." A group of people cannot logically be compared to an action.

4. Confirm Your Choice

Choice (C) is correct because it uses "than" to indicate a comparison, and it effectively compares "people who listened to music" to "people who did not" listen to music.

Solving Pronoun/Referent Questions

Music on headphones can also help to block out *external* noise. [3] Not every sound may be blocked by it, but it should dull any nearby conversations. Thus, music can help people focus on their work in a relatively distraction-free environment.

(A) NO CHANGE
(B) The music may not block every sound,
(C) Not every sound will get blocked,
(D) Not all noise,

1. Determine the Question Type ← By quickly reviewing the passage and the answer choices, we can see that the underlined portion must identify the subject of the sentence. Because the subject is a referent of "it," this question mainly tests **pronouns and referents**.

2. Contextualize the Answer Choices ← Use the context of the paragraph to determine what the pronoun "it" refers to. Once we know this, we will know what noun must be in the underlined portion. Looking at the beginning of the paragraph, we can see that "Music…can also help to block out external noise." From this we can infer that "music" would also "dull any nearby conversations," so we can conclude that "it" refers to "music."

3. Use the Process of Elimination ← Eliminate any answer choice that does not mention "music" or a clear synonym of "music":
- Eliminate choices (A), (C) and (D) because none of them makes any reference to "music," so they do not provide a referent for the pronoun "it."

4. Confirm Your Choice ← **Choice (B)** makes "the music" the subject of the sentence, which maintains the focus of the paragraph and provides a logical referent for "it."

Solving Style & Tone Questions

When it comes to cognitively taxing work, music can sometimes [4] get more concentration. For example, when workers use headphones, they are better able to manage *internal* emotional distractions: they can choose soothing rhythms when they are worried, upbeat music when they are tired, and so on.

04

Which choice best maintains the tone established in the passage?
(A) NO CHANGE
(B) bump up
(C) improve
(D) fix

1. Determine the Question Type

Any question that asks you to add information that "maintains the style/tone of the passage" is a **style and tone question**.

2. Contextualize the Answer Choices

Note that we are being instructed to "maintain the tone established in the passage." The language of the passage is formal and academic. It cites research ("according to research"), avoids using the first or second person ("I" or "you"), and discusses the academic topic of productivity in the workplace. Thus, the correct choice will maintain this academic, formal tone.

3. Use the Process of Elimination

Eliminate any answer choice that **does not fit the context** of the passage or that fails to maintain the passage's formal, academic tone:
- Eliminate choice (A); "concentration" cannot be quantified, so one cannot "get more" of something that cannot be measured in the first place.
- Eliminate choice (B): "bump up" is informal, so it does not match the passage's tone.
- Eliminate choice (D): "concentration" can be neither "fixed" nor "broken," so "fix" does not fit the context of the sentence.

4. Confirm Your Choice

"Concentration" can become better or worse given various circumstances, so the verb "improve" can be used to describe "concentration." Since "improve" is not slang, it fits the academic tone of the passage, making **choice (C)** correct.

Solving Passage Organization Questions

-- 1 --

Music can often help people get work done, according to research. A number of studies have looked at the effects of music on workers. One clear finding is that when a job is simple and repetitive, as in assembly-line work music has a marked effect on productivity. In studies, people who listened to music while doing mundane work were happier and more productive  This was especially true if the music was in a major key.

-- 2 --

Music on headphones can also help to block out *external* noise. but it should dull any nearby conversations. Thus, music can help people focus on their work in a relatively distraction-free environment.

-- 3 --

Moreover, researchers suggest listening to familiar music when concentrating on a task. Doing so ensures that the brain does not focus on the novelty of unfamiliar lyrics or rhythms in the music.

-- 4 --

When it comes to cognitively taxing work, music can sometimes  concentration. For example, when workers use headphones, they are better able to manage *internal* emotional distractions: they can choose soothing rhythms when they are worried, upbeat music when they are tired, and so on.

Question asks about the passage as a whole.

05

To make the passage most logical, paragraph 4 should be placed

(A) where it is now.
(B) before paragraph 1.
(C) before paragraph 2.
(D) before paragraph 3.

1. Determine the Question Type

Any question that asks you to (re)place a sentence or paragraph is a **passage organization question**.

2. Contextualize the Answer Choices

Since this question asks you to find the correct placement for an entire paragraph, you must understand how paragraph 4 relates to the passage as a whole. Paragraph 4 discusses how music can mitigate "internal distractions." Paragraph 1 should stay where it is because it introduces the passage's topic: "Music can...help people get work done." Paragraph 2 discusses how music can "also...block out external noises." The word "also" is a clue; it tells us that the information in paragraph 2 should come after a similar discussion, which is not the case now. Placing paragraph 4 before paragraph 2 would create a clear flow of ideas: music can help block "internal distractions" (paragraph 4) and "external noise" (paragraph 2).

3. Use the Process of Elimination

Eliminate any answer choice that does not indicate that paragraph 4 should come before paragraph 2:
- Eliminate choices (A), (B), and (D) because they do not create a logical flow of ideas within the passage.

4. Confirm Your Choice

Choice (C) is correct; as mentioned in step 2, paragraph 4 must come before paragraph 2 because it introduces the topic of music blocking distractions in the workplace, which is continued in paragraph 2.

CHAPTER 4 - Writing & Language Key Strategies | 99

SAT WRITING & LANGUAGE
Key Strategies - Science Passage

Refer to the passage below to answer questions 6 – 10.

Contrary to popular belief, ears are good for more than getting pierced and holding earbuds in place. The vestibular system, [6] a location found in the inner ear, helps the body regulate balance and stabilize vision. The system is named for the Latin word *vestibulum*, which refers to entrance halls—chambers between entrances and interiors of buildings.

[7] We can see a system with three curved, fluid-filled tubes called "semicircular canals," which are joined at right angles. [8] When the head moves in a certain direction, gravity causes the fluid in the tubes to settle at the lowest point. Sensory hair cells that line each tube bend in the direction of the moving fluid, and stimulate nerves to signal the brain.

Each of the three circular tubes specialize in a different type of directional [9] information. Namely, these are up-and-down, side-to-side, or tilted. Signals from the vestibular system interact primarily with ocular structures to help control eye movement, and with various muscle groups that [10] allows us to stay upright and move around without falling.

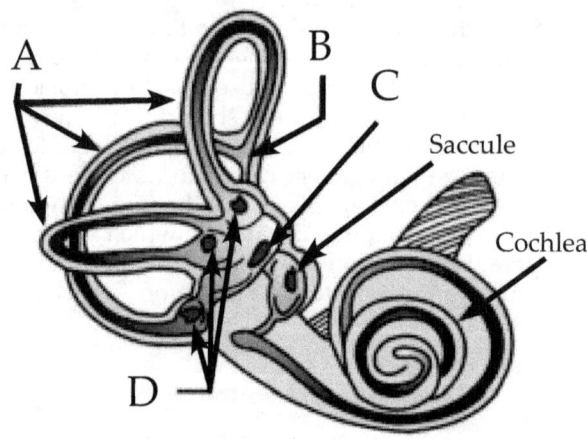

The Vestibular System

Solving Concision Questions

Contrary to popular belief, ears are good for more than getting pierced and holding earbuds in place. The vestibular system, [6] a location found in the inner ear, helps the body regulate balance and stabilize vision. The system is named for the Latin word *vestibulum*, which refers to entrance halls—chambers between entrances and interiors of buildings.

06

(A) NO CHANGE
(B) within
(C) located in
(D) found to be in

1. Determine the Question Type

The answer choices say the same thing in different ways, which generally indicates that you are dealing with a **concision question**.

2. Contextualize the Answer Choices

To solve concision questions, you must determine the clearest way to convey an idea. In this case, the underlined portion needs to show that the inner ear is the location of the vestibular system while still forming a grammatically correct and concise sentence.

3. Use the Process of Elimination

Eliminate any answer choice that does not indicate that the inner ear is the location of the vestibular system:
- Eliminate choices (A) and (D) because the phrases "a location found in" and "found to be in" are unnecessarily wordy; the term "located" conveys the same information using fewer words.
- Eliminate choice (B) because "within the inner ear" is a prepositional phrase, which should not be separated from the rest of the sentence with commas, as is the case in the sentence currently.

4. Confirm Your Choice

Choice (C) is correct because it uses the past participle "located" to introduce a participial phrase that describes the location of the inner ear. Because the participial phrase comes between the sentence's subject and verb, it makes sense to separate it from the rest of the sentence with commas, making "located in" concise and grammatically correct.

Solving Passage Development Questions

Contrary to popular belief, ears are good for more than getting pierced and holding earbuds in place. The vestibular system, [6] a location found in the inner ear, helps the body regulate balance and stabilize vision. The system is named for the Latin word *vestibulum*, which refers to entrance halls—chambers between entrances and interiors of buildings.

[7] We can see a system with three curved, fluid-filled tubes called "semicircular canals," which are joined at right angles. [8] When the head moves in a certain direction, gravity causes the fluid in the tubes to settle at the lowest point. Sensory hair cells that line each tube bend in the direction of the moving fluid, and stimulate nerves to signal the brain.

07

Which choice results in the most effective transition between the previous paragraph and the information that follows?

(A) NO CHANGE
(B) Deep within each ear sits
(C) The "chambers" are essentially
(D) The vestibular system, which helps stabilize the vision, has

---

1. Determine the Question Type

This question is asking you to add a transitional statement, so it is a **passage development question**. Generally, development questions will have you add relevant details and/or remove irrelevant information from a passage.

2. Contextualize the Answer Choices

Take note that we are being instructed to select the "most effective transition" between two paragraphs. Thus, we must decide how to transition from discussing the origins of the name "vestibular system" (end of paragraph 1) to a description of this same system (beginning of paragraph 2). The correct answer should form a link between these ideas.

3. Use the Process of Elimination

Eliminate any answer choice that does not link the etymology of "vestibular system" to a description of its structure:
- Eliminate choice (A) because it does nothing to link the topic of paragraph 1 to paragraph 2.
- Eliminate choices (B) and (D) because they are redundant; paragraph 1 already made both of these statements, so there is no need to repeat either claim in paragraph 2.

4. Confirm Your Choice

Choice (C) effectively links the origin of the term "vestibular system," which is from a Latin word describing a *chamber* at the entrance of a building, to a discussion of the "chambers" within the system.

---

102 | KALLIS' Key to the SAT

Solving Text-Graphic Synthesis Questions

[7] We can see a system with three curved, fluid-filled tubes called "semicircular canals," which are joined at right angles. [8] When the head moves in a certain direction, gravity causes the fluid in the tubes to settle at the lowest point. Sensory hair cells that line each tube bend in the direction of the moving fluid, and stimulate nerves to signal the brain.

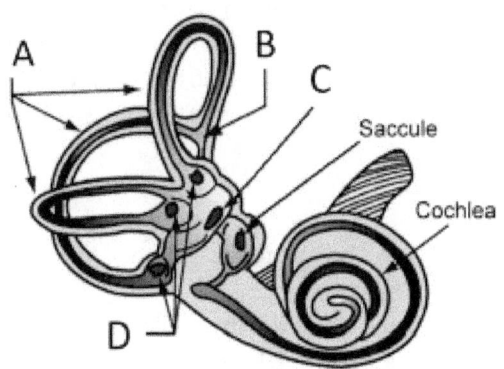

The Vestibular System

08

Based on the information in the passage, which of the following indicates the location of the semicircular canals in the graph on the right?

(A) A
(B) B
(C) C
(D) D

---

1. Determine the Question Type ← This question asks us to apply information from the passage to a graph, chart, or diagram, so it is a **text-graphic synthesis question**.

2. Contextualize the Answer Choices ← Take note that we are being asked to match a written description of "semicircular canals" to its corresponding location on a diagram. From the passage, we know that semicircular canals are "three curved…tubes," so the correct answer will point to three tubes on the diagram.

3. Use the Process of Elimination ← Eliminate any answer choice that does not point to three tubes that "are joined at right angles":
- Eliminate choice (B) because it points to one of the semicircular canals, indicating the convergence of two of the canals, not to the structure as a whole.
- Eliminate choice (C) because it does not point to any tubes or canals.
- Eliminate choice (D) because it indicates structures at the base of the semicircular canals, not the canals themselves.

4. Confirm Your Choice ← **Choice (A)** is correct because it consists of three arrows, each pointing to one of three "curved…tubes" that are "joined at right angles."

Solving Combining Sentences Questions

Each of the three circular tubes specialize in a different type of directional [9] information. Namely, these are up-and-down, side-to-side, or tilted. Signals from the vestibular system interact primarily with ocular structures to help control eye movement, and with various muscle groups that [10] allows us to stay upright and move around without falling.

09

Which choice most effectively combines the sentences at the underlined portion?

(A) information, so
(B) information; including
(C) information that is
(D) information:

1. Determine the Question Type ← Any question that asks you to "combine the sentences at the underlined portion" is a **combining sentences question**.

2. Contextualize the Answer Choices ← Combining sentences questions often require you to identify the most appropriate punctuation and/or conjunction for combining two ideas, so you must understand the grammar and content of the two sentences in question. Here, the second sentence provides an elaboration on the first sentence in the form of a list. Thus, we are looking to combine the sentences using a word or punctuation that indicates that the second sentence elaborates on information in the first sentence.

3. Use the Process of Elimination ← Eliminate any answer choice that does not indicate that the second sentence elaborates on information in the first sentence, and eliminate choices that are grammatically incorrect.
- Eliminate choice (A) because it forms a sentence fragment. The information that follows a comma plus a subordinate conjunction ("so" in this case) must be an independent clause, which is not the case here.
- Eliminate choice (B) because a semicolon separates two independent clauses, and the phrase "including…tilted" is not an independent clause, so a semicolon will not work here.
- Eliminate choice (C) because it forms a run-on sentence; the phrase "that is" would need to be preceded by a long pause, such as a dash or comma, for the sentence to flow smoothly.

4. Confirm Your Choice ← **Choice (D)** is the only grammatical choice, and a colon effectively indicates that what comes after it is an example or elaboration on previous information. Thus, (D) is both grammatically and stylistically appropriate, and is therefore the correct answer.

Solving Verb Questions

Each of the three circular tubes specialize in a different type of directional 9 information. Namely, these are up-and-down, side-to-side, or tilted. Signals from the vestibular system interact primarily with ocular structures to help control eye movement and with various muscle groups that 10 allows us to stay upright and move around without falling.

10

(A) NO CHANGE
(B) allowed
(C) is allowing
(D) allow

1. Determine the Question Type

The answer choices use different tenses and person for the verb "allow," so the question is testing either **verb tense, mood, and voice** and/or **subject-verb agreement**.

2. Contextualize the Answer Choices

The underlined portion is part of a relative clause that defines "muscle groups," so the underlined verb must agree in number (third-person plural) with the term it describes ("muscle groups"). The other verb with a tense in the sentence, "interact," is present-tense because it describes a general process. Nothing in the sentence indicates a change in tense, so the underlined verb should also be in the present tense.

3. Use the Process of Elimination

Eliminate any answer choice that is not a third-person plural, simple present-tense verb:
- Eliminate choice (A) because it requires a singular subject.
- Eliminate choice (B) because it is in the past tense, and nothing in the sentence indicates the need to change to a past tense in the sentence.
- Eliminate choice (C) because it uses the present-progressive aspect ("is + present participle"), and nothing in the sentence indicates the need to change to the present-progressive.

4. Confirm Your Choice

Because **choice (D)**, "allow," is the only available third-person plural, simple present-tense choice, it is the correct answer.

If you don't have time to break a verb question down on such a technical level, at least plug each answer choice into the sentence, rereading the sentence for each answer choice. Often, your ear will tell you which choice "sounds" most natural.

SAT WRITING & LANGUAGE
Key Strategies - Social Science Passage

Refer to the passage below to answer questions 11–15.

England's Industrial Revolution nearly stalled half a century before it began. Factories required machinery (a [11] blueprint of industrial productivity), and machinery had to be forged from iron. However, by the end of the 1600s, iron smelters in England were running out of fuel. England itself lacked enough forests and lumber to supply smelters with the charcoal they needed, and charcoal was too costly to import in large quantities.

As the 18th century dawned, an Englishman named Abraham Darby was experimenting. [12] He knew that malted grains were roasted using coke, a fuel made from coal. He decided to borrow the idea. He set up a smelting facility next to a river in a coal-mining area, and built powerful coke furnaces. Darby's business was the first [13] to be producing high-quality iron using inexpensive fuel. Without such iron, the Industrial Revolution would have been stymied.

[1] Years later, as industrialization was gaining momentum, Darby's grandson, Abraham Darby III, took over the company. [2] Darby III hired a designer [14] and, in 1779 constructed a picturesque cast-iron bridge over the River Severn. [3] The Iron Bridge still stands in Shropshire, England, where it is part of a UNESCO World Heritage Site as well as a popular tourist destination. [4] It was the first iron bridge in the world. [5] Visitors were astounded at its thinness, as bridges had always been made of thick stone or wood. [15]

---★---

Solving Precise Diction Questions

England's Industrial Revolution nearly stalled half a century before it began. Factories required machinery (a  blueprint of industrial productivity), and machinery had to be forged from iron. However, by the end of the 1600s, iron smelters in England were running out of fuel. England itself lacked enough forests and lumber to supply smelters with the charcoal they needed, and charcoal was too costly to import in large quantities.

(A) NO CHANGE
(B) restriction of
(C) prerequisite for
(D) perquisite for

1. Determine the Question Type — The answer choices consist of words with similar meanings. This indicates that we are dealing with a **precise diction question**, and we must determine which word best fits the context of the sentence in which its used.

2. Contextualize the Answer Choices — Review the entire sentence that contains the underlined portion. Here, the underlined term is describing how "machinery" relates to "industrial productivity." Machinery is a major *requirement for* industrial productivity. Thus, the correct term will mean "a requirement for."

3. Use the Process of Elimination — Eliminate any answer choice that does not mean "a requirement for":
- Eliminate choices (A) because a "blueprint" is a design or a technical drawing, which does not have the same meaning as "a requirement for."
- Eliminate choice (B) because a "restriction" is a limit or a constraint, not a requirement.
- Eliminate choice (D) because a "perquisite" is a benefit or a bonus, not a requirement.

4. Confirm Your Choice — **Choice (C)** is correct because a prerequisite is a condition that must be met for something else to happen—a *requirement*, in other words.

Solving Passage Development Questions

As the 18th century dawned, an Englishman named Abraham Darby was experimenting. **12** He knew that malted grains were roasted using coke, a fuel made from coal. He decided to borrow the idea. He set up a smelting facility next to a river in a coal-mining area, and built powerful coke furnaces. Darby's business was the first **13** to be producing high-quality iron using inexpensive fuel. Without such iron, the Industrial Revolution would have been stymied.

12

At this point, the writer is considering adding the following information.
   Darby had been an apprentice at a malt mill.
Should the writer make this addition here?

(A) Yes, because it provides a specific example of Darby's work experience.
(B) Yes, because it explains how Darby gained crucial knowledge.
(C) No, because it interrupts the flow of the paragraph with irrelevant information.
(D) No, because it raises the topic of malt milling which is not explained.

 **1. Determine the Question Type** — This question is asking you whether to keep or delete a portion of the passage, so it is a **passage development question**. Generally, development questions will have you add relevant details and/or remove irrelevant information from a passage.

2. Contextualize the Answer Choices — When deciding whether to add information to a passage, first determine whether the information is relevant to the paragraph's main topic. Here, the paragraph discusses how Darby contributed to the onset of the Industrial Revolution by using coke for smelting, an idea he took from the process for malting grains. The added information clarifies how Darby could have learned that "malting grains were roasted using coke," so it is relevant to the passage.

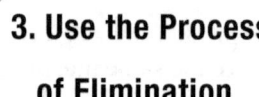 **3. Use the Process of Elimination** — Eliminate any answer choices that are irrelevant or illogical based on the conclusions from step 2:
- Eliminate choice (C) because understanding how Darby learned to use coke as a source of fuel is relevant to the paragraph.
- Eliminate choice (D) because the relationship between malt milling and the Industrial Revolution (the passage's main topic) is explained in the paragraph.

 **4. Confirm Your Choice** — Both (A) and (B) are accurate, but choice (A) implies that the main idea is Darby's work experience. **Choice (B)** is correct because it more clearly states the connection between the added sentence and the topic of the paragraph, that Darby's work experience led to an innovation that was "crucial" to the onset of the Industrial Revolution.

Solving Conventional Expression Questions

As the 18th century dawned, an Englishman named Abraham Darby was experimenting. [12] He knew that malted grains were roasted using coke, a fuel made from coal. He decided to borrow the idea. He set up a smelting facility next to a river in a coal-mining area, and built powerful coke furnaces. Darby's business was the first [13] to be producing high-quality iron using inexpensive fuel. Without such iron, the Industrial Revolution would have been stymied.

13

(A) NO CHANGE
(B) when producing
(C) by producing
(D) to produce

1. Determine the Question Type ← The answer choices consist of variations of a preposition followed by the term "produce." Many questions that ask us to choose the correct phrase from a group of similar phrases is a **conventional expression question**. To answer these, you must be familiar with a variety of phrasal verbs and idioms.

2. Contextualize the Answer Choices ← The correct answer here will be determined by what precedes the underlined portion. In this case, the phrase "was the first" comes right before the underlined portion, which gives us a huge clue. The structure "was the first, second, etc." is generally followed by an infinitive form of the verb ("To + base verb"). Here, "to produce" is the only infinitive choice.

3. Use the Process of Elimination ← Eliminate any answer choices that do not fit the context of the sentence:
- Eliminate choices (A), (B), and (C) because they do not use the conventional infinitive verb after the phrase "was the first, second, etc."

4. Confirm Your Choice ← Choice (D), "to produce," helps convey the information in the sentence clearly and concisely, and it makes sense to say that "Darby's business was the first to produce high-quality iron...".

Solving Phrase/Punctuation Questions

[1] Years later, as industrialization was gaining momentum, Darby's grandson, Abraham Darby III, took over the company. [2] Darby III hired a designer **14** and, in 1779 constructed a picturesque cast-iron bridge over the River Severn. [3] The Iron Bridge still stands in Shropshire, England, where it is part of a UNESCO World Heritage Site as well as a popular tourist destination. [4] It was the first iron bridge in the world. [5] Visitors were astounded at its thinness, as bridges had always been made of thick stone or wood. **15**

(A) NO CHANGE
(B) and—in 1779—
(C) and in 1779
(D) and; in 1779

1. Determine the Question Type — The answer choices consist of differently punctuated versions of the prepositional phrase "in 1779." This is either a **prepositional phrase question**, a **within-sentence punctuation question**, or both.

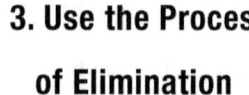 — We can determine what kind of punctuation is needed here if we quickly break down the sentence containing the underlined portion. The subject of the sentence is "Darby," and in the sentence he "hired" and "constructed"—the verbs. When two verbs agree with a single subject in a sentence, as is the case here, no punctuation is needed between the two verbs. And a short prepositional phrase, such as "in 1779," does not need to be punctuated if it comes in the middle of a sentence. So no punctuation is needed.

3. Use the Process of Elimination — Eliminate choices (A), (B), and (D) because they over-punctuate the sentence, which confuses rather than clarifies the intended meaning of the sentence.

 — **Choice (C)** is correct because it is grammatical based on the conclusions drawn in step 2, and because it reads smoothly when plugged back into the sentence, making the relationship between the subject and its verbs clear.

Solving Passage Organization Questions

[1] Years later, as industrialization was gaining momentum, Darby's grandson, Abraham Darby III, took over the company. [2] Darby III hired a designer **14** and, in 1779 constructed a picturesque cast-iron bridge over the River Severn. [3] The Iron Bridge still stands in Shropshire, England, where it is part of a UNESCO World Heritage Site as well as a popular tourist destination. [4] It was the first iron bridge in the world. [5] Visitors were astounded at its thinness, as bridges had always been made of thick stone or wood. **15**

15

To make this paragraph most logical, sentence 3 should be placed

(A) before sentence 1.
(B) after sentence 1.
(C) after sentence 4.
(D) after sentence 5.

---

1. Determine the Question Type ← Any question that asks you to (re)place a sentence or paragraph is a **passage organization question**.

2. Contextualize the Answer Choices ← Determine how the sentence in question relates to the paragraph, which discusses the design, creation, reception, and current status of Darby's Iron Bridge. The paragraph flows chronologically—beginning with the bridge's inception. However, sentence 3 describes the status of the bridge today: it "still stands" and "is part of a UNESCO World Heritage Site." Because the rest of the paragraph uses the past tense to describe the bridge, we can conclude that sentence 3, which uses present-tense verbs, should end the paragraph since it comes last chronologically.

3. Use the Process of Elimination ← Eliminate any answer choice does not indicate that sentence 3 should conclude the paragraph.
- Eliminate choices (A), (B), and (C) because they do not create a logical flow of ideas within the paragraph.

4. Confirm Your Choice ← **Choice (D) is correct;** as mentioned in step 2, sentence 3 should logically conclude the paragraph since it describes the present (the bridge "still stands"), whereas the rest of the paragraph describe past events.

SAT WRITING & LANGUAGE
Key Strategies - Humanities Passage

Refer to the passage below to answer questions 16 – 20.

In the mid-1800s, archaeologists first discovered fossil remains of Neanderthals, [16] a type of hominid. The name "Neanderthal" comes from that first discovery in Germany, in the *Neander* Valley. But before this important paleontological discovery, the name "Neander" was associated in the public mind with music, not fossils.

The valley is named after Joachim Neander, a teacher, songwriter, and [17] theologically. Neander did not own the valley; he lived near it in Düsseldorf during the 1670s. Neander taught Latin, but he was constantly in conflict with leaders at the school where he taught. After only five years, he quit and moved away, and unfortunately died shortly thereafter. But it was said that his frequent walks in the valley had [18] inspired Neander to write dozens of beautiful hymns during his time there.

Neander lived more than a century after the Protestant Reformation began in Europe. As such, his goal was to make church music accessible to common people. His lyrics are in German rather than Latin, and he used familiar folk tunes [19] in addition. Long after his death, his works remained popular; Johann Sebastian Bach even based one of his chorale cantatas on one of [20] his hymns. In 1850, the valley was officially named for him. Six years later, the first fossils were found there, and Neander's name became attached to an entire branch of hominids.

★

Solving Development/Concision Questions

In the mid-1800s, archaeologists first discovered fossil remains of Neanderthals, **16** <u>a type of hominid</u>. The name "Neanderthal" comes from that first discovery in Germany, in the *Neander* Valley. But before this important paleontological discovery, the name "Neander" was associated in the public mind with music, not fossils.

16
- (A) NO CHANGE
- (B) a subspecies of people, but not people like you and me.
- (C) an extinct subspecies of hominid.
- (D) an intriguing species.

1. Determine the Question Type ← The answer choices each provide a definition of the term "Neanderthal." Questions that rephrase the same information are usually **development or concision questions**.

2. Contextualize the Answer Choices ← Because this question does not provide specific instructions, we will assume that we are looking for the clearest, most concise description for a Neanderthal.

3. Use the Process of Elimination ← Eliminate any answer choice that is unnecessarily wordy, redundant, or vague:
- Eliminate choice (B) because it is both vague and wordy. It tells us that Neanderthals are "people," but not where or when they exist or existed.
- Eliminate choice (D) because it is vague; every known living organism is classified by species, so telling us that Neanderthals are a "species" does not provide sufficient information.

4. Confirm Your Choice ← Choices (A) and (C) succinctly provide similar information. However, hominids are a taxonomic family that include humans, so "a type of hominid" is vague. **Choice (C)** informs us that Neanderthals are also extinct, so it provides the most information in an academic and concise manner, making (C) the correct choice.

Solving Parallel Structure Questions

The valley is named after Joachim Neander, a teacher, songwriter, and **17** theologically. Neander did not own the valley; he lived near it in Düsseldorf during the 1670s. Neander taught Latin, but he was constantly in conflict with leaders at the school where he taught. After only five years, he quit and moved away, and unfortunately died shortly thereafter. But it was said that his frequent walks in the valley had **18** inspired Neander to write dozens of beautiful hymns during his time there.

17

(A) NO CHANGE
(B) theologian.
(C) theological studies.
(D) he engaged in theology.

1. Determine the Question Type

The answer choices each provide a different version of the listed element that describes "Joachim Neander." Because this question deals with choosing the correct form of a listed word, we can determine that it is a **parallel structure question**. These questions ask you to maintain the grammatical structure established by other listed elements.

2. Contextualize the Answer Choices

The underlined portion must match the structure of the other listed elements, "teacher" and "songwriter." Both of these words are nouns that describe a profession, so we can infer that the correct choice will maintain this pattern and also be a profession.

3. Use the Process of Elimination

Eliminate any answer choice that is not a profession (and a noun):
- Eliminate choice (A) because "theologically" is an adverb, not a noun or a profession.
- Eliminate choice (C) because the listed elements describe what Neander is—"a teacher" and "songwriter"—and it does not make sense to say that "Neander is a theological studies." So while (C) provides a noun, it does not fit the context of the sentence.
- Eliminate choice (D) because it is unnecessarily wordy: one who engages in theology is, by definition, a theologian.

4. Confirm Your Choice

Choice (B) is correct because it concisely conveys Neander's third profession by identifying him as a "theologian," which matches the word pattern established by "teacher" and "songwriter."

Solving Precise Diction Questions

The valley is named after Joachim Neander, a teacher, songwriter, and  theologically. Neander did not own the valley, but he lived near it in Düsseldorf during the 1670s. Neander taught Latin, but he was constantly in conflict with leaders at the school where he taught. After only five years, he quit and moved away, and unfortunately died shortly thereafter. But it was said that his frequent walks in the valley had  inspired Neander to write dozens of beautiful hymns during his time there.

18

(A) NO CHANGE
(B) forced
(C) exhilarated
(D) invigorated

1. Determine the Question Type

By quickly reviewing the passage and the answer choices, we can see that the answer choices consist of words with similar meanings. This indicates that we are dealing with a **precise diction question**, and we must determine which word best fits the context of the sentence in which its used.

2. Contextualize the Answer Choices

Review the entire sentence that contains the underlined portion. Doing so reveals that Neander's walks in the valley did something that caused him to "write dozens of beautiful hymns." From this, we can infer that the underlined portion is a verb conveying that the walks "caused Neander to create hymns."

3. Use the Process of Elimination

Eliminate any answer choice that does not indicate that walks in the valley caused Neander to create works of art.
- Eliminate choice (B) because "to force" someone means to use coercion or violence, which does not fit the context.
- Eliminate choice (C) because "to exhilarate" is to excite or thrill, which is positive but does not directly link to the production of art.
- Eliminate choice (D) because "to invigorate" is to energize or refresh, which does not directly relate to art.

4. Confirm Your Choice

Choice (A) is correct because "to inspire" is to give someone the desire to feel a certain way or to create something, which fits perfectly in the context of the sentence.

Solving Passage Development Questions

Neander lived more than a century after the Protestant Reformation began in Europe. As such, his goal was to make church music accessible to common people. His lyrics are in German rather than Latin, and he used familiar folk tunes 19 in addition. Long after his death, his works remained popular; Johann Sebastian Bach even based one of his chorale cantatas on one of 20 his hymns. In 1850, the valley was officially named for him. Six years later, the first fossils were found there, and Neander's name became attached to an entire branch of hominids.

19

Which choice best supports the claim made in the previous sentence?

(A) NO CHANGE
(B) that people could easily memorize and sing.
(C) which extolled the beauty of the valley.
(D) to cement his artistic legacy.

1. Determine the Question Type	This question is asking you choose the most effective addition to the passage, so it is a **passage development question**. Generally, development questions will have you add relevant details and/or remove irrelevant information from a passage.
2. Contextualize the Answer Choices	Take note that we are being instructed to select the claim that best supports the previous sentence. The sentence that precedes the underlined portion says that Neander wanted his music to be "accessible to the common people," so the correct choice will likely have something to do with this.
3. Use the Process of Elimination	Eliminate any answer choices that do not fully answer the question: • Eliminate choice (A) because it does not add any new information to the sentence. • Eliminate choice (C) because the preceding sentence is about making music "accessible to the common people," not the beauty of the valley. • Eliminate choice (D) because it does not relate to the topic of the previous sentence.
4. Confirm Your Choice	**Choice (B)** is correct because music that is easy to "memorize and sing" is very accessible, so this choice fits with the topic of the previous sentence.

Solving Pronoun/Referent Questions

Neander lived more than a century after the Protestant Reformation began in Europe. As such, his goal was to make church music accessible to common people. His lyrics are in German rather than Latin, and he used familiar folk tunes 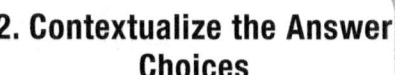 in addition. Long after his death, his works remained popular; Johann Sebastian Bach even based one of his chorale cantatas on one of 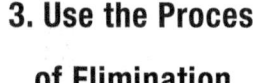 his hymns. In 1850, the valley was officially named for him. Six years later, the first fossils were found there, and Neander's name became attached to an entire branch of hominids.

20

(A) NO CHANGE
(B) their
(C) Bach's
(D) Neander's

---

1. Determine the Question Type ← Because the answer choices consist of nouns and pronouns, we are likely dealing with a **pronoun/referent question**.

2. Contextualize the Answer Choices ← Use the context of the sentence to determine how the underlined portion fits. The sentence refers to "his death" and "his works," referring to Neander's. And it says that Bach based a piece of music on *someone*'s hymn. Thus, whoever wrote the hymn on which Bach based his own work is the correct answer.

3. Use the Process of Elimination ← Eliminate any answer choice that cannot be the person who wrote the hymn that influenced Bach.
- Eliminate choices (A) and (C) because "his" would refer to "Bach" in this case, and we can infer that Bach would not base a piece of music on another of his own pieces. And even if that were the case, such a statement would be out of place in a passage about composer Joachim Neander.
- Eliminate choice (B) because the paragraph does not contain any plural nouns to which "their" would refer.

4. Confirm Your Choice ← Choice (C) is correct because it makes sense grammatically and stylistically. Because the passage is about Neander and his hymns, it is relevant to mention that Bach based his work on Neander's.

END OF SECTION 2

SAT MATH
Key Strategies - No Calculator Section

DIRECTIONS

For questions **1 – 7**, find the solution to each problem and select the most appropriate answer from the choices provided. For questions **8 – 9**, find the solution to each problem and write your answer in the space provided. You may use the blank space in your test booklet for scratch work.

NOTES

1. The use of a calculator on any part of this section is forbidden.
2. Unless otherwise indicated, all variables and expressions used in this test represent real numbers.
3. Unless otherwise indicated, all figures used in this test are drawn to scale.
4. Unless otherwise indicated, all figures used in this test lie on a plane.
5. Unless specified otherwise, a given function, f, has the domain the set of all real numbers x for which $f(x)$ is a real number.

REFERENCE

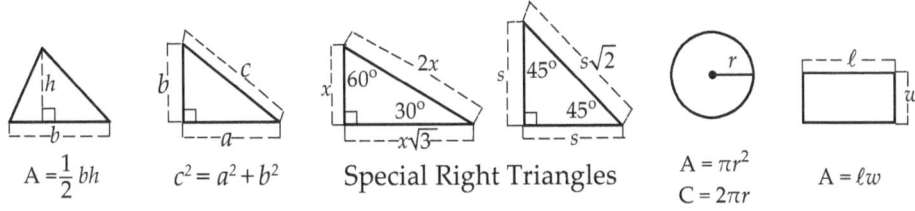

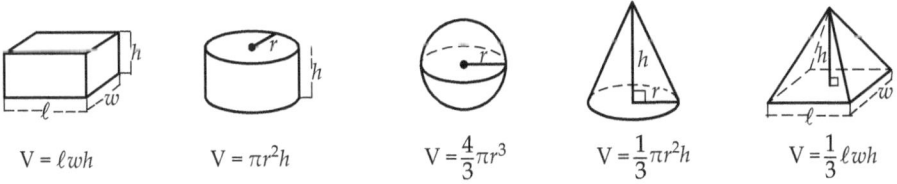

The arc of a circle is 360 degrees or 2π radians.
A triangle has angles that sum to 180 degrees.

CHAPTER 4 - Math Key Strategies | 119

Solving Algebra Questions

01

If $6(p + q) + 5 = 29$, what is the value of $p + q$?

(A) 3
(B) 4
(C) 5
(D) 6

1. Determine What Concepts Are Being Tested ← We are being asked to solve for the expression $p + q$, which indicates that we are dealing with an **algebra question**. Note that many algebra questions will require you to find the value of or relationship between unknown quantities.

2. Plan Your Approach ← Inspecting the question reveals that we must isolate $p + q$ on one side of the equation to find the value of this expression.

3. Solve ←
$$6(p + q) + 5 = 29$$
Subtract 5 from both sides of the equation:
- $6(p + q) = 24$

Divide both sides of the equation by 6:
- $p + q = 4$

4. Confirm Your Choice ← **Choice (B)**, 4, gives the value of $p + q$ and is therefore correct.

Before moving on to the next question, quickly review your work to ensure that you did not make any arithmetic errors.

Solving Function & Graph Questions

02

In the figure to the right, the slope of the line is $\frac{1}{2}$. What is the value of k?

(A) $\frac{1}{2}$

(B) $\frac{3}{2}$

(C) 2

(D) 3

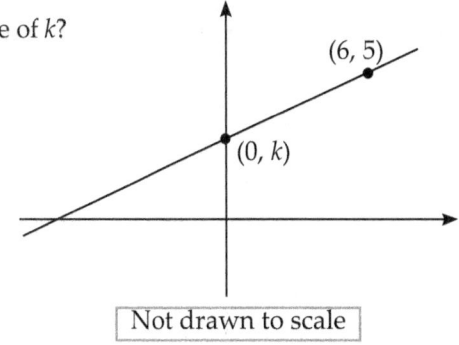

Not drawn to scale

1. Determine What Concepts Are Being Tested

We are being asked to find a missing y-coordinate given a line's slope and three other coordinates, which indicates that we are dealing with a **function and graph question**.

2. Plan Your Approach

Method 1
A line's slope (m) is determined using the formula $m = \frac{y_2 - y_1}{x_2 - x_1}$.

Plug the slope and coordinates provided in the question into the formula above and solve for the missing value to find k.

Method 2
Recognize that the value of k is the line's y-intercept, which is represented by b in the slope-intercept form of a line:

$y = mx + b$.

The slope (m) is given in the question as $\frac{1}{2}$. Solve for b using the point specified on the graph.

3. Solve

Method 1

$\frac{1}{2} = \frac{5-k}{6-0}$ → $\frac{1}{2} = \frac{5-k}{6}$

Cross-multiply and solve for k:

$6 = 2(5-k)$ → $6 = 10 - 2k$ →

$2k = 4$ → $k = 2$

Method 2

$y = mx + b$ →

$5 = \frac{1}{2}(6) + b$ →

$b = 2$

Since $b = k$, $k = 2$.

4. Confirm Your Choice

Choice (C), 2, gives the value of k and is therefore correct.

Before moving on to the next question, quickly review your work to ensure that you did not make any arithmetic errors.

In this case, if time permitted, you could check your work by plugging the value of k into the formula that you did not use to solve. For example, if Method 1 was used to solve, check you work by plugging k into the slope-intercept formula used in Method 2.

Solving Algebra Questions

03

Which of the following is equivalent to the expression $\dfrac{x^2 - 16}{x^3 + x^2 - 20x}$?

(A) $\dfrac{4}{x+5}$

(B) $\dfrac{x+4}{4}$

(C) $\dfrac{x+4}{x+5}$

(D) $\dfrac{x+4}{x^2+5x}$

1. Determine What Concepts Are Being Tested

We are asked to simplify an expression, which indicates that we are dealing with an **algebra question**. These questions will often ask you to determine an unknown value or simplify a complex expression.

2. Plan Your Approach

The numerator of the expression is a difference of squares, and can be factored by recognizing that $a^2 - b^2 = (a-b)(a+b)$.
The denominator looks like it can be factored after the like term, x, is grouped.

3. Solve

Following the procedure outlined above, we get:

$$\dfrac{x^2 - 16}{x^3 + x^2 - 20x} = \dfrac{(x-4)(x+4)}{x(x^2 + x - 20)} = \dfrac{(x-4)(x+4)}{x(x-4)(x+5)} = \dfrac{(x+4)}{x(x+5)} = \dfrac{x+4}{x^2 + 5x}$$

4. Confirm Your Choice

Choice (D), $\dfrac{x+4}{x^2+5x}$, is equivalent to the expression $\dfrac{x^2-16}{x^3+x^2-20x}$ and is therefore correct.

Before moving on to the next question, quickly review your work to ensure that you did not make any arithmetic errors.

Solving Geometry Questions

In the figure to the right, PQRS is a rectangle, and $\overline{TU}$ is the diameter of the circle. If the length of $\overline{RS}$ is 6 centimeters and the length of $\overline{PS}$ is 8 centimeters, what is the value of the shaded area in square centimeters?

(A) $48 - 6\pi$
(B) $48 - 8\pi$
(C) $24 - 6\pi$
(D) $48 - 9\pi$

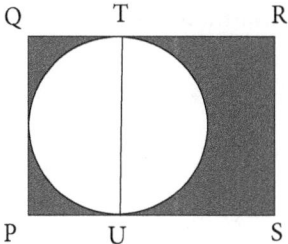

Not drawn to scale

1. Determine What Concepts Are Being Tested

The question provides a diagram containing a circle and a rectangle, and solving this question will require us to determine the relationship between these shapes, all of which indicate that we are dealing with a **geometry question**.

2. Plan Your Approach

Upon inspecting the diagram, it becomes evident that the shaded area that we are trying to determine is the difference between the areas of the rectangle and the circle, which can be expressed as:

$$\text{AREA}_{\text{Shaded}} = \text{AREA}_{\text{PQRS}} - \text{AREA}_{\text{circle}}$$

To solve the equation above, we must determine the area of each shape.

3. Solve

Let's determine the area of the circle first. Its diameter is 6 centimeters and its radius is 3 centimeters, so the area of the circle is:

- $\text{AREA}_{\text{circle}} = \pi r^2 = \pi(3)^2 = 9\pi$

The area of the rectangle is found by multiplying its width, which is 6 cm (the same as the diameter of the circle), and its length, which is given in the question as 8 cm.

- $\text{AREA}_{\text{PQRS}} = wl = (6 \times 8) = 48$

Using the equation in step 2, we can calculate the area of the shaded region as:

- $\text{AREA}_{\text{Shaded}} = 48 - 9\pi$

4. Confirm Your Choice

Thus, **choice (D)**, $48 - 9\pi$, gives us the area of the shaded region.

Before moving on to the next question, quickly review your work to ensure that you did not make any arithmetic errors.

Solving Ratio/Percentage/Rate Questions

Matthew slices a pie into p equal slices and eats three of them. In terms of p, what percentage of the pie is left?

(A) $100(p-3)\%$

(B) $\dfrac{100(p-3)}{p}\%$

(C) $\dfrac{100}{p-3}\%$

(D) $\dfrac{p-3}{100}\%$

1. Determine What Concepts Are Being Tested

This question is asking us to determine a percentage, so it is a **ratio/percentage/rate question.** These questions will generally ask you to find the ratio between two quantities, or the rate at or amount by which a quantity changes.

2. Plan Your Approach

To calculate the amount of remaining pie as a percentage, we must first create a proportion that expresses how much pie is left in terms of p. Eating three of p total slices can be expressed as $p-3$, so the proportion of slices left is: . For example, if the pie began with 8 slices, and three were eaten, then $\dfrac{5}{8}$ of the pie remains. To convert a proportion to a percentage, simple multiply it by 100%.

3. Solve

The proportion of slices left is
To convert this into percentage:

$$\left(\dfrac{p-3}{p}\right) \times 100\% = \dfrac{(p-3)100}{p}\%$$

4. Confirm Your Choice

Thus, **choice (B)**, , expresses the amount of pie left as a percentage in terms of p.

Before moving on to the next question, quickly review your work to ensure that you did not make any arithmetic errors.

Solving Geometry Questions

06

The radius of the circle shown is 9 units. If the area of the shaded sector is 9π square units, what is the length of $\overset{\frown}{ACB}$?

(A) 2π

(B) 15π

(C) 16π

(D) 18π

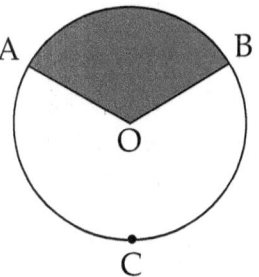

Not drawn to scale

1. Determine What Concepts Are Being Tested

The question provides a diagram containing a circle and requires that we determine arc length, all of which indicate that we are dealing with a **geometry question**.

2. Plan Your Approach

This question requires us to recognize that the area and arc length of a segment are both proportional to the central angle. Thus, the area of the shaded sector and its corresponding arc length are proportional to the area and circumference, respectively, of the circle. If we determine the length of $\overset{\frown}{AB}$, then we can subtract it from the circumference to find $\overset{\frown}{ACB}$.

3. Solve

Using the radius of 9 provided in the question, we can determine that the circumference of the circle is 18π and its area is 81π.

Use this information to complete the proportion that follows:

$$\frac{\text{area of arc } AB}{\text{area of circle}} = \frac{\text{length of } AB}{\text{circumference of circle}} \rightarrow \frac{9\pi}{81\pi} = \frac{\text{length } AB}{18\pi}$$

All answer choices are expressed using π, so let's leave it out as we cross-multiply to find the length of $\overset{\frown}{AB}$, and then add it back when selecting the answer:

$9(18) = 81(\overset{\frown}{AB}) \rightarrow 162 = 81(\overset{\frown}{AB}) \rightarrow \overset{\frown}{AB} = 2$

Remembering to add back π, we know that $\overset{\frown}{AB} = 2\pi$ units. $\overset{\frown}{ACB}$ can be found by subtracting $\overset{\frown}{AB}$ from the circle's circumference, 18π: $18\pi - 2\pi = 16\pi$.

4. Confirm Your Choice

Thus, **choice (C)**, 16π, gives us the length of $\overset{\frown}{ACB}$.

Before moving on to the next question, quickly review your work to ensure that you did not make any arithmetic errors.

Solving Number Rules Questions

$$(2a + b) + (3 - 5a)i = 1 + 8i$$

If a and b are integers such that the equation above is true, what is their sum?

(A) –3

(B) –2

(C) –1

(D) 2

1. Determine What Concepts Are Being Tested

This question includes the imaginary number i, indicating that it is a **number rules question**. These questions generally require you to solve algebra questions that incorporate complex or imaginary numbers.

2. Plan Your Approach

Notice that i will be distributed to both terms in the expression $3 - 5a$. This allows us to redistribute the terms of the equation such that $(3 - 5a)i = 8i$ and $2a + b = 1$.

Solving for a in the equation containing i and then plugging that value into the equation with b should give us the values of a and b.

3. Solve

$(3 - 5a)i = 8i$ can be simplified by dividing out the i, giving $3 - 5a = 8$.

Sovling for a: $3 - 5a = 8$ → $-5a = 8 - 3$ → $-5a = 5$ → $a = -1$

Using the value of a, solve for b in the other equation:
$2(-1) + b = 1$ → $b = 3$

Calculate their sum: $a + b = -1 + 3 = 2$

4. Confirm Your Choice

Thus, **choice (D)**, 2, gives us the value of $a + b$.

Before moving on to the next question, quickly review your work to ensure that you did not make any substitution or arithmetic errors.

Solving Algebra Questions

08

If $x^2 + 7x - 33 = 11$, and $x > 0$, what is the value of $x + 11$?

ANSWER: _____

1. Determine What Concepts Are Being Tested ← We are being asked to solve for the expression $x + 11$, which indicates that we are dealing with an **algebra question**. Note that many algebra questions will require you to find the value of or relationship between unknown quantities.

2. Plan Your Approach ← Based on the information given, we must set the quadratic expression equal to zero and factor it to find a nonnegative value for x. Adding this quantity to 11 will give us the answer.

3. Solve ← We must ensure that our quadratic equation is equal to zero before we factor it:
$x^2 + 7x - 33 = 11 \rightarrow x^2 + 7x - 44 = 0$

Then factor the quadratic equation: $(x + 11)(x - 4) = 0$

Therefore, $x = -11, 4$

Since $x > 0$, $x = 4$

Therefore, $x + 11 = 15$.

4. Confirm Your Choice ← Bubble in the correct value of $x + 11$, which is **15**.

Before moving on to the next question, quickly review your work to ensure that you did not make any arithmetic errors.

CHAPTER 4 - Math Key Strategies | 127

Solving Ratio/Percentage/Rate Questions

09

Eight people working together can build a house in 12 days. How many days would it take six people working together to build the same house?

ANSWER: _____

1. Determine What Concepts Are Being Tested ← This question asks us to identify the rate at which a group of people can build a house, so it is an algebraic word problem that requires an understanding of **rates** and **ratios**.

2. Plan Your Approach ← We can use the information, "Eight people working together can build a house in 12 days" to determine what portion of a house one person finishes in one day. We can then use the rate at which one person works to determine how long it will take six people to build a house.

3. Solve ← Eight people build one-twelfth of a house in one day. One person builds one-eighth of one-twelfth of a house in one day:

Work done by one person in one day = $\left(\dfrac{1}{8}\right)\left(\dfrac{1}{12}\right) = \dfrac{1}{96}$ of a house

In one day, six people can build $\dfrac{6}{96}$, or $\dfrac{1}{16}$ of a house.

Therefore, six people take 16 days to build a house.

4. Confirm Your Choice ← It takes six people **16** days to build a house working together.

Before moving on to the next question, quickly review your work to ensure that you did not make any arithmetic errors.

END OF SECTION 3

SAT MATH
Key Strategies - Calculator Section

DIRECTIONS

For questions **1 – 15**, find the solution to each problem and select the most appropriate answer from the choices provided. For questions **16 – 19**, find the solution to each problem and write your answer in the space provided. You may use the blank space in your test booklet for scratch work.

NOTES

1. The use of a calculator on any part of this section is allowed.
2. Unless otherwise indicated, all variables and expressions used in this test represent real numbers.
3. Unless otherwise indicated, all figures used in this test are drawn to scale.
4. Unless otherwise indicated, all figures used in this test lie on a plane.
5. Unless specified otherwise, a given function, f, has the domain the set of all real numbers x for which $f(x)$ is a real number.

REFERENCE

$A = \frac{1}{2}bh$

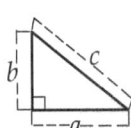
$c^2 = a^2 + b^2$

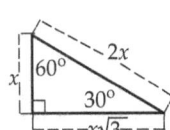
Special Right Triangles

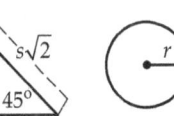
$A = \pi r^2$
$C = 2\pi r$

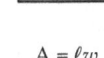
$A = \ell w$

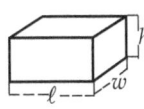
$V = \ell w h$

$V = \pi r^2 h$

$V = \frac{4}{3}\pi r^3$

$V = \frac{1}{3}\pi r^2 h$

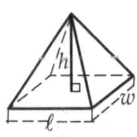
$V = \frac{1}{3}\ell w h$

The arc of a circle is 360 degrees or 2π radians.
A triangle has angles that sum to 180 degrees.

Solving Algebra Questions

01

If $x + 3 = 12$, then $(x + 7)^2 =$

(A) 144

(B) 169

(C) 196

(D) 256

1. Determine What Concepts Are Being Tested

We are being asked to determine an unknown value (x) so that we can substitute it into another equation, all of which indicates that we are dealing with an **algebra question**. Note that many algebra questions will require you to find the value of or relationship between unknown quantities.

2. Plan Your Approach

To find the value of x, simply subtract 3 from both sides of the equation.

Once the value of x is determined, plug it into the second equation, adding seven to it and squaring the sum.

3. Solve

Solve for x: $x + 3 = 12 \rightarrow x + 3(-3) = 12(-3) \rightarrow x = 9$

Plug x's value into the second equation: $(9 + 7)^2 = 16^2 = 256$

4. Confirm Your Choice

Choice (D), 256, is equal to $(x + 7)^2$ and is therefore correct.

Before moving on to the next question, quickly review your work to ensure that you did not make any arithmetic errors.

Solving Function & Graph Questions

On the coordinate plane, the line $\overline{AB}$ passes through the origin. If $\overline{AB} \perp \overline{CD}$ and they intersect at (10, 6), where does $\overline{CD}$ cross the x-axis?

(A) (0, 12)

(B) $(0, 22\frac{2}{3})$

(C) $(13\frac{3}{5}, 0)$

(D) (20, 0)

1. Determine What Concepts Are Being Tested

We are being asked to find a line's x-intercept given one of its points and some information about a perpendicular line, all of which indicate that we are dealing with a **function and graph question**.

2. Plan Your Approach

Before we begin doing any actual math, we can eliminate choices (A) and (B) because they provide y-intercepts, and we must find an x-intercept in this case.

In the question we are given two points on $\overline{AB}$: (0, 0) and (10, 6). We can use these to find the slope of $\overline{AB}$. $\overline{CD}$ is perpendicular to $\overline{AB}$ so its slope will be a negative reciprocal.

Once we have the slope of $\overline{CD}$, we can determine its intercepts.

3. Solve

Using the two points on $\overline{AB}$ that we are given, calculate the slope of $\overline{AB}$: $m_{AB} = \frac{6}{10} = \frac{3}{5}$

The slope of $\overline{CD}$ is the negative reciprocal of the slope of $\overline{AB}$:

$m_{CD} = -\frac{5}{3}$

Since we know $\overline{CD}$ passes through (10, 6), we can determine the equation for the line and then its x-intercept:

$6 = -\frac{5}{3}(10) + b \rightarrow b = \frac{68}{3}$. $\overline{CD}$'s equation is $y = -\frac{5}{3}x + \frac{68}{3}$.

As we are looking for the x-intercept, we substitute zero for y:

$0 = -\frac{5}{3}x + \frac{68}{3} \rightarrow 5x = 68 \rightarrow x = 13\frac{3}{5}$

4. Confirm Your Choice

Choice (C), $(13\frac{3}{5}, 0)$, is the point at which $\overline{CD}$ crosses the x-intercept and is therefore correct.

Before moving on to the next question, quickly review your work to ensure that you did not make any arithmetic errors.

Solving System of Equality Word Problems

03

At an electronics store, Aiden bought USB drives at $8.00 each and Connor bought USB drives at $13.00 each. If they bought a combined eight USB drives and spent $89.00 between them, how many USBs did Connor buy?

(A) 2
(B) 3
(C) 4
(D) 5

1. Determine What Concepts Are Being Tested

Here we must translate a paragraph of text into mathematical equations, which we will then solve to determine how many $13 USB drives were purchased. Because we must create two or more equations, determine their relationship, and solve, this is a **system of equality word problem**.

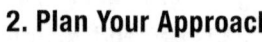
2. Plan Your Approach

This question requires us to create two equations, one describing the number of USB drives purchased and the other describing total money spent. Expressing the information in the question mathematically gives:
- x = number of $8 USBs
- y = number of $13 USBs

Thus, number of USBs purchased is expressed as $x + y = 8$, and total money spent is expressed as $8x + 13y = 89$. We need to solve for y and can do this either of two ways.

Method 1 - Substitution
Solve for x in the first equation ($x + y = 8$) and substitute this value into the second equation to determine the value of y.

Method 2 - Elimination
Multiply the first equation by 8, and then subtract the product from the second equation to eliminate the x variable. Then solve for y.

3. Solve

Method 1 - Substitution
$x + y = 8 \rightarrow x = 8 - y$
Replace x with $(8 - y)$ *in* the second equation and solve for y.
$8(8 - y) + 13y = 89$
$64 - 8y + 13y = 89$
$5y = 25$
$y = 5$

Method 2 - Elimination
Multiplying the first equation by gives:
$8(x + y = 8) \rightarrow 8x + 8y = 64$
Subtract the first equation from the second and solve for y:

$8x + 13y = 89$
$-)8x + 8y = 64$
$\overline{5y = 25}$
$y = 5$

4. Confirm Your Choice

Choice (D), 2, gives the value of y, which describes the number of USBs that Connor purchased, and is therefore correct. Before moving on to the next question, quickly review your work to ensure that you did not make any arithmetic errors.

In this case, if time permits, solve for y using the method not used to solve. For example, if substitution was used to solve, try using the elimination method to check your work.

Solving Algebraic Word Problems

Dani receives a paycheck every two weeks for $750. Every month, she must pay $800 in rent and $450 in bills. She has also committed to putting 15% of her monthly income into a savings account. What is the most she can allocate to other expenses each month?

(A) $0
(B) $25
(C) $100
(D) $250

1. Determine What Concepts Are Being Tested

Here we must translate a paragraph of text into a mathematical equation, which we will then solve to determine how much Dani "can allocate to other expenses each month." Because we must create an equation and then solve it, this question must be an **algebraic word problem**.

2. Plan Your Approach

When solving word problems, start by determining what information you need and what information you have. Here, we need to determine how much money Dani has left over at the end of each month, and we know her:
- bi-monthly income: $750
- monthly rent: $800
- monthly bills: $450
- monthly savings: 15% of her income

Thus, we must use this information to find our answer, which is the difference between her income and expenses:

monthly income − monthly expenses = answer

3. Solve

As indicated in the question, the correct answer will be a dollar amount accumulated monthly, so we must convert all our given values to dollars per month in order to find our solution.

- Calculate Dani's **monthly** income:

$$= \frac{\$750}{2 \; weeks} \times \frac{4 \; weeks}{1 \; month} = \$1,500$$

- Then convert her monthly savings to a dollar amount:
  (0.15)($1500) = $225

- Use the equation *monthly income − monthly expenses = answer* to calculate Dani's leftover income:

  $1,500 − ($800 + $450 + $225) = $25

4. Confirm Your Choice

Choice (B), $25, gives us the value of "the most she [Dani] can allocate to other expenses each month."

Before moving on to the next question, quickly review your work to ensure that you did not make any arithmetic errors.

Solving System of Equality/Inequality Questions

05

If $y = 2x - 3$ and $23y - 15y = 30$, what is the value of x?

(A) $\frac{3}{2}$

(B) 2

(C) $\frac{5}{2}$

(D) $\frac{27}{8}$

1. Determine What Concepts Are Being Tested

We are asked to find a value given two equations, so this is a **system-of-equality/inequality question**. These questions ask you to find one or more unknown value(s) given two or more equations or inequalities.

2. Plan Your Approach

Your top priority when solving system-of-equality questions should be determining how the equations relate to each other and, in this case, how this relationship can help you find x.

Notice that x only appears in the first equation, and that simplifying the second equation will give us the value of y. Once we have the value of y, we can plug it into the first equation, which will in turn give us the value of x.

3. Solve

Solve the equation using the strategy outlined in the previous step:

- Find the value of y:

$$23y - 15y = 30 \rightarrow 8y = 30 \rightarrow y = \frac{30}{8} = \frac{15}{4}$$

- Substitute the value of y into the first equation to find x:

$$y = 2x - 3$$

$$\frac{15}{4} = 2x - 3 \rightarrow 2x = \frac{27}{4} \rightarrow x = \frac{27}{8}$$

4. Confirm Your Choice

Choice (D), $x = \frac{27}{8}$, gives the value of x and is therefore correct. Before moving on to the next question, quickly review your work to ensure that you did not make any arithmetic errors.

If you have time, plug the values of x and y back into the first equation to double-check your answer:

- $\frac{15}{4} = 2\left(\frac{27}{8}\right) - 3 \rightarrow \frac{15}{4} = \frac{27}{4} - \frac{12}{4} \rightarrow \frac{15}{4} = \frac{15}{4}$

Solving Concentration/Density Questions

06

A chemist has 80 pints of a 20-percent salt solution. How many pints of pure salt must be added to produce a solution that is 30 percent salt?

(A) 4.6

(B) 8

(C) 11.4

(D) 16

1. Determine What Concepts Are Being Tested

This question is asking us to change the concentration of salt in a solution, so it is a **concentration/density question.** These questions will generally ask you to calculate the concentration of a substance in a solution or determine the density of a material.

2. Plan Your Approach

In order to determine how much salt we need for a 30 percent salt solution, we must first determine how much salt is already in the 20 percent solution. Once we have this value, we must add x pints of salt to the solution, where x is the amount of salt needed to create a 30 percent salt solution.

3. Solve

The amount of salt in the solution is calculated as follows:

$(0.2)(80) = 16$ pints

Thus, the 20 percent salt solution contains 16 pints of salt. To increase the concentration of salt to 30 percent, add x lb. of salt, but note that this increases the volume of the sample to $80 + x$ pints:

$$0.3 = \frac{16 + x}{80 + x}$$

$24 + 0.3x = 16 + x$

$x = 11.4$

4. Confirm Your Choice

Thus, **choice (C)**, 11.4 pounds, expresses amount of pure salt that must be added to produce a solution that is 30 percent salt.

Before moving on to the next question, quickly review your work to ensure that you did not make any arithmetic errors.

Solving Geometry Questions

What is the area of the trapezoid BCDE?

(A) $16\sqrt{3}$

(B) $\dfrac{45}{2}\sqrt{3}$

(C) $8 + 4\sqrt{3}$

(D) $4 + 12\sqrt{3}$

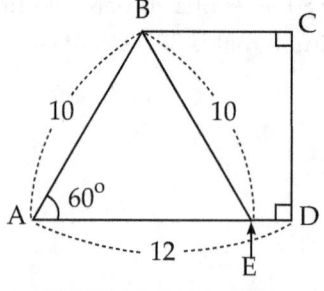

Not drawn to scale

1. Determine What Concepts Are Being Tested

The question provides a diagram containing a triangle and a trapezoid, and solving this question will require us to determine the relationship between these shapes, all of which indicate that we are dealing with a **geometry question**.

2. Plan Your Approach

We must determine what information we have and what information we need in order to determine the trapezoid's area. The base angles $\angle BAE = \angle BEA = 60°$, which means that $\angle ABE = 60°$, $\triangle ABE$ is an equilateral triangle, and $BA = BE = AE = 10$. Therefore: $ED = AD - AE = 12 - 10 = 2$

Because $\triangle ABE$ is an isosceles (and equilateral) triangle, the altitude from the peak angle to the base bisects the base into two segments of 5 units each. As $BC \parallel AD$, we can infer that: $BC = 5 + ED = 5 + 2 = 7$

BC and ED are the two bases of the trapezoid BCDE.
Using this information to solve for the height, and then the area, of the trapezoid will give us our answer.

3. Solve

Calculate the altitude of the trapezoid using the Pythagorean theorem:
$\text{Altitude}^2 + 5^2 = 10^2 \rightarrow \text{Altitude}^2 = 75 \rightarrow \text{Altitude} = \sqrt{75} = 5\sqrt{3}$
The area of the trapezoid is:

$\text{Area}_{BCDE} = \left(\dfrac{BC + ED}{2}\right)(\text{Altitude})$

$\left(\dfrac{7+2}{2}\right)(5\sqrt{3}) = \dfrac{45}{2}\sqrt{3}$

4. Confirm Your Choice

Thus, **choice (B)**, $\dfrac{45}{2}\sqrt{3}$, gives us the area of the trapezoid.
Before moving on to the next question, quickly review your work to ensure that you did not make any arithmetic errors.

Solving Unit Conversion Questions

08

An administrative assistant had a typing speed of 55 words per minute. After practicing, he raised his typing speed to 4,620 words per hour. By what percent did the assistant's typing speed increase?

(A) 10%

(B) 20%

(C) 30%

(D) 40%

1. Determine What Concepts Are Being Tested

We are being asked to find a percent increase, which will require us to convert words per hour to words per minute, and then to calculate a percent increase. Although this question will involve percentages, it is fundamentally testing your understanding of **unit conversion**.

2. Plan Your Approach

Before we can calculate percent increase, we must first make sure all our information is expressed using the same units. In this case it will be easier to deal with words per minute since it gives us smaller quantities to work with.

Once we know what 4,620 words per hour is in minutes, we can subtract the original typing speed (55 wpm) from the new speed, and then we can calculate percent increase using the formula:

$$\text{percent increase} = \frac{\text{amount increased}}{\text{original amount}} \times 100\%$$

3. Solve

Convert words per into words per minute:

$$\text{Typing speed} = \frac{4,260 \text{ words}}{\text{hour}} \times \frac{\text{hour}}{60 \text{ minutes}} = \frac{77 \text{ words}}{\text{minute}}$$

Calculate the percent increase:

$$\text{Percent increase} = \frac{22 \text{ words per minute}}{55 \text{ words per minute}} \times 100\% = 40\%$$

4. Confirm Your Choice

Choice (D), 40%, describes the assistant's typing speed increase as a percent.

Before moving on to the next question, quickly review your work to ensure that you did not make any arithmetic errors.

Solving Geometry Questions

09

In the figure to the right, the cube is divided into 27 smaller cubes of equal volume. If 12 of these smaller cubes have a combined volume of 36 cubic units, what is the volume in cubic units of the entire cube?

(A) 54

(B) 81

(C) 108

(D) 135

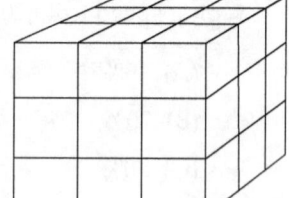

1. Determine What Concepts Are Being Tested

We are being asked to determine the volume of a solid given the volume of a subsection of that solid. Therefore, we are dealing with a **geometry** question that also tests your knowledge of **ratios and proportions**.

2. Plan Your Approach

Set up a ratio to express the relationship between the 12 cubes and their volumes, setting this value equal to the volume of all 27 cubes divided by the total volume of the large cube:

$$\frac{12 \text{ cubes}}{36 \text{ units}^3} = \frac{27 \text{ cubes}}{x}$$

3. Solve

The most effective way to find a missing value in a ratio is to cross multiply and isolate the unknown term:

$$12x = 27 \times 36 \quad \rightarrow \quad x = \frac{27}{12} \times 36 \text{ units}^3 = 81 \text{ units}^3$$

4. Confirm Your Choice

Choice (B), 81, is equal to the volume of the large cube and is therefore the correct answer.

Before moving on to the next question, quickly review your work to ensure that you did not make any arithmetic errors.

Solving Geometry Questions

10

In the figure to the right, $\overline{SQ} = 4$, $\overline{SP} = 8$, $\overline{QR} = 15$, and $\overline{ST}$ is parallel to $\overline{PR}$. What is the length of $\overline{TR}$?

(A) 8
(B) 9
(C) 10
(D) 12

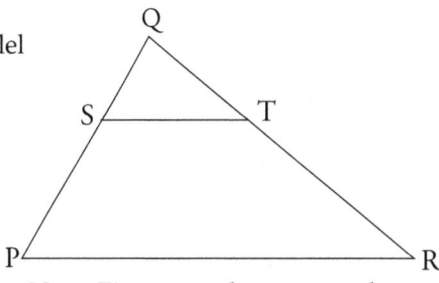

Note: Figure not drawn to scale

1. Determine What Concepts Are Being Tested
The question asks us to determine the length of a line segment based on the lengths of other line segments and information about the relationships between the lines. Therefore, this is a **geometry question**.

2. Plan Your Approach
To find the length of the unknown line segment, use the Triangle Side-splitter Theorem, which states that lines within a triangle and parallel to one side of the triangle divide the sides of that triangle into proportional segments. Thus, we can create the following ratio to express this relationship:

$$\frac{\overline{SP}}{\overline{QP}} = \frac{\overline{TR}}{\overline{QR}} \quad \rightarrow \quad \frac{8}{12} = \frac{\overline{TR}}{15}$$

3. Solve
Solve for $\overline{TR}$ using cross multiplication:

$$\frac{8}{12} = \frac{\overline{TR}}{15} \quad \rightarrow \quad (12)(\overline{TR}) = (8)(15) \quad \rightarrow \quad \overline{TR} = \frac{120}{12} \quad \rightarrow \quad \overline{TR} = 10$$

4. Confirm Your Choice
Choice (C), 10, is the length of $\overline{TR}$.

Before moving on to the next question, quickly review your work to ensure that you did not make any arithmetic errors.

Solving Algebraic Word Problems

11

Janina handles finances for her band. They are currently touring, and have an arrangement whereby they receive 20 percent of ticket sales. If tickets are $15 each, and she hopes to make $300 per show, how many people need to attend each show for her to meet her goal?

(A) 100
(B) 350
(C) 400
(D) 500

1. Determine What Concepts Are Being Tested

This question asks us to determine the number of ticket sales, an unknown value, from given information. Because we must set up an equation using a variable (x), this is an **algebra word problem**.

2. Plan Your Approach

To find the minimum number of tickets Janina needs to sell to meet her goals, set up an equation using x for the unknown value (number of tickets):

Revenue = $(0.20)(\$15)x$

3. Solve

Because the band must make at least $300 per show, set revenue greater than or equal to $300:

$(0.20)(\$15)x \geq \$300$

Solve for x:

$x \geq \dfrac{\$300}{(0.20)(\$15)} \rightarrow x \geq 100$

4. Confirm Your Choice

Choice (A) gives the minimum number of attendees at each show for the band to meet its goals and is therefore the correct answer.

Before moving on to the next question, quickly review your work to ensure that you did not make any arithmetic errors.

Solving Algebraic Word Problems

12

If a bus averages 60 miles per hour on a certain route, it will arrive at the terminal two hours early. If the bus averages 40 miles per hour on the same route, it will arrive two hours late. What is the distance of the trip?

- (A) 9 miles
- (B) 90 miles
- (C) 125 miles
- (D) 480 miles

1. Determine What Concepts Are Being Tested

We are being asked to determine the distance of a route given the times and speeds of two trips along that route. Because we must set up an equation to find an unknown quantity (x), we are dealing with an **algebra word problem**.

2. Plan Your Approach

Note that we are given the times of the two trips in relation to each other; therefore, we must set the scheduled time for the bus equal to x. Use the distance formula, distance = (velocity)(time), to create the following relationship between the two trips:

$60(x - 2) = 40(x + 2)$

3. Solve

Simplify the equation to solve for x, the scheduled duration of the bus trip:

$60x - 120 = 40x + 80$

$20x = 200$

$x = 10$ hours

Plug this value into one of the original equations to solve for distance:

Distance = $60(8) = 480$ miles

4. Confirm Your Choice

The distance of this route is 480 miles, or **choice (D)**.

Before moving on to the next question, quickly review your work to ensure that you did not make any arithmetic errors.

Solving Measure of Center & Spread Problems

13

The shoe sizes of 10 men are 8, 10, 9, 12, 7, 10, 10, 11, 6, and 7. How much greater is the mode than the median?

(A) 0
(B) 0.5
(C) 5
(D) 9.5

1. Determine What Concepts Are Being Tested

We are given a list of values and asked to compare the median and mode of that dataset. Therefore, this is a **measure of center and spread problem**.

2. Plan Your Approach

Because the question asks us to compare the median and mode, we should start by rearranging the values in ascending order:

6, 7, 7, 8, 9, 10, 10, 10, 11, 12

3. Solve

Now we can easily determine that the mode is 10 (because it appears three times while other values appear only once or twice).

Because there are an even number of values, the median is the average of the middle two shoe sizes:

$$\text{Median} = \frac{9 + 10}{2} = 9.5$$

The difference between these two values is:

Mode − Median = 10 − 9.5 = 0.5

4. Confirm Your Choice

Choice (B), 0.5, is equal to the difference between the mode and median. Therefore, this is the correct answer.

Before moving on to the next question, quickly review your work to ensure that you did not make any arithmetic errors.

Solving Data Analysis/Ratios Questions

14

Questions 14 and 15 refer to the information to the right.

The table to the right displays high-speed Internet customers for a cable company in four states in the years 2000 and 2010. The number of customers in Kentucky in 2000 was approximately what percent of the number of customers in Ohio in the same year?

(A) 15%
(B) 20%
(C) 25%
(D) 30%

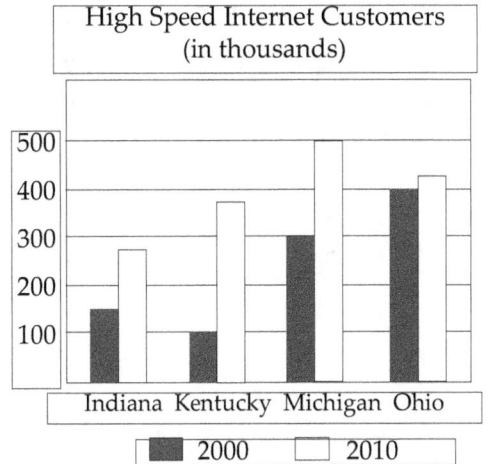

High Speed Internet Customers (in thousands)

1. Determine What Concepts Are Being Tested

This question asks us to analyze information from a graphic, compare two data points, and calculate a percentage. The question tests multiple topics, including **ratios and percentages** and **data analysis**.

2. Plan Your Approach

Start by analyzing the two points mentioned in the question, that is the number of customers in Kentucky in 2000 and the number of customers in Ohio in 2000.

3. Solve

The number of customers in Kentucky in 2000 was 100,000.
The number of customers in Ohio in 2000 was 400,000.

To determine the ratio of customers in Kentucky to customers in Ohio as a percent:

Customers in Kentucky = (x%)(Customers in Ohio) → $x = 25\%$
100,000 = (x%) (400,000)

4. Confirm Your Choice

Choice (C) correctly relates the ratio of customers in Kentucky to customers in Ohio.

Before moving on to the next question, quickly review your work to ensure that you did not make any arithmetic errors.

CHAPTER 4 - Math Key Strategies

Solving Data Analysis/Ratios Questions

Questions 14 and 15 refer to the information to the right.

From 2000 to 2010, the total number of high-speed Internet customers in the four states increased by approximately what percent?

(A) 25%

(B) 33%

(C) 50%

(D) 67%

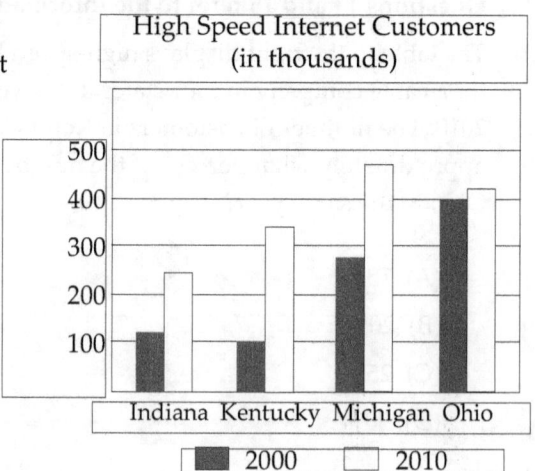

1. Determine What Concepts Are Being Tested

We are being asked to calculate the percent increase in total customers over the ten-year period. Like the previous question, this is a **ratios and percentages** and **data analysis**.

2. Plan Your Approach

Start by adding up the total number of customers for the years 2000 and 2010, then calculate the difference between the two points.

Total customers in 2000 = 125,000 + 100,000 + 275,000 + 400,000

Total customers in 2010 = 250,000 + 350,000 + 475,000 + 425,000

Increase = customers in 2010 − customers in 2000

3. Solve

Total customers in 2000 = 900,000

Total customers in 2010 = 1,500,000

Increase = 1,500,000 − 900,000 = 600,000

% Increase = $\dfrac{\text{change}}{\text{base line}} \times 100\% = \dfrac{600,000}{900,000} \times 100\% = 67\%$

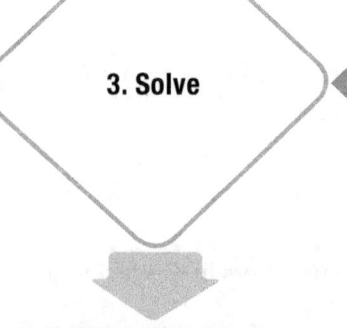

4. Confirm Your Choice

Choice (D) is equal to 67%, which is the percentage increase of the total high-speed internet customers from 2000 to 2010.

Before moving on to the next question, quickly review your work to ensure that you did not make any arithmetic errors.

Solving System of Equality/Inequality Questions

16

At a convenience store, two candy bars and two bags of potato chips cost $4.00, and three candy bars and two bags of potato chips cost $4.75. What is the price, in dollars, of one bag of potato chips?

ANSWER: _____

1. Determine What Concepts Are Being Tested ← We are asked to find a value given two equations, so this is a **system of equality/inequality question**. These questions ask you to find one or more unknown value(s) given two or more equations or inequalities.

2. Plan Your Approach ← Since this question is a word problem, we must first create two equations: one that mathematically describes the $4.00 purchase and another that describes the $4.75 purchase. Given these equations, we can eliminate our variable for the price of a candy bar, isolating the price of a bag of potato chips and giving us our answer.

3. Solve ← Let b be the price of one candy bar and c be the price of one bag of chips.
$2b + 2c = 4$
$3b + 2c = 4.75$

Subtracting the first equation from the second eliminates c and gives $b = 0.75$

According to the first equation, the cost of one candy bar, in dollars, is $2c = 4 - 2b$, which simplifies to $c = 2 - b$. Therefore, $c = 1.25$ or $\frac{5}{4}$

4. Confirm Your Choice ← The price of a bag of potato chips, in dollars, is **1.25**. Expressing this using the equivalent form $\frac{5}{4}$ is also acceptable.
Before moving on to the next question, quickly review your work to ensure that you did not make any arithmetic errors.

Solving Geometry Questions

17

The base of a pyramid has the same area as the base of a cylinder, and the cylinder is twice the height of the pyramid. What is the ratio of the volume of the pyramid to the volume of the cylinder?

ANSWER: _____

1. Determine What Concepts Are Being Tested

Although this question requires us to express our answer as a ratio, it is a **geometry question** because it requires us to determine the volume of two shapes.

2. Plan Your Approach

First, determine what formulas we need to use in order to solve. The formulas for the volumes of both a pyramid ($V = \frac{1}{3}lwh$) and a cylinder ($V = \pi r^2 h$) are located in the "Reference" section at the beginning of the SAT Math Tests.

Since the height of the cylinder (h_c) is twice that of the pyramid (h_p), we can conclude that $h_c = 2h_p$. Use this information to create a ratio that gives $\frac{\text{volume of pyramid}}{\text{volume of cylinder}}$.

3. Solve

Since the area of the cylinder's base is equal to the area of the pyramid's base, we can simplify our formulas as follows:
Let b be the area of the base for both the cylinder and the pyramid
Cylinder volume: $V = bh$
Pyramid volume: $V = \frac{1}{3}bh$
The cylinder has a height twice the height of the pyramid: $h_c = 2h_p$
The ratio of the volume of the pyramid to the volume of the cylinder is:

$$\frac{\text{volume of pyramid}}{\text{volume of cylinder}} = \frac{\frac{1}{3}bh_p}{bh_c} = \frac{\frac{1}{3}h_p}{2h_p} = \frac{1}{6}$$

4. Confirm Your Choice

The correct answers can be expressed as $\frac{1}{6}$, **0.166**, or **0.167**. Before moving on to the next question, quickly review your work to ensure that you did not make any arithmetic errors.

Solving Algebraic Word Problems

PART 1

Karen runs a flower shop. She determines that it takes her two hours of online marketing to bring in five new orders. If each order bills an average of $30, what is the minimum number of hours of marketing necessary to raise *at least* $10,000? (Round your answer to the nearest hour.)

ANSWER: _____

1. Determine What Concepts Are Being Tested

We are being asked to determine how many hours of marketing Karen must do to generate at least $10,000. Because we must set up an equation to find an unknown quantity (x), we are dealing with an **algebra word problem**.

2. Plan Your Approach

We must first extract all necessary information from the word problem:

Two hours of marketing brings in five orders at $30 each. Thus, two hours of marketing bring in $150 of business.

We can extrapolate on this information to determine how many hours of marketing are needed for $10,000 in sales.

3. Solve

If x is the number of marketing hours needed to bill $10,000, and if 2 hours bring in $150, then

$$x = 2 \times \left(\frac{10,000}{150}\right)$$

$$x = 133.3$$

We must find the number of hours needed to raise *at least* $10,000, and it takes 133.3 hours to raise exactly $10,000. Thus, it takes 134 hours to raise an amount of money greater than $10,000.

4. Confirm Your Choice

Make sure you round your answer, 133.3, up to indicate that Karen must raise *at least* $10,000, so the correct answer is **134** hours.

Before moving on to the next question, quickly review your work to ensure that you did not make any arithmetic errors.

Solving Algebraic Word Problems

PART 2

Karen hires a marketing assistant to bolster her online presence, and finds that it now takes only one hour of online marketing to bring in five new orders. If she pays her assistant $15 per hour, and the cost to fill an order is $5, how many hours must her assistant work each month for Karen's business to make a monthly profit of $10,000? (Round your answer to the nearest hour.)

ANSWER: _____

1. Determine What Concepts Are Being Tested

We are being asked to determine how many hours of marketing Karen's assistant must do to generate $10,000 per month. Because we must set up an equation to find an unknown quantity (x), we are dealing with an **algebra word problem**.

2. Plan Your Approach

We must first extract all necessary information from the word problem:

Profit: One hour of marketing generates five orders at $30 each. Thus, each hour of marketing bring in $150 of business.

Expenses: Each hour of marketing, Karen must spend $15 to pay her assistant and $5 to fill each of five orders. Thus, Karen must spend $15 + (\$5)(5) = \$40$ each hour.

We can extrapolate on this information to determine how many hours of marketing are needed for $10,000 in sales.

3. Solve

Each hour worked by the assistant costs $15 in wages and $25 to fill orders (five orders at $5 each). Each hour worked by the assistant brings in $150 in billings (five orders at $30 each). The profit to the business per hour is:

Profit by hour = $150 - (15 + 25) = 110$

To bill $10,000 in a month:

Hours worked = $\dfrac{10,000}{110} = 90.9$

Rounded to the nearest integer, hours worked = 91.

4. Confirm Your Choice

Make sure you round your answer, 90.9, to the nearest hour before you fill in the answer, which is **91** hours.

Before moving on to the next question, quickly review your work to ensure that you did not make any arithmetic errors.

END OF SECTION 4

KEY TO THE SAT

Practice Tests

Reading Test Scoring Guide

Number correct on the SAT Reading Test: _____
(Raw Score)

Raw Score	Scaled Score
52 – 51	400
50 – 49	390
48	380
47	370
46 – 45	360
44 – 43	350
42 – 41	340
40 – 38	330
37	320
36 – 35	310
34 – 33	300
32 – 30	290
29 – 28	280
27	270
26	260
25 – 24	250
23 – 22	240
21	230
20 – 19	220
18	210
17 – 16	200
15	190
14	180
13 – 12	170
11	160
10 – 9	150
8	140
7	130
6	120
5	110
4 – 1	100

Writing and Language Test Scoring Guide

Number correct on the SAT Writing and Language Test: _____
(Raw Score)

Raw Score	Scaled Score
44	400
43	390
42	380
41	370
40 – 38	360
37	350
36	340
35 – 34	330
33 – 32	320
31	310
30 – 28	300
27 – 26	290
25 – 24	280
23 – 22	270
21	260
20	250
19	230 – 240
18	220
17	210
16	200
15	190
14	180
13	170
12	160
11	150
10	140
9	130
8	120
7	110
6 – 1	100

Math Test Scoring Guide

Number correct on the SAT Math Test: _____
(Raw Score)

Raw Score	Scaled Score
58 – 57	800
56 – 55	790
54	780
53	770
52	750
51	740
50	730
49	710
48	700
47	690
46	680
45	670
44	660
43	650
42	640
41	630
40 – 39	620
38 – 37	610
36 – 34	600
33 – 32	590
31 – 30	570
29	560
28 – 27	550
26	530
25	510
24 – 23	500
22 – 21	490
20	480
19	470
18 – 17	460
16	450
15 – 14	440
13	420 – 430
12 – 11	400 – 410
10 – 9	380 – 390
8 – 6	350 – 370
5 – 4	310 – 340
3	290 – 300
2	250 – 280
1	210 – 240
0	200

Reading Test Scaled Score: _____

\+

Writing Test Scaled Score: _____

\+

Math Test Scaled Score: _____

=

Total SAT Practice Test Score: _____

KALLIS

SAT® Practice Test #1

IMPORTANT REMINDERS:

 When you take the official SAT, you will need to use a No. 2 pencil. Do not use a pen or a mechanical pencil.

 On the official SAT, sharing any of the questions on the test violates the College Board's policies and may result in your scores being canceled.

(This cover is modeled after the cover you'll see when you take the official SAT.)

UNAUTHORIZED REPRODUCTION OR USE OF ANY PART OF THIS TEST IS PROHIBITED.

© 2019 KALLIS EDU

YOUR NAME (PRINT) _____
                        LAST   FIRST   MI

TEST CENTER _____
                  NUMBER   NAME OF TEST CENTER   ROOM NUMBER

TEST BOOKLET

- You may open the booklet to ONLY the section that is currently being tested. You may NOT browse upcoming sections, nor can you review your answers in past sections.
- You MAY write in your test booklet., but you will not receive any credit for answers that you indicate in the booklet. When the time for a section is over, you may NOT transfer answers from your booklet to the answer sheet.
- You may NOT take any part of the test booklet out of the room.

ANSWER SHEET

- Machines will scan your answer sheet by checking your pencil marks. Using a No. 2 pencil, fill in the circles that correspond to your answers completely and darkly.
- Do not make any marks on the answer sheet outside of these circles. If you need to erase anything, make sure to do it thoroughly.

SCORING

- Each correct answer is worth one point.
- There is no penalty for incorrect answers. Even if you are unsure about a particular answer, it is a good strategy to mark one of the choices.

9 | TEST ID (Copy from back of test book.)

8 | FORM CODE (Copy and grid as on back of test book.)

Ideas contained in passages for this test, some of which are excerpted or adapted from published material, do not necessarily represent the opinions of KALLIS EDU.

DO NOT OPEN THIS BOOK UNTIL THE TEST ADMINISTRATOR TELLS YOU TO DO SO.

SAT Practice Test Answer Sheet

Remove (or photocopy) this answer sheet and use it to complete the SAT Practice Test. See the answer key and explanations following the test when finished. For printable versions of these answer sheets, visit kallisedu.com's "Resources" page.

Start with number 1 for each section.
If a section has fewer questions than answer spaces, leave the extra spaces blank.

SECTION 1

1. Ⓐ Ⓑ Ⓒ Ⓓ
2. Ⓐ Ⓑ Ⓒ Ⓓ
3. Ⓐ Ⓑ Ⓒ Ⓓ
4. Ⓐ Ⓑ Ⓒ Ⓓ
5. Ⓐ Ⓑ Ⓒ Ⓓ
6. Ⓐ Ⓑ Ⓒ Ⓓ
7. Ⓐ Ⓑ Ⓒ Ⓓ
8. Ⓐ Ⓑ Ⓒ Ⓓ
9. Ⓐ Ⓑ Ⓒ Ⓓ
10. Ⓐ Ⓑ Ⓒ Ⓓ
11. Ⓐ Ⓑ Ⓒ Ⓓ
12. Ⓐ Ⓑ Ⓒ Ⓓ
13. Ⓐ Ⓑ Ⓒ Ⓓ
14. Ⓐ Ⓑ Ⓒ Ⓓ
15. Ⓐ Ⓑ Ⓒ Ⓓ
16. Ⓐ Ⓑ Ⓒ Ⓓ
17. Ⓐ Ⓑ Ⓒ Ⓓ
18. Ⓐ Ⓑ Ⓒ Ⓓ
19. Ⓐ Ⓑ Ⓒ Ⓓ
20. Ⓐ Ⓑ Ⓒ Ⓓ
21. Ⓐ Ⓑ Ⓒ Ⓓ
22. Ⓐ Ⓑ Ⓒ Ⓓ
23. Ⓐ Ⓑ Ⓒ Ⓓ
24. Ⓐ Ⓑ Ⓒ Ⓓ
25. Ⓐ Ⓑ Ⓒ Ⓓ
26. Ⓐ Ⓑ Ⓒ Ⓓ
27. Ⓐ Ⓑ Ⓒ Ⓓ
28. Ⓐ Ⓑ Ⓒ Ⓓ
29. Ⓐ Ⓑ Ⓒ Ⓓ
30. Ⓐ Ⓑ Ⓒ Ⓓ
31. Ⓐ Ⓑ Ⓒ Ⓓ
32. Ⓐ Ⓑ Ⓒ Ⓓ
33. Ⓐ Ⓑ Ⓒ Ⓓ
34. Ⓐ Ⓑ Ⓒ Ⓓ
35. Ⓐ Ⓑ Ⓒ Ⓓ
36. Ⓐ Ⓑ Ⓒ Ⓓ
37. Ⓐ Ⓑ Ⓒ Ⓓ
38. Ⓐ Ⓑ Ⓒ Ⓓ
39. Ⓐ Ⓑ Ⓒ Ⓓ
40. Ⓐ Ⓑ Ⓒ Ⓓ
41. Ⓐ Ⓑ Ⓒ Ⓓ
42. Ⓐ Ⓑ Ⓒ Ⓓ
43. Ⓐ Ⓑ Ⓒ Ⓓ
44. Ⓐ Ⓑ Ⓒ Ⓓ
45. Ⓐ Ⓑ Ⓒ Ⓓ
46. Ⓐ Ⓑ Ⓒ Ⓓ
47. Ⓐ Ⓑ Ⓒ Ⓓ
48. Ⓐ Ⓑ Ⓒ Ⓓ
49. Ⓐ Ⓑ Ⓒ Ⓓ
50. Ⓐ Ⓑ Ⓒ Ⓓ
51. Ⓐ Ⓑ Ⓒ Ⓓ
52. Ⓐ Ⓑ Ⓒ Ⓓ

☐ #right in Section 1

☐ #wrong in Section 1

SECTION 2

1. Ⓐ Ⓑ Ⓒ Ⓓ
2. Ⓐ Ⓑ Ⓒ Ⓓ
3. Ⓐ Ⓑ Ⓒ Ⓓ
4. Ⓐ Ⓑ Ⓒ Ⓓ
5. Ⓐ Ⓑ Ⓒ Ⓓ
6. Ⓐ Ⓑ Ⓒ Ⓓ
7. Ⓐ Ⓑ Ⓒ Ⓓ
8. Ⓐ Ⓑ Ⓒ Ⓓ
9. Ⓐ Ⓑ Ⓒ Ⓓ
10. Ⓐ Ⓑ Ⓒ Ⓓ
11. Ⓐ Ⓑ Ⓒ Ⓓ
12. Ⓐ Ⓑ Ⓒ Ⓓ
13. Ⓐ Ⓑ Ⓒ Ⓓ
14. Ⓐ Ⓑ Ⓒ Ⓓ
15. Ⓐ Ⓑ Ⓒ Ⓓ
16. Ⓐ Ⓑ Ⓒ Ⓓ
17. Ⓐ Ⓑ Ⓒ Ⓓ
18. Ⓐ Ⓑ Ⓒ Ⓓ
19. Ⓐ Ⓑ Ⓒ Ⓓ
20. Ⓐ Ⓑ Ⓒ Ⓓ
21. Ⓐ Ⓑ Ⓒ Ⓓ
22. Ⓐ Ⓑ Ⓒ Ⓓ
23. Ⓐ Ⓑ Ⓒ Ⓓ
24. Ⓐ Ⓑ Ⓒ Ⓓ
25. Ⓐ Ⓑ Ⓒ Ⓓ
26. Ⓐ Ⓑ Ⓒ Ⓓ
27. Ⓐ Ⓑ Ⓒ Ⓓ
28. Ⓐ Ⓑ Ⓒ Ⓓ
29. Ⓐ Ⓑ Ⓒ Ⓓ
30. Ⓐ Ⓑ Ⓒ Ⓓ
31. Ⓐ Ⓑ Ⓒ Ⓓ
32. Ⓐ Ⓑ Ⓒ Ⓓ
33. Ⓐ Ⓑ Ⓒ Ⓓ
34. Ⓐ Ⓑ Ⓒ Ⓓ
35. Ⓐ Ⓑ Ⓒ Ⓓ
37. Ⓐ Ⓑ Ⓒ Ⓓ
38. Ⓐ Ⓑ Ⓒ Ⓓ
39. Ⓐ Ⓑ Ⓒ Ⓓ
40. Ⓐ Ⓑ Ⓒ Ⓓ
41. Ⓐ Ⓑ Ⓒ Ⓓ
42. Ⓐ Ⓑ Ⓒ Ⓓ
43. Ⓐ Ⓑ Ⓒ Ⓓ
44. Ⓐ Ⓑ Ⓒ Ⓓ

☐ #right in Section 2

☐ #wrong in Section 2

Remove (or photocopy) this answer sheet and use it to complete the SAT Practice Test.

Start with number 1 for each section.
If a section has fewer questions than answer spaces, leave the extra spaces blank.

SECTION 3

1. Ⓐ Ⓑ Ⓒ Ⓓ
2. Ⓐ Ⓑ Ⓒ Ⓓ
3. Ⓐ Ⓑ Ⓒ Ⓓ
4. Ⓐ Ⓑ Ⓒ Ⓓ
5. Ⓐ Ⓑ Ⓒ Ⓓ
6. Ⓐ Ⓑ Ⓒ Ⓓ
7. Ⓐ Ⓑ Ⓒ Ⓓ
8. Ⓐ Ⓑ Ⓒ Ⓓ
9. Ⓐ Ⓑ Ⓒ Ⓓ
10. Ⓐ Ⓑ Ⓒ Ⓓ
11. Ⓐ Ⓑ Ⓒ Ⓓ
12. Ⓐ Ⓑ Ⓒ Ⓓ
13. Ⓐ Ⓑ Ⓒ Ⓓ
14. Ⓐ Ⓑ Ⓒ Ⓓ
15. Ⓐ Ⓑ Ⓒ Ⓓ

right in Section 3

16. 17. 18. 19. 20.

[grid-in answer boxes]

#wrong in Section 3

SECTION 4

1. Ⓐ Ⓑ Ⓒ Ⓓ
2. Ⓐ Ⓑ Ⓒ Ⓓ
3. Ⓐ Ⓑ Ⓒ Ⓓ
4. Ⓐ Ⓑ Ⓒ Ⓓ
5. Ⓐ Ⓑ Ⓒ Ⓓ
6. Ⓐ Ⓑ Ⓒ Ⓓ
7. Ⓐ Ⓑ Ⓒ Ⓓ
8. Ⓐ Ⓑ Ⓒ Ⓓ
9. Ⓐ Ⓑ Ⓒ Ⓓ
10. Ⓐ Ⓑ Ⓒ Ⓓ
11. Ⓐ Ⓑ Ⓒ Ⓓ
12. Ⓐ Ⓑ Ⓒ Ⓓ
13. Ⓐ Ⓑ Ⓒ Ⓓ
14. Ⓐ Ⓑ Ⓒ Ⓓ
15. Ⓐ Ⓑ Ⓒ Ⓓ
16. Ⓐ Ⓑ Ⓒ Ⓓ
17. Ⓐ Ⓑ Ⓒ Ⓓ
18. Ⓐ Ⓑ Ⓒ Ⓓ
19. Ⓐ Ⓑ Ⓒ Ⓓ
20. Ⓐ Ⓑ Ⓒ Ⓓ
21. Ⓐ Ⓑ Ⓒ Ⓓ
22. Ⓐ Ⓑ Ⓒ Ⓓ
23. Ⓐ Ⓑ Ⓒ Ⓓ
24. Ⓐ Ⓑ Ⓒ Ⓓ
25. Ⓐ Ⓑ Ⓒ Ⓓ
26. Ⓐ Ⓑ Ⓒ Ⓓ
27. Ⓐ Ⓑ Ⓒ Ⓓ
28. Ⓐ Ⓑ Ⓒ Ⓓ
29. Ⓐ Ⓑ Ⓒ Ⓓ
30. Ⓐ Ⓑ Ⓒ Ⓓ

#right in Section 4

#wrong in Section 4

31. 32. 33. 34. 35.

[grid-in answer boxes]

SECTION 4

36.　　　　37. (PART 1)　　　38. (PART 2)

Remove (or photocopy) this answer sheet and use it to complete the SAT Practice Test.

Section 5 is the Optional Essay test.

SECTION 5

Reading Test 1

65 MINUTES, 52 QUESTIONS

Turn to Section 1 of your answer sheet to answer the questions in this section.

DIRECTIONS

Each passage or pair of passages is accompanied by 10 or 11 questions. Read each passage or pair of passages, and then select the most appropriate answer to each question. Some passages may include tables or graphs that require additional analysis.

Refer to the passage below to answer questions 1 – 10.

This passage is adapted from Stephen Arr, *Mr. President*, originally published in 1953.

   George Wong stood pale and silent by the video screen, listening to the election returns, a long-stemmed glass of champagne clutched forgotten in his trembling right hand.
5 The announcer droned on: "—latest returns from Venus, with half of the election districts reporting, give three billion four hundred and ninety-six million votes for Wong, against one billion, four hundred million for Thompson, one
10 billion one hundred million for Miccio, and nine hundred million for Kau. These results, added to the almost complete returns from Earth and the first fragmentary reports from Mars, clearly indicate a landslide vote for Wong as the next
15 President of the Solar Union. The two billion votes from Ganymede* and Callisto*, which will be received early tomorrow morning, cannot appreciably affect the results. The battle for the twenty-five Vice-Presidents is less clear. It is
20 certain that Thompson, Miccio, Kau, Singh, and DuLavier will all be among those elected, but in what order is not yet...."
   Wong leaned over and snapped the video off. His shoulders sagged. He leaned against
25 the console as though too tired to move, a slight, narrow-shouldered man with a very high forehead and thin receding black hair.
   "I'm sorry, truly sorry," Michael Thompson said sympathetically, placing a friendly arm
30 across the narrow shoulders of the successful candidate. They were alone in the living room of the hotel suite in New Geneva, which they had shared for the campaign. "The people chose well. After the wonderful job you did in organizing
35 the colonization of Io* and Europa*, you were the logical man. And then you do have the fantastic Responsibility Quotient of 9.6 out of 10. Anyway," he added with a weary shrug, "don't feel too bad—it looks as though I'll be First Vice-
40 President."
   A brief ghost of a smile crossed George Wong's face. "We who are about to die salute you," he said, lifting his glass in a bitter toast to the blank video screen.
45   Thompson, the man who was to be First Vice-President, silently joined him.
   Wong had already eaten breakfast and was dressed in an inconspicuous tweed suit for the inauguration when the chimes sounded, telling
50 him that they were at the door. Slowly, he walked to the door and opened it.
   "Good morning, Mr. President," the man outside said cheerily, flashing his famous grin. George Wong immediately recognized Al Grimm,
55 the man who had been personal secretary to sixty-three Presidents. He was one of the vast army of civil servants who kept the wheels of government turning smoothly until Presidents were able to make the decisions that would create policy.
60   "Good morning, Al," George Wong said. "I am afraid I'll have to place myself completely in your hands for these first few days. Do we go to the Executive Mansion for the inauguration now?"
65   "Yes, sir. Then, after your inauguration, to the office. Messages of condolence have been pouring in all night, but I don't think you want to bother with them. However, I am afraid we will have to bring up some of the problems that have
70 arisen in the two weeks since President Reynolds left office."
   "How is he?" Wong asked. "I knew him, you know. He taught at Venus University at the same time I did. He was a fine man."
75   "I'm afraid he's no better," Al said, shaking his head. "We're doing all we can for him, but he won't even speak to his wife. You know how difficult it is."
   "Yes, I know," Wong said.
80   They rode downstairs in silence and walked to the Presidential Copter parked in the street in front of the house. A few guards loitered in the vicinity, but there were no crowds. They entered the plush copter, which rose smoothly under
85 its whirling blades and carried them over the city, landing finally on the lawn of the Executive

Mansion.
   Chief Justice Herz met them, dressed in a blue business suit, and after they shook hands he administered the oath.
   "Do you, George Wong," he asked, "swear to make every decision you are asked to make as President of the Solar Union for the benefit of the people of the Union and in accord with what you believe to be fair and just, fully cognizant of the fact that the welfare of seventy-five billion citizens of the Union is dependent on you?"
   "I do," George Wong said, through a painfully dry throat that would barely permit the words to come out…

* *Ganymede, Callisto, Io, Europa: the four largest moons of Jupiter*

01

George Wong's attitude throughout the passage is best described as

A) haughty.
B) indifferent.
C) melancholic.
D) relieved.

02

Which choice provides the best evidence for the answer to the previous question?

A) Lines 23 – 25 ("Wong leaned…to move")
B) Lines 36 – 37 ("And then…of 10")
C) Lines 42 – 44 ("'We who…screen")
D) Lines 47 – 50 ("Wong had…the door")

03

The description of vote counts from the Solar Union in paragraph 2 (lines 5 – 22) mainly serves to

A) provide information about the main character.
B) create suspense about the election's outcome.
C) introduce the size and scale of an imagined future society.
D) set up a conflict between George Wong and Michael Thompson.

04

The statement in lines 42 – 43, "'We who are about to die salute you,'" seems to be addressed to

A) those who voted.
B) Michael Thompson.
C) the former President.
D) George Wong himself.

05

Based on the information in the passage, what can be inferred about most Presidents of the Solar Union?

A) They rely on their Vice Presidents to do much of the work.
B) They do not stay in office for very long.
C) They remain in office until their deaths.
D) They serve in isolation and secrecy.

06

Which choice provides the best evidence for the answer to the previous question?

A) Lines 38 – 40 ("'don't…Vice-President'")
B) Lines 54 – 56 ("George Wong…Presidents")
C) Lines 68 – 71 ("'I am…office'")
D) Lines 98 – 100 ("'I do…out'")

07

As used in line 48, "inconspicuous" most nearly means

A) concealed.
B) indifferent.
C) modest.
D) discreet.

08

As used in line 66, "condolence" most nearly means

A) sympathy.
B) charity.
C) mercy.
D) dejection.

09

It can be inferred from lines 72 – 79 that President Reynolds

A) was forced to forfeit the presidency because of his wife.
B) was removed from office for committing a heinous crime.
C) was greatly disappointed when he was not reelected as President.
D) was overwhelmed by his experiences while in office.

10

The chief justice's question and George Wong's reaction in lines 91 – 100 most nearly imply that Presidents of the Solar Union

A) often find it onerous to make decisions affecting so many people.
B) struggle to keep up with the constant demands of their staff.
C) usually want more power over the citizens than they are allowed.
D) tend to be careless leaders who must be forced to complete tasks.

Refer to the passage below to answer questions 11 – 21.

This passage is adapted from Frederick Douglass, *Narrative of the Life of Frederick Douglass*, originally published in 1845.

line

If at any one time of my life more than another, I was made to drink the bitterest dregs of slavery, that time was during the first six months of my stay with Mr. Covey. We were
5   worked in all weathers. It was never too hot or too cold; it could never rain, blow, hail, or snow, too hard for us to work in the field. Work, work, work, was scarcely more the order of the day than of the night. The longest days were
10 too short for him, and the shortest nights too long for him. I was somewhat unmanageable when I first went there, but a few months of this discipline tamed me. Mr. Covey succeeded in breaking me. I was broken in body, soul, and
15 spirit. My natural elasticity was crushed, my intellect languished, the disposition to read departed, the cheerful spark that lingered about my eye died; the dark night of slavery closed in upon me; and behold a man transformed into a
20 brute!

Sunday was my only leisure time. I spent this in a sort of beast-like stupor, between sleep and wake, under some large tree. At times I would rise up, a flash of energetic freedom
25 would dart through my soul, accompanied with a faint beam of hope, that flickered for a moment, and then vanished. I sank down again, mourning over my wretched condition. I was sometimes prompted to take my life, and that of
30 Covey, but was prevented by a combination of hope and fear. My sufferings on this plantation seem now like a dream rather than a stern reality.

Our house stood within a few rods of
35 the Chesapeake Bay, whose broad bosom was ever white with sails from every quarter of the habitable globe. Those beautiful vessels, robed in purest white, so delightful to the eye of freemen, were to me so many shrouded
40 ghosts, to terrify and torment me with thoughts of my wretched condition. I have often, in the deep stillness of a summer's Sabbath, stood all alone upon the lofty banks of that noble bay, and traced, with saddened heart and tearful
45 eye, the countless number of sails moving off to the mighty ocean. The sight of these always affected me powerfully. My thoughts would compel utterance; and there, with no audience but the Almighty, I would pour out my soul's
50 complaint, in my rude way, with an apostrophe to the moving multitude of ships:—

"You are loosed from your moorings, and are free; I am fast in my chains, and am a slave! You move merrily before the gentle gale, and I
55 sadly before the bloody whip! You are freedom's swift-winged angels, that fly round the world; I am confined in bands of iron! O that I were free! O, that I were on one of your gallant decks, and under your protecting wing! Alas! betwixt me
60 and you, the turbid waters roll. Go on, go on. O that I could also go! Could I but swim! If I could fly! O, why was I born a man, of whom to make a brute! The glad ship is gone; she hides in the dim distance. I am left in the hottest hell of unending
65 slavery. O God, save me! God, deliver me! Let me be free! Is there any God? Why am I a slave? I will run away. I will not stand it. Get caught, or get clear, I'll try it. ...Let but the first opportunity offer, and, come what will, I am off. Meanwhile,
70 I will try to bear up under the yoke. ... It may be that my misery in slavery will only increase my happiness when I get free. There is a better day coming."

Thus I used to think, and thus I used to
75 speak to myself; goaded almost to madness at one moment, and at the next reconciling myself to my wretched lot.

11

Douglass' statement in lines 9 – 10, "The longest days were too short for [Mr. Covey]," suggests that Mr. Covey

A) had an unusual amount of energy each day.
B) scolded slaves when they took rest breaks.
C) was never satisfied with the plantation's production.
D) expected slaves to labor for unreasonably long periods.

12

In paragraph 1 (lines 1 – 20), Douglass characterizes Mr. Covey as

A) demanding and unsympathetic.
B) unpredictable and dangerous.
C) harsh but fair.
D) intelligent but cruel.

13

In paragraph 1 (lines 1 – 20), Douglass describes his transformation from being

A) content to uneasy.
B) dependable to unreliable.
C) spirited to despondent.
D) confident to anxious.

14

Which choice provides the best evidence for the answer to the previous question?

A) Lines 1 – 4 ("If at…Covey")
B) Lines 7 – 9 ("Work…night")
C) Lines 11 – 12 ("I was…there")
D) Lines 15 – 18 ("My natural…died")

15

Douglass uses the term "brute" in line 20 to

A) explain his unusual attitude.
B) emphasize the importance of adequate rest.
C) describe the effects of constant forced labor.
D) refer to an increase in physical strength.

16

The white sails described in lines 34 – 38 serve which function for Douglass?

A) They lighten his mood.
B) They rouse him to reflect on his situation.
C) They create a diversion.
D) They frighten him into inaction.

17

Which choice provides the best evidence for the answer to the previous question?

A) Lines 34 – 37 ("Our house…globe")
B) Lines 37 – 41 ("Those…condition")
C) Lines 41 – 46 ("I have often … ocean")
D) Lines 46 – 47 ("The sight … powerfully")

18

As used in line 48, "compel utterance" most nearly means

A) apply pressure.
B) require pronouncement.
C) force obedience.
D) urge caution.

19

Which choice most closely captures the meaning of the "turbid waters" referred to in line 60?

A) The impact of travelers
B) Douglass' exhaustion
C) Punishments for slaves
D) Threatening barriers

20

In paragraph 4 (lines 52 – 73), Douglass' thoughts shift from

A) longing to planning.
B) hoping to despairing.
C) planning to relinquishing.
D) envying to reflecting.

21

The final paragraph (lines 74 – 77) primarily serves to

A) recount Douglass' sudden loss of sanity.
B) reiterate the dehumanizing effects of slavery.
C) describe how Douglass' attitude transformed because of Mr. Covey's cruelty.
D) summarize Douglass' attitudes in the previous paragraph.

Refer to the passage below to answer questions 22 – 32.

This passage is adapted from Felicia Chou, "NASA's Kepler Mission Discovers Bigger, Older Cousin to Earth," July 2015.

line

NASA's Kepler [orbiting space telescope] mission has confirmed the first near-Earth-size planet in the "habitable zone" around a sun-like star. This discovery and the introduction of 11
5 other new small habitable-zone candidate planets mark another milestone in the journey to finding another "Earth."

The newly discovered Kepler-452b is the smallest planet to date discovered orbiting in the
10 habitable zone—the area around a star where liquid water could pool on the surface of an orbiting planet—of a G2-type star, like our sun. The confirmation of Kepler-452b brings the total number of confirmed planets to 1,030.
15 "On the 20th anniversary year of the discovery that proved other suns host planets, the Kepler exoplanet explorer has discovered a planet and star which most closely resemble the Earth and our Sun," said John
20 Grunsfeld, associate administrator of NASA's Science Mission Directorate at the agency's headquarters in Washington. "This exciting result brings us one step closer to finding an Earth 2.0."

Kepler-452b is 60 percent larger in diameter
25 than Earth and is considered a super-Earth-sized planet. While its mass and composition are not yet determined, previous research suggests that planets the size of Kepler-452b have a good chance of being rocky.
30 While Kepler-452b is larger than Earth, its 385-day orbit is only 5 percent longer. The planet is 5 percent farther from its parent star Kepler-452 than Earth is from the Sun. Kepler-452 is 6 billion years old, 1.5 billion years older than our sun, has
35 the same temperature, and is 20 percent brighter and has a diameter 10 percent larger.

"We can think of Kepler-452b as an older, bigger cousin to Earth, providing an opportunity to understand and reflect upon Earth's evolving
40 environment," said Jon Jenkins, Kepler data analysis lead at NASA's Ames Research Center in Moffett Field, California, who led the team that discovered Kepler-452b. "It's awe-inspiring to consider that this planet has spent 6 billion
45 years in the habitable zone of its star; longer than Earth. That's substantial opportunity for life to arise, should all the necessary ingredients and conditions for life exist on this planet."

To help confirm the finding and better
50 determine the properties of the Kepler-452 system, the team conducted ground-based observations at the University of Texas at Austin's McDonald Observatory, the Fred Lawrence Whipple Observatory on Mt. Hopkins, Arizona,
55 and the W. M. Keck Observatory atop Mauna Kea in Hawaii. These measurements were key for the researchers to confirm the planetary nature of Kepler-452b, to refine the size and brightness of its host star and to better pin down the size of the
60 planet and its orbit.

The Kepler-452 system is located 1,400 light-years away in the constellation Cygnus. In addition to confirming Kepler-452b, the Kepler team has increased the number of new
65 exoplanet candidates by 521 from their analysis of observations conducted from May 2009 to May 2013, raising the number of planet candidates detected by the Kepler mission to 4,696. Candidates require follow-up observations and
70 analysis to verify they are actual planets.

Twelve of the new planet candidates have diameters between one to two times that of Earth, and orbit in their star's habitable zone. Of these, nine orbit stars that are similar to our sun in size
75 and temperature.

"We've been able to fully automate our process of identifying planet candidates, which means we can finally assess every transit signal in the entire Kepler dataset quickly and uniformly,"
80 said Jeff Coughlin, Kepler scientist at the SETI Institute in Mountain View, California, who led the analysis of a new candidate catalog. "This gives astronomers a statistically sound population of planet candidates to accurately determine the
85 number of small, possibly rocky planets like Earth in our Milky Way galaxy."

Scientists now are producing the last catalog based on the original Kepler mission's four-year data set. The final analysis will be conducted
90 using sophisticated software that is increasingly sensitive to the tiny telltale signatures of Earth-size planets.

22

The passage is primarily concerned with

A) comparing the findings of ground- and space-based observatories.
B) announcing conclusions based on new data.
C) refuting an assumption based on earlier data.
D) stating the primary goal of NASA's Kepler mission.

23

Over the course of the passage, the author's focus shifts from

A) a general description of exoplanets to an investigation of one particular exoplanet.
B) an analysis of NASA's Kepler mission to a criticism of its findings.
C) the discovery of one particular exoplanet to a summary of others.
D) the success of one NASA mission to the challenges faced by its predecessors.

24

The purpose of the phrase "the area…orbiting planet" (lines 10 – 12) is to

A) challenge an earlier claim.
B) validate a hypothesis.
C) define a term.
D) provide an example.

25

According to the passage, the confirmation of Kepler-452b is a result of discoveries including that

A) the majority of solar systems contain Earth-like planets.
B) space telescopes are more effective than ground-based observatories.
C) most stars in our galaxy are approximately the same size as the Sun.
D) planets exist outside of our solar system.

26

The description of Kepler-452b as a "cousin to Earth" in line 38 refers to

A) identical compositions of the planets.
B) similarities between the two planets.
C) the galaxy that the planets share in common.
D) vast distance between the two planets.

27

It can reasonably be inferred from the passage that one aspiration of the researchers studying Kepler-452b is to

A) communicate with the planet's inhabitants.
B) obtain mineral resources from the planet.
C) gather data about its size and structure.
D) travel to the planet.

28

Which choice provides the best evidence for the answer to the previous question?

A) Lines 43 – 47 ("'It's awe-inspiring… arise'")
B) Lines 49 – 56 ("To help…Hawaii")
C) Lines 61 – 62 ("The Kepler-452… Cygnus")
D) Lines 71 – 73 ("Twelve of the… zone")

29

As used in line 71, "candidates" most nearly means

A) applicants.
B) aspirants.
C) possibilities.
D) successors.

30

Which choice provides evidence for the claim that researchers cannot actually see Kepler-452b with telescopes?

A) Lines 26 – 29 ("While its…rocky")
B) Lines 31 – 34 ("The planet…old")
C) Lines 71 – 73 ("Twelve of the…zone")
D) Lines 87 – 89 ("Scientists now…set")

31

As used in line 91, "signatures" most nearly means

A) indications.
B) autographs.
C) designations.
D) trademarks.

32

The passage suggests that an Earth-like planet is likely to

A) orbit a star that is the same size and age of our sun.
B) be more massive than Earth.
C) be older than Earth.
D) contain liquid water.

Refer to the passage and graphic below to answer questions 33 – 42.

This passage is adapted from Kallis Edu, "What's showing on the big screen?" published in 2016.

It is unlikely that the 2014 film *Transformers: Age of Extinction* will go down in history as a great—or even a good—film. The Michael Bay-directed project was panned by critics, [5] and the most notable awards it garnered were Raspberry Awards for Worst Director and Worst Supporting Actor. Nevertheless, the fourth film in the *Transformers* series was the highest grossing film of 2014, bringing in over [10] $1.1 billion worldwide. How did a nominee for 2014's Worst Picture become the top-earning film that year?

Transformers: Age of Extinction is an American film, yet its popularity has little to do [15] with American filmgoers. The film grossed just $245 million domestically, while it raked in $858 million—80 percent of its earnings—from foreign box offices. *Transformers* is only one example of an American-made film that generated [20] disproportionate amounts of money from international audiences. American blockbusters often draw audiences even in places with robust filmmaking industries of their own, such as China and India.

[25] The shift occurred over at least a decade. At the turn of the millennium, in 2000, Hollywood still earned about as much from its domestic audiences as it did abroad. But the tide kept turning. Globally, theater audiences expanded [30] while domestic movie theaters were struggling, as many Americans started watching movies at home on video and DVD. By 2009, foreign ticket sales dominated the market; Hollywood was earning twice as much from movie theaters [35] outside the U.S. as it was inside. Indeed, the top-grossing American film from each year since 2008 has earned considerably more from foreign markets than from domestic ones.

The cultural impact of the shift will [40] necessarily be subjective. Critics will no doubt fill many pages giving their views on whether the shift magnifies the influence of American films abroad in terms of exporting American values, for better or for worse. On the other [45] hand, many will ponder whether American films have become less, well, "American," for better or for worse.

Some studies have attempted to gather hard data regarding the causes and effects of [50] the "internationalization" of Hollywood films. In a 2012 study published in the *Journal of Media Economics*, researchers from the University of Calgary and the University of Sydney analyzed the types of films released between 1997 and [55] 2007. They examined the revenue generated from about 2,000 U.S. films in Australia, Europe, and Mexico, as well as in the United States and Canada.

Researchers sorted each country's ticket sales [60] according to several categories (genre, sequels, and well-known actors) and then noted whether more movies geared toward foreign markets were released subsequently. The data showed that people in different countries, even if they share a [65] border, are more likely to buy movie tickets based on different factors. For example, the French tend to favor dramas, while the Spanish are more often drawn to big-name stars. Romantic comedies do well in Germany and Austria, while only [70] Americans tend to favor American comedies.

The data also suggested that American film companies are indeed keeping their focus on foreign markets. In other words, the data suggest that Hollywood is "sacrificing some U.S. box [75] office appeal" in order to appeal to ticket-buyers elsewhere, according to the study. The researchers concluded that the "growing relative size of the foreign market may be providing an incentive for the production of films that maximize worldwide [80] profitability, which necessarily leads to a trade-off between what appeals to the domestic market and what appeals to foreign markets."

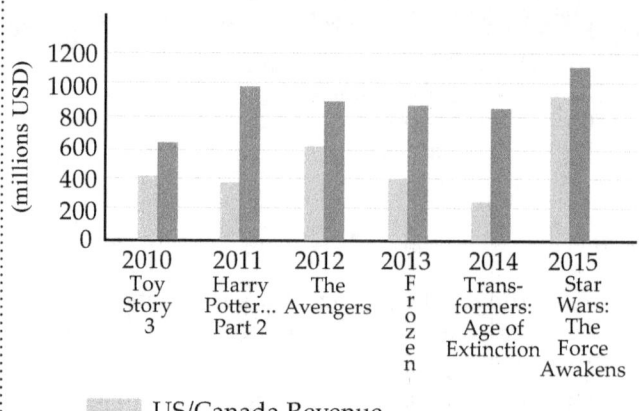

Revenue From Top-Grossing Hollywood Films

33

The author discusses *Transformers: Age of Extinction* in paragraphs 1 and 2 (lines 1 – 24) primarily to

A) illustrate the shift that is the central focus of the passage.
B) criticize a type of film-making popular among Hollywood producers.
C) introduce an analysis of the film preferences of foreign and American audiences.
D) address some common themes in American action films.

34

Which choice provides the best evidence for the answer to the previous question?

A) Lines 1 – 3 ("It's unlikely…film")
B) Lines 7 – 10 ("Nevertheless…worldwide")
C) Lines 15 – 18 ("The film…offices")
D) Lines 18 – 21 ("*Transformers*…audiences")

35

In paragraph 1 (lines 1 – 12), the author suggests that a film is generally regarded as "good" or "bad" based on its

A) foreign box-office earnings.
B) domestic box-office earnings.
C) critical reception and the awards it receives.
D) ability to attract repeat viewers.

36

As used in line 22, "robust" most nearly means

A) unshakable.
B) booming.
C) resilient.
D) strapping.

37

Paragraph 3 (lines 25 – 38) suggests that, from 2000 to 2009,

A) the average budget for a Hollywood film increased significantly.
B) Hollywood produced an increasing number of films that targeted a domestic audience.
C) the number of foreign filmgoers increased significantly.
D) the number of foreign filmgoers remained relatively unchanged.

38

The 2012 study discussed in lines 48 – 82 suggests that

A) most American comedies are not shown in foreign countries.
B) many Spanish actors have become as famous as American actors.
C) France, Spain, Germany, and Austria are the largest foreign markets for American films.
D) American comedies are an exception to the trend discussed throughout the passage.

39

As used in line 77, "relative" most nearly means

A) moderate.
B) reasonable.
C) connected.
D) comparative.

40

According to the passage, the international popularity of American films

A) indirectly affects America's domestic film market.
B) primarily benefits high-ranking Hollywood executives.
C) has encouraged foreign filmmakers to seek work in America.
D) negatively affects the overall quality of many American movies.

41

The data in the graph provide most direct support for which statement from the passage?

A) Lines 10 – 12 ("How…year?")
B) Lines 21 – 24 ("American…India")
C) Lines 33 – 35 ("Hollywood…inside")
D) Lines 35 – 38 ("Indeed…ones")

42

According to the graph, in which year was there the greatest difference between U.S./Canada revenues and international revenues for a top grossing film?

A) 2010
B) 2011
C) 2013
D) 2015

Refer to the passage pair below to answer questions 43 – 52.

Passage 1 is adapted from Frederic A. Lucas, *Animals of the Past*, originally published in 1901. Passage 2 is adapted from "Origin of birds," Wikipedia, 2016.

Passage 1

line   For a long time our knowledge of Dinosaurs was very imperfect and literally fragmentary, depending mostly upon scattered teeth, isolated vertebra, or fragments of bone picked up on the
5   surface or casually encountered in some mine or quarry. Now, however, thanks mainly to the labors of American paleontologists, thanks also to the rich deposits of fossils in our Western States, we have an extensive knowledge of the Dinosaurs,
10   of their size, structure, habits, and general appearance.
   There are to-day no animals living that are closely related to them; none have lived for a long period of time, for the Dinosaurs came to an end
15   in the Cretaceous, and it can only be said that the crocodiles, on the one hand, and the ostriches, on the other, are the nearest existing relatives of these great reptiles.
   For, though so different in outward
20   appearance, birds and reptiles are structurally quite closely allied, and the creeping snake and the bird on which it preys are relatives, although any intimate relationship between them is of the serpent's making, and is strongly objected to by
25   the bird.
   But if we compare the skeleton of a Dinosaur with that of an ostrich—a young one is preferable—and with those of the earlier birds, we shall find that many of the barriers now existing
30   between reptiles and birds are broken down, and that they have many points in common. In fact, save in the matter of clothes, wherein birds differ from all other animals, the two great groups are not so very far apart.

Passage 2

35   *Archaeopteryx*, the first good example of a "feathered dinosaur," was discovered in 1861. The first specimen was found in the Solnhofen limestone in southern Germany, which is a *lagerrstätte*, a rare and remarkable geological
40   formation known for its superbly detailed fossils. *Archeopteryx* is a transitional fossil, with features clearly intermediate between those of non-avian therapod dinosaurs and birds. Discovered just two years after Darwin's seminal *Origin of*
45   *Species*, its discovery spurred the nascent debate between proponents of evolutionary biology and creationism. This early bird is so dinosaur-like that, without a clear impression of feathers in the surrounding rock, at least one specimen was
50   mistaken for *Compsognathus*.
   Since the 1990s, a number of additional feathered dinosaurs have been found, providing even stronger evidence of the close relationship between dinosaurs and modern birds. The
55   feathers were initially described as simple filamentous *protofeathers*, which were reported in dinosaur lineages as primitive as compsognathids and tyrannosauroids. However, feathers indistinguishable from those of modern birds
60   were soon after found in non-avialan dinosaurs as well.
   A small minority of researchers have claimed that the simple filamentous "protofeather" structures are simply the result of the
65   decomposition of collagen fiber under the dinosaurs' skin or in fins along their backs, and that species with unquestionable feathers, such as oviraptorosaurs and dromaeosaurs are not dinosaurs, but true birds unrelated to dinosaurs.
70   However, a majority of studies have concluded that feathered dinosaurs are in fact dinosaurs, and that the simpler filaments of unquestionable theropods represent simple feathers. Some researchers have demonstrated the presence of
75   color-bearing melanin in the structures—which would be expected in feathers but not collagen fibers. Others have demonstrated, using studies of modern bird decomposition, that even advanced feathers appear filamentous when subjected to the
80   crushing force experienced during fossilization, and that the supposed "protofeathers" may have been more complex than previously thought. Detailed examination of the "protofeathers" of *Sinosauropteryx prima* showed that individual
85   feathers consisted of a quill (*rachis*) with thinner barbs branching off from it, similar to but more primitive in structure than modern bird feathers.

"Origin of birds" is licensed under CC BY 4.0. For more information, see page 511.

43

As used in line 3, "isolated" most nearly means

A) atypical.
B) lone.
C) inaccessible.
D) secluded.

44

The clause, "although any intimate…by the bird," in lines 22 – 25 primarily serves to

A) interject humor into an otherwise academic passage.
B) question the anatomical similarities between birds and dinosaurs.
C) comment on the dispositions of different animal species.
D) point out the physical differences among biologically related species.

45

It can be inferred that the "clothes" mentioned in line 32 refer to

A) anatomies.
B) feathers.
C) barriers.
D) skeletons.

46

The author of Passage 1 contends that ostriches are related to dinosaurs

A) because both have historically been preyed upon by snakes.
B) because both evolved from a common ancestor: the crocodile.
C) on the basis of skeletal similarities between the two groups.
D) on the basis of dietary similarities between the two groups.

47

Based on the information in Passage 2, which choice most effectively summarizes the relationship between dinosaurs and feather development?

A) Lines 35 – 36 ("*Archaeopteryx*…1861")
B) Lines 67 – 69 ("species with…dinosaurs")
C) Lines 70 – 73 ("a majority…feathers")
D) Lines 83 – 86 ("Detailed…from it")

48

It can reasonably be inferred from Passage 2 that *Compsognathus*

A) was first discovered in a *lagerrstätte*.
B) was first discovered after 1861.
C) is a very close relative of *Archaeopteryx*.
D) is a species of dinosaur.

49

The author of Passage 2 mentions "A small minority of researchers" (line 62) primarily to

A) introduce a counterargument that is later refuted.
B) undermine the claim that birds and reptiles are closely related.
C) describe the process by which "protofeathers" became modern bird feathers.
D) suggest that very few researchers study feathered dinosaur evolution.

50

In relation to Passage 1, Passage 2

A) takes a more historical and less scientific approach to the same topic.
B) provides a modern and more nuanced overview of the same general topic.
C) uses different pieces of evidence to arrive at the same conclusion.
D) goes into greater detail regarding the relationship between birds and reptiles.

51

The author of Passage 1 would likely respond to the claim in Passage 2 that some dinosaurs had feathers (lines 70 – 71) with

A) surprise, because Lucas presumed that feathers were unique to birds.
B) protest, because this assertion is based on very limited evidence.
C) indifference, because Lucas was only interested in dinosaur behaviors.
D) irritation, because Lucas disproved this theory in Passage 1.

52

Which choice provides the best evidence for the answer to the previous question?

A) Lines 12 – 13 ("There are… to them")
B) Lines 15 – 18 ("it can…reptiles")
C) Lines 19 – 21 ("For, though…allied")
D) Lines 31 – 34 ("In fact…apart")

STOP

Writing & Language Test 1
35 MINUTES, 44 QUESTIONS

Turn to Section 2 of your answer sheet to answer the questions in this section.

DIRECTIONS

Each of the following passages is accompanied by approximately 11 questions. Some questions will require you to revise the passages in order to improve coherence and clarity. Other questions will require you to correct grammatical errors. Passages may be accompanied by graphs, charts, or tables that you must consider when making revisions. For most questions, you may select the "NO CHANGE" option if you believe that portion of the passage is clear, concise, and grammatically correct as is.

Within the passages, highlighted numbers followed by underlined text indicate which part of the text corresponds with each question. Bracketed numbers [1] indicate sentence number. These bracketed numbers are only relevant to problems that require you to add or rearrange sentences in a paragraph.

Questions 1-11 are based on the following passage.

America's Booze Ban

In 1919, the United States Congress passed a law prohibiting the transportation, production, and sale of alcoholic beverages. This followed decades of grassroots movements led by temperance societies across the nation. Some states and counties were already free from alcohol, or "dry." **1** <u>Whereas</u> the federal law went into effect, most people assumed that local authorities would be able to enforce it. **2** <u>Therefore,</u> a strong consumer demand for alcohol persisted, resulting in an extensive black market that no police agency could handle.

After the ban took effect, people began looking for ways to circumvent it. Because the law prohibited distribution, sales, and production of alcoholic beverages **3** , Americans were free to own and consume personal supplies of alcohol. In fact, **4** <u>wealthier Americans purchased personal stockpiles of liquor immediately before the law took effect, often buying out entire warehouses or breweries.</u> Others began illegally brewing their own beer and distilling spirits colloquially known as "moonshine" or "bathtub gin." Grape farmers produced and sold a juice concentrate that, if left to ferment, would turn to wine in a few weeks. Some individuals even smuggled liquor from Canada and Mexico.

1
A) NO CHANGE
B) Although
C) When
D) Because

2
A) NO CHANGE
B) Then,
C) Likewise,
D) However,

3

At this point the author is considering adding the following information:

(but not ownership)

Should the author make this change?

A) Yes, because it sets up the distinction elaborated on later in the paragraph.
B) Yes, because it provides an example of how people circumvented the law.
C) No, because these details about the law have already been outlined in the passage.
D) No, because it confuses readers with irrelevant technical details about a law.

The black market that formed was so prominent that alcohol consumption was only marginally reduced during Prohibition. Appearing in major U.S. cities, [5] illegal clubs known as "speakeasies" forced saloons and bars to close their doors, effectively replacing them. These establishments [6] distinctly sold liquor and quickly became popular places for people to get together and drink. Police agencies regularly raided these risky [7] businesses, however— the profits were so great that another establishment would simply replace one that had been shut down.

Gangs often formed around illegal alcohol enterprises, and the mafia broadened [8] their market to include alcohol. Crime rates increased [9] as much up to 25 percent in some major cities shortly after Prohibition took effect. Local police agencies, which had been charged with enforcing Prohibition laws, were overwhelmed. Many municipalities saw police spending increase by 10 percent or more during Prohibition. Some counties refused to penalize alcohol-related crime and subsequently avoided inflating their law enforcement budgets.

The problems introduced by the banning of alcohol far outweighed its benefits, and in 1933 Congress repealed Prohibition. Some counties opted to retain local Prohibition laws, and many dry counties still [10] existed in southern states such as Texas and Mississippi. Criminal alcohol organizations quickly converted to legitimate operations and began providing local, state, and federal governments with steady tax revenues. Today, the law is largely seen as a [11] flop for the unforeseen negative consequences of its enactment.

---★---

4

Which choice provides the most relevant detail?

A) NO CHANGE
B) Budweiser continued to operate during Prohibition years, producing a non-alcoholic brew to conform with the law.
C) beverages containing less than 0.5% alcohol by volume were not considered "intoxicating."
D) many churches were allowed to keep wine for religious ceremonies.

5

A) NO CHANGE
B) the shut doors of saloons and bars opened doors for illegal clubs called "speakeasies," which were replacing them.
C) so-called "speakeasies" (i.e. illegal clubs) replaced saloons and bars, which had been forced to close their doors.
D) saloons and bars, being forced to shut their doors, were rapidly replaced by so-called "speakeasies" (i.e. illegal clubs).

6

A) NO CHANGE
B) deliberately
C) discretely
D) discreetly

7

A) NO CHANGE
B) businesses; however,
C) businesses, however,
D) businesses, however:

8

A) NO CHANGE
B) they're
C) its
D) it's

9

A) NO CHANGE
B) as much as
C) as many as
D) up to as many as

10

A) NO CHANGE
B) have existed
C) are in existence
D) exist

11

Which choice best maintains the style and tone of the passage?

A) NO CHANGE
B) failure
C) bungle
D) slip-up

Questions 12-22 are based on the following passage.

Heavy Lifting: Balloons Take Flight

Buoyancy is a force exerted on an object immersed in a fluid. For [12] aerostats, which include balloons, zeppelins, and blimps, the fluid is air. The buoyant force exerted on the craft by the surrounding atmospheric gases [13] was equal to the weight of air displaced by the vessel. When the buoyant force on the aerostat is greater than the weight of the craft, lift is achieved.

A typical hot air balloon achieves lift when the air inside the balloon is heated. When [14] heated air becomes less dense and, thus, lighter. As the air temperature inside the balloon rises, the weight of this air decreases until the buoyant force on the balloon exceeds the balloon's own weight. An average passenger balloon can generate about 700 kg of lift when heated to a standard operating temperature of 99°C. [15]

Greater lift can also be achieved by increasing the size of the balloon. A larger balloon contains a greater volume of heated air, so it loses more weight when the air inside is heated; [16] in addition, it experiences greater lift. Another simple way to increase lift is to operate the balloon in cold [17] weather, as the external temperature decreases, the density of atmospheric air increases, intensifying the buoyant force exerted on the balloon. Thus, a balloon operating at the same 99°C will experience greater lift as the atmospheric temperature drops.

[12]

A) NO CHANGE
B) airplanes,
C) watercraft,
D) submarines,

[13]

A) NO CHANGE
B) has been
C) are
D) is

[14]

A) NO CHANGE
B) heated, air
C) heated, air,
D) heated air,

[15]

At this point, the author is considering adding the following sentence to the paragraph.

> This is enough to keep the balloon and five passengers afloat, but higher temperatures are required for takeoff.

Should the author include this information?

A) Yes, because it provides an illustrative counterargument to the previous claim.
B) Yes, because it helps explain the significance of the previous statement.
C) No, because this information is irrelevant to the discussion of lift.
D) No, because the transportation of passengers is beyond the scope of the passage.

[16]

A) NO CHANGE
B) but,
C) therefore,
D) for example,

[17]

A) NO CHANGE
B) weather:
C) weather
D) weather…

Not all balloons utilize heated air to achieve lift, and many rely on a lighter-than-air gas, typically helium. These buoyant gases are naturally less dense than the surrounding [18] atmosphere. They achieve lift under normal environmental conditions. Because the buoyant gas does not need to be heated, [19] gas balloons can remain aloft for much longer than standard hot air balloons. However, gas balloons gain and lose altitude as environmental conditions vary, and the pilot must drop ballast* to maintain buoyancy at night; in addition, warmer temperatures during the day can cause the gas to heat slightly, increasing lift. In order to maintain a safe altitude, the pilot [20] must have vented some of this excessive gas.

A special type of balloon, a Rozière, uses a combination of hot air and a non-heated, buoyant gas. Rozière balloons have a separate chamber for the buoyant gas, usually located above the main chamber of heated air. A Rozière requires a much smaller volume of hot air, because the non-heated gas generates the majority of the [21] crafts' lift under mild atmospheric conditions. At night, when the gas cools and becomes more dense—thereby reducing the amount of lift generated—burners are used to heat the main chamber. [22]

* ballast: a heavy material used to stabilize an airship, and which can be dropped to gain altitude.

---

[18]

Which choice provides the best combination of the sentences at the underlined portion?

A) atmosphere, but they
B) atmosphere because they
C) atmosphere, they
D) atmosphere, so they

[19]

Which choice provides the most relevant detail?

A) NO CHANGE
B) gas balloons are better suited for scientific applications than standard hot air balloons.
C) gas balloons can be operated in any weather.
D) gas balloons do not require special licensing to pilot.

[20]

A) NO CHANGE
B) will need to vent
C) had to have vented
D) must vent

[21]

A) NO CHANGE
B) crafts
C) craft's
D) craft

[22]

At this point, the writer is considering adding the following sentence to the paragraph.

> Because Rozière balloons do not need to vent excessive gas, they offer the pilot a greater deal of control over the balloon's altitude without sacrificing operating time.

Should the writer make this addition here?

A) Yes, because it provides an informative comparison to another type of balloon discussed in the passage.
B) Yes, because it provides an effective summary of the passage.
C) No, because the discussion of piloting a balloon is beyond the scope of this passage.
D) No, because the writer fails to support this claim with quantitative data.

Questions 23-33 are based on the following passage and supplementary material.

Market Research Analyst

[23] A fashion buyer must decide whether to order short skirts; an appliance maker has to predict whether people will want toaster ovens; a mobile phone manufacturer needs a good idea of what size phone people want in the near future. While some companies may rely on intuition when trying to foresee consumers' demands, most probably prefer [24] to consider as much data as they possibly can. The task of amassing and making sense of such data often falls to specialists known as market research analysts.

[1] Market research analysts look for various indicators of market trends. [2] These processes give analysts a sense of what products people prefer – or would prefer if they were offered to them at the right price. [3] By looking at current sales figures, they estimate "market share" – what percentage of a type of product is already being sold by which competitors. [4] To gather clues about current consumer tastes, they may conduct in-person focus groups or surveys, or scour social media. [5] Of course, they keep their eyes on the overall economy to gauge [25] its affect on buying power. [26]

[27] Analysts collect relevant data and a report is compiled integrating all the information. They translate data into visuals such as graphs and charts.

23

Which choice most effectively introduces the passage?

A) Some professionals become accustomed to taking risks.
B) Selling goods involves accurately predicting what people want to buy.
C) Sales in many fields are sensitive to trends.
D) Market research analysts must convey the "big picture" to clients.

24

A) NO CHANGE
B) to consider using data.
C) using data.
D) data usage.

25

A) NO CHANGE
B) it's affect
C) its effect
D) it's effect

26

For the sake of the cohesion of this paragraph, sentence 2 should be placed

A) where it is now.
B) before sentence 1.
C) after sentence 3.
D) after sentence 5.

27

A) NO CHANGE
B) Analysts collect data and write reports
C) Analysts collect data and written reporting
D) Data is collected and reports are written

[28] For example, an analyst might prepare a report for a global apparel company that is trying to decide whether to open retail shops in India. The report might include a general section with descriptions and graphs of India's growing middle class and shopping trends, and then [29] it will turn to a more specific focus on trends in clothing sales. The report will likely include a chart of the competition: the clothing retailers already operating in the country. The digestible report makes it easier for company executives to discuss whether to open shops in India, and if [30] it does, what exactly to offer for sale.

[31] Most market research analysts hold a bachelor's or master's degree in marketing, economics, math, or statistics. Backgrounds in sociology and psychology are also helpful for understanding consumer behavior. Communications and computer classes may be invaluable, as well.

As of 2018, there were 681,900 market research analysts in the United States, according to the U.S. Bureau of Labor Statistics (BLS). Market research [32] analysts job outlook is promising; [33] the field will definitely grow. The bureau says the growth will be driven by the trend in all industries to make more use of data.

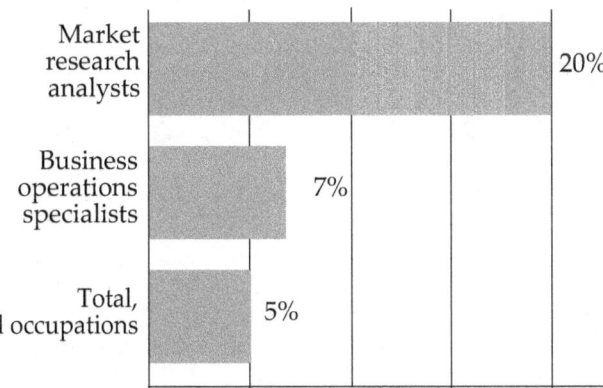

Market Research Analysts
Percent change in employment, projected 2018-28

Market research analysts 20%
Business operations specialists 7%
Total, all occupations 5%

Note: All Occupations includes all occupations in the U.S. Economy.
Source: U.S. Bureau of Labor Statistics, Employment Projections program

---★---

28

A) NO CHANGE
B) Imagine, for example, a report
C) They prepare reports such as
D) There would be plenty of data

29

A) NO CHANGE
B) turned
C) is going to turn
D) turn

30

A) NO CHANGE
B) it is so,
C) they do,
D) one does,

31

Which choice most effectively provides a transition for the new paragraph?

A) Such ability to gather and interpret market data requires a solid academic background.
B) Certainly, it is recommended that interested students pursue a college education.
C) Studying math is essential to obtaining a job as a market research analyst.
D) Market research analysts must be logical, rational thinkers with a dash of creativity.

32

A) NO CHANGE
B) analysts'
C) analyst
D) analyst's

33

The writer wants to conclude the sentence with evidence of the improving job outlook for market research analysts. Which choice best accomplishes this goal with data from the graph?

A) NO CHANGE
B) job experts within the BLS are optimistic that graduates will find jobs in the growing field.
C) according to the BLS, there will be 139,200 new market research analyst jobs by 2022.
D) the BLS predicts that the number of jobs in the occupation will increase 20 percent by 2022

Questions 34-44 are based on the following passage.

Philosophy and Fiction: Philip K. Dick's *Ubik*

Philip K. Dick is often regarded as one of the most influential science fiction writers of the 20th century. Among his most critically acclaimed novels is 1969's *Ubik*, [34] one of *Time* magazine's 100 greatest novels since 1923. The novel features psychic phenomena, human colonization of the moon, and suspended animation after death. The most exciting element of the story, however, is the jarring shift in reality experienced by the main characters after an explosion kills their boss.

[35] Initially, the characters notice gradual changes to the world around them: perishable food products begin spoiling sooner, television stations broadcast only static, and paper money loses its value. As the novel progresses, several characters die mysteriously, and the remaining group members are inexplicably torn backward in time, eventually [36] arriving at 1939. The group also receives [37] esoteric messages from their deceased employer, [38] he attempts to contact them via an infomercial recorded prior to his death.

34

The writer is considering removing the underlined portion and ending the sentence after "*Ubik*." Should the writer make this change?

A) Yes, because *Time* magazine is not central to the passage.
B) Yes, because the remaining 99 novels are not mentioned.
C) No, because it provides relevant support to the author's previous claim.
D) No, because the passage focuses on *Ubik*'s awards and critical reception.

35

Which choice provides the best transition to the details that follow?

A) NO CHANGE
B) Despite this, the world changes inexplicably for the characters:
C) However, changing the world takes time:
D) In addition, the characters are living in the past:

36

A) NO CHANGE
B) being in
C) arriving in
D) being at

37

A) NO CHANGE
B) cryptic
C) blurry
D) arcane

38

A) NO CHANGE
B) who
C) whom
D) him

[1] Joe Chip, the last survivor of the group, later learns that he and his companions are actually in a state of suspended **39** animation, they have been killed in the explosion. [2] This "half-life" they experience is a result of having their consciousnesses artificially preserved after death. [3] Joe's boss, contacting him from the living world, advises Joe to purchase Ubik, an aerosol product purported to prevent the continued deterioration of the half-life world. [4] Despite continued adversity, Joe finds a can of Ubik and uses it to save himself. [5] The novel concludes with a disconcerting shift to Joe's boss in the real world which leaves the reader uncertain as to the authenticity of either reality. **40**

Ubik shares many themes common to Dick's fiction. Most notable among these is the question central to understanding *Ubik's* plot: What is real? Throughout the story, Joe Chip and his colleagues **41** becomes immersed with an illusory reality and struggle to discover its true nature. The novel's conclusion urges readers to question the novel's reality, as well as Joe's reliability as a narrator. The truth is never fully revealed, and the author leaves an audience to draw **42** its own conclusion.

43 Because of this uncertainty, Dick also interspersed his stories with biblical allusions. Present throughout the story is a classic struggle between good and evil, exemplified by Joe's battle with a mysterious force that prevents him from finding Ubik. Dick's former wife commented on the novel, stating that Ubik represents God, and the restorative power of the spray can is a **44** hyperbole for faith; only through the power of belief is Joe able to find Ubik and combat the evil forces inhabiting his half-life reality.

★

39

A) NO CHANGE
B) animation and they have been
C) animation; they having been
D) animation, having been

40

The best placement for sentence 4 is

A) where it is now.
B) after sentence 1.
C) after sentence 2.
D) after sentence 5.

41

A) NO CHANGE
B) become immersed in
C) become immersed into
D) becomes immersed within

42

A) NO CHANGE
B) it's
C) their
D) his or her

43

Which choice provides the most effective transition from the previous paragraph?

A) NO CHANGE
B) In addition to metaphysics, Dick uses religion extensively in his work; this is also a major theme of *Ubik*.
C) Dick's predisposition with metaphysics is evidenced by a family history of mental illness.
D) Another theme central to many of Dick's works, including *Ubik*, is faith and religious belief.

44

A) NO CHANGE
B) simile
C) metaphor
D) double entendre

NO TEST MATERIAL ON THIS PAGE

Math Test 1 – No Calculator

 25 MINUTES, 20 QUESTIONS

Turn to Section 3 of your answer sheet to answer the questions in this section.

DIRECTIONS

For questions **1 – 15**, find the solution to each problem and select the most appropriate answer from the choices provided. For questions **16 – 20**, find the solution to each problem and write your answer in the space provided. You may use the blank space in your test booklet for scratch work.

NOTES

1. The use of a calculator on any part of this section is forbidden.
2. Unless otherwise indicated, all variables and expressions used in this test represent real numbers.
3. Unless otherwise indicated, all figures used in this test are drawn to scale.
4. Unless otherwise indicated, all figures used in this test lie on a plane.
5. Unless specified otherwise, a given function, f, has the domain the set of all real numbers x for which $f(x)$ is a real number.

REFERENCE

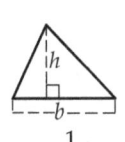
$A = \frac{1}{2}bh$

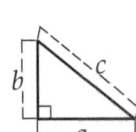
$c^2 = a^2 + b^2$

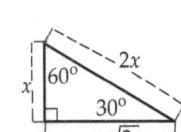
Special Right Triangles

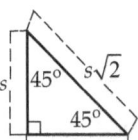
$A = \pi r^2$
$C = 2\pi r$

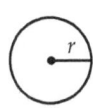
$A = \ell w$

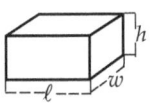
$V = \ell w h$

$V = \pi r^2 h$

$V = \frac{4}{3}\pi r^3$

$V = \frac{1}{3}\pi r^2 h$

$V = \frac{1}{3}\ell w h$

The arc of a full circle is 360 degrees or 2π radians.
A triangle has angles that sum to 180 degrees.

3

1

Maria is reviewing her algebra quiz. She knows that one of the following solutions is incorrect, but does not know which one. Which one is incorrect?

A) $2x + 5(x - 1) = 9$, $x = 2$
B) $p - 3(p - 5) = 10$, $p = 2.5$
C) $4y + 3y = 28$, $y = 4$
D) $t + 2t + 3t = 32$, $t = 8$

2

$$2x + y = 8$$
$$y = -2x + 5$$

Which statement correctly describes the graphs of the equations above?

A) They are two parallel lines.
B) They are two perpendicular lines.
C) They are two lines that intersect at (2, 4).
D) They are two lines that intersect at (−2, 9).

3

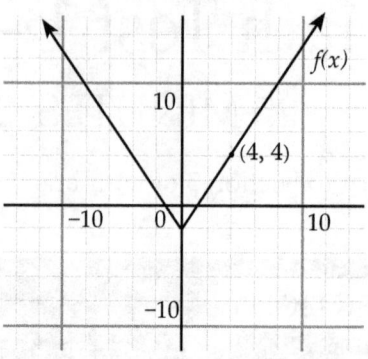

Which of the following functions corresponds to the graph above?

A) $f(x) = \frac{2}{3} |x - 3|$

B) $f(x) = \left|\frac{2}{3}\right| x - 2$

C) $f(x) = \left|\frac{3}{2} x\right| - 2$

D) $f(x) = \left|\frac{3}{2} x - 3\right|$

4

What is the highest value of the function $f(x) = 3 - (x + 1)^2$?

A) −3
B) −1
C) 1
D) 3

5

$$\sqrt{x-y} = \frac{x^x}{27}$$

Which of the following can be a solution to the equation above when $y = 2$?

A) −2
B) 0
C) 1
D) 3

6

Which of the following is a factor of $\frac{a^2}{16} - \frac{4b^2}{9}$?

A) $\frac{a}{4} + \frac{2b}{9}$

B) $\frac{a}{4} - \frac{2b}{3}$

C) $\frac{a}{2} + \frac{2b}{3}$

D) $\frac{a}{2} - \frac{2b}{3}$

7

If $p \nabla q = \frac{2p - q}{p - 2q}$, what is the value of $6 \nabla 2$?

A) 2
B) 3
C) 5
D) 8

8

If $-x - y = -2$ and $2x - y = -11$, what is the value of x?

A) −13
B) −9
C) −3
D) 3

9

The following question is adapted from the Bakhshali Manuscript, the oldest extant South Asian mathematical manuscript.

One merchant has seven Asava horses (*A*), a second has nine Haya horses (*H*), and a third has ten camels (*C*). When each merchant gives two of his animals away—one to each other merchant—the combined value of each merchant's animals is the same. Assume that the values of the animals are integers, and each of the merchants now owns a total of *X* currency worth of animals, where $X - (A + C + H) = 168$. Calculate the value of $A + C + H$, the combined value of owning one of each animal.

A) 89
B) 94
C) 131
D) 262

10

William has 20 jellybeans in his pocket: 8 red, 8 green, and 4 blue. If he pulls jellybeans from his pocket without looking, what is the maximum number of jellybeans he would need to remove from his pocket for him to pull at least one of each color?

A) 4
B) 12
C) 13
D) 17

11

If the equation $x^2 + bx + 4 = 0$ has exactly one solution, which of the following must be true?

A) b is equal to 4.
B) b is equal to –4.
C) b is equal to 4 or –4.
D) b is equal to –2.

12

If $f(x) = |x^2 - 50|$, what is the value of $f(-5)$?

A) 75
B) 25
C) 0
D) –25

13

$$f(x) = 2(x^2 - 6x + 5) - 3(x - q)$$

In the function defined above, q is a constant. If $f(2) = 0$, what is the value of q?

A) –3
B) –2
C) 0
D) 4

14

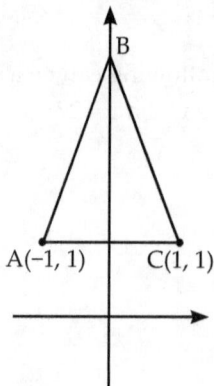

In the figure above, triangle ABC is an equilateral triangle. If BC is a line of the form $y = mx + b$, what is the value of m?

A) –60
B) $-\dfrac{1}{2}$
C) $-\sqrt{3}$
D) 60

15

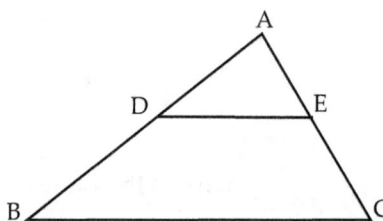

In the figure above, AD = DB, DE is parallel to BC, and the area of triangle ABC is 96 square units. What is the area of triangle ADE in square units?

A) 10
B) 15
C) 24
D) 30

Student-Produced Responses   3

DIRECTIONS

For questions **16 – 20**, find the solution to the problem and enter your answer as demonstrated on the right.

1. Only the answer that is bubbled in on the answer sheet will be credited. The blank spaces above the bubbles are for you to record your answers for accuracy.
2. Only fill in one bubble in any given column.
3. None of the answers on this portion of the test are negative values.
4. If a problem appears to have more than one answer, only enter one answer. If the answer you enter is one of the correct solutions, you will receive full credit for that question.
5. If the correct answer can be expressed as a mixed number, it must be entered as a decimal or an improper fraction.
6. If the correct answer is a decimal that cannot fit into the grid space, you must fill the grid with enough digits to completely fill the space. The number can be rounded or simply shortened but must fill every blank space.

Answer: $\frac{5}{36}$

Answer: 4.5

← Fraction line
← Decimal point

Write answer in boxes.
Grid in result.

Acceptable ways to grid $\frac{1}{6}$ are:

Answer: 302 – either position is correct

NOTES

Begin entering answers in any column that accommodates your answer. If you do not need a column do not enter anything in that column.

CONTINUE

16

If $\frac{8}{x} = \frac{6}{7}$ and $\frac{3x}{a} = \frac{7}{2}$, what is the value of a?

ANSWER: _____

17

Elena splits her time between attending college and working. She works for 25 hours each week, earning $11 per hour. Every four weeks, Elena must pay $600 for college tuition. After paying tuition, how much of her monthly earnings, in dollars, is Elena left with?

ANSWER: _____

18

If $x - 3$ is a factor of $x^2 - 2px + p$, where p is a constant, what is the value of p?

ANSWER: _____

19

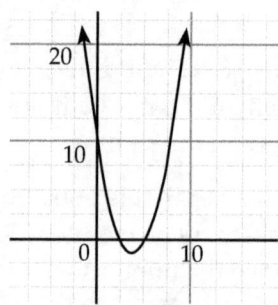

The figure above is the graph of the function $f(x) = k(x - 4)^2 - 2$, where k is a constant and $f(0) = 10$. What is the value of k?

ANSWER: _____

20

The product of three integers is 144. The largest number is 1 greater than the sum of the other two numbers. If the two smaller numbers have the same value, what value results when the larger number is multiplied by the sum of the smaller two numbers?

ANSWER: _____

Math Test 1 – Calculator

 4

55 MINUTES, 38 QUESTIONS

Turn to Section 4 of your answer sheet to answer the questions in this section.

DIRECTIONS

For questions **1 – 30**, find the solution to each problem and select the most appropriate answer from the choices provided. For questions **31 – 38**, find the solution to each problem and write your answer in the space provided. You may use the blank space in your test booklet for scratch work.

NOTES

1. The use of a calculator on any part of this section is allowed.
2. Unless otherwise indicated, all variables and expressions used in this test represent real numbers.
3. Unless otherwise indicated, all figures used in this test are drawn to scale.
4. Unless otherwise indicated, all figures used in this test lie on a plane.
5. Unless specified otherwise, a given function, f, has the domain the set of all real numbers x for which $f(x)$ is a real number.

REFERENCE

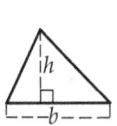
$A = \frac{1}{2}bh$

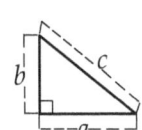
$c^2 = a^2 + b^2$

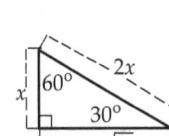
Special Right Triangles

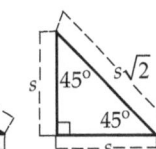

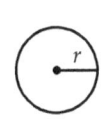
$A = \pi r^2$
$C = 2\pi r$

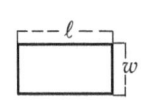
$A = \ell w$

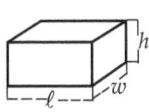
$V = \ell w h$

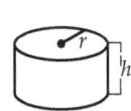
$V = \pi r^2 h$

$V = \frac{4}{3}\pi r^3$

$V = \frac{1}{3}\pi r^2 h$

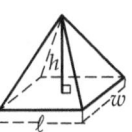
$V = \frac{1}{3}\ell w h$

The arc of a circle is 360 degrees or 2π radians.
A triangle has angles that sum to 180 degrees.

1

Alonzo and Jorge work together to paint skateboards. Alonzo paints 20 more than twice the number of skateboards that Jorge paints. Together they paint 125 skateboards. If Jorge paints x skateboards, which of the following equations could be used to find the value of x?

A) $2x + 20 = 125$
B) $3x + 20 = 105$
C) $3x - 20 = 125$
D) $3x + 20 = 125$

2

Lynn can swim across a lake in p minutes. In terms of p, what percentage of the swim can she complete in 5 minutes?

A) $\frac{5}{p} \times 100\%$

B) $(p - 5) \times 100\%$

C) $(p + 5) \times 100\%$

D) $\frac{p}{5} \times 100\%$

3

Which of the following expressions is equivalent to $12c^2 + cd - 6d^2$?

A) $(4c + 3d)(3c - 2d)$
B) $(4c - 3d)(3c + 2d)$
C) $(6c + d)(2c - 6d)$
D) $6(2c - d)(c + d)$

4

Abandoned mines frequently fill with water. Before an abandoned mine can be reopened, the water must be pumped out. The size of the pump needed for this task depends on the depth of the mine; a mine that is D feet deep requires a pump that removes a minimum of $\frac{D^2}{25} + 4D - 250$ gallons per minute. How many gallons would a pump need to remove per minute to clear a mine that is 150 feet deep?

A) 362
B) 500
C) 800
D) 1250

5

A computer discounted 20% off the regular price is on sale for $1600. What is the regular price?

A) $1800
B) $1900
C) $2000
D) $2100

6

Which of the following is equivalent to the expression $\frac{\sqrt{32}}{2} + \frac{2\sqrt{3}}{3}$?

A) $4 + 2\sqrt{3}$

B) $4 + \frac{2\sqrt{3}}{3}$

C) $\frac{6\sqrt{2} + 2\sqrt{3}}{3}$

D) $\frac{2\sqrt{35}}{5}$

7

Which of the following inequalities is true for all real numbers?

$$\text{I. } x^2 - 2x - 3 > 0$$
$$\text{II. } x^2 - 4x + 4 > 0$$
$$\text{III. } x^2 - x - 6 > 0$$

A) I

B) II

C) II and III

D) Neither I, II, nor III

8

A picture is copied onto a sheet of paper that is 8.5 inches by 10 inches. A 1.5-inch margin is left all around. What is the total area of the copied picture in square inches?

A) 38.5

B) 49

C) 59.5

D) 65

9

A woman stands five feet from a lamppost and casts a shadow four feet long. If the lamppost were two feet taller, her shadow would be a foot shorter. How tall is the woman?

A) $\dfrac{9}{2}$ feet

B) $\dfrac{16}{3}$ feet

C) $\dfrac{14}{3}$ feet

D) $\dfrac{24}{5}$ feet

10

Two lines with equations $y = ax + b$ and $y = cx + a$ are perpendicular to each other. Which of the following must be true?

A) $ac = -1$

B) $a = c, b \neq a$

C) $a = c, b = a$

D) $c = b$

11

Let $f(x) = \dfrac{x+3}{x-1}$ for any x such that $x \neq 1$. Which of the following is equivalent to $f(x) - 1$?

A) $\dfrac{x+2}{x-1}$

B) $\dfrac{4}{x-1}$

C) $\dfrac{2x+4}{x-1}$

D) $\dfrac{2}{x-1}$

12

If $\dfrac{3}{x-3} + \dfrac{5}{2x-6} = \dfrac{11}{2}$, what is the value of $2x - 6$?

A) 2

B) 6

C) 8

D) 12

13

Which of the following expressions is equivalent to $\dfrac{14c^3d^2 - 21c^2d^3}{14cd^2}$?

A) $c^2 - \dfrac{3cd}{2}$

B) $c^2 - \dfrac{3c^2d}{2}$

C) $c^2 - 21c^2d^2$

D) $c^2d - \dfrac{3cd}{2}$

14

Ellen is thinking of two numbers whose sum is 9 and whose difference is 3. What is their product?

A) 6
B) 12
C) 15
D) 18

15

Which of the following is equivalent to the sum of the solutions of the equation $12x^2 + 19x + 5 = 0$?

A) $-\dfrac{1}{3}$

B) $-\dfrac{5}{4}$

C) $-\dfrac{19}{12}$

D) $-\dfrac{5}{12}$

Questions 16 and 17 refer to the following information.

The chart below provides information on how bonuses were distributed among the employees of a business:

Bonus paid to an employee ($)	Number of employees
50	7
100	37
150	4
200	2

16

What was the average bonus per employee?

A) $81
B) $91
C) $100
D) $101

17

If the median bonus is m dollars, the average bonus is a dollars, and the mode bonus is p dollars, which of the following must be true?

A) $m < a < p$
B) $m < a = p$
C) $m = p < a$
D) $m < p < a$

18

Seven integers are ordered from lowest to highest. If the median of the integers is 9 and the mode is 7, what is the smallest possible range for the seven integers?

A) 3
B) 4
C) 5
D) 7

19

A student has an average grade of 82 on three exams. If all exams are weighted equally, what must the student score on the next exam to bring her average score up to 86?

A) 92
B) 94
C) 96
D) 98

20

If $y - 3x = 9$, what does $\dfrac{27^x}{3^{\frac{y}{3}}}$ simplify to?

A) $27x^{\left(\frac{1}{3}\right)^{3y}}$

B) 3^{2x-3}

C) $9^{\frac{xy}{3}}$

D) $27\dfrac{x}{y}$

21

If $(3^x)^2 = 27^{x-1}$, what is the value of x?

A) $\dfrac{3}{2}$

B) 3

C) $\dfrac{5}{2}$

D) 2

22

What is the domain of the function

$$f(x) = \dfrac{x^2 - 21}{x(x+2)}?$$

A) $\{x \neq 0, -2\}$
B) $\{x \neq -2\}$
C) $\{x \neq 0\}$
D) $\{x = 0\}$

23

A high-school cafeteria makes tuna salad by adding two pounds of mayonnaise to every three pounds of tuna. Tuna costs $1.50 per pound and mayonnaise costs $0.75 per pound. How many pounds of tuna salad can be prepared with $100?

A) $33\frac{1}{3}$

B) 50

C) 75

D) $83\frac{1}{3}$

24

If (x, y) is a point on the graph of $f(x)$, which of the following must be a point on the graph of $-f(x)$?

A) $(-x, -y)$
B) $(-x, y)$
C) (y, x)
D) $(x, -y)$

Questions 25 and 26 refer to the following information.

The scatterplot below charts the estimated number of proteins coded on human chromosomes as a function of their lengths.

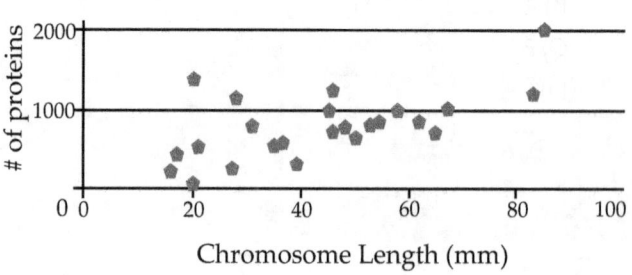

25

Which of the following best describes the relationship between number of proteins on a chromosome and chromosome length?

A) No relationship
B) Negative and linear
C) Positive and linear
D) Positive and exponential

26

The five shortest chromosomes code for an estimated 225, 431, 45, 1,399, and 533 proteins and have an average length of 18.8 mm. The five longest chromosomes code for an estimated 2012, 1,203, 1,040, 718, and 849 proteins and have an average length of 72.4 mm. If the means of these groups are used to create a linear approximation of the relationship between length and protein number, which of the following represents the slope?

A) 11.9 mm/protein
B) 0.08 mm/protein
C) 11.9 proteins/mm
D) 0.08 proteins/mm

27

Which of the following expressions is equivalent to $\dfrac{a^3 - b^3}{b^2 - a^2}$?

A) $a - b$

B) $b - a$

C) $\dfrac{a^2 + ab + b^2}{a + b}$

D) $-\dfrac{a^2 + ab + b^2}{a + b}$

28

A right circular cylinder has a volume of 81π cubic meters. If the circumference of the base is 6π meters, what is the height of the cylinder?

A) 3 meters

B) 6 meters

C) 9 meters

D) 27 meters

29

Which of the following is NOT a solution to the function $f(x) = \dfrac{3(x^2 - 9)}{x^2 - 4}$?

A) $x = -3$

B) $x = -2$

C) $x = 0$

D) They are all solutions to the function.

30

Which of the following is equivalent to $12 - \sqrt{-121}$?

A) 1

B) $12 - 11i$

C) $12 + 11i$

D) 23

4   Student-Produced Responses

DIRECTIONS

For questions **31 – 38**, find the solution to the problem and enter your answer as demonstrated on the right.

1. Only the answer that is bubbled in on the answer sheet will be credited. The blank spaces above the bubbles are for you to record your answers for accuracy.
2. Only fill in one bubble in any given column.
3. None of the answers on this portion of the test are negative values.
4. If a problem appears to have more than one answer, only enter one answer. If the answer you enter is one of the correct solutions, you will receive full credit for that question.
5. If the correct answer can be expressed as a mixed number, it must be entered as a decimal or an improper fraction.
6. If the correct answer is a decimal that cannot fit into the grid space, you must fill the grid with enough digits to completely fill the space. The number can be rounded or simply shortened but must fill every blank space.

NOTES

Begin entering answers in any column that accommodates your answer. If you do not need a column do not enter anything in that column.

31

If $2^{n+1} = 16$, what is the value of n?

ANSWER: _____

33

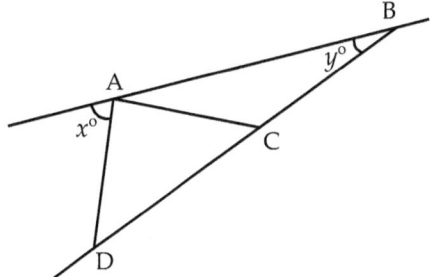

In the figure above, line segments AD = AC = BC. If $y = 20$, what is the value of x?

ANSWER: _____

32

The average weight of four boys is 120 pounds. If three boys each weigh 115 pounds, what is the weight, in pounds, of the fourth person?

ANSWER: _____

34

$$x^2 + y^2 = 5$$
$$x + y = 1$$

(x_1, y_1) and (x_2, y_2) are the solutions to the system of equations above. What is the value of $x_1 + x_2$?

ANSWER: _____

35

In a class of 60, $\frac{2}{3}$ are girls, and $\frac{2}{5}$ of the class are taking music lessons. What is the lowest possible number of girls that could be taking music lessons?

ANSWER: _____

36

If $f(x) = (13 - x)^{\frac{3}{2}}$ and $n = f(4)$, what is the value of $2n$?

ANSWER: _____

Questions 37 and 38 are based on the information below.

A man deposits P_0 dollars into an account at the beginning of each year for n years. The amount of money in the account, P, is determined by the following formula:

$$P = \frac{P_0}{r}[(1+r)^n - 1],$$

where r is an interest rate expressed as a decimal and calculated annually.

37

Suppose the man deposits $300 a year for 12 years at an interest rate of 6%. If no additional deposits or withdrawals are made, what is the balance at the end of 12 years? (Round your answer to the nearest dollar.)

ANSWER: _____

38

What is the smallest amount of money that the man needs to deposit annually for there to be an account balance of over $15,000 at 6% interest after 12 years? (Round your answer up to the nearest dollar.)

ANSWER: _____

NO TEST MATERIAL ON THIS PAGE

Essay Test 1

  50 MINUTES, Prompt-based essay

Turn to Section 5 of your answer sheet to answer the question in this section.

DIRECTIONS

As you read the passage below, consider how Atif Kukaswadia uses
- evidence, such as facts or examples, to support claims.
- reasoning to develop ideas and to connect claims and evidence.
- stylistic or persuasive elements, such as word choice or appeals to emotion, to add power to the ideas expressed.

Adapted from "Science is political and we ignore that at our peril" by Atif Kukaswadia, published on April 25, 2017.

This weekend, citizens around the world joined together and marched for science. Thousands marched in the US as well as internationally in cities like Tokyo and Durban. However, there are those who believe marching is an activity scientists shouldn't be engaging in, and that it risks painting scientists as activists rather than as objective researchers.

This is a viewpoint that ignores a simple fact: Science is already political.

Almost everything we do is influenced by science. The food we eat, the water we drink, this is all managed and controlled by governmental regulations developed through scientific inquiry. The cars we drive, the gas we burn, this was all informed by research and engineering. The medications we use were developed through the hard work of scientists. However, for these findings to be used, someone had to champion the cause and bring it to the attention of the public. Someone had to believe that these findings were worthwhile and then take it through the system, through levels of government to ensure that it led to change.

However, somewhere along the way we forgot that this is part of the scientific process. After the introduction, methods, results, and conclusion should come the "so what" which tells people why they should care. For those who aren't researchers in the field, why should they care? What are the benefits of this work, and what can we do with it? This is especially important in the current US political climate, as there is no top science advisor, and the US Surgeon General was recently let go. Since there is no one at the top to champion these causes, it falls on the populace to make sure that their voices are heard and that their elected officials represent their viewpoints.

Now the question remains: how far do scientists take this process, and how far should they? Should scientists be actively campaigning for candidates in elections, and should they be speaking out when the facts are misrepresented, or worse, ignored altogether? The media has crafted an image of scientists as overreaching zealots who want nothing better than to dictate exactly what you should and should not do, often with limited (or no) social skills, with a desire to eliminate discourse and dissent. So while some may advocate for leaving "politics to the politicians," this is a dangerous gambit, especially when so much funding and support is tied directly to the political will *du jour*. If we do nothing, we risk the narrative being driven by forces who don't believe in the scientific method, choosing dogma over research, and opinions over facts. An excellent piece by Andrew Jewett takes this idea further:

My concern is the opposite of the usual objection. The March for Science, I believe, is not political enough. I do not mean that the marchers should campaign for Democratic or Republican candidates or take stands on contentious issues such as immigration reform. Rather, I hope that they will come to grasp much more clearly how political power works, how it intersects with social conflicts, and how policies emerge from this nexus.

Marching can show solidarity, and it can bring attention to an issue. However, it is the start of a political journey, and not the end result. Now that the march is over, we need to continue to hold our elected officials accountable, which can involve letter writing and calling when issues come up that you feel strongly about, and canvassing for those you support. It's a brave new world for scientists, and one that is currently riding an organized and motivated wave of support. Channeling and turning that energy into action can result in political change, leading to investments that can put us at the forefront of innovation and science.

Write an essay in which you explain how Atif Kukaswadia builds an argument to persuade his audience that science should influence politics. In your essay, analyze how the author uses one or more of the features listed in the box above (or features of your own choice) to strengthen the logic and persuasiveness of his argument. Be sure that your analysis focuses on the most relevant features of the passage.

Your essay should not explain whether you agree with the author's claims, but rather explain how the author builds an argument to persuade his audience.

---

* *Sample response found in the "Answers and Explanations" section of this study guide.*

"Science is political and we ignore that at our peril" is licensed under CC BY 4.0. For more information, see page 511.

KALLIS

SAT® Practice Test #2

IMPORTANT REMINDERS:

 When you take the official SAT, you will need to use a No. 2 pencil. Do not use a pen or a mechanical pencil.

 On the official SAT, sharing any of the questions on the test violates the College Board's policies and may result in your scores being canceled.

(This cover is modeled after the cover you'll see when you take the official SAT.)

UNAUTHORIZED REPRODUCTION OR USE OF ANY PART OF THIS TEST IS PROHIBITED.

© 2019 KALLIS EDU

Reading Test 2

65 MINUTES, 52 QUESTIONS

Turn to Section 1 of your answer sheet to answer the questions in this section.

DIRECTIONS

Each passage or pair of passages is accompanied by 10 or 11 questions. Read each passage or pair of passages, and then select the most appropriate answer to each question. Some passages may include tables or graphs that require additional analysis.

Refer to the passage below to answer questions 1 – 11.

This passage is adapted from Arnold Bennett, *Your United States: Impressions of a First Visit*, originally published in 1912.

The elevator ejects you. You are taken into dazzling daylight, into what is modestly called a business office; but it resembles in its grandeur no European business office, save such
5 as may have been built by an American. You look forth from a window, and lo! New York and the Hudson are beneath you, and you are in the skies. And in the warmed stillness of the room you hear the wind raging and whistling,
10 as you would have imagined it could only rage and whistle in the rigging of a three-master at sea. There are, however, a dozen more stories above this story. You walk from chamber to chamber, and in answer to inquiry learn that
15 the rent of this one suite—among so many—is over thirty-six thousand dollars a year! And you reflect that, to the beholder in the street, all that is represented by one narrow row of windows, lost in a diminishing chess-board of windows. And
20 you begin to realize what a sky-scraper is, and the poetry of it.

More romantic even than the sky-scraper finished and occupied is the sky-scraper in process of construction. From no mean height,
25 listening to the sweet drawl of the steam-drill, I have watched artisans like dwarfs at work still higher, among knitted steel, seen them balance themselves nonchalantly astride girders swinging in space, seen them throwing rivets to one another
30 and never missing one; seen also a huge crane collapse under an undue strain, and, crumpling like tinfoil, carelessly drop its load onto the populous sidewalk below. That particular mishap obviously raised the fear of death among a
35 considerable number of people, but perhaps only for a moment. Anybody in America will tell you without a tremor (but with pride) that each story of a sky-scraper means a life sacrificed. Twenty stories—twenty men snuffed out; thirty stories—
40 thirty men. A building of some sixty stories is now going up—sixty corpses, sixty funerals, sixty domestic hearths to be slowly rearranged, and the registrars alone know how many widows, orphans, and other loose by-products!
45 And this mortality, I believe, takes no account of the long battles that are sometimes fought, but never yet to a finish, in the steel webs of those upper floors when the labor-unions have a fit of objecting more violently
50 than usual to non-union labor. In one celebrated building, I heard, the non-unionists contracted an unfortunate habit of getting crippled; and three of them were indiscreet enough to put themselves under a falling girder that killed
55 them, while two witnesses who were ready to give certain testimony in regard to the mishap vanished completely out of the world, and have never since been heard of. And so on. What more natural than that the employers should form a
60 private association for bringing to a close these interesting hazards? You may see the leading spirit of the association. You may walk along the street with him. He knows he is shadowed, and he is quite cheerful about it. His revolver is always
65 very ready for an emergency. Nobody seems to regard this state of affairs as odd enough for any prolonged comment. There it is! It is accepted. It is part of the American dailiness. Nobody, at any rate in the comfortable clubs, seems even to
70 consider that the original cause of the warfare is aught but a homicidal cussedness on the part of the unions.... I say that these accidents and these guerrillas mysteriously and grimly proceeding in the sky fabric of metal-ribbed constructions, do
75 really form part of the poetry of life in America— or should it be the poetry of death? Assuredly they are a spectacular illustration of that sublime, romantic contempt for law and for human life which, to a European, is the most disconcerting
80 factor in the social evolution of your States. I have sat and listened to tales from journalists and other learned connoisseurs till—But enough!

CONTINUE

1

1

The primary purpose of the passage is to

A) romanticize America's lifestyles and booming city centers.
B) contrast the different work attitudes of Americans and Europeans.
C) recount the author's impressions of New York skyscrapers and construction workers.
D) describe the idiosyncratic lifestyles and attitudes of Americans.

2

In paragraph 1 (lines 1 – 21), the author suggests that, compared to European office buildings, American business offices are

A) cramped and hot.
B) overwhelming.
C) sunny and impressive.
D) full of ornate decorations.

3

The author uses the second person ("you") throughout paragraph 1 (lines 1 – 21) primarily to

A) immerse the reader in the scene he describes.
B) indicate that his intended audience is businesspeople living in New York.
C) target readers who have visited skyscrapers before.
D) create an intimate relationship with his reader.

4

As used in line 18, "lost" most nearly means

A) wandering.
B) indistinguishable.
C) unclaimed.
D) confused.

5

The author's tone in lines 24 – 33 ("From no mean…below") shifts from

A) alertness to distraction.
B) geniality to defensiveness.
C) admiration to morbidity.
D) enthusiasm to weariness.

6

In lines 36 – 38 ("Anybody in America… sacrificed"), the author characterizes Americans' attitudes toward skyscraper-related deaths as that of

A) astonished sorrow.
B) ignorant complacence.
C) proud acceptance.
D) content indifference.

7

The passage implies that members of labor unions

A) tend to be safer on the job than non-union construction workers.
B) are more likely to rely upon each other to help break unhealthy habits.
C) can be blamed for most accidents that occur during the building of skyscrapers.
D) sometimes purposely injure or kill non-union construction workers.

8

Which choice provides the best evidence for the answer to the previous question?

A) Lines 38 – 41 ("Twenty stories…funerals")
B) Lines 50 – 55 ("In one…them")
C) Lines 58 – 61 ("What more…hazards")
D) Lines 63 – 64 ("He knows…about it")

9

The passage suggests that some American employers

A) arm themselves to respond to any violence.
B) form secretive societies to battle labor unions.
C) hire mainly non-union workers to build skyscrapers.
D) show little concern for safety issues.

10

Which choice provides the best evidence for the answer to the previous question?

A) Lines 61 – 65 ("You may see…emergency")
B) Lines 65 – 67 ("Nobody seems…comment")
C) Lines 68 – 72 ("Nobody, at…unions")
D) Lines 72 – 75 ("these accidents…America")

11

As used in lines 77 – 78, "sublime, romantic contempt" most nearly describes a feeling of

A) heavenly bliss.
B) affectionate disregard.
C) wistful love.
D) quixotic disdain.

Refer to the passage below to answer questions 12 – 21.

This passage is adapted from Ernest Hawkes, *The Dance Festivals of the Alaskan Eskimo*, originally published in 1914.

    The ceremonial dance of the Alaskan
Eskimo is a rhythmic pantomime—the story in
gesture and song of the lives of the various Arctic
animals on which they subsist and from whom
5 they believe their ancient clans are sprung. The
dances vary in complexity from the ordinary
social dance, in which all share promiscuously
and in which individual action is subordinated
to rhythm, to the pantomime totem dances
10 performed by especially trained actors who hold
their positions from year to year according to
artistic merit. Yet even in the totem dances the
pantomime is subordinate to the rhythm, or rather
superimposed upon it, so that never a gesture or
15 step of the characteristic native time is lost.
    This is a primitive beat based on the double
roll of the chorus of drums. Time is kept, in the
men's dances, by stamping the foot and jerking
the arm in unison, twice on the right, then
20 twice on the left side, and so on, alternately.
Vigorous dancers vary the program by leaping
and jumping at intervals, and the shamans are
noted for the dizzy circles which they run round
the *púgyarok*, the entrance hole of the dance hall.
25 The women's dance has the same measure and
can be performed separately or in conjunction
with the men's dance, but has a different and
distinctly feminine movement. The feet are kept
on the ground, while the body sways back and
30 forth in graceful undulations to the music and
the hands with outspread palms part the air with
the graceful stroke of a flying gull. Some of their
dances are performed seated. Then they strip to
the waist and form one long line of waving arms
35 and swaying shoulders, all moving in perfect
unison….
    There appears to be no restriction against
the women taking part in the men's dances. They
also act as assistants to the chief actors in the
40 Totem Dances, three particularly expert and richly
dressed women dancers ranging themselves
behind the mask dancer as a pleasing background
of streaming furs and glistening feathers. The only
time they are forbidden to enter the *kásgi* is when
45 the shaman is performing certain secret rites.
They also have secret meetings of their own when
all men are banished. I happened to stumble on to
one of these one time when they were performing
certain rites over a pregnant woman, but being
50 a white man, and therefore unaccountable, I was
greeted with a good-natured laugh and sent about
my business.
    On the other hand, men are never allowed
to take part in the strictly women's dances,
55 although nothing pleases an Eskimo crowd more
than an exaggerated imitation by one of their
clowns of the movements of the women's dance.
The women's dances are practiced during the
early winter and given at the *Aiyáguk*, or Asking
60 Festival, when the men are invited to attend as
spectators. They result in offers of temporary
marriage to the unmarried women, which is
obviously the reason for this rite. Such dances,
confined to the women, have not been observed
65 in Alaska outside the islands of Bering Sea, and I
have reason to believe are peculiar to this district,
which, on account of its isolation, retains the old
forms which have died out or been modified on
the mainland.

12

The passage primarily provides

A) an exhaustive guide explaining how to perform certain ceremonial dances.
B) an attempt to preserve in writing a rapidly disappearing culture.
C) academic observations of gender roles in particular cultural traditions.
D) a detailed account of a foreigner participating in ancient rituals.

13

As used in line 4, "subsist" most nearly means

A) respect.
B) depend.
C) stand.
D) subvert.

14

According to the traditions described in the passage, one aspect unique to women's dance styles is

A) imitating arctic animals.
B) stamping to the rhythm of the drums.
C) keeping feet on the ground.
D) quick, sharp movement of the arms.

15

As used in line 41, "ranging" most nearly means

A) fluctuating.
B) arranging.
C) reaching.
D) differing.

16

It is reasonable to infer that, in the community observed by the author, the meetings that are off-limits to men include

A) drumming and dancing ceremonies.
B) political meetings led by female shamans.
C) rites regarding fertility and childbirth.
D) rehearsals for the Asking Festival.

17

Which choice provides the best evidence for the answer to the previous question?

A) Lines 25 – 28 ("The women's…movement")
B) Lines 32 – 36 ("Some of their…unison")
C) Lines 43 – 45 ("The only time…rites")
D) Lines 47 – 52 ("I happened…business")

18

In paragraph 4 (lines 53 – 69), the author indicates that the main purpose of the Asking Festival is providing opportunities for

A) single people to meet potential spouses.
B) women to take the leading roles in performances.
C) friendly competition among women of far-flung communities.
D) popular clowns to entertain by mimicking female dancers.

19

Which choice provides the best evidence for the answer to the previous question?

A) Lines 53 – 54 ("On the other…dances")
B) Lines 55 – 57 ("nothing pleases…dance")
C) Lines 58 – 61 ("The women's…spectators")
D) Lines 61 – 63 ("They result…rite")

20

In lines 63 – 69, the author suggests that women-only dances on Bering Sea islands may

A) someday change to incorporate the participation of men.
B) be something that few cultural anthropologists know about.
C) help explain a crucial cultural adaptation to the environment of the islands.
D) represent a tradition that was once practiced over a wider area.

21

Overall, the passage implies that, in Alaskan Native culture, women and men traditionally

A) have interchangeable roles in dance ceremonies and rituals.
B) dance only during certain seasons of the year.
C) share in most dance activities together.
D) remain in fairly separate spheres during festivals.

Refer to the passage below to answer questions 22 – 31.

This passage is adapted from Mary Bates, "Why Sloths Live in the Slow Lane," originally published July 25, 2016.

Forests cover more than one-third of the land on Earth, yet few vertebrates make the canopy their home, and even fewer subsist solely on a diet of tree leaves.

In a new study in *American Naturalist*, researchers from the University of Wisconsin–Madison explain why this lifestyle is so rare and why animals that live in trees and eat leaves tend to live life at a slower pace.

Those species that do take advantage of this niche do not often radiate afterwards; that is, they do not diversify and take on a variety of specialized forms. The energetic constraints of a leafy diet are thought to prevent such adaptive radiation.

Leaves are an energetically and nutritionally poor food source. Most animals that live off plant leaves tend to be large, such as moose, elk, and deer.

"Leaves are everywhere, but you need pretty complex gut machinery to be able to extract energy and nutrients from them," says Jonathan Pauli, one of the study's authors. "Most herbivores are big-bodied and they carry around big guts to break down and detoxify plant leaves."

But animals that live in the treetops cannot be too big, or else the branches will not support their body weight. So how do they make it on a nutritionally challenging diet?

Pauli and Zachariah Peery, along with co-authors Emily Fountain and William Karasov, set out to answer this question by measuring the daily energy expenditure of both two-toed and three-toed sloths in Costa Rica.

Both species of sloth are at the extreme end of specialization for a tree-dwelling, leaf-eating, lifestyle. Pauli, Peery, and colleagues found that both sloth species expended very little energy, but three-toed sloths were especially slothful. Three-toed sloths expended as little as 460 kilojoules of energy a day, the equivalent of burning only 110 calories. It is the lowest measured energetic output for any mammal.

Three-toed sloths use both behavioral and thermal strategies to limit their energy output. "They really are a slothful bunch," says Pauli. "While two-toed sloths have bigger home ranges and move around quite a bit, three-toed sloths have very small home ranges and spend most of their time in just one or a few individual trees. To limit energy costs, three-toed sloths find a good tree and camp out for a while and eat from it."

Pauli, Peery, and colleagues concluded that much of the difference in metabolic rate between two-toed and three-toed sloths is due to regulation of body temperature. Three-toed sloths relax control over their body temperatures, letting them fluctuate quite a bit for a mammal. They often ascend to the top of the canopy in the morning, presumably to warm in the sun, and descend into the shade as daytime temperatures increase.

The researchers then compared their sloth data to similar studies of other tree-dwelling, leaf-eating species from around the world. Overall, the more specialized for the niche an animal was, the lower its daily energy expenditure. While these species had lower metabolic rates than most mammals in general, they also relied heavily on thermoregulation and behavioral strategies to reduce their energetic expenditure.

The findings support the idea that tree-dwelling, leaf-eating mammals are tightly constrained by the poor nutritional quality of their diet, and thus, exhibit extremely low energetic output.

"Arboreal folivores have all these oddities— anatomical, behavioral, and physiological – that enable them to exploit this lifestyle," says Pauli. "One of the ways they are able to survive in this energetically stark niche is they have evolved a whole suite of adaptations. They require all these unique adaptations to live in the trees and survive solely on leaves."

The researchers believe this impedes the opportunity for organisms to rapidly radiate into this niche. For tree-dwelling, leaf-eating animals, there is a whole series of key innovations that are needed before they can crack into that open niche.

Sloths are the poster children for making a living in the treetops by saving energy. For them, slothfulness is a necessary virtue, not a deadly sin.

22

The author suggests that Jonathan Pauli and Zachariah Peery's study about sloths

A) provides insight into other species that thrive under the same circumstances.
B) makes a case for further research that is focused on three-toed sloths.
C) proves that "slothfulness" in humans is natural and respectable.
D) demonstrates the importance of sloths in maintaining forest habitat.

"Why Sloths Live in the Slow Lane" is licensed under CC BY 4.0. For more information, see page 511.

23

Which choice provides the best evidence for the answer to the previous question?

A) Lines 1 – 4 ("Forests cover…leaves")
B) Lines 16 – 19 ("Leaves are…deer")
C) Lines 31 – 35 ("Pauli and…Costa Rica")
D) Lines 64 – 68 ("The researchers… expenditure")

24

As used in line 21, "gut machinery" refers to

A) kitchen appliances.
B) biotechnical devices.
C) digestive organs.
D) abdominal muscles.

25

The author of the passage would most likely explain the large bodies of herbivorous giraffes as an adaptation to support

A) competing with sloths in gathering leaves.
B) internal processing of vegetative sources of energy.
C) storing large amounts of herbivorous material in the stomach.
D) finding food in a larger geographic area.

26

As used in line 48, "ranges" most nearly means

A) fields.
B) varieties.
C) ridges.
D) territories.

27

According to Pauli and Peery, three-toed sloths' basic survival strategy is to

A) move around the forest as little as possible.
B) relax control over their immediate environment.
C) sleep as high as possible in the tree canopy.
D) eat all the leaves on a single tree.

28

The study suggests that, compared to two-toed sloths, three-toed sloths have lower energy needs because they

A) maintain a lower body temperature.
B) have less offspring to care for and feed.
C) expend less energy on thermoregulation.
D) have larger, more efficient digestive systems.

29

The researcher mentions "oddities" (line 78) in arboreal folivores in order to

A) emphasize how specialized they must be to fill their ecological niche.
B) demonstrate how unique they are compared to other mammals.
C) illustrate that a wide variety of species fill the niche.
D) explain the unexpected findings of the research study.

30

Which of the following does the author indicate about the evolution of sloths?

A) Sloths are the only mammals that have adapted to living in trees and eating leaves.
B) Sloths' nutritionally limited diets constrain their evolutionary diversity.
C) The general term "sloth" can refer to a wide array of species in the sloth family.
D) Competition with other species for edible leaves has greatly influenced sloth evolution.

31

Which choice provides the best evidence for the answer to the previous question?

A) Lines 10 – 15 ("Those species…radiation")
B) Lines 27 – 30 ("But animals…diet")
C) Lines 38 – 40 ("Pauli, Peery…slothful")
D) Lines 73 – 77 ("The findings…output")

Refer to the pair of passages to answer questions 32 – 42.

Passage 1 is adapted from the publication "Obsessive Compulsive Disorder: When Unwanted Thoughts Take Over," National Institute of Mental Health (NIMH), accessed in 2016. Passage 2 is adapted from "OCD at School/How OCD Affects Studies and Grades," Anxiety and Depression Association of America (ADAA), www.adaa.org, accessed in 2016.

Passage 1

line

The thoughts and rituals associated with obsessive compulsive disorder (OCD) cause distress and get in the way of daily life. The frequent upsetting thoughts are called
5   obsessions. To try to control them, a person will feel an overwhelming urge to repeat certain rituals or behaviors called "compulsions."
    People with OCD generally have repeated thoughts or images about many different things,
10 such as fear of germs, dirt, or intruders; acts of violence; hurting loved ones; sexual acts; conflicts with religious beliefs; or being tidy. They may do the same rituals over and over, such as washing hands, locking and unlocking
15 doors, counting, keeping unneeded items, or repeating the same steps again and again. The rituals may give them brief relief from the anxiety the thoughts cause.
    OCD is generally treated with psycho-
20 therapy, medication, or both. A type of psychotherapy called cognitive behavioral therapy (CBT) is especially useful for treating OCD. It teaches a person different ways of thinking, behaving, and reacting to situations
25 that help him or her better manage obsessive thoughts, reduce compulsive behavior, and feel less anxious. One specific form of CBT, exposure and response prevention, has been shown to be helpful in reducing the intrusive thoughts and
30 behaviors associated with the disorder.

Passage 2

OCD is associated with unwanted and often overwhelming fears, doubts, anxieties and/or urges as well as a need to perform corresponding rituals. This continuous loop
35 of obsessions and compulsions may be relentless and, while all this is going on, it is just about impossible to feel—or even act—"normal." In fact, a student who has OCD often cannot "hear" what the teacher is saying because of
40 the OCD messages coursing through his or her brain.
    Students with OCD may appear to be daydreaming, distracted, noncompliant, disinterested, or even lazy. They may seem
45 unfocused and lacking in the ability to concentrate. In truth, they are very busy—focusing on the nagging urges or confusing, stressful and sometimes terrifying OCD thoughts and images. An example of what OCD "sounds
50 like" is:
    "Uh-oh. What if I forgot my homework for the next class? I think it's in my book bag. But I don't know for sure. I thought it was in my book bag, but it might not be. I think I checked last night, but maybe I
55 moved it. If it's not there, I'll get in trouble and nobody will understand that I forgot it. They might think I did that on purpose. I did the work, but I didn't pack it in the bag. Wait...maybe I didn't actually DO my homework. What if I forgot to do it last night? Oh,
60 no. Now I really WILL be in trouble. I might not have done it. Only bad students don't do their homework. I must be bad. I can't look in my book bag to see if my homework is there because the bag is in my locker. Did I forget my homework? What if I did forget it...now I'm
65 in trouble. I'm going to get punished. I wish I had done my homework. If I could only check and see if maybe it really IS in my book bag. Ooooh. But what if my book bag isn't in my locker? Did I forget my book bag? No, I think I brought it. But what if I didn't?"
70 With thoughts and worries like these running through the student's mind, there is little chance that the voice of the teacher will penetrate the OCD "noise." At best, it might sound as if you tried to watch two television channels
75 simultaneously—you can listen to only one or the other. In the case of OCD, the disorder may be so insidious (and so insistent) that the child will most likely be "tuned in" to the OCD instead of the teacher or the class work.
80 OCD's impact on learning cannot be underestimated. Students may not be able to read without their minds being drawn away from the words and into a world of relentless worries. They may also be unable to read because
85 of the need to perform rituals (e.g., count every fifth word in each sentence or each paragraph). They may not be able to pay attention to visuals very well because of lack of focus on anything other than the mental stream of worries, urges or
90 compulsions. When they leave the classroom to carry out rituals (e.g., going to the bathroom to perform washing rituals), they may miss out on potentially important academic information.
    In addition, students may be extremely tired
95 because of the strain and effort of trying to fight OCD, which can sap one's energy. They may miss out on important instruction when tardiness and school absenteeism became a problem due to OCD symptoms (e.g., carrying out washing, dressing,
100 eating rituals before school; not attending school because of triggers in that environment). They become adept at...avoiding people, places and activities that might trigger their symptoms.

32

The primary purpose of Passage 1 is to

A) present the causes of and cures for a disabling condition.
B) introduce a public health topic via definitions and facts.
C) discuss widespread misconceptions about OCD.
D) analyze specific terms used in the psychiatric field.

33

Passage 1 suggests that people with OCD may repeat behaviors such as handwashing to gain

A) total perfection.
B) cautious optimism.
C) practical solutions.
D) temporary reassurance.

34

Which choice provides the best evidence for the answer to the previous question?

A) Lines 5 – 7 ("To try… 'compulsions'")
B) Lines 8 – 12 ("People with…tidy")
C) Lines 13 – 16 ("They may…again")
D) Lines 16 – 18 ("The rituals…cause")

35

As used in line 29, "intrusive" most nearly means

A) interfering.
B) inquisitive.
C) annoying.
D) impertinent.

36

Over the course of lines 51 – 69, the first-person narrator becomes increasingly

A) confused about his or her next class.
B) unsure about his or her recent actions.
C) disrespectful toward the teacher.
D) self-critical regarding social interactions.

37

As used in line 82, "drawn" most nearly means

A) stretched.
B) deduced.
C) sketched.
D) pulled.

38

In lines 80 – 93 the author of Passage 2 primarily describes

A) how to diagnose the disorder.
B) the appearance of all students with the disorder.
C) possible consequences of invasive thoughts and compulsive behaviors.
D) the repercussions of not being able to "hear" the teacher.

39

The author of Passage 2 implies that, without treatment, OCD sufferers may feel like

A) the least intelligent person in class.
B) aliens in a foreign landscape.
C) victims of a constant struggle.
D) heroes in a meaningful battle.

40

Which choice provides the best evidence for the answer to the previous question?

A) Lines 51 – 55 ("Uh-oh…moved it'")
B) Lines 80 – 81 ("OCD's…underestimated")
C) Lines 94 – 96 ("Students may…energy")
D) Lines 96 – 101 ("They may…environment")

41

Which choice best states the relationship between the two passages?

A) Passage 2 explains important points raised in Passage 1.
B) Passage 2 elaborates on treatment options for OCD introduced in Passage 1.
C) Passage 2 focuses on particular impacts of OCD more than Passage 1 does.
D) Passage 2 raises questions about the validity of the information in Passage 1.

42

The author of Passage 1 would most likely characterize the behaviors outlined in the final paragraph of Passage 2 (lines 94 – 103) as

A) typical examples of the disorder getting in the way of daily life.
B) the reasons that OCD sufferers should be allowed to stay home.
C) frequent outcomes of spoiling children with OCD.
D) most adolescents' natural biorhythms and tendencies.

Refer to the passage below to answer questions 43 – 52.

This passage is adapted from Marianne Olney-Hamel, "Pumas, Wolves, and Eagles, Oh My! Early Captive Carnivore Remains Found in Ancient Mexican Ruins," published on December 16, 2015.

From Roman gladiatorial combat to Egyptian animal mummification, capturing and manipulating wild carnivores has long been a way for humans to demonstrate state or
5 individual power. Historians and scientists alike have attempted to determine when humans first began to use carnivores to establish their place on the social ladder. In the Americas, the Aztec Emperor Moctezuma kept a zoo in his capital of
10 Tenochtitlan, which was described by Spanish conquistadors in about 1520 CE. But a recent study provides evidence that Mesoamericans were keeping carnivores in captivity more than 1,000 years before Moctezuma.
15 The ancient city of Teotihuacan reached the height of its influence and power in about 450 CE, long before the Aztec Empire. In its time, it was one of the largest and most powerful cities in Mesoamerica, heavily influencing Mayan
20 culture, and was home to at least 125,000 people. Its architects designed massive temples to show off the city's power. The ruins of three of these incredible temples still stand: the Temple of Quetzalcoatl, the Pyramid of the Sun, and
25 the Pyramid of the Moon.
 During excavations from 1998-2004, researchers in Teotihuacan found rare artifacts and sacrificial human and animal remains in chambers in the Pyramids of the Sun and the
30 Moon. For their study, anthropologists Nawa Sugiyama and Andrew Somerville analyzed the remains of 194 animals in the laboratory.
 Of particular interest to the authors were the remains of carnivores like wolves, eagles,
35 jaguars, and pumas, as we have little information about how humans related to carnivores prior to the Aztec zoo in Tenochtitlan. Using isotope analysis and visual inspection of the bones, the authors were able to draw possible conclusions
40 about the relationship between the carnivores in the chambers and the ancient inhabitants of Teotihuacan.
 Visual examination of the animal skeletons suggested that at least some of the carnivores
45 were kept in captivity for some period of time. The authors found bone breaks and stress characteristic of captive animals — for example, three eagle skeletons showed stress on the lower part of the legs, where they may have been
50 tied to a perch. Other deformities in the animal skeletons, such as bone fusion or abnormal growth, were evidence of infection, which typically only occur when animals are kept close together in captivity.

55 Isotope analysis provided further evidence of captivity. This technique involves studying the elements present in organic remains; certain isotopes can make their way into an animal's bones based on what they eat or drink. Analysis of
60 the ancient carnivores' bones showed that many of the animals found in the Pyramids had high levels the carbon isotope C14, which is known to be present in corn (or maize) — a food cultivated and consumed by humans living in Teotihuacan,
65 and not likely consumed by wild carnivores.
 The authors also tested the animal bones for nitrogen isotopes. Level of nitrogen isotopes can reflect an animal's place in the food chain. Animals that eat only plants have lower levels of
70 nitrogen isotopes, while carnivores like eagles, big cats, and wolves, have higher levels of nitrogen isotopes.
 The bones of two pumas found in the Pyramids had very high levels of both carbon and
75 nitrogen isotopes. According to the authors, the presence of carbon isotopes may suggest that the cats ate maize fed to them by human caretakers. Carbon may also have been introduced if the cats were fed rabbits or other herbivores who
80 ate maize that were kept in captivity by humans. In addition, high levels of nitrogen in the puma bones suggest that they ate omnivores that were higher up the food chain — perhaps dogs, or even humans. Taken together, the authors believe that
85 this evidence shows that the pumas were kept in captivity, and may have eaten humans as a part of an ancient ritual. Historians believe that carnivores were often linked to human sacrificial ceremonies throughout ancient Mesoamerica
90 based on art throughout the region. Art found at Teotihuacan includes this type of imagery, including a drawing thought to depict a puma eating human hearts.
 While we cannot know for certain whether
95 the carnivores found in the ruins of Teotihuacan were ever fed human sacrificial victims, the bones of the animals in the city's ruins may provide the earliest example of carnivores kept in captivity in the Americas. According to the authors,
100 their findings also provide insight into ancient Mesoamerican culture, and suggest a perceived connection between keeping powerful predatory animals in captivity and power of the state.

"Pumas, Wolves, and Eagles, Oh My!" is licensed under CC BY 4.0. For more information, see page 511.

43

The author uses "Roman gladiatorial combat" and "Egyptian animal mummification" (lines 1 – 2), as references to ancient cultures that

A) used cats as symbols.
B) required sacrifices in public.
C) kept exotic animals in captivity.
D) showcased control over wild animals.

44

As used in line 5, "power" most nearly means

A) might.
B) energy.
C) capacity.
D) competence.

45

The author's attitude toward Teotihuacan is best described as one of

A) aversion.
B) skepticism.
C) esteem.
D) apathy.

46

According to the passage, which of the following is true of isotope analysis?

A) It provided insights into the diets of the investigated animals.
B) It yielded more valuable information than visual examination did.
C) It highlighted valuable genetic abnormalities in the investigated animals.
D) It proved that the investigated animals ate human sacrifices.

47

Which choice provides the best evidence for the answer to the previous question?

A) Lines 46 – 50 ("The authors…a perch")
B) Lines 59 – 65 ("Analysis of…carnivores")
C) Lines 69 – 72 ("Animals that…isotopes")
D) Lines 87 – 90 ("Historians…region")

48

As used in line 68, "reflect" most nearly means

A) reverse.
B) echo.
C) contemplate.
D) indicate.

49

According to the author, researchers reasoned that high levels of C14 isotopes in puma bones supports a scenario in which

A) pumas suffered from skeletal abnormalities associated with infections.
B) pumas were most likely to be trapped and captured alive in maize-growing regions.
C) keepers fed the pumas maize, or fed them other animals that were fed maize.
D) captive pumas were fed a mixture of captive rabbits and other herbivores.

50

According to the author, which statement about captive pumas in ancient Teotihuacan could explain the high levels of nitrogen isotopes in puma bones?

A) Pumas ingested the flesh of animals that also ate meat.
B) Pumas were used in human sacrifice rituals.
C) Ancient depictions of pumas eating human hearts were accurate.
D) Even big cats such as pumas were kept in captivity in chambers of temples.

51

The author implies that leaders in Teotihuacan may have kept live carnivores in an attempt to

A) induce fear and wonder in others.
B) protect leaders in the afterlife.
C) substitute human sacrifice for animal sacrifice.
D) inspire artists to imagine horrific scenes.

52

Which choice provides the best evidence for the answer to the previous question?

A) Lines 2 – 5 ("capturing and…power")
B) Lines 26 – 30 ("During…Moon")
C) Lines 84 – 87 ("Taken together…ritual")
D) Lines 87 – 90 ("Historians…region")

STOP

Writing & Language Test 2
35 MINUTES, 44 QUESTIONS

Turn to Section 2 of your answer sheet to answer the questions in this section.

DIRECTIONS

Each of the following passages is accompanied by approximately 11 questions. Some questions will require you to revise the passages in order to improve coherence and clarity. Other questions will require you to correct grammatical errors. Passages may be accompanied by graphs, charts, or tables that you must consider when making revisions. For most questions, you may select the "NO CHANGE" option if you believe that portion of the passage is clear, concise, and grammatically correct as is.

Within the passages, highlighted numbers followed by underlined text indicate which part of the text corresponds with each question. Bracketed numbers [1] indicate sentence number. These bracketed numbers are only relevant to problems that require you to add or rearrange sentences in a paragraph.

Questions 1-11 are based on the following passage and supplementary material.

In Good Company

In today's workplace, employee turnover is relatively high. **1** Women typically stay at their jobs longer than men. As a result, employers face difficulties filling **2** vacancies. Many full-time workers are actively seeking new opportunities. In order to attract potential employees and retain existing talent, companies are competing to provide the best employment experience for their workers.

In addition to monetary rewards, employees are drawn to firms with an established and cordial company culture. People are more likely to stay with a company that promotes group activities and employee bonding. Google, for example, encourages collaboration both to inspire innovation and improve happiness. **3** Therefore, the technology company offers its employees many unconventional perks to foster a fun and friendly workplace. These practices promote good day-to-day work experiences and reduce employee turnover. For Google, this culture has paid **4** off and the company consistently retains much of its top talent and is known as one of the best places to work.

1

Which choice provides the most accurate detail based on the information in the graphic on the following page?

A) NO CHANGE
B) Teenagers rarely work full-time.
C) U.S. workers never keep a job for very long.
D) Few workers stay with a company for more than five years.

2

Which choice most effectively combines the sentences at the underlined portion?

A) vacancies, and so many
B) vacancies; thus, many
C) vacancies; furthermore, many
D) vacancies: for example, many

3

A) NO CHANGE
B) In addition,
C) Then,
D) However,

4

A) NO CHANGE
B) off the
C) off, the
D) off: the

212

[1] Though company culture is important, it's not the only factor in a person's decision to stay with a business. [2] Competitive employers must accommodate these wishes by providing flexible working hours as well as ample opportunities to take time off for vacations. [3] Many are drawn to flexible schedules and opportunities which allow them to work from home. [4] Values are changing, and people want to spend more time with family, traveling, and participating in community events. [5] Businesses that offer workers the freedom to balance the demands of their personal lives with [5] them of their professional lives [6] have tended to experience less turnover. [7]

Another strategy to retain talent and attract potential employees is to minimize dress codes. Though it may seem minor, adopting a business casual dress policy makes workers more comfortable and, in turn, happier. Thus, [8] a peachy work environment contributes to a person's decision to stay with a company or seek other opportunities for employment.

Hiring practices also affect a potential employee's decision to apply for a particular business. Over the past ten years, competition for some positions increased greatly, and human resources departments across the country lacked the time and energy to respond to every candidate. This tactic left a bad impression on [9] job-seekers, many of whom shared their experiences with others on websites [10] such as glassdoor.com. As a result, some companies now face difficulties receiving applications from qualified candidates and have started sending rejection notifications to avoid deterring future interest from denied applicants.

As markets continue to grow, [11] businesses face new challenges to find and retain their top professionals. Competitive firms must adapt to changing values in society and offer employees a rewarding employment experience.

Average tenure at current job of U.S. workers from 2006, in years

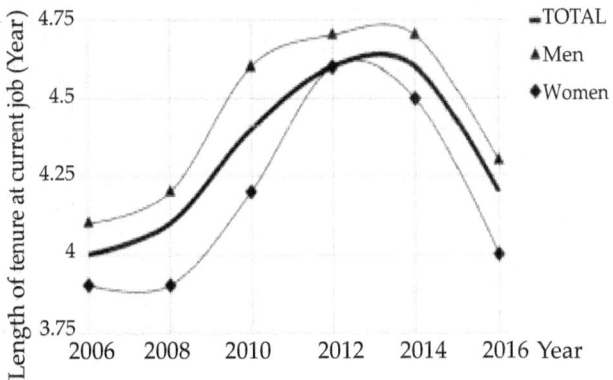

5

A) NO CHANGE
B) they of
C) those of
D) DELETE the underlined portion.

6

A) NO CHANGE
B) had tended
C) tended
D) tend

7

For the sake of logic, sentence 2 should be placed

A) where it is now.
B) after sentence 3.
C) after sentence 4.
D) after sentence 5.

8

A) NO CHANGE
B) an amenable
C) an opulent
D) a deluxe

9

A) NO CHANGE
B) job-seekers, many of them
C) job-seekers, they
D) job-seekers and

10

The author is considering deleting the underlined portion and ending the sentence after "websites." Should this change be made?

A) Yes, because the intended audience is likely unfamiliar with glassdoor.com.
B) Yes, because the author fails to elaborate on the services provided on glassdoor.com.
C) No, because the example provides context for the statement as a whole.
D) No, because it supports the author's central point about employee retention.

11

A) NO CHANGE
B) business faces
C) business' face
D) businesses faces

Questions 12-22 are based on the following passage.

The Science of Solitude

— 1 —

Social interactions are a regular part of most mammals' daily lives, but scientists still understand very little about how the brain handles sociability, or how it copes with isolation. Several areas in the medial prefrontal cortex have been associated with socializing. Particularly of interest are the prelimbic and infralimbic regions. [12] To gain insight into how these structures affect behavior, a team of researchers in Kyoto, Japan recently analyzed the brains of rats during social activities. Researchers reared an experimental group in isolation and compared the social behaviors and neural activity of its members to [13] that of a control group.

— 2 —

Researchers noticed that rats reared in isolation engaged in a greater [14] frequency of contact behaviors; that is, the total number of contacts was increased. However, the duration of each contact was greatly [15] reduced, and these rats spent less total time exhibiting contact behaviors than rats in the control group. Unsurprisingly, rats from the experimental group engaged in sole behavior for a significantly longer amount of time than rats from the control group.

12

At this point, the writer is considering adding the following diagram:

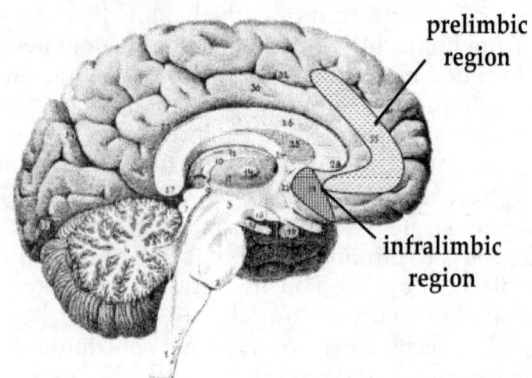

Mesial View of the Human Brain

Should the writer make this addition here?

A) Yes, because it connects the discussion of social interactions to human cognition.
B) Yes, because it helps the reader visualize the anatomical similarities between rats and humans.
C) No, because it is not directly related to the experiment described in the passage.
D) No, because it does not reveal how these brain regions affect human behavior.

13

A) NO CHANGE
B) those of
C) these of
D) DELETE the underlined portion.

14

A) NO CHANGE
B) preponderance
C) oscillation
D) persistence

15

A) NO CHANGE
B) reduced and
C) reduced when these rats
D) reduced, these rats

— 3 —

The team categorized four types of social interactions regularly observed in rats and recorded the duration and frequency of each behavior for each rat during planned social situations: approaching behavior occurs when one rat moves toward another rat; contact occurs when two rats are in close [16] contact—e.g. sniffing or boxing—leaving behavior occurs when a rat moves away from another rat; [17] and sole behavior occurs when both rats behave independently of each other.

— 4 —

In addition to observing and categorizing behavior, researchers attached electrodes containing wireless transmitters to the [18] rat's head and performed brain scans during these experiments. [19] Two critical regions involved in social interactions, the prelimbic and infralimbic regions of the prefrontal cortex, had their neural activity monitored by scientists. Scientists discovered that normal rats exhibited an increase in neural activity in the prelimbic region during contact. During leaving behavior, these same rats showed increased activity in the infralimbic region. In contrast, isolation-reared rats showed no increase in brain activity during leaving behavior. [20] Thus, this group displayed only a slight increase in prelimbic activity during contact; this increase was so slight that the overall activity levels between groups was statistically significant.

— 5 —

The difference in brain activity between the two groups [21] provide researchers with insight into the mechanisms that underlie social experiences in mammals. These experiments help to highlight the ways specific brain regions operate during typical social interactions. Scientists hope this research contributes to a better understanding of how isolation can impact the sociability of humans, and how it affects individuals with psychological disorders. [22]

---★---

Question [22] asks about the previous passage as a whole.

16

A) NO CHANGE
B) contact, e.g. sniffing or boxing,
C) contact e.g. sniffing or boxing;
D) contact (e.g. sniffing or boxing);

17

Which choice provides the most relevant detail based on the experiment described in the passage?

A) NO CHANGE
B) and grooming occurs when one rat cleans itself or another rat.
C) and food-seeking behavior occurs when one or both rats forage.
D) and defensive behavior occurs when one or both rats flee from predators.

18

A) NO CHANGE
B) rat's heads
C) rats' head
D) rats' heads

19

A) NO CHANGE
B) The relative activity level in the prelimbic and infralimbic regions of the prefrontal cortex, two critical regions involved in social interactions, was recorded by them.
C) Recording the relative activity level in two critical regions involved in social interactions, the prelimbic and infralimbic regions of the prefrontal cortex, were scientists.
D) They recorded the relative activity level in the prelimbic and infralimbic regions of the prefrontal cortex, two critical regions involved in social interactions.

20

A) NO CHANGE
B) For example,
C) Besides,
D) Furthermore,

21

A) NO CHANGE
B) provides
C) provided
D) providing

22

The best placement for paragraph 2 is

A) where it is now.
B) after paragraph 3.
C) after paragraph 4.
D) after paragraph 5.

Questions 23-33 are based on the following passage.

An Appetite for Nostalgia

Road trips are popular among American families on vacation. No matter the final destination, travelers make many stops along the way for food and gasoline. In 1969, a salesman for Shell [23] Oil, Dan Evins, saw the growing popularity of road trips and launched a roadside restaurant and gift store in the hopes of increasing gasoline sales. The first Cracker Barrel was conveniently located near Interstate 109 in Lebanon, Tennessee, and offered traditional Southern cuisine to a nation in transit.

The restaurant was [24] successful, and by 1977, the company had expanded to 13 locations in the Southern United States. [25] It included on-site gas stations and, like the original store, were located near interstate highways. Each location also included a gift store stocked with [26] toys, novelty items, baking mixes, country music tapes, and classic television recordings. In 1981, Cracker Barrel became a publicly traded company and continued to [27] grow, their reaching 50 locations by 1987. [28] Today, Cracker Barrel operates more than 600 restaurants in 43 U.S. states.

23

A) NO CHANGE
B) Oil Dan Evins,
C) Oil, Dan Evins
D) Oil Dan Evins

24

A) NO CHANGE
B) successful and
C) successful and,
D) successful. And

25

A) NO CHANGE
B) Many of these
C) Much of it
D) Locations

26

A) NO CHANGE
B) toys:
C) toys;
D) toys—

27

A) NO CHANGE
B) grow, reaching
C) grow, they reached
D) grow; they reaching

28

The writer is considering adding the following sentence to the paragraph.

> During the 1990s, Cracker Barrel began opening locations outside the South, some of which included regional menus in addition to the Southern cuisine that made the chain popular.

Should the writer make this addition here?

A) Yes, because it illustrates a change to company policies as a result of its public offering.
B) Yes, because it provides the next event in a chronological account of the company's history.
C) No, because it provides only a minor detail that blurs the focus of the passage.
D) No, because the passage is only concerned with the company's growth throughout the Southern United States.

The popularity of Cracker Barrel is in part due to the unique appearance and atmosphere of the chain. Each restaurant resembles an old-fashioned general store, with an expansive porch lined with wooden rocking chairs. [29] However, the stores are decorated with authentic American artifacts and antiques from the early 1900s. Included in these displays are obsolete tools and appliances, black-and-white photographs, old signs, and peg solitaire games. Every restaurant has a stone fireplace with a deer head and shotgun above its mantle. Individual stores have regional decorations to distinguish one [30] from another.

The items used to decorate Cracker Barrel restaurants are collected and stored in a warehouse in Lebanon, Tennessee, near the [31] chains first restaurant. The team that manages this warehouse purchases, catalogs, and [32] works on restoring antiques for use in new locations. When a store is ready to open, the team selects the individual items for that location and prepares them for shipping. To acquire these objects, the inventory management team searches for collectors willing to sell particular pieces to the company. [33] Over the years, however, the popularity of the chain has encouraged individuals to sell directly to Cracker Barrel, reducing the number of searches and inquiries needed to fit the company's demands.

As Cracker Barrel continues to grow, more American travelers are being exposed to relics of a bygone era. In a culture obsessed with progress and modernity, Cracker Barrel invites customers to slow down, relax, and appreciate its simple, American pleasures.

———————★———————

[29]

A) NO CHANGE
B) For instance,
C) Moreover,
D) Otherwise,

[30]

A) NO CHANGE
B) restaurant from another restaurant.
C) store from all other restaurants.
D) against the others.

[31]

A) NO CHANGE
B) chains'
C) chain's
D) chain

[32]

A) NO CHANGE
B) restoring
C) restores
D) can restore

[33]

At this point, the author is considering adding the following sentence.

> At first, the team used methods popularized by the television series *American Pickers* in order to find many of the pieces used in Cracker Barrel stores.

Should the author add this statement at this point in the passage?

A) Yes, because it provides an example of the type of work performed by the inventory management team.
B) Yes, because it emphasizes the importance of "picking" in American culture
C) No, because the inventory management team began "picking" before *American Pickers* debuted.
D) No, because the discussion of *American Pickers* is not given enough context to provide effective support.

Questions 34-44 are based on the following passage.

Turkish Percussion

Today, it is difficult to imagine a drum kit without cymbals, or to think of a triangle or tambourine as "exotic". But these instruments were latecomers to the Western music scene. They [34] have come to Europe from the Ottoman Empire, which ruled in Turkey from the 14th to the 20th centuries.

The Ottoman military struck fear into the hearts of Europeans for hundreds of years. As tensions gradually [35] stopped during the 18th century, Europeans were swept up in *turquerie*, a craze for the fashions, coffees, and decorative motifs of their former enemy. [36] At the heart of *turquerie* was music.

Ottoman military marching bands were legendary. Known as *mehters*, they emphasized percussion, using two-sided bass drums that they carried on straps, cymbals, triangles, bells, and tambourines. Wind instruments usually added piercing melody. As military forces have long [37] known during marches, percussive rhythms keep soldiers together and boost their moods. Ottomans also used the *mehter* when heading into battle, where the [38] shrieking and pounding music could have an intimidating effect.

Europeans could not help admiring the *mehters*. Ottoman Sultan Ahmed III sent a *mehter* to King Augustus II of Poland as a gift in 1720. Not to be outdone, Empress Anna of Russia obtained a *mehter* for [39] their court. Soon European leaders were buying *mehter* instruments for military bands of their own.

34

A) NO CHANGE
B) will come
C) came
D) are coming

35

A) NO CHANGE
B) lightened
C) eased
D) numbed

36

A) NO CHANGE
B) In the center
C) The body
D) Factors

37

A) NO CHANGE
B) known, during
C) known: during
D) known. During

38

The writer is considering deleting the underlined portion. Should it be kept or deleted?

A) Kept, because it provides supportive details about effective sounds that *mehter* could make
B) Kept, because the sentence would be illogical without the phrase.
C) Deleted, because it contradicts the claim made earlier that *mehters* helped soldiers march.
D) Deleted, because it mentions shrieking, which can also be accomplished with the voice.

39

A) NO CHANGE
B) theirs
C) them
D) her court

[40] Due to an unfortunate lack of vision, Turkish percussion instruments were largely ignored in Western music during the 1700s. European composers considered timpani—kettle drums, also originally from the eastern Mediterranean—to be standard in an orchestra. [41] But bass drums, cymbals, and other Iinstruments were only for music *alla Turca*. This phrase referred to special "Turkish" effects in operas and symphonies. Most notably, Wolfgang Amadeus Mozart and Joseph Haydn included imitations of *mehter* music in operas with Arab settings. *Alla Turca* referred to an exhilarating and strident style, and a sound that was [42] legibly "Eastern".

By the early 1800s, after Ludwig van Beethoven emphasized timpani and even a bit of the *alla Turca* sound in his general works, a few composers experimented with using *mehter* instruments even more generally. In 1830, Hector Berlioz integrated drums, cymbals and bells into the overall texture of his *Symphonie fantastique*. Franz Liszt's *Piano Concerto No. 1*, first performed in 1855, gives a triangle [43] a major role. Berlioz and Liszt endured criticism for using these percussion instruments, which were thought to be too simple and lowly for an orchestra. However, their experiments helped pave the way for the "Turkish" instruments to [44] gain equal footing with timpani.

———————★———————

40

Which choice best connects the sentence with the previous paragraph?

A) NO CHANGE
B) Perhaps due to quite limited trade between Turkey and Europe,
C) Thus relegated to military pageantry,
D) Within the music of Europe's Classical Era,

41

Which choice most effectively combines the underlined sentences?

A) Referring only to "Turkish" effects, *alla Turca* was how bass drums, cymbals, and other *mehter* instruments were used when they were in symphonies and operas.
B) Bass drums, cymbals, and other *mehter* instruments were only in operas and symphonies for music *alla Turca*, however: this phrase referred to special "Turkish" effects.
C) Used in music with Turkish effects, or *alla Turca*, was how *mehter* instruments such as bass drums and cymbals were used in operas and symphonies.
D) But in symphonies and operas, *mehter* instruments such as bass drums and cymbals served only to create music *alla Turca*— music with Turkish effects.

42

A) NO CHANGE
B) decidedly
C) understandably
D) minutely

43

Which choice results in a sentence that best supports the point developed in this paragraph?

A) NO CHANGE
B) a single tap
C) a solo *alla Turca*
D) to the audience

44

A) NO CHANGE
B) gain the respect that they deserve.
C) cement their reputations in music history.
D) become embraced in the music of the West.

NO TEST MATERIAL ON THIS PAGE

Math Test 2 – No Calculator

25 MINUTES, 20 QUESTIONS

Turn to Section 3 of your answer sheet to answer the questions in this section.

DIRECTIONS

For questions **1 – 15**, find the solution to each problem and select the most appropriate answer from the choices provided. For questions **16 – 20**, find the solution to each problem and write your answer in the space provided. You may use the blank space in your test booklet for scratch work.

NOTES

1. The use of a calculator on any part of this section is forbidden.
2. Unless otherwise indicated, all variables and expressions used in this test represent real numbers.
3. Unless otherwise indicated, all figures used in this test are drawn to scale.
4. Unless otherwise indicated, all figures used in this test lie on a plane.
5. Unless specified otherwise, a given function, f, has the domain the set of all real numbers x for which $f(x)$ is a real number.

REFERENCE

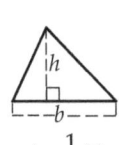
$A = \frac{1}{2}bh$

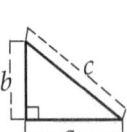
$c^2 = a^2 + b^2$

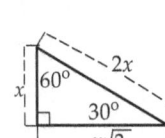
Special Right Triangles

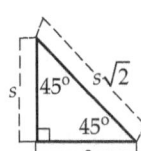

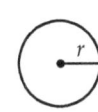
$A = \pi r^2$
$C = 2\pi r$

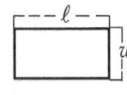
$A = \ell w$

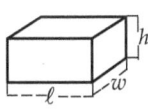
$V = \ell w h$

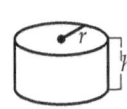
$V = \pi r^2 h$

$V = \frac{4}{3}\pi r^3$

$V = \frac{1}{3}\pi r^2 h$

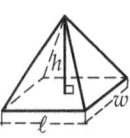
$V = \frac{1}{3}\ell w h$

The arc of a full circle is 360 degrees or 2π radians.
A triangle has angles that sum to 180 degrees.

1

A number, x, is multiplied by six and divided by seven. The result of these operations is added to five. Which of the following expressions represents the description above?

A) $\frac{6}{7}(x+5)$

B) $\frac{6x}{7}+5$

C) $6\left(\frac{x}{7}+5\right)$

D) $\frac{6x+5}{7}$

2

Which of the following expressions gives the range of possible values of x which satisfy the inequality $11 - x < 15$?

A) $x < 4$

B) $x < 2$

C) $x > -4$

D) $x > 4$

3

$$3x + 2y = 7$$
$$2x + 2y = 9$$

If (x, y) is a solution to the system of equations above, what is the value of x?

A) -2

B) 2

C) 7

D) 9

4

If $\frac{8y}{3} - 4 = \frac{1}{6}$, what is the value of $\frac{1}{y}$?

A) 16

B) $\frac{25}{16}$

C) $\frac{2}{3}$

D) $\frac{16}{25}$

5

In a class of 78 students, 41 are taking French, 22 are taking German and 9 of those students are taking both French and German. How many students are enrolled in neither French nor German?

A) 6

B) 15

C) 24

D) 33

6

If $f(3) = 15$ and $f(5) = 45$, which of the following could be the function $f(x)$?

A) $2x^2 - 2x$

B) $3x + 6$

C) $2x^2 - x$

D) $2x^2 - 5$

7

The equation of line *l* in the coordinate plane is $y = 3x + 2$. What is the equation of the line *m*, which is a reflection of line *l* across the *x*-axis?

A) $y = -3x + 2$
B) $y = 3x + 2$
C) $y = -3x - 2$
D) $y = 3x - 2$

8

If $|x| + |y| \leq 1$, which of the following is a possible solution (x, y) to the inequality?

A) $\left(-\frac{1}{3}, \frac{1}{2}\right)$

B) $\left(-\frac{2}{3}, \frac{1}{2}\right)$

C) $\left(\frac{3}{5}, -\frac{1}{2}\right)$

D) $\left(-\frac{1}{2}, -\frac{2}{3}\right)$

9

Jose takes a bus from Santa Fe to New Orleans, spends three nights in New Orleans, and then takes a bus to New York. The bus ticket to New Orleans is $70, the hotel costs $66 per night plus tax, and the ticket to New York is $84. In addition, the bus company and the hotel have a deal where a customer receives a 15% discount off the taxed total of the hotel stay if he presents a bus receipt at check-in. If the tax on the room is 9%, which of the following represents the total cost of the trip?

A) $154 + (66)(3)(1.09)(0.85)$
B) $154 + (70)(3)(1.09)(0.85)$
C) $154 + (66)(3)(1.09)(1.15)$
D) $154 + (66)(3)(0.85)$

10

An arithmetic sequence is a sequence of numbers in which the difference between consecutive terms is a constant. If $x + 3$, $2x + 1$ and $5x + 3$ are the first, second, and third terms of an arithmetic sequence respectively, what is the difference, *d*, between consecutive terms?

A) -4
B) -2
C) 4
D) It cannot be determined.

11

An athletic club charges a monthly membership fee of $65. Members can also take classes for an additional $15 per class. For this month only, the club has a special that includes two free classes for all new members. Which of the following functions expresses the cost for the month for new members who take *x* classes this month, where $x \geq 2$?

A) $C(x) = 2x + 65$
B) $C(x) = 15x + 65$
C) $C(x) = 2(x - 15) + 65$
D) $C(x) = 15(x - 2) + 65$

12

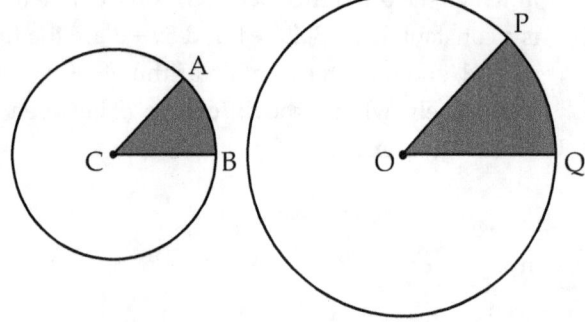

The radius of the circle with center O is twice the radius of the circle with center C. Additionally, ∠ACB ≅ ∠POQ. If the shaded area of the smaller circle is 6 cm², then what is the area of the shaded portion of the larger circle in cm²? (Note: The area of a sector is equal to half its arc length multiplied by the circle's radius.)

A) 12
B) 18
C) 24
D) 36

13

If the expression $\frac{4x^2}{2x-1}$ is written in the equivalent form $\frac{1}{2x-1} + A$, what is A in terms of x?

A) $2x + 1$
B) $2x - 1$
C) $4x^2$
D) $4x^2 - 1$

14

Which of the following expressions is equivalent to the complex expression $\dfrac{\dfrac{1}{x-2} - \dfrac{1}{x+2}}{\dfrac{2}{x+2} + \dfrac{2}{x-2}}$?

A) $-\dfrac{1}{2}$

B) $\dfrac{4x}{x+2}$

C) $\dfrac{1}{x}$

D) $\dfrac{4x}{x-2}$

15

Jack works as a car salesman. He makes 8 dollars for each hour he works, plus he receives a 9 percent commission for every car he sells. During one pay period, Jack works for 100 hours, and he sells 4 cars for an average of x dollars per car. Which of the following expressions gives Jack's gross pay, P, for this pay period?

A) $P = \dfrac{4(0.09x)}{8(100)}$

B) $P = 8(1.09x) + 100(4)$

C) $P = \dfrac{8(100)}{4(1.09x)}$

D) $P = 8(100) + 4(0.09x)$

Student-Produced Responses 3

DIRECTIONS

For questions **16 – 20**, find the solution to the problem and enter your answer as demonstrated on the right.

1. Only the answer that is bubbled in on the answer sheet will be credited. The blank spaces above the bubbles are for you to record your answers for accuracy.
2. Only fill in one bubble in any given column.
3. None of the answers on this portion of the test are negative values.
4. If a problem appears to have more than one answer, only enter one answer. If the answer you enter is one of the correct solutions, you will receive full credit for that question.
5. If the correct answer can be expressed as a mixed number, it must be entered as a decimal or an improper fraction.
6. If the correct answer is a decimal that cannot fit into the grid space, you must fill the grid with enough digits to completely fill the space. The number can be rounded or simply shortened but must fill every blank space.

Answer: $\frac{5}{36}$

Answer: 4.5

← Fraction line
← Decimal point

Write answer in boxes.
Grid in result.

Acceptable ways to grid $\frac{1}{6}$ are:

Answer: 302 – either position is correct

NOTES

Begin entering answers in any column that accommodates your answer. If you do not need a column do not enter anything in that column.

16

The axis of symmetry for the quadratic function $f(x) = -9x^2 + 12x + 1$ is the line $x = k$. What is the value of k?

ANSWER: _____

17

In a game of 60 questions, a score is calculated by subtracting twice the number of wrong answers from the number of correct answers. If a player attempted all questions and received a final score of 45, how many questions did he or she get wrong?

ANSWER: _____

18

If $f(x) = -1 + 8x$, what is the value of $\dfrac{f(x+h) - f(x)}{h}$?

ANSWER: _____

19

n	$n+1$	$n+2$	$n+3$
245	500	1,010	2,030

The sequence above can be expressed as the function $f(n+1) = a\,f(n) + k$. What is the value of $a + k$?

ANSWER: _____

20

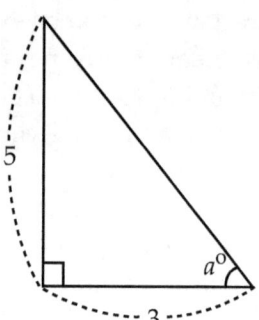

What is the value of $\tan(90° - a°)$?

ANSWER: _____

Math Test 2 – Calculator

 55 MINUTES, 38 QUESTIONS

Turn to Section 4 of your answer sheet to answer the questions in this section.

DIRECTIONS

For questions **1 – 30**, find the solution to each problem and select the most appropriate answer from the choices provided. For questions **31 – 38**, find the solution to each problem and write your answer in the space provided. You may use the blank space in your test booklet for scratch work.

NOTES

1. The use of a calculator on this section is allowed.
2. Unless otherwise indicated, all variables and expressions used in this test represent real numbers.
3. Unless otherwise indicated, all figures used in this test are drawn to scale.
4. Unless otherwise indicated, all figures used in this test lie on a plane.
5. Unless specified otherwise, a given function, f has the domain the set of all real numbers x for which $f(x)$ is a real number.

REFERENCE

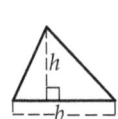
$A = \frac{1}{2}bh$

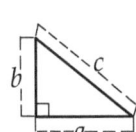
$c^2 = a^2 + b^2$

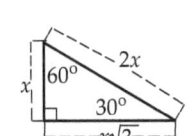
Special Right Triangles

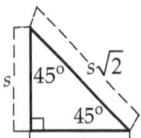
$A = \pi r^2$
$C = 2\pi r$

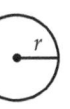
$A = \ell w$

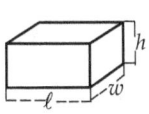
$V = \ell w h$

$V = \pi r^2 h$

$V = \frac{4}{3}\pi r^3$

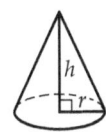
$V = \frac{1}{3}\pi r^2 h$

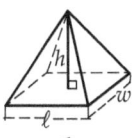
$V = \frac{1}{3}\ell w h$

The arc of a circle is 360 degrees or 2π radians.
A triangle has angles that sum to 180 degrees.

1

During a five-day festival, the number of visitors tripled each day after the first. If the festival opened on a Thursday with 345 visitors, what was the attendance on Sunday?

A) 1,035
B) 1,725
C) 3,105
D) 9,315

2

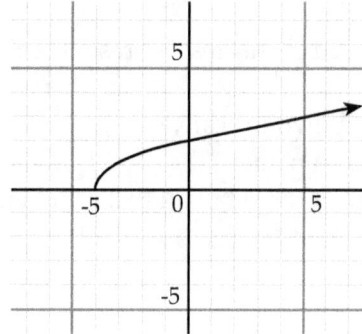

The graph above is of the function $f(x) = \sqrt{x+4}$. What is the function's domain?

A) All real numbers $x \geq -4$
B) All real numbers $x > -4$
C) All real numbers $x \geq 4$
D) All real numbers $x < -4$

3

Which of the following expressions is equivalent to $\dfrac{(2x^{-3}y^4)^3}{(4xy)^2}$ for all $x \neq 0$ and $y \neq 0$?

A) $\dfrac{y^{10}}{2}$

B) $\dfrac{2y^{10}}{x^{10}}$

C) $\dfrac{y^{10}}{2x^{11}}$

D) $\dfrac{y^{10}}{2x^7}$

4

Yearly sales for a new business are 3 million dollars more in the second year than in the first, and sales in the third year double those in the second. If sales in the third year total $38 million, what were sales, in millions of dollars, in the first year?

A) 13
B) 16
C) 17.5
D) 22

5

If $\dfrac{f}{g} = \dfrac{1}{4}$ and $\dfrac{g}{h} = \dfrac{2}{5}$, which of the following is equivalent to $f : h$?

A) 1 : 6
B) 1 : 8
C) 1 : 10
D) 10 : 1

6

A movie theater containing 1,152 seats sells movie tickets for 8 dollars each. On Tuesdays, children aged 10 and under get into the theater for free. During one Tuesday film showing, the theater made $7,920 and filled every seat in the theater. How many children aged 10 and under were in attendance?

A) 144
B) 152
C) 160
D) 162

7

Fifteen percent of a number is 12. What is 35 percent of the same number?

A) 5
B) 12
C) 28
D) 33

8

Which of the following expressions is equivalent to $\sqrt{250x^9y^4}$ for all $x \geq 0$ and $y \geq 0$?

A) $3x\sqrt{28y^7}$
B) $5x^4y^2\sqrt{10x}$
C) $10x^2y^2\sqrt{5x^2y}$
D) $5x^3y^2\sqrt{3}$

9

If $5^{\left(x-\frac{1}{5}\right)^2} = 1$, what is the value of x?

A) $\frac{1}{5}$
B) $\frac{1}{3}$
C) 3
D) 5

10

Vincent arrives at work at 8:15 a.m. and leaves at 10:30 p.m., taking an hour lunch break at noon. He gets paid $10 an hour for the first eight hours, and one-and-a-half his hourly wage for any time worked past eight hours. He is not paid for his lunch break. What was he paid for the day?

A) $120.25
B) $158.75
C) $173.75
D) $180.00

11

The mean of three numbers is V. If the three numbers are X, Y, and Z, what is X in terms of Y, Z, and V?

A) $ZY - V$
B) $\frac{Z}{V} - V - 3$
C) $\frac{Z}{3} - V - Y$
D) $3V - Z - Y$

12

Rachel's gross pay, P, is given below as a function of overtime hours worked, h. Overtime hours are defined as the number of weekly hours worked past 40:

$$P = \$503.60 + \$18.51h$$

How many total hours does Rachel need to work to make at least $910 for the week?

A) 21
B) 61
C) 62
D) 72

13

Which of the following statements is true regarding the rate of change of the function $f(x) = -3x - 8$?

A) The function has a varying rate of change.
B) The function has a constant negative rate of change.
C) The function has a constant positive rate of change.
D) The function has a constant rate of change for $x \geq 8$, and a varying rate of change for $x < 8$.

14

Which of the following binomials is a factor of the quadratic trinomial $3x^2 + 2x - 5$?

A) $3x - 1$
B) $x - 1$
C) $3x - 5$
D) $x - 5$

15

If $\sin\theta = 0.57$, what is the value of $\sin(\pi - \theta)$?

A) −0.57
B) −0.43
C) 0.43
D) 0.57

16

x	4	5	6	7
$f(x)$	17	26	37	50

The table above gives values for a function $f(x)$. Which of the following could be the function $f(x)$?

A) $f(x) = 4x + 1$
B) $f(x) = 6x - 4$
C) $f(x) = x^2 + 1$
D) $f(x) = x^2 - 1$

17

Number of Accidents	Number of Drivers
0	17
1	13
2	21
3	4
4	2
5	2
6	1

A group of drivers were polled on the number of car accidents in which they had been involved over the past five years. The results of the survey are given in the table above. Based on these results, what is the median number of accidents per driver?

A) 0.5
B) 1
C) 1.5
D) 2

18

How many solutions are there for the equation $|2x - 2| = x$?

A) 1
B) 2
C) 3
D) An infinite number of solutions

19

If $3^{5-x} = 81^{x+1}$, what is the value of x?

A) $\frac{1}{3}$

B) 3

C) $\frac{4}{5}$

D) $\frac{1}{5}$

20

Sammy the banana slug travels 13 meters every 1,020 seconds. Approximately how many minutes would it take him to travel 115.5 meters up a sequoia tree?

A) 113
B) 151
C) 177
D) 205

21

Five-sixths of the students in a math class are passing with a grade of C− or better. Three-fourths of the students in the same class are passing with a grade of B− or better. What fraction of the class is passing with a grade higher than C− but lower than a B−?

A) $\frac{5}{8}$

B) $\frac{1}{12}$

C) $\frac{1}{6}$

D) $\frac{1}{4}$

22

Which of the following choices is the solution to the inequality $\frac{x+1}{x-3} \geq 0$?

A) $-1 \leq x < 3$
B) $x \leq -1$ or $x > 3$
C) $x \leq -3$ or $x \geq 1$
D) $x \neq 3$

23

In which quadrant do the graphs of equations $3x - 5y + 2 = 0$ and $y = 0.6x + 0.4$ intersect?

A) I
B) II
C) III
D) Quadrants I, II, and III: they are the same line.

24

If $\frac{1-x}{x} = \frac{4-4x}{x}$, what is the value of $\frac{1-x}{x}$?

A) -1
B) 0
C) $\frac{1}{4}$
D) 1

25

Chocolate Froyo (f) has x fewer calories than Chocolate Ice Cream (c), cup for cup, such that $3x + 28 = f$ calories and $4x + 28 = c$ calories. Given that $c + f + 8 = 8x$, find x.

A) 18
B) 42
C) 60
D) 64

Questions 26 and 27 refer the following information.

The force between two electrically charged particles is given by Coulomb's Law:

$$F = \frac{1}{4\pi\varepsilon_0} \cdot \frac{q_1 q_2}{r^2}$$

where F is force, which is measured in Newtons (N), ε_0 is a constant with value 8.85×10^{-12}, q_1 and q_2 are the charges on the two particles, which are measured using Coulombs (C), and r is the distance between the particles in meters (m).

26

If we rework the equation above to equal ε_0, which of the following expressions could represent the units of ε_0?

A) $\frac{C^2}{m^2 \cdot N}$

B) $\frac{N \cdot m^2}{C^2}$

C) $\frac{C^2 \cdot m^2}{N}$

D) It cannot be determined.

27

If two charged particles with $q_1 = q_2 = 1.6 \times 10^{-19}$ C are 1 meter apart, what is the electrostatic force between them?

A) 0
B) 2.3×10^{-29}
C) 1.4×10^{-28}
D) 2.3×10^{-28}

28

Which one of the following statements is always FALSE?

A) Doubling the base of a rectangle doubles its area.
B) Doubling the height of a triangle doubles its area.
C) Doubling the radius of a circle doubles its area.
D) Doubling a number results in another number of lower value.

29

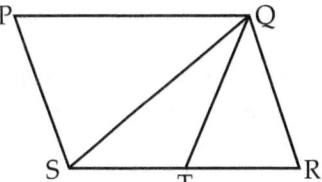

PQRS is a parallelogram and T is the midpoint of $\overline{SR}$. What is the ratio of the area of triangle QST to the area of the parallelogram?

A) 1 : 2
B) 1 : 3
C) 1 : 4
D) 1 : 5

30

If A = −2 + 4i and B = 3 − 2i, which of the following is equivalent to (A − B)?

A) −5 + 6i
B) −1 + 6i
C) 1 − 6i
D) 5 − 6i

4 Student-Produced Responses

DIRECTIONS

For questions **31 – 38**, find the solution to the problem and enter your answer as demonstrated on the right.

1. Only the answer that is bubbled in on the answer sheet will be credited. The blank spaces above the bubbles are for you to record your answers for accuracy.
2. Only fill in one bubble in any given column.
3. None of the answers on this portion of the test are negative values.
4. If a problem appears to have more than one answer, only enter one answer. If the answer you enter is one of the correct solutions, you will receive full credit for that question.
5. If the correct answer can be expressed as a mixed number, it must be entered as a decimal or an improper fraction.
6. If the correct answer is a decimal that cannot fit into the grid space, you must fill the grid with enough digits to completely fill the space. The number can be rounded or simply shortened but must fill every blank space.

NOTES

Begin entering answers in any column that accommodates your answer. If you do not need a column do not enter anything in that column.

Answer: $\frac{5}{36}$ — Write answer in boxes. Grid in result.

Answer: 4.5 — ← Fraction line ← Decimal point

Acceptable ways to grid $\frac{1}{6}$ are:

Answer: 302 – either position is correct

31

If $\dfrac{x+3}{2} + \dfrac{2x}{7} = 7$, what is the value of x?

ANSWER: _____

32

The graph of the equation $2x^2 - y^2 = 8$ passes through the points $(6, p)$ and $(6, -p)$. What is the value of p if $(p > 0)$?

ANSWER: _____

33

After 22 percent of Homer's gross pay is deducted for federal income tax, Homer is left with a $792 check. Rounded to the nearest dollar, how much did Homer earn in gross pay before tax?

ANSWER: _____

34

The line $y = 5$ intersects a circle with center $(4, 4)$ and radius 3 at two points. If the x-coordinate of one point of intersection is 1.17, what is the x-coordinate of the other point of intersection?

ANSWER: _____

35

A charity sells greetings cards in packs costing $10 or $2.50 each. At a fair, a total of 75 packs were sold for a total of $375. How many of the $2.50 packs were sold?

ANSWER: _____

36

x	0	1	2
$f(x)$	4	6	q

The table above gives values for the exponential function $f(x)$. What is one possible value of q?

ANSWER: _____

Questions 37 and 38 are based on the information below.

Any object that has a temperature higher than the temperature of its surroundings will cool until it reaches the same temperature as its surroundings. A hotter object will cool at a faster rate than a cooler object. The relationship between the rate of cooling and the initial temperature of an object is given by the formula:

$$T_t = T_s + (T_0 - T_s)e^{-rt}$$

where T_t is the temperature of the object at a time t in seconds, T_s is the temperature of the surrounding environment, T_0 is the initial temperature of the object, and r is a constant, and $e \approx 2.718$. All temperatures are in degrees Celsius.

37

If an object at 150 degrees Celsius is placed into an ice bath of zero degrees Celsius, what is the value, in degrees Celsius, of T_s in the equation above?

ANSWER: _____

38

A chemical solution at 50 degrees Celsius is placed in an incubator that maintains a temperature of 25 degrees Celsius. What is the temperature of the solution after it has been in the incubator for one minute if the value of r is 0.01? (Round your answer to the nearest degree Celsius.)

ANSWER: _____

NO TEST MATERIAL ON THIS PAGE

Essay Test 2

 50 MINUTES, Prompt-based essay

Turn to Section 5 of your answer sheet to answer the question in this section.

> **DIRECTIONS**
>
> As you read the passage below, consider how Nicholas Buffie uses
> - evidence, such as facts or examples, to support claims.
> - reasoning to develop ideas and to connect claims and evidence.
> - stylistic or persuasive elements, such as word choice or appeals to emotion, to add power to the ideas expressed.

Adapted from "Women Earn Less than Men in 302 of 311 Occupations" by Nicholas Buffie, published on October 5, 2015.

In his 2014 State of the Union address, President Obama discussed the fact that women workers are paid far less than their male colleagues: "That is wrong. And in 2014, it's an embarrassment. Women deserve equal pay for equal work!"

Some commentators have criticized President Obama's statement, arguing that the gender pay gap doesn't account for occupational choices or differences in hours worked. Consider the critique about occupational choices: if women *choose* to work in low-paying occupations, a substantial gender pay gap can exist *even if* women are paid the same as men in every occupation. If this is true, we can't honestly argue that women are being treated worse than men.

This argument can be disproved by a closer look at the data. Earlier this year, the Census Bureau published an extensive dataset which gives the 2013 median annual earnings of full-time, year-round workers by occupation. Moreover, the data is available not only by occupation but by "*Detailed* Occupation"—for instance, under the more general occupational title "Installation, Maintenance, and Repair Occupations," we see a list of 36 sub-occupations such as "Avionics technicians," "Control and valve installers and repairers," "Radio and telecommunications equipment installers and repairers," etc. Because the data give such detailed breakdowns, we are allowed to isolate the effect of occupation on the gender pay gap; and because the data are for "full-time, year-round workers," it already controls for hours worked to a substantial degree.

If men and women received equal pay for equal work, we'd expect the data to show that the two groups are paid equally *within each occupation*. And insofar as any pay discrepancies *did* exist, we'd expect that the distribution of such discrepancies would be fairly equal—that is, if men were paid substantially more than women in ten occupations, we'd expect that women would be paid substantially more than men in ten occupations as well. However, this isn't what we see in the Census data. The Bureau has data on

525 occupations. Of these occupations, 214 have such low employment that we can't reliably estimate the occupation's gender earnings gap. That leaves us with 311 occupations. And of those 311, women make more than men in only *nine*. This means that men make more than women in 97.1 percent of all occupations.

Furthermore, in the few occupations in which women *do* make more, they often don't make *substantially* more. In two of the nine occupations in which women make more, they earn 0.17 percent more than men; in another occupation, they earn 0.47 percent more. By contrast, in about 90 percent of all occupations, women make *at least* 5 percent less than men.

Nonetheless, it may be worth honing in on the definition of "full-time, year-round worker." The Census Bureau's definition of this term is "A person who worked full time (35 or more hours per week) and year round (50 or more weeks) during the previous calendar year or in the past twelve months." This definition leaves a bit of wiggle room in terms of hours worked. For example, if a woman were to work 35 hours a week and a man were to work 50 hours a week, we'd expect the full-time male worker to receive greater weekly earnings than the full-time female worker even if they were paid the same hourly wage.

Fortunately, the Bureau of Labor Statistics has data on the weekly hours of both male and female full-time workers.* In 2013, full-time women worked an average of 41.0 hours per week; full-time men worked an average of 43.7 hours. If this discrepancy holds across occupations (we don't have data on hours that correspond to the occupations given by the Census), then even in the case of equal *hourly* pay, we'd expect women to earn 93.8 percent of what men earn.

Yet even if we apply this adjustment for hours worked, it turns out that men make more than women in the vast majority of occupations. Overall, women earn at least 93.8 percent of what men earn in just 35 out of 311 occupations (11.3 percent).

So the idea that women are paid less than men because of occupational choices is clearly wrong. When you look inside various occupations themselves, it turns out that women doing equal work receive less than equal pay.

The BLS and the Census Bureau have the same definition for "full-time worker," so we need not worry about conflating incompatible datasets.

Write an essay in which you explain how Nicholas Buffie builds an argument to persuade his audience that, on average, women are paid less than men for equal work. In your essay, analyze how the author uses one or more of the features listed in the box above (or features of your own choice) to strengthen the logic and persuasiveness of his argument. Be sure that your analysis focuses on the most relevant features of the passage.

Your essay should not explain whether you agree with the author's claims, but rather explain how the author builds an argument to persuade his audience.

* Sample response found in the "Answers and Explanations" section of this study guide.

"Women Earn Less than Men in 302 of 311 Occupations" is licensed under CC BY 4.0. For more information, see page 511.

KALLIS

SAT® Practice Test #3

IMPORTANT REMINDERS:

 When you take the official SAT, you will need to use a No. 2 pencil. Do not use a pen or a mechanical pencil.

 On the official SAT, sharing any of the questions on the test violates the College Board's policies and may result in your scores being canceled.

(This cover is modeled after the cover you'll see when you take the official SAT.)

UNAUTHORIZED REPRODUCTION OR USE OF ANY PART OF THIS TEST IS PROHIBITED.

© 2019 KALLIS EDU

Reading Test 3

 65 MINUTES, 52 QUESTIONS

Turn to Section 1 of your answer sheet to answer the questions in this section.

DIRECTIONS

Each passage or pair of passages is accompanied by 10 or 11 questions. Read each passage or pair of passages, and then select the most appropriate answer to each question. Some passages may include tables or graphs that require additional analysis.

Refer to the passage below to answer questions 1 – 10.

This passage is from Shara Yurkiewicz, "Time of death," published July 19, 2015.

<pre>
line   I really hoped she was dead.
            It wasn't personal. It was as far from
       personal as possible. I had never met the patient
       while she was alive.
   5   Every four days, my team and I are on call
       at the hospital. For about 16 hours, we must
       make decisions about people we have never met.
       The people range from sick and stable (patients
       from other medical teams and new admissions),
  10   sick and unstable (rapid responses for acute
       changes in mental status or vital signs), dying
       (cardiopulmonary resuscitation and/or emergency
       intubation), and dead (pronouncements).
            My last name and pager number were
  15   plastered on the oncology floor, which increased
       the odds that pages I received would be about the
       dying or dead. The first one was.
            "I need you to pronounce," said the nurse
       when I called her back.
  20   As a two-week-old intern with a largely
       theoretical knowledge base and minimal
       understanding of a new hospital's electronic and
       interpersonal quirks, I appreciate algorithms. "If
       x, then y" gives me relatively secure footing to
  25   rest decision-making upon, mainly because the
       decisions are pre-determined.
            There's not much that's more algorithmic
       than a pronouncement. If called for one, go into
       the patient's room. If the family is there, say that
  30   you're sorry for their loss. Then verify that the
       patient is dead. Shine a penlight into the eyes and
       note that the pupils are fixed and dilated. Place
       a stethoscope on the chest and note the lack of
       breathing and heart sounds. Place a finger on the
  35   carotid artery and note the lack of pulse. Look at
       the clock. Pronounce the patient dead at the given
       time. Repeat again to the family that you are
       sorry for their loss. Ask them (and remind them
       that you must do this for everyone) if they want
  40   to do an autopsy. Leave the room, document the
       encounter.
            My co-intern and I had debated if we
       preferred the family present or absent during the
</pre>

<pre>
       process.
  45   Absent, I said. I had no desire to walk into
       a stranger's funeral as a stethoscope-wielding
       technician who offered stock condolences.
            But my colleague had done several without
       the family present and described it as something I
  50   didn't expect.
            "It's creepy," he said. "It's just you and… you
       know." That stranger on the other end of a one-
       sided interaction. He had almost had to bring the
       nurse in the room with him for company.
  55   I had laughed then.
            "The family was here last night, but they're not
       here right now," the nurse told me as I approached.
            After getting a brief history of the patient's
       medical course from the nurse and the chart, I
  60   opened the door to her room.
            The efforts of the palliative care team were
       obvious. The shades were drawn, and the room was
       quiet except for the sounds of a waterfall playing
       in the background. I closed the door behind me
  65   to keep out the florescent lighting and beeping
       monitors and chatting of the nurses.
            But with the closing of the door, I also kept out
       the sounds of the living. The intern had been right.
            I inwardly cursed him and every horror movie
  70   I had seen to date. I cursed my reptilian brain for
       its very strong impulse to back away from the bed.
       I cursed my irrational thoughts that maybe she
       wasn't dead after all, and wouldn't it be terrifying
       if she sat up while I was trying to find her pulseless
  75   carotid.
            I really hoped she was dead.
            I watched 120 seconds tick by on the clock.
       This woman's time of death was being delayed
       because I was too stupidly scared to confirm it.
  80   I was not going to call the nurse for company.
            Finally, a combination of embarrassment and
       obligation kicked in. I was called for x, so I did
       y. Then I left the room and did z. I wrote a note,
       making sure I used the word "dead" (required). I
  85   called the primary provider. I filled out the death
       certificate.
            I called the patient's family, and they sobbed
       into the phone. Physical presence or absence was
       irrelevant, I realized. I felt like a stethoscope-
  90   wielding technician who offered stock condolences.
            I'm thankful for the algorithms so carefully
</pre>

"Time of death" is licensed under CC BY 4.0. For more information, see page 511.

outlined in my resident handbook. Their explicitness is exactly what a new intern needs. But pre-determination does not preclude
95 meaning. Unwritten between steps are a grieving family's pain, a messenger's fear, and a stranger whom I will never meet.

If x, then y. But…x is really, really hard.

To my first pronounced patient: your time of
100 death was five minutes earlier. I'm so sorry for the delay. It wasn't in the algorithm.

★

1

As used in line 10, "acute" most nearly means

A) fierce.
B) dire.
C) negligible.
D) shrewd.

2

Throughout the passage, the author suggests that she likes following step-by-step procedures because doing so

A) helps compensate for her lack of job experience.
B) reduces her risk of harming a patient.
C) distinguishes her from the other interns.
D) makes her feel more comfortable around the deceased.

3

Which choice provides the best evidence for the answer to the previous question?

A) Lines 20 – 23 ("As…algorithms")
B) Lines 48 – 50 ("But…expect")
C) Lines 81 – 86 ("Finally…certificate")
D) Lines 99 – 101 ("To my…algorithm")

4

The main purpose of paragraph 7 (lines 27 – 41) is to

A) criticize the formal protocol that the narrator must follow.
B) list the sequential steps of a professional duty.
C) instruct the reader about how to complete a difficult task.
D) explain how to interact with grieving families.

5

The narrator probably includes the information about laughing at what her co-intern says in lines 51 – 54 because it is

A) revealing; it highlights the narrator's dry wit and sharp sense of humor.
B) perplexing; the co-intern is discussing a very serious and personal issue.
C) amusing; it underscores her warm friendship with her co-intern.
D) ironic; the narrator later has a similar reaction during her own pronouncement.

6

The atmosphere in the patient's room, as described in lines 61 – 66, is

A) tranquil.
B) unsettling.
C) sterile.
D) disorienting.

7

As used in line 61, "palliative" most nearly means

A) restorative.
B) maintenance.
C) funereal.
D) soothing.

8

The narrator's initial attitude toward the woman's corpse can best be described as one of

A) unexpected grief.
B) uncontrollable panic.
C) profound hope.
D) instinctive recoiling.

9

Which choice provides the best evidence for the previous question?

A) Lines 52 – 53 ("That stranger…interaction")
B) Lines 67 – 68 ("But with…living")
C) Lines 69 – 71 ("I inwardly…bed")
D) Line 76 ("I really…dead")

10

The narrator calls herself a "stethoscope-wielding technician" (lines 46 – 47) mainly to imply that she

A) must play an impersonal role in a sensitive situation.
B) feels proud of her technical education and learned skills.
C) wants the procedure to be as formal and as fact-based as possible.
D) worries that the family will not believe her or trust her.

Refer to the passage below to answer questions 11 – 21.

This passage is adapted from a speech by President Franklin D. Roosevelt, "Address at the Dedication of Boulder Dam," delivered on September 30, 1935. The Boulder Dam, now called the Hoover Dam, spans the Colorado River and is located on the Arizona-Nevada border. It was the largest dam of its kind when it was constructed.

line
   Ten years ago the place where we are gathered was an unpeopled, forbidding desert. In the bottom of a gloomy canyon, whose precipitous walls rose to a height of more than
5 a thousand feet, flowed a turbulent, dangerous river. The mountains on either side of the canyon were difficult of access with neither road nor trail, and their rocks were protected by neither trees nor grass from the blazing heat of the sun. The
10 site of Boulder City was a cactus-covered waste. The transformation wrought here in these years is a twentieth-century marvel.
   We are here to celebrate the completion of the greatest dam in the world, rising 726 feet
15 above the bed-rock of the river and altering the geography of a whole region; we are here to see the creation of the largest artificial lake in the world—115 miles long, holding enough water, for example, to cover the State of Connecticut to
20 a depth of ten feet; and we are here to see nearing completion a power house which will contain the largest generators and turbines yet installed in this country, machinery that can continuously supply nearly two million horsepower of electric
25 energy.
   All these dimensions are superlative. They represent and embody the accumulated engineering knowledge and experience of centuries; and when we behold them it is
30 fitting that we pay tribute to the genius of their designers. We recognize also the energy, resourcefulness and zeal of the builders, who, under the greatest physical obstacles, have pushed this work forward to completion two
35 years in advance of the contract requirements. But especially, we express our gratitude to the thousands of workers who gave brain and brawn to this great work of construction.
   Beautiful and great as this structure is, it
40 must also be considered in its relationship to the agricultural and industrial development and in its contribution to the health and comfort of the people of America who live in the Southwest.
   To divert and distribute the waters of an arid
45 region, so that there shall be security of rights and efficiency in service, is one of the greatest problems of law and of administration to be found in any Government. The farms, the cities, the people who live along the many thousands of
50 miles of this river and its tributaries —all of them depend upon the conservation, the regulation, and the equitable division of its ever-changing water supply.
   What has been accomplished on the
55 Colorado in working out such a scheme of distribution is inspiring to the whole country. Through the cooperation of the States whose people depend upon this river, and of the Federal Government which is concerned in the general
60 welfare, there is being constructed a system of distributive works and of laws and practices which will insure to the millions of people who now dwell in this basin, and the millions of others who will come to dwell here in future generations,
65 a just, safe and permanent system of water rights.
   Last year a drought of unprecedented severity was visited upon the West. The watershed of this Colorado River did not escape. In July the canals of the Imperial Valley went dry. Crop
70 losses in that Valley alone totaled $10,000,000 that summer. Had Boulder Dam been completed one year earlier, this loss would have been prevented, because the spring flood would have been stored to furnish a steady water supply for the long dry
75 summer and fall.
   Across the San Jacinto Mountains southwest of Boulder Dam, the cities of Southern California are constructing an aqueduct to cost $220,000,000, which they have raised, for the purpose of
80 carrying the regulated waters of the Colorado River to the Pacific Coast 259 miles away.
   Across the desert and mountains to the west and south run great electric transmission lines by which factory motors, street and household lights
85 and irrigation pumps will be operated in Southern Arizona and California. Part of this power will be used in pumping the water through the aqueduct to supplement the domestic supplies of Los Angeles and surrounding cities.

11

How do the words "forbidding," "gloomy," and "dangerous" (lines 1 – 5) in the first paragraph help set the tone of the speech?

A) They provide an important factual base on which to build a convincing argument.
B) They set the scene for a speech about sobering societal problems.
C) They create a negative image to heighten the sense of triumph over adversity.
D) They provide a contrast with the "blazing heat of the sun" image that follows.

12

As used in line 30, "genius" most closely means

A) mastermind.
B) brilliance.
C) specialty.
D) expert.

13

In paragraph 2 (lines 13 – 25) President Roosevelt provides specific measurements primarily to

A) suggest that the Boulder Dam project has been too costly.
B) emphasize the enormity of the Boulder Dam project.
C) demonstrate his understanding of public works projects.
D) challenge those who doubt the value of the Boulder Dam.

14

In paragraph 4 (lines 39 – 43), President Roosevelt shifts from discussing the Boulder Dam itself to focusing on

A) its effects on the economics and welfare of the region's inhabitants.
B) its potential for stemming anxieties about water.
C) descriptions of the people who will benefit from it.
D) details about how water will be allocated among different types of users.

15

President Roosevelt indicates that those who govern a hot, dry region

A) should study the aqueducts built in connection with Boulder Dam.
B) should not share water with neighboring territories.
C) must bring about agricultural and industrial growth.
D) must be largely concerned with managing water distribution.

16

Which choice provides the best evidence for the answer to the previous question?

A) Lines 11 – 12 ("The transformation…marvel")
B) Lines 44 – 48 ("To divert…Government")
C) Lines 57 – 65 ("Through the…rights")
D) Lines 76 – 79 ("Across the…raised")

17

As used in line 74, "furnish" most nearly means

A) put.
B) stock.
C) yield.
D) equip.

18

According to the passage, the Boulder Dam is inspiring partly because

A) people have already made laws and agreements about using what it produces.
B) it is permanent and guaranteed never to fail those who depend on it.
C) it can prevent droughts such as the one in the preceding year.
D) it can bring millions of people into the Southwest in future generations.

19

President Roosevelt mentions crop losses from the drought primarily to

A) show his empathy to the American public.
B) support his central claim about the value of the dam.
C) emphasize the difficulty of farming in the West.
D) list another major expense in the dam's construction cost.

20

Which choice provides the best evidence for the answer to the previous question?

A) Lines 66 – 67 ("Last year…West")
B) Lines 71 – 75 ("Had Boulder…and fall")
C) Lines 79 – 81 ("for the…away")
D) Lines 82 – 86 ("Across the…California")

21

It can be inferred from the passage that cities in Southern California will

A) take most of the water from the Colorado River.
B) build the longest aqueduct in history.
C) become more populous as a result of better water access.
D) become at least partly dependent on water and power from the dam.

Refer to the passage below to answer questions 22 – 32.

This passage is adapted from E. Walter Maunder, *Are the Planets Inhabited*, originally published in 1913.

line   Many writers on the subject of the habitability of other worlds, from contemplating the rich and apparently limitless variety of the forms of life, and the diversity of the conditions
5   under which they exist, have been led to assume that the basis of life must itself also in like manner be infinitely broad and infinitely varied. In this they are mistaken. As we have seen, the elements entering into the composition of organic
10 bodies are, in the main, few in number. The temperatures at which they can exist are likewise strictly limited. But, above all, that circulation of matter which we call Life—the metabolism of vital processes—requires for its continuance the
15 presence of one indispensable factor—water....
    Water is the compound of oxygen and hydrogen in the proportion of two atoms of hydrogen to one of oxygen. It is familiar to us in three states: solid, liquid, and gaseous, or
20 ice, water, and steam. But it is only in the liquid state that water is available for carrying on the processes of life. This fact limits the temperatures at which the organic functions can be carried on, for water under terrestrial conditions is
25 only liquid for a hundred degrees; it freezes at 0° Centigrade, it boils at 100° Centigrade. Necessarily, our experiences are mostly confined within this range, and therefore we are apt unconsciously to assume that this range is all
30 the range that is possible, whereas it is but a very small fraction of the range conceivable, and indeed existing, in cosmical space....
    Water is, then, indispensable for the living organism; but there are two great divisions of
35 such organisms—plants and animals. Animals are generally, but not universally, free to move, and therefore to travel to seek their food. But their food is restricted; they cannot directly convert inorganic matter to their own use; they can only
40 assimilate organic material. The plant, on the other hand, unlike the animal, can make use of inorganic material. Plant life, therefore, requires an abundant supply of water in which the various substances necessary for its support can
45 be dissolved; it must either be in water, or, if on land, there must be an active circulation of water both through the atmosphere and through the soil, so as to bring to it the food that it requires. Animal life presupposes plant life, for it is always
50 dependent upon it.
    Many writers have assumed that life is very widely distributed in connection with this planet. The assumption is a mistaken one, as has been well pointed out by Garrett P. Serviss, a
55 charming writer on astronomical subjects: "*On the Earth we find animated existence confined to the surface of the crust of the globe, to the lower and denser strata of the atmosphere, and to the film of water that constitutes the oceans.*
60 *It does not exist in the heart of the rocks forming the body of the planet nor in the void of space surrounding it outside the atmosphere. As the Earth condensed from the original nebula, and cooled and solidified, a certain quantity of*
65 *matter remained at its surface in the form of free gases and unstable compounds, and, within the narrow precincts where these things were, lying like a thin shell between the huge inert globe of permanently combined elements below, and the*
70 *equally unchanging realm of the ether above, life, a phenomenon depending upon ceaseless changes, combinations and re-combinations of chemical elements in unstable and temporary union, made its appearance, and there only we find it at the*
75 *present time.*"
    "The huge inert globe of permanently combined elements below, and the equally unchanging realm of the ether above," offer no home for the living organism; least of all for the
80 highest of such organisms—Man. Both must be tempered to a condition which will permit and favor continual change, the metabolism which is the essential feature of life.
    "*...Between the earth and man arose the leaf.*
85 *Between the heaven and man came the cloud. His life being partly as the falling leaf and partly as the flying vapor.*"
    The leaf and the cloud are the signs of a habitable world. The leaf—that is to say, plant
90 life, vegetation—is necessary because animal life is not capable of building itself up from inorganic material. This step must have been previously taken by the plant. The cloud, that is to say water-vapour, is necessary because the plant in its turn
95 cannot directly assimilate to itself the nitrogen from the atmosphere. The food for the plant is brought to it by water, and it assimilates it by the help of water. It is, therefore, upon the question of the presence of water that the question of the
100 habitability of a given world chiefly turns. In the physical sense, man is "born of water," and any world fitted for his habitation must "stand out of the water and in the water."

22

The main function of lines 1 – 7 ("Many... varied") is to

A) establish the author's main argument.
B) present a popular viewpoint that the author rejects.
C) reveal compelling evidence that supports the author's hypothesis.
D) challenge the scientific community to broaden a definition.

23

As used in line 21, "carrying on" is closest in meaning to

A) maintaining.
B) bringing.
C) persevering.
D) demanding.

24

In paragraph 3 (lines 33 – 50), the author suggests that animal life

A) is more versatile and variable than plant life on Earth.
B) depends heavily on the conversion of organic materials to inorganic materials.
C) creates the conditions that allow plant life to thrive.
D) can only thrive in conditions where plant life already exists.

25

Which choice provides the best evidence for the answer to the previous question?

A) Lines 35 – 37 ("Animals are…their food")
B) Lines 37 – 40 ("but their…material")
C) Lines 42 – 45 ("Plant life…dissolved")
D) Lines 49 – 50 ("Animal life…upon it")

26

As used in line 49, "presupposes" most nearly means

A) accepts.
B) predates.
C) requires.
D) superimposes.

27

The quote by Serviss that begins on line 55 primarily serves to

A) refute a common misconception.
B) shed light on a confusing process.
C) elaborate on a definition.
D) provide evidence for an assumption.

28

The author suggests that life thrives

A) under conditions of extreme chaos.
B) under virtually any condition.
C) in a mutable environment.
D) in a static environment.

29

Which choice provides the best evidence for the answer to the previous question?

A) Lines 8 – 10 ("As we…in number")
B) Lines 27 – 32 ("our experiences…space")
C) Lines 62 – 66 ("As the…compounds")
D) Lines 80 – 83 ("Both…life")

30

In paragraph 5 (lines 76 – 83), the author implicitly agrees with Serviss' contention that

A) life will never be found on any other planet.
B) much of the universe is in stasis.
C) plants with leaves were the first living organisms.
D) Earth's oceans are relatively shallow.

31

The primary purpose of the quote in lines 84 – 87 ("'Between…vapor'") is to

A) summarize the author's argument using metaphor.
B) refute a claim from the previous paragraph.
C) highlight that scientific writing can include poetic qualities.
D) introduce a piece of evidence that supports the author's viewpoint.

32

Throughout the passage, the author implies that

A) scientists have attempted to replicate the processes that created life on Earth.
B) life can probably only thrive under the conditions found on Earth.
C) classifying all living organisms is too large a task for scientists of his era.
D) there is a general consensus regarding the prerequisites for life.

Refer to the passage and graph below to answer questions 33 – 42.

This passage is adapted from Stefanie Knoll, "Waging war on poverty: Historical trends using the Supplemental Poverty Measure," published January 24, 2014.

  The question of how the government can alleviate poverty has long been disputed in the United States. In a 1986 radio address, President Ronald Reagan urged that the welfare system set
5 up to help the poor was itself to blame for their plight. "We spend vast amounts on a system that perpetuates poverty," he said. Ten years later, President Bill Clinton signed a bill "ending welfare as we know it," abolishing the federal Aid
10 to Families with Dependent Children and shifting control of welfare programs to the states. The bill required recipients of benefits to work and limited aid to five years.
  Critics of anti-poverty programs point out
15 that significant progress has not been made in eliminating poverty in recent decades. Indeed, the overall poverty rate has hovered around 12% to 15% since the 1970s. Without a doubt, poverty and inequality continue to be significant problems
20 in the United States, and the economic recession of 2007 and 2008 led to levels of hardship not seen since the Great Depression. But how one defines and thus measures "poverty" is also central to the debate over anti-poverty programs
25 and their effectiveness. The Census Bureau's Official Poverty Measure is based on metrics that are little changed from the 1960s, and it has been criticized for using outdated poverty thresholds that do not vary geographically,
30 and for neglecting government policies that include non-cash transfers, such as food stamps, subsidized childcare, and housing. In response, the U.S. Census Bureau in 2011 began formally experimenting with a new poverty paradigm, the
35 Supplemental Poverty Measure (SPM).
  A 2014 study for the National Bureau of Economic Research, "Waging War on Poverty: Historical Trends in Poverty Using the Supplemental Poverty Measure," focuses on the
40 effectiveness of government anti-poverty policies since 1967, using the SPM. The scholars—Liana Fox from the Swedish Institute for Social Research and Irwin Garfinkel, Neeraj Kaushal, Jane Waldfogel and Christopher Wimer of Columbia
45 University—use data from the Annual Social and Economic Supplement, the Current Population Survey and the Consumer Expenditure Survey in order to construct the Supplemental Poverty Measure for the years 1967 to 2012. They then
50 use the measures to estimate what poverty rates would have been had certain government policies not been enacted.
  Based on the Supplemental Poverty Measure, government programs were more effective
55 in reducing poverty than previous estimates suggested. Whereas the Official Poverty Rate showed almost no reduction in poverty between 1967 and 2012, "estimates using SPM show that without government programs, poverty
60 would have risen from 25% to 31%, while with government benefits poverty has fallen from 19% to 16%. Thus government programs today are cutting poverty nearly in half (from 31% to 16%) while in 1967 they cut poverty by only a quarter
65 (from 25% to 19%)."
  Tax credits and food and nutrition programs have been especially effective in reducing poverty. Among all transfers, the impact of food and nutrition programs has been the largest in the last
70 few years. The Official Poverty Measure misses this effect since it only takes into account cash transfers.
  Because the Official Poverty Measure fails to take into account non-cash transfers,
75 such as childcare and food stamp assistance, it underestimates the important role that government programs play in alleviating child poverty. The study reveals, "Taken together, government programs in 2012 reduced child
80 poverty by 12 percentage points, and deep child poverty by 11 percentage points, versus 3 and 5 percentage points respectively in 1967."

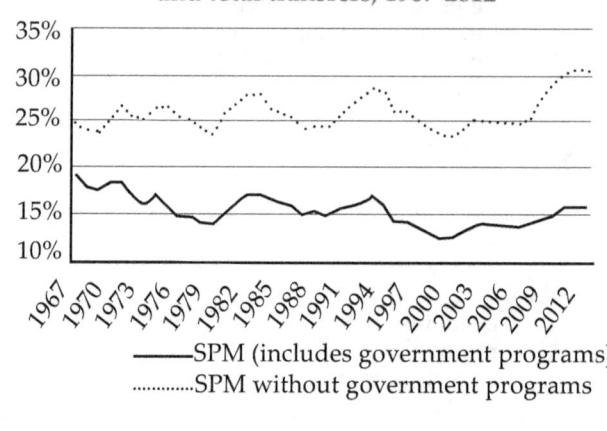

Overall poverty, with and without SPM and total transfers, 1967-2012

——— SPM (includes government programs)
·········· SPM without government programs

"Waging war on poverty: Historical trends using the Supplemental Poverty Measure" is licensed under CC BY 4.0. For more information, see page 511.

33
As used in line 7, "perpetuates" most nearly means

A) enshrines.
B) safeguards.
C) prolongs.
D) immortalizes.

34
It can reasonably be inferred from paragraph 1 (lines 1 – 13) that President Clinton

A) reduced federal involvement in social welfare programs.
B) challenged President Reagan's criticisms of the U.S. welfare system.
C) eliminated the majority of welfare programs meant to help poor children.
D) increased the length of time that people could receive federal aid.

35
According to the author, public assistance

A) is largely ineffective in addressing poverty nationally.
B) has often been criticized as failing to reduce overall poverty.
C) leads to continued poverty and inequality.
D) has been seen by many as absolutely necessary.

36
The sentence in lines 16 – 18 ("Indeed...1970s") primarily serves to

A) refute the preceding information about welfare programs.
B) concede the apparent accuracy of a counterargument.
C) substantiate the author's central claim with specific figures.
D) introduce a new topic regarding the causes of poverty.

37
As used in line 29, "thresholds" most nearly means

A) entrances.
B) speculations.
C) new beginnings.
D) defining points.

38
According to the passage, the Supplemental Poverty Measure differs from the Official Poverty Measure mainly by

A) reflecting more data.
B) using higher estimates.
C) engaging in abstraction.
D) focusing on non-cash assistance only.

39
Which choice provides the best evidence for the answer to the previous question?

A) Lines 32 – 35 ("In response...Measure")
B) Lines 45 – 49 ("data from...2012")
C) Lines 49 – 52 ("They then...enacted")
D) Lines 53 – 56 ("Based on...suggested")

40
The passage and the figure are in agreement that

A) tax credits and programs that provide food are especially helpful for the impoverished.
B) government programs have reduced overall poverty rates in the U.S. for nearly half a century.
C) government programs have reduced child poverty by 12 percentage points.
D) food and nutrition programs have had the most impact during recent years.

41
Which statement is best supported by the figure?

A) Non-cash aid such as food stamps has risen by more than 10 percent since 1967.
B) As of 2012, government assistance has cut estimated poverty rates by about 50 percent.
C) The Supplemental Poverty Measure fluctuates more than the Official Poverty Measure.
D) The Supplemental Poverty Measure is more accurate than the Official Poverty Measure.

42
Which choice provides the best support for the information in the graph?

A) Lines 33 – 35 ("the U.S. Census...Measure")
B) Lines 58 – 62 ("'estimates...16%")
C) Lines 68 – 70 ("Among all...years")
D) Lines 78 – 82 ("'Taken...1967'")

Refer to the pair of passages below to answer questions 43–52.

Passage 1 is adapted from "Ghosts of the Prairie: The Reintroduction of the Black-footed Ferret," 2016, U.S. Department of the Interior. Passage 2 is adapted from "15 Facts About Our National Mammal: the American Bison," 2016, U.S. Department of the Interior.

Passage 1

line
    Black-footed ferrets—agile creatures with masked faces and droopy whiskers—once roamed the prairies in 12 western states, stretching from Canada to Mexico. By the 1960s,
5 their numbers had plummeted because of habitat loss, a decline in prey, and plague. But with the help of a farm dog and years of recovery efforts, these nocturnal mammals have made their way back home.
10   Recently the Wyoming Game and Fish Department and U.S. Fish and Wildlife Service partnered to reintroduce the species to the place where they were rediscovered after being believed to be extinct.
15   In 1981, a dog named Shep tussled with a weasel-like creature at the Hogg family's ranch near Meeteetse, Wyoming. Shep's owners, John and Lucille Hogg, found the small creature's carcass the next day and brought it to the town's
20 taxidermist, who correctly identified the animal as the thought-to-be extinct black-footed ferret.
    After an extensive search of the surrounding area, conservationists determined that the nearby Pitchfork Ranch was sustaining
25 the last remaining wild black-footed ferrets on the planet. At this time, the species was considered the rarest mammal in the world.
    In an effort to save the species, these last ferrets were captured and placed in a captive
30 breeding program, which has been highly successful in expanding the population.
    Over the course of the next 35 years, 50 federal, state, Tribal, nonprofit and other local partners joined forces to enable the ferret's
35 recovery. These efforts have resulted in the successful reintroduction of the ferret at 28 sites across its historic range.
    Perhaps the most meaningful and symbolic of these efforts occurred in May of 2016, when
40 black-footed ferrets finally returned home to the ranch in Meeteetse, where they were rediscovered 35 years ago.
    At one time, the black-footed ferret was nothing more than a memory—a ghost of the
45 prairie, believed to have gone the way of the dodo. But what was once considered the last holdout of the black-footed ferret will now be the beginning of an anticipated stronghold.

Passage 2

    Buffalos, more accurately called "bison,"
50 are the largest mammal in North America. Male bison weigh up to 2,000 pounds and stand 6 feet tall, while females weigh up to 1,000 pounds and reach a height of 4-5 feet. Bison may be big, but they're also fast. They can run up to 35 miles per
55 hour. Plus, they're extremely agile. Bison can spin around quickly, jump high fences and are strong swimmers. They primarily eat grasses and leafy plants—typically foraging for 9 to 11 hours a day. That's where the bison's large protruding shoulder
60 hump comes in handy during the winter. It allows them to swing their heads from side-to-side to clear snow—especially for creating foraging patches.
    In prehistoric times, millions of bison roamed North America, from the forests of Alaska and the
65 grasslands of Mexico to Nevada's Great Basin and the eastern Appalachian Mountains. The history of bison and Native Americans are intertwined. Bison have been integral to tribal culture, providing them with food, clothing, fuel, tools, shelter and
70 spiritual value. But by the late 1800s, there were only a few hundred bison left in the United States after European settlers pushed west, reducing the animal's habitat and hunting the bison to near extinction. Had it not been for a few private
75 individuals working with tribes, states and the Interior Department, the bison would be extinct today.
    Years before he became a U.S. president, Teddy Roosevelt traveled to the Dakota Territory to
80 hunt bison. He bought a ranch and ended up living on it for a couple of years. Roosevelt returned to New York with a new outlook on life. As president from 1901 to 1909, he paved the way for the conservation movement, and in 1905, formed the
85 American Bison Society with William Hornaday to save the disappearing bison. Supporting a breeding program at the New York City Zoo (today, the Bronx Zoo,) the American Bison Society had enough bison by 1913 to restore a free-ranging
90 bison herd. Working with Interior, they donated 14 bison to Wind Cave National Park in South Dakota. More than 100 years later, the bison from Wind Cave have helped reestablishing other herds across the United States and most recently in Mexico.
95 Public lands managed by Interior support 17 bison herds—or approximately 10,000 bison—in 12 states, including Alaska.
    Yellowstone National Park is the only place in the U.S. where bison have continuously lived
100 since prehistoric times. What makes Yellowstone's bison so special is that they're the pure descendants (free of cattle genes) of early bison that roamed our country's grasslands. As of July 2015, Yellowstone's bison population was estimated at 4,900—making
105 it the largest bison population on public lands.

43

The author of Passage 1 indicates that, by the 1960s, black-footed ferrets had become rare partly because

A) they were overhunted by early settlers in the region.
B) their natural resources became increasingly scarce.
C) they had become too widely dispersed.
D) farm dogs hunted too many of them.

44

According to Passage 1, Pitchfork Ranch is significant primarily because it

A) is where the Hogg family found a black-footed ferret carcass.
B) acted as the headquarters for black-footed ferret revival efforts.
C) is a research facility for the reintroduction of endangered species.
D) was home to the only surviving members of a particular species.

45

As used in line 35, "recovery" is closest in meaning to

A) replenishment.
B) retrieval.
C) resuscitation.
D) recuperation.

46

It can be inferred from lines 43 – 46 of Passage 1 ("At one...dodo") that "the dodo" is

A) a now-extinct prey species of the black-footed ferret.
B) another animal species that was reintroduced in North America.
C) an example of an extinct animal species.
D) a species whose population has seen a steep decline in recent decades.

47

As used in line 72, "pushed" most nearly means

A) forced.
B) urged.
C) advanced.
D) sent.

48

The author of Passage 2 implies which of the following about bison?

A) They can survive freezing temperatures.
B) They are distantly related to the black-footed ferret.
C) A typical bison once traveled thousands of miles a year.
D) They occasionally take shelter in caves such as the Wind Cave.

49

Which choice provides the best evidence for the answer to the previous question?

A) Lines 50 – 53 ("Male bison...feet")
B) Lines 55 – 57 ("Bison can...swimmers")
C) Lines 57 – 58 ("They primarily...day")
D) Lines 59 – 62 ("That's where...patches")

50

The author of Passage 1 likely views Teddy Roosevelt's actions in lines 82 – 90 of Passage 2 ("As president...herd") with

A) skepticism, because Roosevelt hunted the threatened bison.
B) approval, because he helped create a model for saving other endangered species.
C) foreboding, because the bison species is still struggling after a century of efforts.
D) disappointment, because so many of today's bison carry cattle genes.

51

Which choice provides the best evidence for the answer to the previous question?

A) Lines 15 – 17 ("In 1981...Wyoming")
B) Lines 26 – 27 ("At this time...world")
C) Lines 28 – 31 ("In an...population")
D) Lines 38 – 42 ("Perhaps the...ago")

52

The primary purpose of each passage is to

A) celebrate successful efforts to breed and reintroduce an endangered grassland mammal.
(B) praise individuals who rediscovered a species that was believed extinct.
C) describe the process by which members of an endangered species are released into the wild.
D) criticize American developers for driving native animal species from their habitats.

STOP

Writing & Language Test 3
35 MINUTES, 44 QUESTIONS

Turn to Section 2 of your answer sheet to answer the questions in this section.

DIRECTIONS

Each of the following passages is accompanied by approximately 11 questions. Some questions will require you to revise the passages in order to improve coherence and clarity. Other questions will require you to correct grammatical errors. Passages may be accompanied by graphs, charts, or tables that you must consider when making revisions. For most questions, you may select the "NO CHANGE" option if you believe that portion of the passage is clear, concise, and grammatically correct as is.

Within the passages, highlighted numbers followed by underlined text indicate which part of the text corresponds with each question. Bracketed numbers [1] indicate sentence number. These bracketed numbers are only relevant to problems that require you to add or rearrange sentences in a paragraph.

Questions 1-11 are based on the following passage.

The Architecture of Kings

Kings in 17th-century Europe were consolidating power, usually at the expense of aristocratic landholders. But to keep their thrones, monarchs needed to constantly reinforce **1** the public's acceptance, and assumption, of their greatness. Architecture and design often served such a purpose. Monarchs commissioned the construction of palaces that rendered viewers awestruck and spread word of the royal family's magnificence **2** far and wide. Consequently, the social elite utilized an expressive style now called **3** "baroque." The baroque style influenced art, music, and architecture. Baroque artists rebelled against tranquility; they wanted to excite passions. Sculpted figures are caught in movement, often twisting their bodies, reaching out, running, or fighting. **4** The style originated within the Catholic Church in Rome. In architecture, baroque style is elaborately embellished; decorations seem to overflow their boundaries. Rulers of the era found that the style was perfect for extolling their own glory.

1

A) NO CHANGE
B) their subjects' attitudes for greatness.
C) their prestige.
D) an acceptance and assumption of greatness.

2

A) NO CHANGE
B) widely and far.
C) far away.
D) farther and wider.

3

Which choice most effectively combines the underlined sentences?

A) "baroque," which
B) "baroque," it
C) "baroque" as it
D) "baroque," and

4

Which choice provides a second example that most effectively supports the claim made in the paragraph?

A) NO CHANGE
B) Sculptors paid special attention to cloaks, skirts, and hair.
C) Painters generally used patches of light and shadow within the composition.
D) Paintings often depict the most dramatic point in some well-known story.

252

CONTINUE

King Louis XIV of France became perhaps the most famous purveyor of baroque [5] style: through his 700-room palace at Versailles. Started in 1661, the palace still stands, bearing witness to Louis XIV's claim to be the "Sun King." Its high, curved ceilings and vast interior spaces dwarf visitors. In addition, the [6] excessive ornamentation on walls and furnishings is meant to dazzle viewers. The opulence [7] is likely intimidating to even the wealthy lords and ladies of the Sun King's reign.

Baroque décor provided a theatrical backdrop for the king and his family to carry out their daily lives in the presence of an audience. Members of the aristocracy were forced to live at the palace and serve as that reverent audience. For example, Louis XIV's bedroom was [8] glamorous, covered in gold and draped with gold-brocaded red velvet curtains. About 100 courtiers attended a ceremony to wake up and dress the king each morning, most of them standing behind a gold railing. More nobles could await the king in the Hall of Mirrors. The hall is designed so that natural light reflects from mirrored, polished, bronzed, and gilded surfaces. [9] It provided a spectacular promenade for the Sun King.

A special setting was created for foreign visitors as well. Baroque buildings were often designed with dramatic entry halls for ceremonial welcomes; Versailles originally featured [10] one with a huge skylight known as the Ambassadors' Stair. Already diminished in the cavernous space, a visitor would have to look up to his host, the king, standing at the head of the grand staircase. [11] Thereby the king could expect to impress even the greatest of visiting dignitaries.

★

5

A) NO CHANGE
B) style, through
C) style through
D) style. Through

6

The writer wants to maintain a descriptive yet neutral tone. Which choice best accomplishes this goal?

A) NO CHANGE
B) profuse
C) splendid
D) immoderate

7

A) NO CHANGE
B) probably was being
C) was surely
D) is doubtless

8

Which choice provides information that best supports the claim made in this paragraph?

A) NO CHANGE
B) in effect a stage,
C) at the very center of the palace,
D) formal,

9

The writer is considering deleting the underlined sentence. Should the writer make this change?

A) Yes, because it introduces distracting information about promenades.
B) Yes, because it fails to add new information about the Hall of Mirrors.
C) No, because it provides information that will be explained in the next paragraph.
D) No, because it explains the underlying purpose of the Hall of Mirrors.

10

A) NO CHANGE
B) a grand, sky-lit entry hall known as the Ambassador's Stair.
C) an entry hall with a big skylight—known as the Ambassador's Stair.
D) an "Ambassador's Stair," as it was known, with a huge skylight.

11

A) NO CHANGE
B) Similarly,
C) Nevertheless,
D) Afterward

Questions 12-22 are based on the following passage.

The Cursed Villages

In the Cappadoccia region of Turkey, doctors wondered for decades about the noticeably short lifespans in three particular [12] villages—Tuzköy, Karain, and Sanhidir. Many of the villagers seemed to suffer from tuberculosis (TB) but did not respond to TB treatment. [13] Some village residents believed they lived under a curse. Lifespans were so short that there was even a common saying: "I cannot remember my father, and he cannot remember his father."

[1] Outside of the three villages, inhabitants of the region had ordinary lifespans. [2] For centuries, the Cappadoccia region has been settled by various peoples seeking safety within its arid peaks and valleys. [3] Early settlers discovered that the surrounding rock was relatively [14] soft and yielding and used it for building and plastering. [4] They even carved into the rock to create cave homes, churches, mosques, and underground cities for emergencies. [5] Today, Cappadoccia is renowned for its rock-hewn architecture dating from ancient times. [6] Their descendants continued these practices. [15]

12
A) NO CHANGE
B) villages; the villages being
C) villages, including
D) villages, which would be

13

At this point, the writer is considering adding the following sentence.

> Even people who moved away from the villages died at a relatively young age.

Should the writer make this addition here?

A) Yes, because it implies that many villagers sought to move away from the villages.
B) Yes, because it reinforces the paragraph's claim about the mysterious nature of the premature deaths.
C) No, because it fails to support the connection between the premature deaths and particular locations.
D) No, because it fails to describe how many villagers moved, and to where.

14
A) NO CHANGE
B) softly yielding
C) soft
D) soft in composition

15

The most logical placement for sentence 6 is

A) where it is now.
B) after sentence 1.
C) after sentence 2.
D) after sentence 3.

The [16] danger behind the three "cursed" villages was eventually identified. Doctors found that a rare and deadly cancer, mesothelioma, was causing 50 percent of all deaths there. In modernized countries, mesothelioma tends to be caused by exposure to [17] insulating material asbestos, but asbestos had never been used in the villages. Researchers discovered that the rock surrounding the three villages contained erionite, a rock crystal that is also linked to mesothelioma. Thus, the prime suspect for generations of premature deaths in the three villages turned out to be the rock that [18] they built with, lived in, and walked on.

Each time residents disturbed the powdery rock, they had no idea that they were raising small clouds of erionite dust containing microscopic crystal needles. When inhaled or ingested, the erionite "needles" may lodge in the soft tissue that lines [19] the lungs, abdomen, and heart. Exposure as a child may lead to cancer after a long latency period. This sobering fact explains why even villagers who [20] moved away had unusually short lifespans.

Efforts to help the villages and learn more about the disease continue. Recent research has suggested that genetics plays a significant role in susceptibility to mesothelioma, because some village families had high rates of the [21] disease when considering others. The Turkish government built new housing for the villagers away from the erionite. Regular blood testing helps to catch the disease in its early stages. [22] Meanwhile, public health officials are taking a closer look at other erionite deposits around the globe. In many places, they are trying to halt any disturbances of the deposits.

16

A) NO CHANGE
B) peril of
C) predominate effect on
D) threat to

17

A) NO CHANGE
B) asbestos, an insulating material,
C) an insulating material asbestos
D) insulation material, asbestos,

18

A) NO CHANGE
B) the three of them
C) villagers
D) had been

19

A) NO CHANGE
B) lungs, abdomen, and additionally the heart.
C) lungs, the abdomen and the heart.
D) lungs, abdomen, heart.

20

A) NO CHANGE
B) have moved away had
C) had moved away were having
D) moved away had been having

21

A) NO CHANGE
B) disease.
C) disease, but not everybody.
D) disease while others had none.

22

Which choice best combines the underlined sentences?

A) Public health officials, taking a closer look at other erionite deposits around the globe, are meanwhile trying to prevent the deposits from being disturbed in many places.
B) Meanwhile, taking a closer look at other erionite deposits, in many places around the globe public health official are trying to prevent the deposits from being disturbed.
C) Meanwhile, public health officials are taking a closer look at many other erionite deposits around the globe and trying to prevent them from being disturbed.
D) To prevent erionite deposits around the globe from being disturbed, meanwhile, in many places public health officials are taking a closer look at them.

Questions 23-33 are based on the following passage and supplementary material.

A Jury of Your Peers

[23] In this passage I will describe how I once served on a jury for a criminal case. After reporting to the local courthouse for "jury duty," I was randomly selected to serve. I really did not want to, but I understood the principle. If I were accused of a crime, I would want a jury to decide my case, because a jury of 12 disparate [24] people are more likely to make a [25] tenable judgment than any one individual.

During courtroom proceedings, individual jurors must absorb information in a kind of isolation. [26] They are not even allowed to talk about it with their spouses or friends. At the appropriate time, members of the jury solemnly discuss the evidence with each other and try to reach a consensus. [27] Either the charges are supported, and the defendant is found guilty; or, there is a reasonable level of uncertainty, and the defendant is found not guilty.

In the case I mentioned, the defendant was a young husband. The alleged crimes occurred when his wife, along with one of her [28] friends, "Ashley," and another couple, a man and a woman, ebulliently entered his apartment late one night after being in a pub. The husband/defendant was upset about being awakened, especially by the other couple [29] who he did not know. Ashley testified that the defendant lost all self-control and, completely unprovoked, inflicted serious injuries on the others.

23

Which choice most effectively introduces the passage?

A) NO CHANGE
B) Because no one in my family works in law enforcement,
C) Believe me, I know about the American jury system, because
D) Like about one in every four Americans,

24

A) NO CHANGE
B) peoples are
C) people's is
D) people is

25

A) NO CHANGE
B) transparent
C) sound
D) consequential

26

The writer wants to add a supporting detail to indicate the extent of jurors' solitude. Which choice best accomplishes this goal?

A) NO CHANGE
B) Attorneys for each side present evidence and question witnesses.
C) Jurors must decide whether to believe testimony of witnesses and defendants.
D) Sometimes they may take notes as long as they leave them in the courtroom during breaks.

27

A) NO CHANGE
B) They must determine whether the prosecution has proved the defendant's guilt "beyond a reasonable doubt."
C) Juries try to decide if there is a "reasonable doubt" of the defendant's guilt regarding each charge, and if there is not, they must find the defendant "guilty" of that charge.
D) They try to agree that the defendant is guilty of a charge and that any doubts are not "reasonable," or that the defendant is possibly innocent, or more strictly "not guilty."

28

A) NO CHANGE
B) friends, "Ashley" and another couple, a man and a woman
C) friends, "Ashley" and another couple, a man and a woman
D) friends, "Ashley," and another couple, a man, and a woman,

The defendant admitted to trying to eject his wife's friends, but testified that the incident was being exaggerated and misinterpreted. The alleged victims—the defendant's own wife and the other couple—surprisingly agreed with him. That left the prosecution to prove that Ashley's perceptions were clearer than [30] all the other people involved. Based mainly on her testimony, the prosecution claimed that the defendant's actions amounted to criminal battery, assault, and false imprisonment.

In the jury room, [31] we weighed the conflicting interpretations; truth seemed amorphous. Eventually, we agreed that reasonable doubts did exist for most of the charges. For example, in the context of a loud brawl, the defendant's pulling his wife inside did not seem to amount to "false imprisonment," especially since she went out again. [32] One charge, however, seemed like you couldn't deny it. We agreed to find the defendant guilty of assault for pounding the other man's head on the sidewalk. It seemed plain that such an action crossed a line into criminal behavior.

Juries are not usually involved in sentencing criminals, so I never found out what sentence the defendant received. He may have appealed the case to a higher court. Our jury disbanded; it is likely that we each occasionally ask ourselves [33] if we made the right decisions? Hopefully, we lived up to the meaning of "common sense."

---------★---------

[29]

A) NO CHANGE
B) that
C) which
D) whom

[30]

A) NO CHANGE
B) those of all the
C) those
D) of all those

[31]

The writer is considering deleting the underlined information. Should the writer make this change?

A) Yes, because it blurs the main focus of the paragraph.
B) Yes, because it creates a sentence that is wordy and redundant.
C) No, because it serves as a transition from the preceding paragraphs.
D) No, because it makes a claim that is supported in the body of the paragraph.

[32]

A) NO CHANGE
B) However, there was one exception.
C) On only one matter, our adjudication diverged.
D) There was this one thing that we couldn't get over.

[33]

A) NO CHANGE
B) whether our decisions were the right ones.
C) whether or not we did the right thing?
D) if our decisions were tenable and based upon a preponderance of evidence.

Questions 34-44 are based on the following passage.

Classic Job Training: Apprenticeships

An apprenticeship offers an individual the opportunity to learn a trade while working in his or her chosen field. An apprentice receives on-the-job training in exchange for a lower wage. Upon completion of the apprenticeship, the apprentice gains professional certification in his or her industry and is eligible for increased wages.

Apprenticeships were first formalized during the Middle [34] Ages. A time when skilled labor was regulated by guilds. The apprenticeship system allowed governing bodies to hold workers accountable and set a standard for craftsmen. It also gave young people the opportunity to learn a trade and become recognized as journeymen. This was important, because only journeymen or master crafters were allowed to join guilds and [35] scrape by from their craft.

These days, apprenticeships are often partnerships between governments and private organizations that allow a new generation of workers to gain the skills necessary for a competitive job market. Apprentices [36] deign to accept lower wages while working under the supervision of journeymen for a number of years [37] before becoming journeymen themselves. Apprentices must also attend weekly classroom lectures on subjects relevant to their chosen profession. Apprenticeships are common in trades such as carpentry, plumbing, and engineering.

In the United States, there are regulations to ensure that apprentices receive adequate training and [38] preparing for the full responsibilities of [39] they're occupations once the apprenticeships are over. Often, when an apprentice becomes a journeyman, he or she receives some manner of formal certification. This allows journeymen to

34

A) NO CHANGE
B) Ages, a
C) Ages; a
D) Ages a

35

A) NO CHANGE
B) become a breadwinner
C) make a living
D) get dough

36

A) NO CHANGE
B) see fit to
C) make the terribly difficult decision to
D) DELETE the underlined portion.

37

At this point the writer is considering adding the following information.

   (usually five to seven)

Should the writer include this information here?

A) Yes, because it clarifies an ambiguous statement.
B) Yes, because it highlights an important feature of apprenticeships.
C) No, because it fails to elaborate on the process of becoming a journeyman.
D) No, because it blurs the focus of the paragraph with irrelevant details.

38

A) NO CHANGE
B) have preparation
C) are prepared
D) had prepared

39

A) NO CHANGE
B) there
C) their
D) his or her

prove their abilities to <u>40 perspective</u> employers. However, a new journeyman may elect to continue working for the company that sponsored him or <u>41 her. He</u> or she will work more independently and receive a higher wage.

Apprenticeships are popular in many countries and provide entry to careers that may otherwise be difficult to pursue. <u>42 Moreover,</u> some contemporary industries are starting to offer apprenticeships; for example, many software companies are encouraging potential employees to participate in apprenticeships. Combined with the growth in traditional apprenticeships, <u>43 these programs are expected to increase the average wages of apprentices in the United States by 50 percent over the next three years.</u>

Growth in these programs can be economically beneficial, as apprenticeships provide opportunities for individuals of every education level. Also, apprenticeship programs are often administered in cooperation with labor unions, which helps apprentices gain access to larger professional networks. <u>44 In general, apprentices spend less time than college graduates seeking employment.</u>

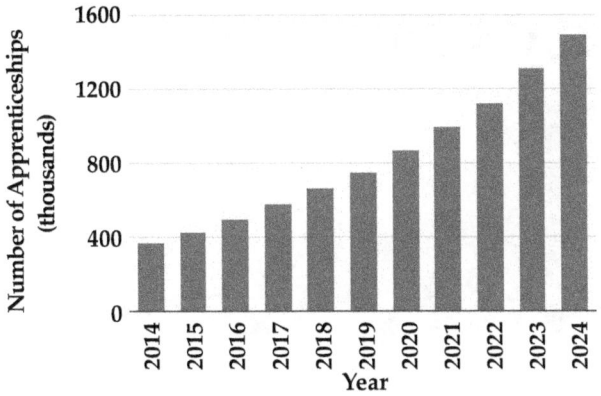

Number of Apprenticeships Predicted in the United States

40

A) NO CHANGE
B) prospective
C) aspiring
D) contingent

41

Which provides the best combination of the two sentences at the underlined portion?

A) her; in this case, he
B) her, but he
C) her: he
D) her; he

42

A) NO CHANGE
B) However,
C) Next,
D) Thus,

43

Which choice provides the most relevant detail based on the information in the graphic?

A) NO CHANGE
B) these programs are expected to reduce government spending on apprenticeships by 50 percent over the next three years.
C) these programs are expected to increase the total number of apprenticeships in the United States by 50 percent over the next three years.
D) these programs are expected to reduce the duration of apprenticeship by 50 percent over the next three years.

44

Which of the following most effectively concludes the passage?

A) NO CHANGE
B) Therefore, apprentices will gain an economic advantage over those not participating in apprenticeships.
C) Finally, journeymen attend long-term professional development courses to stay competitive after completing an apprenticeship.
D) Overall, apprenticeships provide aspiring professionals with the knowledge and experience necessary to compete in today's job market.

NO TEST MATERIAL ON THIS PAGE

Math Test 3 – No Calculator

 25 MINUTES, 20 QUESTIONS

Turn to Section 3 of your answer sheet to answer the questions in this section.

DIRECTIONS

For questions **1 – 15**, find the solution to each problem and select the most appropriate answer from the choices provided. For questions **16 – 20**, find the solution to each problem and write your answer in the space provided. You may use the blank space in your test booklet for scratch work.

NOTES

1. The use of a calculator on any part of this section is forbidden.
2. Unless otherwise indicated, all variables and expressions used in this test represent real numbers.
3. Unless otherwise indicated, all figures used in this test are drawn to scale.
4. Unless otherwise indicated, all figures used in this test lie on a plane.
5. Unless specified otherwise, a given function, f, has the domain the set of all real numbers x for which $f(x)$ is a real number.

REFERENCE

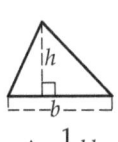
$A = \frac{1}{2}bh$

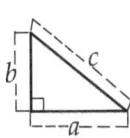
$c^2 = a^2 + b^2$

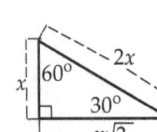
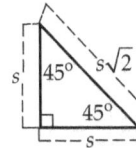
Special Right Triangles

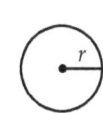
$A = \pi r^2$
$C = 2\pi r$

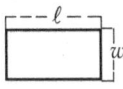
$A = \ell w$

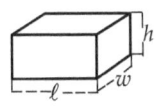
$V = \ell w h$

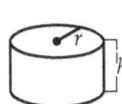
$V = \pi r^2 h$

$V = \frac{4}{3}\pi r^3$

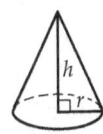
$V = \frac{1}{3}\pi r^2 h$

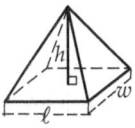
$V = \frac{1}{3}\ell w h$

The arc of a full circle is 360 degrees or 2π radians.
A triangle has angles that sum to 180 degrees.

3

1

If $\dfrac{2x + 3y - 19}{y + 5} = 3$, what is the value of x?

A) −9
B) 9
C) 17
D) It cannot be determined.

2

An isosceles triangle has a perimeter of 36 inches. The length of the two equal sides, b, is related to the length of the third side, a, by the equation $a = 36 - 2b$. What is b in terms of a?

A) $b = 2(a + 36)$

B) $b = \dfrac{36 + a}{2}$

C) $b = 2(a - 36)$

D) $b = \dfrac{a - 36}{-2}$

3

A subscription to an online book archive costs $35 per year. This fee gives the subscriber unlimited web access to an online library. If the subscriber wants to download a book (as opposed to reading it online), the cost is $1.99 per download. Which of the following equations describes the total dollar cost per year, p, for a subscriber who downloads m books?

A) $p = 1.99 + 35m$
B) $p = 35 + 1.99m$
C) $p = 35(1.99m)$
D) $p = 35 - 1.99m$

4

Which of the following expressions is numerically equivalent to $\left(\sqrt[7]{\sqrt[10]{7}}\right)^{35}$?

A) $\dfrac{1}{7}$

B) $\sqrt{7}$

C) 7

D) $7\sqrt{7}$

5

The following was developed in the Bakhshali manuscript four centuries before it was replicated in Europe.

Two page-boys are attendants of a king. The first is paid $\dfrac{13}{6}$ dinaras a day and the other receives $\dfrac{3}{2}$ dinaras a day. The first must pay back a debt to the second totaling 10 dinaras. If the first gives the second all of his income until his debt is repaid, after how many days of work will the two have an equal number of dinaras?

A) 30
B) 25
C) 21
D) 15

6

If $2x - 3y = 3x + 3y = 30$, what is the value of x?

A) 5
B) 10
C) 12
D) 50

CONTINUE

7

Which of the following equations has no y-intercepts?

A) $x = 7$
B) $y = 0$
C) $y = x$
D) $x = 0$

8

If Tweedledee can move 100 rocks in 6 hours, and Tweedledum can move the same number of rocks in 4 hours, how long will it take for them to move 100 rocks working together?

A) 2 hours and 24 minutes
B) 3 hours and 12 minutes
C) 3 hours and 44 minutes
D) 4 hours and 10 minutes

9

A Colombian coffee at $8.00 per pound is mixed with an Ethiopian coffee at $3.00 per pound to make a blend worth $5.00 per pound. How many pounds of the Colombian coffee is needed to make 50 pounds of the blend?

A) 20
B) 25
C) 30
D) 35

10

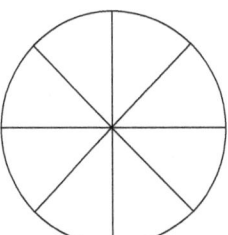

Assuming each piece of the pie above measures $\frac{81\pi}{8}$ inches², what is the diameter of the pie?

A) 2π inches
B) 18 inches
C) $\frac{36}{\pi}$ inches
D) $\frac{2}{\pi\sqrt{\pi}}$ inches

11

The slope and y-intercept of a line are $\frac{1}{2}$ and 3, respectively. What is its x-intercept?

A) $x = -6$
B) $x = 0$
C) $x = \frac{3}{2}$
D) $x = 6$

12

Sloan has driven p miles of a 202-mile trip. If her average speed is below 65 miles per hour for the rest of the trip, which of the following inequalities represents the time in hours t it will take her to reach her destination?

A) $t < \frac{202-p}{65}$
B) $t > \frac{65}{202-p}$
C) $t < \frac{65}{202-p}$
D) $t > \frac{202-p}{65}$

13

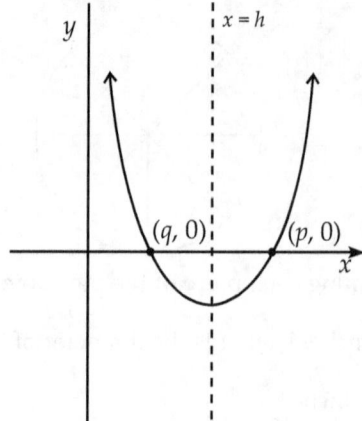

The parabola above has x-intercepts $(p, 0)$ and $(q, 0)$ and a line of symmetry $x = h$. What is q in terms of p and h?

A) $q = p - 2h$

B) $q = \dfrac{p - h}{2}$

C) $q = \dfrac{p + h}{2}$

D) $q = 2h - p$

14

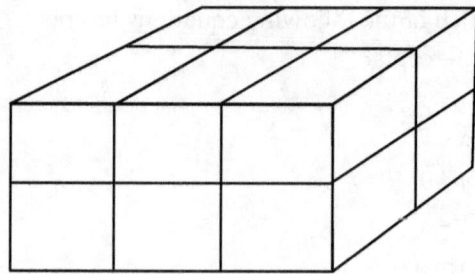

A large brick is composed of identical smaller bricks as shown in the figure above. The smaller bricks are cubes with length 2 inches. What is the absolute difference, in square inches, between the surface area of the large brick and the combined surface area of its constituent bricks?

A) 68
B) 80
C) 136
D) 160

15

Line l passes through the point $(3, -2)$ and has a y-intercept of 4. Line m passes through the origin and has slope 3. The two lines intersect at point (d, e). What is the value of $e - d$?

A) $-\dfrac{8}{5}$

B) $\dfrac{4}{5}$

C) $\dfrac{8}{5}$

D) $\dfrac{12}{5}$

Student-Produced Responses 3

DIRECTIONS

For questions **16 – 20**, find the solution to the problem and enter your answer as demonstrated on the right.

1. Only the answer that is bubbled in on the answer sheet will be credited. The blank spaces above the bubbles are for you to record your answers for accuracy.
2. Only fill in one bubble in any given column.
3. There are no negative answers in this portion of the test.
4. If a problem appears to have more than one answer, only enter one answer. If the answer you enter is one of the correct solutions, you will receive full credit for that question.
5. If the correct answer can be expressed as a mixed number, it must be entered as a decimal or an improper fraction.
6. If the correct answer is a decimal that cannot fit into the grid space, you must fill the grid with enough digits to completely fill the space. The number can be rounded or simply shortened but must fit within the space provided.

NOTES

Begin entering answers in any column that accommodates your answer. If you do not need a column do not enter anything in that column.

Answer: $\frac{5}{36}$

Answer: 4.5

← Fraction line
← Decimal point

Acceptable ways to grid $\frac{1}{6}$ are:

Answer: 302 – either position is correct

16.

A sequence of numbers is generated by doubling the previous number and adding 3. The first number of the sequence is 5. What is the fourth?

ANSWER: _____

17.

Theresa has three pet snakes named Mister Slithers, Coil, and Sir Hiss-a-lot. Once a week, she feeds the snakes a total of 110 crickets. Mister Slithers eats twice as many crickets as Coil does, and Mister Slithers eats 10 fewer crickets than Sir Hiss-a-lot does. How many crickets does Coil eat?

ANSWER: _____

18.

A college football team has 12 wins and 6 losses during the season. If it wins all of its remaining games, it will have a win percentage of 75%. What is the total number of games?

ANSWER: _____

19.

The amount of time it takes to paint a house is inversely proportional to the number of people working the job. If it takes five painters three days to paint the house, how much longer, in days, will it take for two workers to complete the same task?

ANSWER: _____

20.

A cylinder whose base has a diameter of 4 inches and a height of $\frac{12}{\pi}$ inches is filled two-thirds of the way up with a cleaning solution that contains three parts water to one part bleach. How many cubic inches of water are in the container?

ANSWER: _____

Math Test 3 – Calculator

 55 MINUTES, 38 QUESTIONS

Turn to Section 4 of your answer sheet to answer the questions in this section.

DIRECTIONS

For questions **1 – 30**, find the solution to each problem and select the most appropriate answer from the choices provided. For questions **31 – 38**, find the solution to each problem and write your answer in the space provided. You may use the blank space in your test booklet for scratch work.

NOTES

1. The use of a calculator on any part of this section is allowed.
2. Unless otherwise indicated, all variables and expressions used in this test represent real numbers.
3. Unless otherwise indicated, all figures used in this test are drawn to scale.
4. Unless otherwise indicated, all figures used in this test lie on a plane.
5. Unless specified otherwise, a given function, f, has the domain the set of all real numbers x for which $f(x)$ is a real number.

REFERENCE

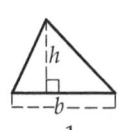 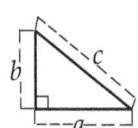 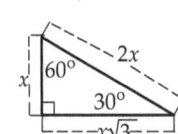 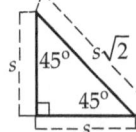 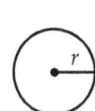 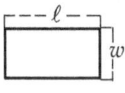

$A = \frac{1}{2}bh$ $c^2 = a^2 + b^2$ Special Right Triangles $A = \pi r^2$ $A = \ell w$
$C = 2\pi r$

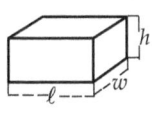 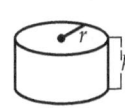   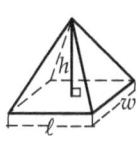

$V = \ell wh$ $V = \pi r^2 h$ $V = \frac{4}{3}\pi r^3$ $V = \frac{1}{3}\pi r^2 h$ $V = \frac{1}{3}\ell wh$

The arc of a circle is 360 degrees or 2π radians.
A triangle has angles that sum to 180 degrees.

1

x	1	2	3	4
f(x)	14	10	6	2

The table above gives values for a function $f(x)$. What is the value of $f(16)$?

A) −28

B) −32

C) −46

D) −64

2

A typical high school student consumes 67.5 pounds of sugar every year. As part of a nutrition plan, each member of a high school track team plans to reduce the amount sugar he or she consumes by 20% for the coming year. Assuming each member consumed typical amount of sugar last year, what is the maximum number of pounds of sugar he or she can consume this coming year?

A) 14

B) 44

C) 48

D) 54

3

Michael takes 45 minutes to complete two laps of a running track. If the track is 3 miles long, what is his average speed in miles per hour?

A) 6

B) 8

C) 10

D) 12

4

Research suggests that ~88% of the global population was illiterate in 1800, while only ~15% illiteracy was recorded in 2014. Approximately how many more people, in millions, were illiterate in 2014 than in 1800, given that the global populations were 7.3 billion and 900 million respectively? (1 billion = 1,000 million)

A) 53

B) 303

C) 660

D) 1,560

5

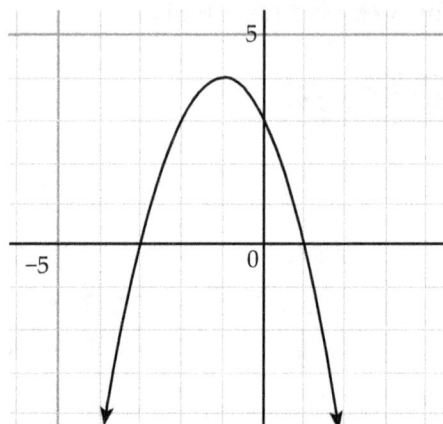

Which of the following equations describes the graph above?

A) $f(x) = -x^2 - 2x - 3$

B) $f(x) = -x^2 + 2x + 3$

C) $f(x) = -x^2 - 2x + 3$

D) $f(x) = -x^2 - 6x + 3$

6

Week	1	2	3
Distance (mi)	8	9.6	11.52

Tobi is training for a marathon. The table above gives the number of miles Tobi runs during each of her first three weeks of training. If her training continues to progress at the same rate, which of the following could model the number of miles run, a_n, where n corresponds to the nth week of training?

A) $a_n = 8 + 2(n - 1)$
B) $a_n = 10n^2$
C) $a_n = 1.2\, a_{n-1}$
D) $a_n = 1.6 + a_{n-1}$

7

Which of the following has the same value as the expression $(3^{-1} + 2^{-1})^{-1}$?

A) 5

B) $\dfrac{5}{6}$

C) $\dfrac{6}{5}$

D) $\dfrac{1}{5}$

8

Combined Elephant Population By Year For Etosha National Park and the Northwestern Namibia

Year	Base Year	Number of Elephants
1998	3	3,354
2000	5	3,469
2002	7	3,588
2004	9	3,711

The elephant population in northwestern Namibia and the Etosha National Park is modeled by the expression $3{,}189(1.017)^t$, where t is the base year, that is, the number of years since 1995. What is the meaning of the value 3,189?

A) The increase in the number of elephants per year
B) The number of elephants in the region in 1995
C) The year in which the elephant population is expected to stop increasing
D) The percentage by which the elephant population increases each year

9

A and B are positive integers such that one-third of A is B minus one-half of A. Which of the following could be the value of A?

A) 15
B) 21
C) 24
D) 26

10. Which of the following is equivalent to the expression $\dfrac{24x^4z^{-2}}{8x^{-3}z}$?

A) $\dfrac{3x}{z}$

B) $\dfrac{16x^2}{z}$

C) $\dfrac{3x^7}{z^3}$

D) $16xz$

11. If $2a$ is a solution to the inequality $9x - 10 > x + 4$, then which of the following is a possible value of a?

A) -1

B) 0

C) $\dfrac{1}{2}$

D) 1

12.
$$-9(x - 3) + 2x \geq 2(4 - x)$$

Which of the following is the solution to the inequality above?

A) $x \leq -1$

B) $-1 \leq x$

C) $x \leq \dfrac{19}{5}$

D) $\dfrac{19}{5} \leq x$

13. The equation $5\sqrt{x + 4} = x + 10$ has two solutions. What is their product?

A) -5

B) 0

C) 5

D) 10

14. Which of the following is equivalent to the expression $\dfrac{x}{x-1} - \dfrac{2}{1-x}$?

A) $\dfrac{x + 2}{x - 1}$

B) $\dfrac{x - 2}{x - 1}$

C) $\dfrac{x - 2}{x^2 - 1}$

D) $x + 2$

15. A ball is thrown in the air. The height in feet, h, of the ball above the ground t seconds after it is thrown is given by the expression $h = -16t^2 + 40t + 5$. What is the meaning of the number 5 in this expression?

A) The time it takes the ball to reach its maximum height
B) The time takes the ball to fall to the ground
C) The height from which the ball was first thrown
D) The angle at which the ball is thrown

16

The shortest distance required for a moving car to come to a stop is directly proportional to the square of its velocity when it begins braking. If a car moving at 15 kilometers per hour can come to a stop in 112.5 meters, at least how many meters are needed for a car moving at 25 kilometers per hour to come to a complete stop?

A) 250.75
B) 298.00
C) 312.50
D) 337.50

17

Which of the following is the quotient of $\dfrac{2x^4 + 5x^3 - 20x^2 - 16x + 35}{x^2 + 3x - 5}$?

A) $2x^4 + 5x^3 + 5x^2 + 2x - 7$
B) $2x^4 + 5x^3 + 2x - 16x - 7$
C) $2x^2 + 5x - 7$
D) $2x^2 - x - 7$

Questions 18–20 refer to the following information.

Acquisition of Public Domain 1781–1867 (in square acres)

	Land (acres)	Water (acres)	Cost
Louisiana Purchase (1803)	523,446,400	6,465,280	$23,213,568
Oregon Compromise (1846)	180,644,480	2,741,760	$6,674,057
Mexican Cessation (1848)	334,479,360	4,201,600	$16,295,149
Alaska Purchase (1867)	365,333,120	12,909,440	$7,200,000

18

Of the four acquisitions above, which was the most expensive, disregarding inflation, in terms of cost per acre?

A) Louisiana Purchase
B) Oregon Compromise
C) Mexican Cessation
D) Alaska Purchase

19

Assuming the cost of land and water rights were the same, how much did the United States pay for the acquisition of just water in the Alaska Purchase?

A) $200,578
B) $245,736
C) $356,780
D) $507,435

20

The total acreage of the United States is 2.27 billion acres. If one acre is equal to 43,560 square feet, and one foot is equal to 0.305 meters, what is the total area of the United States in square kilometers?

A) 5.6 million
B) 9.2 million
C) 56 million
D) 9.2 billion

21

$$z = x^2 + 3x + \frac{y^2 + 2xy}{x+2}$$

If $x = 2$ for the equation above, what is z in terms of y?

A) $\dfrac{y^2 + 4y + 10}{4}$

B) $\dfrac{y^2 + 4y + 32}{4}$

C) $\dfrac{y^2 + 4y + 40}{4}$

D) $y^2 + y + 10$

22

Which of the following values of x satisfy the inequality $|x^3 - 3| < 7$?

A) $-2 < x < 3.16$
B) $-1.59 < x < 2.15$
C) $x > 2.15$ or $x < -1.59$
D) $x > 3.16$ or $x < -2$

23

A scientist observes an 8.25 gram sample of a radioactive element with a half-life of 4 days. The amount of the sample in grams left after d days, $R(d)$, is given by the function $R(d) = 8.25\left(\dfrac{1}{2}\right)^{\frac{d}{4}}$.

Which of the following must be true?

A) An equivalent function is $R(d) = 8.25(0.125)^d$.
B) An equivalent function is $R(d) = 8.25(0.841)^d$.
C) The element decays at a rate of 0.125 grams per day.
D) The the element decays at a rate of 0.841 grams per day.

24

Twelve pints of a 20 percent alcohol solution are mixed with eight pints of a 10 percent alcohol solution. What is the percent of alcohol concentration of the new solution?

A) 13
B) 14
C) 15
D) 16

25

A triangle has one side of length 16 centimeters and a second side of length 10 centimeters. Which of the following could be the area of the triangle?

    I. 96 cm^2
    II. 80 cm^2
    III. 60 cm^2

A) I only
B) II only
C) II and III only
D) I, II and III

26

Which of the following equations will maintain the same solutions when x is replaced by $-x$?

A) $2x^2 + 2x - 1 = 0$
B) $2x^2 - 3x = 0$
C) $x^4 + x^2 = 0$
D) $x^4 - 3x^2 + x + 1 = 0$

27

Line m is tangent to the circle with equation $x^2 + y^2 = 1$ at the point $\left(\frac{3}{5}, \frac{4}{5}\right)$. What is the y-intercept of line m?

A) 0.80
B) 1
C) 1.20
D) 1.25

28

Carol invests $12,000 in a savings bonds account. After t years, the amount of money in the account is found by calculating the product of one plus the interest rate of the investment times t. If, after five years, there is $15,000 in the account and no additional deposits or withdrawls have been made, what is the interest rate on the investment?

A) 4%
B) 5%
C) 6%
D) 7%

29

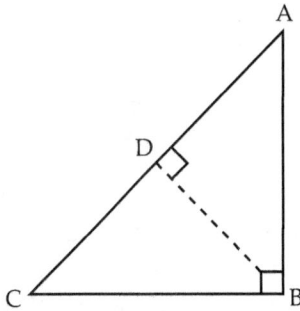

In the figure above, AC = 5, CB = 3. What is the length of DB?

A) $\frac{9}{5}$
B) $\frac{12}{5}$
C) $\frac{16}{5}$
D) It cannot be determined.

30

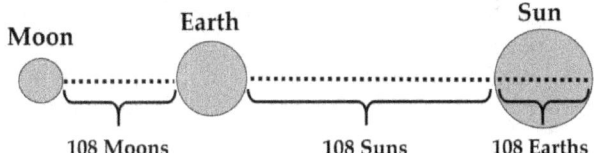

The average distance between the Earth and the Moon is equal to a line of 108 moons. The average distance between the Earth and the Sun is equal to a line of 108 Suns. The diameter of our Sun is equal to a line of 108 Earths. Given the Moon's diameter is roughly 27% that of Earth, calculate the distance to the nearest integer in Moons from the Moon to the other side of the Sun when the three celestial bodies are lined up as above.

A) 44,113
B) 43,758
C) 43,712
D) 43,269

4 Student-Produced Responses

DIRECTIONS

For questions **31 – 38**, find the solution to the problem and enter your answer as demonstrated on the right.

1. Only the answer that is bubbled in on the answer sheet will be credited. The blank spaces above the bubbles are for you to record your answers for accuracy.
2. Only fill in one bubble in any given column.
3. None of the answers on this portion of the test are negative values.
4. If a problem appears to have more than one answer, only enter one answer. If the answer you enter is one of the correct solutions, you will receive full credit for that question.
5. If the correct answer can be expressed as a mixed number, it must be entered as a decimal or an improper fraction.
6. If the correct answer is a decimal that cannot fit into the grid space, you must fill the grid with enough digits to completely fill the space. The number can be rounded or simply shortened but must fill every blank space.

NOTES

Begin entering answers in any column that accommodates your answer. If you do not need a column do not enter anything in that column.

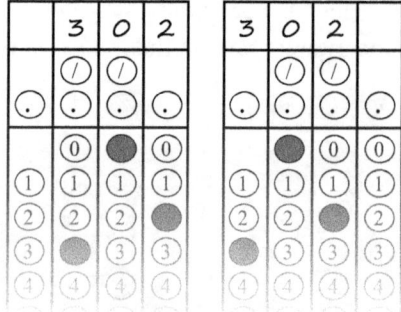

31

If the average of 5 and x is 7, and the average of 3 and y is 5, what is the average of x and y?

ANSWER: _____

32

$$y = 5x$$
$$-4x^2 + 3y^2 = 284$$

If (x, y) is a solution to the system of equations above, what is the value of x^2?

ANSWER: _____

33

A box contains 22 chocolates, 5 with soft centers, 10 with nut centers, and 7 with hard centers. Three people take turns taking a chocolate out of the box at random. If the probability that all three people pick a chocolate with a soft centers is $\frac{1}{x}$, what is the value of x?

ANSWER: _____

34

A company's profit curve is modeled by the function $p(x) = 2 + 10x - x^2$, where $p(x)$ is profit and x is the number of products sold. What is the highest profit possible according to this curve?

ANSWER: _____

35

The graph of the equation $y = 2x^2 - 5x + 2$ has two x-intercepts. What is the value of the smaller of these?

ANSWER: _____

36

The volume of a pyramid with a square base is equal to 16 units^3. What will the volume of the pyramid be, in units^3, if the sides of the base are tripled, and the height is reduced by half?

ANSWER: _____

Questions 37 and 38 are based on the information below.

An object attached to a spring will exhibit a type of motion, called periodic motion, in which a path of motion is repeated over a set interval of time. The interval T, called a period and measured in seconds, is calculated according to the formula

$$T = 2\pi\sqrt{\frac{m}{k}}$$

where m is the mass of the object in kilograms and k is a constant determined by the spring in units $\frac{kg}{sec^2}$.

37

If an object of mass 20 kilograms is attached to a spring with $k = 0.2\pi^2 \frac{kg}{sec^2}$, what is the value, in seconds, of T?

ANSWER: _____

38

If the object in the previous equation is replaced by another object with a quarter of its mass, what is the absolute difference, in seconds, between the periods of the two objects?

ANSWER: _____

NO TEST MATERIAL ON THIS PAGE

Essay Test 3

50 MINUTES, Prompt-based essay

Turn to Section 5 of your answer sheet to answer the question in this section.

DIRECTIONS

As you read the passage below, consider how President Barack Obama uses
- evidence, such as facts or examples, to support claims.
- reasoning to develop ideas and to connect claims and evidence.
- stylistic or persuasive elements, such as word choice or appeals to emotion, to add power to the ideas expressed.

Adapted from "Speech on the BP Oil Spill," delivered by President Barack Obama on June 15, 2010.

For decades, we have known the days of cheap and easily accessible oil were numbered. For decades, we've talked and talked about the need to end America's century-long addiction to fossil fuels. And for decades, we have failed to act with the sense of urgency that this challenge requires. Time and again, the path forward has been blocked -- not only by oil industry lobbyists, but also by a lack of political courage and candor.

The consequences of our inaction are now in plain sight. Countries like China are investing in clean energy jobs and industries that should be right here in America. Each day, we send nearly $1 billion of our wealth to foreign countries for their oil. And today, as we look to the Gulf, we see an entire way of life being threatened by a menacing cloud of black crude.

We cannot consign our children to this future. The tragedy unfolding on our coast is the most painful and powerful reminder yet that the time to embrace a clean energy future is now. Now is the moment for this generation to embark on a national mission to unleash America's innovation and seize control of our own destiny.

This is not some distant vision for America. The transition away from fossil fuels is going to take some time, but over the last year and a half, we've already taken unprecedented action to jumpstart the clean energy industry. As we speak, old factories are reopening to produce wind turbines, people are going back to work installing energy-efficient windows, and small businesses are making solar panels. Consumers are buying more efficient cars and trucks, and families are making their homes more energy-efficient. Scientists and researchers are discovering clean energy technologies that someday will lead to entire new industries.

Each of us has a part to play in a new future that will benefit all of us. As we recover from this recession, the transition to clean energy has the potential to grow our economy and create millions of jobs—but only if we accelerate that transition. Only if we seize the moment. And only if we rally together and act as one nation—workers and entrepreneurs; scientists and citizens; the public and private sectors.

When I was a candidate for this office, I laid out a set of principles that would move our country towards energy independence. Last year, the House of Representatives acted on these principles by passing a strong and comprehensive energy and climate bill—a bill that finally makes clean energy the profitable kind of energy for America's businesses.

Now, there are costs associated with this transition. And there are some who believe that we can't afford those costs right now. I say we can't afford not to change how we produce and use energy—because the long-term costs to our economy, our national security, and our environment are far greater.

So I'm happy to look at other ideas and approaches from either party—as long they seriously tackle our addiction to fossil fuels. Some have suggested raising efficiency standards in our buildings like we did in our cars and trucks. Some believe we should set standards to ensure that more of our electricity comes from wind and solar power. Others wonder why the energy industry only spends a fraction of what the high-tech industry does on research and development—and want to rapidly boost our investments in such research and development.

All of these approaches have merit, and deserve a fair hearing in the months ahead. But the one approach I will not accept is inaction. The one answer I will not settle for is the idea that this challenge is somehow too big and too difficult to meet. You know, the same thing was said about our ability to produce enough planes and tanks in World War II. The same thing was said about our ability to harness the science and technology to land a man safely on the surface of the moon. And yet, time and again, we have refused to settle for the paltry limits of conventional wisdom. Instead, what has defined us as a nation since our founding is the capacity to shape our destiny—our determination to fight for the America we want for our children. Even if we're unsure exactly what that looks like. Even if we don't yet know precisely how we're going to get there. We know we'll get there.

> Write an essay in which you explain how President Barack Obama builds an argument to persuade his audience that America must reduce its dependence on fossil fuels. In your essay, analyze how the author uses one or more of the features listed in the box above (or features of your own choice) to strengthen the logic and persuasiveness of his argument. Be sure that your analysis focuses on the most relevant features of the passage.
>
> Your essay should not explain whether you agree with the author's claims, but rather explain how the author builds an argument to persuade his audience.

* *Sample response found in the "Answers and Explanations" section of this study guide.*

KALLIS

SAT® Practice Test #4

IMPORTANT REMINDERS:

When you take the official SAT, you will need to use a No. 2 pencil. Do not use a pen or a mechanical pencil.

On the official SAT, sharing any of the questions on the test violates the College Board's policies and may result in your scores being canceled.

(This cover is modeled after the cover you'll see when you take the official SAT.)

UNAUTHORIZED REPRODUCTION OR USE OF ANY PART OF THIS TEST IS PROHIBITED.

© 2019 KALLIS EDU

Reading Test 4

65 MINUTES, 52 QUESTIONS

Turn to Section 1 of your answer sheet to answer the questions in this section.

DIRECTIONS

Each passage or pair of passages is accompanied by 10 or 11 questions. Read each passage or pair of passages, and then select the most appropriate answer to each question. Some passages may include tables or graphs that require additional analysis.

Refer to the passage below to answer questions 1 – 11.

This passage is adapted from Stephen Crane, *The Open Boat and Other Stories*, originally published in 1898. The story is based on the author's experiences as an American journalist traveling in Cuba.

None of them knew the color of the sky. Their eyes glanced level, and were fastened upon the waves that swept toward them. These waves were of the hue of slate, save for the tops, which were of
5 foaming white, and all of the men knew the colors of the sea. The horizon narrowed and widened, and dipped and rose, and at all times its edge was jagged with waves that seemed thrust up in points like rocks.
10 Many a man ought to have a bath-tub larger than the boat which here rode upon the sea. These waves were most wrongfully and barbarously abrupt and tall, and each froth-top was a problem in small boat navigation.
15 The cook squatted in the bottom and looked with both eyes at the six inches of gunwale which separated him from the ocean. His sleeves were rolled over his fat forearms, and the two flaps of his unbuttoned vest dangled as he bent to bail
20 out the boat. Often he said: "Gawd! That was a narrow clip." As he remarked it he invariably gazed eastward over the broken sea.
The oiler, steering with one of the two oars in the boat, sometimes raised himself suddenly to
25 keep clear of water that swirled in over the stern. It was a thin little oar and it seemed often ready to snap.
The correspondent, pulling at the other oar, watched the waves and wondered why he was
30 there.
The injured captain, lying in the bow, was at this time buried in that profound dejection and indifference which comes, temporarily at least, to even the bravest and most enduring when, willy
35 nilly, the firm fails, the army loses, the ship goes down. The mind of the master of a vessel is rooted deep in the timbers of her, though he commanded for a day or a decade, and this captain had on him the stern impression of a scene in the greys of
40 dawn of seven turned faces, and later a stump of a top-mast with a white ball on it that slashed to and fro at the waves, went low and lower, and down. Thereafter there was something strange in his voice. Although steady, it was deep with mourning, and of a
45 quality beyond oration or tears.
"Keep 'er a little more south, Billie," said he.
"'A little more south,' sir," said the oiler in the stern.
A seat in this boat was not unlike a seat upon a
50 bucking Broncho, and, by the same token, a Broncho is not much smaller. The craft pranced and reared, and plunged like an animal. As each wave came, and she rose for it, she seemed like a horse making at a fence outrageously high. The manner of her scramble over
55 these walls of water is a mystic thing, and, moreover, at the top of them were ordinarily these problems in white water, the foam racing down from the summit of each wave, requiring a new leap, and a leap from the air. Then, after scornfully bumping a crest, she would slide,
60 and race, and splash down a long incline, and arrive bobbing and nodding in front of the next menace.
A singular disadvantage of the sea lies in the fact that after successfully surmounting one wave you discover that there is another behind it just as important
65 and just as nervously anxious to do something effective in the way of swamping boats. In a ten-foot dingy one can get an idea of the resources of the sea in the line of waves that is not probable to the average experience which is never at sea in a dingy. As each salty wall of
70 water approached, it shut all else from the view of the men in the boat, and it was not difficult to imagine that this particular wave was the final outburst of the ocean, the last effort of the grim water. There was a terrible grace in the move of the waves, and they came in
75 silence, save for the snarling of the crests.
In the wan light, the faces of the men must have been grey. Their eyes must have glinted in strange ways as they gazed steadily astern. Viewed from a balcony, the whole thing would doubtlessly have been weirdly
80 picturesque. But the men in the boat had no time to see it, and if they had had leisure there were other things to occupy their minds. The sun swung steadily up the sky, and they knew it was broad day because the color of the sea changed from slate to emerald-green, streaked with
85 amber lights, and the foam was like tumbling snow. The process of the breaking day was unknown to them. They were aware only of this effect upon the color of the waves that rolled toward them.
In disjointed sentences the cook and the
90 correspondent argued as to the difference between a life-saving station and a house of refuge. The cook had said: "There's a house of refuge just north of the

Mosquito Inlet Light, and as soon as they see us, they'll come off in their boat and pick us up."
95 "As soon as who see us?" said the correspondent.
"The crew," said the cook.
"Houses of refuge don't have crews," said the correspondent. "As I understand them, they are
100 only places where clothes and grub are stored for the benefit of shipwrecked people. They don't carry crews."
"Oh, yes, they do," said the cook.
"No, they don't," said the correspondent.
105 "Well, we're not there yet, anyhow," said the oiler, in the stern.
"Well," said the cook, "perhaps it's not a house of refuge that I'm thinking of as being near Mosquito Inlet Light. Perhaps it's a life-saving station."
110 "We're not there yet," said the oiler, in the stern.

01

The passage mainly discusses

A) the consequences of a ship's crew disobeying a captain's orders.
B) the dangers of setting sail during a storm.
C) a group of friends learning to coordinate their activities in a boat.
D) the crew of a shipwreck trying to survive in rough waters.

02

The primary purpose of paragraph 1 (lines 1 – 9) is to

A) bring in background expository material.
B) introduce the story's characters.
C) establish the passage's overall mood and setting.
D) put the story in historical context.

03

As used in line 13, "abrupt" most nearly means

A) unexpected.
B) truncated.
C) terse.
D) disjointed.

04

As used in line 22, "broken" most nearly means

A) weakened.
B) feeble.
C) ruined.
D) turbulent.

05

In lines 28 – 30 ("The correspondent...was there"), the author suggests that the correspondent

A) does not have much strength left in him.
B) is not a part of the ship's regular crew.
C) blames the captain for the situation he is in.
D) feels better when he looks at the waves.

06

The narrator indicates that the captain's "profound dejection and indifference" (lines 32 – 33) are a result of the

A) incompetence of his crew.
B) seriousness of his injury.
C) loss of his ship.
D) storm's ferocity.

07

The men's attitude toward the sunrise can best be described as

A) resentful.
B) oblivious.
C) unappreciative.
D) anxious.

08

Throughout the passage, the author implies that the waves

A) appear to be actively trying to sink the small boat.
B) are becoming larger and more frequent over time.
C) are carrying the small boat away from its intended destination.
D) must be navigated around because of their massive size.

09

Which choice provides the best evidence for the answer to the previous question?

A) Lines 1 – 3 ("None...toward them")
B) Lines 11 – 13 ("These waves...and tall")
C) Lines 63 – 66 ("after successfully...boats")
D) Lines 73 – 74 ("There was...waves")

10

Which choice best indicates the crew's tenuous control over their vessel?

A) Lines 6 – 9 ("The horizon...like rocks")
B) Lines 10 – 11 ("Many a man...the sea")
C) Lines 23 – 27 ("The oiler...to snap")
D) Lines 80 – 82 ("But the men...their minds")

11

The oiler's replies to both the cook and the correspondent in the conversation in lines 89 – 111 reveal the oiler's

A) assumption that they will not be rescued.
B) unwillingness to speculate about details.
C) penchant for annoying others on the boat.
D) desire to make peace with the cook and the correspondent.

Refer to the passage below to answer questions 12 – 21.

This passage is adapted from Samuel Adams Drake, *The Battle of Gettysburg 1863*, originally published in 1892. Drake recounts events during the American Civil War (1861 – 1865) between the North and the South. Here, the southern (Confederate) General Robert E. Lee marches troops into a northern (Union) state, Pennsylvania.

A very unusual thing in war it is to see an army which has just been acting strictly on the defensive suddenly elude its adversary for the purpose of carrying the war into that enemy's
5 country! It marks a new epoch in the history of that war, and it supposes wholly altered conditions. In this particular instance Lee's moves were so bold as almost to savor of contempt.
10 It is enough to know that Lee was now in Pennsylvania, at the head of seventy thousand men, before our army reached the Potomac* in pursuit of him, if following at a respectful distance be called a pursuit.
15 At no period of the war, their own officers said, had the Confederates been so well equipped, so well clothed, so eager for a fight, or so confident of success; and we may add our own conclusions, that never before had this army taken
20 the field so strong in numbers, or with such a powerful artillery.
The infantry were armed with Enfield rifles, fresh from British workshops, and it is probable that no equal number of men ever knew
25 how to use them better. Indeed, we consider it indisputable that the Confederates greatly excelled the Union soldiers as marksmen. Most of them were accustomed to the use of firearms from boyhood; in some sections they were noted
30 for their skill with the rifle. The Confederates, therefore, were nearly always good shots before they went into the army, while the Union soldiers mostly had to acquire what skill they could after going into the ranks. In the South the habit of
35 carrying arms was almost universal: in the North it was not only unusual, but unpopular as well as unlawful.
Man for man, the Confederate cavalry was also superior to the Union horse, because in one
40 section riding is a custom, in the other a pastime rarely indulged in. Consequently, it took months to teach a Union cavalryman how to ride,—a costly experiment when your adversary is already prepared,—whereas if there is anything
45 a Southerner piques himself upon, it is his horsemanship.
Lee's cavalry had preceded the infantry by nearly a week, reaching Chambersburg on the 16th, seizing horses and provisions for the
50 use of the army behind them, and spreading consternation to the gates of Harrisburg* itself. Having loaded themselves with plunder unopposed, they then fell back upon the main army, thus leaving it in some doubt whether this
55 raid accomplished all it designed, or was only the prelude to something for which it was serving as a mask.
All doubts were set at rest, however, when, on the 23d, Ewell's dust-begrimed infantry
60 came tramping into Chambersburg, regiment after regiment, hour after hour, until the streets fairly swarmed with them. Though the houses were shut up, a few citizens were in the streets, or looking out of their windows at the passing
65 show, as men might at the gathering of a storm-cloud about to burst with destructive fury upon them; and though the time was hardly one for merriment, we are assured that some of these lookers-on could not refrain from "pointing
70 and laughing at Hood's ragged Jacks" as they marched along to the tune of "Dixie's Land." "This division," remarks the partial narrator, "well known for its fighting qualities, is composed of Texans, Alabamians, and Arkansians, and they
75 certainly are a queer lot to look at. They carry less than any other troops; many of them have only got an old piece of carpet or rug as baggage; many have discarded their shoes in the mud; all are ragged and dirty, but full of good-humor
80 and confidence in themselves and their general. They answered the numerous taunts of the Chambersburg ladies with cheers and laughter." To the scowling citizens the Confederates would call out from the ranks, "Well, Yank, how far
85 to Harrisburg? How far to Baltimore? What's the charge at the Continental?" or some such innocuous bits of irony as came into heads turned, no doubt, at the thought of standing unchallenged on Northern soil, where nothing but themselves
90 recalled war or its terrors, or at sight of the many evidences of comfort and thrift to which they themselves were strangers. But we shall meet these exultant ragamuffins ere long under far different circumstances.

* *The Potomac River: a 400-mile long river that divided Union and Confederate territories.*

* *Harrisburg: the capital city of the state of Pennsylvania.*

12

The passage is primarily concerned with

A) praising the bravery and resourcefulness of General Lee and his troops.
B) describing a pivotal tactical move made by Confederate forces.
C) pointing out major differences between Union and Confederate troops.
D) documenting a major turning point near the end of the American Civil War.

13

As used in lines 8 – 9, "to savor of contempt" most nearly means to

A) relish a challenge.
B) appear disdainful.
C) initiate a feint.
D) take pleasure in another's failure.

14

The author is writing from the perspective of a

A) member of the Union reflecting on the American Civil War.
B) Confederate troop involved in combat.
C) non-political, unbiased commentator.
D) Union soldier spying on the Confederate troops.

15

Which choice provides the best evidence for the answer to the previous question?

A) Lines 10 – 13 ("It is enough…of him")
B) Lines 25 – 27 ("Indeed…marksmen")
C) Lines 47 – 52 ("Lee's cavalry…itself")
D) Lines 79 – 80 ("all are…general")

16

The author suggests that, in general, Confederate troops

A) received better equipment and more military training than Union troops.
B) greatly outnumbered Union troops.
C) were less organized and less disciplined than Union troops.
D) were better prepared for combat than Union troops.

17

Which choice provides the best evidence for the answer to the previous question?

A) Lines 15 – 18 ("At no…of success")
B) Lines 30 – 34 ("The Confederates…the ranks")
C) Lines 52 – 57 ("Having loaded…mask")
D) Lines 75 – 78 ("They carry…the mud")

18

In paragraph 7 (lines 58 – 94), the author characterizes the Confederate troops as

A) disheveled yet self-assured.
B) well-loved by the people of Chambersburg.
C) confident yet cautious.
D) rude and unkempt.

19

As used in line 90, "recalled" most nearly means

A) thought of.
B) brought.
C) evoked.
D) returned.

20

The author suggests that the people of Chambersburg regarded the Confederate troops with

A) fear and admiration.
B) curiosity and derision.
C) scorn and envy.
D) apathy and disregard.

21

The author's overall attitude toward the Confederate troops is one of

A) envy.
B) disgust.
C) contempt.
D) respect.

Refer to the passage and supplementary material below to answer questions 22 – 33.

This passage is adapted from Sarah Gibson, "Happy Fins: Plesiosaurs Flapped like Penguins," published December 18, 2015.

One of the most infuriating things about being a paleontologist is being able to study some of the coolest organisms that have ever inhabited the Earth, yet never being able to see one in life.
[5] We'll never know with complete surety what color they were, what they sounded like, and how they moved. Thankfully, new technology has allowed paleontologists to test hypotheses about these ancient animals, allowing us to get closer and
[10] closer to fully understanding the biota of a time long past.

One such group of organisms that has puzzled paleontologists for over 200 years are the plesiosaurs, a group of Mesozoic marine reptiles
[15] that first showed up in the Jurassic and persisted as apex predators until their demise in the Late Cretaceous. Paleontologists have debated for decades about how they swam, as no such living analogous animal has a body plan identical to
[20] these long-necked, four-flipper critters.

Many modern tetrapods have evolved their own ways of swimming as they transitioned from living on land to living in the ocean: penguins, sea turtles, sea lions, and whales, for example.
[25] Previous studies have compared the possible swimming stroke and gait of plesiosaurs to the flight stroke seen in penguins and turtles, or even compared the movement to a rowing stroke like oars of a boat. And while all of these hypotheses
[30] are plausible, based on the musculature and anatomy of plesiosaurs, they still can't fully explain how the four flippers of a plesiosaur moved in relation to each other. Did they move together in synchrony, or alternate between front
[35] and hind limbs? Likewise, did the propulsion come from the forelimbs or the hindlimbs? Or the steering? So many unanswered questions!

The closest thing to four-flipper swimming would assumedly be sea turtles, but even then
[40] they are constrained by their shells and would unlikely move in a way similar to plesiosaurs. So the debate has continued, without an entirely satisfactory answer for most interested parties.

A new study published by researchers at the
[45] Georgia Institute of Technology led by Greg Turk, in collaboration with paleontologist Adam Smith at Wollaston Hall, Nottingham Natural History Museum, has taken a stab at solving the decades-old question of how plesiosaurs swam.
[50] This study uses computer simulation to build virtual three-dimensional models of a plesiosaur within a liquid, to provide a way to test different modes of swimming. They built a virtual life-sized plesiosaur model based on *Meyerasaurus victor*, a
[55] small (3.35 m) plesiosaur from the Lower Jurassic of Germany. *Meyerasaurus* presents a generalized morphotype for plesiosaurs, with a moderately long neck (as plesiosaurs have both long- and short-neck varieties). The skeleton was built
[60] using fossil data, and muscles, cartilage, skin, etc., were built upon it using evidence from other taxa.

The team had to address a seemingly endless multitude of variables and parameters in
[65] order to assure that the model is moving under realistic and biologically plausible conditions. For example, each limb on a plesiosaur has one single mobile joint: the glenohumeral joint in the forelimbs, and the acetabulum-femoral joint in
[70] the hindlimbs. The team had to take into account the maximum and minimum allowable up/down and forward/backward movement of each fin before the joint would dislocate (which helps no one, really, especially the plesiosaur), as well as
[75] the possible amount of pronation/supination of each limb. Other factors had to be considered as well, such as how the neck and tail might move and influence the movement of the organism. In this instance, the team remained conservative
[80] and prevented movement in the model of the neck and tail, focusing more on the movement of the limbs.

The team ran multiple simulations under different conditions: all four flippers moving
[85] synchronously, flippers alternating, or each set moving while the other remains immobile, for example. They even conducted tests with different weights of the plesiosaur, in hopes of testing how that might influence the motion.
[90] In total, the team ran thousands of different simulations, each with changes to the variables and parameters.

The study found that the most effective motion for plesiosaur swimming is an
[95] underwater flight motion, not dissimilar to modern-day penguins.

"Our results show that the front limbs provide the powerhouse for plesiosaur propulsion, while the hindlimb are more
[100] passive," said Smith.

Their study concludes that the rear flippers really played little role in the propulsion of the plesiosaur, but may have more likely been used for steering and stability.
[105] The team will likely continue this study, with future computer simulations testing the degree of agility plesiosaurs gain from their rear flippers. The method can also be applied to understand the swimming motion of other
[110] prehistoric animals.

"Plesiosaur swimming has remained a mystery for almost 200 years, so it was exciting to see the plesiosaur come alive on the computer screen," said Smith.
[115] So while the very thing that all paleontologists want, to see their organisms "come alive," may not be attainable through the outlandish methods seen in movies such as "Jurassic Park," they just may very well be
[120] attainable through the digital world.

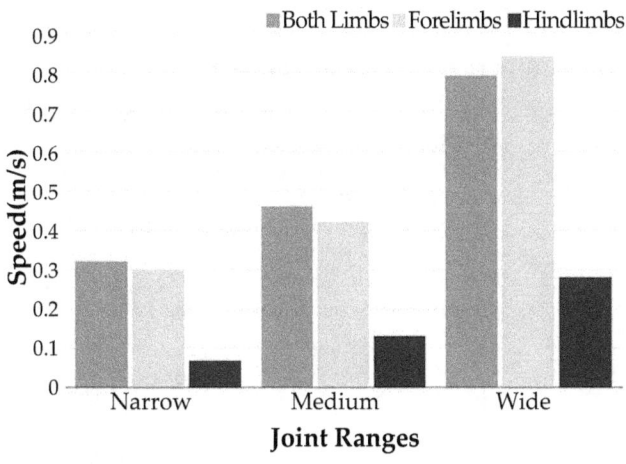

Plesiosaur Speed in Relation to Range of Motion

"Happy Fins: Plesiosaurs Flapped like Penguins" is licensed under CC BY 4.0. For more information, see page 511.

22

The primary purpose of the passage is to

A) discuss some of the largest challenges faced by modern paleontologists.
B) praise the use of computer simulations in paleontological research.
C) highlight the unique characteristics of an extinct animal group.
D) describe an experiment and its conclusion.

23

The reference to "over 200 years" (line 13) implies that, at that time,

A) the last of the plesiosaurs became extinct.
B) plesiosaur fossils were discovered and classified.
C) a living plesiosaur was discovered and captured for study.
D) the closest living relatives of plesiosaurs were discovered.

24

It can reasonably be inferred from paragraph 3 (lines 21 – 37) that

A) plesiosaurs evolved from land-dwelling animals.
B) both penguins and turtles descended from plesiosaurs.
C) different species of plesiosaur likely had different swimming strokes.
D) most modern aquatic animals have a similar swimming stroke.

25

The statement in line 37 ("So many unanswered questions!") primarily serves to

A) invite readers to come up with plesiosaur-related questions of their own.
B) accuse other paleontologists of not conducting enough research.
C) reiterate the sense of exasperation introduced in paragraph 1.
D) express excitement over the prospect of discovery.

26

As used in line 48, "taken a stab at solving" most nearly means

A) finally resolved.
B) attempted to answer.
C) refused to acknowledge.
D) killed all discussion regarding.

27

As used in lines 56 – 57, "a generalized morphotype" probably describes an organism

A) whose characteristics represent many other members of the same taxonomic group.
B) that represents the link between a species and all related species.
C) whose anatomy varies greatly from one member to another.
D) whose physical characteristics are similar to those of many living species.

28

The most likely purpose of the parenthetical information in lines 73 – 74 is to

A) define a term.
B) offer a humorous aside.
C) amend a previous claim.
D) elaborate on a hypothesis.

29

Which choice best explains why the researchers created virtual plesiosaur models for their study?

A) Lines 18 – 20 ("no such...critters")
B) Lines 21 – 23 ("Many modern...ocean")
C) Lines 25 – 27 ("Previous...turtles")
D) Lines 38 – 39 ("The closest...turtles")

30

It can reasonably be inferred from the passage that the team of researchers

A) concluded that plesiosaurs changed their modes of swimming from the Jurassic Period to the Late Cretaceous Period.
B) assumed that nearly all plesiosaurs were approximately the same size and weight.
C) determined that plesiosaurs swam by using both hindlimbs and forelimbs equally.
D) have not yet quantified how plesiosaur neck and tail movement affected limb movement.

31

Which choice provides the best evidence for the answer to the previous question?

A) Lines 53 – 56 ("They built...Germany")
B) Lines 78 – 82 ("In this...limbs")
C) Lines 93 – 96 ("The study...penguins")
D) Lines 97 – 100 ("'Our results...passive'")

32

Data in the graph most strongly support which of the following statements?

A) Using both limbs achieves the fastest swimming speed for all joint ranges.
B) The fastest plesiosaur swimming speed was achieved using only the forelimbs.
C) Plesiosaurs probably never used their hindlimbs for propulsion.
D) Using only forelimbs and a wide joint range allowed plesiosaurs to swim with the greatest efficiency.

33

Data in the graph provide the most direct support for which idea in the passage?

A) The size of a plesiosaur may have affected its swimming stroke.
B) Plesiosaur hindlimbs were likely used to maneuver and stabilize the animal.
C) It is likely that plesiosaurs swam similarly to modern-day penguins.
D) Plesiosaur forelimbs provided most of the propulsion when swimming.

THIS PAGE HAS INTENTIONALLY BEEN LEFT BLANK

Section 1 continues on the next page.

Refer to the pair of passages below to answer questions 34 – 43.

Passage 1 is adapted with permission from "Extremist Files/Anti-Muslim Hate Groups," Southern Poverty Law Center, accessed in 2016 at www.splcenter.org. Passage 2 is adapted with permission from Scott Plous, "The Psychology of Prejudice: An Overview," accessed in 2016 at www.understandingprejudice.org.

Passage 1

Brigitte Gabriel founded ACT! for America in 2007 at a time when the anti-Muslim movement was beginning to take shape in the United States. In the years since, the group has grown to become
5 the largest grassroots anti-Muslim group in America, claiming 280,000 members and over 1,000 chapters.

Gabriel claims ACT! was launched as a response to the 9/11 attacks and "educates citizens
10 and elected officials to impact policy involving national security and defeating terrorism." Throughout its existence, ACT! has actually worked to advance anti-Muslim legislation at the local and federal level while flooding
15 the American public with wild hate speech demonizing Muslims.

Even before she created ACT!, Gabriel, a Christian originally from Lebanon, was vocally critical of Islam and Muslims and repeatedly
20 made statements conflating all Muslims with terrorists. "Islamic terrorists … are really just very devout followers of Muhammad," she wrote in 2006. "They are following his example and doing exactly what the Koran teaches and their mullahs
25 exhort them to do." In 2004, she angered a Jewish audience during a speech in which she reportedly referred to Arabs as "barbarians," prompting a public apology from her hosts. In 2006 Gabriel released *Because They Hate: A Survivor of Islamic
30 Terror Warns America*. The book was a call to action based on the "truth" behind Islam that Gabriel says she learned as a child during the civil war in Lebanon.

In 2007, Gabriel gave a lecture to the Defense
35 Department's Joint Forces Staff College as part a course on Islam. She reportedly told U.S. military and national security personnel that Muslims should be prohibited from serving in public office on the basis of their faith. "If a Muslim who has
40 — who is — a practicing Muslim who believes the word of the Koran to be the word of Allah, who abides by Islam, who goes to mosque and prays every Friday, who prays five times a day — this practicing Muslim, who believes in the teachings
45 of the Koran, cannot be a loyal citizen to the United States of America," she said.

In 2008, a year after forming ACT!, Gabriel published a second book, *They Must Be Stopped: Why We Must Defeat Radical Islam and How We Can
50 Do It*. A line from the book's introduction reads, "In the Muslim world, extreme is mainstream."

Passage 2

In the language of social psychology, an "ingroup" is a group to which someone belongs, and an "outgroup" is a group to which the person
55 does not belong. Research on the "outgroup homogeneity effect" has found that when it comes to attitudes, values, personality traits, and other characteristics, people tend to see outgroup members as more alike than ingroup members.
60 As a result, outgroup members are at risk of being seen as interchangeable or expendable, and they are more likely to be stereotyped. This perception of sameness holds true regardless of whether the outgroup is another race, religion, nationality,
65 college major, or other naturally occurring group (Linville, 1998).

In one of the first studies to document the outgroup homogeneity effect, Princeton University researchers asked students in four
70 different "eating clubs" to rate members of their own group and members of three other groups on personality dimensions (Jones, Wood, & Quattrone, 1981). The results showed that students tended to rate members of their own group as
75 more varied in personality than members of the outgroup—regardless of which group students were in.

Why are outgroups generally seen as more homogeneous than ingroups? One possible
80 reason is that people usually have less contact with outgroup members than ingroup members, and indeed, there is good evidence for this explanation (Islam & Hewstone, 1993; Linville & Fischer, 1993). But contact alone cannot explain
85 the outgroup homogeneity effect, because some studies have found that the effect is unrelated to the number of ingroup or outgroup members a person knows (e.g., Jones, Wood, & Quattrone, 1981). Furthermore, perceptions of outgroup
90 homogeneity are sometimes found among groups that have extensive contact with each other, such as females and males (Park & Rothbart, 1982; Park & Judd, 1990). When men complain that "women are all alike" and women complain that "men are
95 all alike," their charges rarely stem from a lack of contact.

The best explanation is that a variety of factors produce the outgroup homogeneity effect. In addition to the fact that people usually
100 have more contact with ingroup members, they tend to organize and recall information about ingroups in terms of persons rather than abstract characteristics (Ostrom, Carpenter, Sedikides, & Li, 1993; Park & Judd, 1990). In many cases, people
105 are also more motivated to make distinctions among ingroup members with whom they will have future contact (Linville, 1998). When these factors operate together, the end result is often an ingroup that appears to have a diverse assortment
110 of individuals, and an outgroup that appears relatively homogeneous and undifferentiated.

34

It can reasonably be inferred that the author of Passage 1

A) has a close personal relationship with Brigitte Gabriel.
B) does not understand why ACT! has achieved such popularity.
C) does not share the views espoused by ACT!
D) used to be a member of ACT!

35

Which choice provides the best evidence for the answer to the previous question?

A) Lines 4 – 7 ("In the…chapters")
B) Lines 12 – 16 ("ACT! has…Muslims")
C) Lines 17 – 19 ("Even before…Muslims")
D) Lines 36 – 39 ("She reportedly…faith")

36

As used in line 10, "impact" most nearly means

A) affect.
B) reveal.
C) strike.
D) contact.

37

In line 31 of Passage 1, the author places the word "truth" in quotation marks to

A) suggest that the term has multiple meanings.
B) refer to other "truths" about Islam mentioned in the passage.
C) emphasize the importance of the term.
D) indicate that it does not reflect the author's views.

38

The author of Passage 2 mentions contact between "females and males" in lines 89 – 96 primarily to

A) suggest that such contact is crucial to the formation of ingroups and outgroups.
B) provide support for the outgroup homogeneity effect.
C) challenge a hypothesis presented earlier in the paragraph.
D) introduce a groundbreaking experiment in social psychology.

39

As used in line 95, "charges" most nearly means

A) demands
B) accusations.
C) burdens.
D) attacks.

40

The author of Passage 2 indicates that the outgroup homogeneity effect can prove problematic because

A) those who are most affected by it choose not to acknowledge its effects.
B) it facilitates the development of stereotypes among members of an ingroup.
C) it often prevents people of different races, religions, nationalities, and professions from communicating.
D) it can lead people to make detrimental generalizations about outgroups.

41

Which of the following best describes the relationship between the two passages?

A) Passage 1 gives an extreme example of the concept discussed in Passage 2.
B) Passage 1 supports a cause, and Passage 2 provides a psychological basis for this support.
C) Passage 1 poses a question, which Passage 2 answers using scientific research.
D) Passage 1 provides controversial evidence for the hypothesis of Passage 2.

42

According to the information in both passages, Brigitte Gabriel would likely claim that

A) heterogeneous groups are much more dangerous than homogeneous groups.
B) regarding outgroups as highly heterogeneous encourages cooperation.
C) ACT! members are more homogeneous than Muslims.
D) Muslims are more homogeneous than ACT! members.

43

Which choice provides the best evidence for the answer to the previous question?

A) Lines 8 – 11 ("Gabriel claims…terrorism'")
B) Lines 17 – 21 ("Even before…terrorists")
C) Lines 30 – 33 ("The book…Lebanon")
D) Lines 50 – 51 ("A line…mainstream'")

Refer to the passage below to answer questions 44 – 52.

This passage is adapted from Mary Bates, "Bats and Wind Turbines," originally published July 8, 2016.

line
        In laudable efforts to counter climate change, many countries around the world are turning to renewable energy sources, such as wind. Wind energy is one of the fastest-growing
5 industries in the world, with wind turbines being installed in large numbers across the globe. Yet these efforts may come at a great cost for wildlife.
        Evidence from the U.S., Canada,
10 and Europe shows that wind turbines are responsible for an unprecedented number of bat fatalities. Estimates of bat deaths at wind turbines range from the tens of thousands to the hundreds of thousands each year.
15   But this does not mean we should abandon wind energy altogether. Scientists are studying how bats behave near wind farms to better understand how to mitigate the risk.
        In a new study, an international team of
20 researchers used miniaturized GPS devices to track the movements of common noctule bats (Nyctalus noctula) around wind farms in Germany. These bats hunt flying insects in open spaces and fly relatively high above ground;
25 they also make up the majority of bat fatalities at wind turbines in Germany.
        The researchers found that during midsummer, female bats made long journeys over open landscapes, repeatedly coming close
30 to wind farms and foraging near wind turbines. They often flew at heights above ground that would put them on a collision course with wind turbines. Male bats recorded earlier in the summer, on the other hand, made short, straight
35 trips between their roosts and foraging grounds and tended to fly lower than turbine blades. The researchers suggest that females may be searching for additional foraging grounds or mates in midsummer, and hunting insects along
40 the way, while males in early summer follow a nightly routine of commuting to established foraging sites. All of the bats preferred areas with bodies of water, perhaps because of the abundance of insect prey in those areas.
45   The findings demonstrate the potential threat of wind turbines to these bats and illuminate specifics about the bats' behavior that could help conservation efforts. The authors suggest that future wind turbines sites should
50 not be built in habitats preferred by these bats, such as water bodies, as well as flight corridors between roosting sites and foraging grounds.
        Why so many bats die at wind turbines is still a mystery, but some clues can be found in
55 the patterns of fatalities. Most of the bats killed by wind turbines are so-called "tree bats," species that roost in trees throughout the year and often migrate long distances. Additionally, the majority of bat fatalities at wind turbines occur
60 during late summer and autumn. This coincides with both migration and mating season for tree bats.
        Some studies suggest that tree bats may mistake wind turbines for tall trees. The bats may
65 actually be attracted to the turbines as they seek shelter, mating opportunities, and insects.
        Are there ways to minimize the risk to bats before turbines are built, or to repel them from existing turbines?
70   One of the most promising options is turning turbines down or off on low-wind nights in the summer and fall, when bats are most active. In one study, such small changes to turbine operations reduced bat deaths by 44 to 93
75 percent, with minimal losses in power generation. Researchers are also testing the use of ultrasonic "boom boxes" and UV light emitters to deter bats from wind turbines.
        Bats rarely collide with other tall, human-
80 made structures, so it appears there is something unique about wind turbines. Scientists are currently looking at the hypothesis that bats are attracted to wind turbines, as well as determining the optimal times to run wind turbines so that
85 they don't interfere with bat migration patterns. Even more basic research also needs to be done – population estimates are needed to get a sense of what proportion of different bat species are killed by wind turbines.
90   Wind power holds great promise for future renewable energy production. A better understanding of bat populations, habitats, and behaviors will help us grow wind energy without so many needless bat casualties.

44

The primary purpose of the passage is to

A) challenge a common assumption by citing recent research.
B) describe an issue and explore possible solutions.
C) raise awareness about declining bat populations in Europe and North America.
D) explore the factors that limit the spread of renewable energy sources.

45

Paragraph 5 (lines 27 – 44) suggests that, in Germany,

A) more bats are injured in summer than in every other season combined.
B) female bats are at a higher risk of injury by wind turbines than male bats are.
C) a lack of food causes bats to range further during nighttime hunts.
D) wind turbines are taller than elsewhere, making them especially hazardous to bats.

46

It is reasonable to conclude that the primary goal of the "international team of researchers" (lines 19 – 20) is to

A) determine how to reduce the number of bat fatalities caused by wind turbines.
B) understand how bats' flight patterns vary from season to season.
C) discover how wind turbines' locations affect bats' feeding habits.
D) learn why so many species of bats mistake wind turbines for trees.

47

As used in line 86, "basic" most nearly means

A) intrinsic.
B) adequate.
C) fundamental.
D) severe.

48

Researchers hope to repel bats from existing wind turbines by

A) altering the appearance of wind turbines so they look less like bat roosting locations.
B) removing any existing lights on wind turbines that might attract bats.
C) broadcasting specific visual and audio deterrents.
D) changing the trajectories of bats' flight paths.

49

The author's attitude toward the continued use of wind energy is best described as one of

A) censure.
B) optimism.
C) apprehension.
D) indifference.

50

Which choice provides the best evidence for the answer to the previous question?

A) Lines 9 – 12 ("Evidence…fatalities")
B) Lines 15 – 16 ("But this…altogether")
C) Lines 79 – 81 ("Bats rarely…turbines")
D) Lines 90 – 91 ("Wind…production")

51

The passage strongly suggests that

A) certain species of tree bats are in danger of becoming extinct because of wind turbine-related fatalities.
B) the majority of wind turbines interfere with bat migration paths or block bat feeding grounds.
C) wind turbines cause the vast majority of bat fatalities in the U.S., Canada, and Europe.
D) researchers are unable to measure the exact number of annual wind turbine-related bat fatalities.

52

Which choice provides the best evidence for the answer to the previous question?

A) Lines 9 – 12 ("Evidence from…fatalities")
B) Lines 12 – 14 ("Estimates…each year")
C) Lines 48 – 52 ("The authors…foraging grounds")
D) Lines 55 – 58 ("Most of…distances")

Writing & Language Test 4
35 MINUTES, 44 QUESTIONS

Turn to Section 2 of your answer sheet to answer the questions in this section.

DIRECTIONS

Each of the following passages is accompanied by approximately 11 questions. Some questions will require you to revise the passages in order to improve coherence and clarity. Other questions will require you to correct grammatical errors. Passages may be accompanied by graphs, charts, or tables that you must consider when making revisions. For most questions, you may select the "NO CHANGE" option if you believe that portion of the passage is clear, concise, and grammatically correct as is.

Within the passages, highlighted numbers followed by underlined text indicate which part of the text corresponds with each question. Bracketed numbers [1] indicate sentence number. These bracketed numbers are only relevant to problems that require you to add or rearrange sentences in a paragraph.

Questions 1-11 are based on the following passage.

Visiting Lecturer: Isabel Allende

Isabel Allende, a well-known Latin American writer, was a guest lecturer at my college last week. She spoke about her life in Chile, politics, her writing, and her foundation. I was excited to see her speak because I'd read *The House of the* **1** <u>*Spirits*, one of her most famous novels</u> in high school. I was thrilled when Allende discussed the story and how it relates to her own life.

The House of the Spirits, as Allende explained, began as a letter to be read by her dying grandfather. The story follows four generations of the fictional Trueba family as their country **2** <u>understands</u> significant political change. **3** <u>Much</u> of the events outlined in the novel are fictionalized accounts of Chilean history, and much of the novel is autobiographical. Allende's family, as it turns out, was actively involved in politics, and one of her cousins became the president of Chile in 1970. **4**

1

A) NO CHANGE
B) *Spirits* one of her most famous novels,
C) *Spirits*, one of her most famous novels,
D) *Spirits* one of her most famous novels

2

A) NO CHANGE
B) underscores
C) undermines
D) undergoes

3

A) NO CHANGE
B) Many
C) Little
D) Any

4

At this point, the writer is considering adding the following sentence.

> However, he was violently removed from office in 1973, and Allende had to live in exile.

Should the writer make this addition here?

A) Yes, because it reiterates an important point from Allende's lecture.
B) Yes, because it provides an effective transition to the next paragraph.
C) No, because the novel centers around the Allende family's rise to power, not its demise.
D) No, because it distracts from the paragraph's focus on Allende's autobiography.

It's not only Allende's personal experiences that make her novel engaging. She also relies heavily on elements of magical realism, a style of literature in which ordinary events are presented alongside mystical occurrences. For example, one of the main characters in *The House of the Spirits* [5] have telekinetic powers and can prophesize the future. Allende uses magical realism to immerse the reader in the drama and explain situations in her life for which she had no other explanation.

Allende also spoke about her memoir, *Paula*, and its context. The book focuses on Allende's [6] daughter, Paula, that fell into a coma. [7] Allende began writing letters for Paula to read when she awoke. Sadly, Paula died; eventually Allende adapted the material as a memoir. Like *The House of the Spirits*, *Paula* draws heavily on Allende's personal experiences and blends biography with supernatural phenomena.

After the publication of the memoir, Allende founded the Isabel Allende Foundation. Allende explained that, after Paula's death, she felt compelled to honor her daughter's memory. Paula was dedicated to improving the lives of impoverished families in Venezuela and [8] Spain. Allende started the foundation as a way to support local and international programs that empower underprivileged women and children.

[1] Though she has received numerous awards for her literature, Allende was very humble when asked about her honors. [2] She talked about accepting the Presidential Medal of Freedom, giving a TED talk, and [9] when she was a flag bearer in the 2006 Winter Olympics. [3] At the end of her lecture, Allende answered questions from the audience. [4] Her gratitude for fans and supporters stuck with me; she insisted that [10] she would be nowhere without them. [11]

★

5

A) NO CHANGE
B) having
C) had
D) has

6

A) NO CHANGE
B) daughter, Paula, who
C) daughter, Paula
D) daughter, and Paula

7

Which choice provides the most relevant detail?

A) NO CHANGE
B) Allende worked as a journalist long before she became a novelist.
C) Allende wrote letters in Spanish, her native language.
D) Paula was only 27 when she fell into the coma in 1991.

8

Which choice provides the best combination of the two sentences at the underlined portion?

A) Spain; for instance, Allende
B) Spain, so Allende
C) Spain when Allende
D) Spain, but Allende

9

A) NO CHANGE
B) when she was bearing one of the flags
C) bearing one of the flags
D) how she was a flag bearer

10

A) NO CHANGE
B) she was incredibly grateful for their support.
C) she appreciates the support of her fans.
D) she is thankful to all of her supporters.

11

What is the most logical placement of sentence 3?

A) Where it is now
B) Before sentence 1
C) After sentence 1
D) After sentence 4

2

Questions 12-22 are based on the following passage.

A Hot Topic

Yellowstone National Park sits over a geological "hot spot," a region where molten magma swells up beneath the Earth's crust. [12] Most visitors want to see the park's lower elevations. Each spring, the nearby Rocky Mountains shed melted snow, drenching Yellowstone's valleys with icy water. Deep beneath the surface, groundwater becomes super-heated by the magma below and the pressure of the melted snow above. As the groundwater reaches a boiling point and converts to steam, it rises to the surface through cracks in the rock.

Any obstruction in the steam's path causes the pressure to increase [13] while blocked, as when a can of soda is shaken and then opened. The bursts of water form Yellowstone's famous geysers. In contrast, unobstructed vents allow steam and water to seep out peacefully.

One of Yellowstone's seeping vents is the Grand Prismatic Spring. The spring is "grand" partly because of its sizable diameter of 370 [14] feet; but more marvelous are its rings of surprising color, which contrast sharply with the surrounding mudflat. The spring is so hot that it essentially sterilizes the water, resulting in a center of clear, reflected blue. The steaming water spreads out from the center as it [15] surfaces, cooling slightly along the way. In the process, it creates different habitats.

12

Which choice results in the most effective introduction to the main idea of the passage?

A) NO CHANGE
B) It is most interesting at
C) The heat dramatically affects
D) Forests and meadows cover

13

Which choice most effectively sets up the example that follows?

A) NO CHANGE
B) and forces water to spray out,
C) and creates substantial risk,
D) to an uncontainable level,

14

A) NO CHANGE
B) feet, but even more
C) feet but more
D) feet even though more

15

A) NO CHANGE
B) surfaces in order to be
C) surfaces and
D) surfaces

[16] As the water would kill a human almost instantly, at a certain radius it becomes just cool enough for hardy thermophiles, including certain species of the cyanobacteria *Synechococcus*, to survive. These cyanobacteria live on sunlight. Like plants, they contain chlorophyll to transform light into chemical energy, [17] and like plants, usually green.

However, summer presents a predicament for microbes that ordinarily love heat and light. [18] Plants cannot grow near the hot water, so there is a complete absence of shade. Summer's blistering sunlight can be overwhelming even for the tough *Synechococcus*. As an adaptation to the [19] severe conditions, the bacteria manufacture yellow pigments that absorb harmful ultraviolet (UV) rays from the sun. They survive the summer in [20] there brilliant yellow cloaks. In colder weather, they shed their cloaks, and *Synechococcus* reverts to green.

Toward the edge of the steaming spring, the temperature range supports more diverse microbes. Some of these thermophiles contain beta-carotene, the same pigment seen in carrots. [21] The overall mix of microbes at this range appears orange. The microbes spread into the mud in flows that resemble rays or tentacles. The spring's blue, green, yellow, and orange hues thus present a beautiful and rare opportunity [22] for you to view living creatures adapting to an extreme environment.

★

16

Which choice forms the most effective transition to the ideas that follow?

A) NO CHANGE
B) As long as
C) Considering that
D) Whereas

17

A) NO CHANGE
B) therefore it is
C) the corresponding hues are
D) and like plants, they are

18

The writer is considering deleting the underlined sentence. Should the writer make this change?

A) Yes, because it provides information that is not relevant to *Synechococcus*.
B) Yes, because it makes a claim that is unsupported in the paragraph.
C) No, because it explains why only bacteria live in the spring.
D) No, because it provides insight into the adaptation discussed in the paragraph.

19

A) NO CHANGE
B) calamitous
C) inopportune
D) strenuous

20

A) NO CHANGE
B) they're
C) their
D) its

21

At this point, the writer is considering adding the following diagram:

Skeletal Formula of a Beta-Carotene Molecule

Should the writer make this addition here?

A) Yes, because it clarifies the connection between thermophiles and carrots.
B) Yes, because it helps explain why orange coloration is beneficial to an organism.
C) No, because a discussion of molecular structures is beyond the scope of the passage.
D) No, because an academic diagram does not fit with the conversational tone of the passage.

22

A) NO CHANGE
B) to view
C) and view
D) viewing

Questions 23-33 are based on the following passage.

Going Pro

Watching a sports event is infinitely more absorbing if one chooses a side; the event becomes an "us vs. them" experience. Fans rally behind their respective teams in hopes that, by the season's end, they will be able to call themselves "league champions." During each game, they feel a sense of collective purpose: cheer, shout advice to players, and [23] slam game officials, whether from the stands or from their own living rooms. Spectator sports allow fans to join a kind of heroic [24] quest an experience that many people value and are willing to pay for. In fact, Forbes magazine has predicted fast growth in the North American sports market, for a total worth of $73.5 billion by 2019.

[1] The term "professional sports team" conjures images of athletes, naturally. [2] Yet players, and even their coaches and trainers, are the proverbial tip of the iceberg. [3] After all, professional teams are big businesses that can generate millions and even billions of dollars of revenue each year. [4] A professional team may rely upon hundreds of employees. [5] For example, the Washington Post has reported that the Washington D.C. baseball team, the Nationals, controls 200 players from the minor and major [25] leagues, yet, the team employs more than 1,000 other people. [26]

One could argue that professional sports teams [27] depend more on the efforts of their front offices than on the skills of their current players. A baseball team like the Nationals travels to around 80 games a year, so it needs logistical experts to keep the traveling organized. The team can expect to host 80 home games, so it needs sales and marketing experts to fill the 40,000-seat stadium each time. It also needs people to manage corporate sponsorships and television contracts. It needs people to [28] make sure that the bills are paid and the computers work. Like any business, its operations depend on people with diverse talents.

[23]
A) NO CHANGE
B) rate
C) reprimand
D) berate

[24]
A) NO CHANGE
B) quest, but an
C) quest, an
D) quest and an

[25]
A) NO CHANGE
B) leagues—yet
C) leagues yet
D) leagues, yet—

[26]
To improve the cohesion and flow of this paragraph, the writer wants to add the following sentence.

Spectators never see the bulk of the team.

The sentence would most logically be placed after

A) sentence 1.
B) sentence 2.
C) sentence 3.
D) sentence 4.

[27]
Which choice best supports the point developed in this paragraph?

A) NO CHANGE
B) must place more monetary value on the skills of employees
C) rely more on comfortable team buses
D) succeed more based on aggressive marketing

[28]
A) NO CHANGE
B) make sure that they pay the bills and repair their computers.
C) make sure the bills are paid and the computers are worked upon.
D) pay the bills and repair the computers.

That said, most jobs in sports are not with sports teams. Many are in the fields that support [29] the spectator experience. Stadiums and sports arenas require vast numbers of employees to keep fans comfortably entertained. As for sports broadcasting, viewers see only the announcers and commentators who appear on their television screens, but just as important are the production crews, advertising sales people, and countless others [30] who work to support the announcers and commentators.

Other general professions can attract a mainly sports-related clientele; sports medicine is a good example. Public relations agencies and law firms may specialize in sports clients. [31] Some professional athletes even earn advanced degrees in order to more easily find work once they retire. Being part of the sports world does not necessarily mean throwing a 90 mile-per-hour fastball. Nor does it mean driving a basketball [32] passed giants, or any other extraordinary feat. Essentially, any person who loves sports [33] has many options for pursuing a sports-related career.

★

29

A) NO CHANGE
B) spectators experiences.
C) the spectator's experiences.
D) the experiences of spectator's.

30

A) NO CHANGE
B) who work to help and support them.
C) whose work supports them.
D) DELETE the underlined portion and put a period after "others."

31

Which example best supports the claim made by this paragraph?

A) NO CHANGE
B) Even at the professional level, cheerleading is a seasonal, part-time job.
C) Language interpreters may specialize in helping athletes from abroad.
D) In some professional sports leagues, umpires and referees are full-time employees.

32

A) NO CHANGE
B) passing
C) pass
D) past

33

At this point, the writer is considering adding the following information.

—but is not a star athlete—

Should the writer make this addition here?

A) Yes, because it links the concluding sentence to the rest of the paragraph.
B) Yes, because it provides information that is essential to understanding the sentence.
C) No, because it raises a new topic that goes unexplained.
D) No, because it interrupts the flow of the sentence with contradictory information.

Questions 34-44 are based on the following passage and supplementary material.

Oil Shock: The Energy Crises of the 1970s

During the 1970s, the United States and many other developed countries faced serious energy crises related to extreme fluctuation in global oil prices. At the peaks of the two crises, gas shortages were common, and the U.S. government imposed fuel rations on motorists. The fluctuations were caused by a number of economic factors, including a war in the oil-rich Middle East. Combined with the [34] dwindling of U.S. domestic oil reserves, this led to a drastic decrease in the supply of petroleum products and, consequently, a substantial increase in price.

In 1973, several members of the Organization of the Petroleum Exporting Countries (OPEC) agreed to reduce oil production and raise the price of oil. They also imposed an embargo on oil exports to any country supporting Israel in the Yom Kippur War. The United States, in particular, [35] were targeted for supplying the Israeli military. At this time OPEC had a strong influence because [36] it controlled about half of the global oil market. Its reduction in supply sent the price of petroleum products skyrocketing. In the U.S., when millions of panicked drivers rushed to fill up their tanks and gas cans before gasoline prices climbed even [37] higher, they drained the supply, causing more panic. The U.S. swiftly negotiated Israeli troop withdrawals that led to the cancellation of the embargo. [38] In addition, the effects of the oil crisis were long-lasting.

In order to conserve fuel during the crisis, the U.S. government enforced a maximum speed limit of 55 miles per hour, which lasted until 1995. In addition, daylight savings time was used year-round to help reduce energy consumption in the evenings. Also, automakers ceased making large domestic cars, and focused [39] to more fuel-efficient models. [40] Finally, it was during this time that people became interested in alternative energy sources.

34

A) NO CHANGE
B) decay
C) weakening
D) disrepair

35

A) NO CHANGE
B) are
C) is
D) was

36

The writer wants to support the proposition about OPEC's influence. Which choice best accomplishes this goal?

A) NO CHANGE
B) it represented 12 nations.
C) it had first been formed in 1960.
D) it negotiated with major oil companies.

37

A) NO CHANGE
B) higher they drained the supply,
C) higher, they drained the supply
D) higher they drained the supply

38

A) NO CHANGE
B) Next,
C) However,
D) Therefore,

39

A) NO CHANGE
B) on
C) with
D) DELETE the underlined portion

40

The writer is considering deleting the underlined sentence. Should the writer delete this portion?

A) Yes, because it distracts from the discussion of automakers.
B) Yes, because it provides a minor detail that blurs the focus of the passage.
C) No, because it supports the author's central claim that the crisis spurred technological advancements in the energy industry.
D) No, because it provides an effective transition to the next paragraph.

Despite this budding interest, America's perpetual dependence on foreign oil sources led to a second oil crisis in [41] 1979, following the Iranian Revolution, oil exports from Iraq and Iran were severely reduced, and once again, the price of oil increased dramatically. [42] However, the price for a gallon of gasoline actually decreased, and mass panic ensued, as in 1973. Prices rose disproportionately to the decrease in supply, and investors doubted the longevity of the petroleum business. As a result, the U.S. faced another oil shortage. Gas was rationed, and motorists waited in long lines to buy fuel; many gas stations sold out their entire stock and were forced to close until [43] it could resupply.

Though the crisis itself was as short-lived as its predecessor had been, it had a lasting impact on the economy. Specifically, American automakers were in [44] big trouble as demand for fuel-efficient vehicles attracted consumers to smaller, foreign cars. As these companies adapted to a changing market, many faced bankruptcy, and several smaller manufacturers merged with larger ones.

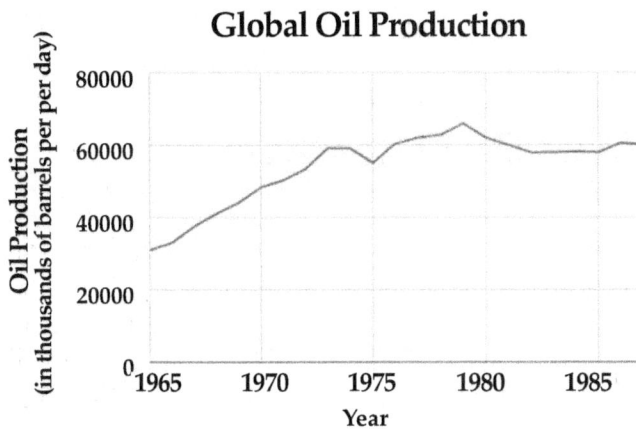

41

A) NO CHANGE
B) 1979. Following
C) 1979 and following
D) 1979—therefore—following

42

Which of the following provides the most accurate information based on the graph?

A) NO CHANGE
B) Thus, the decrease in oil production was drastic, and
C) Although the global oil supply increased overall between 1973 and 1979,
D) In spite of the global oil supply having doubled by the late 1970s,

43

A) NO CHANGE
B) they could
C) their ability to
D) they're able to

44

A) NO CHANGE
B) a mess
C) a pickle
D) a tough situation

NO TEST MATERIAL ON THIS PAGE

ps://mymostructor.com# Math Test 4 – No Calculator

 25 MINUTES, 20 QUESTIONS

Turn to Section 3 of your answer sheet to answer the questions in this section.

DIRECTIONS

For questions **1 – 15**, find the solution to each problem and select the most appropriate answer from the choices provided. For questions **16 – 20**, find the solution to each problem and write your answer in the space provided. You may use the blank space in your test booklet for scratch work.

NOTES

1. The use of a calculator on any part of this section is forbidden.
2. Unless otherwise indicated, all variables and expressions used in this test represent real numbers.
3. Unless otherwise indicated, all figures used in this test are drawn to scale.
4. Unless otherwise indicated, all figures used in this test lie on a plane.
5. Unless specified otherwise, a given function, f, has the domain the set of all real numbers x for which $f(x)$ is a real number.

REFERENCE

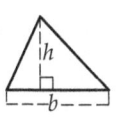
$A = \frac{1}{2}bh$

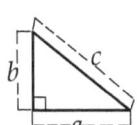
$c^2 = a^2 + b^2$

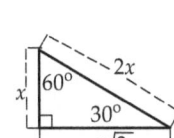
Special Right Triangles

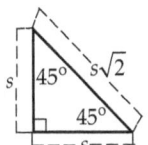

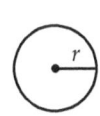
$A = \pi r^2$
$C = 2\pi r$

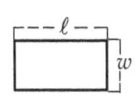
$A = \ell w$

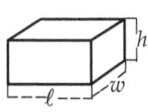
$V = \ell w h$

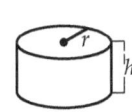
$V = \pi r^2 h$

$V = \frac{4}{3}\pi r^3$

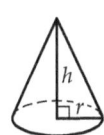
$V = \frac{1}{3}\pi r^2 h$

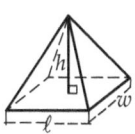
$V = \frac{1}{3}\ell w h$

The arc of a full circle is 360 degrees or 2π radians.
A triangle has angles that sum to 180 degrees.

3

1

$$7x - 5 < 13 + 4x$$

Which of the following is the solution to the inequality above?

A) $x > 18$
B) $x > 6$
C) $x < 6$
D) $x < \dfrac{17}{3}$

2

What is the set of solutions to the equation $\sqrt{2x+3} + \sqrt{x+1} = 1$?

A) $\{-1, 3\}$
B) $\{1, -3\}$
C) $\{-1\}$
D) $\{3\}$

3

If $\dfrac{m}{3m-n} = \dfrac{1}{5}$, what is the value of $\dfrac{n}{m}$?

A) -2
B) $-\dfrac{1}{2}$
C) $\dfrac{1}{2}$
D) 2

4

Which of the following is equivalent to the expression $(x+3)^2 - (x-3)^2$?

A) 9
B) 18
C) $12x$
D) $2x^2 + 18$

5

The operation designated by the symbol $\triangledown$ is defined for any three real numbers as $a \triangledown b \triangledown c = a(c - b)$. If $2 \triangledown 1 \triangledown x = 10$, what is the value of x?

A) -6
B) -4
C) 5
D) 6

6

The formula for the speed of sound [S(T)] in meters per second as a function of the air temperature (T) in degrees Celsius is shown below. What is the speed of sound, in meters per second, in Antarctica, where the average temperature is approximately −55° C?

$$S(T) = \frac{3T}{5} + 331.4$$

A) 265.4
B) 273.4
C) 298.4
D) 301.4

7

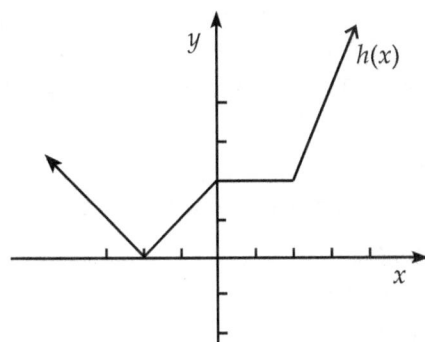

Which of the following is the greatest rate of increase for the piecewise function $h(x)$?

A) $\frac{3}{5}$

B) $\frac{2}{3}$

C) 2

D) 5

8

Which of the following is equivalent to $(\sqrt{2} - \sqrt{3})^2$?

A) $5 - 2\sqrt{6}$
B) $5 - \sqrt{6}$
C) $1 - 2\sqrt{6}$
D) $1 - \sqrt{2}$

9

Which of the following values of b will give integer solutions to the equation $x^2 + bx - 16 = 0$?

A) −8
B) −6
C) 4
D) 12

10

The shortest distance, in feet, over which a car traveling at x miles per hour is able to come to a complete stop corresponds to the function $f(x) = x + \frac{x^2}{20}$. What is the increase in this distance if a car increases its speed from 20 to 30 miles per hour?

A) 35
B) 40
C) 75
D) 80

11

$8f + 12g = 27$ and $5f + 6g = 15$. What is the value of $f + g$?

A) $\dfrac{5}{4}$

B) $\dfrac{11}{4}$

C) $\dfrac{3}{2}$

D) $\dfrac{7}{2}$

12

If $\dfrac{n}{x^2 - 36} = \dfrac{1}{x-6} + \dfrac{1}{x+6}$, what is n in terms of x?

A) x
B) $2x$
C) $2(x + 6)$
D) $2(x - 6)$

13

A right circular cylinder has a volume of 81π cm³. If the circumference of the base of the cylinder is 6π cm, what is its height?

A) 6 cm
B) 9 cm
C) 12 cm
D) 13.5 cm

14

Tyler is currently three times as old as Isabella. If Tyler's age is t years, how many years in the future will Tyler be twice as old as Isabella?

A) $\dfrac{t}{3}$

B) $\dfrac{t}{2}$

C) $\dfrac{2t}{3}$

D) t

15

A band decides to go on tour. They will play at 26 different venues over the course of d days. Each venue agrees to pay the band x dollars up front, plus 50 percent of ticket sales. Each venue attracts an average of y attendees. Which of the following factors does NOT affect how much money the band can earn?

A) The average price per concert ticket
B) The value of d
C) The value of y
D) The value of x

Student-Produced Responses   3

DIRECTIONS

For questions **16 – 20**, find the solution to the problem and enter your answer as demonstrated on the right.

1. Only the answer that is bubbled in on the answer sheet will be credited. The blank spaces above the bubbles are for you to record your answers for accuracy.
2. Only fill in one bubble in any given column.
3. None of the answers on this portion of the test are negative values.
4. If a problem appears to have more than one answer, only enter one answer. If the answer you enter is one of the correct solutions, you will receive full credit for that question.
5. If the correct answer can be expressed as a mixed number, it must be entered as a decimal or an improper fraction.
6. If the correct answer is a decimal that cannot fit into the grid space, you must fill the grid with enough digits to completely fill the space. The number can be rounded or simply shortened but must fill every blank space.

Answer: $\frac{5}{36}$ Answer: 4.5

Write answer in boxes.
← Fraction line
← Decimal point
Grid in result.

Acceptable ways to grid $\frac{1}{6}$ are:

Answer: 302 – either position is correct

NOTES

Begin entering answers in any column that accommodates your answer. If you do not need a column do not enter anything in that column.

16

The function $f(x)$ is defined as follows:

$$f(x) = 5x - 1 \text{ for } x \geq 5$$
$$f(x) = 1 - 5x \text{ for } x < 5$$

What is the value of $f(5) + f(-3)$?

ANSWER: _____

17

If $\dfrac{x+4}{7} = \dfrac{4}{9}$, what is the value of $|x|$?

ANSWER: _____

18

The function $f(x)$ is defined as $f(x) = ax^2 + bx + c$ for all real numbers x. If $f(0) = 2$ and $f(1) = 3$, what is the value of $a + b$?

ANSWER: _____

19

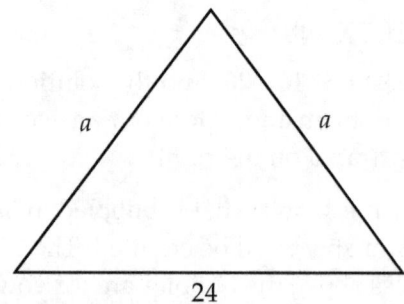

The triangle above has an area of 108. What is its perimeter?

ANSWER: _____

20

If $f(x) = \dfrac{1}{2}x^2 - 8$ for $-4 \leq x \leq 4$, what is the highest possible value of $|f(x)|$?

ANSWER: _____

Math Test 4 – Calculator

 55 MINUTES, 38 QUESTIONS

Turn to Section 4 of your answer sheet to answer the questions in this section.

DIRECTIONS

For questions **1 – 30**, find the solution to each problem and select the most appropriate answer from the choices provided. For questions **31 – 38**, find the solution to each problem and write your answer in the space provided. You may use the blank space in your test booklet for scratch work.

NOTES

1. The use of a calculator on any part of this section is allowed.
2. Unless otherwise indicated, all variables and expressions used in this test represent real numbers.
3. Unless otherwise indicated, all figures used in this test are drawn to scale.
4. Unless otherwise indicated, all figures used in this test lie on a plane.
5. Unless specified otherwise, a given function, f, has the domain the set of all real numbers x for which $f(x)$ is a real number.

REFERENCE

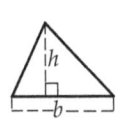 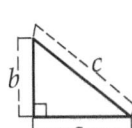 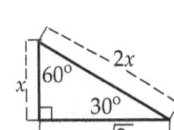 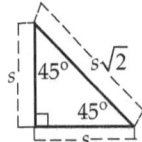 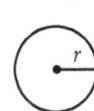 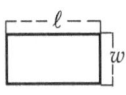

$A = \frac{1}{2}bh$ $c^2 = a^2 + b^2$ Special Right Triangles $A = \pi r^2$ $A = \ell w$
$C = 2\pi r$

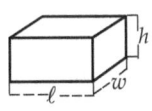 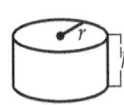  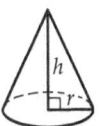 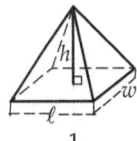

$V = \ell w h$ $V = \pi r^2 h$ $V = \frac{4}{3}\pi r^3$ $V = \frac{1}{3}\pi r^2 h$ $V = \frac{1}{3}\ell w h$

The arc of a circle is 360 degrees or 2π radians.
A triangle has angles that sum to 180 degrees.

4

1

A group of 400 teenagers participated in a taste survey in which each participant was given four samples of different sodas (labeled A, B, C, and D) and asked to pick a favorite. Their responses are given in the table below:

	A	B	C	D	Total
Boys	90	50	60	40	240
Girls	50	20	60	30	160
Total	140	70	120	70	400

Based on the information in the table, which of the following statements is NOT true?

A) 40% of the participants were girls.

B) 70% of the participants preferred "A."

C) $\frac{1}{6}$ of the boys preferred "D."

D) $\frac{2}{7}$ of the participants who preferred "B" were girls.

2

Which of the following is the domain of the function $f(x) = \frac{3-x}{\sqrt{x^2-9}}$?

A) $-3 \leq x \leq 3$

B) $-3 < x < 3$

C) $x < -3$, or $x > 3$

D) $x \leq -3$, or $x \geq 3$

3

Olivia saved $45 by buying a sweater that is discounted 25% from the retail price. How much did she pay for the sweater?

A) $135

B) $160

C) $180

D) $210

4

Section	1	2	3	4	5
Frequency	12	9	10	11	8

John spins a spinner 50 times and records his results in the table above. The spinner has five sections, numbered 1, 2, 3, 4, and 5. If the spinner continues to land on each of the sections with the same frequencies as the first 50 spins, how many times will the spinner land on 3 or 4 if it is spun 300 times?

A) 60

B) 66

C) 126

D) 132

5

$$y = \frac{1}{2}x - 3$$
$$2y = x - 6$$

If the system of equations above is graphed on a coordinate plane, which of the following must be true?

A) The two lines will be perpendicular.
B) There is only one line.
C) The two lines intersect once at (2, −1).
D) The two lines intersect once at (−2, −4).

6

A car dealer sells an SUV for $39,000, which represents a 25% markup over the car's cost to the dealer. What was the cost of the SUV to the dealer?

A) $29,250
B) $31,200
C) $32,500
D) $33,800

7

In 2014, Gerry pumped 200 gallons of gas. In 2015, Gerry pumped 250 gallons of gas at an average cost per gallon 75 cents lower than in 2014. Each year, he spent the same amount on gas. How much did he spend on gas in 2014?

A) $525.00
B) $675.00
C) $750.00
D) $900.00

8

In 1994, the average price of a new domestic car was $16,930. In 2002, the average price was $19,126. Based on a linear model, what is the predicted average price for 2008?

A) $22,969
B) $21,322
C) $20,773
D) $18,577

9

Which of the following is the factored form of the expression $a^3 - a^2 b - ab^2 + b^3$?

A) $(a^2 - b^2)(a + b)$
B) $(a^2 + b^2)(a + b)$
C) $(a - b)(a + b)^2$
D) $(a - b)^2(a + b)$

10

MOST POPULAR BOY NAMES IN 1995

Rank	Name	Number
1	Michael	21
2	Jacob	19
3	Timothy	17
4	John	15
5	Kevin	13

The table above lists the most popular names for boys born in 1995 in one city in the United States. On the basis of this information, a student concludes that 20 percent of the boys born in the town that year were named Timothy. Why is the student incorrect?

A) The student did not consider names for girls.
B) The student did not consider popular names in entire the United States.
C) The student did not consider names given to boys in other years.
D) The student did take into consideration that there were other names given to boys born in that city in 1995.

11

Which of the following sets of values satisfies the inequality $|7 - 3x| > 2$?

A) $x < \frac{5}{3}$ or $x > 3$

B) $\frac{5}{3} < x < 3$

C) $x < \frac{5}{3}$

D) $x > -3$

12

A number, n, is increased by 8. If the cube root of that result is -0.5, what is the value of n?

A) -15.625
B) -8.794
C) -8.125
D) 7.875

13

Results from Filing Taxes	Number of Single Adults
Received a return of more than $500	20
Received a return of less than $500	35
Had to pay less than $500	28
Had to pay more than $500	17

The table above gives the results of a survey of 100 single adults on their tax filings from the previous year. Based on the information above, how many adults out of a group of 900 would expect to receive a return of less than $500?

A) 315
B) 320
C) 325
D) 330

14

Which of the following is equivalent to the expression $\frac{7+20x-3x^2}{2x^2-11x-21}$?

A) $-\frac{3x+1}{2x+3}$

B) $\frac{3x+1}{2x+3}$

C) $\frac{1}{2}(3x+1)$

D) $-2(x-7)$

15

Jim can shear thirty sheep in 30 minutes. Dolly can do the same job in 45 minutes, and Antonio in an hour and a half. How quickly can they shear thirty sheep working together?

A) 12 minutes
B) 15 minutes
C) 21 minutes
D) 23 minutes

16

The graph of the function $h(x)$ is equivalent to the graph of the function $f(x)$ shifted down 4 units and to the right 2 units. If $f(x) = x^3$, which of the following is $h(x)$?

A) $h(x) = (x - 2)^3 + 4$
B) $h(x) = (x + 2)^3 - 4$
C) $h(x) = (x - 2)^3 - 4$
D) $h(x) = (x - 4)^3 - 2$

17

A market sells pears, apples, and oranges. If 1 pear and 3 apples cost $1.90; 1 pear, 1 apple, and 1 orange cost $1.60; and 2 apples and 1 orange cost $1.70, what is the price of one apple?

A) $0.40
B) $0.45
C) $0.50
D) $0.52

18

Julia and Grace, working together, can paint the exterior of a house in six days. Julia, by herself, can complete the job five days faster than it would take Grace to complete the job by herself. How long would it take Grace to paint the house alone?

A) 10 days
B) 15 days
C) 18 days
D) 20 days

19

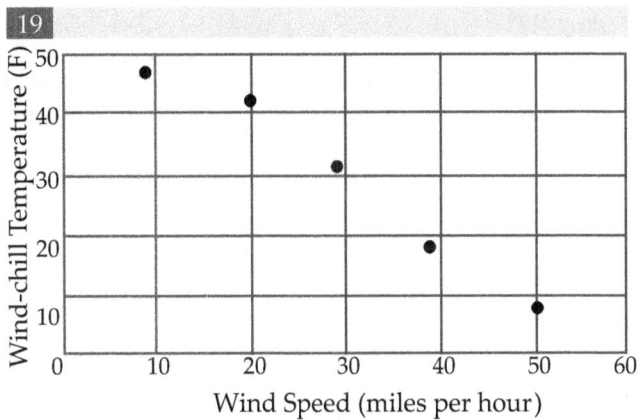

The graph above shows wind-chill temperature in New York City as a function of wind speed. Which of the following equations best approximates the line of best fit?

A) $y = -x + 60$
B) $y = -5x + 60$
C) $y = -3x + 55$
D) $y = 5x + 60$

20

What are the values of x that satisfy the inequality $\frac{2x}{3} - 4 \leq -1 + \frac{2x}{3}$?

A) $x \leq -\frac{15}{5}$

B) $x \geq -\frac{9}{4}$

C) $x \leq \frac{9}{4}$

D) All real numbers

21

If the graph of the equation $y = x^2 + mx + n$ passes through the points (1, 12) and (3, 28), what is the value of mn?

A) 20
B) 36
C) –40
D) 28

22

Each of the following scenarios describes two numerical quantities. For which of these scenarios would you expect the two quantities to exhibit a negative correlation?

A) The number of students in a high school and the average student GPA

B) The age of a car and its resale value

C) The price of an item and the amount of tax on that item

D) The speed of a car and the distance traveled in a fixed time

23

What is the domain of the function $f(x) = \frac{x+1}{x} - \frac{3}{\sqrt{5-x}}$?

A) $x \neq 0$
B) All real numbers
C) $x > 5$, and $x \neq 0$
D) $x < 5$, and $x \neq 0$

24

How many degrees does the hour hand of a clock move between noon and 2:30 pm on the same day?

A) 60
B) 65
C) 75
D) 195

25

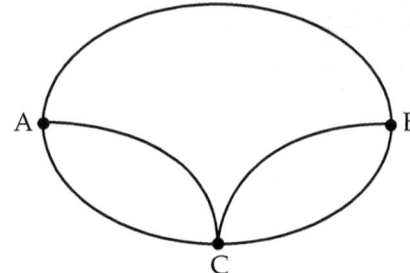

Amy, who lives in town A, visits neighboring towns B and C. The roads connecting these three towns are represented in the diagram above. How many different routes can Amy take, beginning at A and returning to A, and passing through B and C in any order but not more than once through each?

A) 4
B) 6
C) 8
D) 10

26

One wheel has a diameter of x inches and a second wheel has a diameter of y inches. The first wheel covers a distance of d feet per 100 revolutions. How many revolutions does the second wheel make in covering the same distance?

A) $100xy$

B) $100y - x$

C) $\dfrac{100y}{x}$

D) $\dfrac{100x}{y}$

27

At what point does the graph of $5x + 4y = 12$ intersect the y-axis?

A) (0, 3)
B) (0, −3)
C) (3, 0)
D) (5, 0)

Questions 28-30 are based on the information below.

Children per woman(Total Fertility Rate), 1955 to 2015
Total fertility rate (TFR) is the number of children that would be born to a woman if she were to live to the end of her childbearing years and bore children in accordance with age-specific fertility rates of the specified year.

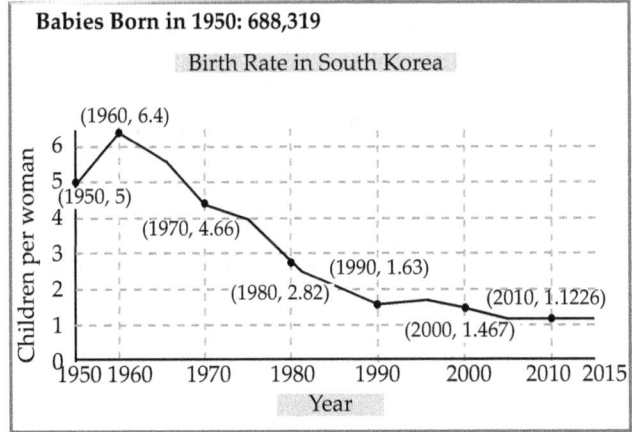

Babies Born in 1950: 688,319

Name and Population Chart for 1950			
Boys		Girls	
Romanized Name	Percent of Baby Boys with Name	Romanized Name	Percent of Girls Born with Name
Young-soo	1.68%	Young-sook	1.44%
Young-ho	1.54%	Jung-sook	1.39%
Sung-soo	1.35%	Young-hee	1.29%
Young-chul	1.25%	Jung-hee	1.17%
Jung-ho	1.20%	Myung-sook	1.11%
Sung-ho	1.18%	Hyun-sook	1.05%
Young-sik	0.97%	Kyung-sook	1.04%
Percent of Babies Born Male	50.80%	Percent of Babies Born Female	49.20%

28

Given the data above, about how many of the popularly named 1950s newborns had Young in their names?

A) 13,144
B) 28,166
C) 56,029
D) 826,568

29

If all the popularly named female babies born in 1950 lived to bear the total fertility ratio (TFR) at age 30, how many babies would they produce to the nearest baby?

A) 81,079
B) 680,793
C) 1,371,024
D) 8,026,288

30

Which of the following conclusions can be drawn from the data above?
  I) Hospitals in 1960 had better birth procedures
  II) The range of TFR from 1950 to 2015 is ~4

A) I only
B) II only
C) I and II
D) Neither I nor II

4 Student-Produced Responses

DIRECTIONS

For questions **31 – 38**, find the solution to the problem and enter your answer as demonstrated on the right.

1. Only the answer that is bubbled in on the answer sheet will be credited. The blank spaces above the bubbles are for you to record your answers for accuracy.
2. Only fill in one bubble in any given column.
3. None of the answers on this portion of the test are negative values.
4. If a problem appears to have more than one answer, only enter one answer. If the answer you enter is one of the correct solutions, you will receive full credit for that question.
5. If the correct answer can be expressed as a mixed number, it must be entered as a decimal or an improper fraction.
6. If the correct answer is a decimal that cannot fit into the grid space, you must fill the grid with enough digits to completely fill the space. The number can be rounded or simply shortened but must fill every blank space.

NOTES

Begin entering answers in any column that accommodates your answer. If you do not need a column do not enter anything in that column.

Answer: $\frac{5}{36}$ — Write answer in boxes. Grid in result.

Answer: 4.5 — ← Fraction line, ← Decimal point

Acceptable ways to grid $\frac{1}{6}$ are:

Answer: 302 – either position is correct

31

Three gallons of a fluid mixture contain antifreeze and fuel in a ratio of one part antifreeze to five parts fuel. To this mixture, one gallon of another mixture, made up of one part antifreeze to one part fuel, is added. What is the percentage of fuel in the final mixture?

ANSWER: _____

32

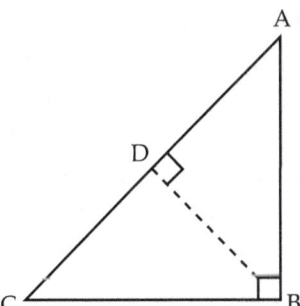

Triangle ABC is a right triangle. Also AC = 10, CB = 6, and ∠ADB is a right angle. What is the length of DB?

ANSWER: _____

33

If p and q are positive integers, and $\left(pq^{\frac{3}{2}}\right)^2 = 108$, what is the value of pq?

ANSWER: _____

34

If $(3x + 2)(2x - 5) = ax^2 + kx + n$, where n and k are constants, what is the value of $a - n + k$?

ANSWER: _____

4

35

A stone is thrown directly upwards at a speed of 40 feet per second. The height of the stone h, in feet, is given by the equation $h = 40t - 16t^2$, where t is the time in seconds after the stone is thrown. How many seconds after being thrown does the stone hit the ground?

ANSWER: _____

36

The quotient $\frac{x}{y}$ is recalculated by decreasing x by 25% and increasing y by 25%. What percentage of the old quotient is the new?

ANSWER: _____

Questions 37 and 38 are based on the information below.

In epidemiology (the study of disease across populations), the incidence rate (IR) is a measure of the number of new cases of a disease in a population over a set period of time:

$$IR = \frac{\text{Number of new cases}}{\text{Number of people at risk}} \times 100\%$$

37

Disease X affects exclusively children between the ages 3 and 6. If 62 new cases of this disease are reported over a period of 3 years, and the number of children in the population between 3 and 6 years of age is 4,000, what is the incidence rate in percentage over this period?

ANSWER: _____

38

A new law requires all children in this age demographic to receive a vaccine for this disease. In the 3 years following the period above, the incidence falls by 67% compared to the previous 3 years. How many fewer cases of the disease are reported during the 3 years after the vaccine is introduced (round to the nearest whole number)?

ANSWER: _____

NO TEST MATERIAL ON THIS PAGE

Essay Test 4

 50 MINUTES, Prompt-based essay

Turn to Section 5 of your answer sheet to answer the question in this section.

> **DIRECTIONS**
> As you read the passage below, consider how Susanna Heckman uses
> - evidence, such as facts or examples, to support claims.
> - reasoning to develop ideas and to connect claims and evidence.
> - stylistic or persuasive elements, such as word choice or appeals to emotion, to add power to the ideas expressed.

This passage is adapted from Susanna Heckman, "Genetic Engineering: Past, Present, Future."

There was a time, more than 10,000 years ago in what is now China, when small groups of humans regularly waded around in swamps to find a special plant. They collected the plant's thin little seeds to cook and eat. Eventually, they figured out that they could raise the grass themselves all in one place, and that planting the largest seeds resulted in plants that tended to produce large seeds. Unwittingly, they were selecting one set of genes over another. Over millennia, the domestication process led to the plump, starchy grain that we now call "rice." Half the world's population depends upon rice as a staple food.

People have altered most of the crops and livestock that we now consume to the point that they bear little resemblance to the original. A case in point: the swamp-grass species that served as the ancestor for rice, *Oryza rufipogon*, is now considered a noxious weed in several states in the U.S.

Yet some people fear that we have gone way, way too far by using methods of genetic engineering to alter the DNA of plants we eat.

In 1994, the Flavr Savr tomato was the first Genetically Modified Organism (GMO) product to hit food markets. The tomato stayed fresh longer because a gene responsible for an enzyme that promoted ripening was isolated, reversed, cloned, and added to bacteria that was then absorbed by the plant, whose seeds were sold to farmers. To some consumers, the process seemed too impossibly unnatural to be healthy. Another outcry occurred when it was made public that a gene for cold-tolerance had been added to some strawberries so that they could be grown in more northern climates. The gene came from a species of fish. Consumers mistakenly expected fishy-tasting strawberries.

Some activist groups such as Greenpeace have fought all GMO products, claiming that meddling with Nature can have unexpected consequences. The fears they stoked have not been assuaged by hundreds of peer-reviewed, published studies that indicate otherwise. Today, 64 countries and several states in the U.S. require special labeling of GMO products. Chipotle restaurants and Trader Joe's markets advertise that they never use GMO ingredients. Field tests of GMO crops have even been vandalized in many places in the world.

Agriculture, however, has embraced GMOs. By 2013, nearly all the corn, cotton, and soybeans grown in America were from GMO seed. Much has been made of large corporations such as Monsanto using GMO technology for dubious purposes. But farmers have embraced GMO seeds for a large variety of reasons. As William Saletan of Slate Magazine has written, "Genetic engineering isn't a thing. It's a process that can be used in different ways to create different things."

Crops can be engineered with very precise gene changes to resist insects and viruses; to survive droughts or floods; to grow in less-than-ideal soils; to produce larger fruits; to withstand temperature extremes. Scientists have worked on many ideas for increasing the nutrients in crops. For example, bioengineers have developed "golden rice," a vitamin-A-infused grain that could help prevent widespread cases of blindness and even death among millions of children in Southeast Asia every year.

Scientific consensus supports the GMO products available today. The U.S. Food and Drug Administration (FDA) insists that there is no inherent danger to genetically engineered (GE) foods. "Foods from GE plants must meet the same food safety requirements as foods derived from traditionally bred plants," it says on its website. "GE plant varieties marketed to date are as safe as comparable, non-GE foods."

It is urgent that the global community, including the American public, learns more about the science behind GMO foods. We cannot afford to dismiss GMOs out of hand for one very big reason: 9 billion people. That is the expected population on Earth by 2050, compared to 7 billion today, about 800 million of whom already experience chronic undernourishment .

Farmers realize the financial benefits of improving yields from every square meter of cultivated land. In this, what is in their self-interest is in ours, too. There is not enough undeveloped arable land to grow food for 9 billion people. Unless we increase the productivity of land that is already in cultivation, the world will experience untold suffering.

M.S. Swaminathan, an agronomist who is considered the father of India's Green Revolution, has put it quite bluntly: "There should be no relaxation of yield-enhancing research, since there is no other way of meeting global food needs."

Write an essay in which you explain how Susanna Heckman builds an argument to persuade her audience that genetic engineering of food crops should be more widely accepted. In your essay, analyze how Heckman uses one or more of the features in the directions that precede the passage (or features of your own choice) to strengthen the logic and persuasiveness of her argument. Be sure that your analysis focuses on the most relevant features of the passage.
Your essay should not explain whether you agree with Heckman's claims, but rather explain how Heckman builds an argument to persuade her audience.

* Sample responses found in the "Answers and Explanations" section of this study guide.

KALLIS

SAT® Practice Test #5

IMPORTANT REMINDERS:

When you take the official SAT, you will need to use a No. 2 pencil. Do not use a pen or a mechanical pencil.

On the official SAT, sharing any of the questions on the test violates the College Board's policies and may result in your scores being canceled.

(This cover is modeled after the cover you'll see when you take the official SAT.)

UNAUTHORIZED REPRODUCTION OR USE OF ANY PART OF THIS TEST IS PROHIBITED.

© 2019 KALLIS EDU

Reading Test 5

65 MINUTES, 52 QUESTIONS

Turn to Section 1 of your answer sheet to answer the questions in this section.

DIRECTIONS

Each passage or pair of passages is accompanied by 10 or 11 questions. Read each passage or pair of passages, and then select the most appropriate answer to each question. Some passages may include tables or graphs that require additional analysis.

Refer to the passage below to answer questions 1–10.

This passage is adapted from Zane Grey, *The Young Pitcher*, originally published in 1911.

Ken Ward had not been at the big university many days before he realized the miserable lot of a freshman.

At first he was sorely puzzled. College
5 was so different from what he had expected. At the high school of his home town, which, being the capital of the State, was no village, he had been somebody. Then his summer in Arizona, with its wild adventures, had given him a self-
10 appreciation which made his present situation humiliating.

There were more than four thousand students at the university. Ken felt himself the youngest, the smallest, the one of least
15 consequence. He was lost in a shuffle of superior youths. In the forestry department he was a mere boy; and he soon realized that a freshman there was the same as anywhere. The fact that he weighed nearly one hundred and sixty pounds,
20 and was no stripling, despite his youth, made not one whit of difference.

Unfortunately, his first overture of what he considered good-fellowship had been made to an upper-classman, and had been a grievous mistake.
25 Ken had not yet recovered from its reception. He grew careful after that, then shy, and finally began to struggle against disappointment and loneliness.

Outside of his department, on the campus and everywhere he ventured, he found things still
30 worse. There was something wrong with him, with his fresh complexion, with his hair, with the way he wore his tie, with the cut of his clothes. In fact, there was nothing right about him. He had been so beset that he could not think of anything
35 but himself. One day, while sauntering along a campus path, with his hands in his pockets, he met two students coming toward him. They went to right and left, and, jerking his hands from his pockets, roared in each ear, "How dare you walk
40 with your hands in your pockets!"

Another day, on the library step, he encountered a handsome bareheaded youth with a fine, clean-cut face and keen eyes, who showed the true stamp of the great university.
45 "Here," he said, sharply, "aren't you a freshman?"

"Why—yes," confessed Ken.

"I see you have your trousers turned up at the bottom."
50 "Yes—so I have." For the life of him Ken could not understand why that simple fact seemed a crime, but so it was.

"Turn them down!" ordered the student. Ken looked into the stern face and flashing
55 eyes of his tormentor, and then meekly did as he had been commanded.

"Boy, I've saved your life. We murder freshmen here for that," said the student, and then passed on up the steps.
60 In the beginning it was such incidents as these that had bewildered Ken. He passed from surprise to anger, and vowed he would have something to say to these upper-classmen. But when the opportunity came Ken always felt
65 so little and mean that he could not retaliate. This made him furious. He had not been in college two weeks before he could distinguish the sophomores from the seniors by the look on their faces. He hated the sneering "Sophs," and
70 felt rising in him the desire to fight. But he both feared and admired seniors. They seemed so aloof, so far above him. He was in awe of them, and had a hopeless longing to be like them. And as for the freshmen, it took no second glance for
75 Ken to pick them out. They were of two kinds— those who banded together in crowds and went about yelling, and running away from the Sophs, and those who sneaked about alone with timid step and furtive glance.
80 Ken was one of these lonesome freshmen. He was pining for companionship, but he was afraid to open his lips. Once he had dared to go into Carlton Hall, the magnificent club-house which had been given to the university by a famous
85 graduate. The club was for all students—Ken had read that on the card sent to him, and also in the papers. But manifestly the upper-classmen had a different point of view. Ken had gotten a glimpse

CONTINUE

into the immense reading-room with its open fireplace and huge chairs, its air of quiet study and repose; he had peeped into the brilliant billiard-hall and the gymnasium; and he had been so impressed and delighted with the marble swimming-tank that he had forgotten himself and walked too near the pool. Several students accidentally bumped him into it. It appeared the students were so eager to help him out that they crowded him in again. When Ken finally got out he learned the remarkable fact that he was the sixteenth freshman who had been accidentally pushed into the tank that day.

So Ken Ward was in a state of revolt. He was homesick; he was lonely for a friend; he was constantly on the lookout for some trick; his confidence in himself had fled; his opinion of himself had suffered a damaging change; he hardly dared call his soul his own.

★

01

The passage is best described as

A) a contrast between freshmen and sophomore university life.
B) a social commentary on the state of American colleges.
C) an introduction to a social hierarchy using multiple anecdotes.
D) an illustration of the joys and frustrations of college life.

02

Ken's transitional experience in college as a freshman in paragraph 2 (lines 4 – 11) can best be likened to

A) a soldier who returns home only to find that his family has moved.
B) a big fish in a small pond that becomes a small fish in a big pond.
C) a boastful professional wrestler who has finally met his match.
D) a school bully who finally gets his comeuppance.

03

As used in line 20, "stripling" most nearly means

A) native.
B) weakling.
C) scholar.
D) loudmouth.

04

The statement in lines 30 – 35 ("There was something…but himself") primarily serve to show Ken Ward's

A) lack of money for clothing.
B) ever-changing appearance.
C) empathy toward other freshmen.
D) feelings of inadequacy.

05

As used in lines 65, "mean" most nearly means

A) inferior.
B) average.
C) brazen.
D) unkind.

06

Ken regards the sophomores and seniors of the university with

A) brotherly affection.
B) thinly veiled hatred.
C) loathing and deference respectively.
D) indifference and fascination respectively.

07

Which choice provides the best evidence for the answer to the previous question?

A) Lines 13 – 16 ("Ken felt…youths")
B) Lines 54 – 56 ("Ken looked…commanded")
C) Lines 61 – 63 ("He passed…upper-classmen")
D) Lines 69 – 71 ("He hated…seniors")

08

Ken learns to identify other freshmen by

A) their size.
B) their treatment of others.
C) their clothing choices.
D) the size of their social groups.

09

Which choice provides the best evidence for the answer to the previous question?

A) Lines 18 – 21 ("The fact…difference")
B) Lines 41 – 44 ("Another day…university")
C) Lines 66 – 69 ("He had…their faces")
D) Lines 73 – 79 ("And as…glance")

10

In lines 97 – 100 ("When Ken…that day"), the author implies that

A) the students who bumped people into the tank felt sorry.
B) the freshmen were intentionally being pushed into the tank.
C) Ken was pushed into the tank sixteen separate times.
D) Ken accidentally bumped other freshmen into the tank.

Refer to the passage below to answer questions 11 – 20.

This passage is adapted from Devon Maylie, "Violent media and real-world behavior: Historical data and recent trends," published February 18, 2015.

line
    Since the release of the PC game *Grand Theft Auto* in 1997, the *Grand Theft Auto* (*GTA*) franchise—which now includes seven games and
5 a handful of expansions available on a number of consoles—has sold over 185 million copies, making it one of the most successful video game series of all time. Part of the series' success comes from its open-ended gameplay: players customize their characters while exploring a massive and
10 immersive in-game world. And as the series' title implies, exploring these worlds invariably involves perpetrating acts of theft and violence. Players are free to steal cars, assault pedestrians, and deal drugs. Not surprisingly, the *GTA* series
15 has been accused of inspiring countless acts of real-world violence and has come under intense scrutiny on a number of occasions.
    As indicated by the astounding success and harsh criticisms of the *GTA* series, Americans
20 have ambivalent attitudes toward violent media; the films and video games that are devoured by American consumers are demonized once they can be linked to acts of violence. Although the relationship between violent media and real-
25 world violence has been the subject of extensive debate and considerable academic research, the core question is far from answered. Do violent games and movies encourage more violence, less, or is there no effect?
30   Many have attempted to correlate appalling acts of violence with the consumption of violent media. They are quick to highlight that Adam Lanza and James Holmes — respectively, the perpetrators of the Newtown and Aurora mass
35 shootings — both played violent video games. Yet so do millions of law-abiding Americans. Clearly, correlation is not necessarily causation, and the relationship between media violence and real-world violence cannot be demonstrated so easily.
40   A 2014 study in *Psychology of Popular Media Culture* found no evidence of an association between violent crime and video game sales and the release dates of popular violent video games. "Unexpectedly, many of the results
45 were suggestive of a *decrease* in violent crime in response to violent video games," write the researchers, based at Villanova and Rutgers. Although this study seems to negate claims that media violence inspires real-world violence, its
50 results remain "suggestive." It seems that even the most rigorous studies remain riddled with ambiguities.
    A 2014 study in *Journal of Communication*, "Does Media Violence Predict Societal Violence?
55 It Depends on What You Look at and When," builds on prior research to look closer at media portrayals of violence and rates of violent behavior. The research, by Christopher J. Ferguson of Stetson University, had two parts:
60 The first measured the frequency and graphicness of violence in movies between 1920 and 2005 and compared it to homicide rates, median household income, policing, population density, youth population and GDP over the same period. The
65 second part looked at the correlation between the consumption of violent video games and youth behavior from 1996 to 2011.
    "Results from the two studies suggest that socialization models of media violence
70 may be inadequate to our understanding of the interaction between media and consumer behavior at least in regard to serious violence," Ferguson concludes. Given that effects on individual users may differ widely, Ferguson
75 suggests that policy discussion should be more focused on "more pressing" issues that influence violence in society such as poverty or mental health.
    With this last statement, Ferguson exposes
80 the debate over the effects of violent media on real-world violence for what it is: a red herring. Blaming violent media for acts of real-world violence has obvious appeal—it invites the simple solution of banning or heavily regulating
85 depictions of violence. Yet while simple solutions may appeal to much of the public, they do little to nothing to address the complex and sensitive societal issues addressed by Ferguson.

★

"Violent media and real-world behavior: Historical data and recent trends," is licensed under CC BY 4.0. For more information, see page 511.

11

Paragraph 1 (lines 1 – 17) primarily contrasts the *Grand Theft Auto* series'

A) cartoonish graphics with its shockingly obscene themes.
B) popularity with the controversy that it has inspired.
C) financial success with its critical failure.
D) relentless violence with its overall positive message.

12

As used in line 20, "ambivalent" most nearly means

A) uninformed.
B) incomplete.
C) uncertain.
D) disparaging.

13

The author mentions "millions of law-abiding Americans" in line 36 primarily to

A) expand the scope of the passage from the individual to the societal.
B) explain which group is most affected by depictions of violence in media.
C) reinforce her main argument regarding depictions of violence in media.
D) undermine a connection made in the previous sentence.

14

As used in line 49, "inspires" most nearly means

A) engenders.
B) incentivizes.
C) affects.
D) galvanizes.

15

Ferguson's study (lines 53 – 67) differs from the study outlined in lines 40 – 52 in that it

A) focuses specifically on the effects of violent media on youth behavior.
B) draws more definitive conclusions regarding the link between violent media and real-world violence.
C) considers how social and economic factors may influence violent behavior.
D) fails to account for unreported violent crimes.

16

In lines 77 – 78, the author uses "poverty" and "mental health" as examples of

A) personal factors that contribute to widespread societal paranoia.
B) social issues that are traditionally studied alongside the effects of violent media.
C) issues that may be caused by exposure to violent media.
D) societal factors that impact violent crime rates.

17

The author strongly implies that "a red herring" (line 81) is

A) a complex issue that lacks a single discernible cause or factor.
B) something that distracts from a more pressing or relevant issue.
C) a missing piece of information required for forming a conclusion.
D) an issue that has been ignored by the media.

18

Which choice best summarizes Ferguson's stance on studying the effects of violent media?

A) Lines 48 – 50 ("Although...'suggestive'")
B) Lines 64 – 67 ("The second...2011")
C) Lines 75 – 78 ("policy...mental health")
D) Lines 82 – 83 ("Blaming...appeal")

19

It can reasonably be inferred that the author would react to claims that media violence inspires real-world violence with

A) resignation.
B) skepticism.
C) justified resentment.
D) enthusiastic agreement.

20

Which choice provides the best evidence for the answer to the previous question?

A) Lines 18 – 20 ("As indicated...media")
B) Lines 36 – 39 ("Clearly...so easily")
C) Lines 53 – 58 ("A 2014...behavior")
D) Lines 82 – 83 ("Blaming...appeal")

Refer to the passage and supplementary material below to answer questions 21 – 32.

This passage is adapted from John Munro, *The Story of Electricity*, originally published in 1915.

line   A schoolboy who rubs a stick of sealing wax on the sleeve of his jacket, then holds it over dusty shreds or bits of straw to see them fly up and cling to the wax, repeats without knowing
5   it the fundamental experiment of electricity. In rubbing the wax on his coat, he has electrified it, and the dry dust or bits of wool are attracted to it by reason of a mysterious process which is called "induction."
10   Electricity, like fire, was probably discovered by some primeval savage. According to Humboldt*, the Indians of the Orinoco sometimes amuse themselves by rubbing certain beans to make them attract wisps of the wild cotton, and
15 the custom is doubtless very old. Certainly the ancient Greeks knew that a piece of amber had when rubbed the property of attracting light bodies. Thales of Miletus*, wisest of the Seven Sages, and father of Greek philosophy, explained
20 this curious effect by the presence of a "soul" in the amber, whatever he meant by that. Thales flourished 600 years before the Christian era….
    Amber, the fossil resin of a pine tree, was found in Sicily, the shores of the Baltic, and other
25 parts of Europe. It was a precious stone then as now, and an article of trade with the Phoenicians, those early merchants of the Mediterranean. The attractive power might enhance the value of the gem in the eyes of the superstitious ancients, but
30 they do not seem to have investigated it, and beyond the speculation of Thales, they have told us nothing more about it.
    Towards the end of the sixteenth century Dr. Gilbert of Colchester, physician to Queen
35 Elizabeth, made this property the subject of experiment, and showed that, far from being peculiar to amber, it was possessed by Sulphur, wax, glass, and many other bodies which he called electrics, from the Greek word *elektron*,
40 signifying amber. This great discovery was the starting-point of the modern science of electricity. That feeble and mysterious force which had been the wonder of the simple and the amusement of the vain could not be slighted any longer as
45 a curious freak of nature, but assuredly none dreamt that a day was dawning in which it would transform the world.
    Otto von Guericke, burgomaster of Magdeburg, was the first to invent a machine for
50 exciting the electric power in larger quantities by simply turning a ball of Sulphur between the bare hands. Improved by Sir Isaac Newton and others, who employed glass rubbed with silk, it created sparks several inches long. The ordinary frictional
55 machine is now made with a disc of plate glass mounted on a spindle and turned by hand…. Machines of this sort have been made with plates 7 feet in diameter, and yielding sparks nearly 2 feet long.

60 The properties of the "electric fire," as it was now called, were chiefly investigated by du Fay*. To refine on the primitive experiment let us replace the shreds by a pithball hung from a support by a silk thread. If we rub the glass rod
65 vigorously with a silk handkerchief and hold it near, the ball will fly toward the rod. Similarly we may rub a stick of sealing wax, a bar of Sulphur, indeed, a great variety of substances, and by this easy test we shall find them electrified. Glass
70 rubbed with glass will not show any sign of electrification, nor will wax rubbed on wax; but when the rubber is of a different material to the thing rubbed, we shall find, on using proper precautions, that electricity is developed. In fact,
75 the property which was once thought peculiar to amber is found to belong to all bodies. The electricity thus produced is termed frictional electricity. Of course there are some materials, such as amber, glass, and wax, which display
80 the effect much better than others, and hence its original discovery.

* *Alexander von Humboldt: a 19th century German biologist*

* *Thales of Miletus: a seventh century BCE Greek philosopher*

* *Charles du Fay: an 18th century French chemist*

Triboelectric Series

Interpreting this chart: *The following chart shows what type of charge (positive or negative) a material acquires when touched to an oppositely charged material. The farther away two materials are from each other in the chart, the greater the charge transferred.*

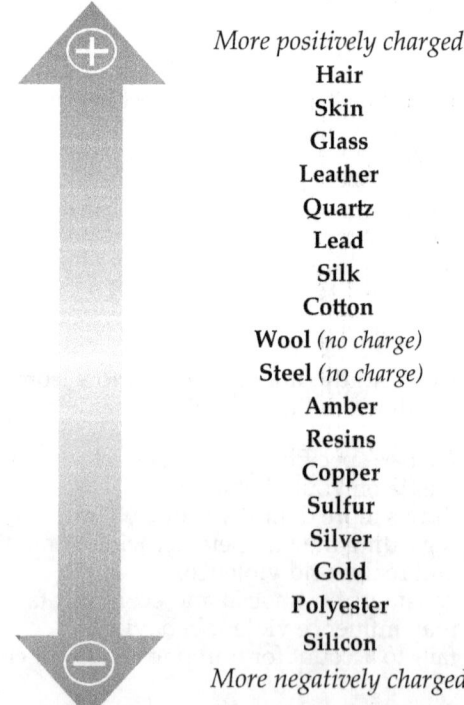

More positively charged
Hair
Skin
Glass
Leather
Quartz
Lead
Silk
Cotton
Wool *(no charge)*
Steel *(no charge)*
Amber
Resins
Copper
Sulfur
Silver
Gold
Polyester
Silicon
More negatively charged

21
Paragraph 1 (lines 1 – 9) can best be described as a

A) personal reflection.
B) startling statistic.
C) rhetorical question.
D) hypothetical occurrence.

22
The passage's structure is best characterized as

A) a critical study on a scientific phenomenon.
B) a chronological-historical account.
C) a cause and effect analysis.
D) a personal narrative.

23
The author probably puts the term "soul" in quotes (line 20) in order to

A) emphasize the importance of the term.
B) indicate that he is quoting from an ancient source that he holds in high regard.
C) suggest his skepticism regarding Thales of Miletus' conclusion.
D) imply that he is providing a simplified explanation of Thales of Miletus' conclusion.

24
As used in line 28, "attractive power" most nearly means

A) scientific value.
B) electrical properties.
C) financial worth.
D) pleasing appearance.

25
As used in line 44, "slighted" most nearly means

A) offended.
B) realized.
C) denied.
D) dismissed.

26
The passage strongly suggests that Dr. Gilbert of Colchester

A) was among the first to formally investigate the properties of electricity.
B) built on the experiments conducted by past academics, such as Thales of Miletus.
C) disproved many previously existing assumptions regarding electricity.
D) was inspired by the research of Otto von Guericke to investigate electricity.

27
Which choices provides the best evidence for the answer to the previous question?

A) Lines 5 – 9 ("In rubbing…electricity")
B) Lines 40 – 41 ("This great…electricity")
C) Lines 45 – 47 ("but assuredly…the world")
D) Lines 48 – 52 ("Otto…hands")

28
According to the passage, Otto von Guericke's invention was

A) funded by Queen Elizabeth.
B) begun by Dr. Gilbert of Colchester.
C) refined by Sir Isaac Newton.
D) perfected by Charles du Fay.

29
Which choice best summarizes the discovery made by Charles du Fay?

A) Soft materials electrify better than do hard materials.
B) The properties of electrification are equal in all substances.
C) Like materials are electrified when they are rubbed together.
D) Any material, when rubbed against a different material, can become electrified.

30
Which choice provides the best evidence for the answer to the previous question?

A) Lines 66 – 69 ("Similarly…electrified")
B) Lines 69 – 71 ("Glass…on wax")
C) Lines 72 – 74 ("when the…developed")
D) Lines 78 – 81 ("Of course…discovery")

31
According to the chart, rubbing which two materials together would create the strongest charge?

A) Steel rubbed against hair
B) Leather rubbed against quartz
C) Gold rubbed against skin
D) Silicon rubbed on silk

32
Using the chart, it can be inferred that "turning a ball of Sulphur between the bare hands" (lines 51 – 52) produces frictional electricity because

A) sulfur's negative charge cancels out skin's positive charge.
B) sulfur and skin acquire opposite charges when rubbed together.
C) skin acquires a stronger charge than any material other than hair.
D) sulfur acquires a strong charge when touched to any material.

Refer to the passage below to answer questions 33 – 42.

This passage is adapted from Edward Gibbon, *The History of the Decline and Fall of the Roman Empire*, originally published in 1836.

line
Agriculture is the foundation of manufactures; since the productions of nature are the materials of art. Under the Roman empire, the labor of an industrious and ingenious people was
5 variously, but incessantly, employed in the service of the rich. In their dress, their table, their houses, and their furniture, the favorites of fortune united every refinement of conveniency, of elegance, and of splendor, whatever could soothe their pride or
10 gratify their sensuality. Such refinements, under the odious name of luxury, have been severely arraigned by the moralists of every age; and it might perhaps be more conducive to the virtue, as well as happiness, of mankind, if all possessed
15 the necessaries, and none the superfluities, of life. But in the present imperfect condition of society, luxury, though it may proceed from vice or folly, seems to be the only means that can correct the unequal distribution of property.
20 The diligent mechanic, and the skillful artist, who have obtained no share in the division of the earth, receive a voluntary tax from the possessors of land; and the latter are prompted, by a sense of interest, to improve those estates, with whose
25 produce they may purchase additional pleasures. This operation, the particular effects of which are felt in every society, acted with much more diffusive energy in the Roman world. The provinces would soon have been exhausted of
30 their wealth, if the manufactures and commerce of luxury had not insensibly restored to the industrious subjects the sums which were exacted from them by the arms and authority of Rome. As long as the circulation was confined within the
35 bounds of the empire, it impressed the political machine with a new degree of activity, and its consequences, sometimes beneficial, could never become pernicious.
    But it is no easy task to confine luxury
40 within the limits of an empire. The most remote countries of the ancient world were ransacked to supply the pomp and delicacy of Rome. The forests of Scythia afforded some valuable furs. Amber was brought over land from the shores of
45 the Baltic to the Danube; and the barbarians were astonished at the price which they received in exchange for so useless a commodity. There was a considerable demand for Babylonian carpets, and other manufactures of the East; but the most
50 important and unpopular branch of foreign trade was carried on with Arabia and India. Every year, about the time of the summer solstice, a fleet of a hundred and twenty vessels sailed from Myos-hormos, a port of Egypt, on the Red Sea.
55 By the periodical assistance of the monsoons, they traversed the ocean in about forty days. The coast of Malabar, or the island of Ceylon, was the usual term of their navigation, and it was in those markets that the merchants from the more remote
60 countries of Asia expected their arrival.
    The return of the fleet of Egypt was fixed to the months of December or January; and as soon as their rich cargo had been transported on the backs of camels, from the Red Sea to the Nile, and
65 had descended that river as far as Alexandria, it was poured, without delay, into the capital of the empire. The objects of oriental traffic were splendid and trifling; silk, a pound of which was esteemed not inferior in value to a pound of gold;
70 precious stones, among which the pearl claimed the first rank after the diamond, and a variety of aromatics, that were consumed in religious worship and the pomp of funerals.
    The labor and risk of the voyage was
75 rewarded with almost incredible profit; but the profit was made upon Roman subjects, and a few individuals were enriched at the expense of the public. As the natives of Arabia and India were contented with the productions and
80 manufactures of their own country, silver, on the side of the Romans, was the principal, if not the only instrument of commerce. It was a complaint worthy of the gravity of the senate, that, in the purchase of female ornaments, the
85 wealth of the state was irrecoverably given away to foreign and hostile nations. The annual loss is computed, by a writer of an inquisitive but censorious temper, at upwards of eight hundred thousand pounds sterling. Such was the style of
90 discontent, brooding over the dark prospect of approaching poverty. And yet, if we compare the proportion between gold and silver, as it stood in the time of Pliny, and as it was fixed in the reign of Constantine, we shall discover within that
95 period a very considerable increase. There is not the least reason to suppose that gold was become more scarce; it is therefore evident that silver was grown more common; that whatever might be the amount of the Indian and Arabian exports,
100 they were far from exhausting the wealth of the Roman world; and that the produce of the mines abundantly supplied the demands of commerce.

33

The author regards luxury and decadence as

A) fascinating and inevitable.
B) distasteful but necessary.
C) reprehensible and outdated.
D) socially significant but politically problematic.

34

As used in line 26, "operation" most nearly means

A) maneuver.
B) performance.
C) campaign.
D) process.

35

As used in line 29, "exhausted" most nearly means

A) depleted.
B) consumed.
C) overworked.
D) fatigued.

36

Paragraph 2 (lines 20 – 38) describes a mutually beneficial relationship between

A) the Roman empire and its neighbors.
B) mechanics and artists.
C) farmers and aristocrats.
D) artisans and landowners.

37

Beginning in paragraph 3 (lines 39 – 60), the author suggests that Roman trade with Arabia and India

A) provided valuable luxury goods but was extremely time-consuming and dangerous.
B) introduced exotic foods to the Roman world but was very expensive to fund.
C) allowed Roman merchants to travel extensively but was not particularly profitable.
D) strengthened Rome's political ties but required the efforts of many merchants.

38

Which choice provides the best evidence for the answer to the previous question?

A) Lines 51 – 54 ("Every year…Myos-hormos")
B) Lines 58 – 60 ("it was…their arrival")
C) Lines 67 – 69 ("The objects…of gold")
D) Lines 74 – 75 ("The labor…profit")

39

In line 84, the phrase "female ornaments" most nearly refers to

A) materials used during religious ceremonies and funerals.
B) luxury goods imported from Arabia and India.
C) small, decorative objects crafted by Roman women.
D) the inferior manufactured products created by non-Roman craftspeople.

40

The author references "Pliny" (line 93) and "Constantine" (line 94) primarily to

A) provide examples of frugal Roman leaders.
B) name two Romans who expanded the trade of gold and silver.
C) serve as chronological points of reference.
D) compare their economic successes and failures.

41

According to the passage, the primary complaint that Romans had against Roman trade and commerce was that

A) valuable resources were traded for expensive objects of little to no utility.
B) the purchase of luxury goods from Arabia and India depleted Roman gold stores.
C) overseas trade journeys were excessively costly and dangerous.
D) Roman manufacturers and artisans were overtaxed in order to fund commerce.

42

Which choice provides the best evidence for the answer to the previous question?

A) Lines 20 – 23 ("The diligent…land")
B) Lines 49 – 51 ("the most…India")
C) Lines 67 – 68 ("The objects…trifling")
D) Lines 82 – 86 ("It was…nations")

Refer to the passage pair below for questions 43 – 52.

Passage 1 is excerpted from a press release by the United Nations (UN) News Centre, "Knowledge Saves Lives, UN Stresses on International Day for Disaster Reduction," published on October 13, 2015. Passage 2 is from Carolina T. de Freitas, Glenn H. Shepard, Jr, and Maria T. F. Piedade, "The Floating Forest: Traditional Knowledge and Use of *Matupá* Vegetation Islands by Riverine Peoples of the Central Amazon," published in PLoS ONE on April 2, 2015.

Passage 1

United Nations Secretary General Ban Ki-moon today stressed the "indispensable" power of traditional, indigenous and local knowledge in his message on this year's observance of the
5   International Day for Disaster Reduction.
    "Traditional and indigenous knowledge is the indispensable information base for many societies seeking to live in harmony with nature and adapt to disruptive weather events, a
10 warming globe and rising seas," Mr. Ban said in his message on the International Day.
    The Secretary-General recalled a conversation he had earlier in the year with the President of Vanuatu at the opening of the
15 Third UN World Conference on Disaster Risk Reduction in Sendai, Japan. Vanuatu was at that time being hit hard by Cyclone Pam.
    "The force of the storm led to expectations that there would be great loss of life.
20 Thankfully, this was not the case. One reason was that cyclone shelters built in the traditional style from local materials saved many lives," explained Mr. Ban.
    "Resilience is the sum of many such acts of
25 disaster risk reduction at the local level," said the UN chief, noting in another example that the low-tech local knowledge in Cameroon passed down from generation to generation, helped farmers to cope with drought and protect their
30 crops from pests.
    Based on the impacts of climate changes in the Arctic, which can expand to all humanity, the Secretary-General said: "Local knowledge of the impacts of urbanization, population
35 growth, eco-system decline and greenhouse gas emissions is especially important in an era when more and more disasters are climate- and weather-related."
    The Sendai Framework for Disaster
40 Risk Reduction, said the Secretary-General, underlines how traditional knowledge can complement scientific knowledge in disaster risk management.
    He said that building resilience to disasters
45 is also a key feature of the newly adopted Sustainable Development Goals, the framework that will guide U.N. efforts to end poverty and promote shared prosperity on a healthy planet by 2030.

Passage 2

50 *Matupá* is a local term in the Brazilian Amazon for free-floating islands of vegetation growing on blocks of soil that can be as much as 3 meters thick, in sizes ranging from a few square meters to several hectares, and supporting a variety of plant
55 communities from aquatic herbs to shrubs and trees. They are found in *várzea* lakes distributed along the floodplains of white-water river systems rich in nutrients and sediments. *Matupás* are formed through a series of natural successional
60 stages beginning with the agglomeration of aquatic and semi-aquatic plants, and the consequent accumulation of organic substrate where free-standing herbs, shrubs and even trees can later grow. Larger, thicker *matupás* with substantial
65 vegetation are sturdy enough for people to walk on.
    Despite anecdotal references in scientific literature to *matupás* as nesting ground for *caimans* and shelter for manatees, there is exceedingly
70 little published information on their ecological characteristics and relevance. Most of what is currently known about *matupás* is found in just two scientific publications, both concerning flooded environments generally. Nonetheless, during
75 exploratory research in the Amanã Sustainable Development Reserve (RDSA; central Brazilian Amazon), we realized that local people made use of *matupás* both for fishing and agriculture, and appeared to have detailed knowledge about the
80 ecology of these floating forest islands.
    Traditional ecological knowledge can provide insights for studying ecological systems that are important to the livelihoods of local populations. Such knowledge accumulates from generation
85 to generation through daily interactions with the environment and can be especially useful for understanding ecological processes that occur at temporal or spatial scales not easily observed by conventional scientific research.
90 Studies of traditional ecological knowledge first emerged within the fields of ethnobotany and ethnobiology, eventually developing into an independent field called ethnoecology. Recently, landscape ethnoecology has emerged as a
95 multidisciplinary paradigm for understanding traditional knowledge of the environment at broad spatial and temporal scales.
    Drawing on these various methodological and theoretical advances, we expected that
100 traditional people living near *matupás* could help us better understand the ecology of these poorly studied floating islands, especially regarding those aspects that require long-term field observation. By conducting interviews with traditional people
105 of the RDSA, we sought to obtain information about how *matupás* are formed; what conditions contribute to their occurrence in some places but not others; what plants and animals occur on them; and what uses, ecological function and
110 other significance or importance they have in local peoples' eyes.

Passage 2 is licensed under CC BY 4.0. For more information, see page 511.

43
The author of Passage 1 most likely uses the extended quotation in lines 18 – 23 to

A) introduce a view that contrasts with the author's.
B) prove that the information is true.
C) characterize the speaker as a disaster-relief expert.
D) emphasize the passage's main focus with a supporting example.

44
In Passage 1, the U.N. Secretary-General implies that

A) local knowledge must be combined with modern technology to improve disaster reduction.
B) environmental changes are making traditional knowledge increasingly essential.
C) the use of local knowledge renders modern disaster reduction measures ineffective.
D) local knowledge often helps improve the health of the surrounding ecosystems.

45
Which choice provides the best evidence for the answer to the previous question?

A) Lines 20 – 22 ("'One reason...lives'")
B) Lines 24 – 25 ("'Resilience...local level'")
C) Lines 33 – 38 ("'Local...weather-related'")
D) Lines 44 – 49 ("He said...2030")

46
As used in line 59, "successional" most nearly means

A) elevated.
B) inherited.
C) cyclical.
D) sequential.

47
Passage 2 is structured as

A) an introduction to an ethnoecological research project.
B) a recap of an ethnoecological research team's recent findings.
C) an appeal for other cultures to adapt traditional Amazonian fishing practices.
D) a general survey of traditional customs and practices in the Brazilian Amazon.

48
The authors of Passage 2 strongly suggest that traditional knowledge

A) exists to some extent in virtually every society.
B) may be able to explain the protracted processes that shape an environment.
C) is often used by native people to alter a region's ecological systems.
D) often provides more information to ethnoecologists than formal experiments do.

49
Which choice provides the best evidence for the answer to the previous question?

A) Lines 67 – 71 ("Despite...relevance")
B) Lines 74 – 78 ("during...agriculture")
C) Lines 84 – 89 ("Such knowledge...research")
D) Lines 99 – 103 ("we expected...observation")

50
The main purpose of both passages is to

A) discuss the role of local and traditional knowledge in disaster reduction.
B) explore how local and traditional knowledge has been incorporated into modern practices.
C) update local and traditional knowledge using modern scientific research.
D) compile and categorize local and traditional knowledge from several cultures.

51
It can reasonably be inferred that the authors of both passages would advocate for

A) more frequent interactions between traditional societies from different regions.
B) an abandonment of all modern practices in favor of local and traditional ones.
C) more government funding for disaster reduction.
D) more academic attention towards local and traditional knowledge.

52
Which choice best describes the relationship between the two passages?

A) One describes policy while the other describes academic methodology.
B) Each comes to a different conclusion regarding how to gather local and traditional knowledge.
C) One praises local knowledge while the other approaches it with skepticism.
D) One focuses on general and the other on specific knowledge.

Writing & Language Test 5
35 MINUTES, 44 QUESTIONS

Turn to Section 2 of your answer sheet to answer the questions in this section.

DIRECTIONS

Each of the following passages is accompanied by approximately 11 questions. Some questions will require you to revise the passages in order to improve coherence and clarity. Other questions will require you to correct grammatical errors. Passages may be accompanied by graphs, charts, or tables that you must consider when making revisions. For most questions, you may select the "NO CHANGE" option if you believe that portion of the passage is clear, concise, and grammatically correct as is.

Within the passages, highlighted numbers followed by underlined text indicate which part of the text corresponds with each question. Bracketed numbers [1] indicate sentence number. These bracketed numbers are only relevant to problems that require you to add or rearrange sentences in a paragraph.

Questions 1-11 are based on the following passage.

Writing from Experience

The 18th- and 19th-century Industrial Revolution in Great Britain created unprecedented opportunities for acquiring wealth. People **1** eagerly scrambled to open factories and manufacture products that they could sell at a profit. But author Charles Dickens (1812 – 1870) spent his literary career trying to illuminate the dark side of that scrambling.

Dickens **2** published 15 novels: *Oliver Twist, A Christmas Carol*, and *Great Expectations*. His work inspired social reform because he often depicted young people caught in desperate circumstances due to poverty and social class. The youths are innocent and naïve, so they are easily exploited by more self-serving characters. **3** Dickens published his novels one segment at a time in newspapers, keeping readers on pins and needles about the fates of the young characters. Few people knew at the time that Dickens identified with miserable children because he **4** was one of them.

1

Which choice most effectively sets up the contrasting viewpoints on the Industrial Revolution presented in the paragraph?

A) NO CHANGE
B) dutifully
C) cautiously
D) grudgingly

2

A) NO CHANGE
B) published 15 novels;
C) published 15 novels, including
D) published 15 novels such as

3

At this point, the author is considering adding the following information.

> For example, *Oliver Twist* follows the story of a young orphan who falls into the hands of murderous thieves.

Should the writer make this addition here?

A) Yes, because it provides a specific example that supports the previous statement.
B) Yes, because it explains the basic plot of one of Dickens' most important novels.
C) No, because it adds information that is not relevant to the paragraph's claim.
D) No, because it fails to address the plots of the other novels mentioned earlier.

4

A) NO CHANGE
B) was being
C) has been
D) had been

Charles was the second of eight children born to a family that lived comfortably in the English countryside. But when Charles was 10, his father, a British Navy clerk, was transferred to [5] London. Where the family began sliding into debt. They gradually sold [6] they're treasured books there, and most other belongings as well.

Recognizing their plight, a cousin [7] offered to employ Charles in a shoe-polish factory. At the time, it was quite normal for poor children to spend their days toiling in factories. Charles' parents accepted the offer on his behalf. Suddenly, Charles found himself working six days a week, morning till night, pasting labels on bottles of shoe polish. [8] The factory was in an old house on a riverbank, decaying and full of rats. Charles was in shock; many years later, he wrote that he still found it hard to believe that no relative or family friend stepped forward to provide any alternative.

Charles' father was soon thrown into a debtor's prison, a common practice at the time. [9] As well, Charles' mother gave up their home and moved into the prison, and his siblings. Charles had to lodge with an acquaintance. In the evenings he wandered about London, hungry, lonely, and shabby. He said later that he could have easily become a "little robber" at that point.

Then his luck took yet another turn. Charles' father came into an inheritance and was able to pay off his debts and move his family out of debtors' prison. He arranged for Charles to quit working and go back to school. Charles' mother [10] declined; she hated to see him give up the factory job. To Charles, his mother's stance seemed yet another shocking betrayal from which he never recovered. His feeling of emotional abandonment and the sudden changes in his fortunes [11] stayed with him even after he married and had 10 children of his own.

---------- ★ ----------

[5]

A) NO CHANGE
B) London, where
C) London, when
D) London; when

[6]

A) NO CHANGE
B) there treasured books there,
C) their treasured books they're
D) their treasured books there,

[7]

At this point, the writer is considering adding the following information.

   by marriage who had once lived with the family

Should the writer make this addition here?

A) Yes, because it improves the logical sequence of events in the paragraph.
B) Yes, because it provides a necessary context for the information that follows.
C) No, because it fails to explain the quality of the family's relationship with the cousin.
D) No, because it blurs the focus of the paragraph by focusing on irrelevant details.

[8]

A) NO CHANGE
B) The factory, an old house on a riverbank, was decaying and full of rats.
C) The factory was an old house, on a riverbank, and was decaying and full of rats.
D) The factory was in an old house on a riverbank. It was decaying and full of rats.

[9]

A) NO CHANGE
B) Into the prison moved Charles' mother and siblings as well, who gave up their home.
C) Charles' mother and siblings gave up their home and moved into the prison as well.
D) Giving up their home, moving into the prison as well, were Charles' mother and siblings.

[10]

A) NO CHANGE
B) withstood;
C) objected;
D) accepted;

[11]

Which choice best concludes the passage by restating the main claim in the introduction?

A) NO CHANGE
B) informed his writing for the rest of his life.
C) made him an insecure person in adulthood.
D) ironically led him to acquire wealth as a writer.

Questions 12-22 are based on the following passage.

Current Events

California has a history of long droughts followed by periods of severe flooding. In an attempt to manage the state's water budget, meteorologists have examined many factors that contribute to rainfall in California. [12] Among these, the behaviors of atmospheric rivers can greatly affect the state's variable rainfall.

An atmospheric river is a relatively thin strip of concentrated water vapor in the air. Atmospheric rivers carry water vapor out of the tropics in huge quantities—one atmospheric river can contain as much water as the Amazon River. When the system reaches [13] land it cools and the water vapor condenses to rain or snow. [14] Atmospheric rivers contain a large volume of water. These events often cause flooding and landslides.

However, the amount of water in an atmospheric river varies greatly, as does the amount of rainfall it provides. [15] Therefore, a majority of California's rainfall comes directly from atmospheric rivers; unfortunately, the rainfall from these rivers is inconsistent, sometimes [16] it leaving California in a long-term drought, and flooding the parched state when storms finally arrive. Predicting the frequency and strength of atmospheric rivers and ensuing storms in any given year can be difficult. This makes it tough for the state to manage [17] it's water resources and increases the risk for droughts and floods.

[12]

Which of the following provides the best introduction to the topic of the passage?

A) NO CHANGE
B) The weather pattern known as El Niño is responsible for the unpredictable storms that flood the state each year.
C) Researchers have discovered that tidal patterns can influence the amount of rain the state receives.
D) Global warming has reduced the total amount of rainfall in California while increasing the number of extreme flooding events.

[13]

A) NO CHANGE
B) land, it cools
C) land it cools,
D) land, it cools,

[14]

Which choice provides the best combination of the two underlined sentences?

A) Although atmospheric rivers often cause flooding and landslides, they typically contain a large volume of water.
B) Because of the large volume of water contained in one atmospheric river, these phenomena often cause flooding and landslides.
C) With a large volume of water typically contained in one atmospheric river, these phenomena are to blame for the majority of floods and landslides.
D) The number of floods and landslides caused by atmospheric rivers has led researchers to believe they contain a large volume of water.

[15]

A) NO CHANGE
B) In addition,
C) For example,
D) Next,

[16]

A) NO CHANGE
B) it leaves
C) leaving
D) they leave

[17]

A) NO CHANGE
B) its
C) their
D) there

California is not the only place to experience heavy rainfall due to atmospheric rivers. In fact, a handful of these bands exist around the globe at any given time. Though [18] small in number, atmospheric rivers contain nearly 90 percent of Earth's total water vapor. Concentrated over a small area, this moisture is capable of producing severe storms, primarily in coastal regions. In addition to the Western United States, Western Europe and parts of West Africa are also particularly [19] vulnerable to these weather patterns.

An example of a well-known atmospheric river is a so-called "Pineapple Express." This system brings moisture from Hawaii to the west coast of the United States. Pineapple Express weather patterns are responsible for many major floods in California and the Pacific Northwest. They also [20] result from the Madden-Julian oscillation and have even contributed to severe rainstorms in Alaska.

Despite the importance of atmospheric rivers in the global water [21] cycle, meteorologists have much to learn about their formation. By understanding the processes that cause atmospheric rivers, scientists may be better able to predict storms and major flooding events. Though consistent rainfall will never likely be a reality for California, a greater understanding of [22] those phenomena will make it easier for the state to manage its water supply.

---- ★ ----

18

A) NO CHANGE
B) few
C) little
D) diminutive

19

A) NO CHANGE
B) weak
C) liable
D) influential

20

Which choice provides information that is most consistent in style and content with the information about Alaska?

A) NO CHANGE
B) are sometimes referred to a Chinook Wind in the Pacific Northwest
C) provide much of the snowfall for the Sierra Nevadas
D) have caused many power outages in California

21

A) NO CHANGE
B) cycle;
C) cycle:
D) cycle—

22

A) NO CHANGE
B) them
C) that
D) these

Questions 23-33 are based on the following passage.

Jobs in Quiet Places

[23] Do the benefits of moving to the wilderness outweigh the risks? Living amidst natural beauty, far from traffic jams and office cubicles, may seem an unrealistic goal. But it is now more realistic than ever, as the Internet has increased access to information about jobs in far-flung places. [24] At the same time, the Internet has also increased competition for such jobs.

Perhaps the most extreme example occurred in 2009, when an Australian state tourism agency [25] listed an opening for a temporary caretaker on an island in the Great Barrier Reef. The listing called the caretaker/blogger position "The Best Job in the World." For a salary of $134,000 over six months, the duties entailed living in a villa on a tropical island and [26] to upload a few blogs about it. Simply intending to draw attention to the islands, the travel agency [27] bemoaned beaches. On the first day, so many people submitted applications for the job that the agency's website crashed.

23

Which choice provides the most effective introduction to the passage?

A) NO CHANGE
B) Some people may dream of becoming closer to nature with a wistful sigh.
C) Naomi Judd once said, "solitude is creativity's best friend."
D) Asphalt freeways are an indispensable part of modern life, as are offices.

24

A) NO CHANGE
B) As always,
C) Of more concern,
D) Certainly,

25

A) NO CHANGE
B) advertised for someone to temporarily take care of an island in the Great Barrier Reef.
C) listed a job that was taking care of a Great Barrier Reef island temporarily.
D) sought a temporary caretaker for a Great Barrier Reef island.

26

A) NO CHANGE
B) blog
C) report
D) posting

27

Which choice most effectively conveys the idea that the job listing was meant to advertise the islands?

A) NO CHANGE
B) emphasized
C) undermined
D) mentioned

[28] The person who finally got the job was British adventurer Ben Southall. He beat out 34,000 other applicants from across the globe. Southall relished the work, and blogged regularly about his adventures jet-skiing and diving. He admitted that the sun-drenched days away from civilization were [29] blissful. At one point when he was in the sea, he was stung by an Irukandji, a tiny jellyfish whose sting can be lethal. Southall had access to medical care and quickly recovered, but the incident was a reminder that living in remote areas requires extra attention to safety.

While "The Best Job in the World" was primarily a publicity stunt, island-caretaker jobs do exist. An example would be a wealthy family buying a small tropical island for private vacations. The family [30] needs to hire someone to live on the island year-round to maintain the buildings and grounds. It may sound like a life in paradise, but ironically, island caretakers may need plenty of vacation time off the island.

Tranquility does not have to mean complete isolation; there are countless places in the world where small groups of people live ordinary lives in extraordinary settings. Remote communities often need to recruit newcomers to fill jobs. The Scottish island of Muck is a good example. [31] Noted for its seal and porpoise populations as well as its natural beauty, the island is home to about 30 people, most of whom raise sheep and cattle. When the islanders needed a new teacher for the eight children residing on the [32] island, they used social media to get the word out. The posting cheerfully acknowledged Muck's isolation and fierce weather; it stipulated that applicants should have "a love of the outdoors and good waterproofs." The community was shocked when [33] it received hundreds of applications from teachers who said they would love to try living on Muck.

★

---

[28]

Which choice most effectively combines the underlined sentences?

A) Getting the job at last was Ben Southall, a British adventurer, from among 34,000 applicants.
B) British adventurer Ben Southall eventually beat out 34,000 other applicants to get the job.
C) Thirty-four thousand other applicants were eventually beat out for the job by British adventurer Ben Southall.
D) Finally beating out 34,000 other applicants, the person who got the job was British adventurer Ben Southall.

[29]

Which choice most effectively links the sentence to the information that follows in the passage?

A) NO CHANGE
B) ominously dangerous.
C) not without trade-offs.
D) costly.

[30]

A) NO CHANGE
B) always needed
C) would need
D) has a need

[31]

Which choice most effectively establishes Muck as an extraordinary setting, as implied earlier in the passage?

A) NO CHANGE
B) Likely named after the Gaelic word for "porpoise,"
C) Serviced by only two ferries,
D) Owned by the MacEwen family since 1896,

[32]

A) NO CHANGE
B) island
C) island:
D) island, and

[33]

A) NO CHANGE
B) one
C) they
D) their

Questions 34-44 are based on the following passage.

Culture Shock

Many people feel anxious when they find themselves in an unfamiliar environment and culture. [34] The degree of stress from totally new surroundings has been suggested by the metaphor of the "fish out of water." Even if one has sought the move and prepared for it, some degree of shock—"culture shock"—is nearly unavoidable.

In 1954, cultural anthropologist Kalervo Oberg famously [35] shared his personal insights into culture shock. Oberg was invited to speak to a group of women from English-speaking countries who were living in Rio de Janeiro, Brazil. Based on his own lifetime of experience adjusting to [36] different cultures, Oberg offered empathy, humor, and [37] advise. His speech was later widely disseminated.

Oberg said that most people find a new place and culture fascinating initially. They revel in new foods, drinks, and customs, and they are "shown the show places." Visitors may stay at [38] hotels, where staff members speak their language and are anxious to please them.

Enthusiasm quickly dissipates, however, with the realities of daily life in a foreign place. Housing and transportation may be costly or uncomfortable, [39] unlikeable food may sit on the table, the weather may be unbearable, and so on.

34

A) NO CHANGE
B) The metaphor of the "fish out of water" —feeling shocked and unable to breathe— conveys the feeling.
C) In totally new surroundings, the intensity of the feeling is suggested by the metaphor of the "fish out of water."
D) A degree of stress, to the point of feeling breathless, was summed up as "fish out of water."

35

Which choice provides the most appropriate introduction to the paragraph?

A) NO CHANGE
B) gave a fiery speech on
C) provided conclusions based on research about
D) argued for a wider definition of

36

A) NO CHANGE
B) an assortment of different
C) a varied assortment of
D) a myriad of different

37

A) NO CHANGE
B) advice
C) adverse
D) adversity

38

A) NO CHANGE
B) hotels:
C) hotels—
D) hotels

39

Which choice best maintains the pattern already established in the sentence?

A) NO CHANGE
B) you might not like the food,
C) the food may be tiresome on a daily basis,
D) hosts may be serving inedible dishes,

40 Whatever the discomforts, native inhabitants are most likely indifferent to them. This only adds to newcomers' sense of frustration. Facing daily hassles is made even more difficult when newcomers become emotionally exhausted trying to understand the people around them. Social interactions are full of mysterious new "cues" such as facial expressions, hesitations, or **41** words. Cultures may have assumptions about "good manners," resulting in occasional awkwardness or even hurt feelings.

During the alienating "crisis" stage, Oberg said, it is not uncommon for visitors to seek out other people from their own culture. Together, they tend to commiserate and complain about the host culture, depicting it as **42** much lesser perfect than their own.

Oberg assured the audience that time tends to heal culture shock. He said that if **43** a newcomer stays, they typically begin learning the language and getting around on their own. Oberg said that at this stage they may still be ethnocentric, but they are not as easily upset by differences. They are more likely to laugh than to criticize. Moreover, by unconsciously projecting a friendlier attitude to everyone they meet, they find people in the host country reacting more positively toward them.

In the end, Oberg said, fully overcoming culture shock requires communication. **44** By learning the language, newcomers gain a window into "a new world of cultural meanings," Oberg said. They become familiar with what the local people are interested in. Over time, they gain perspective. They see the host culture and their native culture objectively, as simply products of different histories.

★

40

Which choice best combines the underlined sentences?

A) Whatever the discomforts, native inhabitants add to newcomers' sense of frustration most likely by being indifferent.
B) Adding to newcomers' sense of frustration, native inhabitants most likely treat the discomforts with indifference.
C) Native inhabitants add to the newcomers' sense of frustration with indifference
D) Native inhabitants, by being indifferent to the newcomers, add to their sense of frustration about whatever the discomforts are.

41

Which choice provides the best additional example to the sentence?

A) NO CHANGE
B) gestures.
C) outfits.
D) birthdays.

42

A) NO CHANGE
B) much less perfect
C) least perfect
D) most imperfect

43

A) NO CHANGE
B) newcomers stayed,
C) a newcomer stayed,
D) newcomers stay,

44

At this point, the writer is considering adding the following sentence.

> Mastering the language helps newcomers feel more connected.

Should the writer make this addition here?

A) Yes, because it provides a necessary transition between ideas in the paragraph.
B) Yes, because it supports the conclusion drawn in the following sentence.
C) No, because it shifts the focus away from steps newcomers can take to overcome culture shock.
D) No, because it contradicts a claim about emotional exhaustion made earlier in the passage.

NO TEST MATERIAL ON THIS PAGE

Math Test 5 – No Calculator

25 MINUTES, 20 QUESTIONS

Turn to Section 3 of your answer sheet to answer the questions in this section.

DIRECTIONS

For questions **1 – 15**, find the solution to each problem and select the most appropriate answer from the choices provided. For questions **16 – 20**, find the solution to each problem and write your answer in the space provided. You may use the blank space in your test booklet for scratch work.

NOTES

1. The use of a calculator on any part of this section is forbidden.
2. Unless otherwise indicated, all variables and expressions used in this test represent real numbers.
3. Unless otherwise indicated, all figures used in this test are drawn to scale.
4. Unless otherwise indicated, all figures used in this test lie on a plane.
5. Unless specified otherwise, a given function, f, has the domain the set of all real numbers x for which $f(x)$ is a real number.

REFERENCE

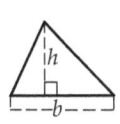
$A = \frac{1}{2}bh$

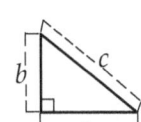
$c^2 = a^2 + b^2$

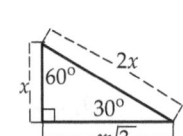
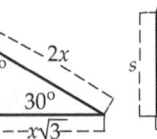
Special Right Triangles

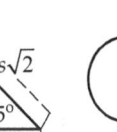
$A = \pi r^2$
$C = 2\pi r$

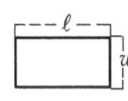
$A = \ell w$

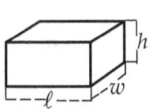
$V = \ell w h$

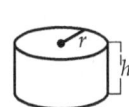
$V = \pi r^2 h$

$V = \frac{4}{3}\pi r^3$

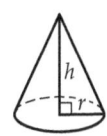
$V = \frac{1}{3}\pi r^2 h$

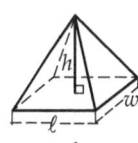
$V = \frac{1}{3}\ell w h$

The arc of a circle is 360 degrees or 2π radians.
A triangle has angles that sum to 180 degrees.

3

1. If $-5 < m < 10$ and $2 < n < 4$, which of the following must be true for $m + n$?

A) $-3 < m + n < 14$
B) $-7 < m + n < 6$
C) $-5 < m + n < 12$
D) $8 < m + n < 14$

2. $$f(x) = \frac{\sqrt{3x}}{b}$$

In the function $f(x)$, b is a constant and $f(3) = 3$. What is the value of b?

A) 3
B) 1
C) $\frac{1}{3}$
D) -1

3. A machine puts c caps on bottles in m minutes. If each bottle receives one cap, how many hours will it take to put caps on b bottles?

A) $\frac{60bm}{c}$
B) $\frac{bm}{60c}$
C) $\frac{bc}{60m}$
D) $\frac{60b}{cm}$

4. Janet and Maria purchased flowers at the same store. Janet purchased 5 roses for x dollars each and 4 daisies for y dollars each and spent $32 total on the flowers. Maria purchased 1 rose for x dollars and 6 daisies for y dollars each and spent $22. The system of equations below represents this situation.

$$5x + 4y = 32$$
$$x + 6y = 22$$

Which statement is true?

A) A rose costs $1 more than a daisy.
B) Janet spent $4 on each daisy.
C) Janet spent more on daisies than she did on roses.
D) Maria spent more on daisies than Janet spent on roses.

5. Solve $\dfrac{x^2}{x-4} = \dfrac{16}{x-4}$.

A) $\{-4, 4\}$
B) $\{0\}$
C) $\{4\}$
D) $\{-4\}$

6. Which of the following is the point at which the graph of $5x + 4y = 12$ intersects the y-axis?

A) $(0, 3)$
B) $(0, -3)$
C) $(3, 0)$
D) $(5, 0)$

7

Which of the following is equivalent to the expression $(5x + 4)(7x + 1)$?

A) $33x + 4$
B) $35x^2 + 5x$
C) $35x^2 + 23x + 4$
D) $35x^2 + 33x + 4$

8

Solve the equation for x: $x + \sqrt{x-4} = 4$.

A) 5
B) 4
C) 0 and 4
D) 4 and 5

9

If x and y are positive integers, $x^2 + y^2 = 25$, and $x^2 - y^2 = 7$, then what is y?

A) 3
B) 4
C) 5
D) 16

10

Which of the following statements best describes the relationship between the graphs of $y = 2$ and $y = 2x + 5$?

A) The lines have the same slope.
B) The lines are perpendicular.
C) The lines intersect at exactly one point.
D) The lines intersect at more than one point.

11

$$3x - y + 5 = 0$$
$$2x + 3y - 4 = 0$$

What is the solution to this system of equations above?

A) $x = -1, y = -2$
B) $x = -1, y = 2$
C) $x = 2, y = -1$
D) $x = 2, y = 1$

12

Noah has a set of data to study. He adds one more data value to the set and as a result, the range increases. Which of the following statements MUST be true?

A) The median also increased.
B) The mean also increased.
C) The mode also increased.
D) The mode did not change.

13

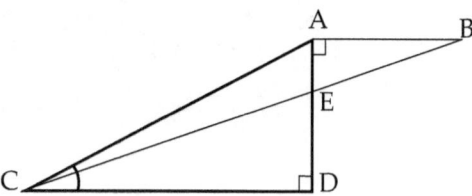

In the figure above, $\triangle ABE \sim \triangle EDC$, $AD = 4$, $AB = 3$ and $CD = 9$. What is the area of the triangle AEC?

A) 18
B) 13.5
C) 9
D) 4.5

14

The function $y = -x^2 + 4x + 5$ has a y-intercept of (0, 5). Which of the following is the reflection of the y-intercept across the function's line of symmetry?

A) (0, −5)
B) (2, 5)
C) (2, 9)
D) (4, 5)

15

All the dots in the array are 2 units apart vertically and horizontally. What is the length of the longest line segment that can be drawn joining any two points in the array without passing through any other point?

A) 2

B) $2\sqrt{20}$

C) 3

D) $\sqrt{20}$

Student-Produced Responses   3

DIRECTIONS

For questions **16 – 20**, find the solution to the problem and enter your answer as demonstrated on the right.

1. Only the answer that is bubbled in on the answer sheet will be credited. The blank spaces above the bubbles are for you to record your answers for accuracy.
2. Only fill in one bubble in any given column.
3. None of the answers on this portion of the test are negative values.
4. If a problem appears to have more than one answer, only enter one answer. If the answer you enter is one of the correct solutions, you will receive full credit for that question.
5. If the correct answer can be expressed as a mixed number, it must be entered as a decimal or an improper fraction.
6. If the correct answer is a decimal that cannot fit into the grid space, you must fill the grid with enough digits to completely fill the space. The number can be rounded or simply shortened but must fill every blank space.

Answer: $\frac{5}{36}$ Answer: 4.5

Write answer in boxes. Grid in result.

← Fraction line
← Decimal point

Acceptable ways to grid $\frac{1}{6}$ are:

Answer: 302 – either position is correct

NOTES

Begin entering answers in any column that accommodates your answer. If you do not need a column do not enter anything in that column.

3

16

If $6j - 5k = 11$ and $5j - 6k = -22$, then what is the value of $2j + 2k$?

ANSWER: _____

17

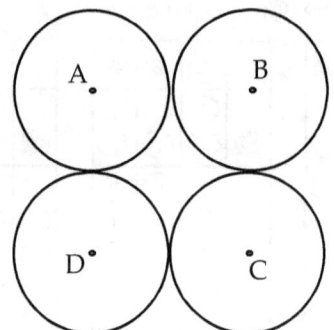

Four circles of diameter $\sqrt{2}$ are placed tangent to each other as shown above. What is the distance from point A to point C?

ANSWER: _____

18

If $ab = \dfrac{1}{2}$, $bc = 4$ and $ac = 8$, what is the value of abc (if $abc > 0$)?

ANSWER: _____

19

If $x^2 - y^2 = 45$ and $x - y = 5$, what is the value of y?

ANSWER: _____

20

Let x be a positive integer. If $a = x^2 + 4x + 4$ and $\sqrt{a} = 4$, what is the value of x?

ANSWER: _____

Math Test 5 – Calculator

 55 MINUTES, 38 QUESTIONS

Turn to Section 4 of your answer sheet to answer the questions in this section.

DIRECTIONS

For questions **1 – 30**, find the solution to each problem and select the most appropriate answer from the choices provided. For questions **31 – 38**, find the solution to each problem and write your answer in the space provided. You may use the blank space in your test booklet for scratch work.

NOTES

1. The use of a calculator on any part of this section is allowed.
2. Unless otherwise indicated, all variables and expressions used in this test represent real numbers.
3. Unless otherwise indicated, all figures used in this test are drawn to scale.
4. Unless otherwise indicated, all figures used in this test lie on a plane.
5. Unless specified otherwise, a given function, f, has the domain the set of all real numbers x for which $f(x)$ is a real number.

REFERENCE

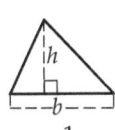 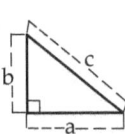 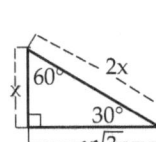 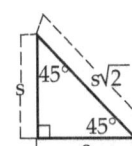 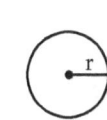 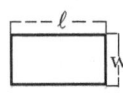

$A = \frac{1}{2}bh$ $c^2 = a^2 + b^2$ Special Right Triangles $A = \pi r^2$; $C = 2\pi r$ $A = \ell w$

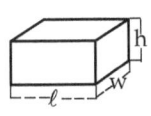 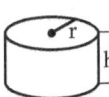   

$V = \ell wh$ $V = \pi r^2 h$ $V = \frac{4}{3}\pi r^3$ $V = \frac{1}{3}\pi r^2 h$ $V = \frac{1}{3}\ell wh$

The arc of a full circle is 360 degrees or 2π radians.
A triangle has angles that sum to 180 degrees.

4

1

A streaming service has a $25 sing-up fee. Each video that is rented costs $2.50. Let v represent the number of videos rented. Write a rule in function notation for the situation.

A) $f(v) = 25v + 2.5$
B) $f(v) = 25v - 2.5$
C) $f(v) = 2.5v + 25$
D) $f(v) = 2.5v - 25$

2

Solve for x: $3(2x + 5) - 4(x - 2) = 3(2x + 2) + 1$.

A) 9
B) 3
C) 4
D) −5

3

What is the 50th term of the arithmetic sequence 4, 10, 16, 22, …?

A) 202
B) 206
C) 294
D) 298

Questions 4 and 5 refer to the following information.

Two companies charge different rates for painting lines on a road.
- Company A charges $0.60 per foot of line painted and no base price.
- Company B charges a base price of $120 plus $0.25 per foot of line painted.

4

Which of the following expressions gives the charge, in dollars, for painting x feet of line if company A does the job?

A) $0.30x$

B) $0.60x$

C) $x + 0.60$

D) $\dfrac{x}{0.60}$

5

Which of the following graphs could show the relation between the length of line painted and the charge if company B does the job and cost is represented on the y-axis and feet painted on the x-axis?

A) 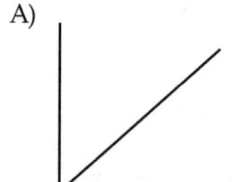 B)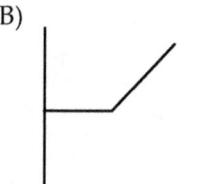

C) 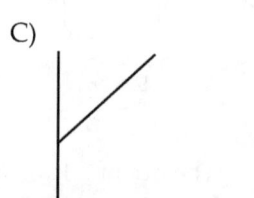 D)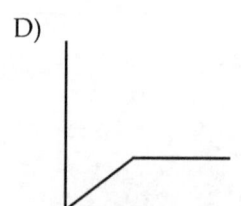

6

After having to pay increased income taxes this year, Edmond has to sell his BMW. Edmond bought the car for $49,000, but he sold it for 20% less. For how much did Edmond sell the car?

A) $28,900
B) $35,600
C) $37,300
D) $39,200

7

If $i^2 = -1$, what is the value of $5 + 6i$ multiplied by $3 - 2i$?

A) 27
B) 27i
C) 27 + 8i
D) 15 + 8i

8

The graph below charts snowfall in Buffalo, NY from 1960 – 1970.

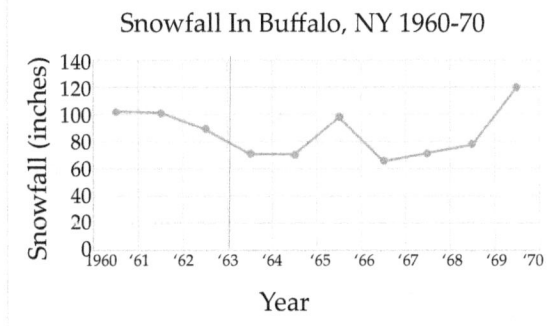

Based on the graph, which choice best describes the snowfall pattern from 1960 to 1964?

A) Snowfall remained steady with a single peak.
B) Snowfall decreased steadily.
C) Snowfall remained steady with a peak at the end of the period.
D) Snowfall rose steadily.

9

Rearrange the following equation so there are no radicals in the denominator: $\dfrac{\sqrt{3}+1}{\sqrt{3}-1}$

A) $2 + 2\sqrt{3}$

B) $2 - 2\sqrt{3}$

C) $2 - \sqrt{3}$

D) $2 + \sqrt{3}$

10

One store sold four red pens for a dollar and three yellow pens for a dollar. A second store sold four red pens for a dollar and six yellow pens for a dollar. What is the greatest number of pens that Jason can purchase with ten dollars, assuming he spends at least one dollar on each color of pen?

A) 31
B) 40
C) 58
D) 60

11

Solve completely for x: $3^{x^2} = 9^8$.

A) –2, 2
B) –4, 4
C) 8
D) –16, 16

12

Let $f(x) = ax^2$ and $g(x) = bx^4$ for any value of x. If a and b are positive constants, for how many values of x does $f(x) = g(x)$?

A) None
B) One
C) Two
D) Three

13

In the board game "Silly Bills," there are $1, $2, and $3 bills. There are 11 more $2 bills than $1 bills. There are 18 fewer $3 bills than $1 bills. If there is 101 bills in total, then how many $1 bills are there in the board game?

A) 11
B) 14
C) 33
D) 36

14

The Apollo 11 mission used 770,000 liters of kerosene and 1,200,000 liters of liquid hydrogen to propel a space shuttle to the moon. Kerosene has an average energy density of 37.4 Megajoules per liter $\left(\frac{MJ}{l}\right)$, and hydrogen has an average energy density of 8.5 $\frac{MJ}{l}$. One kilocalorie is equal to 4184 Joules. Given that one gram of sugar contains 4 kilocalories, and 1 cup of sugar contains about 200 grams of sugar, approximately how many cups of sugar does it take to get to the moon? (Note: 1 Megajoule is equal to 1-million Joules.)

A) 11.7 million
B) 11.7 billion
C) 9.3 million
D) 9.3 billion

15

Twenty students have each sampled one or more of three kinds of candy bars that a school store sells. If 3 students have sampled all three kinds, and 5 have sampled exactly two kinds, how many of these students have sampled only one kind?

A) 8
B) 12
C) 15
D) 17

16

If $f(x, y) = \frac{1}{4}x - y$, then which of the following is equal to $f(8, 3)$?

A) $f(12, 2)$
B) $f(16, 6)$
C) $f(2, 1)$
D) $f(-12, -2)$

17

Solve for x: $2(x - 5)(x + 3) = -28$.

A) $\{-2, 5\}$
B) $\{-3, 14\}$
C) $\left\{\frac{4 \pm \sqrt{3}}{2}\right\}$
D) $\{1 \pm \sqrt{2}\}$

18

The operation Φ is defined for all real numbers a and b as $a \, \Phi \, b = a^{-b} - 3b$.

If $n \, \Phi - 2 = 70$, which of the following could equal n?

A) 7
B) 9
C) −8
D) 8.7

19

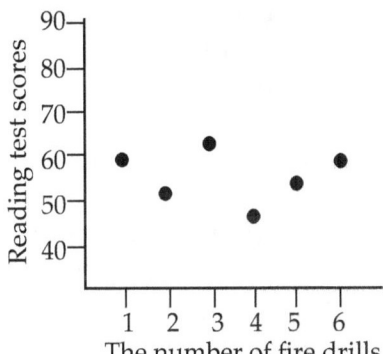

One state did a study to see if last year's reading test scores were related to the number of fire drills each school conducted. The data is shown on the scatter plot above. Which of the following is the best conclusion of the study?

A) The fewer fire drills a school conducted, the lower the test scores.
B) The more fire drills a school conducted, the higher the test scores.
C) The more fire drills a school conducted, the lower the test scores.
D) There was no relationship found between fire drills and test scores.

Questions 20 and 21 refer to the following table.

PROJECTED SALES FOR GAME X

Price of Game X	Projected # of Games Sold
$55	52,500
$35	98,000
$15	153,000

20

Based on the projections, how much more money would be received from sales of game X when the price is $35 than when the price is $55?

A) $54,250
B) $532,000
C) $542,500
D) $1,135,000

21

Which of the following descriptions would best represent a graph (not shown) of the relationship between the price of game X and the projected number of games sold, as indicated by the table?

A) Directly proportional
B) Inversely proportional
C) Exponential
D) Constant

4 Student-Produced Responses

DIRECTIONS

For questions **31 – 38**, find the solution to the problem and enter your answer as demonstrated on the right.

1. Only the answer that is bubbled in on the answer sheet will be credited. The blank spaces above the bubbles are for you to record your answers for accuracy.
2. Only fill in one bubble in any given column.
3. None of the answers on this portion of the test are negative values.
4. If a problem appears to have more than one answer, only enter one answer. If the answer you enter is one of the correct solutions, you will receive full credit for that question.
5. If the correct answer can be expressed as a mixed number, it must be entered as a decimal or an improper fraction.
6. If the correct answer is a decimal that cannot fit into the grid space, you must fill the grid with enough digits to completely fill the space. The number can be rounded or simply shortened but must fill every blank space.

NOTES

Begin entering answers in any column that accommodates your answer. If you do not need a column do not enter anything in that column.

Answer: $\frac{5}{36}$ Answer: 4.5

Write answer in boxes.
Grid in result.
← Fraction line
← Decimal point

Acceptable ways to grid $\frac{1}{6}$ are:

Answer: 302 – either position is correct

31

Two people set off by car on a rally and take the same route which is 50 miles long. If A drives at an average speed of 100 miles per hour, and B at an average speed of 120 miles per hour, how much longer, in minutes, will it take A to cover the course than it takes B?

ANSWER: _____

32

At one point in a game, the shooting team has a ratio of hits to misses of 5 : 1. After the team misses the next three shots, which are the last in the game, its ratio of hits to misses is 5 : 2. What is the total number of shots taken by the team in the game?

ANSWER: _____

33

Andy, Maddie and Jack all have their birthdays today, but Andy is more than twice as old as Maddie and Maddie is more than four years older than Jack. If the sum of their ages is less than 24 years old, what is the maximum value for Maddie's age in years?

ANSWER: _____

34

Line l and line m lie on the same plane but have no points in common. They are both tangent to a circle of area 9π. What is the shortest distance between any point on l and any point on m?

ANSWER: _____

35

A projectile is fired vertically upward with the initial speed of 32 feet per second.

The height of the projectile is given by $h(t) = vt - 16t^2$, where v is the initial speed and t is the time in seconds. What will be the maximum height that the projectile reaches?

ANSWER: _____

36

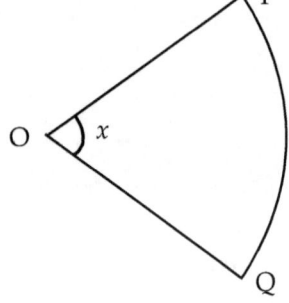

In the figure above, the arc has center O and radius 12. If the length of arc $\overset{\frown}{PQ}$ is between 6 and 18, what is the one possible integer value of angle x in radians?

ANSWER: _____

Questions 37 and 38 refer to the following information.

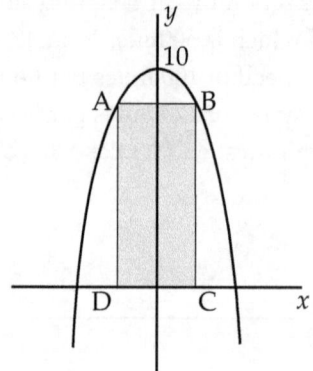

As shown above, rectangle ABCD has vertices C and D on the x-axis and vertices A and B on the part of the parabola $y = 10 - x^2$ that is above or on the line $y = 1$.

37

What is the interval length of the possible domain of the perimeter function?

ANSWER: _____

38

For what value of x is the perimeter a maximum?

ANSWER: _____

NO TEST MATERIAL ON THIS PAGE

Essay Test 5

 50 MINUTES, Prompt-based essay

Turn to Section 5 of your answer sheet to answer the question in this section.

> **DIRECTIONS**
>
> As you read the passage below, consider how Konrad Graf uses
> - evidence, such as facts or examples, to support claims.
> - reasoning to develop ideas and to connect claims and evidence.
> - stylistic or persuasive elements, such as word choice or appeals to emotion, to add power to the ideas expressed.

This passage is adapted from Konrad S. Graf, "SpaceX can get there, but biology a probable Mars residence limiter," published on September 29, 2016.

[SpaceX Founder Elon] Musk's aim is to make humanity a multiplanetary species. He envisions a city of a million people on Mars that could become "self-sustaining"...

Most of the technical issues with Mars habitation can be addressed with technical means. Radiation can be shielded against. Water, air, and regulated temperatures can be produced, and chemical plants such as for ship propellant can be built. Psychological and other factors in long-term, small-scale hab confinement have already been under study both in space and in remote desert sims.

However, the harshest sticking point for a colonization plan could be something that Musk mentioned, but characterized only as a source of fun—38% Earth gravity on Mars. He presented images of jumping high and lifting heavy things with ease.

The possible problems would only appear, as they so often do, over the longer term. Research on the health effects of low gravity has already begun to suggest a quite unfavorable pattern. Much of this research has been done in zero g, but long-term exposure to 38% Earth gravity—Mars g—could well produce many similar effects along the same spectrum, just more slowly.

Zero g has been found to produce not only the expected muscle atrophy in astronauts, but a host of other health issues, which isometrics and exercise bikes can only partially limit. Research on both astronauts and lab animals point to falling bone mineral density and circulatory issues, including impaired heart health.

Thus, limited research to date already suggests negative effects on three major physical systems. Yet muscular, skeletal, and circulatory systems are hardly footnotes to transporting brains... Moreover, there is no reason to expect nervous and reproductive systems to get free passes, especially over years and decades.

Studies of zero-g animal embryonic development raise concerns for long-term Mars colonization. Reproduction among spacefaring rodents has gone quite badly. Experiments with mice on a Space Shuttle mission resulted in normal embryos for the earthside controls and no growing embryos in zero g. Rat groups sent into orbit produced some weightless pregnancies, but with no resulting births. The pregnancies spontaneously terminated—all of them...

The so-far unquestioned constant has been that all earthly life has evolved in 1g (with very tiny variations) and every embryonic developmental process has evolved to take place in this 1g.

What about adaptation? As powerful a force as evolution by natural selection is, it tends to require extremely long time scales, on the order of thousands and more generations, especially for larger-scale adaptations. Too great a change—or an entirely unprecedented type of change—and a species will simply not make it.

Adaptations to something so pervasive and otherwise constant as gravity would have to proceed in steps. If a hypothetical planet's gravity were to (somehow) shift to 38% of its former level, but do so over several million years or more, then life there would have a decent chance of adapting because any given generation would only be subject to minute changes... In contrast, evolution copes far less well with sudden large jumps, which tend to be associated with mass extinctions.

Temperature variation is a variable to which earthly life is widely adapted, both across species and to a lesser degree within each organism. Temperature has changed remarkably and continuously throughout Earth's 4.5-billion-year history and it also varies starkly with season and geography. Temperature adaptation therefore has a vast range of evolutionary precedent. Atmospheric composition, pressure, and radiation levels have also changed back and forth over geologic history.

What earthly life has never had to do, not even once, is what a Mars relocation would ask of it. Low g is something that evolution has had no opportunity to tackle. One of the few rough constants throughout the 3 billion or more years of earthly life has been 1g.

This still does not make some degree of individual gravity adaptation impossible now, but it does suggest that this could be a very serious issue for colonization and a potential deal-breaker for both indefinite stays on Mars and natural reproduction of future generations there.

For long-term extra-terrestrial colonization, artificial structures capable of producing artificial gravity that approximate 1g seem more promising….

Given the grave potential health and reproductive risks of long-term exposure to zero g and/or Mars g for Earth-evolved organisms, those interested in space colonization ought to assign a high priority, alongside ongoing engineering work, to low- and zero-g health research. Critical for colonization are three research areas: effects of Mars g on the health of Earth-leavers, likely health of long-term Mars residents upon potential return to Earth, and effects of low and no g on embryonic and childhood development.

Getting people to Mars is an engineering challenge. Musk, SpaceX, and collaborators are up to the task and well on their way. But the length of time that hopeful new Martian arrivals can expect to live there, in what state of health, and with what likelihood of producing healthy offspring, are critical questions in need of serious research and consideration in relation to any developing colonization plans. Early animal and astronaut studies combined with an evolutionary perspective suggest that shorter-term Mars visits are likely to be far more feasible from a health perspective, that natural reproduction among colonists might well be out of the question, and that the development of spacecraft and stations with artificial gravity is likely to be a biological priority for any future long-term extra-terrestrial residents.

Write an essay in which you explain how Konrad Graf builds an argument to persuade his audience that efforts to colonize Mars should focus on low gravity research. In your essay, analyze how Graf uses one or more of the features in the directions that precede the passage (or features of your own choice) to strengthen the logic and persuasiveness of his argument. Be sure that your analysis focuses on the most relevant features of the passage.
Your essay should not explain whether you agree with Graf's claims, but rather explain how Graf builds an argument to persuade his audience.

---

* Sample responses found in the "Answers and Explanations" section of this study guide.

"SpaceX can get there, but biology a probable Mars residence limiter" is licensed under CC BY 4.0. For more information, see page 511.

KALLIS

SAT® Practice Test #6

IMPORTANT REMINDERS:

When you take the official SAT, you will need to use a No. 2 pencil. Do not use a pen or a mechanical pencil.

On the official SAT, sharing any of the questions on the test violates the College Board's policies and may result in your scores being canceled.

(This cover is modeled after the cover you'll see when you take the official SAT.)

UNAUTHORIZED REPRODUCTION OR USE OF ANY PART OF THIS TEST IS PROHIBITED.

© 2019 KALLIS EDU

Reading Test 6

65 MINUTES, 52 QUESTIONS

Turn to Section 1 of your answer sheet to answer the questions in this section.

DIRECTIONS

Each passage or pair of passages is accompanied by 10 or 11 questions. Read each passage or pair of passages, and then select the most appropriate answer to each question. Some passages may include tables or graphs that require additional analysis.

Refer to the passage below to answer questions 1 – 10.

This passage is adapted from Herman Melville, *Typee*, originally published in 1846.

    Six months at sea! Yes, reader, as I live, six months out of sight of land; cruising after the sperm whale beneath the scorching sun of the Line, and tossed on the billows of the wide-
[5] rolling Pacific—the sky above, the sea around, and nothing else! Weeks and weeks ago our fresh provisions were all exhausted. There is not a sweet potato left; not a single yam. Those glorious bunches of bananas which once decorated our
[10] stern and quarter-deck, have, alas, disappeared! and the delicious oranges which hung suspended from our tops and stays—they, too, are gone! Yes, they are all departed, and there is nothing left us but salt-horse and sea-biscuit.
[15]   Oh! for a refreshing glimpse of one blade of grass—for a snuff at the fragrance of a handful of the loamy earth! Is there nothing fresh around us? Is there no green thing to be seen? Yes, the inside of our bulwarks is painted green; but what a vile
[20] and sickly hue it is, as if nothing bearing even the semblance of verdure could flourish this weary way from land. Even the bark that once clung to the wood we use for fuel has been gnawed off and devoured by the captain's pig; and so long
[25] ago, too, that the pig himself has in turn been devoured.
    There is but one solitary tenant in the chicken-coop, once a gay and dapper young cock, bearing him so bravely among the coy hens. But
[30] look at him now; there he stands, moping all the day long on that everlasting one leg of his. He turns with disgust from the moldy corn before him, and the brackish water in his little trough. He mourns no doubt his lost companions, literally
[35] snatched from him one by one, and never seen again. But his days of mourning will be few; for Mungo, our black cook, told me yesterday that the word had at last gone forth, and poor Pedro's fate was sealed. His attenuated body will be laid
[40] out upon the captain's table next Sunday, and long before night will be buried, with all the usual ceremonies, beneath that worthy individual's vest. Who would believe that there could be any one so cruel as to long for the decapitation of the
[45] luckless Pedro; yet the sailors pray every minute, selfish fellows, that the miserable fowl may be brought to his end. They say the captain will never point the ship for the land so long as he has in anticipation a mess of fresh meat. This unhappy
[50] bird can alone furnish it; and when he is once devoured, the captain will come to his senses. I wish thee no harm, Peter; but as thou art doomed, sooner or later, to meet the fate of all thy race; and if putting a period to thy existence is to be the
[55] signal for our deliverance, why—truth to speak—I wish thy throat cut this very moment; for, oh! how I wish to see the living earth again! The old ship herself longs to look out upon the land from her hawseholes once more, as Jack Lewis said right
[60] the other day when the captain found fault with his steering.
    "Why, d'ye see, Captain Vangs," says bold Jack, "I'm as good a helmsman as ever put hand to spoke; but none of us can steer the old lady
[65] now. We can't keep her full and bye, sir: watch her ever so close, she will fall off; and then, sir, when I put the helm down so gently and try like to coax her to the work, she won't take it kindly, but will fall round off again; and it's all because she knows
[70] the land is under the lee, sir, and she won't go any more to windward." Ay, and why should she, Jack? didn't every one of her stout timbers grow on shore, and hasn't she sensibilities as well as we?
[75]   Poor old ship! Her very looks denote her desires: how deplorable she appears! The paint on her sides, burnt up by the scorching sun, is puffed out and cracked. See the weeds she trails along with her, and what an unsightly bunch of these
[80] horrid barnacles has formed about her stern-piece; and every time she rises on a sea, she shows her copper torn away or hanging in jagged strips.

01

The main purpose of the passage is to

A) provide a detailed description of the layout of a whaling vessel.
B) describe the hardships of a long journey at sea.
C) criticize the callousness and indifference of a ship's captain.
D) express the narrator's lifelong love of sailing.

02

As used in line 4, "billows" most nearly means

A) gases.
B) clouds.
C) swells.
D) storms.

03

In lines 15 – 17 ("Oh!...loamy earth"), the speaker's tone is best described as

A) grateful.
B) scornful.
C) alarmed.
D) wistful.

04

In lines 17 – 18 ("Is there nothing…be seen") the speaker asks questions primarily to

A) complain to fellow sailors.
B) reinforce a tone of desperation.
C) pose a philosophical conundrum.
D) criticize the unpleasant color of the ship's paint.

05

The speaker's attitude toward Pedro could best be described as

A) condescending.
B) violent.
C) indifferent.
D) sympathetic.

06

Which choice provides the best evidence for the answer to the previous question?

A) Lines 27 – 29 ("There is…hens")
B) Lines 39 – 43 ("His attenuated…vest")
C) Lines 43 – 45 ("Who would…Pedro")
D) Lines 49 – 51 ("This unhappy…senses")

07

According to the passage, the captain has not ordered the boat ashore because

A) the boat is too damaged to steer.
B) the boat is sailing in unfamiliar waters.
C) he has not yet eaten Pedro.
D) he is pursuing a sperm whale.

08

In paragraph 4 (lines 62 – 74), Jack Lewis implies that

A) the ship steers of its own volition.
B) the ship's steering mechanism is damaged.
C) he is the only person capable of steering the ship.
D) Captain Vangs does not know how to operate the ship.

09

As used in line 76, "deplorable" most nearly means

A) wretched.
B) heinous.
C) unforgivable.
D) diabolical.

10

Which choice best summarizes the narrator's overall outlook?

A) Lines 1 – 2 ("as I…land")
B) Lines 13 – 14 ("they…sea-biscuit")
C) Lines 51 – 52 ("I wish…Peter")
D) Lines 56 – 57 ("how…again")

Refer to the passage below to answer questions 11 – 20.

This passage is adapted from Benjamin Franklin, *Autobiography of Benjamin Franklin*, originally published in 1791.

In this piece it was my design to explain and enforce this doctrine, that vicious actions are not hurtful because they are forbidden, but forbidden because they are hurtful, the nature
5 of man alone considered; that it was, therefore, everyone's interest to be virtuous who wished to be happy even in this world; and I should, from this circumstance (there being always in the world a number of rich merchants, nobility, states, and
10 princes, who have need of honest instruments for the management of their affairs, and such being so rare), have endeavored to convince young persons that no qualities were so likely to make a poor man's fortune as those of probity and integrity.
15 My list of virtues contained at first but twelve; but a Quaker friend having kindly informed me that I was generally thought proud; that my pride showed itself frequently in conversation; that I was not content with being
20 in the right when discussing any point, but was overbearing, and rather insolent, of which he convinced me by mentioning several instances; I determined endeavoring to cure myself, if I could, of this vice or folly among the rest, and I added
25 *Humility* to my list, giving an extensive meaning to the word.
    I cannot boast of much success in acquiring the *reality* of this virtue, but I had a good deal with regard to the *appearance* of it. I made it a
30 rule to forbear all direct contradiction to the sentiments of others, and all positive assertion of my own. I even forbid myself, agreeably to the old laws of our Junto, the use of every word or expression in the language that imported a fixed
35 opinion, such as *certainly*, *undoubtedly*, etc., and I adopted, instead of them, I *conceive*, I *apprehend*, or I *imagine* a thing to be so or so; or it *so appears to me at present*. When another asserted something that I thought an error, I denied myself the pleasure
40 of contradicting him abruptly, and of showing immediately some absurdity in his proposition; and in answering I began by observing that in certain cases or circumstances his opinion would be right, but in the present case there *appeared* or
45 *seemed* to me some difference, etc. I soon found the advantage of this change in my manner; the conversations I engaged in went on more pleasantly. The modest way in which I proposed my opinions procured them a readier reception
50 and less contradiction; I had less mortification when I was found to be in the wrong, and I more easily prevailed with others to give up their mistakes and join with me when I happened to be in the right.
55 And this mode, which I at first put on with some violence to natural inclination, became at length so easy, and so habitual to me, that perhaps for these fifty years past no one has ever heard a dogmatical expression escape me. And to
60 this habit (after my character of integrity) I think it principally owing that I had early so much weight with my fellow-citizens when I proposed new institutions, or alterations in the old, and so much influence in public councils when I became
65 a member; for I was but a bad speaker, never eloquent, subject to much hesitation in my choice of words, hardly correct in language, and yet I generally carried my points.
    In reality, there is, perhaps, no one of our
70 natural passions so hard to subdue as *pride*. Disguise it, struggle with it, beat it down, stifle it, mortify it as much as one pleases, it is still alive, and will every now and then peep out and show itself; you will see it, perhaps, often in this history;
75 for, even if I could conceive that I had completely overcome it, I should probably be proud of my humility.

———————★———————

11

In paragraph 1 (lines 1 – 14), Franklin suggests that acting virtuously

A) is very difficult for people who also possess probity and integrity.
B) must begin when a person is young in order to guarantee happiness.
C) is a quality possessed by many of the world's merchants, nobility, and princes.
D) can lead to financial success because those who do so are in high demand.

12

The primary purpose of paragraph 2 (lines 15 – 26) is to

A) explain how Franklin arrived at a conclusion.
B) present a controversial viewpoint that Franklin defends.
C) reveal that Franklin has little regard for others' opinions.
D) describe how Franklin managed to overcome an obstacle.

13

As used in line 34, "imported" most nearly means

A) derived.
B) brought.
C) obtained.
D) expressed.

14

In paragraph 3 (lines 27 – 54), Franklin implies that

A) humility is largely demonstrated through one's manner of speaking.
B) humility was the most difficult virtue for him to master.
C) few people took notice of his attempts at showing humility.
D) many people demonstrate humility without realizing it.

15

According to Franklin, disagreeing with someone in a polite manner results in

A) more dishonesty among friends.
B) less embarrassment from one's own mistakes.
C) stress and strain from tolerating absurd ideas.
D) a reputation for always being correct.

16

Which choice provides the best evidence for the answer to the previous question?

A) Lines 48 – 51 ("The modest … wrong")
B) Lines 55 – 59 ("And this … escape me")
C) Lines 59 – 65 ("And to … member")
D) Lines 65 – 68 ("for I was … points")

17

As used in line 56, "violence to natural inclination" most nearly means

A) self-harm.
B) difficulty.
C) adaptation.
D) destruction.

18

Paragraph 5 (lines 69 – 77) mainly serves to

A) point out a humorous contradiction.
B) highlight the extent of Franklin's humility.
C) refer to the conversation in paragraph 2.
D) refute the claim that humility is not a virtue.

19

According to the passage, Franklin believes that

A) pride is the most harmful and problematic quality that one can possess.
B) acting with humility and being humble are distinct.
C) virtues must be acquired over the course of many years.
D) one cannot develop humility without first possessing integrity.

20

Which choice provides the best evidence for the answer to the previous question?

A) Lines 27 – 29 ("I cannot…of it")
B) Lines 55 – 59 ("And this…me")
C) Lines 59 – 63 ("And to…institutions")
D) Lines 69 – 70 ("In reality…*pride*")

Refer to the passage and supplementary material below to answer questions 21 – 30.

This passage is adapted from Yoo Jung Kim, "Why Statistics Should Be A Mandatory Part of High School Education," published on August 18, 2016.

Back in 2007, the Advertising Standards Authority (ASA) in Britain ruled that the oral health manufacturing giant Colgate could not use its claim that "More than 80% of dentists
[5] recommend Colgate" or that its brand was "used and recommended by most dentists." These bans were based on the finding that Colgate had used deceptive statistics to derive its numbers.
   For instance, when reading the original
[10] claim, consumers would likely think that four out of five dentists had recommended Colgate over its competitors. Instead, ASA found that dentists in the study were allowed to recommend more than one toothpaste. The numbers were less impressive
[15] than Colgate had made them sound.
   The ASA explained that "The claim would be understood by readers to mean that 80 per cent of dentists recommend Colgate over and above other brands, and the remaining 20 percent
[20] would recommend different brands. [...] Because we understood that another competitor's brand was recommended almost as much as the Colgate brand by the dentists surveyed, we concluded that the claim misleadingly implied 80 per cent
[25] of dentists recommend Colgate toothpaste in preference to all other brands."
   This sort of fact-fudging is concerning because numbers permeate our lives. Sports fans pore over statistics of their favorite teams and
[30] players. Consumers are bombarded with product information on billboards, TV, and the Internet. Pundits and politicians rattle off figures to tell voters how much better or worse things have gotten. People tune into the weather channel
[35] to see the chance of rain. Some data are truly informative, some are twisted to support a point, and others are outright fabricated. And yet, every day, we are inundated with a deluge of numbers we must continually process.
[40]   So how can we make sense of it all?
   According to Charles Wheelan, a senior lecturer and policy fellow at Dartmouth College and bestselling author of *Naked Economics*, one of the best tools that we have to separate the
[45] wheat from the chaff is statistics, a system used to gather, organize, and interpret data. In short, statistics helps us to conceptualize information by allowing individuals to understand how data is collected and how it can be interpreted and
[50] communicated. Wheelan states, "Statistics is one of those things that people need to understand in order to be an informed citizen, especially the use and abuse of data."
   Given its importance, descriptive statistics
[55] ought to ascend from its status as an elective (where it currently resides along with precalculus and calculus) to the pantheon of required high school mathematics, next to the trinity of algebra, geometry, and trigonometry. Statistics is "also
[60] more intuitive and applied than other kinds of high school math courses (e.g. calculus or trig)," states Wheelan, "so it certainly strikes me as sensible to make basic statistics an integral part of any high school math curriculum."
[65]   In doing so, students will be better prepared to make informed decisions as adults over a wide range of subjects. For instance, as consumers, students will learn to question and be skeptical of advertisement claims. As voters, they will be able
[70] to interpret basic socioeconomic data touted or slammed by candidates, understand how surveys and polls work, and be aware of how data can be skewed—intentionally or unintentionally— through bias.
[75]   By incorporating more knowledge of statistics into our everyday lives, we will be able to foster an educated citizenry, helping future generations to make sense of our increasingly data-deluged world.

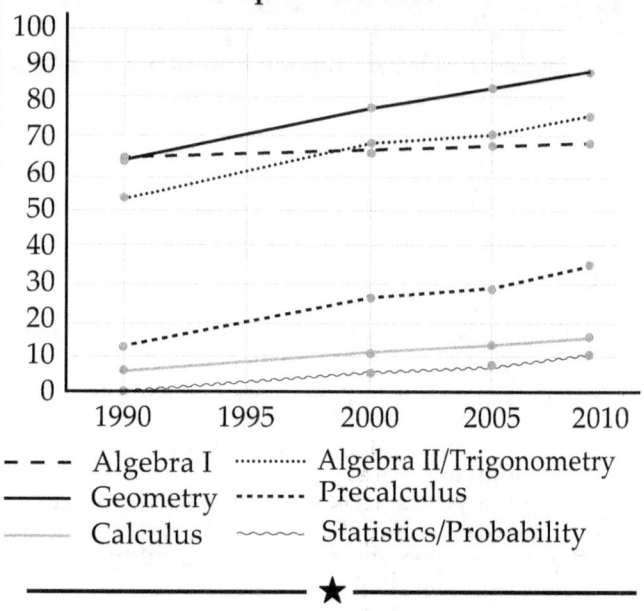

Percent of High-School Graduates that Completed Course

- - - Algebra I .... Algebra II/Trigonometry
―― Geometry - - - - Precalculus
―― Calculus ～～ Statistics/Probability

"Why Statistics Should Be A Mandatory Part of High School Education" is licensed under CC BY 4.0. For more information, see page 511.

21

The first three paragraphs (lines 1 – 26) primarily serve to

A) condemn an establishment.
B) describe a process.
C) exemplify an issue.
D) praise a ruling.

22

In the passage, the author strongly suggests that

A) statistics should replace all other subjects in high school math.
B) people encounter more data in their daily lives than they can process.
C) the majority of statistical data encountered in daily life is misleading or fabricated.
D) many people would benefit by improving their grasp of statistical analysis.

23

Which choice provides the best evidence for the answer to the previous question?

A) Lines 35 – 37 ("Some data…fabricated")
B) Lines 37 – 39 ("every day…process")
C) Lines 62 – 64 ("'it certainly…curriculum'")
D) Lines 75 – 77 ("By incorporating…citizenry")

24

The primary purpose of paragraph 4 (lines 27 – 39) is to

A) transition from a specific example to a broad discussion.
B) condemn the use of misleading or deceptive statistics.
C) provide examples of non-deceptive statistics.
D) challenge the conclusions of the Advertising Standards Authority.

25

As used in line 55, "status" most nearly means

A) regard.
B) esteem.
C) position.
D) prominence.

26

As used in line 70, "touted" most nearly means

A) solicited.
B) extolled.
C) implied.
D) revealed.

27

The quotations by Charles Wheelan (lines 50 – 53 and 59 – 64) primarily serve to

A) criticize the use of deceptive statistics.
B) clarify a potentially confusing concept.
C) reinforce a theory presented by the author.
D) strengthen the passage's main argument.

28

The author suggests that an understanding of statistics will prove especially useful in the future because

A) an increasing number of advertisers use deceptive statistics to market products.
B) statistics will soon become a required math course for high-school students.
C) political statistics are becoming increasingly biased.
D) the amount of data people must process in their daily lives is increasing.

29

According to the passage and graph information,

A) fewer than half of the high-school students who graduated in 2000 completed an elective math course.
B) nearly 90 percent of students failed statistics/probability in 2010.
C) calculus has maintained the steadiest completion rate from 1990 – 2010.
D) algebra, geometry, and trigonometry completion rates are expected to decrease in the near future.

30

Using information from the passage and the graph, it can reasonably be inferred that, in high school,

A) since 1990 an increasing number of students have opted to take statistics/probability instead of calculus.
B) enrollment in elective math classes has increased considerably since 1990.
C) geometry has always been the most studied math course.
D) students generally find calculus to be easier than statistics/probability, which accounts for calculus' higher enrollment rates.

Refer to the passage below to answer questions 31 – 40.

This passage is adapted from a speech by Elizabeth Cady Stanton, "The Solitude of Self," first delivered in 1892.

line

The strongest reason for giving woman all the opportunities for higher education, for the full development of her faculties, her forces of mind and body; for giving her the most enlarged
5   freedom of thought and action; a complete emancipation from all forms of bondage, of custom, dependence, superstition; from all the crippling influences of fear—is the solitude and personal responsibility of her own individual life.
10   The strongest reason why we ask for woman a voice in the government under which she lives; in the religion she is asked to believe; equality in social life, where she is the chief factor; a place in the trades and professions, where she may earn
15   her bread, is because of her birthright to self-sovereignty; because, as an individual, she must rely on herself. No matter how much women prefer to lean, to be protected and supported, nor how much men desire to have them do so, they
20   must make the voyage of life alone, and for safety in an emergency, they must know something of the laws of navigation. To guide our own craft, we must be captain, pilot, engineer; with chart and compass to stand at the wheel; to watch the
25   winds and waves, and know when to take in the sail, and to read the signs in the firmament over all. It matters not whether the solitary voyager is man or woman; nature, having endowed them equally, leaves them to their own skill and
30   judgment in the hour of danger, and, if not equal to the occasion, alike they perish.

We ask for the complete development of every individual, first, for his own benefit and happiness. In fitting out an army, we give each
35   soldier his own knapsack, arms, powder, his blanket, cup, knife, fork and spoon. We provide alike for all their individual necessities; then each man bears his own burden....Seeing, then, that life must ever be a march and a battle that each
40   soldier must be equipped for his own protection, it is the height of cruelty to rob the individual of a single natural right.

To throw obstacles in the way of a complete education is like putting out the eyes; to deny the
45   rights of property is like cutting off the hands. To refuse political equality is to rob the ostracized of all self-respect; of credit in the market place; of recompense in the world of work, of a voice in choosing those who make and administer
50   the law, a choice in the jury before whom they are tried, and in the judge who decides their punishment.

An uneducated woman trained to dependence, with no resources in herself,
55   must make a failure of any position in life. But society says women do not need a knowledge of the world, the liberal training that experience in public life must give, all the advantages of collegiate education; but when for the lack of all
60   this, the woman's happiness is wrecked, alone she bears her humiliation; and the solitude of the weak and the ignorant is indeed pitiable. In the wild chase for the prizes of life, they are ground to powder.
65   The talk of sheltering woman from the fierce storms of life is the sheerest mockery, for they beat on her from every point of the compass, just as they do on man, and with more fatal results, for he has been trained to protect himself, to
70   resist, and to conquer. Such are the facts in human experience, the responsibilities of individual sovereignty.

We see reason sufficient in the outer conditions of human beings for individual liberty
75   and development, but when we consider the self-dependence of every human soul, we see the need of courage, judgment and the exercise of every faculty of mind and body, strengthened and developed by use, in woman as well as man.
80   Whatever may be said of man's protecting power in ordinary conditions, amid all the terrible disasters by land and sea, in the supreme moments of danger, alone woman must ever meet the horrors of the situation. The Angel of Death
85   even makes no royal pathway for her. Man's love and sympathy enter only into the sunshine of our lives. In that solemn solitude of self, that links us with the immeasurable and the eternal, each soul lives alone forever. Such is individual life. Who, I
90   ask you, can take, dare take on himself the rights, the duties, the responsibilities of another human soul?

31

Stanton's main argument is that

A) a lack of political equality is the biggest issue faced by women.
B) men need to be more sympathetic toward the plights of women.
C) women should be given the same opportunities as men.
D) female explorers and soldiers are models of self-sufficiency.

32

Which choice provides the best evidence for the answer to the previous question?

A) Lines 20 – 22 ("for safety…navigation")
B) Lines 32 – 34 ("We ask…and happiness")
C) Lines 70 – 72 ("Such are…sovereignty")
D) Lines 87 – 89 ("In that solemn…alone forever")

33

Stanton strongly suggests that men

A) have deprived women of the opportunities that instill self-sufficiency.
B) do not consider why they feel the need to protect women.
C) should assume more "domestic" roles to understand the difficulties faced by women.
D) often ignore the social and political contributions made by women.

34

As used in line 3, "forces" most nearly means

A) efforts.
B) powers.
C) groups.
D) pressures.

35

The primary function of the list in lines 10 – 15, ("The strongest…bread") is to

A) emphasize the extent of women's involvement in society.
B) summarize the differences between the roles of men and women in society.
C) list the roles that women are generally forced to assume.
D) compare the limited rights of women to the extensive rights of men.

36

As used in line 54, "resources" most nearly means

A) reserves.
B) supplies.
C) ruses.
D) capabilities.

37

In the passage, Stanton claims that depriving women of knowledge and responsibility

A) always results in them making unfortunate choices.
B) has a negative effect on the entire family.
C) means that they become a financial burden.
D) positions them for failure and reproach.

38

Which choice provides the best evidence for the answer to the previous question?

A) Lines 43 – 44 ("To throw…eyes")
B) Lines 59 – 61 ("but when…humiliation")
C) Lines 65 – 68 ("The talk of…results")
D) Lines 70 – 72 ("Such are…sovereignty")

39

Based on the information in the passage, which choice best describes Stanton's overall outlook on life?

A) Most lives are a continuous struggle.
B) Earning a living is challenging.
C) Disaster is inescapable.
D) Difficult experiences can have unexpected rewards.

40

Stanton's rhetorical question in lines 89 – 92 ("Who, I ask … human soul") primarily serves to

A) provide context for all her previous statements.
B) share her own individual experience with the audience.
C) change the topic to focus on philosophical issues.
D) encourage deeper reflections on the nature of autonomy.

Refer to the passage pair below for questions 41 – 52.

Passage 1 is adapted from Maggie Brown, "Sanitation is Key in Controlling Worm Diseases," published in 2012. Passage 2 is adapted from Dr. Mohammad Razai, "Ending Tuberculosis in Afghanistan: working together towards a common goal," published in 2016.

Passage 1

Diarrhea, abdominal pain, malaise, anemia, and delayed child development: these are the debilitating effects of one group of diseases, the worms referred to as "soil-transmitted
5   helminths" (STHs). As indicated by the name, these diseases are transmitted via contaminated soil; as such, good sanitation has a key role in prevention. However, because sanitation systems vary greatly, their impact is difficult to study.
10 Now, a systematic review and meta-analysis (a reanalysis of data from already published studies), by Ziegelbauer and coauthors, quantifies the benefits of sanitation: for all three of the STHs, when sanitation was both available
15 and regularly used, the odds of getting a worm disease was cut in half.
    One billion of the world's people experience a diminished ability to work, learn, and thrive as a result of infection by these parasites –
20 roundworm, whipworm, and hookworm. The resulting losses in quality of life and productivity can trap people in a cycle of poverty and stigma and diminish their ability to care for themselves and their families.
25 Currently, the primary approach to the problem is repeat drug treatment. As important as drugs are, though, they also have limitations: reinfection in endemic areas; possible reduced efficacy and development of resistance; and
30 supply, delivery, and compliance problems. Drug administration can go only so far, and currently many programmatic goals are not being met. For the STHs, many authors argue that integrated control is the only hope for lasting improvement.
35 Integrated control of infectious diseases involves not only drug treatment to knock down the illness itself, but preventive measures such as education of at-risk communities, surveillance and research, strong healthcare systems, vector
40 control, safe water supplies, good hygiene practices, and adequate sanitation systems.
    Thus, Ziegelbauer and coauthors urge, drug treatment should be only part of efforts toward STH control; sanitation should also
45 be emphasized. And the authors point out something that drug treatment does not do: "Implementation of sanitation facilities and integrated control approaches go far beyond the prevention and control of intestinal helminths;
50 they impact other neglected tropical diseases, such as schistosomiasis, trachoma, and diarrhea."

Policy and funding support for integrated control that includes good sanitation should be a focus as the world fast approaches the deadline
55 for the Millennium Development Goals with disappointing progress toward the goal to "Halve, by 2015, the proportion of the population without sustainable access to safe drinking water and basic sanitation."

Passage 2

60 Afghanistan is one of 22 countries with a high burden of tuberculosis (TB) according to the World Health Organisation (WHO). The estimated number of new cases each year is a staggering 53,000 and as many as 12,000 afflicted by this
65 curable infection lose their lives each year. For a large number of those infected, a timely diagnosis and effective treatment is out of reach due to high levels of poverty, lack of access to effective healthcare, and ongoing conflict in large parts of
70 the country. It is not a surprise that a significant number of victims are women and children due to their vulnerable status in a society ravaged by decades of war, drought and migration. Some of these challenges such as poverty and lack of
75 access to healthcare facilities are not unique to Afghanistan, but it is the only country, out of 22 that account for 80% of TB cases in the world, that has been utterly decimated by over four decades of war and migration.
80 Despite the challenges, the Afghan government and its international partners have made some progress with the implementation of the National Tuberculosis Control Program (NTCP). In 2011 an estimated 97% of people
85 had access to TB facilities. But access to facilities is one small part of the answer. The quality of diagnosis, treatment and outreach is much more important when dealing with one of the most persistent diseases known. The causative pathogen,
90 mycobacterium tuberculosis, can remain in an asymptomatic form for a long time. Even after treatment is started, bacteria can easily develop resistance to drugs if they are not administered appropriately.
95 The public health challenge of treating TB in Afghanistan is that most of those affected are extremely hard to reach, public awareness of the illness and its mode of transmission is very poor, and treatment programs are quite ineffective,
100 giving rise to a large burden of multi-drug resistant TB (MDR-TB). According to WHO, in 2014, one in four of the estimated 480,000 people worldwide with a new MDR infection received a diagnosis.
    Fortunately, the recently updated WHO
105 guidelines offer hope for patients in countries like Afghanistan in the form of shorter, cheaper treatment regimens and rapid diagnostic tests. This

is an opportunity to focus all efforts on improving the quality of diagnosis as an important public
110 health matter and tackling the MDR-TB through this novel treatment regimen with better reported success rates.

Inadequate treatment of MDR-TB is in fact a big part of the problem. All stakeholders
115 must work together to address the increasing prevalence of MDR-TB and the slow progress in its detection and access to care. MDR-TB cannot be managed via national programs alone without addressing the issue of private and other
120 healthcare providers in Afghanistan. Evidence has consistently shown that, in countries with high burden of TB, engaging all healthcare providers working in partnership through Public-Private Mix (PPM) has improved all aspects
125 of patient care including better case detection, improved treatment outcomes, increased cost-effectiveness and more effective outreach.

The hope is that by rapid diagnosis, shorter treatment regimen and involvement of all
130 providers through PPM initiative, Afghanistan will make significant progress towards achieving the WHO's End TB Strategy.

★

Passages 1 and 2 are licensed under CC BY 4.0. For more information, see page 511.

41

As used in line 3, "debilitating" most nearly means

A) deadly.
B) concerning.
C) impairing.
D) widespread.

42

The primary purpose of paragraph 2 of Passage 1 (lines 17 – 24) is to

A) applaud the effectiveness of repeat drug treatment for treating STHs.
B) trace the origins of poverty to the spread of STHs.
C) explain what differentiates roundworms, whipworms, and hookworms from other parasites.
D) emphasize the need to improve STH treatment methods.

43

As presented in Passage 1, the study by Ziegelbauer and coauthors relied upon

A) information from the Millenium Development Goals project.
B) interviews with people trapped in a cycle of poverty due to STHs.
C) data from other published studies about sanitation and STHs.
D) data gathered by Ziegelbauer in STH-contaminated areas.

44

Passage 1 implies that integrated control of STHs

A) may completely eliminate soil-transmitted helminths.
B) requires educational and public health initiatives.
C) will completely replace drug treatment as the primary form of soil-transmitted helminth treatment.
D) should eliminate many other tropical diseases caused by poor sanitation.

45

Which choice provides the best evidence for the answer to the previous question?

A) Lines 30 – 32 ("Drug…met")
B) Lines 32 – 34 ("For the…improvement")
C) Lines 35 – 39 ("Integrated…systems")
D) Lines 47 – 51 ("'Implementation… diarrhea'")

46

According to paragraph 1 of Passage 2, which of the following distinguishes Afghanistan from the other countries with "a high burden of tuberculosis" (lines 60 – 61)?

A) Its recent history of socio-political turbulence
B) Its lack of modern healthcare facilities
C) Its high rates of poverty
D) Its recent and drastic increase in reported cases of tuberculosis

47

In paragraph 2 of Passage 2 (lines 80 – 94), the author indicates that

A) people with TB can be unaware that they are infected.
B) over 95 percent of those with TB have received a diagnosis.
C) every TB patient must receive an individualized treatment regimen.
D) TB has the highest rate of infection among infectious diseases.

48

Which choice provides the best evidence for the answer to the previous question?

A) Lines 84 – 85 ("In 2011…facilities")
B) Lines 85 – 89 ("But access…known")
C) Lines 89 – 91 ("The causative…time")
D) Lines 91 – 94 ("Even…appropriately")

49

The author of Passage 2 implies that treatment of TB in Afghanistan has tended to

A) rely primarily on government programs.
B) take place mainly in private clinics.
C) be scattered and disorganized.
D) be inefficient and wasteful.

50

Both passages primarily discuss

A) the role of the World Health Organization in improving worldwide sanitation.
B) the inherent difficulties of diagnosing and treating newly discovered diseases.
C) American efforts to improve public health in impoverished countries.
D) methods for the prevention and treatment of widespread diseases.

51

Passage 1 and Passage 2 are written from the perspective of

A) opponents of current disease response programs.
B) proponents of specific shifts in public health policy.
C) researchers advocating the development of new drugs.
D) health educators spreading information about disease prevention.

52

Both authors identify which of the following as a major hindrance to infectious disease treatment?

A) The development of drug-resistant diseases
B) The non-compliance of local governments
C) A lack of effective sanitation facilities
D) Arduous treatment regimens for patients

STOP

NO TEST MATERIAL ON THIS PAGE

Writing & Language Test 6

35 MINUTES, 44 QUESTIONS

Turn to Section 2 of your answer sheet to answer the questions in this section.

DIRECTIONS

Each of the following passages is accompanied by approximately 11 questions. Some questions will require you to revise the passages in order to improve coherence and clarity. Other questions will require you to correct grammatical errors. Passages may be accompanied by graphs, charts, or tables that you must consider when making revisions. For most questions, you may select the "NO CHANGE" option if you believe that portion of the passage is clear, concise, and grammatically correct as is.

Within the passages, highlighted numbers followed by underlined text indicate which part of the text corresponds with each question. Bracketed numbers [1] indicate sentence number. These bracketed numbers are only relevant to problems that require you to add or rearrange sentences in a paragraph.

Questions 1-11 are based on the following passage.

Grammelot: A Universal Language

[1] In theater, the tone that an actor uses when delivering a line arguably communicates as much as the line **1** itself; researchers have studied the effects of tone of voice on comprehension. [2] Some plays even call for actors to rely entirely on tone by making up words. [3] Suppose that an actor slowly pressed down three fingers, one by one, while saying "Ahh—opp. Nahh—opp. Chop." [4] You would understand that she was counting to three. [5] If the audience members know the context, they may be able to decode meaning from tone, rhythm of speech, mimed actions, facial expressions, and so on. **2**

3 Now, nonsense language has served a practical purpose. In Europe in the Middle Ages, there was a tradition of traveling performers in open-air markets or carnivals using nonsense language and onomatopoeic sounds, such as "bloop, bloop" for boiling water. At the time, the dialect spoken in one village may have been different than **4** the one spoken in the village down the road; traveling performers had to find a way to communicate wherever they went.

1

Which choice adds the most relevant support?

A) NO CHANGE
B) itself since, as is often said, "Actions speak louder than words."
C) itself, although the use of monotone may sometimes be used for special effect by an impersonal cyber being, for example.
D) itself, as when actors convey the meaning of Elizabethan English to modern audiences.

2

To make this paragraph most logical, sentence 5 should be placed

A) where it is now.
B) before sentence 1.
C) after sentence 2.
D) after sentence 3.

3

A) NO CHANGE
B) In some cases,
C) To be sure,
D) In the end,

4

A) NO CHANGE
B) the village down the road
C) people in the village down the road
D) down the road

Nonsense words also came in handy when troubadours wanted to satirize the [5] powerful such as kings and nobles, a risky yet timeless pursuit. For example, acting the role of a peasant greeting an official, a performer might bow while earnestly pronouncing "Gazooooom, BeeSweeee-bitty!" From the silliness of the words, the audience could recognize that the official was being mocked, [6] even though the words do not have specific meanings.

Theatrical gibberish has been called "grammelot" by the Italian playwright and actor Dario Fo, who [7] publicized its use in modern times. In 1969, Fo began touring with his one-man play, *Mistero Buffo*. The play satirized the way that organized religion often presented biblical characters as perfect. Fo imagined new characters in the stories and gave them down-to-earth reactions. Using nonsense language allowed him more artistic freedom to interpret the stories. [8] Fo later received the Nobel Prize for [9] Literature, with the Nobel committee citing his influential "blend of laughter and gravity."

Film and television producers are more likely to employ nonsense language purely for laughs. In the 1977 film *Star Wars*, for example, the burbling and squealing robot R2D2 adds comic relief to the science-fiction battles. In 2010's *Despicable Me*, the "Minions" babble [10] unintelligibly; viewers can focus on their antics rather than their thoughts. Not only are viewers liberated from trying to remember which Minion is which, [11] but the Minions surprise us all the more with their zany reactions.

★

---

[5]

A) NO CHANGE
B) powerful such as kings, (and nobles)
C) powerful, such as (kings and nobles),
D) powerful (such as kings and nobles),

[6]

Which choice provides the best supporting example for the main idea of the paragraph?

A) NO CHANGE
B) but a real-life official would have a hard time proving it
C) and may or may not become upset as a result.
D) often eliciting laughter and applause.

[7]

A) NO CHANGE
B) popularized
C) globalized
D) immortalized

[8]

At this point, the writer is considering adding the following sentence.

　　Fo performed it for 30 years, while also working on other projects.

Should the writer make this addition here?

A) Yes, because it adds a specific context for the sentence that follows.
B) Yes, because it supports the main claim of the paragraph.
C) No, because it repeats information offered earlier in the paragraph.
D) No, because it provides contradictory and confusing details.

[9]

A) NO CHANGE
B) Literature. With
C) Literature–
D) Literature thus

[10]

A) NO CHANGE
B) unintelligibly; viewers perceive
C) unintelligibly, highlighting
D) unintelligibly to focus viewers on

[11]

A) NO CHANGE
B) except
C) notwithstanding
D) DELETE the underlined word.

Questions 12-22 are based on the following passage.

Nicotine in Nature

Nicotine is a mild stimulant produced naturally in the leaves of tobacco plants. Because of its ability to interact with the nervous system, nicotine can be toxic to many [12] animals. Pure nicotine is a potent insecticide. Though much research has been done, little is known about nicotine in its natural environment.

One group of researchers sought to determine the role of nicotine in the wild tobacco plant. Scientists mutated several plants, preventing them from producing nicotine. Then, they compared the growth of mutant plants to [13] that of normal tobacco. With the exception of nicotine, the two groups displayed no noticeable differences in growth or biosynthesis of any metabolites (substances involved in chemical changes within cells). [14] Finally, researchers observed the eating behaviors of herbivores that were allowed to choose between the different plant types studied.

Scientists discovered that the nicotine-free mutated plants had a much higher [15] quota of predation in a laboratory. One of tobacco's primary pests, a moth larva, showed a preference for these plants. When allowed to feed solely on the mutated plants, the moth larvae grew faster, suggesting that nicotine [16] slowed insect growth. However, the caterpillars studied were not entirely [17] inimical to the unmutated tobacco plants, leading scientists to believe that nicotine resistance may have developed in some species to combat the toxicity of a valuable food source.

12

Which choice provides the best combination of the two sentences at the underlined portion?

A) animals, so pure
B) animals and pure
C) animals, pure
D) animals; then pure

13

A) NO CHANGE
B) it of
C) those of
D) DELETE the underlined portion.

14

The author is considering deleting the underlined sentence. Should the writer make this change?

A) Yes, because the discussion of insect eating patterns is beyond the scope of the passage.
B) Yes, because it distracts from the passage's focus on the role of nicotine in tobacco plants.
C) No, because it sets up the controversial argument that follows in the next paragraph.
D) No, because it describes a crucial feature of the experiment.

15

A) NO CHANGE
B) incidence
C) incidents
D) recurrence

16

A) NO CHANGE
B) slows
C) was slowing
D) is slowing

17

A) NO CHANGE
B) critical
C) scrupulous
D) averse

Researchers followed up on their initial findings and transplanted study groups in the field, [18] they used the same treatments and the same controls. Again, the mutated plants were the primary targets for pests in the plant's natural habitat. [19] Furthermore, normal tobacco plants incurred reduced pest activity. The group's findings indicate that nicotine acts as an effective defensive compound for the [20] native tobacco plant in its natural environment.

However, other metabolites besides nicotine may discourage insects from eating the plants. To find out, the researchers subjected both the mutant and normal tobacco plants to a treatment that stimulates the production of abnormally high levels of defensive compounds within cells. They found that the treatment resulted in decreased herbivore activity for both the normal plants and the nicotine-free mutants. This suggests that the overall increase in defensive molecules compensated for the lack of nicotine in these mutants. In addition, the data indicates that these compounds may not naturally be present in sufficient quantities to defend against pests.

This research helps scientists understand the complex processes underlying the relationships between plants and their predators. Furthermore, it highlights the evolutionary importance of secondary [21] metabolites (such as nicotine), which are not necessary for an organism's growth or survival, but nevertheless contribute to health in other ways. Finally, it establishes the relevance of laboratory findings by confirming [22] researchers' theories with field data.

18
A) NO CHANGE
B) they are using
C) used
D) using

19
A) NO CHANGE
B) Necessarily,
C) While
D) Next,

20
A) NO CHANGE
B) indigenous
C) domestic
D) DELETE the underlined portion.

21
A) NO CHANGE
B) metabolites (such as nicotine)
C) metabolites; such as nicotine;
D) metabolites: such as nicotine,

22
A) NO CHANGE
B) researchers
C) researcher's
D) researcher

Questions 23-33 are based on the following passage.

Automation and Jobs

— 1 —

Our great-grandparents [23] lived in a different world. Ladies in a "typing pool" used manual typewriters to produce copies. Men sawed blocks of ice out of frozen lakes to cool food in far-away kitchens. Bakers kneaded bread dough for hours. In contrast, today copying, refrigerating, and bread-baking have been largely "automated." Machines can now do these tasks.

— 2 —

The ongoing automation of work causes some people to fear that nearly all jobs will someday become obsolete. They point to revolutionary and perhaps alarming developments: robots performing surgery, vehicles driving themselves, [24] instructional computer programs. It is impossible to know whether consumers will embrace all automated changes, however; in some cases, they may prefer face-to-face interactions with other humans. For example, a chain of grocery stores opened in Southern California with only self-pay scanners for customers to use on their own. However, the stores failed. Customers reported that shopping there was too [25] impersonal.

— 3 —

[26] Whether jobs will become obsolete is unknowable. History, however, can provide some clues. The Paris-based international Organization for Economic Cooperation and Development (OECD), which studies global economies, says that historically, when automation wipes out some jobs, it generates others. Agriculture provides a dramatic example. When fields were tilled and harvested by hand, nearly 100 percent of the workforce worked on farms. Gradually, hand-tools were replaced by horse-drawn steel plows and mechanical [27] devices, that could do the work of many people. [28] The process of automating farm tasks continued, of course, so that now farming employs less than 2 percent of the U.S. workforce. Since about 95 percent of U.S. workers are currently employed, clearly many non-farming jobs were created as farming jobs disappeared.

[23]

Which choice most effectively sets up the main contrast described in the paragraph?

A) NO CHANGE
B) likely had jobs that required physical skills and stamina.
C) probably wanted something different for future generations.
D) did not have computers or the Internet.

[24]

A) NO CHANGE
B) instruction via computer programming.
C) computer programs instructing students.
D) students taught by computer programs.

[25]

Which choice most effectively supports the central point of the paragraph?

A) NO CHANGE
B) time-consuming.
C) expensive.
D) frightening.

[26]

A) NO CHANGE
B) What will happen to jobs down the road
C) The nature of the jobs that will be done
D) The question of jobs in the future

[27]

A) NO CHANGE
B) devices–
C) devices and
D) devices

[28]

At this point, the writer is considering adding the following sentence.

> By 1870, agriculture employed only about half of the American workforce.

Should the writer make this addition?

A) Yes, because it provides a numerical benchmark for the decrease in farm labor.
B) Yes, because it explains a crucial detail about 19th century agriculture.
C) No, because it fails to describe automation in agriculture at the time.
D) No, because it focuses too precisely on a particular year.

— 4 —

After looking at all the evidence, [29] automation is more likely to change work than to end it. Many occupations require a "bundle of tasks," the OECD report points out, and automating one of the tasks does not necessarily obliterate the occupation. For example, although there are no longer "typing pools," there are still office jobs. Typing quickly still matters, but it is only one of many specialized skills required of today's administrative [30] assistance.

— 5 —

The OECD and many other economic researchers stress that occupations of the future will generally require more education than those of the past. [31] In agriculture, for example, farms will need very few manual laborers. Instead, farms may need workers who can design and run automated greenhouses, select the best robotic bees, or program drones to [32] keep tabs on crops. Workers will need scientific and technological skills. [33]

---★---

Question [33] asks about the previous passage as a whole.

[29]
A) NO CHANGE
B) automation can be seen as something that
C) one can conclude that automation
D) encouraging automation

[30]
A) NO CHANGE
B) assistant's.
C) assistants.
D) assists.

[31]
A) NO CHANGE
B) Agriculturally, farms will need
C) For example, in agriculture, the need of farmers will be for
D) Farms, for example, will need

[32]
A) NO CHANGE
B) monitor
C) keep them apprised of
D) check out

Consider the passage as a whole as you answer question 33.

[33]
To make the passage most logical, paragraph 4 should be placed

A) where it is now.
B) after paragraph 1.
C) after paragraph 2.
D) after paragraph 5.

Questions 34-44 are based on the following passage and supplementary material.

Violence Interrupters

[34] Protocols shift in some hospital emergency rooms in the United States. According to a new routine, when young victims arrive with gunshot or stab wounds that may stem from neighborhood conflicts, hospital staff members call an "interrupter" to help in the healing process.

Interrupters are [35] outreach worker's. They may be from the victim's own community and may have had a violent past themselves. The interrupter does not share information with law [36] enforcement. The patient may feel comfortable sharing whatever he knows about who attacked him, and why. Frequently, the violence stems from an ongoing conflict. The interrupter offers the patient support, including helping with restarting education, getting a job, and [37] new interpersonal skills. Meanwhile, the interrupter meets with a team of fellow interrupters who can reach out to the perpetrators and the victim's friends. The short-term goal is to prevent retaliation.

"Interrupting" violence is part of [38] a novel public health approach developed by Gary Slutkin, a doctor and professor of epidemiology. Research has shown that when people are exposed to violence in their homes and communities, they tend to "catch" the behavior; they become [39] traumatized. Dr. Slutkin reasoned that such a clear case of contagion could be met with the same epidemiological response used for diseases such as tuberculosis (TB), HIV, and Ebola. He hypothesized that violence is primarily a health issue.

34

A) NO CHANGE
B) Shifted protocols
C) Protocols are shifted
D) Protocols have shifted

35

A) NO CHANGE
B) outreach workers'.
C) outreach workers.
D) an outreach worker.

36

Which choice most effectively combines the underlined sentences?

A) enforcement, so the patient
B) enforcement, indicating that the patient
C) enforcement although the patient
D) enforcement because the patient

37

A) NO CHANGE
B) how to develop
C) the development of
D) developing

38

A) NO CHANGE
B) an unfamiliar
C) an arcane
D) an obscure

39

Which choice most effectively explains the contagion theory as applied to violence?

A) NO CHANGE
B) more likely to commit violence.
C) embarrassed.
D) more likely to become a victim of violence.

[1] In 2000, Dr. Slutkin [40] launched a program called CeaseFire in a violent Chicago neighborhood. [2] CeaseFire staff members tried to halt contagion by identifying and resolving minor conflicts in the community. [3] Secondly, outreach workers identified individuals with the highest risk for spreading the contagion of violence and worked with them personally to change their behaviors, as in the hospital visit described above. [4] They organized community vigils and protests at the sites of shootings or stabbings. [5] Changing community norms is crucial because research has shown that a major factor in whether people commit violent acts is peer expectations. [41]

During the first year of the CeaseFire program, the rate of violent crime in the neighborhood dropped by 67 percent. [42] Attracting notice for such results, hospitals and local governments began contacting CeaseFire. Public awareness grew with the 2011 release of an award-winning documentary film, *The Interrupters*.

Dr. Slutkin eventually founded Cure Violence, a non-profit research and training organization. [43] They help public health agencies launch epidemiological responses to violence. Cure Violence estimates that about 50 urban centers in the U.S. and elsewhere are using the "interrupter" approach to address violence. In some cases, data showed decreased rates of violence not only in the target community but also in surrounding communities, [44] thereby lending support to the "contagion" theory of violence.

40

Which choice provides the most effective link to the previous paragraph?

A) NO CHANGE
B) tested out his epidemiological approach with CeaseFire, an interrupter program
C) garnered public funding to launch an anti-violence non-profit agency, CeaseFire,
D) founded CeaseFire, a professional outreach organization to address violence

41

To improve the cohesion and flow of this paragraph, the writer wants to add the following sentence.

  Finally, outreach workers tried to change the assumptions and norms of the entire community.

The sentence would most logically be placed

A) after sentence 1.
B) after sentence 2.
C) after sentence 3.
D) after sentence 5.

42

A) NO CHANGE
B) They were attracted to these results;
C) Attracting such noticeable results,
D) Such results attracted notice;

43

A) NO CHANGE
B) It helps
C) They helped
D) It was helping

44

Which choice most clearly concludes the passage with a restatement of its main proposition?

A) NO CHANGE
B) which causes one to wonder why such an approach was not implemented sooner.
C) showing the importance of collecting hard data on community-based programs.
D) a fact that proves the level of skill of the interrupters.

NO TEST MATERIAL ON THIS PAGE

Math Test 6 – No Calculator

25 MINUTES, 20 QUESTIONS

Turn to Section 3 of your answer sheet to answer the questions in this section.

DIRECTIONS

For questions **1 – 15**, find the solution to each problem and select the most appropriate answer from the choices provided. For questions **16 – 20**, find the solution to each problem and write your answer in the space provided. You may use the blank space in your test booklet for scratch work.

NOTES

1. The use of a calculator on any part of this section is forbidden.
2. Unless otherwise indicated, all variables and expressions used in this test represent real numbers.
3. Unless otherwise indicated, all figures used in this test are drawn to scale.
4. Unless otherwise indicated, all figures used in this test lie on a plane.
5. Unless specified otherwise, a given function, f, has the domain the set of all real numbers x for which $f(x)$ is a real number.

REFERENCE

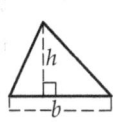
$A = \frac{1}{2}bh$

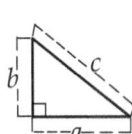
$c^2 = a^2 + b^2$

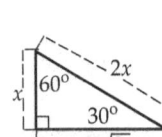
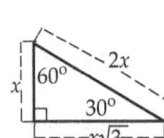
Special Right Triangles

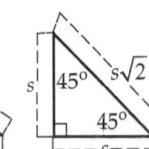

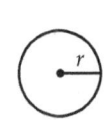
$A = \pi r^2$
$C = 2\pi r$

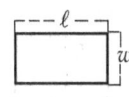
$A = \ell w$

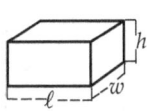
$V = \ell w h$

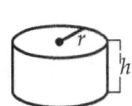
$V = \pi r^2 h$

$V = \frac{4}{3}\pi r^3$

$V = \frac{1}{3}\pi r^2 h$

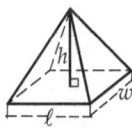
$V = \frac{1}{3}\ell w h$

The arc of a full circle is 360 degrees or 2π radians.
A triangle has angles that sum to 180 degrees.

3

1

If $\dfrac{400}{100(x+3)} = 4$, then what does x equal?

A) -4
B) -3
C) -2
D) -1

2

A kilowatt-hour (kWh) is a unit of energy equivalent to one kilowatt of power expended for one hour. For example, an electrical load rated at 1 kW that operates for 1 hour uses 1 kWh of energy. Electricity in a certain city costs $0.18 per kilowatt-hour, and a light bulb rated at 80 W operates in that city for two hours every day for 200 consecutive days. If 1 kW equals 1,000 W, which equation best models the cost in dollars, c, of the light bulb over this time period?

A) $c = \dfrac{80}{1000} \cdot 400 \cdot 0.18$

B) $c = \dfrac{1000}{80} \cdot 400 \cdot 0.18$

C) $c = \dfrac{80}{1000} \cdot \dfrac{400}{0.18}$

D) $c = 80 \cdot 1000 \cdot 400 \cdot 0.18$

3

$$7 - 8(x - 2) = ax + 5$$

In the equation shown above, a is a constant. Which of the following values of a results in an equation with exactly one solution?

A) 7
B) 8
C) Neither (A) nor (B)
D) Both (A) and (B)

4

The equations $2x + 2y = 6$ and $-7x - 7y = -21$ are graphed in the xy-plane. Which of the following must be true of the graphs of the two equations?

A) The slope of the graph of $2x + 2y = 6$ is 1 and the slope of the graph of $-7x - 7y = -21$ is -1.
B) The graphs of the two equations are perpendicular lines.
C) The y-intercept of the graph of $-7x - 7y = -21$ is -21.
D) The graphs of the two equations are the same line.

5

A dress on sale in a shop is marked at D dollars. During the discount sale, its price is reduced by 15%. Staff are allowed a further 10% reduction on the discounted price. If a staff member buys the dress, what will she have to pay in terms of D?

A) 0.75D
B) 0.76D
C) 0.765D
D) 0.775D

6

If $4r + 3s = 7$, $2r + s = 1$, and $2r + 2s = t - 4$, what is the value of t?

A) 6
B) 8
C) 10
D) 12

7

A 3 by 4 rectangle is inscribed in a circle. What is the circumference of the circle?

A) 2.5π
B) 3π
C) 5π
D) 6

8

At a juice bar, Steven can prepare 20 drinks in 5 minutes, Ashley can prepare 20 drinks in 10 minutes, and Ethan can prepare 20 drinks in 15 minutes. How much time will it take for all 3 of them to work together to prepare 20 drinks?

A) 2 minutes and 2 seconds
B) 2 minutes and 44 seconds
C) 3 minutes and 10 seconds
D) 3 minutes and 26 seconds

9

In a sports club with 30 members, 17 members play badminton, 19 members play tennis, and 2 members play neither. How many members play both badminton and tennis?

A) 7
B) 8
C) 9
D) 10

10

Half the people on a bus get off at each stop after the first, and no one gets on after the first stop. If only one person gets off at stop number 7, how many people got on at the first stop?

A) 128
B) 64
C) 32
D) 16

11

In 2000, approximately 19.5% of seats in a national parliament were held by women. Between 2000 and 2014, this percentage increased at a constant rate of about 3 percentage points every 4 years. If t is the year when approximately 28% of the seats in the national parliaments were held by women, which of the following equations best models the situation?

A) $19.5 + 3t = 28$

B) $19.5 + \frac{3}{4}t = 28$

C) $19.5 + 3(t - 2000) = 28$

D) $19.5 + \frac{3}{4}(t - 2000) = 28$

12

The minimum value of $f(x) = x^2 + x + 4$ is

A) 2
B) -2
C) 4
D) $\frac{15}{4}$

13

What is the reciprocal of $6 + i$? ($i = \sqrt{-1}$)

A) $\frac{1}{6}$

B) $\frac{6-i}{35}$

C) $\frac{6+i}{36}$

D) $\frac{6-i}{37}$

14

What is the domain of $f(x) = \sqrt{9 - x^2}$?

A) $x \leq 3$
B) $x \geq -3$
C) $-3 \leq x \leq 3$
D) $x \leq 3$ or $x \geq -3$

15

$$\frac{x}{x-2} + \frac{x}{(x-2)(x-3)} = \frac{4}{x-3}$$

What are the solutions to the above equation?

A) 2 only
B) 4 only
C) 2 and 3
D) 2 and 4

3 Student-Produced Responses

DIRECTIONS

For questions **16 – 20**, find the solution to the problem and enter your answer as demonstrated on the right.

1. Only the answer that is bubbled in on the answer sheet will be credited. The blank spaces above the bubbles are for you to record your answers for accuracy.
2. Only fill in one bubble in any given column.
3. None of the answers on this portion of the test are negative values.
4. If a problem appears to have more than one answer, only enter one answer. If the answer you enter is one of the correct solutions, you will receive full credit for that question.
5. If the correct answer can be expressed as a mixed number, it must be entered as a decimal or an improper fraction.
6. If the correct answer is a decimal that cannot fit into the grid space, you must fill the grid with enough digits to completely fill the space. The number can be rounded or simply shortened but must fill every blank space.

NOTES

Begin entering answers in any column that accommodates your answer. If you do not need a column do not enter anything in that column.

Answer: $\frac{5}{36}$ Answer: 4.5

Acceptable ways to grid $\frac{1}{6}$ are:

Answer: 302 – either position is correct

16

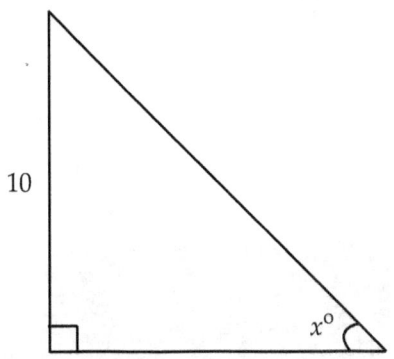

If the area of the right triangle above is 50 units², what is the value of x?

ANSWER: _____

17

If $3^{5-x} = 81^{x+1}$, what does x equal?

ANSWER: _____

18

The population of South Korea, p, in millions of people at time t, where negative values of t represent a number of years before January 1st, 2005 and positive values of t represent a number of years after January 1st, 2005, is projected as:

$$p = 132 - 0.024(t - 8.25)^2$$

According to this projection, during which year does South Korea reach its maximum population?

ANSWER: _____

19

$$k + 3 = \sqrt{a - k}$$

For what value of the constant a does the above equation have k = 2 as the only solution?

ANSWER: _____

20

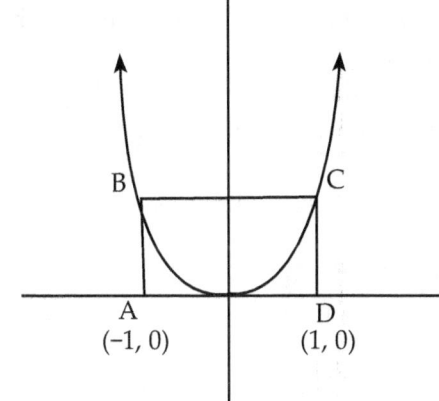

ABCD is a rectangle. Points B and C lie on the graph of $y = px^2$, where p is a constant. If the perimeter of ABCD is 10, what is the value of p?

ANSWER: _____

Math Test 6 – Calculator

 55 MINUTES, 38 QUESTIONS

Turn to Section 4 of your answer sheet to answer the questions in this section.

DIRECTIONS

For questions **1 – 30**, find the solution to each problem and select the most appropriate answer from the choices provided. For questions **31 – 38**, find the solution to each problem and write your answer in the space provided. You may use the blank space in your test booklet for scratch work.

NOTES

1. The use of a calculator on any part of this section is allowed.
2. Unless otherwise indicated, all variables and expressions used in this test represent real numbers.
3. Unless otherwise indicated, all figures used in this test are drawn to scale.
4. Unless otherwise indicated, all figures used in this test lie on a plane.
5. Unless specified otherwise, a given function, f, has the domain the set of all real numbers x for which $f(x)$ is a real number.

REFERENCE

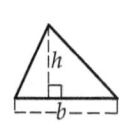 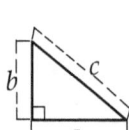 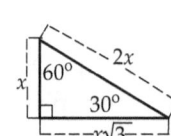 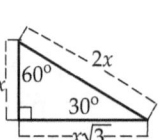 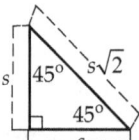 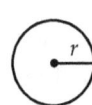

$A = \frac{1}{2}bh$ $c^2 = a^2 + b^2$ Special Right Triangles $A = \pi r^2$ $A = \ell w$
                                                                                       $C = 2\pi r$

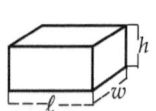 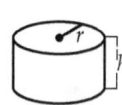   

$V = \ell wh$ $V = \pi r^2 h$ $V = \frac{4}{3}\pi r^3$ $V = \frac{1}{3}\pi r^2 h$ $V = \frac{1}{3}\ell wh$

The arc of a circle is 360 degrees or 2π radians.
A triangle has angles that sum to 180 degrees.

1

The air temperature decreases by about 5°F for every 1,500 feet of elevation gained. On a certain day, the air temperature outside an airplane flying above Newark is −62°F, and the ground level temperature in Newark is 68°F. If x is the height, in feet, at which the plane is flying, which of the following best models the situation?

A) $68 = -\dfrac{5}{1500}x - 62$

B) $68 = \dfrac{5}{1500}x - 62$

C) $-62 = -5x + 68$

D) $-62 = 5x + 68$

2

Drew slices a pie into p equal pieces and eats two pieces. In terms of p, what percent of the pie is left?

A) $100(p-2)\%$

B) $\dfrac{100(p-2)}{p}\%$

C) $\dfrac{100}{p-2}\%$

D) $\dfrac{p-2}{100}\%$

3

Ricardo wants to determine whether a greater proportion of people at his school have brown or black hair. He observes a total of 282 people; 109 students have brown hair, and the number of students with black hair is 21 greater than the number of students with brown hair. Approximately what percent of observed students have NEITHER black nor brown hair?

A) 7
B) 15
C) 39
D) 43

4

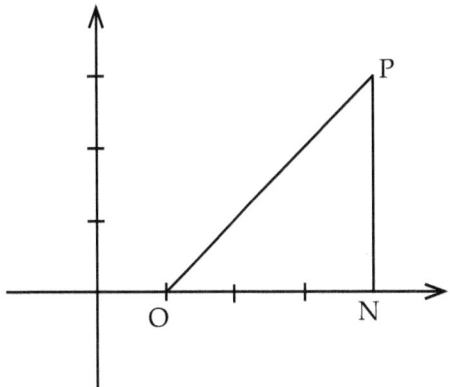

In the figure above, for which of the following coordinates of a point Q (not shown) will △OQN have the same perimeter as △OPN?

A) (0, 3)
B) (1, −3)
C) (2, 3)
D) (3, −1)

5

An electronics company has modeled its profits, in dollars, from the sale of smart phones by the quadratic function $P(x) = -0.06x^2 + 1{,}200x$ where x is the number of units sold. Which of the following equivalent expressions displays the number of units that must be sold to maximize profit?

A) $P(x) = -0.06(x^2 + 20{,}000x)$
B) $P(x) = -0.06(x - 10{,}000)^2 + 6{,}000{,}000$
C) $P(x) = -0.06x(x - 20{,}000)$
D) $P(x) = -0.06(x^2 - 6{,}000x) + 840x$

6

If p and q are positive, then what is x in the equation $\dfrac{qx}{p-x} = 1$?

A) $\dfrac{p}{q+1}$

B) $\dfrac{p+1}{q+1}$

C) $\dfrac{q-1}{p}$

D) $\dfrac{q+1}{p}$

7

When each side of a given square is lengthened by 2 inches, the square's area is increased by 80 square inches. What is the length, in inches, of a side of the original square?

A) 14
B) 16
C) 18
D) 19

8

A cellphone plan costs 2 dollars per month plus 10 cents per minute of talk time used. If the total talk time used in a month is m minutes, what is the total cost in dollars?

A) $10 + 2m$
B) $2 + 10m$
C) $0.1 + 2m$
D) $2 + 0.1m$

9

Week	1	2	3	4	5
Plant Height (cm)	1.2	2.0	2.8	3.95	4.6

If the information in the table above were graphed on a coordinate plane in which the x-axis is number of weeks and the y-axis is plant height, which of the following functions best approximates the line of best fit?

A) $y = x^2 + 0.2$
B) $y = 0.65x^2 + 1.2$
C) $y = 0.8x$
D) $y = 0.85x + 0.35$

10

$$4x - y = 3y + 7$$
$$x + 8y = 4$$

Based on the system of equations above, what is the product of xy?

A) $-\dfrac{3}{2}$

B) $\dfrac{1}{4}$

C) $\dfrac{1}{2}$

D) $\dfrac{11}{9}$

Questions 11–12 refer to the table below.

The chart shows the amount paid in bonuses to the employees of a certain firm.

Bonus paid to an employee ($)	50	100	150	200
Number of employees	7	37	4	2

11

The median bonus per employee is

A) 81
B) 91
C) 100
D) 101

12

If median bonus amount is m, mean bonus amount n, and mode bonus amount p, which of the following represents the correct ordering of m, n, and p?

A) $m < n < p$
B) $m < n = p$
C) $m = p < n$
D) $p < m < n$

13

$$4 \times |9 + 3x| - 39 \leq -3$$

Which of the following best describes the solutions to the inequality shown above?

A) $-18 \leq x \leq 0$
B) $-6 \leq x \leq 0$
C) $x \leq -6$ or $x \geq 0$
D) No solution

14

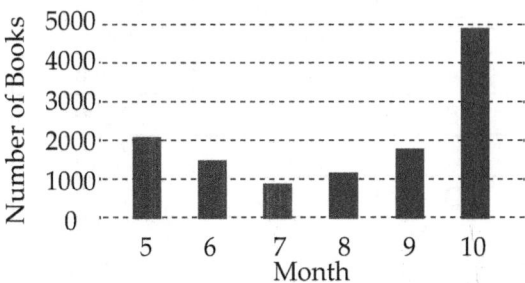

Paige's Bookstore Sales

According to the graph above, during which of the following two-month periods did Paige's Bookstore sell the least number of books?

A) September and October (months 9 and 10)
B) August and September (months 8 and 9)
C) July and August (months 7 and 8)
D) June and July (months 6 and 7)

15

If $a_1 = 1$, $a_2 = 3$, and $\dfrac{2a_{n-1} + 3}{a_{n-2}} = a_n$, then $a_5 =$

A) 9
B) 7
C) $\dfrac{13}{6}$
D) $\dfrac{17}{9}$

16

NUMBER OF CAR RENTAL LOCATIONS

Company	United States Locations	Foreign Locations
A	1,500	4,200
B	1,400	3,500
C	1,250	4,400
D	1,050	1,900

The table above shows the number of car rental locations for four car rental companies. For which of the four companies is the ratio of the number of foreign locations to the number of United States locations the greatest?

A) A
B) B
C) C
D) D

17

A piece of wire 47 cm long is cut so that the two pieces can be formed into a square and an equilateral triangle. The sum of the lengths of a side of the square and a side of the triangle is 15 cm. How long is the side of the square?

A) 1 cm
B) 2 cm
C) 8 cm
D) 9.75 cm

Questions 18 – 19 refer to the following graph.

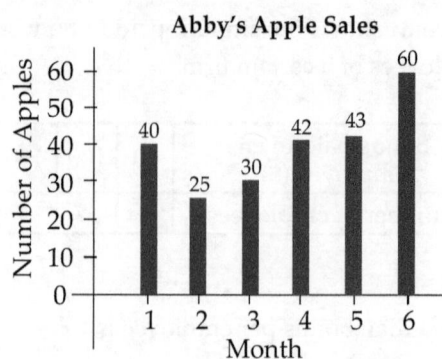

The bar graph above shows the number of apples Abby sold in each of the first six months of 2008.

18

How many more apples did Abby sell in June (month 6) than in February and March (months 2 and 3) combined?

A) 2
B) 5
C) 10
D) 24

19

If the apple sales data from these six months were illustrated by a circle graph (a pie chart), what would be the measure of the central angle of the sector that represents January (month 1)?

A) 30°
B) 40°
C) 54°
D) 60°

20

The number of distinct real values x which satisfy the equation $(x^2 - 6x + 9)^{(x^2 - 8x + 12)} = 1$ is:

A) 0
B) 1
C) 2
D) 3

21

Let a and b be numbers such that $30 < a < 40$ and $50 < b < 70$. Which of the following represents all the possible values of $a - b$?

A) $-40 < a - b < -20$
B) $-40 < a - b < -10$
C) $-30 < a - b < -20$
D) $-20 < a - b < -10$

22

If w is a positive integer and $w^3 = 9w$, then what is w^5 equal to?

A) 59,049
B) 243
C) 1,024
D) 3,125

23

Solve the formula $E = mc^2$ for c.

A) $c = \sqrt{Em}$
B) $c = \dfrac{\sqrt{Em}}{m}$
C) $c = \dfrac{E}{m^2}$
D) $c = \dfrac{\sqrt{E}}{m}$

24

Assuming $a \neq 0$, which of the following equations is equal to $\dfrac{5 - \frac{1}{a}}{a^{-1}}$?

A) $5a - 1$
B) $\dfrac{5a - 1}{a^2}$
C) 4
D) $\dfrac{1 - 5a}{a^2}$

25

$$E(n) = 8.25n - 110{,}000{,}000$$

The function above shows a movie's earnings, $E(n)$, as a function of its ticket sales, n, minus its budget. Approximately how many tickets must the movie sell for the film's earnings to double its budget?

A) 4,000,000
B) 13,333,333
C) 26,666,667
D) 40,000,000

26

Year	Low-Budget Airlines' Share of Low-Cost Seats
2002	24%
2004	34%
2006	47%
2008	66%
2010	92%

The table above shows low-budget airline companies' percentage share of all low-cost seats in a country compared to other airline companies. Which of the following statements best describes the growth of low-budget airlines' percentage share of low-cost seats in the country?

A) The growth is approximately linear, since the percentage share of low-cost seats increases by roughly 13% every year.
B) The growth is approximately linear, since the percentage share of low-cost seats increases by roughly 13% every 2 years.
C) The growth is approximately exponential, since the percentage share of low-cost seats grows at an average rate of 40% per year.
D) The growth is approximately exponential, since the percentage share of low-cost seats grows at an average rate of 40% every 2 years.

27

The graph of $f(x) = x^3$ is translated 6 units up, 2 units right, and reflected over the x-axis. If the resulting graph represents $g(x)$, then what is $g(-1)$?

A) -21
B) 5
C) 14
D) 21

28

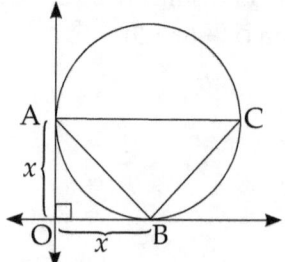

The axes above with an origin at O are tangent to the circle at points A and B, $\angle BCA = \angle OAB$. Which of the following must be true?

 I. $\angle CBA = \angle OAB$
 II. The x-axis is parallel to $\overline{AC}$
 III. $\triangle ABC$ is isosceles

A) I only
B) II only
C) I and II
D) II and III

29

If $\sin 2x = \cos x$, then what is the value of x?

A) $-\dfrac{\pi}{6}$
B) $\dfrac{\pi}{6}$
C) $\dfrac{\pi}{3}$
D) $-\dfrac{\pi}{3}$

30

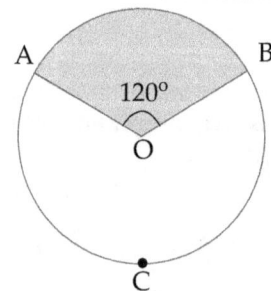

In the figure above, AB is the arc of a circle with center O. If the length of arc AB is 12π, what is the area of sector AOB?

A) 54π
B) 72π
C) 108π
D) 216π

Student-Produced Responses

DIRECTIONS

For questions **31 – 38**, find the solution to the problem and enter your answer as demonstrated on the right.

1. Only the answer that is bubbled in on the answer sheet will be credited. The blank spaces above the bubbles are for you to record your answers for accuracy.
2. Only fill in one bubble in any given column.
3. None of the answers on this portion of the test are negative values.
4. If a problem appears to have more than one answer, only enter one answer. If the answer you enter is one of the correct solutions, you will receive full credit for that question.
5. If the correct answer can be expressed as a mixed number, it must be entered as a decimal or an improper fraction.
6. If the correct answer is a decimal that cannot fit into the grid space, you must fill the grid with enough digits to completely fill the space. The number can be rounded or simply shortened but must fill every blank space.

NOTES

Begin entering answers in any column that accommodates your answer. If you do not need a column do not enter anything in that column.

Answer: $\frac{5}{36}$

Answer: 4.5

← Fraction line
← Decimal point

Write answer in boxes.
Grid in result.

Acceptable ways to grid $\frac{1}{6}$ are:

Answer: 302 – either position is correct

31

$f(x) = \frac{3}{2}x - 2$ and $g(x) = \frac{2}{3}x + 1$. If $f(k) = g(k)$, what is the value of k?

ANSWER: _____

32

Over the course of one week, Andrew spends 42 fewer hours commuting to and from work than he spends working. The time he spends working and commuting that week totals 60 hours. How much time, in hours, did Andrew spend commuting that week?

ANSWER: _____

33

A right triangle has perimeter 30 and sides x, $x + 7$, and $x + 8$. What is the area of the triangle?

ANSWER: _____

34

Emma's test scores on a number of academic subjects are as follows: History is 76, Geography is 74, Math is 92, English is 81, and Chemistry is 80. If the average (arithmetic mean) score is M and the median score is m, what is the value of $M - m$?

ANSWER: _____

35

J donates 15 percent of his current salary to charity. If his pay is increased by 10 percent and he continues to donate 15 percent of the salary, by what percentage do his charity contributions increase?

ANSWER: _____

36

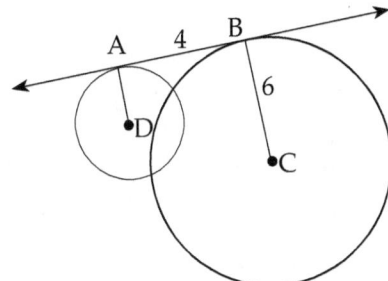

The line through AB is tangent to two circles with centers D and C and whose areas are in the ratio 4 : 1. If AB = 4 and BC = 6, what is the length of line segment DC?

ANSWER: _____

Questions 37 – 38 refer to the following information.

The table shows the amount, $A(t)$, in grams of the radioactive element present after t years. Suppose that $A(t)$ decays exponentially.

t	0	2	4	6	8	10
$A(t)$	320	226	160	113	80	57

37

What is the half-life of the element, in years?

ANSWER: _____

38

About how much element will be present after 16 years, in grams?

ANSWER: _____

Essay Test 6

50 MINUTES, Prompt-based essay

Turn to Section 5 of your answer sheet to answer the question in this section.

DIRECTIONS

As you read the passage below, consider how Dean Baker uses
- evidence, such as facts or examples, to support claims.
- reasoning to develop ideas and to connect claims and evidence.
- stylistic or persuasive elements, such as word choice or appeals to emotion, to add power to the ideas expressed.

This passage is adapted from Dean Baker, "Bill Gates Is Clueless on the Economy," published on February 27, 2017.

Last week Bill Gates called for taxing robots. He argued that we should impose a tax on companies replacing workers with robots and that the money should be used to retrain the displaced workers. As much as I appreciate the world's richest person proposing a measure that would redistribute money from people like him to the rest of us, this idea doesn't make any sense.

Let's skip over the fact of who would define what a robot is and how, and think about the logic of what Gates is proposing. In effect, Gates wants to put a tax on productivity growth. This is what robots are all about. They allow us to produce more goods and services with the same amount of human labor. Gates is worried that productivity growth is moving along too rapidly and that it will lead to large scale unemployment.

There are two problems with this story. First, productivity growth has actually been very slow in recent years. The second problem is that if it were faster, there is no reason it should lead to mass unemployment. Rather, it should lead to rapid growth and increases in living standards.

Starting with the recent history, productivity growth has averaged less than 0.6 percent annually over the last six years. This compares to a rate of 3.0 percent from 1995 to 2005 and also in the quarter century from 1947 to 1973. Gates' tax would slow productivity growth even further.

It is difficult to see why we would want to do this. Most of the economic problems we face are implicitly a problem of productivity growth being too slow. The argument that budget deficits* are a problem is an argument that we can't produce enough goods and services to accommodate the demand generated by large budget deficits.

The often-told tale of a demographic nightmare with too few workers to support a growing population of retirees is also a story of inadequate productivity growth. If we had rapid productivity growth then we would have all the workers we need.

In these and other areas, the conventional view of economists is that productivity growth is too slow. From this perspective, if Bill Gates gets his way then he will be making our main economic problems worse, not better.

Gates' notion that rapid productivity growth will lead to large-scale unemployment is contradicted by both history and theory. The quarter century from 1947 to 1973 was a period of mostly low unemployment and rapid wage growth. The same was true in the period of rapid productivity growth in the late 1990s.

Moreover, theory refutes Gates' proposal because low productivity growth implies fewer goods and services to meet demand. Consequently, prices increase and both demand and job growth stagnate as a result.

Instead of taxing productivity, we can look to boost demand by running large budget deficits. We can spend money on long neglected needs, like providing quality child care, education, or modernizing our infrastructure. Remember, if we have more output potential because of productivity growth, the deficits are not a problem.

We can also look to take advantage of increases in productivity growth by allowing workers more leisure time. Workers in the United States put in 20 percent more hours each year on average than workers in other wealthy countries like Germany and the Netherlands. In these countries, it is standard for workers to have five or six weeks a year of paid vacation, as well as paid family leave. We should look to follow this example in the United States as well.

If we pursue these policies to maintain high levels of employment then workers will be well-positioned to secure the benefits of higher productivity in higher wages. This was certainly the story in the quarter century after World War II when real wages rose at a rate of close to two percent annually.

Of course these policies will not ensure that no workers ever suffer from automation. While we can never guarantee that no worker is harmed by improvements in technology in a dynamic economy, we can look to soften the impact.

One obvious policy would be to require severance pay, for example two weeks of pay for each year worked. This would both give displaced workers somewhat of a cushion and changes the incentives for employers. If a company knows that it faces large payout if it lays off a number of long-term employees, then it has more incentive to think about modernizing its facilities and retraining workers. This would be a win-win where the company has an interest in ensuring that its workers are as productive as possible while the workers get to keep their jobs.

In short, there is no reason that productivity growth should ever be viewed as the enemy of workers. We just need the right set of policies to ensure that they share in the gains.

budget deficits: an indicator of financial health in which spending exceeds revenue

> Write an essay in which you explain how Dean Baker builds an argument to persuade his audience that governments should not tax companies that replace employees with robots. In your essay, analyze how Baker uses one or more of the features in the directions that precede the passage (or features of your own choice) to strengthen the logic and persuasiveness of his argument. Be sure that your analysis focuses on the most relevant features of the passage.
>
> Your essay should not explain whether you agree with Baker's claims, but rather explain how Baker builds an argument to persuade his audience.

Sample response found in the "Answers and Explanations" section of this study guide.

"Bill Gates Is Clueless on the Economy" is licensed under CC BY 4.0. For more information, see page 511.

ANSWERS & Explanations

TESTS 1-6

SAT Practice Test 1: Answers & Explanations

Reading Test

1.	C	6.	B	11.	D	16.	B	21.	D	26.	B	31.	A	36.	B	41.	D	46.	C	51.	A
2.	A	7.	C	12.	A	17.	B	22.	B	27.	C	32.	D	37.	C	42.	B	47.	C	52.	D
3.	C	8.	A	13.	C	18.	B	23.	C	28.	B	33.	A	38.	D	43.	B	48.	D		
4.	A	9.	D	14.	D	19.	D	24.	C	29.	C	34.	D	39.	D	44.	A	49.	A		
5.	B	10.	A	15.	C	20.	A	25.	D	30.	A	35.	C	40.	C	45.	B	50.	B		

1) ➡ C
Concept(s) Tested: Attitude and Tone
Choice (C) is correct. Throughout the passage, George Wong's actions and demeanor indicate that he is unhappy with his present circumstances. In line 1, he is described as standing "pale and silent," and in line 25, the narrator claims that Wong appears "too tired to move." These descriptions indicate that Wong is physically and/or emotionally drained, and that he appears to feel sadness, making "melancholic" the most accurate choice. Choice (A) is incorrect because "haughty" means "arrogant" or "vain," and there is no evidence that Wong is either. Choice (B) is incorrect because, based on the passage, Wong seems sad and bothered by his present circumstances, not uncaring or "indifferent." Choice (D) is incorrect because "relieved" means "reassured" or "thankful," while Wong appears to be stressed.

2) ➡ A
Concept(s) Tested: Citation
Choice (A) is correct because it provides clues that suggest Wong's melancholic attitude: his shoulders "sagged" and he appears "too tired to move." Choice (B) is incorrect because this choice characterizes Wong as responsible, yet the correct choice proves that he is melancholy. Choice (C) is incorrect because it mentions that Wong is "bitter," not sad or melancholic. Choice (D) is incorrect because it describes Wong's actions, but does not reveal his attitude.

3) ➡ C
Concept(s) Tested: Purpose
Choice (C) is correct. Paragraph 2 informs the reader that the story takes place in the future, when humans have inhabited much of the solar system. Without the information in paragraph 2, a reader would have great difficulty determining the overall setting of the story, so you can infer that the paragraph serves to "introduce...an imagined future society." Choice (A) is incorrect because the main character, George Wong, is briefly mentioned in paragraph 2, but the focus of the paragraph is not providing information about Wong. Choice (B) is incorrect because the paragraph reveals that the election is "a landslide vote for Wong" (line 14), and a landslide is a clear victory, not a suspenseful one. Choice (D) is incorrect because paragraph 2 does not reveal anything about the relationship between Wong and Thompson.

4) ➡ A
Concept(s) Tested: Inference
Choice (A) is correct. Lines 43 – 44 reveal that Wong is toasting "the blank video screen," which had just recently been relaying election results. Thus, we can infer that he is saluting the people who have just voted him into office.

5) ➡ B
Concept(s) Tested: Inference
Choice (B) is correct. Lines 54 – 56 reveal that Al Grimm has served "sixty-three Presidents." Because there is no indication that Grimm is incredibly old, these lines suggest that there is a fast presidential turnover rate. Choice (A) is incorrect because the passage does not elaborate on the responsibilities of the Vice-Presidents, and there is no indication in the passage that they must do more work than the President. Choice (C) is incorrect because lines 68 – 78 reveal that the former President is still alive, disproving (C)'s claim. There is no evidence to support (D).

6) ➡ B
Concept(s) Tested: Citation
Choice (B) is correct. These lines reveal that Al Grimm has served "sixty-three Presidents"; the passage does not suggest that Grimm is exceedingly old, so we can infer that he has been secretary to so many Presidents because they "do no stay in office for very long." Choices (A), (C), and (D) are incorrect because they do not allow the reader to make any generalizations about all Presidents of the Solar Union.

7) ➡ C
Concept(s) Tested: Words in Context
Choice (C) is correct. In the context of the passage, "inconspicuous" describes Wong's suit. Of the available choices, "modest," meaning "proper" or "unassuming," provides the most logical description for a suit. Choice (A) is incorrect because Wong is wearing the "inconspicuous" suit, so describing it as "concealed," or "hidden," does not make sense. Choice (B) is incorrect because indifference is an attitude, and suits do not have attitudes. Choice (D) is incorrect because "discreet" means "cautious" or "subtle," which is not as accurate a description for a suit as is "modest."

8) ➡ A
Concept(s) Tested: Words in Context
Choice (A) is correct; throughout the passage, the narrator indicates that being President of the Solar Union is undesirable: Wong appears sad and drained throughout the passage, Vice-President Thompson speaks "sympathetically" (lines 29) to Wong, and voters send "messages of condolence" to the Presidential winner. Based on

404 | KALLIS' Key to the SAT

this information, you can infer that "condolence" means "sympathy" because the passage has already revealed that people are acting with sympathy towards Wong.

9) ➡ D
Concept(s) Tested: Inference
Choice (D) is correct because the passage suggests on multiple occasions that being President of the Solar Union is extremely taxing and stressful, and that Reynolds was overwhelmed by his presidential responsibilities and is "no better" even weeks after leaving office. Choice (A) is incorrect because there is no evidence for it; the passage reveals that Reynolds is not speaking, not even to his wife, but that does not imply that he forfeited the presidency because of her. Similarly, there is no evidence for choice (B), making it incorrect. Choice (C) is incorrect because the passage reveals that Reynolds left office two weeks ago, and that the election occurred more recently, suggesting that Reynolds was uninvolved in the recent election.

10) ➡ A
Concept(s) Tested: Inference
Choice (A) is correct because the question in lines 91 – 97 highlights the incredible amount of responsibility placed on the President of the Solar Union, and Wong's reaction reveals his nervousness and reluctance to accept such responsibility. Thus, you can infer that Wong (and Reynolds before him) finds it "onerous" (incredibly difficult) to bear the responsibility of making "decisions affecting so many people." Choice (B) is incorrect because lines 91 – 100 do not discuss the relationship between the President and his staff. Choice (C) is incorrect because Wong is characterized as nervous, not greedy or desirous of power. Choice (D) is incorrect because the passage reveals that Wong is responsible (lines 36 – 37), which is the opposite of "careless."

11) ➡ D
Concept(s) Tested: Summary
Choice (D) is correct because the phrase in lines 10 – 11 suggests that even the longest days of working did not satisfy Mr. Covey, so you can infer that he had unreasonable expectations. Choice (A) is incorrect because paragraph 1 does not mention Mr. Covey's energy levels, instead focusing on his harshness and cruelty. Choice (B) is incorrect because Douglass does not make any references to taking breaks in this paragraph. Choice (C) is incorrect because the passage does not provide enough information about Mr. Covey for the reader to determine how happy or unhappy he is with overall production.

12) ➡ A
Concept(s) Tested: Attitude and Tone
Choice (A) is correct; lines 9 – 11 ("The longest…for him") characterize Covey as *demanding*, as he forced his slaves to work extremely long hours. Moreover, lines 13 – 14, "Mr. Covey succeeded in breaking me," reveal that he is harsh and *unsympathetic* towards slaves. Choice (B) is incorrect because there is no evidence in the passage that Mr. Covey is "unpredictable." In fact, Douglass suggests that Covey is fairly predictable in that he is consistently demanding and cruel. Choice (C) is incorrect because Douglass never suggests that Covey is "fair." Choice (D) is incorrect because the passage does not provide any information about Covey's intelligence, so this choice is unsupported.

13) ➡ C
Concept(s) Tested: Passage Organization
Choice (C) is correct; lines 15 – 20 reveal that Douglass was spirited, intelligent, and cheerful before living under Covey, and was "broken" by his experiences as a slave to Covey. Thus, he goes from being "spirited" to being "despondent." Choices (A) and (D) are incorrect because "uneasy" and "anxious" do not convey the extent to which Covey "succeeded in breaking" Douglass' spirit. Choice (B) is incorrect because Douglass' dependability is not mentioned in paragraph 1.

14) ➡ D
Concept(s) Tested: Citation
Choice (D) is correct because it effectively conveys that Douglass was "spirited" ("the cheerful spark that lingered about my eye"), but that Covey "crushed" his spirit, driving Douglass to despondency. Choice (A) is incorrect because it does not suggest that Douglass was "spirited," only that Covey drove him to despondency. Choice (B) is incorrect because it describes conditions, but not Douglass' transformation. Choice (C) is incorrect because it explains Douglass' mood only in vague terms.

15) ➡ C
Concept(s) Tested: Purpose
Paragraph 1 primarily discusses how Mr. Covey's unreasonable work schedule transformed Douglass from "a man…into a brute," so it can reasonably be inferred that Douglass' transformation into a "brute" is at least in part a result of "constant forced labor." Choice (A) is incorrect because it is unclear what "his unusual attitude" refers to. Choice (B) is incorrect because "the importance of adequate rest" is not directly discussed in the passage. Choice (D) is incorrect because Douglass does not state or imply that he became physically stronger as a result of laboring for Mr. Covey.

16) ➡ B
Concept(s) Tested: Summary, Purpose
Choice (B) is correct because Douglass states in lines 40 – 41 that the sight of the white sails would "torment [him] with thoughts of [his] wretched condition"; in other words, they caused him to "reflect on his situation" as a slave. Choices (A) and (C) are incorrect because Douglass states that the white sails "torment" him, not that they "lighten his mood" or "create diversions." Choice (D) is incorrect because line 47 states that the white sails "affected [Douglass] powerfully," ultimately leading him to vow to escape.

17) ➡ B
Concept(s) Tested: Citation
Choice (B) is correct because this excerpt shows that the sight of white sails causes Douglass to reflect on his situation because they "torment [him] with thoughts of [his] wretched condition" as a slave. Choice (A) is incorrect because it provides a setting, not an analysis of Douglass' feelings. Choices (C) and (D) are incorrect because they indicate that the sight of white sails "affected" Douglass, but they do not as directly describe Douglass' reflection.

18) ➡ B
Concept(s) Tested: Words in Context
Choice (B) is correct. Using the context of the passage, you can determine that his deep emotions inspire the monologue that follows (lines 52 – 73). The only choice that fits the situation is (B) because strong feelings can force speech, or "require pronouncement." The other choices are incorrect because they do not involve being made to speak.

TEST 1: Answers & Explanations | 405

19) D
Concept(s) Tested: Inference
Choice (D) is correct because lines 58 – 60 contrast a ship's "protecting wing" and the "turbid waters" that separate Douglass from this protection. Because Douglass is seeking protection under the ship's sails, you can infer that the "turbid waters" look dangerous enough to deter Douglass from escaping, making "threatening barriers" the most appropriate choice. Choices (A) and (B) are incorrect because they are irrelevant to the main topic of the paragraph, and choice (C) is incorrect because it is not clear from the text how "punishments for slaves" would be indicated by "turbid waters."

20) A
Concept(s) Tested: Passage Organization
Choice (A) is correct because in the first part of paragraph 4, Douglass addresses the ships in the bay with longing, wishing to stand on their "gallant decks" (line 58). At the end of the paragraph, he begins to plan his future: "I will run away" (line 67), and "There is a better day coming" (line 72 – 73). Thus, over the course of the paragraph, Douglass goes from "longing to planning." Choice (B) is incorrect because Douglass goes from despairing to hoping, not the other way around. Choice (C) is incorrect because Douglass does not "relinquish" at the end of the paragraph; rather, he ends with optimism, claiming that "There is a better day coming." Choice (D) is incorrect because at the end of the paragraph, Douglass is planning his future, not "reflecting" on his past.

21) D
Concept(s) Tested: Purpose
Choice (D) is correct. Douglass reveals that he is summarizing the previous paragraph in lines 74 – 77 ("Thus…lot"), and then recaps his feelings of fury and resolve. Choice (A) is incorrect because it overstates Douglass' madness. Douglass claims he was "goaded almost to madness," (line 75) meaning he *nearly* went insane, so a "sudden loss of sanity" is not supported by the passage. Choice (B) is incorrect; while the "dehumanizing effects of slavery" is a theme throughout the passage, it is not the main purpose of the final paragraph, making (B) too broad. Choice (C) is also a theme of the passage, but is not applicable to the final paragraph.

22) B
Concept(s) Tested: Primary Purpose
Choice (B) is correct. The first sentence establishes a focus on discovery based on new data (gathered from the Kepler mission). Choice (A) is incorrect because comparing findings using different observatories is a minor point in the passage (lines 49 – 60). Choice (C) is incorrect because the passage does not "refute" any assumptions; rather, it elaborates on a recent discovery. Choice (D) is incorrect because the passage never explicitly states the Kepler mission's main goal, so this choice is not supported by the passage.

23) C
Concept(s) Tested: Passage Organization
Choice (C) is correct. The passage begins by announcing the discovery of Kepler-452b ("one particular exoplanet"), and then, around line 61, the focus of the passage shifts to a discussion of the 4,696 planet candidates that have been detected by Kepler ("a summary of others"). Choice (A) is incorrect because it reverses the organization of the passage. Choice (B) is incorrect because the passage does not discuss the goals of the Kepler mission in great detail, and it does not offer any criticisms of the mission. Choice (D) is incorrect because the passage does not mention any "challenges faced by" past NASA missions.

24) C
Concept(s) Tested: Purpose
Choice (C) is correct because the information contained within the em-dashes defines the term "habitable zone," as it is a technical term with which the author did not expect all readers to be familiar. All other choices are incorrect because they do not relate to defining or elaborating on a term, making them unsupported by the passage.

25) D
Concept(s) Tested: Summary
Choice (D) is correct because it provides an accurate summary of the quote in lines 15 – 19 ("'On the…Sun'"). Choices (A) and (C) are not supported anywhere in the passage, and are therefore incorrect. Choice (B) is incorrect because the passage never states or implies that the Kepler telescope is more effective than the ground-based observatories mentioned in lines 51 – 56.

26) B
Concept(s) Tested: Inference
Choice (B) is correct because calling Kepler-452b Earth's "cousin" implies that the two planets are related or have similar features and qualities. This claim is supported by the comments in lines 37 – 40. Choice (A) is incorrect because the passage states that the planet's "mass and composition are not yet determined." Choice (C) is incorrect because it is not distinctive that the planets share the same galaxy. Choice (D) is incorrect because calling something a relative, or "cousin," indicates some sort of closeness or similarity, not "vast distance."

27) C
Concept(s) Tested: Inference
Choice (C) is correct because lines 26 – 27 reveal that the planet's size and composition are unknown and lines 49 – 51 reveal that researchers are studying the properties (which likely include planetary size and composition) of Kepler-452b's system.

28) B
Concept(s) Tested: Citation
Choice (B) is correct because these lines indicate that the properties (which likely include size and composition) of Kepler-452b interest researchers, providing support for the answer to the previous question. The other choices fail to mention or imply "aspirations of the researchers studying Kepler-452b," making them incorrect.

29) C
Concept(s) Tested: Words in Context
Choice (C) is correct. Lines 69 – 70 state that planet "candidates require follow-up observations and analysis to verify they are actual planets." In other words, "candidate planets" are those that researchers think may possibly exist. Choices (A), (B), and (D) are incorrect because "applicants," "aspirants," and "successors" all imply agency and do not make sense in the context.

30) A
Concept(s) Tested: Citation
Choice (A) is correct because it reveals that researchers do not know Kepler-452b's "mass or composition," which implies that the planet

was detected indirectly rather than through visual, telescopic observation. Choice (B) is not evidence because it simply describes the planet's sun and distance from the sun. Choices (C) and (D) are incorrect because they are irrelevant to the discussion of Kepler-452b observations.

31) **A**
Concept(s) Tested: Words in Context
Choice (A) is correct. The context in which the word appears suggests that "signatures" are signs or "indications" of other planets that can be picked up by observatories and telescopes. All other choices are incorrect because "autographs," "designations," and "trademarks" do not clearly relate to "Earth-sized planets," so these choices do not fit the context of the passage.

32) **D**
Concept(s) Tested: Inference
Choice (D) is correct because paragraphs 1 and 2 imply that Earth-like planets are those that fall in the habitable zone, where liquid water can form. Thus, you can safely assume that Earth-like planets are expected to "contain liquid water."

33) **A**
Concept(s) Tested: Purpose
Choice (A) is correct because paragraph 2's primary focus is linking the discussion of the *Transformers* film to a wider discussion of domestic and foreign box offices, which is the "central focus of the passage." Choice (B) is incorrect because, while the author discusses criticisms of the *Transformers* film itself, he or she does not "criticize a type of film-making," so this choice is unsupported by the passage. Choices (C) and (D) are irrelevant to those lines.

34) **D**
Concept(s) Tested: Citation
Choice (D) is correct because it directly states that the *Transformers* film in question provides an example of the phenomenon discussed in the passage. Choices (A) and (B) are incorrect because they only discuss the *Transformers* film, and do not include "the shift that is the central focus of the passage." Although choice (C) does describe the example, it does not tie the example into a trend or a generalized shift.

35) **C**
Concept(s) Tested: Inference
Choice (C) is correct because in paragraph 1, the author claims that *Transformers* will not "go down in history as a great…film" because it "was panned by critics" and did not win any prestigious awards (lines 1 – 7), all of which provides support for choice (C). Choice (A) is incorrect because the author indicates that *Transformers* gathered huge foreign box office earnings despite being considered a "bad" film. Choice (B) is incorrect because the author does not imply that box office earnings anywhere correlate with a film's artistic merits. Choice (D) is incorrect because "repeat viewers" are not discussed in the passage.

36) **B**
Concept(s) Tested: Words in Context
Choice (B) is correct because "robust" describes "filmmaking industries" such as those in China and India. "Booming" is often used to describe growing or successful industries and therefore fits the context of the sentence, making (B) the best choice. Although "unshakable," "resilient," and "strapping" are all close in meaning, they do not fit the context of the passage because they would not quite make sense to describe growing industries.

37) **C**
Concept(s) Tested: Summary
Choice (C) is correct because lines 29 – 30 state, "Globally, theater audiences expanded" after 2000, and lines 32 – 33 state, "By 2009, foreign ticket sales dominated the market," both of which support the claim in choice (C). All other choices are incorrect because they are not mentioned or suggested in paragraph 3.

38) **D**
Concept(s) Tested: Inference
Choice (D) is correct because lines 69 – 70 state, "only Americans tend to favor American comedies." Moreover, it can reasonably be inferred that the "trend discussed throughout the passage" mentioned in choice (D) refers to the growing international audiences for American movies. Thus, you can infer that American comedies are an exception to this trend. Choice (A) is incorrect because the passage discusses preferences of moviegoers, but it does not comment on the types of films shown in foreign countries. Choices (B) and (C) are incorrect because there is no textual evidence supporting them.

39) **D**
Concept(s) Tested: Words in Context
Choice (D) is correct because, in the context of the sentence, "relative" means "in relation to, or compared to, the American market," so "comparative" is the choice with the closest meaning. The other choices do not fit the context of the sentence.

40) **A**
Concept(s) Tested: Inference
Choice (A) is correct because lines 74 – 75 claim that "Hollywood is 'sacrificing some U.S. box office appeal.'" From this, you can conclude that as the "international popularity of American films" grows, some "U.S. box office appeal" will be sacrificed to cater to foreign audiences, which "affects America's domestic film market." All other choices are incorrect because there is no textual evidence supporting them.

41) **D**
Concept(s) Tested: Graph Synthesis, Citation
The graph compares sources of revenue for particular films. Neither (A) nor (B) offers a related text. Choice (C) is incorrect because it offers a general observation. Only choice (D) can be supported; the graph illustrates revenue from top-grossing films only.

42) **B**
Concept(s) Tested: Graph Analysis
Choice (B) is correct because, according to the graph, the top grossing film of 2011 earned approximately 600 million dollars more abroad than it did in the U.S. and Canada. Choice (A) is incorrect because the top grossing film from 2010 made just 200 million dollars more abroad than it did in the U.S. and Canada. Choice (C) is incorrect because the top grossing film from 2013 made approximately 400 million dollars more abroad than it did in the U.S. and Canada. Choice (D) is incorrect because the top grossing film from 2015 made approximately 150 million dollars more abroad than it did in the U.S. and Canada.

43) **B**
Concept(s) Tested: Words in Context

44) **A**
Concept(s) Tested: Purpose
Choice (B) is correct because, along with "scattered teeth" and "fragments of bone," "isolated vertebra" contribute to the "literally fragmentary" knowledge of dinosaurs described in the first paragraph. The image is of a piece of something, and "lone" fits this description best. Choices (A), (C), and (D) are incorrect because they would not describe single pieces of dinosaur bones or teeth.

44) **A**
Concept(s) Tested: Purpose
Choice (A) is correct because in these lines, the author is using subtle understatement and word play to juxtapose the fact that birds and snakes are biological "relatives," and yet the "relationship" between the two is one of predator and prey. The use of such word play indicates that the author is inserting dry humor into the passage, making (A) the best choice. Choice (B) is incorrect because lines 22–25 do not pose a question. Choice (C) is incorrect because the lines comment on the relationship between, not the dispositions of, different species. And choice (D) is incorrect because the lines do not mention physical characteristics.

45) **B**
Concept(s) Tested: Inference
Choice (B) is correct because, as used in line 32, "clothes" describes a supposedly unique feature of birds. From this information, we can infer that "clothes" refers to feathers, as both clothes and feathers are worn on the outside of the body, and feathers are generally considered to be unique to birds. Choices (A) and (D) are incorrect because "anatomies" and "skeletons" refer to bodies, not body coverings. Choice (C) is incorrect because it does not make sense in the context of the passage.

46) **C**
Concept(s) Tested: Summary
Choice (C) is correct because it is an accurate summary of lines 26–31, making it fully supportable based on the passage information. Choice (A) is incorrect because Passage 1 does not indicate that dinosaurs were preyed upon by snakes. Choice (B) is incorrect because Passage 1 argues that reptiles and birds evolved from dinosaurs, not that birds and dinosaurs evolved from crocodiles. Choice (D) is incorrect because Passage 1 does not discuss the diets of dinosaurs or birds.

47) **C**
Concept(s) Tested: Citation
Choice (C) is correct because it explains the position of "a majority of studies" regarding dinosaurs and feather development, making it the most effective summary. Choice (A) is incorrect; although it mentions "feathered dinosaurs," it does not explain how, when, or why dinosaurs developed feathers, making it less thorough than choice (C). Choice (B) is incorrect because it summarizes the views of "a small minority of researchers" (line 62), implying that the theory expressed is not as widely accepted as the one expressed in (C). Choice (D) is incorrect; although it describes the "protofeathers" possessed by one type of dinosaur, it does not explain how, when, or why dinosaurs developed them.

48) **D**
Concept(s) Tested: Inference
Choice (D) is correct because Passage 2 claims that *Archaeopteryx* was "so dinosaur-like" (line 47) that it was once "mistaken for *Compsognathus*." Thus, you can assume that *Compsognathus* is a dinosaur because the "dinosaur-like" *Archaeopteryx* was once mistaken for it. Choices (A) and (B) are incorrect because there is no evidence for them in the passage. Choice (C) is incorrect because the passage does not discuss to what extent the two species are related.

49) **A**
Concept(s) Tested: Purpose
Choice (A) is correct because paragraph 3 of Passage 2 begins with a theory held by "A small minority of researchers," which is later countered by the theory held by "a majority of studies" (line 70). Thus, the "majority of studies" essentially dismiss the "small minority of researchers." Choice (B) is incorrect because Passage 2 never discusses the taxonomic relationship between birds and reptiles. Choice (C) is incorrect because the "small minority of researchers" appear to reject the idea that protofeathers became modern bird feathers. Choice (D) is incorrect because the author mentions the "small minority" of researchers in terms of a specific debate, and makes no mention of the field as a whole.

50) **B**
Concept(s) Tested: Text Synthesis
Choice (B) is correct because—to a certain extent—both passages discuss the evolutionary connection between birds and dinosaurs. Moreover, while Passage 1 argues that skeletal similarities support a link between birds and dinosaurs, Passage 2 cites subtler evolutionary clues and was written over a century after Passage 1, so you can infer that Passage 2 "provides a more modern and nuanced overview" of dinosaur-bird evolution than does Passage 1.

51) **A**
Concept(s) Tested: Text Synthesis
Choice (A) is correct because Passage 1 claims that "birds differ from all other animals" in that they have feathers, which is disproven by the claims in Passage 2. Thus, the author of Passage 1 would probably be *surprised* by developments in paleontology which reveal that birds are not unique for their feathers. Choice (B) is incorrect because Passage 2 does not indicate that the feathered dinosaur theory lacks evidence: while a "small minority of researchers" have argued against feathered dinosaurs, the general consensus is that feathered dinosaurs did exist. Choice (C) is incorrect because Lucas shows interest in the relationship between dinosaurs, reptiles, and birds. (D) is completely unsupported by either passage, and is therefore incorrect.

52) **D**
Concept(s) Tested: Citation
Choice (D) is correct because it provides evidence that Lucas believes that *only* birds have feathers, which indicated that he would be surprised by any developments that indicated otherwise. Other choices are incorrect because they discuss the differences between birds and reptiles, but do not mention dinosaurs or feathers.

SAT Writing & Language Test 1 : Answers & Explanations

Writing & Language Test

1. C	5. C	9. B	13. D	17. B	21. C	25. C	29. D	33. D	37. B	41. B
2. D	6. D	10. D	14. B	18. D	22. A	26. D	30. C	34. C	38. B	42. A
3. A	7. B	11. B	15. B	19. A	23. B	27. B	31. A	35. A	39. D	43. D
4. A	8. C	12. A	16. C	20. D	24. C	28. A	32. B	36. C	40. A	44. C

1) ➡ C
Concept(s) Tested: Conjunction Use
Choice (C) is correct because it clarifies that two events are occurring in sequence. Choices (A) and (B) are incorrect because they imply contrast, which is not the relationship in the sentence. Choice (D) is incorrect because the the law itself did not cause people to assume that local authorities would be able to enforce it, which is the relationship implied by "because."

2) ➡ D
Concept(s) Tested: Transition Words and Phrases
Choice (D) is correct because the sentence containing the underlined portion contrasts with the previous sentence, as the previous sentence claims that local authorities were expected to enforce Prohibition, which is contrasted by the fact that the increase in crime made Prohibition un-enforceable. All other choices are incorrect because they fail to convey this contrast, instead conveying cause-and-effect, sequence, or agreement, respectively.

3) ➡ A
Concept(s) Tested: Passage Development
Choice (A) is correct because the paragraph focuses on ways that Americans circumvented Prohibition, and the fact that Americans could still legally own and consume alcohol is a major detail in this circumvention. Thus, the added portion provides an important distinction, and should be added to the passage.

4) ➡ A
Concept(s) Tested: Passage Development
The underlined portion should relate to the previous sentence, which clarifies that Americans were allowed to own and consume liquor despite other Prohibition restrictions, and choice (A) does this most effectively. The other choices are incorrect because they detail how large institutes, such as churches and corporations, dealt with Prohibition laws, whereas the paragraph is focused on how citizens reacted to Prohibition.

5) ➡ C
Concept(s) Tested: Dangling Modifiers
We can infer that the participial phrase that precedes the underlined portion is describing the "speakeasies" that appeared shortly after Prohibition. Because a participial phrase that begins a sentence must always be followed by the noun it describes, choices (B) and (D) can be eliminated. Choice (A) is incorrect because it suggests that illegal clubs closed saloons and bars, which does not make sense. Thus, choice (C) is the best answer.

6) ➡ D
Concept(s) Tested: Precise Diction
We can infer that, because they were illegal businesses, speakeasies sold liquor in a secret or surreptitious way, and the word with the closest meaning is choice (D), "discreetly." Choices (A) and (B) are incorrect because they do not make sense given what the reader knows about speakeasies. Choice (C) is incorrect because, although it looks and sounds very similar to choice (D), "discretely" means individually, which does not make sense in the context of the sentence.

7) ➡ B
Concept(s) Tested: In-Sentence Punctuation
Choice (B) is correct because it is the only choice that effectively separates two independent clauses using a semicolon. All other choices form run-on sentences, making them incorrect.

8) ➡ C
Concept(s) Tested: Pronoun Use, Commonly Confused Words
Choice (C) is correct because the underlined pronoun refers to "the mafia," a singular noun, and it shows possession over "market." Thus the singular possessive pronoun "its" is correct. Choices (A) and (B) are incorrect because they incorrectly refer to the mafia in the plural. Choice (D) is incorrect because it is a contraction of "it is," which does not make sense in the context of the sentence.

9) ➡ B
Concept(s) Tested: Concision, Correlative Conjunctions
Choice (B) is correct because "as much as" is a standard phrase that means "up to." Although (C), "as many as," conveys the same meaning, the underlined portion is referring to an amount of *crime*, which is an uncountable noun, making "much" the appropriate determiner. ("Many" is used to modify countable quantities.) Choices (A) and (D) are incorrect because it is redundant to use "up to" and "as many/much as" to refer to the same quantity.

10) ➡ D
Concept(s) Tested: Verb Tense, Concision
The simple present tense is correct because the word "still" indicates that dry counties persist in the present. Choice (C) is grammatically correct, but is wordier than choice (D) and therefore incorrect. Choices (A) and (B) are incorrect because they use an inappropriate tense that does not coincide with "still."

11) ➡ B
Concept(s) Tested: Passage Tone, Precise Diction
Only "failure" maintains the academic, neutral tone of the passage as a whole, making (B) the correct choice. All other choices are too casual or colloquial to fit the tone of the rest of the passage, making them incorrect.

12) **A**
Concept(s) Tested: Precise Diction
The correct choice is (A) because "aerostats" accurately describes the list of nouns that follows. (B) is incorrect because balloons cannot be classified as "airplanes." (C) and (D) are incorrect because the passage focuses on vessels that operate in air, not water.

13) **D**
Concept(s) Tested: Verb Tense, Subject-Verb Agreement
The sentence describes a universal physical phenomenon; therefore, the verb must be in the simple present tense. The subject of the sentence is "the buoyant force," which is a singular noun. Thus, (D) is the correct choice.

14) **B**
Concept(s) Tested: In-Sentence Punctuation
The correct choice is (B) because it effectively separates the prepositional phrase from the remainder of the sentence without adding unnecessary punctuation.

15) **B**
Concept(s) Tested: Passage Development
The correct answer is (B) because the added sentence provides information that helps the reader understand the preceding statement. The added statement provides an example to explain the significance of "700 kg of lift."

16) **C**
Concept(s) Tested: Transition Words and Phrases
The information following the semicolon explains a conclusion based on the information preceding the semicolon. "Therefore" best expresses this cause-and-effect relationship, so (C) is the correct choice.

17) **B**
Concept(s) Tested: In-Sentence Punctuation
The information in the second half of the sentence clarifies the claim made in the first half, so a colon is most appropriate to separate these two ideas, and (B) is the correct choice.

18) **D**
Concept(s) Tested: Combining Sentences
The second sentence describes an effect of the information in the first sentence. The best combination of these two sentences is (D) because it accurately expresses this cause-effect relationship. (C) is incorrect because joining two independent clauses requires a coordinating conjunction as well as a comma.

19) **A**
Concept(s) Tested: Passage Development
The paragraph as a whole describes details of operating gas balloons "under normal environmental conditions." Length of time that a balloon could stay aloft would be a relevant operating detail, and thus (A) is correct. Choices (B), (C), and (D) are unsupported and fall outside the scope of the paragraph.

20) **D**
Concept(s) Tested: Verb Tense
The sentence describes a routine or process, so the verb must be in the simple present tense, and (D) is the correct choice.

21) **C**
Concept(s) Tested: Possession
"Craft" is being used as a possessive noun, so the apostrophe and "s" are necessary. Because "craft" is first introduced as a singular noun ("a Roziere"), (C) is the correct choice.

22) **A**
Concept(s) Tested: Passage Development
Choice (A) is correct because the added sentence provides a useful comparison that relates the information in the final paragraph to the information presented earlier in the passage. (D) is incorrect because the information in the final paragraph supports the claim made in the added sentence, and quantitative data is unnecessary in this case.

23) **B**
Concept(s) Tested: Passage Development
The first paragraph discusses the importance of companies anticipating consumers' preferences. A good opening sentence should introduce this idea, so (B) is the correct choice. (A) is incorrect because the paragraph's emphasis is on prediction, not risk-taking, in business. Choice (C) is not the best choice because it is less specific than choice (B). (D) would be disorganized because it would name the job before the concept was developed.

24) **C**
Concept(s) Tested: Concision
Choices (A), (B), and (C) convey approximately the same information, but (C) presents it most concisely, so it is the best choice. Choice (D) is incorrect because it is not clear who would be undertaking the "data usage."

25) **C**
Concept(s) Tested: Commonly Confused Words, Pronoun Use
(C) is correct because the pronoun at the underlined portion is replacing a possessive noun: the economy's "effect on buying power." Thus, we must use the possessive form of the pronoun "it", which is "its". Choices (B) and (D) incorrectly use the contracted form of "it is". Furthermore, choices (A) and (B) are incorrect because they use a verb ("affect") where a noun ("effect") is required.

26) **D**
Concept(s) Tested: Paragraph Organization
In sentence 2 of paragraph 2, the author states that "these processes" give market analysts a sense of what people prefer. The succeeding sentences mention several data-collection processes. Sentence 2 should be placed after the sentences about the processes, where it nicely sums them up. Thus, it should go after sentence 5.

27) **B**
Concept(s) Tested: Voice, Syntax
The active voice is often preferable to the passive voice; in other words, the subject of the sentence should come first, followed by the subject's action. Only choice (B) offers the active voice here. Choice (A) is incorrect because it shifts voice mid-sentence. Choice (C) produces a run-on sentence and confusion about who is writing. Choice (D) is not the best choice because its passive-voice construction omits the subject of the sentence and of the paragraph.

28) **A**
Concept(s) Tested: Precise Diction, Style & Tone
The options to replace choice (A) would not offer enough information for clear meaning. Moreover, (B) addresses the reader directly ("Imagine... ") which is inconsistent with the passage's more formal style.

29) **D**
Concept(s) Tested: Verb Tense
Choice (D) is correct because it supports the conditional modal "might" in the sentence. The subject of the sentence ("the report") *might include ….*, and then (*might*) *turn* to ….. All other choices create inconsistencies in verb tense.

30) **C**
Concept(s) Tested: Pronoun Use, Subject-Verb Agreement
There are two possible referents for the pronoun in this "if" clause: "The digestible report" and "company executives." The pronoun must refer to the latter because it would make sense to substitute "and if *company executives* (they) (do) *open shops in India,…* " Thus, (C) is correct.

31) **A**
Concept(s) Tested: Passage Development
Choice (A) most effectively transitions from the previous topic of what market research analysts do to the new paragraph's topic: what they need ("a solid academic background"). (B) is incorrect because there is no apparent reason for the emphatic "Certainly," followed by a vague statement. Choices (C) and (D) each have a different focus than the paragraph.

32) **B**
Concept(s) Tested: Possession
The meaning of the sentence is that the job outlook for *all* market research analysts looks favorable. We could say that *their* job outlook looks favorable. It makes sense to use the plural possessive, as in (B).

33) **D**
Concept(s) Tested: Graph Analysis
The subtitle of the graph is "Percent change in employment…" Thus, choice (D) is correct because it offers specific evidence from the graph. Other choices are vague or are not reflected in the graph.

34) **C**
Concept(s) Tested: Passage Development
The underlined portion is not essential to the meaning of the passage, but it does provide support with a relevant example, making (C) the best choice.

35) **A**
Concept(s) Tested: Passage Development
The paragraph focuses on the progressive nature of the changes experienced by *Ubik*'s main characters. (A) is the only choice that emphasizes the "gradual" aspect of these changes, making it the correct answer. (B) is incorrect because there in no indication that that "gradual changes" occured *despite* the events in the previous paragraph. Both (C) and (D) are abrupt statements that interrupt rather than transition.

36) **C**
Concept(s) Tested: Phrasal Verbs
Choice (C) is correct because the characters have been transported from one point in time to another, making the phrase "arrive in" a point in time most appropriate. (A) is incorrect because one arrives "in" a point in time, not "at" it. (B) and (D) are incorrect because the sentence stresses the characters' transitory nature, making "arrive" a more appropriate verb.

37) **B**
Concept(s) Tested: Precise Diction
Based on the context, the underlined word describes "messages" and should be close in meaning to "obscure" or "mysterious," making (B) the best choice. (A) and (D) are incorrect because these words typically refer to specialized knowledge and do not provide an adequate description of "messages."

38) **B**
Concept(s) Tested: Pronoun Use
The underlined pronoun introduces a relative clause and therefore should be a relative pronoun. Of the choices, only (B) satisfies this requirement, making it the correct answer. (A) is a subjective pronoun, while (C) and (D) are object pronouns, making these choices incorrect.

39) **D**
Concept(s) Tested: Participial Phrases, In-Sentence Punctuation
Choice (D) makes sense because the participial phrase "having been killed in the explosion" extends the description of Joe Chip and his companions. There is no need for the pronoun "they." (A) and (B) are incorrect because two independent clauses can only be separated by a comma and a coordinating conjunction, not just one or the other. (C) is incorrect because a semicolon establishes a new independent clause, but the main verb is in the participle form.

40) **A**
Concept(s) Tested: Passage Organization
The correct choice is (A) because it accurately places the events of the novel in chronological order. Sentence 3 introduces the topic of Ubik spray cans, so it does not make sense to put sentence 4 before sentence 3. Sentence 5 succinctly concludes the discussion of the novel's plot, so it does not make sense to place sentence 4 after sentence 5. Therefore, the only logical placement left is after sentence 3, or choice (A).

41) **B**
Concept(s) Tested: Subject-Verb Agreement
The verb in the correct choice must be in the plural form because "Joe Chip and his colleagues" is a plural noun phrase. Thus, (B) is the correct choice. (C) is incorrect because the preposition "into" is used to describe movement in space and time and is not normally used with the verb "immerse."

42) **A**
Concept(s) Tested: Commonly Confused Words, Pronoun Use
The underlined pronoun is showing possession over "conclusion," and is referencing "an audience" (a singular noun). Therefore, (A) is the correct choice. (D) is incorrect because "an audience" can be a single reader or a group of readers, so it does not make sense to replace this noun with a more specific pronoun.

43) **D**
Concept(s) Tested: Passage Development, Concision
The correct choice should emphasize religion as an additional theme in Dick's fiction and *Ubik* specifically, making (D) the best choice. Choice (B) is incorrect because it is unnecessarily wordy, and it interferes with the paragraph's focus by inserting the terms "metaphysics," which has not been specifically mentioned.

44) **C**
Concept(s) Tested: Precise Diction
The only choice that correctly identifies the literary device being used is (C), because a metaphor often describes symbolic representation, as in Ubik symbolizing God. (A) is incorrect because hyperbole describes excessive exaggeration, which does not make sense here. Similarly, (B) does not make sense because a simile is a type of comparison, and (D) is incorrect because it names a type of expression, not a type of symbol.

SAT Practice Test 1: Answers & Explanations

Math Test

No-Calculator Portion

1. D	7. C	13. D	19. 0.75		
2. A	8. C	14. C	20. 72		
3. C	9. B	15. C			
4. D	10. D	16. 8			
5. D	11. C	17. 500			
6. B	12. B	18. 1.8			

Calculator Portion

1. D	7. D	13. A	19. D	25. C	31. 3	37. 5061		
2. A	8. A	14. D	20. B	26. C	32. 135	38. 890		
3. A	9. D	15. C	21. B	27. D	33. 60			
4. D	10. A	16. D	22. A	28. C	34. 1			
5. C	11. B	17. C	23. D	29. B	35. 4			
6. C	12. A	18. A	24. D	30. B	36. 54			

No-Calculator Portion

1) D
Concept(s) Tested: Algebra
(A), (B), and (C) all contain correct solutions, yet the solution to (D) is incorrect. You can check this by simply substituting the given value into the equation.
Note that $t + 2t + 3t = 32 \rightarrow 6t = 32$
$t = \frac{32}{6} = \frac{16}{3}$, which is not equal to 8.

2) A
Concept(s) Tested: Functions and Graphs
Rewrite both equations in slope-intercept form:
$y = -2x + 8$ & $y = -2x + 5$
Both equations have the same slope, −2, but different y-intercepts, 8 and 5. Thus, they are parallel lines.

3) C
Concept(s) Tested: Functions and Graphs
Note that $f(x) < 0$ for some x values, but the functions in choices (A) and (D) are always nonnegative. Thus, (A) and (D) do not fit with the graph, and we can eliminate those choices. Note that the function in choice (B) forms a line that is not symmetrical with respect to the y-axis, but the given graph is symmetrical with respect to the y-axis, so (B) does not fit with the given graph. Finally, the function (C) fits with the given graph, making (C) the correct answer.

4) D
Concept(s) Tested: Functions and Graphs
Note that $(x + 1)^2$ is always nonnegative, so $(x + 1)^2 \geq 0$. Therefore, $f(x) = 3 - (x + 1)^2$ is always less than or equal to 3. Therefore, the highest value of the function is 3.

5) D
Concept(s) Tested: Number Rules
To give a real-number solution, $\sqrt{x-2}$ must be greater than or equal to 0. Since only (D) gives a values that results in $\sqrt{x-2} > 0$, it is correct.

6) B
Concept(s) Tested: Algebra, Factoring
$\frac{a^2}{16} - \frac{4b^2}{9}$ is a difference of two squares, and
$\frac{a^2}{16} - \frac{4b^2}{9} = \left(\frac{a}{4}\right)^2 - \left(\frac{2b}{3}\right)^2 = \left(\frac{a}{4} + \frac{2b}{3}\right)\left(\frac{a}{4} - \frac{2b}{3}\right)$
Note that (B) has the factor $\left(\frac{a}{4} - \frac{2b}{3}\right)$.

7) C
Concept(s) Tested: Algebra
Substitute $p = 6$ and $q = 2$ to the $p \triangledown q$. It results in the following:
$6 \triangledown 2 = \frac{2(6) - 2}{6 - 2(2)} = 5$

8) C
Concept(s) Tested: Algebra
Solving y in $-x - y = -2$, we get $y = -x + 2$ Substituting this into $2x - y = -11$ results in $x = -3$.

9) B
Concept(s) Tested: Problem Solving, Algebra
First, write a list of what each merchant begins with: 7A, 9H, and 10C respectively.
Next, take two away from each of these starting quantities, and add one of each other animal to the resulting quantity:
$\rightarrow 7A \; (7A - 2A) + H + C$
$\rightarrow A + (9H - 2H) + C$
$\rightarrow A + H + (10C - 2C)$

412 | KALLIS' Key to the SAT

Since we are told that these new quantities of animals are equal in value (X), and each variable is an integer such that X − (A + H + C) = 168, we can set all of the above equations equal to each other and X:
X = 5A + H + C = A + 7H + C = A + H + 8C
Recognize that each of these quantities in the system of equations can have (A + H + C) subtracted from all sides such that the quantities are now each equal to 168, the value of X − (A + H + C):
X − (A + H + C) = (5A − A) + (H − H) + (C − C)
= (A − A) + (7H − H) + (C − C)
= (A − A) + (H − H) + (8C − C) = 168
Therefore,
168 = 4A = 6H = 7C
Next, find the value of each variable by dividing 168 by each coefficient: A, H, and C.
A = 42
H = 28
C = 24
Since we are asked to find the combined value of one of each animal, we can add together our computed values to find:
42 + 28 + 24 = 94, so the correct choice is (B).

10)  D
Concept(s) Tested: Problem Solving, Probability
It is possible, if unlikely, that William would pull all of the red and green jellybeans out of his pocket before pulling out a blue one. Therefore, the maximum would be 8 + 8 + 1 = 17.

11) ▶ C
Concept(s) Tested: Algebra, Factoring
Note that the equation has one solution. This means that the discriminant ($b^2 − 4ac$) will equal zero.
$b^2 − 4(1)(4) = 0$ should hold for the equation $x^2 − bx + 4 = 0$ to have exactly one solution, so $b^2 − 16 = 0 \rightarrow b^2 = 16 \rightarrow b = \pm 4$.

12) ▶ B
Concept(s) Tested: Algebra, Number Rules
$f(−5) = |(−5)^2 − 50| = |25 − 50| = |−25| = 25$

13) ▶ D
Concept(s) Tested: Algebra
If $f(2) = 0$, then: $f(2) = 2(2^2 − 6 \times 2 + 5) − 3(2 − q) = 0$, resulting in $q = 4$.

14) ▶ C
Concept(s) Tested: Functions and Graphs
Let D be the point where the y-axis and the line $\overline{AC}$ meet, so that D = (0, 1). Note that ΔBCD is a right triangle. The length of $\overline{BC}$ = 2 because it is twice the length of $\overline{CD}$, which is 1. By the Pythagorean theorem, the length of $\overline{BD} = \sqrt{3}$, so point B = (0, 1 + $\sqrt{3}$) and C = (1, 1). Thus, using the slope equation, the slope of line $\overline{BC}$ is $m = -\sqrt{3}$.

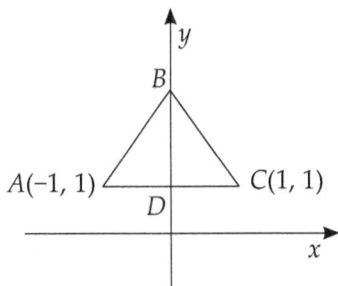

15) ▶ C
Concept(s) Tested: Geometry
Note that the triangles are similar, and that side BA is twice the length of side AD. Since the side lengths of ΔADE are one-half those of ΔABC, the area of ΔABC is 4 times of that of ΔADE.
$S(\triangle ADE) = \frac{1}{4} S(\triangle ABC) = \frac{1}{4} \times 96 = 24$

16)  8
Concept(s) Tested: Algebra
Multiplying $7x$ on both sides of the equation $\frac{8}{x} = \frac{6}{7}$ results in $6x = 56$. Therefore, $3x = 28$.
Substituting $3x = 28$ in the equation $\frac{3x}{a} = \frac{7}{2}$ results in $a = \frac{2}{7} \times (3x) = \frac{2}{7}(28) = 8$

17) ▶ 500
Concept(s) Tested: Algebra
Determine Elena's total monthly earnings:
(25 hours)($11) = $275/week $275 × 4 = $1,100
Then deduct her $600/month tuition fee:
$1,100 − $600 = $500 left over per month.

18) ▶ 1.8 or $\frac{9}{5}$
Concept(s) Tested: Algebra, Factoring
If $x − 3$ is factor of $x^2 − 2px + p = 0$, it means $f(3) = 0$. Therefore, $f(3) = 3^2 − 6p + p = 0$. It results in $p = \frac{9}{5}$.

19) ▶ 0.75 or $\frac{3}{4}$
Concept(s) Tested: Functions and Graphs
Note that $f(0) = 10$. Therefore,
$f(0) = 16k − 2 = 10$. It results in $k = \frac{3}{4}$ or 0.75.

20) ▶ 72
Concept(s) Tested: Problem Solving, Algebra
Let y be the value of the larger number, and x be the value of the two smaller numbers:

$(x)(x)(y) = 144$ and $y = 1 + 2x$
While these equations can be solved using substitution, simply puzzling the relationship between the variable is, in this case, easier.

To start, let's factor 144 into $2 \times 2 \times 2 \times 2 \times 3 \times 3$ Because $x \times x \times y = 144$, two factors must be equal, meaning $x = 2 \times 2 = 4$ and $y = 3 \times 3 = 9$ or $x = 3 \times 2 = 6$ and $y = 2 \times 2 = 4$. Only $x = 4$ satisfies $y = 1 + 2x$. Finally, solve for $(y)(2x) = (9)(8) = 72$.

Calculator Portion

1) D
Concept(s) Tested: Problem Solving
When Jorge paints x skateboards, Alonzo paints $2x + 20$. So when they paint together, $x + (2x + 20) = 3x + 20 = 125$.
Therefore, the answer is (D).

2) A
Concept(s) Tested: Ratios and Percentages
Note that Lynn can swim across the lake in p minutes. Let x be the percentage of the lake's width that Lynn can swim in 5 minutes.
$$\frac{1^{(\text{width})}}{p_{(\text{min})}} = \frac{x^{(\text{width})}}{5_{(\text{min})}}$$
$5 = px$
$x = \frac{5}{p}$
$x = \frac{5}{p} \times 100\%$
Note that we want to find what *percent* of the lake's width she can swim, so we must multiply by 100%.

3) A
Concept(s) Tested: Algebra, Factoring
By multiplying the binomials in the answer choices, we see that the only correct answer is $12c^2 + cd - 6d^2 = (4c + 3d)(3c - 2d)$.
Therefore, the answer is (A).

4) D
Concept(s) Tested: Problem Solving
$\frac{D^2}{25} + 4D - 250$ with $D = 150$ feet results in
$\frac{150^2}{25} + 4 \times 150 - 250 = 1{,}250$ gallons.

5) C
Concept(s) Tested: Ratios and Percentages, Algebra
The question can be solved using the formula:
Regular price − Discount = Sale price
Let x be the regular price:

$x - 0.2x = \$1600$
$x(1 - 0.2) = \$1600$
$x = \$2000$.

6) C
Concept(s) Tested: Number Rules, Algebra
$$\frac{\sqrt{32}}{2} + \frac{2\sqrt{3}}{3} = \frac{4\sqrt{2}}{2} + \frac{2\sqrt{3}}{3}$$
$$= 2\sqrt{2} + \frac{2\sqrt{3}}{3}$$
$$= \frac{6\sqrt{2} + 2\sqrt{3}}{3}$$

7) D
Concept(s) Tested: Algebra
We want to determine if there are x-values that cause the equations to equal zero or any negative value. If so, they are NOT true for all real numbers. The following cases show that none of the inequalities meets the requirements, as they can all be ruled out through substitution:
I. $x^2 - 2x - 3 = (x - 1)^2 - 2 = -2$ for $x = 1$
II. $x^2 - 4x + 4 = (x - 2)^2 = 0$ for $x = 2$
III. $x^2 - x - 6 = (x + 2)(x - 3) = 0$ for $x = -2, 3$
The correct answer is (D).

8) A
Concept(s) Tested: Geometry

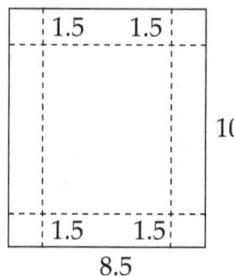

The area of the copy is $8.5 - 1.5 - 1.5$ inches by $10 - 1.5 - 1.5$ inches. Therefore, the area is 38.5 square inches.
$Area = (8.5 - 1.5 - 1.5) \times (10 - 1.5 - 1.5) = 38.5 \text{ in}^2$

9) D
Concept(s) Tested: Geometry, Ratios and Percentages
Let x be the height of the woman, and y be the height of the lamppost. By the triangle side-splitter theorem, line segments $\frac{CG}{AC} = \frac{DE}{AD}$ and $\frac{CG}{BC} = \frac{DF}{BD}$. Therefore, $\frac{x}{4} = \frac{y}{9}$, $\frac{x}{3} = \frac{y+2}{8}$. Both equations result in $x = \frac{24}{5}$ feet.

414 | KALLIS' Key to the SAT

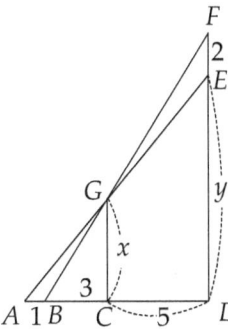

10) ➡ A
Concept(s) Tested: Functions and Graphs
The slope of $y = ax + b$ is a, and the slope of $y = cx + a$ is c. When two lines are perpendicular, the product of their slopes is -1.
Therefore, $ac = -1$.

11) ➡ B
Concept(s) Tested: Functions and Graphs, Algebra
$$f(x) - 1 = \frac{x+3}{x-1} - 1 = \frac{(x+3) - (x-1)}{x-1} = \frac{4}{x-1}$$

12) ➡ A
Concept(s) Tested: Algebra
$$\frac{3}{x-3} + \frac{5}{2x-6} = \frac{2 \times 3}{2(x-3)} + \frac{5}{2x-6} = \frac{11}{2x-6} = \frac{11}{2}$$
Thus, $2x - 6 = 2$.

13) ➡ A
Concept(s) Tested: Algebra
$$\frac{14c^3d^2 - 21c^2d^3}{14cd^2} = \frac{14c^3d^2}{14cd^2} - \frac{21c^2d^3}{14cd^2} = c^2 - \frac{3cd}{2}$$

14) ➡ D
Concept(s) Tested: Problem Solving
If x and y are the two numbers that Ellen is thinking of, it follows that:
$x + y = 9$, $x - y = 3$. Both equations result in $x = 6$, $y = 3$. Therefore, $xy = 18$.

15) ➡ C
Concept(s) Tested: Factoring, Algebra
Factoring $12x^2 + 19x + 5 = 0$ results in $(3x + 1)(4x + 5) = 0$, so:
$3x + 1 = 0$
$4x + 5 = 0$
Thus, $x = -\frac{1}{3}$ and $-\frac{5}{4}$
The sum of the roots is $-\frac{1}{3} - \frac{5}{4} = -\frac{19}{12}$

16) ➡ D
Concept(s) Tested: Measures of Center and Spread, Data Analysis

$$\frac{50 \times 7 + 100 \times 37 + 150 \times 4 + 200 \times 2}{7 + 37 + 4 + 2} = \frac{5050}{50} = \$101$$

17) ➡ C
Concept(s) Tested: Measures of Center and Spread, Data Analysis
Since there are 50 employees, the median is the averages of the bonuses paid to the 25th and 26th employees, which results in $100. Therefore, $m = 100$. We determined that $a = 101$ in number 16, and the most frequently paid bonus is $100, so $p = 100$.
Therefore, $m = p < a$.

18) ➡ A
Concept(s) Tested: Measures of Center and Spread, Problem Solving
For the smallest range, all numbers below the median should be the mode, 7. The number of median values and the number of other numbers above median should be less than 3, respectively. Therefore, {7, 7, 7, 9, 9, 10, 10} is the set with the smallest range. Thus: *the smallest range = max value – min value*, and $10 - 7 = 3$.

19) ➡ D
Concept(s) Tested: Measures of Center and Spread, Problem Solving
Let x be the minimum value required on the next exam to bring her average score up to 86. Then it should hold that $\frac{3 \times 82 + x}{4} = 86$. It results in $x = 98$.

20) ➡ B
Concept(s) Tested: Algebra, Number Rules
Set the equation equal to each variable so that
$y = 9 + 3x$ and $x = \frac{9-y}{-3}$.
Since we want to simplify the second value, let us choose one of our new translations of the equation of x and y to substitute into the y or x values of the unknown quantity. The equation equal to x is more difficult to work with, so let us choose to only insert the value of $y = 9 + 3x$ into the variable y of the second quantity so that:

$$\frac{27^x}{3^{\frac{y}{3}}} \rightarrow \frac{27^x}{3^{\frac{9+3x}{3}}} \rightarrow \frac{(27 = 3 \cdot 3 \cdot 3)^x}{3^{\frac{3(3+x)}{3}}} \rightarrow$$

$$\frac{(3^3)^x}{3^{3+x}} \rightarrow \frac{3^{3 \cdot x}}{3^{3+x}} \rightarrow 3^{3x - (x+3)} = 3^{2x-3}$$

21) ➡ B
Concept(s) Tested: Algebra, Number Rules
The term 27^{x-1} can be transformed to $(3^3)^{x-1}$. Therefore:

$(3^x)^2 = (3^3)^{x-1}$

$(3^x)^2 = 3^{3x-3}$

$2x = 3x - 3$.

$x = 3$.

22) **A**

Concept(s) Tested: Functions and Graphs

The denominator x is not defined when $x(x + 2) = 0$.

Therefore: $x = 0$, and $x + 2 = 0 \rightarrow x = -2$.

Therefore, we exclude the two values, and $\{x \neq 0, -2\}$ is the domain of the function.

23) **D**

Concept(s) Tested: Problem Solving, Algebra

Let t be the quantity of tuna and m be the quantity of mayonnaise. Then it holds that

$1.5t + 0.75m = 100$, $\dfrac{t}{3} = \dfrac{m}{2}$.

Putting $m = \dfrac{2t}{3}$ into $1.5t + 0.75m = 100$

results in $t = 50$, $m = \dfrac{2}{3} \times 50 = \dfrac{100}{3}$. Therefore,

$t + m = 50 + \dfrac{100}{3} = 83\dfrac{1}{3}$.

24) **D**

Concept(s) Tested: Functions and Graphs

Note that $-f(x)$ means $-y$. Therefore, if (x, y) is the point on the graph of $f(x)$, $(x, -y)$ will be the corresponding point on the graph of $-f(x)$.

25) **C**

Concept(s) Tested: Data Analysis

As length increases, the number of proteins also increases linearly. Therefore, the correct answer is (C). Choice (A) is incorrect because the graph has a slightly positive slope, and "no relationship" implies that the coordinates are random. Choice (B) is incorrect because a "negative" relationship implies a negative slope, which is not the case here. And (D) is incorrect because an exponential relationship would include a curved increase.

26) **C**

Concept(s) Tested: Data Analysis, Functions and Graphs

The average of the five shortest chromosomes is

$\dfrac{225 + 431 + 45 + 1399 + 533}{5} = 526.6$,

and the average of the five longest chromosomes is $\dfrac{2012 + 1203 + 1040 + 718 + 849}{5} = 1164.4$.

 KALLIS' Key to the SAT

Thus, $slope = \dfrac{1164.4 - 526.6}{72.4 - 18.8} = 11.9\ proteins/mm$.

27) **D**

Concept(s) Tested: Factoring

$\dfrac{a^3 - b^3}{b^2 - a^2} = \dfrac{(a-b)(a^2 + ab + b^2)}{(b-a)(b+a)} = -\dfrac{a^2 + ab + b^2}{a+b}$

Therefore, the solution is (D).

28) **C**

Concept(s) Tested: Geometry

If r is the radius of the cylinder, and the circumference of the base is $2\pi r = 6\pi$, then $r = 3$. The area of the base is $\pi r^2 = 9\pi$.

If h is the height of the cylinder, and the cylinder's volume (V) is $\pi r^2 h = 9\pi h = 81\pi$, then $h = 9$ meters.

29) **B**

Concept(s) Tested: Number Rules, Functions and Graphs

The denominator $x^2 - 4$ should not be zero. Therefore, $x = 2$ and $x = -2$ are the extraneous solutions, and the answer is (B).

30) **B**

Concept(s) Tested: Number Rules

$12 - \sqrt{-121} = 12 - \sqrt{-(11)^2}$

$= 12 - 11\sqrt{-1}$

$= 12 - 11i$

31) **3**

Concept(s) Tested: Algebra

$16 = 2^4$, so $2^{n+1} = 2^4$, and $n + 1 = 4$. Therefore, $n = 3$.

32) **135**

Concept(s) Tested: Problem Solving, Algebra

Let x be the weight of the fourth person.

The average of the four boys is

$\dfrac{3 \times 115 + x}{4} = 120$. It results in $x = 135$.

33) **60**

Concept(s) Tested: Geometry

Note that AC = BC. This implies that $\triangle ABC$ is isosceles. Therefore, $\angle CAB = y°$. Note that the sum of the angles of triangle $\triangle ABC$ is $180°$.

It is the same with $\angle ACB + \angle ACD$.

Therefore, $\angle ACD = 2y°$. Note that AC = AD implies that $\triangle ACD$ is also an isosceles triangle.

Therefore, $\angle ADC = 2y°$.

The sum of the angles of triangle

$\triangle$ ACD is $2y° + 2y° + \angle CAD = 180°$.
It is the same with $x° + y° + \angle CAD = 180°$.
This implies that $x° + y° = 2y° + 2y°$.
Therefore, $x° = 3y° = 3 \times 20° = 60°$.
It results in $x = 60$.

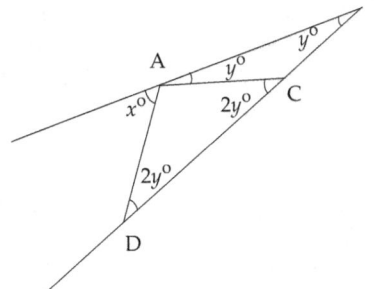

34) ▶ 1

Concept(s) Tested: Algebra

Put $y = -x + 1$ into $x^2 + y^2 = 5$.
It results in $x^2 + (-x + 1)^2 = 2x^2 - 2x + 1 = 5$.
Therefore, $2(x^2 - x - 2) = 0$, and $2(x - 2)(x + 1) = 0$.
The values of x_1 and x_2 are 2 and -1, so
$x_1 + x_2 = 2 - 1 = 1$.

35) ▶ 4

Concept(s) Tested: Problem Solving, Algebra

$\frac{2}{3}(60) = 40$ girls

$\frac{2}{5}(60) = 24$ students taking music lessons

$60 - 40 = 20$ boys

If all of boys take music lessons, only 4 girls can take music lessons because only 24 people take music lessons.

36) ▶ 54

Concept(s) Tested: Algebra

$2n - 2f(4) = 2(13 - 4)^{\frac{3}{2}} = 2 \times 9^{\frac{3}{2}}$

$= 2 \times (3^2)^{\frac{3}{2}} = 2 \times 3^3 = 2 \times 27$

$= 54$

37) ▶ 5061

Concept(s) Tested: Ratios and Percentages, Problem Solving

$P = \frac{P_0}{r}[(1 + r)^n - 1] = \frac{300}{0.06}[(1 + 0.06)^{12} - 1]$

$= 5060.98$

Therefore, the balance, in dollars, at the end of 12 years is $5,061.

38) ▶ 890

Concept(s) Tested: Ratios and Percentages, Problem Solving

$P_0 = \frac{P \times r}{[(1 + r)^n - 1]} = \frac{15000 \times 0.06}{[(1 + 0.06)^{12} - 1]} = 889.16$

Therefore, the smallest amount of money, in dollars, that the man needs to deposit annually is 890.

SAT Practice Test 1: Answers & Explanations

Sample Essay Response

Countless think pieces and debates have argued over the meaning and boundaries of the separation of church and state. However, much less attention is paid to determining the role of scientific inquiry in politics: the separation of lab and state, if you will. Mr. Kukaswadia explores the extent to which scientific development permeates the very fabric of political and social discourse, and uses the recent march for science as a call to action to further "politicize" science.

Mr. Kukaswadia wastes no time revealing his central argument: Science is political. And in the paragraph that follows, he sets the audience up to agree with him. In paragraph 3, he uses examples to present an indisputably true effect: scientific developments have always influenced society. He then reveals that the cause of this universal truth is that science must be political before it can have a social impact. Thus, in the third paragraph, Mr. Kukaswadia uses a cause-effect relationship to get the reader on his side so that he can more easily build his case.

Having proven that "science is political," Mr. Kukaswadia goes on to show that U.S. politics are, presently, not adequately informed by science. It is here that he begins his calls to action, encouraging "the populace to make sure that their voices are heard and that their elected officials represent their viewpoint" (paragraph 4). Because Mr. Kukaswadia has already proven that effective science is inherently political, he now urges the reader to champion this cause, to make its truth known to those in power.

Through much of the rest of the passage, Mr. Kukaswadia unpackages this call to action: science should be political, but not partisan, as stated by Jewett; scientists should "make their voice heard" (paragraph 3) but not embody the "overreaching zealots" the media often portrays them as. Mr. Kukaswadia is here conveying the nuance of the issue, that there is no distinct boundary where science encroaches on politics or vice versa, and that a communication between scientists, politicians, and the general populace can help enact positive change rather than delineate boundaries.

Mr. Kukaswadia concludes the passage by returning to the march for science, continuing his call to action. Although the march (and his article) have ended, he claims that "journey" to keep our politicians accountable is just beginning. And as if to drive this call to action home., Mr. Kukaswadia's conclusion reveals that his passage is itself structured like the "scientific process" he espouses in paragraph 4; if "science is political" is his conclusion, then his final paragraph provides the "so what" that "tells people why they should care" about the future role of science in politics.

Sample Essay Score: 4/3/4

Reading: 3

The response conveys the passage's main arguments, that science is political and that scientists should be politically active: *Having proven that "science is political," Mr. Kukaswadia ... begins his call to action...* The response skillfully describes the author's position: *Mr. Kukaswadia is here conveying the nuance of the issue, that there is no distinct boundary where science encroaches on politics or vice versa...*

The response becomes a bit muddled in paragraph 5 when it says that the author "reveals" the scientific process within the structure of his text by mentioning the significance at the end: *As if to drive this...home, Mr. Kukaswadia's conclusion reveals that his passage is itself structured like the "scientific process" he espouses...* The response's conclusion would have been more relevant if it had summarized the significance (to which the author alludes throughout the passage). Explaining how these important details relate to the main argument would have demonstrated a more thorough comprehension of the text.

Writing: 4

The response is cohesive, with a central claim and with each of its three body paragraphs focused on supporting a topic sentence. The response is virtually free of grammar errors. The sentences are varied in structure, and word choice is highly effective: *Mr. Kukaswadia explores the extent to which scientific development permeates the very fabric of political and social discourse, and uses the recent march for science as a call to further "politicize" science.*

The response could benefit from more control over wordiness and redundancy, as when it says that the author uses a strategy *to get the reader on his side so that he can more easily build his case.* But overall, the student demonstrates advanced writing skills.

Analysis: 3

The student demonstrates effective analytical skills by identifying several of Kukaswadia's persuasive strategies: *In paragraph 3, (Kukaswadia) uses examples to present an indisputably true effect...*; and, *Throughout much of the rest of the passage, Mr. Kukaswadia unpackages this call to action...*

The response includes several well-chosen quotations to support its insights. For example, in paragraph 4, the response makes skillful use of both paraphrasing and partial quotes to succinctly describe the author's specificity: *science should be political but not partisan, as stated by Jewett; scientists should "make their voices heard" (paragraph 3) but not embody the "overreaching zealots" the media often portrays them as.*

While the response includes analysis, in a few places it veers into summary, describing what the material explores, reveals, or shows instead of describing rhetorical strategies. Furthermore, some of the strategies that are identified are insufficiently supported, as when the student writes that *Mr. Kukaswadi uses a cause-effect relationship to get the reader on his side.* Explanation and/or an example would have made the point more convincing.

SAT Practice Test 2: Answers & Explanations

Reading Test

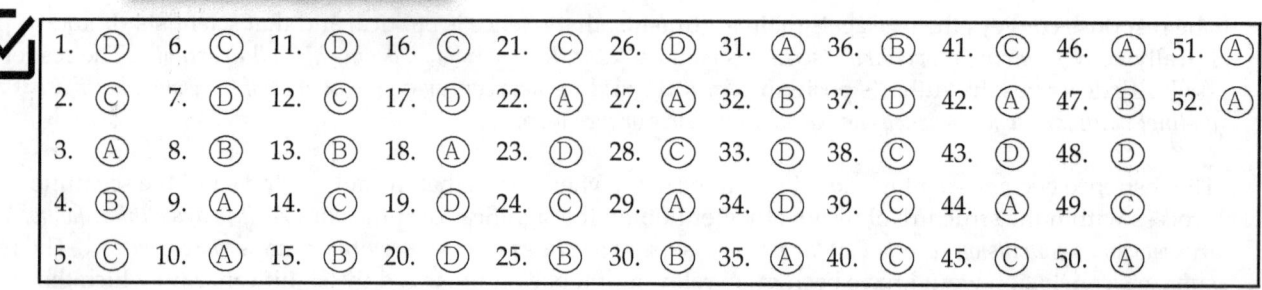

1. D	6. C	11. D	16. C	21. C	26. D	31. A	36. B	41. C	46. A	51. A
2. C	7. D	12. C	17. D	22. A	27. A	32. B	37. D	42. A	47. B	52. A
3. A	8. B	13. B	18. A	23. D	28. C	33. D	38. C	43. D	48. D	
4. B	9. A	14. C	19. D	24. C	29. A	34. D	39. C	44. A	49. C	
5. C	10. A	15. B	20. D	25. B	30. B	35. A	40. C	45. C	50. A	

1) ▶ D
Concept(s) Tested: Purpose
Choice (D) is correct. In lines 3 – 5 and 76 – 80, the author notes lifestyles and values that he says are American and not European, and this focus persists throughout the passage. Choice (A) is incorrect because the author criticizes the construction of skyscrapers and the loss of life associated with them rather than romanticizing American lifestyles. Choice (B) is incorrect because the passage does not address the difference in American and European work attitudes. Choice (C) is incorrect because the author uses his impressions about skyscrapers as an introduction to the critique that follows in lines 72 – 80.

2) ▶ C
Concept(s) Tested: Inference
Choice (C) is correct because in lines 1 – 4 the author mentions "dazzling daylight" and "grandeur" in the offices, implying that they are "sunny and impressive." Choice (A) is incorrect because there is no evidence to suggest that the office is hot or cramped, although "warmed stillness" implies heat. Choice (B) is incorrect because, while the author finds the experience impressive, there is nothing to indicate he is overwhelmed. Choice (D) is incorrect because the author does not comment on the decorations in either American or European offices.

3) ▶ A
Concept(s) Tested: Purpose
Choice (A) is correct; the author uses the second person to invite the audience to share his experience of being in a skyscraper for the first time. Choices (B) and (C) are incorrect because the author does not provide enough information for us to assign such a specific audience. Choice (D) is incorrect because the author does not proceed with personal details, but rather describes a socio-political and cultural phenomenon. Thus, he cannot reasonably be described as trying to create an "intimate" relationship with the reader.

4) ▶ B
Concept(s) Tested: Words in Context
Choice (B) is correct. As used, "lost" describes the way each window in a skyscraper is "indistinguishable" from any other window. Although the other choices are synonyms of "lost," "wandering," "unclaimed," and "confused" fail to fit the specific meaning of the word as used in the passage.

5) ▶ C
Concept(s) Tested: Attitude and Tone
In the beginning of the paragraph, the author describes construction workers with clear admiration; however, his attitude shifts toward morbidity as he transitions to the consequences of their construction. Thus, (C) is the correct choice. Choice (A) is incorrect because the author does not become distracted by the information presented in the second half of the passage. Choice (B) is incorrect because the author never defends the practices used in the construction of skyscrapers, but rather admonishes Americans for their "contempt for ... human life" (line 78). Choice (D) is incorrect; the author's attitude in the first paragraph can be described as enthusiastic, but he transitions into a passionate, not a weary, critique.

6) ▶ C
Concept(s) Tested: Inference
In line 37, the author indicates that Americans acknowledge skyscraper-related deaths "with pride," making (C) the correct choice. Choice (A) is incorrect because there is no evidence to suggest Americans are either astonished or saddened by the loss of life associated with construction. Choice (B) is incorrect because the author does not suggest that Americans are ignorant of the facts presented in the passage. Choice (D) is incorrect because the author implies that Americans are not indifferent about these deaths; rather, the author believes Americans take pride in the losses.

7) ▶ D
Concept(s) Tested: Summary
Choice (D) is correct. In paragraph 3 (lines 45 – 82), the author describes the "long battles" fought on construction sites when the "labor unions have a fit of objecting more violently than usual to non-union labor." The examples that follow imply that union workers "sometimes purposely injure or kill non-union construction workers." Choice (A) is incorrect because the author never suggests the deaths were a result of unsafe work habits. Choice (B) is incorrect because the author never mentions workers' reliance on each other. Choice (C) is incorrect because the author does not discuss "most" accidents during construction.

8) ▶ B
Concept(s) Tested: Citation
Choice (B) is correct. In lines 50 – 55, the author discusses several incidents in which non-union laborers were disabled or killed in workplace accidents. His tone throughout this excerpt indicates that the author believes these accidents were staged by union workers. Choice (A) is incorrect because it fails to mention labor unions. Choices (C) and (D) are incorrect because they both address the employers' response to the "accidents" rather than the violence itself.

9) ▶ A
Concept(s) Tested: Summary
Choice (A) is correct because the author implies that

420 | KALLIS' Key to the SAT

"the leading spirit of the association" is an American employer who has created a private association, and that "his revolver is always very ready for an emergency." This implies that "some American employers arm themselves to respond to any violence." Choice (B) is incorrect because the author does not exactly describe the existence of "secretive" societies that "battle" labor unions. Choice (C) is incorrect because the author implies that hiring non-union workers is "the original cause of the warfare" (line 70), but does not imply that employers are *mainly* hiring non-union workers. Choice (D) is incorrect because the author does not comment on employers' concerns for safety.

10) ▶ A
Concept(s) Tested: Citation
Choice (A) is correct because it demonstrates that some employers are literally armed with pistols, ready to respond violently should the need arise. Choices (B), (C), and (D) are incorrect because none of them addresses American employers or their purported tendencies to arm themselves.

11) ▶ D
Concept(s) Tested: Words in Context
Choice (D) is correct because "romantic contempt" is used to describe antipathy that is somehow enjoyable, which can be expressed as "quixotic disdain." Choice (A) is incorrect because, while "heavenly" is a synonym for both sublime and romantic, the author is describing distaste, not "bliss." Choice (B) is incorrect because "affectionate" fails to capture the superlative quality implied by "sublime." Choice (C) is incorrect because "love" is the opposite of "contempt."

12) ▶ C
Concept(s) Tested: Purpose
The correct choice is (C) because the passage focuses on a discussion of dances common to a group of Alaskan Eskimos. The author spends the majority of the passage describing the differences between the men's and women's dances. Choice (A) is incorrect because the author does not primarily focus on providing instructions for the dances. Choice (B) is incorrect because, while the author notes that the culture has diminished, this is a minor detail and not the passage's focus. Choice (D) is incorrect because the author does not describe himself as participating in the dances.

13) ▶ B
Concept(s) Tested: Words in Context
Choice (B) is correct. In the context of the passage, the Eskimos "subsist" or "survive" on various Arctic animals. In other words, they "depend" on the animals for survival. The remaining answer choices fail to capture the context-specific meaning of the word.

14) ▶ C
Concept(s) Tested: Summary
In lines 25 – 36, the author describes the women's dance and how it differs from the men's. Specifically, the passage states that "the feet are kept on the ground" (line 28 – 29). Thus, (C) is the correct answer choice. Choice (A) is incorrect because the passage suggests that *both* the men's and women's dances include imitations of arctic animals. Choice (B) is incorrect because it is the men who stamp to the rhythm of the drums, while the women keep their feet on the ground. Choice (D) is incorrect because in lines 30 – 34, the women's dances are characterized as having "waving" and "graceful" arm movements, not "quick, sharp movements."

15) ▶ B
Concept(s) Tested: Words in Context
Choice (B) is correct because the author describes the women as "ranging themselves behind the mask dancer." In other words, they are placing, or "arranging," themselves in a specific formation. Choices (A), (C), and (D) are all definitions for "ranging" but fail to fit the specific context in which the word is used in the passage, so these choices are incorrect.

16) ▶ C
Concept(s) Tested: Inference
In lines 46 – 52, the author describes an incident in which he encountered a women-only ritual being performed on a pregnant woman. Being a man, he was asked to leave; thus, we can infer that "rites regarding fertility and childbirth" are considered meetings that are off-limits to men. Therefore, choice (C) is correct. Choices (A) and (B) are incorrect because the author gives no clues about the content of the "rites" upon which he stumbled. Choice (D) is incorrect because the author never mentions a rehearsal for the Asking Festival.

17) ▶ D
Concept(s) Tested: Citation
Choice (D) is correct because it recounts the incident in which the male author was denied access to a specific rite related to pregnancy. Choices (A) and (B) are incorrect because they provide descriptions of women's dances performed in a mixed setting. Choice (C) is incorrect because it mentions a meeting that is off-limits to women, which is the opposite situation.

18) ▶ A
Concept(s) Tested: Summary
In lines 60 – 62, the author explains that the Asking Festival "result[s] in offers of temporary marriage to the unmarried women." Thus, choice (A) is correct. Choice (B) is incorrect because, while women do take the lead in this ritual, the author never suggests that this is the purpose for holding the festival. Choice (C) is incorrect because the author does not discuss any competitive activities taking place during the Asking Festival. Choice (D) is incorrect because clowns are not mentioned in the description of the Asking Festival.

19) ▶ D
Concept(s) Tested: Citation
Choice (D) is correct. In lines 61 – 63, the author states that "offers of temporary marriage… [are] obviously the reason for this rite." Choices (A), (B), and (C) are incorrect because none explains the purpose of the Asking Festival.

20) ▶ D
Concept(s) Tested: Summary
The author explains that the women-only dances on the islands of the Bering Sea may represent "old forms which have died out or been modified on the mainland" (lines 67 – 69), indicating that these practices "represent a tradition that was once practiced over a wider area." Thus, (D) is the correct choice. Choice (A) is incorrect because the author never speculates about the future of Eskimo rituals. Choice (B) is incorrect because the author does not indicate whether knowledge of these rituals is widespread among anthropologists. Choice (C) is incorrect because the author does not describe the dances as a crucial cultural adaptation.

21) ▶ C
Concept(s) Tested: Inference
Choice (C) is correct because the author describes very few gender-specific dances, and indicates that most dances are performed by both men and women. Choice (A) is incorrect because the author discusses specific gender roles within many of the dances, indicating that the roles are not interchangeable. Choice (B) is incorrect because the author describes dances that

occur throughout the year, not just during a certain season. Choice (D) is incorrect because the author describes festivals where "women's dances can be performed separately or in conjunction with men's dance" (lines 25 – 27).

22) **A**
Concept(s) Tested: Inference
Choice (A) is correct because the researchers "compared their sloth data to similar studies of other tree-dwelling, leaf-eating species from around the world" (lines 64 – 66), indicating that this research may "provide insight into other species that thrive under the same circumstances." Choice (B) is incorrect because the author does not raise questions or mention future research on sloths. Choice (C) is incorrect because the researchers do not comment on the quality of "slothfulness" in humans. Choice (D) is incorrect because the passage does not mention the role sloths play in maintaining the forest habitat.

23) **D**
Concept(s) Tested: Citation
Choice (D) is correct because it illustrates that the research described in the passage can be used to examine evolutionary adaptations of similar species. Choice (A) is incorrect because it merely introduces the topic of the passage and does not give any information regarding sloths or research conducted on tree-dwelling, leaf-eating species. Choice (B) is incorrect because it does not discuss Pauli and Peery's research. Choice (C) is incorrect because it merely introduces the research procedure.

24) **C**
Concept(s) Tested: Words in Context
Choice (C) is correct; the author uses the phrase "gut machinery" to describe internal organs of digestion, which can be inferred because the focus of the paragraph containing the phrase is herbivores' digestive processes. Choices (A) and (B) are incorrect because the author is discussing non-human animals that do not have access to kitchen appliances or biotechnological devices. Choice (D) is incorrect because abdominal muscles cannot extract energy from food, so this choice does not make sense in the context in which the phrase is used.

25) **B**
Concept(s) Tested: Summary
In lines 24 – 26, the author indicates that "'Most herbivores are big-bodied and they carry big guts to break down and detoxify plant leaves,'" so we can conclude that large bodies are an adaptation for "internal processing of vegetative sources of energy." Thus, (B) is the correct choice. Choice (A) is incorrect because the author never implies that sloths have to compete for food resources. Choice (C) is incorrect because the author does not explain large bodies as an adaptation for storing food. Choice (D) is incorrect because the author does not discuss large bodies in relation to the area in which the species must search for food.

26) **D**
Concept(s) Tested: Words in Context
Choice (D) is correct. Lines 49 – 51 describe the three-toed sloth's "range" as "one or a few individual trees," so we can infer that "ranges" refers to an animal's home or "territory." Choices (A), (B), and (C) are incorrect because none captures the context-specific meaning as used in the passage.

27) **A**
Concept(s) Tested: Summary
Choice (A) is correct. In lines 49 – 51, the author quotes researchers, saying "'three-toed sloths have very small home ranges and spend most of their time in just one or a few individual trees.'" In other words, their basic survival strategy is to "move around the forest as little as possible." Choice (B) is incorrect because the passage does not suggest that sloths have control over their immediate environment, so this selection does not make sense. Choice (C) is incorrect because the author indicates that sloths sleep in different parts of the tree during different times of day. Choice (D) is incorrect because the author never implies that sloths would eat in this manner.

28) **C**
Concept(s) Tested: Summary
In lines 57 – 58, the author indicates that three-toed sloths "relax control over their body temperatures," suggesting that they "expend less energy on thermoregulation." Thus, (C) is the correct answer choice. Choices (A) and (B) are incorrect because the author never mentions a consistently lower body temperature or sloths' offspring in the passage. Choice (D) is incorrect because the author does not mention the size or efficiency of two-toed or three-toed sloths' digestive systems.

29) **A**
Concept(s) Tested: Purpose
Choice (A) is correct because the word "oddities" brings additional attention to the fact that these adaptations are unique and highly specialized. Choice (B) is incorrect because the researcher is not comparing sloths to other mammals at this point in the passage. Choice (C) is incorrect because, as the author states in lines 1 – 4, a wide variety of species do not fill this niche. Choice (D) is incorrect because the findings are not described as surprising.

30) **B**
Concept(s) Tested: Summary
The correct choice is (B) because, in lines 10 – 11, the author mentions that "species that do take advantage of this niche do not often radiate." This implies that sloths' evolutionary diversity is constrained due to the nutritional limitations of the niche they inhabit. Choice (A) is incorrect because the author never implies that this is the case. Choice (C) is incorrect because the author does not emphasize the ways in which the term "sloth" can be used taxonomically. Choice (D) is incorrect because the passage points out that there is little competition for tree leaves (lines 86 – 88).

31) **A**
Concept(s) Tested: Citation
The best choice is (A) because the excerpt explains how "the energetic constraints of a leafy diet are thought to prevent such adaptive radiation." Because sloths subsist on a diet of leaves, we can infer that "sloths' nutritionally limited diets constrain their evolutionary diversity." Choices (B) and (C) are incorrect because they do not mention the evolutionary constraints placed on sloths as a result of their diet. Choice (D) is incorrect because, while it does discuss the constraints of a leafy diet, the excerpt fails to relate sloths' diets to their limited evolutionary diversity.

32) **B**
Concept(s) Tested: Purpose
Choice (B) is correct because the passage is primarily focused on providing information ("definitions and facts") about OCD (a "public health topic"). Choice (A) is incorrect because the passage does not go into detail about the causes or cures of OCD, but rather provides a brief overview of the topic. Choice (C) is incorrect because the passage does not discuss

misconceptions about OCD. Choice (D) is incorrect because the specific terms used are meant to enhance the reader's understanding of the topic and are not the primary purpose for the passage.

33) ▶ D
Concept(s) Tested: Inference, Summary
Choice (D) is correct. In lines 16 – 18, the author of Passage 1 states, "the rituals may give them brief relief from the anxiety the thoughts cause." In other words, these behaviors provide "temporary reassurance." Choice (A) is incorrect because the author does not discuss perfection. Choice (B) is incorrect because the author never implies that the rituals provide a sense of optimism. Choice (C) is incorrect because the author explains that these rituals are "intrusive" and "get in the way of daily life," and never indicates that they may be "practical solutions."

34) ▶ D
Concept(s) Tested: Citation
The best choice is (D) because the excerpt explains how rituals may provide brief relief from the anxiety experienced by people who suffer from OCD. Choice (A) is incorrect because it does not provide enough information regarding why people who suffer from OCD engage in these behaviors. Choice (B) is incorrect because it only discusses the fears and anxieties associated with OCD, but does not link these anxieties to ritualistic behavior. Choice (C) is incorrect because it discusses the ritual behaviors associated with OCD but does not make the relationship between these behaviors and the fears which drive them clear.

35) ▶ A
Concept(s) Tested: Words in Context
The best choice is (A) because the author explains that these "intrusive" thoughts "get in the way of daily life." In other words, they "interfere" with a person's life. Choices (B), (C), and (D) are all accurate definitions of the word "intrusive", but fail to convey the specific meaning used in this context.

36) ▶ B
Concept(s) Tested: Attitude and Tone
The correct choice is (B) because the narrator expresses doubt about whether or not he or she is prepared for the next class, and his or her worries increase throughout the course of the excerpt. Choice (A) is incorrect because the narrator is worried about homework and never expresses any confusion about any of his or her classes. Choice (C) is incorrect because the narrator never mentions the teacher in the excerpt. Choice (D) is incorrect because the narrator in this example is primarily worried about schoolwork.

37) ▶ D
Concept(s) Tested: Words in Context
Choice (D) is correct because it accurately conveys the idea that the student's mind is being taken away, or "pulled," from his or her schoolwork. The remaining choices are correct definitions of "drawn," but do not fit the specific context in which the word is used.

38) ▶ C
Concept(s) Tested: Summary
Choice (C) is correct. In lines 80 – 81, the author indicates the main purpose of the paragraph is to emphasize that "OCD's impact on learning cannot be underestimated." In other words, he or she details examples of consequences of OCD in school. Choice (A) is incorrect because the author never mentions the criteria necessary to diagnose the disorder. Choice (B) is incorrect because the author does not discuss the appearances of students with OCD. Choice (D) is incorrect because the author discusses multiple consequences of OCD, not just being unable to "hear" the teacher.

39) ▶ C
Concept(s) Tested: Inference/Analogy
Choice (C) is correct because the author describes students who suffer from OCD as being "extremely tired because of the strain and effort of trying to fight OCD" (lines 94 – 96). This implies that they may feel as if engaged in a "constant struggle." Choices (A) and (B) are incorrect because the author never mentions intelligence or a feeling of being alienated. Choice (D) is incorrect because the author does not describe students with OCD as "heroes" nor does he or she argue that this struggle is meaningful.

40) ▶ C
Concept(s) Tested: Citation
Choice (C) is correct because it reflects the author's point that people with OCD must cope continuously with overwhelming and unwanted thoughts. Choice (A) is incorrect because it does not specifically illustrate a "constant" phenomenon. Choice (B) is incorrect because it discusses ramifications of the disorder, but does not address the emotional experience. Choice (D) similarly fails to describe what OCD sufferers may feel.

41) ▶ C
Concept(s) Tested: Text Synthesis
Choice (C) is correct because Passage 1 introduces OCD and many of the terms associated with the disorder while Passage 2 focuses on a particular social implication of the disorder. Choice (A) is incorrect because Passage 2 does not "explain" concepts presented in Passage 1, although it does elaborate on them. Choice (B) is incorrect because Passage 2 does not discuss treatment options at all, instead focusing on the impact of OCD. Choice (D) is incorrect because Passage 2 does not challenge any of the information provided in Passage 1.

42) ▶ A
Concept(s) Tested: Text Synthesis
Choice (A) is correct because the final paragraph of Passage 2 describes a series of behaviors that interfere with daily life. This is an effective example of the ritualistic behavior described in Passage 1. Choice (B) is incorrect because the author of Passage 1 never indicates that he or she believes OCD sufferers should be allowed to stay home. Choice (C) is incorrect because the author of Passage 1 does not discuss possible outcomes of spoiling children. Choice (D) is incorrect because the discussion of biorhythms is outside the scope of both passages.

43) ▶ D
Concept(s) Tested: Purpose
Choice (D) is correct because the introductory paragraph describes several cultures which placed importance on the ability to capture and control wild animals. Choice (A) is incorrect because paragraph 1 does not mention cats. Choice (B) is incorrect because the discussion of sacrifices takes place later in the passage. Choice (C) is incorrect because the author focuses on control of carnivores but never implies that the animals are "exotic."

44) ▶ A
Concept(s) Tested: Words in Context
(A) is the correct choice because it most accurately expresses the idea that control over wild animals demonstrated strength and authority, or "might." Choices (B), (C), and (D) are incorrect because they do not fit the specific context in which "power" is being used.

45) **C**
Concept(s) Tested: Attitude and Tone
In lines 15 – 25, the author describes the city of Teotihuacan as "one of the largest and most powerful cities in Mesoamerica" and describes its temple architecture as "incredible." Thus, she seems to hold the city in high regard, making (C) the best choice. Choice (A) is incorrect because the author indicates an academic interest in the city, and "aversion" is not an attitude typically associated with topics one finds interesting. Choice (B) is incorrect because "skepticism" implies that the author is unsure or questions something about Teotihuacan, and there is no evidence to suggest this is the case. Choice (D) is incorrect because the author's interest in the city precludes the possibility of her "apathy."

46) **A**
Concept(s) Tested: Summary
The correct choice is (A) because lines 57 – 59 state: "certain isotopes can make their way into an animal's bones based on what they eat or drink." This implies that analyzing isotopes can "provide insight into the diets of the investigated animals." Choice (B) is incorrect because the author never compares the value of the information provided by visual analysis to that provided by isotope analysis. Choice (C) is incorrect because the author never indicates that isotope analysis can provide insight into genetic abnormalities. Choice (D) is incorrect because, in lines 94 – 96, the author concedes that "we cannot know for certain whether the carnivores found in Teotihuacan were ever fed human sacrificial victims."

47) **B**
Concept(s) Tested: Citation
Choice (B) is correct because this excerpt explains what type of information isotope analysis yielded. Choice (A) is incorrect because this excerpt deals with visual examination of the bones only and does not mention isotope analysis. Choice (C) is incorrect because it discusses general facts based on isotope analysis, not the study's findings. Choice (D) is incorrect because it concerns conclusion drawn from art, not isotopes.

48) **D**
Concept(s) Tested: Words in Context
The correct choice is (D) because it expresses the idea that isotope levels reveal or "indicate" an animal's position in the food chain. Choices (A), (B), and (C) all provide definitions for "reflect," but do not fit the specific meaning as the word is used in this context.

49) **C**
Concept(s) Tested: Summary
In lines 75 – 80, the author explains that high levels of carbon isotopes "may suggest that the cats ate maize fed to them by human caretakers." The author further indicates that the C14 isotopes may have been introduced "if the cats were fed rabbits or other herbivores who ate maize." Thus, (C) is the best answer choice. Choice (A) is incorrect because visual examination, not isotope analysis, revealed skeletal abnormalities associated with infection. Choice (B) is incorrect because it does not address the pumas' diets, instead focusing only on the locations in which they were captured. Choice (D) is incorrect because it is only partially true; the author speculates that the pumas may have been fed rabbits or maize.

50) **A**
Concept(s) Tested: Summary
Choice (A) is correct. In lines 81 – 84, the author explains that pumas "ate omnivores that were higher up the food chain." Because omnivores also eat meat, we can deduce that "pumas ingested the flesh of animals that also ate meat." Choices (B) and (C) are incorrect because the author expresses doubt about whether or not pumas were fed human sacrifices. Choice (D) is incorrect because the author does not discuss the location of pumas' captivity.

51) **A**
Concept(s) Tested: Inference
Choice (A) is correct because, in lines 1 – 5, the author says, "capturing and manipulating wild carnivores has long been a way for humans to demonstrate state or individual power." Thus, we can infer that she believes the leaders in Teotihuacan sought to control animals for similar reasons, a claim supported by the last sentence of the passage, as well. Choice (B) is incorrect because there is no mention of the afterlife in the passage. Choice (C) is incorrect because the author indicates that human sacrifices were still being made, so there is no evidence to conclude that animal sacrifices replaced human ones. Choice (D) is incorrect because, although art is mentioned in lines 90 – 93, there is no evidence that animals were kept to inspire artists.

52) **A**
Concept(s) Tested: Citation
Choice (A) is correct because it explains the author's opinion about why ancient cultures kept wild carnivores, and can be used to extrapolate the reasons she believes the leaders in Teotihuacan kept wild animals as well. Choices (B), (C), and (D) do not address possible motivations for keeping live carnivores and are therefore incorrect.

SAT Writing & Language Test 2 : Answers & Explanations

Writing & Language Test

1. D	5. C	9. A	13. B	17. A	21. B	25. B	29. C	33. D	37. B	41. D
2. C	6. D	10. C	14. A	18. D	22. B	26. A	30. A	34. C	38. A	42. B
3. B	7. C	11. A	15. A	19. D	23. A	27. B	31. C	35. C	39. D	43. A
4. D	8. B	12. C	16. D	20. D	24. A	28. B	32. C	36. A	40. C	44. D

1) ➡ D
Concept(s) Tested: Graph Synthesis
The best choice is (D) because it accurately summarizes the information from the graph. (A) is incorrect because the graph indicates that, on average, women tend to leave their jobs sooner than men. The graph does not comment on the work habits of teenagers, so (B) cannot be correct. Finally, (C) is an extreme that can easily be disproven by a single counterexample, so this choice is also incorrect.

2) ➡ C
Concept(s) Tested: Precise Diction
The second sentence is different but equitable, which is best indicated by choice (C). Choices (B) and (D) are incorrect because they would create inaccurate meanings. Choice (A) would result in a vague and informal claim that "so many" workers are job-hunting.

3) ➡ B
Concept(s) Tested: Transition Words and Phrases
The information in the sentence *adds to* the passage's discussion of Google and the benefits it provides its employees. Thus, (B) is the best choice. The remaining choices create relationships (cause-and-effect, time, contrast respectively) that aren't present in the passage, so they are all incorrect.

4) ➡ D
Concept(s) Tested: Clauses, Sentence Boundaries, In-Sentence Punctuation
The information in the second clause is an elaboration on the information in the first clause, so a colon is the most appropriate way to separate these two clauses. Thus, (D) is the best choice. (A) and (C) are incorrect because two independent clauses may be separated by a comma and coordinating conjunction, but only one or the other is not adequate. (B) is incorrect because it creates a run-on sentence with no punctuation to separate ideas.

5) ➡ C
Concept(s) Tested: Logical Comparisons
The passage compares "the demands of" one's personal and professional lives. In order to ensure this comparison is logical, the phrase "those of" is often used, making (C) the best choice. (A) and (B) are incorrect because the pronouns "them" and "they" are not appropriate in this context. (D) is incorrect because, without the additional pronoun, the sentence would compare "the demands" with "their professional [lives]," which is an illogical comparison.

6) ➡ D
Concept(s) Tested: Verb Tense
The correct answer is (D) because it uses the simple present tense to express a universal truth or generalization. The remaining choices are incorrect because it is not appropriate to express this statement in any other tense.

7) ➡ C
Concept(s) Tested: Paragraph Organization
Sentence 2 uses the pronoun "these wishes" to reference information that has yet to be presented, so its current placement is incorrect. Because "these wishes" refers to employees' desires ("spend time with family," "traveling," "participating in community events"), it makes the most sense to put sentence 2 after sentence 4, where "these wishes" are introduced. Thus, (C) is the best answer.

8) ➡ B
Concept(s) Tested: Precise Diction, Style & Tone
The underlined word shows a drastic shift from the passage's generally formal tone, so it must be changed. Choice (B) provides the most formal, precise word in context. (C) is incorrect because it is not an appropriate adjective for describing workplace conditions. (D) is incorrect because it, too, strays from the neutral tone maintained throughout.

9) ➡ A
Concept(s) Tested: Clauses, Sentence Boundaries, In-Sentence Punctuation
The information in the second part of the sentence forms a relative clause describing job-seekers, and is correct as is. (B) and (C) are incorrect because both choices create two independent clauses, but fail to separate them appropriately with a comma and coordinating conjunction or a semicolon. (D) is incorrect because the second clause does not have the same subject as the first, so a compound sentence is necessary.

10) ➡ C
Concept(s) Tested: Passage Development
The underlined portion provides an example of websites where job-seekers share their experiences with others. Though the audience may not be familiar with this particular service, the example itself provides context for understanding the author's statement; without it, readers may think job-seekers share this information on random websites. The inclusion of this one website informs the reader about a specific online forum that has contributed to the difficulties faced by employers. Therefore, (C) is the correct answer.

11) ➡ A
Concept(s) Tested: Subject-Verb Agreement, Noun Agreement, Possession
The underlined noun must be plural because it is referenced by a plural pronoun ("they") later in the sentence. The underlined verb must agree with this noun, so (A) is the correct answer.

12) ➡ C
Concept(s) Tested: Passage Development
Choice (C) is correct because the diagram only provides information on the human brain, whereas the passage focuses on rat cognition and social behaviors. The

TEST 2: Answers & Explanations | 425

diagram of a human brain does not contribute to the research described in the passage and should not be added to the passage. Choice (D) is incorrect because the diagram is irrelevant to the passage's main idea, so the fact that it does not "reveal how these [brain] regions affect human behavior" is also irrelevant.

13) **B**
Concept(s) Tested: Logical Comparisons
Choice (B) is correct because the sentence is comparing the "social behaviors and neural activity" of one group to those qualities in another group. Because there are multiple elements being compared, the plural pronoun "those" is appropriate. Choice (D) is incorrect because it would create an illogical comparison ("behaviors" to "control group").

14) **A**
Concept(s) Tested: Precise Diction
Choice (A) is correct because the underlined portion is referring to the "number of" contact behaviors, and "frequency of" is closest in meaning to "number of." Although choice (B), "preponderance," is close in meaning, it indicates that something is prevalent or dominant, which implies a hierarchy that is not present in the passage. Choices (C) and (D) are incorrect because they do not relate to the "frequency" or "number" of occurrences of something.

15) **A**
Concept(s) Tested: In-Sentence Punctuation, Sentence Boundaries
Choice (A) is correct because it effectively combines the sentence's two independent clauses using a comma followed by a coordinating conjunction ("and"). All other choices are incorrect because they form run-on sentences or lack a subject

16) **D**
Concept(s) Tested: In-Sentence Punctuation, Parallel Structure
The sentence containing the underlined portion consists of a lengthy list that separates each element using a semicolon. Thus, the underlined portion must also be separated from the rest of the list by a semicolon, which eliminates choices (A) and (B). Choice (C) is incorrect because examples that are preceded by the abbreviation "e.g" are parenthetical, and must therefore be separated from the rest of the sentence using punctuation, which choice (D) does effectively.

17) **A**
Concept(s) Tested: Passage Development
Choice (A) is correct because the experiment describes the rats' contact behaviors, leaving behaviors, and sole behaviors. Because sole behaviors are not described elsewhere in the passage, they should come at the underlined portion. All other choices are incorrect because they describe behaviors that are not mentioned elsewhere in the passage.

18) **D**
Concept(s) Tested: Possession
The paragraph implies that all of the rats in the control and experimental groups were observed using wireless transmitters, so both "rat" and "head" must be plural to reflect this, making (D) the correct choice. All other choices are incorrect because they fail to maintain this noun agreement between "rats" and "heads."

19) **D**
Concept(s) Tested: Voice, Syntax
Choice (D) is correct because it is the only choice that maintains the active voice, as it makes "they" (the researchers) the subject of the sentence. All other choices are incorrect because their structure confuses rather than clarifies the relationship between the researchers and the experiment they are performing.

20) **D**
Concept(s) Tested: Transition Words and Phrases
Choice (D) is correct because the sentence containing the underlined portion *adds to* the information in the previous sentence. Thus, the relationship is one of addition, and "furthermore" is the most appropriate transition. Choice (A) is incorrect because it links a cause-effect relationship. Choice (B) is incorrect because the "minor increase in prelimbic activity during contact" is not an example of "brain activity during leaving behavior." And choice (C) is incorrect because "besides" indicates a contrast or break from the previous topic, which is not the case here.

21) **B**
Concept(s) Tested: Subject-Verb Agreement, Verb Tense
Choice (B) is correct because the underlined verb must agree in person and number with the third-person singular noun "difference," making "provides" appropriate. Moreover, the verb must be in the simple present tense to match the tense of the rest of the paragraph.

22) **B**
Concept(s) Tested: Passage Organization
Choice (B) is correct because paragraph 3 outlines the experiment, whereas paragraph 2 begins to describe the results of the experiment. Thus, the placement of these paragraphs should switch so that the experiment is presented in chronological order, and paragraph 2 should come after paragraph 3.

23) **A**
Concept(s) Tested: Appositive Phrases
"Dan Evins" is being used as an appositive phrase and must be set apart from the rest of the sentence with a pair of commas, em-dashes, or parentheses. Only (A) correctly uses a pair of punctuation marks to set the phrase apart, so it is the correct choice.

24) **A**
Concept(s) Tested: In-Sentence Punctuation, Sentence Boundaries
The sentence contains two independent clauses, which must be connected using a comma and coordinating conjunction or a semicolon. Only (A) correctly uses a comma and an appropriate conjunction. (D) is incorrect because a conjunction is unnecessary when you split the information into two new sentences.

25) **B**
Concept(s) Tested: Countable/Uncountable Modifiers and Pronouns
The pronoun in the underlined portion is replacing "locations" and must be plural to match the number of the original noun. Because "locations" is a countable noun, the modifier "many" should be used instead of "much." The only choice that correctly uses a plural pronoun and a countable modifier is (B).

26) **A**
Concept(s) Tested: In-Sentence Punctuation
The items in the list after "toys" are not classified as toys, so a comma is more effective here than a colon, making (A) the best choice. (C) is incorrect because the elements of the list are simple and only require commas for separation. Furthermore, the remaining items use commas, so changing the structure for one item doesn't make sense.

27) **B**
Concept(s) Tested: Participial Phrases
The information after the punctuation is a participial phrase, which is indicated by the use of a participle.

The only choice that correctly begins the phrase with a present participle is (B), making it the correct answer. (C) is incorrect because two independent clauses should be separated by both a comma and coordinating conjunction. (D) is incorrect because a semicolon indicates a new independent clause, but the main verb is a participle.

28) ➡ B
Concept(s) Tested: Passage Development
The added sentence provides additional details about Cracker Barrel's growth outside the southern United States. Because the paragraph focuses on Cracker Barrel's history and growth, the added sentence fits nicely without distracting from the main idea. Therefore, (B) is the best choice.

29) ➡ C
Concept(s) Tested: Transition Words and Phrases
The sentence that contains the underlined portion describes another unique feature of the chain, so (C) is the best choice. (B) is incorrect because the sentence containing the underlined portion provides another example, but it does not elaborate on the previous example.

30) ➡ A
Concept(s) Tested: Concision
The correct choice is (A) because it provides the most succinct comparison between restaurants. All other choices are redundant or unnecessarily wordy.

31) ➡ C
Concept(s) Tested: Possession
A "chain" of restaurants refers to the group of all similar restaurants and, as such, is treated as a singular noun. The noun in the underlined portion is being used to show possession over the first restaurant, so the apostrophe is necessary, making (C) the correct choice.

32) ➡ C
Concept(s) Tested: Parallel Structure
The verbs in this sentence are presented in a list and use the simple present tense to describe the duties of the inventory management team. Therefore, the verb in the underlined portion must match this construction in order to maintain parallel structure, so (C) is the best choice.

33) ➡ D
Concept(s) Tested: Passage Development
The added sentence provides a minor detail that is not crucial to the passage, and the discussion of *American Pickers* distracts from the paragraph's focus, so (D) is the best choice.

34) ➡ C
Concept(s) Tested: Verb Tense
It is most appropriate to use the simple past tense here, as in (C), because the action of the instruments "coming" from the Ottoman Empire began and ended in the past. Other choices do not make sense and are not consistent with the other verb in the sentence, "ruled."

35) ➡ C
Concept(s) Tested: Precise Diction
Tensing and easing are opposite processes, so it is logical to say that "tensions eased," as in choice (C). Other choices would not have precise meaning when paired with "tensions."

36) ➡ A
Concept(s) Tested: Conventional Expressions
Choice (A) is correct because idiomatically, being "at the heart of" something is to be an underlying and core part, and it makes sense that music would be that for *turquerie*. Choice (B) is not the best answer because it is unclear what it would mean to be literally "in the center" of a social fad.

37) ➡ B
Concept(s) Tested: In-Sentence Punctuation
Choice (B) is correct because the word "known" comes at the end of a dependent clause. When a dependent clause comes first in a sentence, it must be followed by a comma in order to avoid confusion. Choice (A) is not correct because it appears to mean that the knowing has only taken place during marches, which would not make sense.

38) ➡ A
Concept(s) Tested: Passage Development
The sentence is part of a paragraph describing the music and how it was used. Although the paragraph has already mentioned that the bands consisted of percussion and wind instruments, the added details provide useful elaboration to help the reader imagine how such instruments could be used when heading into a battle. Thus, (A) is correct.

39) ➡ D
Concept(s) Tested: Pronoun Use
The subject of the sentence is "Empress Anna of Russia." Although it is tempting to use plural pronouns because she is acting on behalf of Russians (plural), nevertheless the singular subject must get a singular pronoun, as in (D), "her court."

40) ➡ C
Concept(s) Tested: Passage Development
Choice (C) is correct because we are being asked to connect the sentence with the previous paragraph. Since the previous paragraph is about European leaders importing *mehter* military bands or starting their own with *mehter* instruments, the clearest connect is with C's mention of "military pageantry."

41) ➡ D
Concept(s) Tested: Combining Sentences
Only choice (D) combines the two thoughts into a clear, concise sentence. Moreover, by starting with "But", (D) provides a clear contrast to the preceding sentence about the timpani already having a standard place in European orchestras at the time.

42) ➡ B
Concept(s) Tested: Precise Diction
The sentence is about how the *mehter* sound was used in a stereotypical way, a way that audiences could not fail to see as "Eastern". "Decidedly" can mean "without a doubt," which fits, and thus (B) is the answer. None of the other choices would make sense. "Legibly" means "in a way that can be read;" "understandably" implies sympathy; and "minutely" refers to attention to tiny details.

43) ➡ A
Concept(s) Tested: Passage Development
The paragraph describes how *mehter* instruments, including the triangle, were incorporated into the musical mainstream in Europe. (A) is correct because the composition by Liszt would only be mentioned in that context if the triangle played a noticeably large part. (C) is not correct because the paragraph's main point is that the triangle was not being used *alla Turca*.

44) ➡ D
Concept(s) Tested: Passage Development
The passage begins by talking about how certain familiar instruments were not always a part of the "music scene" of Western Europe. Therefore, (D) is the best choice because it wraps up the passage's explanation of the shift. (A) is not the best choice because parity with the timpani is a minor point in the passage, while (B) and (C) are incorrect because they are vague and less neutral than the passage as a whole.

SAT Practice Test 2: Answers & Explanations
Math Test

 No-Calculator Portion

1. B	7. C	13. A	18. 8		
2. C	8. A	14. C	19. 12		
3. A	9. A	15. D	20. $\frac{3}{5}$		
4. D	10. A	16. $\frac{2}{3}$			
5. C	11. D				
6. C	12. C	17. 5			

 Calculator Portion

1. D	7. C	13. B	19. D	25. D	31. 7	37. 0
2. A	8. B	14. B	20. B	26. A	32. 8	38. 39
3. C	9. A	15. D	21. B	27. D	33. 1015	
4. B	10. B	16. C	22. B	28. C	34. 6.83	
5. C	11. D	17. C	23. D	29. C	35. 50	
6. D	12. C	18. B	24. B	30. A	36. 9	

No-Calculator Portion

1)  B
   Concept(s) Tested: Problem Solving, Algebra
   Starting with x, and then multiplying by 6 gives $6x$. Divide $6x$ by 7 and then add 5 to it. Doing so results in:
   $$\frac{6x}{7} + 5$$

2)  C
   Concept(s) Tested: Algebra
   $11 - x < 15 \rightarrow -x < 4 \rightarrow x > -4$
   Note that when multiflying or dividing by a negative number, the inequality flips.

3)  A
   Concept(s) Tested: Algebra
   Subtracting the second expression from the first results in $x = -2$ as follows:
   $3x + 2y = 7$
   $-)2x + 2y = 9$
   $x = -2$

4) ▶ D
   Concept(s) Tested: Algebra
   $\frac{8y}{3} - 4 = \frac{1}{6} \rightarrow \frac{8y}{3} = \frac{25}{6} \rightarrow y = \frac{25}{16} \rightarrow \frac{1}{y} = \frac{16}{25}$
   Answer (B) is incorrect because it provides the value of y, not that of $\frac{1}{y}$.

5) ▶ C
   Concept(s) Tested: Problem Solving
   Let F be the set of students taking French and G be the set of students taking German. Note that the number of students taking French or German is $n(F \cup G) = n(F) + n(G) - n(F \cap G)$. It results in $n(F \cup G) = 41 + 22 - 9 = 54$. Therefore, the number of students who are not taking either course is $78 - 54 = 24$.

6) ▶ C
   Concept(s) Tested: Functions and Graphs
   Only (C) satisfies (3, 15) and (5, 45). To solve questions like this one, simply plug the values into the choices:
   $2(3)^2 - (3) = 15$
   $2(5)^2 - (5) = 45$

7) ▶ C
   Concept(s) Tested: Functions and Graphs
   A reflection of line l across the x-axis:
   $y' = -y = -(3x + 2) = -3x - 2$
   (A) is a reflection across the y-axis, so it is not the right answer. We can eliminate (B) and (D) as our answer choices since the slopes are the same. Changing the y-intercept only alters the height of the graph.

8) ▶ A
   Concept(s) Tested: Algebra, Number Rules
   Only $\left(-\frac{1}{3}, \frac{1}{2}\right)$ satisfies the equation $|x| + |y| \leq 1$ as follows:
   $|x| + |y| = \left|-\frac{1}{3}\right| + \left|\frac{1}{2}\right| = \frac{1}{3} + \frac{1}{2} = \frac{5}{6} \leq 1$.
   Therefore, the correct answer is (A). The fastest way to solve this problem is by determining that the sum of the absolute values of the correct choice must be less than or equal to one.

428 | KALLIS' Key to the SAT

9) ▶ A
Concept(s) Tested: Problem Solving
The total ticket cost is $70 + $84 = $154.
Stay cost = hotel cost (number of nights) × (1 + tax percentage) × (1 − discount rate) = ($66)(1.09)(0.85). The total cost of the trip is the sum of both the ticket cost and stay cost. Therefore, total cost = $154 + ($66)(3)(1.09)(0.85). The correct answer is (A).

10) ▶ A
Concept(s) Tested: Problem Solving, Algebra
If d is the difference between the consecutive terms, then:
$x + 3 + d = 2x + 1 \rightarrow x - 2 = d$
$2x + 1 + d = 5x + 3 \rightarrow 3x + 2 = d$
Subtracting the first equation from the second equation results in $x = -2$, $d = -4$. Therefore, the correct answer is (A).

11) ▶ D
Concept(s) Tested: Problem Solving
Note that new members take x classes at $15 per class, but 2 classes are free after paying the membership fee of $65. Since 2 classes are free, you subtract 2 from the number of classes must be paid for. Thus, the correct choice is (D).

12) ▶ C
Concept(s) Tested: Geometry
Let l, r, and A be the length of the arc, the radius of the smaller circle, and the area of the smaller arc respectively, and l', r' and A' be the length of the arc, the radius of the larger circle, and the area of the larger arc respectively. Then, $A = \frac{rl}{2}$
For the shaded area of the larger circle:
$l' = 2l$, $r' = 2r \rightarrow A' = 4A = 4(6) = 24$.
Therefore, the area of the shaded portion of the larger circle is 24.

13) ▶ A
Concept(s) Tested: Algebra, Factoring
First, rearrange the given expression so that a 1 can be isolated in the numerator:
$\frac{4x^2}{2x-1} = \frac{4x^2 - 1 + 1}{2x - 1}$
$= \frac{(2x-1)(2x+1)+1}{2x-1}$
$= \frac{(2x-1)(2x+1)}{2x-1} + \frac{1}{2x-1}$
$= 2x + 1 + \frac{1}{2x-1}$

Therefore, $A = 2x + 1$.

14) ▶ C
Concept(s) Tested: Algebra
Simplify the numerator and denominator. Numerator

$= \frac{1}{x-2} - \frac{1}{x+2} = \frac{1}{x-2}\left(\frac{x+2}{x+2}\right) - \frac{1}{x+2}\left(\frac{x-2}{x-2}\right)$
$= \frac{x+2}{(x-2)(x+2)} - \frac{x-2}{(x-2)(x+2)} = \frac{x+2-x+2}{(x-2)(x+2)}$
$= \frac{4}{(x-2)(x+2)}$

Denominator $= \frac{2}{x+2} + \frac{2}{x-2} = \frac{4x}{(x+2)(x-2)}$

Note that once the common factors are removed, the expression is $\frac{1}{x}$.

15) ▶ D
Concept(s) Tested: Problem Solving
Jack's gross pay, P, consists of his hourly wage, $8, times the number of hours he worked, 100, plus the money earned on commission. Jack's commissions can be expressed as 9 percent (0.09) of the average value of each sold car, x, times the number of cars sold, 4, giving: $4(0.09x)$. Thus, Jack's gross pay is the hourly wages, $8(100)$, plus commission earnings, $4(0.09x)$, making (D) the correct choice.

16) ▶ $\frac{2}{3}$ or .666 or .667
Concept(s) Tested: Functions and Graphs
For the quadratic function $f(x) = ax^2 + bx + c$, the axis of symmetry is $-\frac{b}{2a}$. Applying this to the function provided gives $x = -\frac{12}{(2)(-9)} = \frac{2}{3}$. That means $k = \frac{2}{3}$.

17) ▶ 5
Concept(s) Tested: Problem Solving
Let x be the number of correct answers and y be the number of wrong answers. Then it follows that:
$x + y = 60 \rightarrow$ number of questions
$x - 2y = 45 \rightarrow$ player score By elimination, we can conclude that $x = 55$, $y = 5$. The number of questions that the player got wrong, y, is 5.

18) ▶ 8
Concept(s) Tested: Functions and Graphs, Algebra
$\frac{f(x+h) - f(x)}{h}$
$= \frac{-1 + 8(x+h) - (-1 + 8x)}{h}$
$= \frac{8h}{h} = 8$

Thus, this is the derivative of the function $f(x)$.

19) ▶ 12
Concept(s) Tested: Data Analysis, Algebra
Note that $f(n) = 245$ implies $f(n+1) = 500$.
It results in $245a + k = 500$.
Similarly, $f(n) = 500$ implies $f(n+1) = 1,010$.

It results in $500a + k = 1{,}010$.
From both equations that contain a and k, it follows $a = 2, k = 10$. Therefore, $a + k = 12$.

20) ▶ $\frac{3}{5}$ or .6

Concept(s) Tested: Trigonometry
Because the figure is a right triangle, its third angle is equal to $90° - a°$. Thus, $\tan(90° - a°)$ is the length of the opposite side divided by the length of the adjacent side, making $\frac{3}{5}$ the correct answer.

Calculator Portion

1) ▶ D

Concept(s) Tested: Problem Solving
Note that the 3 elapsed days implies that the number of visitors has been tripled 3 times. Therefore, the number of attendees is $345 \times 3^3 = 9{,}315$.

2) ▶ A

Concept(s) Tested: Functions and Graphs
Note that $f(x) = \sqrt{(x+4)}$ has a nonnegative range. This implies that $x + 4 \geq 0$. Therefore, the domain of $f(x)$ is all real numbers $x \geq -4$.

3) ▶ C

Concept(s) Tested: Algebra, Number Rules
$$\frac{(2x^{-3}y^4)^3}{(4xy)^2} = \frac{8x^{-9}y^{12}}{16x^2y^2} = \frac{8y^{12-2}}{16x^{2+9}} = \frac{y^{10}}{2x^{11}}$$
Thus, it is equivalent to the expression in (C).

4) ▶ B

Concept(s) Tested: Problem Solving
Let x be the amount of sales in the first year. Then it follows that $2(x + 3) = 38$. It results in $x = 16$. Therefore, the correct answer is (B).

5) ▶ C

Concept(s) Tested: Ratios and Percentage
$\frac{f}{g} = \frac{1}{4}, \frac{g}{h} = \frac{2}{5}$
$\rightarrow \frac{f}{g} \cdot \frac{g}{h} = \frac{1}{4} \cdot \left(\frac{g}{h}\right)$
$\rightarrow \frac{f}{h} = \frac{1}{4} \cdot \left(\frac{g}{h}\right)$
$\rightarrow \frac{f}{h} = \frac{1}{4} \cdot \left(\frac{2}{5}\right)$
$\rightarrow \frac{f}{h} = \frac{2}{20} = \frac{1}{10}$

6) ▶ D

Concept(s) Tested: Problem Solving
To determine the number of children in the audience, calculate the number of paying adults in the audience, and subtract this value from the total number of seats in the theater.
Let x be the number of paying customers in the theater: $8(x) = 7{,}920$, which gives $x = 990$.
If 990 of the 1,152-person audience were paying customers (over the age of 10), then $1{,}152 - 990 = 162$ audience members were children aged 10 and under.

7) ▶ C

Concept(s) Tested: Ratios and Percentages
Let x be the unknown number. Then it follows that $0.15x = 12$, and $x = 80$. Therefore, 35% of x is $(0.35)(80) = 28$.

8) ▶ B

Concept(s) Tested: Algebra
$= \sqrt{250x^9y^4}$
$= (25 \times 10x^9y^4)^{\frac{1}{2}}$
$= (5x^4y^2) \times (10x)^{\frac{1}{2}}$
$= 5x^4y^2\sqrt{10x}$

9) ▶ A

Concept(s) Tested: Algebra
Note that $a^0 = 1$ for $a > 0$. It implies that the expression $5^{\left(x - \frac{1}{5}\right)^2} = 1$ should satisfy $\left(x - \frac{1}{5}\right)^2 = 0$.
Therefore, $x = \frac{1}{5}$.

10) ▶ B

Concept(s) Tested: Problem Solving
Vincent's working hours are composed of the first 8 hours for regular-pay work, 1 hour for a lunch break, and 5 hours and 15 minutes for overtime work. Therefore, he gets paid $8 \times \$10 + 5.25 \times \$15 = \$158.75$.

11) ▶ D

Concept(s) Tested: Problem Solving, Measures of Center and Spread
$\frac{X + Y + Z}{3} = V \rightarrow X + Z + Y = 3V \rightarrow X = 3V - Z - Y$

12) ▶ C

Concept(s) Tested: Problem Solving
If Rachel's gross pay is at least \$910, then $\$503.60 + \$18.51h \geq \$910$. This results in $h \geq 61.95$. Therefore, the correct answer is (C).

13) ▶ B
Concept(s) Tested: Functions and Graphs
As x increases, y decreases at a constant rate, -3, so the function has a constant negative rate of change. The slope is negative.
Expressed mathematically:
Rate of change = $m = -\frac{3}{1} = \frac{\Delta y}{\Delta x}$

14) ▶ B
Concept(s) Tested: Algebra, Factoring
$3x^2 + 2x - 5 = (3x + 5)(x - 1)$. Thus, $(3x + 5)$ and $(x - 1)$ are factors. Therefore, the correct answer is (B).

15) ▶ D
Concept(s) Tested: Trigonometry
Note that $\sin\theta = \sin(\pi - \theta)$. It results in
$\sin\theta = \sin(\pi - \theta) = 0.57$

16) ▶ C
Concept(s) Tested: Functions and Graphs
Note that $f(x)$ is not increasing linearly, so you can eliminate choices (A) and (B). The table fits with $f(x) = x^2 + 1$. Therefore, the correct answer is (C). The fastest way to solve this problem is by plugging in the values.

17) ▶ C
Concept(s) Tested: Data Analysis, Measures of Center and Spread
Note that the numbers of drivers in the set is 60. Therefore, the median is the average of the two middle values, 1 (the value of 30th) and 2 (the value of 31st), that is, $\frac{1+2}{2} = 1.5$.

18) ▶ B
Concept(s) Tested: Algebra, Number Rules
Note that $|2x - 2| = x$ implies $2x - 2 = x$ and $2x - 2 = -x$. Therefore, $x = 2$, and $x = \frac{2}{3}$, so there are 2 solutions and the correct answer is (B).

19) ▶ D
Concept(s) Tested: Algebra
Note that $81^{x+1} = (3^4)^{x+1} = 3^{4x+4}$. When we set $3^{5-x} = 3^{4x+4}$, we can see that
$5 - x = 4x + 4$. Therefore, $x = \frac{1}{5}$.

20) ▶ B
Concept(s) Tested: Unit Conversion, Algebra
Because our answers are given in minutes, first convert 1,020 seconds to minutes:
$\frac{1,020}{60} = 17$ minutes
Sammy travels 13 meters in 17 minutes. Therefore, the number of minutes it takes him to travel 115.5 meters can be determined using cross-multiplication:
$\frac{13 \text{ meters}}{17 \text{ minutes}} = \frac{115.5 \text{ meters}}{x \text{ minutes}}$
$1,963.5 = 13x \rightarrow x \approx 151$ minutes
It takes Sammy 151 minutes to summit the sequoia.

21) ▶ B
Concept(s) Tested: Problem Solving, Ratios and Percentages
The fraction of students with a grade of C– or better is $\frac{5}{6}$, and a grade of B– or better is $\frac{3}{4}$. Therefore the fraction of students with a grade higher than C– but lower than a B– is $\frac{5}{6} - \frac{3}{4} = \frac{1}{12}$.

22) ▶ B
Concept(s) Tested: Algebra
If $x \leq -1$ or $x > 3$, then $\frac{x+1}{x-3} \geq 0$.
Otherwise, $-1 < x < 3$ and it results in $\frac{x+1}{x-3} < 0$.
Therefore, the correct answer is (B).

23) ▶ D
Concept(s) Tested: Functions and Graphs
Two equations $3x - 5y + 2 = 0$ and $y = 0.6x + 0.4$ are the same, which becomes apparent when $3x - 5y + 2 = 0$ is divided by 5. Note that the graph of the equation $3x - 5y + 2 = 0$ passes through quadrants I, II, and III. Therefore, the correct answer is (D).

24) ▶ B
Concept(s) Tested: Algebra
$\frac{1-x}{x} = \frac{4-4x}{x}$ Thus, it must be true that
$\frac{1-x}{x} - \frac{4-4x}{x} = 0$
$-3(\frac{1-x}{x}) = 0$
Therefore, $\frac{1-x}{x} = 0$.

25) ▶ D
Concept(s) Tested: Problem Solving, Algebra
To calculate the value of x calories, list your given equations:
$c = 4x + 28$
$f = 3x + 28$
$c + f + 8 = 8x$
Substitute the values of c and f in the third equation from the first two equations:
$(4x + 28) + (3x + 28) + 8 = 8x$
Combine like terms and simplify:
$7x + 64 = 8x \rightarrow x = 64$

26) ▶ A
Concept(s) Tested: Problem Solving, Unit Conversion
From Coulomb's law, ε_0 is as follows:

$$F = \frac{1}{4\pi\varepsilon_0} \times \frac{q_1 q_2}{r^2} \quad \rightarrow \quad \varepsilon_0 = \frac{1}{4\pi F} \times \frac{q_1 q_2}{r^2}$$

Since q is expressed using Columbs (C), F using Newtons (N), and r in meters (m), we can determine that the units for ε_0 can be calculated as follows:

$$\varepsilon_0 \text{ unit} = \frac{(q_1 \text{ unit})(q_2 \text{ unit})}{(F \text{ unit})(r \text{ unit})^2} = \frac{C^2}{N \times m^2} = \frac{C^2}{m^2 \cdot N}$$

27) ▶ D
Concept(s) Tested: Problem Solving
Substitute q_1 and q_2 with 1.6×10^{-19}C and r with 1 in the Coulomb's law. It results in the following equation.

$$F = \frac{1}{4\pi\varepsilon_0} \times \frac{q_1 q_2}{r^2} = \frac{(1.6)^2 \times 10^{-19 \times 2}}{4\pi \times 8.85 \times 10^{-12}} =$$

$$\frac{2.56 \times 10^{-38}}{111.156 \times 10^{-12}} = \frac{2.56 \times 100 \times 10^{-40}}{111.156 \times 10^{-12}} =$$

$$\frac{2.56}{111.156} \times \frac{10^{-40}}{10^{-12}} = 2.3 \times 10^{-28}$$

28) ▶ C
Concept(s) Tested: Geometry, Number Rules
Note that the area of the circle is $A = \pi r^2$. Therefore, doubling the radius of a circle quadruples its area. It means that the statement (C) is always FALSE.

29) ▶ C
Concept(s) Tested: Geometry
Note that the area of the parallelogram PQRS is 2 times of the area of the triangle QSR and this value is also 2 times of the area of $\triangle$QST. It implies the area of $\square$PQRS is 4 times of the area of $\triangle$QST. Therefore, the ratio of the area of $\triangle$QST to the area of the $\square$PQRS is 1 : 4.

30) ▶ A
Concept(s) Tested: Algebra, Number Rules
If $A = -2 + 4i$, and $B = 3 - 2i$,
then $A - B = (-2 + 4i) - (3 - 2i) = -5 + 6i$

31) ▶ 7
Concept(s) Tested: Algebra
Convert the denominators on the left side of the equation $\frac{x+3}{2} + \frac{2x}{7} = 7$.

It results in $\frac{7x+21}{14} + \frac{4x}{14} = \frac{11x+21}{14} = 7$.

Therefore, $x = 7$.

32) ▶ 8
Concept(s) Tested: Functions and Graphs
The graph of the equation $2x^2 - y^2 = 8$ passes through $(6, p)$ and $(6, -p)$. Therefore, $2(6)^2 - p^2 = 8$. It results in $p = \pm 8$. Note that p is positive. Therefore, $p = 8$.

33) ▶ 1015
Concept(s) Tested: Problem Solving, Ratios and Percentages
Let g be Homer's gross pay for the pay period:
Total pay − Tax = Paycheck
$g - 0.22(g) = 792$
$g \times (1 - 0.22) = 792$
$g = 1015.38$.
Therefore, the nearest gross pay in dollars is $1,015.

34) ▶ 6.83
Concept(s) Tested: Functions and Graphs, Geometry
Note that the line $y = 5$ intersects with the circle $(x - 4)^2 + (y - 4)^2 = 3^2$. Therefore, putting $y = 5$ into the equation of the circle results in $(x - 4)^2 + 1 = 9$, which solves to $x = 4 \pm 2\sqrt{2}$. Note that $4 - 2\sqrt{2}$ is approximately 1.17. The other point of intersection is $4 + 2\sqrt{2}$, which is approximately 6.83.

35) ▶ 50
Concept(s) Tested: Problem Solving, Algebra
Let x and y be the number of cards in a pack costing $10 and $2.50 respectively.
Then, $x + y = 75$, $10x + 2.5y = 375$ should hold.

$10x + 10y = 750$
$-)10x + 2.5y = 375$
$7.5y = 375 \quad \rightarrow \quad y = 50$

From both equations, $y = 50$, where y is the number of $2.50 packs.

36) ▶ 9
Concept(s) Tested: Functions and Graphs
Let $f(x) = Ca^x$ where C is constant and a is an exponential factor. From $f(0) = 4$, it follows that $C = 4$. From $f(1) = 6$, it follows that $6 = 4a$, so $a = \frac{3}{2}$. It results in $f(x) = 4\left(\frac{3}{2}\right)^x$.

Therefore, $q = f(2) = 4\left(\frac{3}{2}\right)^2 = 3^2 = 9$.

37) ▶ 0
Concept(s) Tested: Problem Solving
Note that T_s is the temperature of the surrounding environment. If an object is placed into an ice bath, the temperature of the surrounding enviroment is zero. Therefore, $T_s = 0$.

38) ▶ 39
Concept(s) Tested: Problem Solving, Algebra
Using the equation $T_t = T_s + (T_0 - T_s)e^{-rt}$, we can conclude that:

$T_1 = 25 + (50 - 25)2.71^{-0.01(60)}$
$T_1 = 25 + (50 - 25)2.71^{-0.6}$
$T_1 = 25 + (25)(0.55) = 38.7°C$.
Round this value to 39.

SAT Practice Test 2: Answers & Explanations

Sample Essay Response

Nicholas Buffie's articles "Women Earn Less Than Men in 302 of 311 Occupations" takes a clinical approach to an often emotionally charged discussion: the gender pay gap. Buffie creates an evidence-based argument by using government data to prove the persistence of a gender pay gap among the vast majority of professions.

After introducing the general topic of the gender pay gap with a quote from Obama, Buffie immediately addresses a counter argument that questions the existence of a pay gap on the basis of women's occupational choices and hours worked. Buffie helps the audience grasp the counter argument by way of conditional statements: "If women choose to work in low-paying occupations..." Buffie's matter-of-fact response, that one can focus on pay within each occupation, undermines the counterargument.

Buffie's argument begins in paragraph 3, where he clarifies that his main goal is to disprove the claims of "some commentators" mentioned in the previous paragraph. And while he did not cite any sources that substantiate the views of "some commentators," Buffie immediately tells the reader where he derived his data: the U.S. Census Bureau. Thus, he weighs the argument in his favor by demonstrating that his claims are based on data from a reliable source, whereas the claims of those he is disproving seem to have been pulled from the ether.

Buffie appeals to the reader's reasoning abilities as he outlines his methodology for interpreting this data. By describing how he structured his study, he allows the reader to work with him; again, his precision and transparency compares favorably with his opposition's unsupported argument. Once Buffie has covered methodology, he begins to interrogate the counterargument by picking apart the conditions he presented in paragraph 2. In paragraphs 4, 5, 6, and 7, Buffie uses the Census Bureau data to account for both "occupational choices" and "hours worked" (the two factors that the counterargument use to question the pay gap), ultimately concluding that, even taking these factors into account, women make less than men. Thus, the conclusions he draws from the data provide the evidence that proves his argument.

Buffie concludes his argument by bringing it full circle: he restates the counter argument and concludes that the data disproves it. Here, he implicitly compares his methodical, data-based approach to the unsubstantiated, "clearly wrong" claims of his opponents.

Student Response Score: 4/4/3

Reading: 4

The student outlines Buffie's argument clearly, referencing all the author's major points. The student references the source text often and makes appropriate use of quotations. The response shows clear understanding of Buffie's central claim without distorting any of the author's ideas.

Writing: 4

The response is organized logically and maintains focus throughout. The student states the central claim of his response in the introduction and then analyzes one critical feature of Buffie's argument in each body paragraph. The conclusion is concise and summarizes the student's claim without restating unnecessary information.

Analysis: 3

The student carefully considers Buffie's use of facts and data as well as his refutation of a common counterargument. He notes the source of Buffie's data as being "authentic" and comments on how this authenticity lends credibility to the author's overall claim. However, the student could benefit from analyzing a more diverse range of literary features from the source.

SAT Practice Test 3: Answers & Explanations

Reading Test

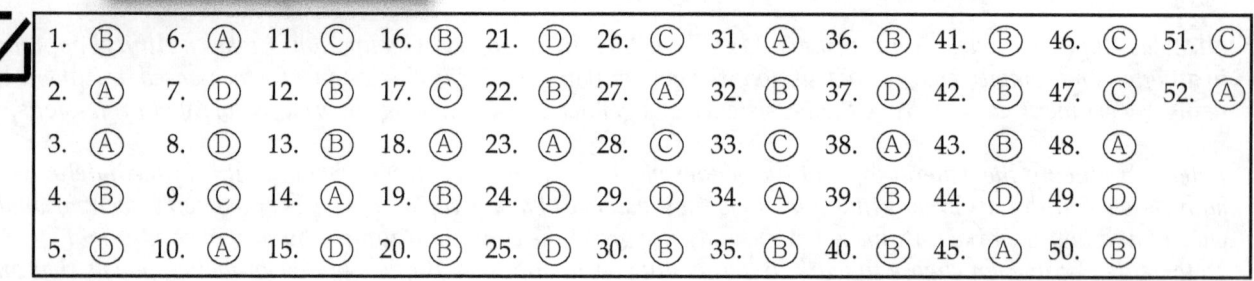

1. B	6. A	11. C	16. B	21. D	26. C	31. A	36. B	41. B	46. C	51. C
2. A	7. D	12. B	17. C	22. B	27. A	32. B	37. D	42. B	47. C	52. A
3. A	8. D	13. B	18. A	23. A	28. C	33. C	38. A	43. B	48. A	
4. B	9. C	14. A	19. B	24. D	29. D	34. A	39. B	44. D	49. D	
5. D	10. A	15. D	20. B	25. D	30. B	35. B	40. B	45. A	50. B	

1) ▶ B
Concept(s) Tested: Words in Context
The correct choice is (B) because "acute" changes in a patient's condition that require immediate attention would be considered urgent, or "dire." Choices (A), (C), and (D) are incorrect because they do not convey the specific meaning used in this context.

2) ▶ A
Concept(s) Tested: Summary
Choice (A) is correct because the author confesses that she has very little experience "as a two-week-old intern with a largely theoretical knowledge base." This lack of experience leads her to appreciate step-by-step procedures. Choice (B) is incorrect because the author never expresses fears about harming patients. Choice (C) is incorrect because the author does not compare herself to other interns. Choice (D) is incorrect because the step-by-step procedures did not make her more comfortable around the deceased patient in the passage.

3) ▶ A
Concept(s) Tested: Citation
Choice (A) is correct. This excerpt explains the author's inexperience and her appreciation for following predetermined courses of action. Choice (B) is incorrect because it does not address the author's inexperience or her desire to follow step-by-step procedures. Choice (C) is incorrect because it does not explain why the author appreciates simple instructions. Choice (D) is incorrect because this excerpt does not provide any insight into the author's motivations.

4) ▶ B
Concept(s) Tested: Purpose
The correct choice is (B) because the paragraph in question describes the exact steps related to pronouncing a patient dead. Choice (A) is incorrect because the author's tone is informative and there is nothing to indicate she is critical of her duties. Choice (C) is incorrect because the author never indicates that a pronouncement is a difficult task. Choice (D) is incorrect because the author spends very little time discussing grieving family members in this paragraph and never explains strategies for interacting with them.

5) ▶ D
Concept(s) Tested: Passage Organization
The correct choice is (D) because the narrator's experience later in the passage—that is, her own fear of the dead body—makes her laughter ironic. Choice (A) is incorrect because this excerpt does not highlight the narrator's sense of humor. Choice (B) is incorrect because the narrator's laughter is not perplexing, as it is directed at her coworker's humorous admission. Choice (C) is incorrect because the quality of her friendship with her co-intern is not the topic of the anecdote and is not described.

6) ▶ A
Concept(s) Tested: Summary
The correct choice is (A) because the room is described as being "quiet except for the sounds of a waterfall playing in the background." Choice (B) is incorrect because the narrator finds nothing unsettling or strange about the room itself. Choice (C) is incorrect because there is no evidence to suggest that the room is sterile. Choice (D) is incorrect because the narrator is not disoriented upon entering the room.

7) ▶ D
Concept(s) Tested: Words in Context
The efforts of the palliative care team included pulling down the shades and playing nature sounds, implying an effort to create a "soothing" environment where death is expected. Thus, (D) is the best answer choice. Choices (A), (B), and (C) are incorrect because they fail to fit the context-specific meaning of the word as it is used in the passage.

8) ▶ D
Concept(s) Tested: Attitude and Tone
The correct choice is (D) because the narrator describes a "very strong impulse to back away from the bed." In other words, she is recoiling instinctively. Choice (A) is incorrect because the author does not indicate any feelings of grief toward the deceased woman, whom she has never met. Choice (B) is incorrect because the narrator delays her task by watching the clock, but does not display "uncontrollable panic." Choice (C) is incorrect because the narrator does not describe any genuine feelings of hope toward the patient.

9) ▶ C
Concept(s) Tested: Citation
The best choice is (C) because this excerpt effectively expresses the narrator's instinct to recoil. Choice (A) is incorrect because it reveals nothing about the narrator's reaction to the corpse. Choice (B) is incorrect because this excerpt does not accurately convey the narrator's emotions. Choice (D) is incorrect because the narrator's hope that the patient is dead does not fully reveal her instinct to back away.

10) ▶ A
Concept(s) Tested: Inference
Choice (A) is correct because the narrator uses this description in the context of saying that she does not want to simply offer surviving friends and family "stock condolences," or impersonal comfort, when a patient dies. Choice (B) is incorrect because the description fails to convey the humility that the

434 | KALLIS' Key to the SAT

narrator feels in the situation. Choice (C) is incorrect because there is no evidence that the narrator describes herself in such a way in order to maintain formalities. Choice (D) is incorrect because there is no evidence that the narrator believes the family will not trust her.

11) **C**
Concept(s) Tested: Attitude and Tone
The correct choice is (C) because Roosevelt uses these words to create a scene of harshness and adversity. The image of a "cactus-covered waste" can then be contrasted with the "marvel" of the dam. Choice (A) is incorrect because the words chosen are descriptive and subjective rather than factual. Choice (B) is incorrect because the speech does not focus on unsolvable, "sobering" societal problems. Choice (D) is incorrect because the image of the "blazing heat of the sun" adds to rather than "contrasts with" the negative and harsh landscape described in the paragraph.

12) **B**
Concept(s) Tested: Words in Context
Choice (B) is correct. Roosevelt's emphasis on the "accumulated knowledge and experience of centuries" suggests "brilliance" is the most fitting choice. Choices (A) and (D) are incorrect because, in the context of the passage, "genius" is used to indicate a quality or character trait, while "mastermind" and "expert" describe people. Choice (C) is incorrect because the emphasis is on the ingenuity of the engineers, not necessarily the specialization of their role.

13) **B**
Concept(s) Tested: Purpose
Choice (B) is correct. In the first sentence of paragraph 2, Roosevelt announces, "We are here to celebrate the completion of the greatest dam in the world." Therefore, we can determine he uses precise measurements to back up this claim and "emphasize the enormity of the Boulder Dam project." Choice (A) is incorrect because Roosevelt does not mention the cost of the project in the second paragraph. Choice (C) is incorrect because Roosevelt's speech focuses on public works themselves, not his knowledge of them. Choice (D) is incorrect because Roosevelt does not defend the value of the Boulder Dam at this point in the speech.

14) **A**
Concept(s) Tested: Summary
The correct choice is (A). In paragraph 4, Roosevelt discusses "agricultural and industrial development" as well as "the health and comfort" of the people who live in the Southwest. Therefore, he is shifting to focus on the effects of the Boulder Dam on the nation's economy and local citizens. Choice (B) is incorrect because Roosevelt does not mention water in this paragraph. Choice (C) is incorrect because Roosevelt does not provide a description of the people who will benefit from the dam in this speech. Choice (D) is incorrect because no details regarding water allocation appear in the paragraph.

15) **D**
Concept(s) Tested: Summary
Choice (D) is correct because Roosevelt emphasizes the widespread dependence on this source of water throughout the region. He believes that "one of the greatest problems of law and of administration" is "to divert and distribute the waters of an arid region." (lines 44 — 47). In other words, governments "that control a hot, dry region must be largely concerned with managing water distribution." Choice (A) is incorrect because Roosevelt does not suggest that anyone study the aqueducts built in connection with the Boulder Dam. Choice (B) is incorrect because Roosevelt never discusses sharing water with neighboring territories. Choice (C) is incorrect because Roosevelt never makes this claim.

16) **B**
Concept(s) Tested: Citation
The correct choice is (B). In this excerpt, Roosevelt puts a great deal of emphasis on a government's responsibility to adequately distribute water to the inhabitants and farmers in a harsh, arid desert. Choice (A) is incorrect because it does not address the role of governments that control desert territories. Choice (C) is incorrect because this excerpt focuses on a specific project, but does not indicate Roosevelt's emphasis on the overall importance of managing water resources in hot, dry regions. Choice (D) is incorrect because it consists of a detail, rather than an overall claim about government's role in water distribution.

17) **C**
Concept(s) Tested: Words in Context
The correct choice is (C) because storing the spring flood provides, or "yields," a constant water supply. The remaining choices are incorrect because they do not fit the context in which the word is used.

18) **A**
Concept(s) Tested: Summary
Choice (A) is correct. Roosevelt praises the plans and laws that already regulate water distribution. He says in lines 55 — 56 that states along the Colorado River and the federal government "working out such a scheme of distribution is inspiring to the whole country." (B) is incorrect because Roosevelt never makes such a claim. Choice (C) is incorrect because, although Roosevelt says that the dam will prevent crop losses during droughts, he does not claim that the dam will prevent droughts. Choice (D) is incorrect because Roosevelt does not imply the Boulder Dam will encourage future generations to reside in the Southwest.

19) **B**
Concept(s) Tested: Purpose
The correct choice is (B). Roosevelt's primary purpose for giving the speech is to argue the Boulder Dam's value to the American people. Therefore, he uses crop losses to emphasize the importance of the dam in storing water. Choice (A) is incorrect because Roosevelt does not discuss or explain individual hardships in the passage. Choice (C) is incorrect because Roosevelt does not address the difficulty of farming in the West. Choice (D) is incorrect because crop losses are not directly related to the cost of the dam.

20) **B**
Concept(s) Tested: Citation
Choice (B) is correct because the excerpt highlights Roosevelt's primary purpose for giving the speech: defending the value of the Boulder Dam. Choice (A) is incorrect because it fails to connect the Boulder Dam to preventing future water shortages. Choice (C) is incorrect because it does not mention the dam in relationship to the regulated water supply. Choice (D) is incorrect because it speculates on future benefits of the electricity generated by the dam, making it less precise than (B).

21) **D**
Concept(s) Tested: Inference
Choice (D) is correct. Roosevelt suggests that thousands of cities and farms along the river "depend upon the conservation, the regulation, and the equitable division of [the Colorado River]" (lines 51 — 53). Because of the importance of the Boulder Dam in securing water and electricity to the inhabitants of this region, we can

infer that these people "will become at least partly dependent on water and power from the dam." Choice (A) is incorrect because Roosevelt does not suggest that the people in California will use more water from the Colorado River than people elsewhere, only that they are constructing an aqueduct. Choice (B) is incorrect because Roosevelt does not indicate that the aqueduct being built is longest aqueduct in history. Choice (C) is incorrect because Roosevelt does not imply that water rights are a driving force behind population expansion.

22) ➡ B
Concept(s) Tested: Purpose
The correct choice is (B). The author spends the majority of the passage discussing the constraints on living organisms, contrasting the point made in the first sentence. Choice (A) is incorrect because the author challenges the view presented in these lines. Choice (C) is incorrect because the author does not present any evidence in this selection. Choice (D) is incorrect because the author does not challenge the scientific community at any point in the passage.

23) ➡ A
Concept(s) Tested: Words in Context
Choice (A) is correct because the author points out that water is necessary for supporting, or "maintaining," life. Choices (B), (C), and (D) all define the phrase "carrying on," but do not fit the specific context in which it is used.

24) ➡ D
Concept(s) Tested: Summary
Choice (D) is correct because the author points out that "animal life presupposes plant life, for it is always dependent upon it." Choice (A) is incorrect because the author does not comment on the variety or versatility of plant and animal life. Choice (B) is incorrect because the author discusses the conversion of inorganic matter to organic matter, not the other way around. Choice (C) is incorrect because the author argues that plant life creates the conditions that support animal life, not the other way around.

25) ➡ D
Concept(s) Tested: Citation
Choice (D) is correct because this excerpt clearly expresses the author's point that animal life is completely dependent upon plant life. Choice (A) is incorrect because the selection does not accurately describe the relationship between plant and animal life. Choice (B) is incorrect because it only supports the theory that animals are dependent upon organic matter, but does not make it clear that the necessary organic components are provided by plants. Choice (C) is incorrect because it highlights the requirements for plant life but fails to describe the necessary components of animal life.

26) ➡ C
Concept(s) Tested: Words in Context
Choice (C) is correct. Animal life is dependent upon plant life; in other words, animal life "requires" plant life. The remaining answer choices do not fit the meaning of the word as it used in this context.

27) ➡ A
Concept(s) Tested: Purpose
Choice (A) is correct. Before introducing the quote, the author of the passage indicates that "the assumption is a mistaken one, as has been well pointed out by Garrett P. Serviss." Therefore, the quote is being used to "refute a common misconception." Choice (B) is incorrect because the author does not indicate that anything in the discussion would be confusing or need clarification from an outside source. Choice (C) is incorrect because the author does not define any terms that need elaboration. Choice (D) is incorrect because the quote refutes the assumption mentioned.

28) ➡ C
Concept(s) Tested: Summary
Choice (C) is correct. The author explains that life thrives under only very specific conditions "which will permit and favor continual change" (lines 81 – 82). Choice (A) is incorrect because the passage never claims that "chaos" favors life. Choice (B) is incorrect because the author suggests life only thrives under specific conditions. Choice (D) is incorrect because this is the opposite of the author's claim.

29) ➡ D
Concept(s) Tested: Citation
Choice (D) is correct because it most clearly expresses the author's claim that life requires constant change. Choices (A), (B), and (C) are incorrect because none of these choices mentions the conditions favorable to living organisms.

30) ➡ B
Concept(s) Tested: Inference
Choice (B) is correct because the author argues that much of the universe "offer[s] no home for the living organism" (lines 78 – 79). He goes on to say that life requires continually changing conditions, implying that much of the universe cannot support life because it is in stasis. (The author was writing before the 1929 discovery that the Universe is expanding and before geological activity on other planets had been observed.) Choice (A) is incorrect because the author argues that life is limited by environmental factors, not that life will never be found on another planet. Choice (C) is incorrect because Serviss does not discuss whether plants or animals arose as the first living organisms. Choice (D) is incorrect because the passage makes no mention of the depth of Earth's oceans.

31) ➡ A
Concept(s) Tested: Purpose
The correct choice is (A) because the quote is a metaphor, and the author explains its relevance to the main argument in the following paragraph. Choice (B) is incorrect because the quote does not refute any claims made in the previous paragraph. Choice (C) is incorrect because the author does not mention this in the passage. Choice (D) is incorrect because the quote does not provide any evidence for any of the author's claims.

32) ➡ B
Concept(s) Tested: Inference
Throughout the passage, the author describes the very specific conditions under which life is possible. The article also mentions that much of the universe is uninhabitable for any living organism, implying that "life can probably only thrive under the conditions found on Earth." Thus, (B) is the correct answer choice. Choice (A) is incorrect because the passage does not discuss attempts to replicate the processes that created life on Earth. Choice (C) is incorrect because the author does not discuss classifying living organisms at any point in the passage. Choice (D) is incorrect because this is outside the scope of this passage.

33) ➡ C
Concept(s) Tested: Words in Context
The correct choice is (C) because, in this context,

"perpetuate" means to increase the duration of, or "prolong." Choices (A), (B), and (D) do not fit the meaning of the word as it is used in the passage.

34) **A**
Concept(s) Tested: Inference
The correct choice is (A) because the passage explains that President Clinton agreed to end a federal program and shift "control of welfare programs to the states" (lines 7 – 11). Thus, we can infer that he reduced federal involvement in such programs. Choice (B) is incorrect because there is no evidence in the passage to suggest President Clinton challenged Reagan's views. Choice (C) is incorrect because the passage implies that many of these programs were not eliminated, but shifted from federal to state control. Choice (D) is incorrect because the passage implies that Clinton reduced the amount of time people were eligible for aid.

35) **B**
Concept(s) Tested: Summary
Paragraph 1 describes two presidents who took measures to limit federal aid programs, and in lines 14 – 16, the author states that "critics of anti-poverty programs point out that significant progress has not been made in eliminating poverty." From this, we can infer that (B) is the correct answer choice. Choice (A) is incorrect because the author argues that public assistance has been more effective than critics realize. Choices (C) and (D) are incorrect because the author's goal is to analyze historical trends rather than to explore opinions.

36) **B**
Concept(s) Tested: Purpose
Choice (B) is correct because, later in the passage, the author argues that welfare programs have been successful. Therefore, this sentence is used to "concede the apparent accuracy of a counterargument" before the author presents her own case. Choice (A) is incorrect because this sentence supports rather than refutes the preceding information. Choice (C) is incorrect because these numbers support the counterargument to the author's central claim and do not provide evidence for the author's main argument. Choice (D) is incorrect because this excerpt does not address the causes of poverty.

37) **D**
Concept(s) Tested: Words in Context
Choice (D) is correct because "thresholds" is being used to describe the upper limits of poverty, or the "defining points." Choices (A) and (C) are both accurate definitions for the word, but they do not fit the context of the sentence. Choice (B) is not a synonym of "thresholds" and does not fit the context of the passage.

38) **A**
Concept(s) Tested: Summary
Choice (A) is correct. In the passage, the author describes the Supplemental Poverty Measure and explains that it "use[s] data from the Annual Social and Economic Supplement, the Current Population Survey and the Consumer Expenditure Survey" (lines 45 — 47). Choice (B) is incorrect because it is not clear what "estimates" it refers to. Choice (C) is incorrect because both studies use numerical data, not abstract measures. Choice (D) is incorrect because the Supplemental Poverty Measure incorporates both cash and non-cash assistance.

39) **B**
Concept(s) Tested: Citation
The correct choice is (B) because this excerpt accurately describes the additional data used to construct the Supplemental Poverty Measure. Choice (A) is incorrect because it introduces the topic of the Supplemental Poverty Measure but gives us no information about what it is or how it differs from the Official Poverty Measure. Choice (C) is incorrect because the selection tells us how the researchers made use of the measures but not how they constructed them. Choice (D) is incorrect because it shows researchers' conclusions but does not mention the data used to create the Supplemental Poverty Measure.

40) **B**
Concept(s) Tested: Graph Synthesis
Based on the graph, estimated poverty levels would be much higher without government programs. Because this is in agreement with one of the main arguments of the passage, (B) is the correct choice. Choices (A) and (D) are incorrect because the graph makes no distinction between the types of programs and which were more or less helpful than others. Choice (C) is incorrect because the graph makes no reference to child poverty levels and only provides an overall poverty measurement.

41) **B**
Concept(s) Tested: Graph Analysis
The correct answer choice is (B) because the graph indicates that, as of 2012, overall poverty was reduced by about 50 percent when both cash aid and non-cash transfers were considered. Choice (A) is incorrect because the graph does not address the amount of aid provided, instead focusing on the impact of public assistance on the overall poverty level. Choice (C) is incorrect because the graph does not use the Official Poverty Measure. Choice (D) is incorrect because the graph makes no claim about the accuracy of either poverty measure.

42) **B**
Concept(s) Tested: Graph Analysis, Citation
The correct choice is (B). In this selection, the author explains the significance of government assistance and provides figures to support her claim. This describes the information presented in the graph, indicating the decrease in poverty over the course of the study as well as the estimated increase in poverty had government assistance not been provided. Choice (A) is incorrect because it gives us no information about the data collected to compare with the graph. Choice (C) is incorrect because this selection is irrelevant to the information presented in the graph. Choice (D) is incorrect because the graph does not distinguish between child poverty and overall poverty.

43) **B**
Concept(s) Tested: Summary
The correct choice is (B) because the decline of the black-footed ferret was primarily due to "habitat loss, a decline in prey, and plague" (lines 5 — 6). In other words, "their natural resources became increasingly scarce." Choice (A) is incorrect because the author of Passage 1 does not indicate that the ferrets were hunted by early settlers. Choice (C) and (D) are incorrect because they are not supported by the passage.

44) **D**
Concept(s) Tested: Summary
According to Passage 1, the last surviving black-footed ferrets were found on Pitchfork Ranch, making (D) the correct choice. Choice (A) is incorrect because the living ferrets, not the ferret carcass, were the primary reason the ranch became significant. Choice (B) is incorrect because the location of the revival efforts was not discussed. Choice (C) is incorrect because such a facility was not described in the passage.

45) ➡ A
Concept(s) Tested: Words in Context
As used in the passage, "recovery" refers to the increase in the black-footed ferret's population. Thus, (A) is the correct choice. The remaining choices fail to communicate the idea that the species is repopulating, so they are all incorrect.

46) ➡ C
Concept(s) Tested: Inference
The correct choice is (C) because the black-footed ferret is being described as a "memory" and then being compared to the dodo. Therefore, it is reasonable to infer that the dodo is a type of animal that exists only in the collective memory of humanity. Choice (A) is incorrect because the passage does not mention which species the ferret preys upon. Choice (B) is incorrect because the author contrasts the reintroduction of the black-footed ferret with the complete disappearance of the dodo. Choice (D) is incorrect because the dodo is "nothing more than a memory," implying that it has been extinct for some time.

47) ➡ C
Concept(s) Tested: Words in Context
(C) is the correct choice because it accurately conveys the idea that settlers were moving, or "advancing," further west. The remaining choices are incorrect because they fail to define the word as it is being used in this context.

48) ➡ A
Concept(s) Tested: Inference
The correct choice is (A). The author of Passage 2 describes bison and their ability to clear snow to create foraging patches during winter, implying that "they can survive freezing temperatures." Choice (B) is incorrect because the author of Passage 2 makes no mention of the black-footed ferret. Choice (C) is incorrect because the author never discusses the distance traveled by a typical bison in a year. Choice (D) is incorrect because the author never indicates that this is true.

49) ➡ D
Concept(s) Tested: Citation
Choice (D) is correct because it describes a feature that allows bison to forage despite freezing temperatures. Choice (A) is incorrect because this excerpt only gives a physical description of bison, but does not give us enough information to know if they can survive cold weather. Choice (B) is incorrect because, again, it does not tell us enough about their ability to survive freezing temperatures. Choice (C) is incorrect because it only provides information about the bison's diet and fails to mention any adaptations for cold winters.

50) ➡ B
Concept(s) Tested: Text Synthesis, Attitude and Tone
The correct choice is (B) because the author of Passage 1 indicates appreciation for the efforts made to save an endangered species. Therefore, this author would approve of Teddy Roosevelt's efforts to save other endangered species. Choice (A) is incorrect because the topic of bison hunting is used merely as an introduction to Roosevelt's more selfless actions discussed later on. Choice (C) is incorrect because Passage 2 does not indicate that the bison is struggling; rather, it implies that reintroduction efforts have been successful. Choice (D) is incorrect because the author of Passage 1 does not present any opinions on genetic purity of endangered species.

51) ➡ C
Concept(s) Tested: Citation
The correct choice is (C) because this selection discusses using captive breeding programs and reintroduction efforts similar to those used with bison. From this excerpt, we can infer that the author of Passage 1 likely views Roosevelt's actions with praise. Choice (A) is incorrect because this selection provides an introduction to later topics, but does not address the author's attitude toward reintroducing and expanding endangered species. Choice (B) is incorrect because it does not reveal any information about the author's attitude toward efforts to save endangered species. Choice (D) is incorrect because it provides a description of ferrets "returning home," but does not directly support the author's approval of models for saving endangered species.

52) ➡ A
Concept(s) Tested: Purpose, Text Synthesis
The correct choice is (A). Both passages focus primarily on describing and celebrating efforts to breed and reintroduce an endangered species. Choice (B) is incorrect because both passages focus on the efforts to expand the populations of endangered species and do not spend much time praising the individuals involved. Choice (C) is incorrect because neither passage discusses the specific procedures involved in reintroducing species to the wild. Choice (D) is incorrect because the issue of American developers is not raised in either passage.

SAT Writing & Language Test 3 : Answers & Explanations

Writing & Language Test

1. C	5. C	9. D	13. B	17. B	21. D	25. C	29. D	33. B	37. A	41. A
2. A	6. B	10. B	14. C	18. C	22. C	26. A	30. B	34. B	38. C	42. A
3. A	7. C	11. A	15. D	19. A	23. D	27. B	31. C	35. C	39. C	43. C
4. D	8. B	12. A	16. D	20. A	24. D	28. A	32. B	36. D	40. B	44. D

1) ➤ C
Concept(s) Tested: Concision
The correct choice is (C) because it conveys the same idea as the other choices, but it is the most concise. The remaining choices are unnecessarily wordy.

2) ➤ A
Concept(s) Tested: Conventional Expression, Sentence Modifiers
The expression "far and wide" means "over a great distance," so (A) is the correct choice. (B) is incorrect because, although both "wide" and "widely" are acceptable adverb forms, only "wide" fits the expression as used in the sentence. Choice (C) is incorrect because something is not usually said to be "spread...far away," and (D) is incorrect because nothing is being compared, so use of the comparative "-er" ending is unnecessary.

3) ➤ A
Concept(s) Tested: Combining Sentences
Choice (A) is correct because it effectively conveys the relationship between the sentences by turning the second sentence into a relative clause that describes the term "baroque." All other choices are incorrect because they form run-ons or do not as clearly convey the same relationship.

4) ➤ D
Concept(s) Tested: Passage Development
The author mentions that baroque artists "wanted to excite passions" and provides an example of movement within baroque sculpture. Therefore, the correct choice should emphasize the excitement of baroque art, making (D) the best choice. (A) is incorrect because the origin of baroque style adds no information about its appeal to emotions. (B) and (C) are incorrect because they simply describe techniques used by baroque artists.

5) ➤ C
Concept(s) Tested: In-Sentence Punctuation
The correct choice is (C) because a prepositional phrase in the middle of a sentence does not require punctuation. (D) is incorrect because it creates a fragment by starting a new sentence with the prepositional phrase.

6) ➤ B
Concept(s) Tested: Precise Diction, Passage Tone
Choice (B) is correct because it conveys the idea that there is much ornamentation without injecting the author's personal opinion about the decorations. (A) and (D) are incorrect because "excessive" and "immoderate" imply that the ornamentation is more than is necessary, so these choices stray from the neutral tone sought. (C) is incorrect because "splendid" implies the author's approval, so this choice also deviates from the desired tone.

7) ➤ C
Concept(s) Tested: Verb Tense
The main verb must be in the simple past tense because the sentence focuses on an effect of the palace on its visitors from centuries ago. Thus, (C) is the best answer. (A) is incorrect because the past progressive is typically used to express an ongoing action that was interrupted.

8) ➤ B
Concept(s) Tested: Passage Development
The paragraph focuses on the "theatrical" nature of the palace at Versailles, as the author later mentions that the king awoke to an "audience" every morning. Therefore, (B) is the correct answer because it supports this claim.

9) ➤ D
Concept(s) Tested: Passage Development
The underlined sentence is necessary to describe the function of the Hall of Mirrors and continues the paragraph's discussion of the dramatic nature of the palace, so (D) is the best choice.

10) ➤ B
Concept(s) Tested: Participial Phrases, Misplaced Modifier
The correct answer is (B) because it is the only choice that accurately places the noun next to its modifier. (A) and (C) are incorrect because they imply that the skylight, not the entry hall, was known as the Ambassador's Stair. (D) is incorrect because it does not specify what the Ambassador's Stair is, creating confusion for the reader.

11) ➤ A
Concept(s) Tested: Transition Words and Phrases
The correct choice should emphasize that the Ambassador's Stair is the means by which the king impressed his guests, which is conveyed effectively by "thereby." (B) is incorrect because the author is not making a comparison with this statement. (C) is incorrect because the information in the final sentence does not contrast with earlier information. (D) is incorrect because the passage does not provide a chronological account of events.

12) ➤ A
Concept(s) Tested: In-Sentence Punctuation
Choice (A) is correct because the information after the em-dash provides an elaboration, namely a list of the three villages. (B) is incorrect because the use of a semicolon here creates a sentence fragment. (C) is incorrect because the word "including" implies a partial list of the group, but all three villages are named.

13) ➤ B
Concept(s) Tested: Passage Development
The added sentence provides insight into the shortened lifespans mentioned, so it should be included in the passage. Thus, (B) is the correct answer.

TEST 3: Answers & Explanations | 439

14) **C**
Concept(s) Tested: Concision
The author indicates that the rock was "soft" and settlers "used it for building," so it is redundant to add a second adjective, making (C) the best choice. The remaining answer choices all add redundant information to the passage, so they are all incorrect.

15) **D**
Concept(s) Tested: Passage Organization
Sentence 6 discusses the continuation of practices mentioned earlier in the paragraph. Therefore, it makes sense to place this sentence after the discussion of the practices of carving rock, so (D) is the correct choice.

16) **D**
Concept(s) Tested: Precise Diction, Preposition Use
The underlined phrase should highlight the fact that the danger affects the villagers, so (D) is the correct answer. (A), (B), and (C) are incorrect because they confuse the reader with vague descriptions.

17) **B**
Concept(s) Tested: Appositive Phrases
Titles before nouns do not require commas, but not every noun can serve as a title. In this case, what is needed is an appositive phrase to explain what asbestos is, and that phrase must be set off by commas, as in (B).

18) **C**
Concept(s) Tested: Pronoun Use
The underlined pronoun is ambiguous; that is, there are multiple referents so it is unclear which noun is being replaced. To avoid confusion, the pronoun should be replaced by a noun, making (C) the correct choice. (D) is incorrect because it is in the passive voice and fails to clarify the sentence's intended meaning.

19) **A**
Concept(s) Tested: Concision, Parallel Structure
Choice (A) is correct because it separates each item in the list with a comma and maintains parallel structure. (B) is incorrect because the final item in the list deviates from parallel structure. (C) is incorrect because the first item in the list does not contain an article. (D) is incorrect because none of the items in the list contains an article.

20) **A**
Concept(s) Tested: Verb Tense
Both verbs in this sentence should be in the simple past tense because there is no comparison between the times at which each event took place. Therefore, (A) is the best choice.

21) **D**
Concept(s) Tested: Syntax, Logical Comparison
Choice (D) is correct because it correctly makes a comparison between families with a high rate of the disease and families without. (A) and (C) are incorrect because they fail to compare the rates of disease among the two groups mentioned. (B) is incorrect because the meaning of the sentence is unclear without a proper comparison.

22) **C**
Concept(s) Tested: Combining Sentences, Syntax
Choice (C) is correct because it includes a clear transition ("Meanwhile") and then starts with the sentence's subject, verb, and object. Thus, it is the clearest in meaning out of all the choices.

23) **D**
Concept(s) Tested: Passage Development
Choice (D) is correct because it provides an informative introduction to the topic of jury duty. The remaining choices are incorrect because they add no additional information about jury duty to the passage. Choice (B) adds information that does not appear to be relevant.

24) **D**
Concept(s) Tested: Subject-Verb Agreement, Noun Agreement
The correct answer is (D) because the subject of the sentence is "a jury," so the the singular form of the verb must be used ("is"). Furthermore, (C) is incorrect because the use of the possessive does not make sense in this context.

25) **C**
Concept(s) Tested: Precise Diction
The underlined word should emphasize the "logical" or "reasonable" nature of the jurors' decision, so (C) is the best answer. (A) is incorrect because a "tenable" conclusion can be supported, but does not have enough evidence to always be the "right" decision. (B) is incorrect because "transparent" implies that the circumstances of the ruling are visible and fails to comment on its accuracy. (D) is incorrect because it conveys a cause and effect relationship, but the author focuses on the accuracy of the judgement.

26) **A**
Concept(s) Tested: Passage Development
Choice (A) is correct because it expresses the degree of jurors' isolation. The remaining choices provide details about courtroom proceedings but fail to mention the topic of solitude, so they are all incorrect.

27) **B**
Concept(s) Tested: Concision, Syntax
The best choice is (B) because it clearly and concisely expresses the information in the underlined portion. (A) and (C) are incorrect because both choices are excessively wordy, and the meaning is convoluted. (D) is incorrect because it confuses the reader and fails to clarify the role of the jury.

28) **A**
Concept(s) Tested: In-Sentence Punctuation
The phrase "a man and a woman" describes "another couple" and must be separated with a pair of commas, em-dashes, or parentheses. Likewise, "'Ashley'" is synonymous with "one of her friends" and must be separated with appropriate punctuation. Therefore, (A) is the correct choice.

29) **D**
Concept(s) Tested: Pronoun Case
Choice (D) is correct because the pronoun in the underlined portion acts as an object and only "whom" is an objective pronoun. (A) is incorrect because "who" is a subjective pronoun.

30) **B**
Concept(s) Tested: Logical Comparison
In this sentence, the author is comparing Ashley's perceptions to the perceptions of other people. The only choice that logically makes this comparison is (B), so it is the correct answer. (A) and (C) are incorrect because they compare Ashley's perceptions to other people, which is an illogical comparison.

31) **C**
Concept(s) Tested: Passage Development
The underlined portion is necessary for understanding the passage because it provides the next event in the courtroom proceedings. Therefore, (C) is the best choice. (D) is incorrect because the underlined portion does not provide a claim, but rather introduces the

paragraph.

32) B
Concept(s) Tested: Passage Tone
The correct choice is (B) because it maintains the formal tone of the passage. Choices (A) and (D) introduce an informal or casual tone and are not appropriate for an academic passage. Choice (C) consists of awkward legal jargon, so it also does not fit the passage's overall tone.

33) B
Concept(s) Tested: Clauses, In-Sentence Punctuation
Choice (B) is correct because it is concise, it maintains the passage's tone, and it ends the sentence with a period. The question marks after choices (A) and (C) are incorrect because the narrator is making a statement, not asking a question. Choice (D) is incorrect because it unnecessarily uses legal jargon, which breaks from the passage's formal, but not technical, tone.

34) B
Concept(s) Tested: In-Sentence Punctuation
Choice (B) is correct because the modifying phrase after the underlined portion describes "the Middle Ages" and must be separated from its noun with a comma. (A) is incorrect because it creates a sentence fragment after the period. (C) is incorrect because a semicolon is typically used to separate two independent clauses, but the information following the semicolon is a modifying phrase. (D) is incorrect because it creates a run-on sentence.

35) C
Concept(s) Tested: Passage Tone
Choice (C) is correct because it maintains the formal tone used throughout the passage. The remaining choices contain informal phrases that do not belong in an academic article, so they are incorrect.

36) D
Concept(s) Tested: Concision
The underlined portion adds no descriptive information to the passage, so it should be removed, making (D) the best choice.

37) A
Concept(s) Tested: Passage Development
The added information is necessary because it helps to explain a vague statement ("a number of years"), so (A) is the best choice. (B) is incorrect because the added information adds a relatively minor detail and does not emphasize important features of apprenticeships.

38) C
Concept(s) Tested: Verb Tense
The sentence is written in the simple present tense because it is part of a relative clause that ultimately describes "regulations," which can be thought of as a general state of being. Thus, (C) is the correct answer. (A) is incorrect because a gerund cannot act as a verb.

39) C
Concept(s) Tested: Possession, Commonly Confused Words, Pronoun Use
The underlined portion is a pronoun showing possession over "occupations," so (C) is the correct choice. (A) is incorrect because "they're" is a contraction for "they are" and is not appropriate in context. (B) is incorrect because "there" is typically used as an adverb or existential pronoun. (D) is incorrect because the pronoun is replacing a plural noun ("apprentices"), but "his" and "her" are both singular pronouns.

40) B
Concept(s) Tested: Precise Diction, Commonly Confused Words
The underlined word should emphasize the potential for future employment, so (B) is the best choice. (A) is incorrect because "perspective" refers to one's point of view or outlook on life, which is not appropriate in context. (C) is incorrect because it implies that the employers, not the journeymen, hope to get hired. (D) is incorrect because "contingent" suggests conditions under which an employment relationship is possible, but no such conditions are mentioned.

41) A
Concept(s) Tested: Combining Sentences
Choice (A) is correct because it clearly expresses the relationship between the two sentences. (B) is incorrect because the information in the two sentences does not contrast. (C) is incorrect because the information after the colon does not provide an explanation or definition of the information that preceded it. (D) is incorrect because the relationship between the two sentences is not self-evident.

42) A
Concept(s) Tested: Transition Words and Phrases
The sentence containing the underlined portion is providing additional information about the popularity of apprenticeships. Choice (A) "moreover" is correct because it is the only choice that indicates that additional, relevant information is to follow. (B) is incorrect because "however" indicates contrast; (C) is incorrect because "next" implies a chronology; and (D) is incorrect because "thus" indicates consequence.

43) C
Concept(s) Tested: Graph Analysis
The graph shows the number of apprenticeships available in the United States as a function of time, so the correct choice is (C) because it is the only choice focused on the number apprenticeships. (A) is incorrect because the graph does not comment on the wages of apprentices. (B) is incorrect because the graph makes no mention of government spending. (D) is incorrect because the graph does not cover the duration of an apprenticeship.

44) D
Concept(s) Tested: Passage Development
Choice (D) is correct because it concludes the passage with a general statement about why apprenticeships are popular and beneficial. (A) is incorrect because the passage never compares college graduates to apprentices in this way. (B) is incorrect because the passage does not mention apprentices' economic successes or failures. (C) is incorrect because this is a minor detail that would best serve as an example in a body paragraph and is not appropriate for a conclusion to the passage.

SAT Practice Test 3: Answers & Explanations

Math Test

✓ No-Calculator Portion

1.	C	7.	A	13.	D	19.	4.5
2.	D	8.	A	14.	D	20.	24
3.	B	9.	A	15.	C		
4.	B	10.	B	16.	61		
5.	A	11.	A	17.	20		
6.	C	12.	D	18.	24		

✓ Calculator Portion

1.	C	7.	C	13.	B	19.	B	25.	C	31.	8	36.	72
2.	D	8.	B	14.	A	20.	B	26.	C	32.	4		
3.	B	9.	C	15.	C	21.	C	27.	D	33.	154	37.	20
4.	B	10.	C	16.	C	22.	B	28.	B	34.	27	38.	10
5.	C	11.	D	17.	D	23.	B	29.	B				
6.	C	12.	C	18.	C	24.	D	30.	C	35.	$\frac{1}{2}$ or 0.5		

No-Calculator Portion

1) ➡ **C**

Concept(s) Tested: Algebra

For the given equation, $\frac{2x + 3y - 19}{y + 5} = 3$, multiply $y + 5$ on both sides.
It results in $2x + 3y - 19 = 3y + 15$.
Therefore, $2x - 19 = 15$, which results in $x = 17$.

2) ➡ **D**

Concept(s) Tested: Algebra, Geometry

If $a = 36 - 2b$, then $b = \frac{a - 36}{-2}$. Therefore, the answer is (D).

3) ➡ **B**

Concept(s) Tested: Problem Solving, Functions and Graphs

Looking at the answer choices reveals that we must create a linear function in slope-intercept form. Note that $35 per year implies that the y-intercept is 35. The cost $1.99 per download implies that the slope is 1.99. It results in $p = 1.99m + 35$. Therefore, the answer is (B).

4) ➡ **B**

Concept(s) Tested: Algebra

$(\sqrt[7]{\sqrt[10]{7}})^{35} = (7^{\frac{1}{7} \times \frac{1}{10}})^{35} = 7^{\frac{1}{7} \times \frac{1}{10} \times 35} = 7^{\frac{1}{2}} = \sqrt{7}$

5) ➡ **A**

Concept(s) Tested: Functions and Graphs, Problem Solving

Let us begin by assigning the page boys sequential variables: A and B for first and second, respectively. Since we know the rate of pay for each, as well as the debt expected and paid by each (10), we can assign each page boy a function of money earned in terms of x days:

Pageboy A : $f(x) = \frac{13}{6}x - 10$

Pageboy B: $g(x) = \frac{3}{2}x + 10$

Since we are asked to find the number of days necessary for the pageboys to have equal amounts, we can set the functions equal to each other in order to solve for x days:

$f(x) = g(x) \rightarrow \frac{13}{6}x - 10 = \frac{3}{2}x + 10$

Multiply both sides by 6 to get

$13x - 60 = 3(3)x + 60$

$13x = 9x + 120$

$4x = 120$

$x = 30$ days

6) ➡ **C**

Concept(s) Tested: Algebra

Adding both equations results in $x = 12$ as follows:

$2x - 3y = 30$
$+)3x + 3y = 30$
$\overline{5x \quad\quad = 60}$

Thus, $x = 12$, and (C) is the answer.

7) ➡ **A**

Concept(s) Tested: Problem Solving, Functions & Graphs

Only (A) cannot have a y-intercept because the line $x = 7$ runs parallel to the y-axis. All other choices will have a y-intercept of 0.

8) ➡ **A**

Concept(s) Tested: Problem Solving

442 | KALLIS' Key to the SAT

Tweedledee can move $\frac{100}{6}$ rocks per hour and Tweedledum can move $\frac{100}{4}$ rocks per hour. So they can move $\frac{100}{6} + \frac{100}{4} = \frac{1000}{24}$ rocks per hour together. Then, it follows that $\frac{1000}{24} = \frac{100}{x}$. By cross-multiplying and solving for x, we get $x = 2.4$ hours. Therefore, it takes 2 hours 24 minutes.

9) ▶ A
Concept(s) Tested: Algebra, Problem Solving
Let C be pounds of Colombia coffee and let E be pounds of Ethiopian coffee.
The composition of the 50 pound blend can be expressed as: $C + E = 50$
The price of the blend can be expressed as $8C + 3E = (\$5)(50\text{ lb.}) = \$250$.
Multiply the first equation by 3, then use elimination to isolate (C).

$$8C + 3E = 250$$
$$-(3C + 3E = 150)$$
$$5C = 100 \rightarrow C = 20$$

10) ▶ B
Concept(s) Tested: Geometry
First, determine the area of the entire pie:
$$\frac{81\pi}{8}(8) = 81\pi$$
Then determine the pie's radius using the formula for the area of a circle: $81\pi = \pi r^2$
$r = 9$ If $d = 2r$, and $r = 9$, then $d = 18$.

11) ▶ A
Concept(s) Tested: Functions and Graphs
The line with slope $\frac{1}{2}$ and y-intercept 3 is $y = \frac{1}{2}x + 3$. Therefore, the x-intercept is obtained by setting $y = 0$ as follows: $0 = \frac{1}{2}x + 3$. It results in $x = -6$.

12) ▶ D
Concept(s) Tested: Problem Solving, Unit Conversions
Note that Sloan has driven p miles of a 202-mile trip. It implies that the remaining trip distance is $202 - p$ miles. Because she drives less than 65mph, it will take her more time, eliminating choices (A) and (C). The answer is (D) because if we divide the distance by 65 mile/hour, the distances cancel out, leaving time.

13) ▶ D
Concept(s) Tested: Functions and Graphs
The symmetry line $x = h = \frac{p+q}{2}$.
Therefore, $q = 2h - p$.

14) ▶ D
Concept(s) Tested: Geometry, Problem Solving
Smaller bricks are cubes with a length of 2 inches. Therefore, the surface area of each of the smaller bricks is $2 \times 2 \times 6 = 24$ square inches. Note that the number of smaller cubes is 12. Therefore, the combined surface area of all smaller cubes is $24 \times 12 = 288$ square inches.

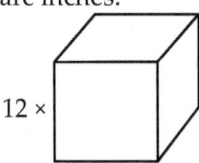

The surface area of large block consists of 4 larger areas of 4×6 and 2 smaller areas of 4×4. Therefore, the surface area of the large block is $(4 \times 6) \times 4 + (4 \times 4) \times 2 = 128$.

Therefore, the difference between the surface area of the large brick and the combined surface area of its constituent bricks is $288 - 128 = 160$.

15) ▶ C
Concept(s) Tested: Functions and Graphs
Using the information from the questions, find the equations of lines l and m:

Line l: $m = \frac{y_2 - y_1}{x_2 - x_1} = \frac{4 - (-2)}{0 - 3} = \frac{6}{-3} = -2$

Thus, the slope-intercept equation of line l is $y = -2x + 4$
Line m: $y = 3x$
Because line m passes through the origin, its y-intercept is 0.
Next, set the equations of lines l and m equal to one another and solve for x to find the x-coordinate of intersection:
$3x = -2x + 4 \rightarrow 5x = 4 \rightarrow x = \frac{4}{5}$

Plug the x-value into one of the line equations and solve for y: $y = (3)(\frac{4}{5}) \rightarrow y = \frac{12}{5}$

Thus, point (d, e) is $(\frac{4}{5}, \frac{12}{5})$, and

$e - d = \frac{12}{5} - \frac{4}{5} = \frac{8}{5}$, making choice (C) correct.

16) ▶ 61
Concept(s) Tested: Problem Solving, Algebra
Note that a sequence of numbers is generated by doubling the previous number and adding 3. The first number $p_1 = 5$. Therefore, the second number $p_2 = 2p_1 + 3 = 13$; the third number $p_3 = 2p_2 + 3 = 29$; and the fourth number $p_4 = 2p_3 + 3 = 61$.

17) ■▶ 20
Concept(s) Tested: Problem Solving, Algebra
Convert the information in the question to equations. Let m be the number of crickets eaten by Mister Slithers, c be the number of crickets eaten by Coil, and s be the number of crickets eaten by Sir Hiss-a-lot:
$m + c + s = 110$
$m = 2c$ and $10 + m = s \rightarrow 10 + 2c = s$
To find the value of c, we must use substitution:
$2c + c + (10 + 2c) = 110 \rightarrow 5c + 10 = 110 \rightarrow c = 20$
Thus, Coil eats 20 crickets.

18) ■▶ 24
Concept(s) Tested: Probability, Ratios and Percentages
Let x be the total number of games. Among them, the number of wins is $x - 6$. Therefore, a win percentage $\frac{x-6}{x} = 0.75$. It results in $0.25x = 6$. Therefore, $x = 24$.

19) ■▶ 4.5 or $\frac{9}{2}$
Concept(s) Tested: Problem Solving, Algebra
Note that the amount of time it takes to paint a house is inversely proportional to the number of people working on the job. Therefore, (the amount of time it takes to paint a house) x (the number of people working the job) = constant. Let x be how many more days it takes for two workers to complete the same task. Then the following should hold. $5 \times 3 = 2 \times (3 + x)$. Therefore, $x = 4.5$ days.

20) ■▶ 24
Concept(s) Tested: Geometry, Ratios and Percentages
First, calculate the volume of the cylinder:
$V = \pi r^2 h$
$r = 2$, $h = \frac{12}{\pi}$, so $V = \pi(2)^2(\frac{12}{\pi}) \rightarrow V = \frac{48\pi}{\pi}$
So $V = 48$ cubic inches. Thus, $\frac{2}{3}$ of the volume of the cylinder is $(\frac{2}{3})(48) = 32$ cubic inches. A ratio of 3 parts water to 1 part bleach means that the solution is $\frac{3}{4}$ water. Thus, the amount of water in the container is $(\frac{3}{4})(32) = 24$ cubic inches.

Calculator Portion

1) ■▶ C
Concept(s) Tested: Functions and Graphs
The coordinates in the table have a linear relationship, so we can use the point-slope formula $f(x) = mx + b$ to find the value of $f(16)$. First we must determine the values of m and b.
The slope, m, is $\frac{14 - 10}{1 - 2} = -4$. Plugging in the value $(1, 14)$ from the table and the slope $m = -4$ gives: $14 = (-4)(1) + b$, so $b = 18$. Thus, the value of $f(16) = (-4)(16) + 18 = -46$.

2) ■▶ D
Concept(s) Tested: Problem Solving, Ratios and Percentages
A typical high school student consumes 67.5 pounds of sugar every year. But the consumption will be reduced for the coming year. Therefore, $67.5 \times (1 - 0.2) = 67.5 \times 0.8 = 54$ pounds of sugar will be consumed per student this coming year.

3) ■▶ B
Concept(s) Tested: Problem Solving, Algebra
The total distance of two laps of the running track is 2×3 miles. The elapsed 45 minutes is equal to 0.75 hour. Therefore, the average speed is as follows:
average = $\frac{\text{distance}}{\text{time}} = \frac{6}{0.75} = 8$ miles per hour.

4) ■▶ B
Concept(s) Tested: Problem Solving, Ratios and Percentages
Calculate the correlating percentages of the given populations and find their difference.
2014 → (15%)(7,300 million) = 1,095 million
1800 → (88%)(900 million) = 792 million
Difference 2014 - 1800 ~ 303 million

5) ■▶ C
Concept(s) Tested: Functions and Graphs
Note that the x-intercepts of the graph are $x = 1$, and $x = -3$, and the y-intercept of the graph is $y = 3$. The graph also opens downwards. It implies that the equation of the graph is as follows:
$f(x) = -(x - 1)(x + 3) = -x^2 - 2x + 3$.
Therefore, the solution is (C).

6) ■▶ C
Concept(s) Tested: Functions and Graphs, Problem Solving
To find the rate by which Tobi increases the distance she runs each week, divide the distance

she ran the second week by the distance she ran during the first week. 8 divided by 9.6 gives 1.2, so $a_1 = 8$ and $a_2 = 1.2a_1$, and it increases at the same rate of 1.2 per week.
Therefore, $a_n = 1.2a_{n-1} = (1.2)^{n-1}a_1 = 8(1.2)^{n-1}$.

7) ▶ C
Concept(s) Tested: Number Rules
$(3^{-1} + 2^{-1})^{-1} = \left(\frac{1}{3} + \frac{1}{2}\right)^{-1} = \left(\frac{5}{6}\right)^{-1} = \frac{6}{5}$

8) ▶ B
Concept(s) Tested: Problem Solving
Note that $3{,}189(1.017)^t$ is the combined elephant population of the given area in the year t since 1995. Set $t = 0$, then, $3{,}189(1{,}017)^0 = 3{,}189$ is the number of elephants in the region in the initial year 1995.

9) ▶ C
Concept(s) Tested: Problem Solving, Number Rules
Note that the equation $\frac{A}{3} = B - \frac{A}{2}$ results in the equation $\frac{5A}{6} = B$. Note that A and B are positive integers. It implies that A should be a multiple of 6. Note that 24 is a multiple of 6. Therefore, the correct answer is (C).

10) ▶ C
Concept(s) Tested: Number Rules
$\frac{24x^4z^{-2}}{8x^{-3}z} = \frac{24}{8} \cdot \frac{x^{4-(-3)}}{z^{1-(-2)}} = \frac{24}{8} \cdot \frac{x^7}{z^3} = \frac{3x^7}{z^3}$

11) ▶ D
Concept(s) Tested: Algebra
To determine a possible value for a, solve the inequality for x: $9x - 10 > x + 4 \rightarrow x > \frac{14}{8}$. Thus, the value of $2a$ must be greater than $\frac{14}{8}$, and a must be greater than $\frac{7}{8}$. Therefore, (D) is correct: $1 > \frac{7}{8}$.

12) ▶ C
Concept(s) Tested: Algebra
$-9(x-3) + 2x \geq 2(4-x) \rightarrow -9x + 27 + 2x \geq 8 - 2x$
$\rightarrow -5x \geq -19$. This results in $x \leq \frac{19}{5}$.

13) ▶ B
Concept(s) Tested: Algebra
Square both sides of the given equation.
$5\sqrt{x+4} = x + 10$.
It results in $25(x+4) = x^2 + 20x + 100$, which gives $x^2 - 5x = x(x-5) = 0$.
Therefore, $x = 0$ or 5. So the product of two solutions is 0.

14) ▶ A
Concept(s) Tested: Number Rules
To combine the denominators in the expression, multiply the second term by $\frac{-1}{-1}$:
$\frac{x}{x-1} - \frac{2}{1-x} = \frac{x}{x-1} - \frac{-2}{x-1} = \frac{x+2}{x-1}$

15) ▶ C
Concept(s) Tested: Functions and Graphs
When $t = 0$, the $h = -16t^2 + 40t + 5 = 5$. So the value 5 is the height from which the ball was first thrown.

16) ▶ C
Concept(s) Tested: Problem Solving, Algebra
Let x be the distance in meters needed for a car moving at 25 kilometers per hour to come to a complete stop and k be a constant. Note that $distance = k \cdot velocity^2$. Therefore, $\frac{112.5}{15^2} = \frac{x}{25^2}$, which results in $x = 312.50$.

17) ▶ D
Concept(s) Tested: Algebra
The expression is as follows:

$$\begin{array}{r}
2x^2 - x - 7 \\
x^2+3x-5 \overline{\smash{)}\, 2x^4 + 5x^3 - 20x^2 - 16x + 35} \\
\underline{-)2x^4 + 6x^3 - 10x^2 } \\
-x^3 - 10x^2 - 16x + 35 \\
\underline{-)-x^3 - 3x^2 + 5x } \\
-7x^2 - 21x + 35 \\
\underline{-)-7x^2 - 21x + 35} \\
0
\end{array}$$

Therefore, the quotient is $2x^2 - x - 7$.

18) ▶ C
Concept(s) Tested: Data Analysis
Of the costs per acre listed in the table, the Mexican cessation is the most expensive:
Cost per acre (Louisiana Purchase) =
$\frac{23{,}213{,}568}{523{,}446{,}400 + 6{,}465{,}280} = \$0.043/$ acre

Cost per acre (Oregon Compromise) =
$\frac{6{,}674{,}057}{180{,}644{,}480 + 2{,}741{,}760} = \$0.036/$ acre

Cost per acre (Mexican cessation) =
$\frac{16{,}295{,}149}{334{,}479{,}360 + 4{,}201{,}600} = \$0.048/$ acre

Cost per acre (Alaska Purchase) =
$\frac{7{,}200{,}000}{365{,}333{,}120 + 12{,}909{,}440} = \$0.019/$ acre

19) **B**
Concept(s) Tested: Data Analysis, Ratios and Percentages
If the United States paid for the acquisition of just water in the Alaska purchase:

$$7,200,000 \times \frac{12,909,440}{365,333,120 + 12,909,440} = \$245,736$$

20) **B**
Concept(s) Tested: Unit Conversion
The total area of the United States in square kilometers is as follows.

$$2.27 \times 10^9 acre \times \frac{43,560\, ft^2}{acre} \times \left(\frac{0.305\, m}{ft}\right)^2 \times \left(\frac{1\, km}{1,000\, m}\right)^2$$
$$= 9,198,424\, km^2$$

It is approximately 9.2-million square kilometers.

21) **C**
Concept(s) Tested: Algebra
Let $x = 2$. The given equation then results in
$$z = 2^2 + 3 \times 2 + \frac{y^2 + 2 \times 2y}{2 + 2} = 10 + \frac{y^2 + 4y}{4}$$
$$= \frac{40}{4} + \frac{y^2 + 4y}{4} = \frac{y^2 + 4y + 40}{4}$$

22) **B**
Concept(s) Tested: Algebra
$|x^3 - 3| < 7$ implies that $-7 < x^3 - 3 < 7$.
Therefore, $-4 < x^3 < 10$ results in $-1.59 < x < 2.15$.

23) **B**
Concept(s) Tested: Number Rules
$$R(d) = 8.25\left(\frac{1}{2}\right)^{\frac{d}{4}} = 8.25\left(\left(\frac{1}{2}\right)^{\frac{1}{4}}\right)^d = 8.25(0.841)^d$$

24) **D**
Concept(s) Tested: Ratios and Percentages
Alcohol quantity in the mixed solution is $(12\ pints \times 0.2) + (8\ pints \times 0.1) = 3.2$ pints.
Note that the total solution quantity is 20 pints. Therefore, the alcohol concentration of the new solution is $\frac{3.2 \times 100}{20} = 16\%$

25) **C**
Concept(s) Tested: Geometry
Using the formula for the area of a triangle, we know that the maximum area of the triangle with sides of length a and b is $\frac{ab}{2}$. Thus, the area of the triangle should be less than or equal to $\frac{16 \times 10}{2} = 80$. Therefore, 80 cm² and 60 cm² could be the area of the triangle.

26) **C**
Concept(s) Tested: Number Rules
(C) is correct because x^2, x^4, and constant terms are independent of the sign of x because multiplying two negatives always makes a positive.

27) **D**
Concept(s) Tested: Geometry

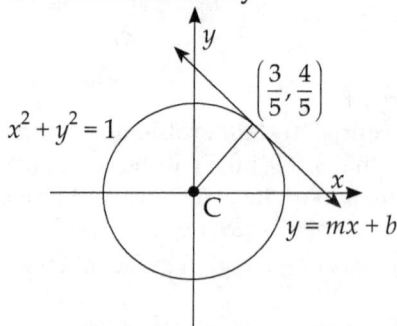

Let l be the line tangent to the circle and p be the line perpendicular to l. Let m and b be the slope and y-intercept of line l, respectively. Line l is perpendicular to the line formed by the radius of the circle in the diagram above (line p); use the coordinates given to find the slope of line p:

$$m = \frac{\frac{4}{5} - 0}{\frac{3}{5} - 0}$$

Thus, the equation of p is $y = \frac{4}{3}x$, The product of the slopes of the both lines $m \times \frac{4}{3} = -1$. It results in $m = -\frac{3}{4}$. Note that line l passes through the point $\left(\frac{3}{5}, \frac{4}{5}\right)$. Substituting this point into line l results in the following equation: $\frac{4}{5} = \left(-\frac{3}{4}\right)\left(\frac{3}{5}\right) + b$

Therefore, $b = 1.25$.

28) **B**
Concept(s) Tested: Problem Solving
Let r be the simple interest rate per year. Then, $15,000 = 12,000(1 + 5r)$. Therefore, $r = 5\%$.

29) **B**
Concept(s) Tested: Geometry
Use the Pythagoran Theorem to determine that the length of $\overline{AB}$ is 4. Then, use the formula for the area of a triangle to find the missing length. Note that the area of $\triangle ABC = \frac{3 \times 4}{2} = \frac{5 \times \overline{DB}}{2}$.
It results in $\overline{DB} = \frac{12}{5}$.

30) **C**
Concept(s) Tested: Problem Solving, Unit Conversion
Since we are finding the distance in "Moon diameter" units from the Moon to the opposite

446 | KALLIS' Key to the SAT

side of the Sun in the above cosmic line, let us begin with the understanding that we are already given 108 "Moon units" (*mu*) between the moon and the Earth; we will add the remaining distance after we calculate the value of the space in mu, given the values in the problem.

Moon Diameter = 1 *mu* = 27% Earth diameter

→ 1 *mu* = Earth diameter $\frac{27}{100}$

→ Earth diameter = $\frac{100\,mu}{27}$

Earth Diameter = 100 *mu* / 27 = $\frac{Sun\ Diameter}{108}$ →

Sun Diameter = (108)(100 *mu*/ 27)
Sun Diameter = 400 *mu*
Now that we have calculated all the given diameters in terms of *mu*, calculate the number of *mu*'s in the line from the Moon to the other side of the Sun.
108 moons + Earth + 108 Suns + 108 Earths =
108 *mu* + 109(100 *mu* / 27) + 108(400 *mu*)
→ 43,308 + 403.7037 ≈ 43,711.7, or 43,712

31) ▶ 8
Concept(s) Tested: Measures of Center and Spread
The average of 5 and x results in $\frac{5+x}{2} = 7$. The average of 3 and y results in $\frac{3+y}{2} = 5$. So, x is 9 and y is 7. The average, $\frac{x+y}{2} = 8$.

32) ▶ 4
Concept(s) Tested: Algebra
Putting $y = 5x$ into the equation
$-4x^2 + 3y^2 = 284$ → $-4x^2 + 3(25x^2) = 284$ → $x^2 = 4$

33) ▶ 154
Concept(s) Tested: Ratios and Percentages
The probability P_1 (the first person picking a chocolate with a soft center) = $\frac{5}{22}$. After that, there are 21 chocolates total with a remaining 4 with soft centers. The probability P_2 (the second person picking chocolate with a soft center) = $\frac{4}{21}$. After that, there are 20 chocolates total and 3 have soft centers. The Probability P_3 (the third person picking a chocolate with soft centers) = $\frac{3}{20}$.

Therefore, $\frac{1}{x} = P_1 P_2 P_3 = \frac{5}{22} \cdot \frac{4}{21} \cdot \frac{3}{20} = \frac{1}{154}$, which results in $x = 154$.

34) ▶ 27
Concept(s) Tested: Functions and Graphs

$p(x) = -x^2 + 10x + 2$ Determine a number that will allow you to create factors. Add the number and its opposite:
= $-x^2 + 10x - 25 + 25 + 2$
= $-(x - 5)^2 + 27$
It implies that the highest profit is 27 when $x = 5$.

35) ▶ $\frac{1}{2}$ or 0.5
Concept(s) Tested: Functions and Graphs, Factoring
The equation $y = 2x^2 - 5x + 2$ can be factored into $y = (2x - 1)(x - 2)$. Therefore, it has two solutions $x = \frac{1}{2}$, $x = 2$. Among them, $x = \frac{1}{2}$ is the smaller value.

36) ▶ 72
Concept(s) Tested: Geometry, Problem Solving
Recall the formula for the volume of a pyramid. Let x be the length of the pyramid's base and y be the pyramid's height. It follows that $16 = \frac{1}{3}x^2 y$ or $48 = x^2 y$. Once the pyramid is modified, we have
$\frac{1}{3}(3x)^2 \left(\frac{1}{2}y\right) = \left(\frac{1}{3}\right)(9x^2)\left(\frac{1}{2}y\right) = \frac{3}{2}x^2 y$.

Substitute $48 = x^2 y$ into the equation above to find
$V = \frac{3}{2}(48) = 72$.

37) ▶ 20
Concept(s) Tested: Algebra
Note that $m = 2$, $k = 0.2$. Put these values to the period formula $T = 2\pi\sqrt{\frac{m}{k}}$. It results in the following value.

$T = 2\pi\sqrt{\frac{20}{0.2\pi^2}} = 2\pi\sqrt{\frac{20}{0.2}} \cdot \sqrt{\frac{1}{\pi^2}} = 2\sqrt{100} = 20$

38) ▶ 10
Concept(s) Tested: Algebra, Problem Solving
The period of the second object, T', is as follows:

$T' = 2\pi\sqrt{\left(\frac{20}{4}\right)\left(\frac{1}{0.2\pi^2}\right)} = 2\sqrt{25} = 10$.

Therefore, the absolute difference between the periods of the two objects is $T - T' = 20 - 10 = 10$.

SAT Practice Test 3: Answers & Explanations

Sample Essay Response

In his "Speech on the BP Oil Spill," President Barack Obama condemns the U.S.'s stubborn dependence on fossil fuels while imploring Americans to aggressively pursue alternative fuel and energy sources. Thus, one of President Obama's main rhetorical devices is the use of contrast to emphasize the cost of inaction versus the benefits of action. Moreover, he conveys this contrast using inclusive language, implying that both action and inaction are national efforts.

The first three paragraphs of Obama's speech explore the idea that the past, wherein there was "a lack of political courage and candor" to end U.S. dependence on fossil fuels, haunts the present and shapes the future. Here, Obama sets up inaction as the enemy--a force that harms America financially, as "we send nearly $1 billion of our wealth to foreign countries for their oil," and environmentally, as "a menacing black cloud of crude" consumes the Gulf (paragraph 2). Having outlined the costs of inaction, Obama transitions in the third paragraph: when Obama states that "the time to embrace a clean energy future is now," (paragraph 3), he asks the audience to shape America's present, in which inaction is the modus operandi, into its future, a time of action. And with this transition, Obama leaves inaction behind and lays out "a future that will benefit us all" (paragraph 5).

Moreover, the future he describes is made all the more attractive because of how severely it contrasts with America's past inactions and present predicaments. When he mentions the "costs associated with this transition" away from fossil fuels (paragraph 7), he immediately contrasts them with the "far greater" cost of inaction. When he discusses the difficulties of deciding on an approach for transitioning away from fossil fuels, he clarifies that the only unacceptable approach is inaction. And finally, Obama links action to national identity with the claim, "what has defined as a nation since our founding is the capacity to shape our destiny" (paragraph 9). This view is supported with allusions to a past in which American cooperation and action surmounted incredible odds.

Indeed, inclusive language, namely Obama's use of "we" and "us," helps strengthen his argument by involving the audience. Rather than placing partisan blame for America's past inactions and present failures, he holds everyone, including himself, accountable: "we have failed to act" (paragraph 2), and "We cannot consign our children to this future" (paragraph 3). By implying that all Americans are part of the problem, he invites each of us to contribute to the solution, claiming, "Each of us has a part to play in a new future" (paragraph 5). Additionally, this inclusive language presents the issue as nonpartisan, something he clarifies in paragraph 8, and something that heightens the contrast between a bleak past of inaction and a bright future of cooperation and progress.

Obama's speech effectively conveys the need for change by convincing the audience that the only way to improve a system is through action. While he recognizes that change is often difficult, he frames it as necessary by contrasting it with the greater cost of inaction. All the while, his use of inclusive first-person plural pronouns reinforces the idea that change is only possible through unity.

Student Response Score: 4/4/4

Reading: 4

The student demonstrates a thorough understanding of the source text. Relevant quotations are used throughout to solidify the student's claims. No misinterpretations are present.

Writing: 4

The response is structured and thoughtful. The student makes a central claim in the first sentence and maintains excellent focus throughout the essay. Ideas are connected logically within the essay. Word choice and sentence structure are varied, and there are no noticeable errors.

Analysis: 4

The response clearly and concisely outlines the speech and its persuasive features. The student analyzes the entire speech sequentially, characterizing Obama's use of contrasting visions and inclusive diction as persuasive strategies.

SAT Practice Test 4: Answers & Explanations

Reading Test

1. D	6. C	11. B	16. D	21. D	26. B	31. B	36. A	41. A	46. A	51. D
2. C	7. B	12. B	17. B	22. D	27. A	32. B	37. D	42. D	47. C	52. B
3. A	8. A	13. B	18. A	23. B	28. B	33. D	38. C	43. B	48. C	
4. D	9. C	14. A	19. C	24. A	29. A	34. C	39. B	44. B	49. B	
5. B	10. C	15. A	20. B	25. C	30. D	35. B	40. D	45. B	50. D	

1) ➡ D
Concept(s) Tested: Summary
Choice (D) is correct because lines 35 – 36, "the ship goes down," indicate that the characters in the passage survived a shipwreck, and most of the passage recounts their attempts to cooperate and survive aboard the small vessel. Choice (A) is incorrect because the captain only speaks once (line 46), and his order is obeyed. Choice (B) is incorrect because there is no indication that the crew set sail during a storm, only that they were caught in a storm. Choice (C) is incorrect because the crew of the vessel are never identified as friends; the narrator implies that they are a disparate group of people stuck in a treacherous situation.

2) ➡ C
Concept(s) Tested: Purpose
Choice (C) is correct because paragraph 1 establishes that the passage takes place on stormy seas, and it establishes the gloomy and stressful mood of the passage by describing the crew's attentiveness to the waves and nothing else. Choice (A) is incorrect because paragraph 1 does not provide any background information; the reader is thrust into the middle of the action, wherein one must extrapolate that the crew has recently survived a shipwreck. Choice (D) is incorrect because paragraph 1 does not mention any historical events.

3) ➡ A
Concept(s) Tested: Words in Context
Choice (A) is correct because "abrupt," along with "tall," describes the waves, which are also mentioned as "a problem in small boat navigation." Since "unexpected" is a synonym of abrupt, and because an "unexpected and tall" wave would prove problematic for a small boat to navigate, we can conclude that "unexpected" is the most effective choice. While the other choices provide accurate synonyms for "abrupt," they do not fit the context of the sentence.

4) ➡ D
Concept(s) Tested: Words in Context
Choice (D) is correct; throughout the passage, the narrator implies that the sea is "turbulent," such as in lines 6 – 7, where he says that from the perspective of the people in the boat, "The horizon narrowed and widened, and dipped and rose." The view is the opposite of a smooth, calm sea where the horizon appears flat; thus, it has a "turbulence" or "broken" quality. "Feeble," which means "weak," is an inaccurate description for the waves because the author frequently describes them as "tall" and "sheer."

5) ➡ B
Concept(s) Tested: Inference
Choice (B) is correct because the passage indicates that the correspondent "wondered why he was there," which suggests that he did not expect to be in his current situation and that he does not feel useful, which implies that he "is not part of the ship's regular crew." This assumption is further supported by his title (correspondent), which implies that he works as a journalist, not a sailor. Choice (A) is incorrect because the provided lines say that he is "pulling at the other oar," but it does not indicate that the exertion has exhausted him. Choice (C) is incorrect because his attitude toward the captain cannot be determined from the information provided. Choice (D) is incorrect because, while the excerpt explains that the correspondent "watched the waves," it does not indicate that the waves helped him "feel better" about his situation.

6) ➡ C
Concept(s) Tested: Summary
Choice (C) is correct because although it is unclear whether there has been loss of life, it is clear that the captain has watched the ship sink "low and lower, and down" (lines 40 – 42) into the ocean. Choice (A) is incorrect because, based on the passage, the crew appears competent, and the captain gives no indication that he is displeased with them. Choice (B) is incorrect because lines 31 – 45 indicate that the captain is mainly in shock over the loss of his ship, although he is injured. Choice (D) is incorrect because the passage does not clarify the captain's attitude towards the storm.

7) ➡ B
Concept(s) Tested: Attitude and Tone
Choice (B) is correct because, when the narrator describes the sunrise in lines 82 – 88, he claims that it was "unknown to them," indicating that the crew is "oblivious" to the sunrise. Choice (A) is incorrect because to be "resentful" toward something is to regard it with anger or annoyance, and there is no indication that the crew even notice the sunrise, much less feel anger toward it. Likewise, choices (C) and (D) are incorrect because the narrator indicates that the crew do not even see the sunrise, which means that they do not have emotional reactions to it.

8) ➡ A
Concept(s) Tested: Inference
Choice (A) is correct because, in lines 62 – 66, the narrator claims that the waves seem as though they are lining up specifically "to do something effective in the way of swamping boats," implying that the waves are actively trying to assault and sink the vessel. Choice (B) is incorrect; the waves are described as massive and intimidating throughout the passage, with no indication that they are becoming larger as the passage progresses. Choice (C) is incorrect because lines 89 onwards reveal that the small boat is traveling to a house of refuge "just north of the Mosquito Inlet Light," yet there is no indication that the waves are carrying the crew away from this house of refuge. Choice (D) is incorrect because lines 54 – 58 state that the small boat must "scramble over these walls of

TEST4: Answers & Explanations | 449

water," indicating that the boat is traveling over, not around, the waves.

9) **C**
Concept(s) Tested: Citation
Choice (C) is correct because this quote gives the waves agency by describing them as "nervously anxious to do something effective in the way of swamping boats," implying that the waves are consciously assaulting the small vessel. While the other choices effectively describe the waves, they fail to give the waves agency, so these choices do not support the claim that the waves are "actively trying to sink" the vessel.

10) **C**
Concept(s) Tested: Citation
Choice (C) is correct because it explains that the small vessel is slowly taking on excess water ("water… swirled in over the stern") and that their "thin little oar" that steers the ship "seemed often ready to snap," indicating that the crew can barely control the vessel in the stormy waters. All other choices are incorrect because they describe the sea, the size of the boat, or the sunrise, none of which describes the "crew's tenuous control" as well as (C) does.

11) **B**
Concept(s) Tested: Inference
Choice (B) is correct because the oiler responds to the correspondent's and cook's speculations with the statement, "we're not there yet," indicating that, while the other crew members are willing to make speculations about the house of refuge, the oiler is "unwilling to speculate about details." All other choices are incorrect because the only phrase spoken by the oiler is, "we're not there yet," and one cannot reasonably extrapolate any of the other choices from this statement alone.

12) **B**
Concept(s) Tested: Purpose
Choice (B) is correct because, in paragraph 1, the author states that the actions taken by the Confederates "mark a new epoch in the history of that war," which indicates that the passage focuses on a "pivotal tactical move." Choice (A) is incorrect because, while the author does imply that he admires the gumption of the Confederates, this is not the primary purpose of the passage, but rather a minor detail. Choice (C) is incorrect because, while paragraphs 4 and 5 focus on the level of combat preparedness of the Confederates and Union troops, this is not the focus of the passage, but rather an aside. Choice (D) is incorrect because nowhere in the passage does the author suggest that the events he is describing take place "near the end of the American Civil War."

13) **B**
Concept(s) Tested: Words in Context
Choice (B) is correct; the phrase "to savor of contempt" describes the bold actions of General Lee, and how they may have been perceived by Union troops. In this context, "savor" is used metaphorically to mean "have a slight taste of" or "have a detectable suggestion of" disdain for his opponents' capabilities. Choices (A) and (C) are incorrect because they do not fit the context of describing a perception. Choice (D) is incorrect because it over-interprets the phrase: there is no evidence that the Union has failed or that Lee has taken pleasure in it.

14) **A**
Concept(s) Tested: Attitude and Tone
Choice (A) is correct; the narrator is recounting the events of the American Civil War in the past tense, which indicates that he is reflecting on the war, and in line 12, he refers to the Union Army as "our army," suggesting that he considers himself a part of the Union. Choice (B) is incorrect because there is no indication that the author has any affiliation with Confederate forces. Choice (C) is incorrect because he repeatedly includes his own opinions regarding the martial skills of the two forces and the demeanor and attitude of the Confederate troops, which indicate that the author is not "unbiased." Choice (D) is incorrect because the passage does not indicate that the author is "spying" on the Confederate troops; rather, the passage suggests that the author gathered much of his information after the events occurred.

15) **A**
Concept(s) Tested: Citation
Choice (A) is correct because in these lines the author refers to the Union forces as "our army," implying that the author considers himself a part of the Union forces, or at the very least a member of the Union. All other choices are incorrect because they do not tell the reader anything about the author's background or identity.

16) **D**
Concept(s) Tested: Inference
Choice (D) is correct because lines 26 – 27 claim that "Confederates greatly excelled the Union soldiers as marksmen," and lines 38 – 39 claim that "the Confederate cavalry was also superior to the Union horse," providing thorough support for (D). Choice (A) is incorrect because, although the author mentions new Enfield rifles (lines 22 – 23), he does not claim that the Confederate troops received better equipment overall than Union troops; indeed, lines 76 – 79 claim that some Confederate troops were shoeless and had "an old piece of carpet or rug as baggage." Choice (B) is incorrect because, while the passage states that the Confederate force entering the town had 70,000 men, it does not tell the reader how many Union troops were in pursuit. Choice (C) is incorrect because, while the author does indicate that the Confederate troops were "ragged and dirty" upon entering Chambersburg (line 79), he does not comment on the organization or discipline of either Confederate or Union troops.

17) **B**
Concept(s) Tested: Citation
Choice (B) is correct because it explicitly states that overall, the Confederate troops were better marksmen than the Union forces, providing effective support for choice (D) of the previous question. Choice (A) is incorrect; although it seems to support choice (D) of the previous question, it does not state that the Confederates were *better* equipped than the Union forces, so it is incorrect. Choices (C) and (D) are incorrect because they do not provide any support for the claim that Confederate troops were "better prepared for combat than Union troops."

18) **A**
Concept(s) Tested: Summary
Choice (A) is correct because the author characterizes the Confederate troops as "ragged and dirty, but full of good-humor and confidence in themselves and their general" (lines 79 – 80), which can effectively be summarized as "disheveled yet self-assured." Choice (B) is incorrect because the author claims that the Confederates, while advancing into enemy territory in the town, endured the "taunts of the Chambersburg ladies" (lines 81 – 82), indicating that the Confederates were *not* "well-loved by the people of Chambersburg." Choice (C) is incorrect because the author does not indicate that the Confederates were "cautious"; rather, he characterizes their actions as bold. Choice (D) is incorrect because the author does not characterize the Confederates as "rude"; rather, he describes them as giddy and "exultant" in response to the "scowling" people of Chambersburg in lines 81 – 86.

19) C
Concept(s) Tested: Words in Context
Choice (C) is correct; "evoked," which means "brought to mind," best fits the situation: an intact town where only the soldiers' presence indicates that there is a war.

20) B
Concept(s) Tested: Attitude and Tone
Choice (B) is correct; lines 62 – 67 support the claim that the people of Chambersburg watched the Confederates from their windows with "curiosity," and lines 67 – 70 support the claim that they pointed and laughed at the Confederates with "derision." Choice (A) is incorrect because, while it can be argued that many of the people of Chambersburg feared the Confederates, there is no indication that they "admired" them. Choice (C) is incorrect because there is no indication that the people of Chambersburg envy the Confederate troops. And choice (D) is incorrect because paragraph 7 details the response of the people of Chambersburg, indicating that they did not "disregard" the troops.

21) D
Concept(s) Tested: Attitude and Tone
Choice (D) is correct because, in paragraphs 4 and 5, the author praises the Confederates' combat skills, and toward the beginning of the passage he praises their general's tactical moves as "bold" and as marking "a new epoch in the history of that war" (lines 5 – 9), which implies that the author has respect for the Confederate forces. All other choices are incorrect because they lack textual support.

22) D
Concept(s) Tested: Purpose
Choice (D) is correct because the passage is structured around the experiment described from line 44 onwards: the first four paragraphs provide background information on the problem that the experiment hoped to shed light on, and the rest of the passage describes the experiment and its conclusions. Choice (A) is incorrect because only the first paragraph discusses the "challenges faced by modern paleontologists," so it is a minor detail that introduces the passage's primary purpose. Choice (B) is incorrect because this point is made only in the last paragraph, so it is a minor detail of the conclusion, not the primary purpose of the passage. Choice (C) is incorrect because the passage focuses on determining how plesiosaurs swam. Because the research concluded that their swimming style was probably similar to that of a penguin, we can conclude that it is not a "unique characteristic," making (C) unsupportable.

23) B
Concept(s) Tested: Inference
Choice (B) is correct because the passage states that paleontologists have been "puzzled" by how plesiosaurs swam "for over 200 years," which implies that they first discovered the animal's fossilized remains, and then attempted to determine how the animal swam based on the fossil evidence. Choice (A) is incorrect because the passage states that the creatures went extinct during the "Late Cretaceous," a period that ended millions, not hundreds, of years ago. Choice (C) is incorrect because the author never states that any living plesiosaur specimens have been "captured for study." Choice (D) is incorrect because the author states that "no such living analogous animal has a body plan identical to" plesiosaurs (lines 18 – 20).

24) A
Concept(s) Tested: Inference
Choice (A) is correct because the author mentions plesiosaur's swimming stroke along with those of "modern tetrapods" that have "transitioned from living on land to living in the ocean." Thus, the author implies that that the ancestors of plesiosaurs were land-dwelling animals. Choices (B) and (C) are incorrect because there is no evidence in paragraph 3 that provides support for them, and choice (D) is incorrect because the passage has a much narrower focus than the vast category "modern aquatic animals."

25) C
Concept(s) Tested: Purpose
Choice (C) is correct because, in paragraph 1 (lines 1 – 11), the author claims that "never being able to see one [extinct species] in real life" is infuriating because it prevents paleontologists from learning more about these species. Thus, the statement in line 37 repeats, or "reiterates," this sense of frustration. Choice (A) is incorrect because the author does not address the reader or invite speculation. Choice (B) is incorrect because the author's tone here is not accusatory, but rather frustrated at a situation with no foreseeable solution. Choice (D) is incorrect because the passage does not describe a "prospect of discovery," but rather the difficulty of answering a basic question.

26) B
Concept(s) Tested: Words in Context
Choice (B) is correct because "to take a stab" at something is an English idiom meaning "to attempt" something, and it makes sense to say that a paleontologist has attempted to solve a long-standing question related to plesiosaurs. All other choices are incorrect because they are not accurate synonyms of "take a stab" and because they do not correspond with the information presented in the passage.

27) A
Concept(s) Tested: Inference
Choice (A) is correct; lines 56 – 59 describe the "generalized morphotype" as having a "moderately long neck" for a plesiosaur. This implies that the "generalized morphotype" is an average or typical example of the species, so its "characteristics represent many other members of the same [group]." Choice (B) is incorrect because there is no indication that the "generalized morphotype" serves as a link to plesiosaur-related species. Choice (C) is incorrect because there is no indication that the "generalized morphotype's" anatomy varied between members of the species. Choice (D) is incorrect because the author does not relate the "generalized morphotype" to any organisms other than plesiosaurs.

28) B
Concept(s) Tested: Purpose
Choice (B) is correct because the casual tone of the parenthetical information breaks from the academic tone of the rest of the passage, and it describes the parameters for an experiment by making the obvious statement that joint dislocation while swimming would be detrimental to plesiosaurs and to the research about them. Choice (A) is incorrect because the parenthetical phrase provides commentary, not definition. Choice (C) is incorrect because the parenthetical phrase is elaborating on a previous statement, not amending or changing it. Choice (D) is incorrect because the parenthetical information comments on an experiment's parameters, not on its hypothesis.

29) A
Concept(s) Tested: Citation
Choice (A) is correct; it can be inferred from the passage that the researchers created a virtual model of a plesiosaur to observe how it swam because they could not observe any plesiosaur-like animals in nature, and lines 18 – 20 support this assumption by stating that no "living analogous animal has a body plan identical to" those of plesiosaurs. All other choices are incorrect because they speculate on how a plesiosaur's swim stroke may have resembled some living creatures', but do not explain why the researchers used a virtual model to simulate plesiosaur swimming.

30) **D**
Concept(s) Tested: Inference
Choice (D) is correct because lines 78 – 82 explain that the researchers "prevented movement in the model of the neck and tail," which implies that they do not yet know how neck and tail movement affected plesiosaur swimming or limb movement. Choice (A) is incorrect because the passage never indicates that plesiosaurs changed their mode of swimming. Choice (B) is incorrect because lines 54 – 56 describe a "small" plesiosaur species, which implies that plesiosaur species varied in size. Choice (D) is incorrect because lines 97 – 104 state that a plesiosaur's hind limbs were likely used for steering, while the forelimbs were used for propulsion, but it is not clear what it would mean to conclude that all four limbs were used simultaneously.

31) **B**
Concept(s) Tested: Citation
Choice (B) is correct because these lines clarify that the researchers did not study plesiosaur head and tail movement, which means they would not have "quantified how…neck and tail movement affects limb movement." All other choices are incorrect because they do not mention plesiosaur neck or tail movement.

32) **B**
Concept(s) Tested: Graph Analysis
Choice (B) is correct because, according to the graph, the fastest plesiosaur swimming speed was achieved using a wide joint range and only forelimbs. Choice (A) is incorrect because using both limbs did not achieve the fastest swimming speed for wide joint ranges. Choice (C) is incorrect because the graph does not provide enough information to make assumptions about plesiosaurs "never" using their hindlimbs. Choice (D) is irrelevant because the graph provides information on plesiosaur swimming speed and joint range, not on its swimming "efficiency."

33) **D**
Concept(s) Tested: Graph Synthesis
Choice (D) is correct because lines 97 – 99 state that "'the front limbs provide the powerhouse for plesiosaur propulsion,'" which corresponds with the graph showing that the fastest plesiosaur swimming speed was achieved using only the forelimbs. Choice (A) is incorrect because neither the passage nor the graph reference plesiosaur size in relation to swimming speed. Choices (B) and (C) are incorrect because they are supported by the passage but are not referenced in the graph.

34) **C**
Concept(s) Tested: Inference
Choice (C) is correct. In lines 15 – 16, the author uses "wild hate speech," a phrase with strong negative connotations, to describe the ideas espoused by ACT!, implying that the author does not condone ACT!'s "hate speech" and does not share the organization's views. Choice (A) is incorrect because there is no indication in the passage that the author has ever interacted with Brigitte Gabriel. Choice (B) is incorrect because, in paragraph 1, the author describes but does not question ACT!'s popularity. Choice (D) is incorrect because it is entirely unsupported by the passage.

35) **B**
Concept(s) Tested: Citation
Choice (B) is correct; in the line numbers referenced, the author refers to the ideas espoused by ACT! as "wild hate speech." This phrase implies that the author views ACT!'s ideas as unfounded and hurtful, which effectively supports the answer to the previous question. All other choices are incorrect; although they describe the actions and beliefs of ACT!'s founder, they do not effectively reveal the author's attitude towards these actions or beliefs.

36) **A**
Concept(s) Tested: Words in Context
Choice (A) is correct because, as used in the context of the passage, "to impact" means "change and/or affect" government policies. All other choices are incorrect because they do not effectively describe how a person or group of people can influence government policies, so they do not fit the context of the passage.

37) **D**
Concept(s) Tested: Purpose
Choice (D) is correct because the author of Passage 1 implies that he or she does not agree with the views of Gabriel or ACT! From this, we can infer that the author puts Gabriel's purported "truth" in quotes to show that Gabriel's words neither reflect the author's views nor what may be considered the norm. Choice (A) is incorrect because the context of the sentence does not imply that "truth" is meant to be ambiguous or nuanced. Choice (B) is incorrect because the passage does not mention other "truths" about Islam. Choice (C) is incorrect because quotation marks do not emphasize the importance of terms.

38) **C**
Concept(s) Tested: Purpose
Choice (C) is correct because the example involving interactions between females and males challenges the theory presented in lines 78 – 84. Choice (A) is incorrect because lines 89 – 96 do not focus on the formation of ingroups and outgroups, but rather they challenge a theory on ingroups and outgroups mentioned earlier. Choice (B) is incorrect because lines 89 – 96 challenge an assumption about the cause(s) of the outgroup homogeneity effect, so they do not simply "provide support" for the existence of the effect. Choice (D) is incorrect because lines 89 – 96 do not mention an experiment.

39) **B**
Concept(s) Tested: Words in Context
Choice (B) is correct because "charges" refers to the claim that members of the opposite sex are all alike. Because these claims accuse members of the opposite sex of homogeneity, we can infer that "charges" are "accusations." Choices (A) and (C) are incorrect because they do not fit the context of the sentence, and (D) is incorrect because "attack" is too strong a term to refer to clichés regarding homogeneity.

40) **D**
Concept(s) Tested: Summary
Choice (D) is correct because lines 60 – 62 explain that ingroups can stereotype outgroups, or make "detrimental generalizations" about them. Choice (A) is incorrect because the passage does not claim that any individuals choose to remain willfully ignorant of the effect. Choice (B) is incorrect because the outgroup homogeneity effect causes members of an ingroup to stereotype others, not one another. Choice (C) is incorrect because the passage does not claim that the outgroup homogeneity effect necessarily prevents communication; rather, the passage maintains that some outgroups have extensive contact with each other.

41) **A**
Concept(s) Tested: Text Synthesis
Choice (A) is correct because Passage 2 describes the outgroup homogeneity effect and how it can lead to ingroups stereotyping perceived outgroups, and Passage 1 provides an example of this by describing the extreme actions of one group's leader. Choice (B) is incorrect because neither passage supports a particular cause. Choice (C) is incorrect because Passage 1 provides a profile of an organization's leader, so it does not primarily "pose a question." Choice (D) is incorrect because there is no indication that anything in Passage 1 can be considered

"controversial evidence."

42) ▶ D
Concept(s) Tested: Text Synthesis
Choice (D) is correct because, according to Passage 1, Brigitte Gabriel is the founder of ACT!, so according to the information in Passage 2, she would view members of ACT! as part of her ingroup. Because ACT! engages in "wild hate speech demonizing Muslims," we can also infer that Gabriel would view Muslims as an outgroup. All other choices are incorrect because they cannot be extrapolated based on the information about Gabriel provided in Passage 1.

43) ▶ B
Concept(s) Tested: Text Synthesis, Citation
Choice (B) is correct because these lines show that Gabriel regards Muslims as homogeneous when she "conflates all Muslims with terrorists." All other choices are incorrect because they do not provide evidence that Gabriel views Muslims as homogeneous or members of ACT! as heterogeneous, so they do not effectively support the answer to the previous question.

44) ▶ B
Concept(s) Tested: Primary Purpose
Choice (B) is correct; paragraph 2 (lines 9 – 14) describes the main issue of the passage (wind-turbine-related bat deaths), and most of the passage after paragraph 2 discusses "possible solutions" to this problem. Choice (A) is incorrect because the passage neither states nor implies that its purpose is to "challenge an assumption." Choice (C) and (D) are incorrect because the passage never discusses overall bat populations or limits on "renewable energy sources."

45) ▶ B
Concept(s) Tested: Summary
Choice (B) is correct because paragraph 5 indicates that female bats make longer journeys than male bats, and that females fly at heights that "put them on a collision course with wind turbines" (lines 32 – 33), so we can conclude that female bats risk injury more often than males do. Choice (A) is incorrect because, while the passage implies that more bat fatalities occur during summer than during other seasons, we cannot extrapolate that there are more injuries in summer than in every other season combined. Choice (C) is incorrect because while female bats may be "searching for additional foraging grounds" (lines 37 – 38), it is not clear that this is due to "a lack of food." Choice (D) is incorrect because there is no evidence that German wind turbines are any taller than turbines anywhere else.

46) ▶ A
Concept(s) Tested: Inference
Choice (A) is correct because, in lines 48 – 52, the team of researchers suggest ways to reduce the number of bat fatalities caused by wind turbines, so it is reasonable to conclude that this is a primary goal of their research. Choices (B) and (C) are incorrect because while the team studied bats' seasonal flight patterns and feeding habits, they were studying them as they related to wind turbines. Choice (D) is incorrect because the researchers in the passage have not yet determined that bats mistake wind turbines for trees, so this idea remains a hypothesis (lines 63 – 64).

47) ▶ C
Concept(s) Tested: Words in Context
Choice (C) is correct. As used in the passage, "basic" describes general research about bat populations; "fundamental" is closest in meaning to "general" and works best as a descriptor of "research." Choice (A) is incorrect because "intrinsic" means "inherent" or "inborn," which does not fit the context of the sentence. Choice (B), "adequate," is incorrect because the passage is commenting on the type of research, whereas "adequate" comments on the quality of the research. Choice (D) is incorrect because "severe" does not fit the context of the sentence.

48) ▶ C
Concept(s) Tested: Summary
Choice (C) is correct because it provides an effective summary of lines 76 – 78, as ultrasonic "boom boxes" are audio deterrents while UV light emitters are visual deterrents. All other choices are incorrect because they are not preventative measures discussed in the passage.

49) ▶ B
Concept(s) Tested: Attitude and Tone
Choice (B) is correct; in lines 90 – 91, the author claims, "Wind power holds great promise for future renewable energy production," which indicates that she is hopeful, or "optimistic," about the continued production of wind energy. Choice (A) is incorrect because "censure" describes a feeling of disapproval, which is the opposite of the author's attitude. Choice (C) is incorrect because "apprehension" means "anxiety" or "uncertainty," which does not summarize the author's attitude. Choice (D) is incorrect because the author expresses an opinion regarding wind energy production, so "indifference" does not describe her attitude.

50) ▶ D
Concept(s) Tested: Citation
Choice (D) is correct; in these lines, the author describes wind power as holding "great promise," which indicates that she is hopeful, or "optimistic," about the continued use of wind energy. Choice (A) is incorrect because it points out a negative result of wind turbine use. Choice (B) is incorrect because, although it advocates for the continued use of wind energy, it does not provide any indication that the author is hopeful or optimistic. Choice (C) is incorrect because it does not provide any textual clues that allow us to infer the author's attitude.

51) ▶ D
Concept(s) Tested: Inference
Choice (D) is correct; lines 12 – 14 explain that the estimated number of turbine-related bat fatalities varies by orders of magnitude, which indicates that researchers do not know exactly how many "annual wind turbine-related bat fatalities" occur. Choices (A) and (C) are incorrect; although the passage indicates that there are thousands of turbine-related bat fatalities, we cannot infer that this means any species are in danger of extinction, or that the vast majority of bat fatalities are caused by wind turbines. Choice (B) is incorrect; lines 27 – 44 suggest that some wind turbines interfere with bat flight paths, but we cannot extrapolate that the majority of wind turbines block flight paths.

52) ▶ B
Concept(s) Tested: Citation
Choice (B) is correct because it reveals that the estimated number of turbine-related bat fatalities varies widely, which provides support for the claim that researchers do not know precisely how many bats are killed. All other choices are incorrect because they do not relate to a lack of exact numbers regarding turbine-related bat fatalities.

SAT Writing & Language Test 4 : Answers & Explanations

Writing & Language Test

1. C	5. D	9. C	13. B	17. D	21. C	25. B	29. A	33. A	37. A	41. B
2. D	6. B	10. A	14. B	18. D	22. B	26. B	30. C	34. A	38. C	42. C
3. B	7. A	11. B	15. A	19. B	23. D	27. A	31. C	35. A	39. B	43. B
4. B	8. B	12. C	16. D	20. C	24. C	28. D	32. D	36. A	40. D	44. D

1) ➡ C
Concept(s) Tested: In-Sentence Punctuation
The noun phrase "one of her most famous novels" is an appositive, meaning it identifies or describes another noun. To avoid confusion, it must be framed by commas, dashes, or parentheses. Only (C) provides two commas.

2) ➡ D
Concept(s) Tested: Precise Diction
Choice (D) is correct because "to undergo" something is to "experience" it, and it makes sense to claim that a country "experiences significant political change." Choice (A) is incorrect because a country cannot be said to "understand" anything. Choice (B) is incorrect because "underscore" means "emphasize," and it is unclear what it would mean for a country to "emphasize political change." Choice (C) is incorrect because "undermine" means to weaken, and "political change" is not something that can be diminished or weakened.

3) ➡ B
Concept(s) Tested: Pronoun Use, Countable/Uncountable Nouns
(A) and (C) are incorrect because the answer must serve as a quantifier for the countable noun "events." Yet "much" or "little" are used for uncountable (necessarily singular) nouns. (D) is incorrect because "any" indicates that something is not particular or specific, while the events in the sentence are particular and specific: they are the ones "outlined in the novel." Therefore, only (B) is correct.

4) ➡ B
Concept(s) Tested: Passage Development
The added sentence mentions some of Allende's personal experiences that informed her writing, so it provides an effective transition to the next paragraph, which starts by referring to "Allende's personal experiences." Choice (A) is incorrect because the sentence does not reiterate any previous point. Choice (C) is incorrect because it misidentifies the novel's focus, and (D) is incorrect because the added sentence maintains the autobiographical focus of the paragraph.

5) ➡ D
Concept(s) Tested: Subject-Verb Agreement, Verb Tense
The answer must be a third-person form of the verb (ie., he has, she has) because it must agree with "one of the main characters." The simple present tense of the verb is correct in this case because it refers to a character in fiction, thereby requiring the literary present tense. Thus, (D) is the correct answer.

6) ➡ B
Concept(s) Tested: Combining Sentences
Choice (B) is correct because it connects the independent clause ending with "Paula" to a relative clause using a comma and the appropriate pronoun, "who." Choice (A) is incorrect because it uses the relative pronoun "that" to indicate a person. Choices (C) and (D) are incorrect because they do not clarify that Paula is Allende's daughter, creating unnecessary confusion.

7) ➡ A
Concept(s) Tested: Passage Development
The paragraph describes the events surrounding Allende's writing of the book *Paula*. The narrative is most supported by (A) because it describes the inadvertent first step in the process. Choices (B) and (C) are incorrect because they stray from discussing steps in the process. Choice (D) is not the best answer because it provides details about the tragedy, but not about the process of writing the memoir.

8) ➡ B
Concept(s) Tested: Combining Sentences
The two sentences can be considered independent clauses and can be joined by a comma and a coordinating conjunction that indicates their relationship. In this case, the relationship is cause and effect, making "so" the most appropriate answer.

9) ➡ C
Concept(s) Tested: Parallel Structure
The underlined portion is part of a list of important experiences in Allende's life so far, and thus should have parallel structure with the first two items on the list. In this case, the list includes *accepting a medal, giving a talk*, and, in (C), *bearing a flag*.

10) ➡ A
Concept(s) Tested: Concision, Redundancy
Choice (A) is correct because it is the only choice that explains *why* Allende is grateful to her fans. All other choices simply restate that she is grateful to her fans and supporters, which is redundant and therefore incorrect.

11) ➡ B
Concept(s) Tested: Passage Organization
Sentence 3 states that Allende answered questions from the audience. The most logical placement would be at the beginning of the paragraph, which elaborates on what she said "when asked about her honors."

12) ➡ C
Concept(s) Tested: Passage Development
The first sentence describes the hot liquid rock that wells up under Yellowstone National Park. The best choice for the next sentence is (C), because it introduces the topic of the heat's effect on the region. The rest of the passage focuses on that impact, not on visitors or plant life in the park.

13) ➡ B
Concept(s) Tested: Passage Development
The example that follows the underlined information is the effect of a can of soda shaken and then opened. Thus, the best phrase to set it up is (B), as it describes the phenomenon of pressurized water spraying out. The other choices more or less describe the pressure but not the spray.

454 | KALLIS' Key to the SAT

14) ➡ B
Concept(s) Tested: In-Sentence Punctuation, Sentence Boundaries
The underlined portion requires the joining of two independent clauses; the writer can use a semicolon alone or a comma and a coordinating conjunction, such as "but." Only (B) includes both correctly. (A) incorrectly uses both a semicolon and "but." (C) and (D) use no punctuation and thus would create a run-on sentence.

15) ➡ A
Concept(s) Tested: In-Sentence Punctuation
In the sentence, the participial phrase "cooling slightly along the way" modifies "the steaming water." Participial phrases should generally be separated from the rest of the sentence by commas, making (A) the only correct answer. (B), (C), and (D) are incorrect because they create confusion.

16) ➡ D
Concept(s) Tested: Transition Words and Phrases
The underlined portion begins a transition to the subject of thermophiles. In this case, "whereas" is the only correct choice. It signals an unexpected fact ahead, ie., the water is deadly—but some bacteria can survive in it. The other choices would not make sense in the sentence.

17) ➡ D
Concept(s) Tested: Style and Tone
Only choice (D) creates a complete sentence, so it is correct. Choice (B) uses the pronoun "it," which has no referent, so (B) is incorrect. Choice (A) doesn't specify *what* is usually green, creating an unclear sentence. Choice (C) forms a run-on and is therefore incorrect.

18) ➡ D
Concept(s) Tested: Passage Development
(D) is correct; the sentence should not be deleted because it helps explain the environmental conditions that *Synechococcus* must survive in summer. Without the sentence, readers would have less context to understand *Synechococcus* adapting by developing a protective yellow pigment.

19) ➡ A
Concept(s) Tested: Precise Diction
The hot spring water from below and the unfiltered summer sunlight from above create an *extremely harsh* environment for life forms. "Severe," as in (A), is the most precise descriptor from among the choices. The other choices do indicate physical difficulty, but they fit different situations.

20) ➡ C
Concept(s) Tested: Pronoun Use, Commonly Confused Words
The plural pronoun "they" in the sentence properly refers to the bacteria in the preceding sentence. Thus, (C) is correct because the plural possessive determiner "their" must be used to describe the bacteria's "cloaks." (A) and (B) are words that sound the same but have different meanings. (D), "its," is the singular form of "their."

21) ➡ C
Concept(s) Tested: Passage Development, Graph Analysis
Choice (C) is correct because the passage as a whole focuses on the general features and ecosystems of the Grand Prismatic Spring, so a detailed diagram of molecular structures is beyond the scope of the passage.

22) ➡ B
Concept(s) Tested: Syntax, Concision
Choice (B) is correct. The information following the underlined portion introduces a phrase that modifies "opportunity," so it makes sense to introduce the phrase with the infinitive verb form "to view," as prepositions, participles, and infinitives often introduce modifying phrases such as this one. Choice (A) is incorrect; although it uses the correct infinitive, it includes the pronoun "you," which breaks from the formal, academic tone throughout the passage. Choices (C) and (D) are incorrect because they do not effectively connect the phrase to the rest of the sentence.

23) ➡ D
Concept(s) Tested: Precise Diction, Style and Tone
(D) is correct because it describes the behavior precisely—fans criticizing game officials—while also maintaining the formal tone of the passage. (A) is incorrect because it uses colloquial diction. (C) is incorrect because "reprimand" conveys an official rebuke, such as an employer reprimanding an employee, making it too formal for the situation. (B) would not make sense in the sentence.

24) ➡ C
Concept(s) Tested: In-Sentence Punctuation
The phrase "an experience that many people value …" describes the "heroic quest" mentioned in the sentence. As a noun phrase describing a noun, it is an appositive phrase, and thus should be separated from the rest of the sentence by a comma. The other choices would create noun confusion.

25) ➡ B
Concept(s) Tested: In-Sentence Punctuation, Sentence Boundaries
The independent clause ending in "minor and major leagues" should be separated with a comma and a conjunction (in this case "yet") from the independent clause that follows. Thus, (C) can be ruled out. Meanwhile, em dashes near the end of sentences emphasize the information that follows. But they are used only in place of other punctuation, such as colons, commas, and parentheses. (A) and (D) can be ruled out because no punctuation would normally follow a conjunction. Thus, (B) is the correct answer.

26) ➡ B
Concept(s) Tested: Passage Development
Sentence 1 of the paragraph describes the public image of sports teams as groups of athletes. Sentence 2 presents the argument that athletes are the "tip of the iceberg." (B) is correct because this would be the most logical place to explain the imagery: just as we never see the bulk of an iceberg, "spectators never see the bulk of the team." (C) and (D) might work, except that adding the sentence after sentence 3 or 4 would interrupt a discussion that has turned away from spectator impressions and toward information about "professional teams."

27) ➡ A
Concept(s) Tested: Passage Development
(A) is correct because it introduces a proposition that is elaborated upon throughout the paragraph: teams depend on their non-playing staff for success. Choice (B) is incorrect because the paragraph does not develop an argument for how much teams should value or pay their employees. Choices (C) and (D) each focus too narrowly on one example that is later described in the paragraph, so they are incorrect.

28) ➡ D
Concept(s) Tested: Concision, Voice
(D) is the best choice because it is clear and concise, and it is written using the active voice. All other choices are excessively wordy and use the passive voice, so they are incorrect.

29) ➡ A
Concept(s) Tested: Possession
"The spectator experience," as in (A), is a generalized reference to the many experiences fans have while watching games, either in person or on television. In (A), the noun "spectator" functions as an adjective. One could also use the plural possessive phrase "spectators' experiences," but there is no choice offered that uses the plural possessive correctly.

30) C
Concept(s) Tested: Concision
Choice (C) is correct because it is the clearest and most concise choice that still includes all necessary information. Choice (A) is incorrect because it is unnecessarily wordy to repeat "announcers and commentators." Choice (B) is incorrect because it is redundant to say, "help and support." Choice (D) is incorrect because the underlined portion is necessary to limit who "countless others" can be.

31) C
Concept(s) Tested: Passage Development
The topic of the sentence is "general professions" that can be centered on sports, such as medicine, public relations, and law. The only example that supports the topic is (C) because it mentions the "general profession" of language interpreting. (A) focuses instead on athletes' career paths; (B) and (D) focus instead on whether certain sports-related jobs are part-time or full-time.

32) D
Concept(s) Tested: Commonly Confused Words
The writer intends to describe a player "driving a basketball" beyond a tall guard on the opposing team. Like "beyond," the underlined word must describe the place or direction of the action with a preposition: a player drives "past" a guard. Choices (A), (B), and (C) are incorrect because they are forms of the verb "to pass."

33) A
Concept(s) Tested: Passage Development
The passage describes various ways to pursue a career in the "sports market." It implies that the business of sports is an alternative to the playing of sports. Thus, choice (A) is correct because the phrase would link the concluding sentence to the main idea of the paragraph (and the entire passage). (B) is incorrect because although the added information would develop the conclusion, it is not essential to the structure of the sentence. (C) and (D) are inaccurate.

34) A
Concept(s) Tested: Precise Diction
The writer describes a "drastic decrease" in oil supply due to Middle Eastern countries exporting less oil and, it is implied, a reduction in oil from within the U.S. ("domestic oil reserves.") Thus, "dwindling" is the most precise term. There are no contextual clues about the reduction being caused by decay or disrepair of anything, ruling out choices (B) and (D). Meanwhile "weakening," as in (C), does not describe quantity.

35) D
Concept(s) Tested: Subject-Verb Agreement, Verb Tense
Nouns that represent groups are known as "collective nouns," and in American English, they are generally singular. Although "the United States" refers to more than one state, by convention the name represents one group and is therefore considered singular. (D) is correct because it is singular. It is also a past-tense verb, and the action in the sentence takes place in the past.

36) A
Concept(s) Tested: Passage Development
The most effective choice is (A) because it explains the size of OPEC's market share, which contributes to readers' understanding about its potentially massive impact on global economies. (B) and (C) are incorrect because they do not convey information about oil production. (D) is not the best answer because it does not indicate how much influence OPEC had with the oil companies.

37) A
Concept(s) Tested: In-Sentence Punctuation
The word "higher" in the underlined section marks the ending of a dependent clause that begins with "when." Thus, "higher" should be followed by a comma to separate it from the rest of the sentence and indicate a natural pause. Next, the independent clause "they drained the supply" is followed by a participial phrase beginning with "causing." The clause and the participial phrase should be separated by a comma to avoid verb confusion.

38) C
Concept(s) Tested: Passage Organization
The paragraph relates the events of 1973. The sentence preceding the underlined portion describes the embargo being "swiftly" brought to an end through negotiations. The last sentence states that the effects were long-lasting. Thus, the transition between the two sentences should indicate contrast, as in (C), "however."

39) B
Concept(s) Tested: Conventional Expressions
"Focus on" is a phrasal verb. When paired, the words have the particular meaning of "to pay attention to" or "to concentrate on." Thus, the pairing is conventional, and other words cannot be substituted for "on."

40) D
Concept(s) Tested: Passage Development
As stated in (D), the sentence should not be deleted; it contributes to a smooth transition between paragraphs. It is relevant to the discussion about conserving oil and gas, because it describes a growing public interest in alternative energy sources. It also helps develop the transition to the next paragraph, where the writer points out that "this budding interest" was not enough to prevent another oil crisis in 1979.

41) B
Concept(s) Tested: Sentence Boundaries, In-Sentence Punctuation
(B) is correct because breaking the information into two sentences avoids creating a long, run-on sentence as in (A). The participial phrase "following the Iranian Revolution" makes a good introduction to the second sentence because it helps explain the information that oil exports from Iran and Iraq declined at the time. Choices (C) and (D) do not work grammatically or conceptually.

42) C
Concept(s) Tested: Graph Analysis
Only (C) provides an accurate and relevant statement based on information in the graph: the global supply rose and fell between 1973 and 1979, but ended up slightly higher, from just below 60 million barrels per day to just above. (A) is incorrect because the graph does not depict information about prices of gasoline; (B) is incorrect because "drastic" is a subjective term rather than a factual one; and (D) is incorrect because it fails to indicate a starting point for the time period it indicates, making it virtually meaningless.

43) B
Concept(s) Tested: Pronoun Use, Commonly Confused Words
The subject of the clause is "many gas stations." The pronoun in the underlined portion representing "many gas stations" must be plural, ruling out (A). Meanwhile, the word "until" only make sense if it is followed by a point in time; (C) would not make sense because "their ability to resupply" is not a point in time. (D) is incorrect because it is in the present tense (they + are), while the events took place in the past.

44) D
Concept(s) Tested: Style and Tone
The choices all offer the same basic meaning. However, the tone of the passage is fairly formal, so it would be inconsistent to use the informal/colloquial expressions in (A), (B), or (C).

SAT Practice Test 4: Answers & Explanations

Math Test

✓ No-Calculator Portion

1. C	7. C	13. B	18. 1
2. C	8. A	14. A	19. 54
3. A	9. B	15. B	20. 8
4. C	10. A	16. 40	
5. D	11. B	17. $\frac{8}{9}$	
6. C	12. B		

✓ Calculator Portion

1. B	7. C	13. A	19. A	25. C	31. 75	35. 2.5
2. C	8. C	14. A	20. D	26. D	32. 4.8	36. 60
3. A	9. D	15. B	21. D	27. A	33. 6	37. 1.55
4. C	10. D	16. C	22. B	28. B	34. 5	38. 42
5. B	11. A	17. C	23. D	29. A		
6. B	12. C	18. B	24. C	30. D		

No-Calculator Portion

1) ▶ C
Concept(s) Tested: Algebra
$7x - 5 < 13 + 4x$ → $3x < 18$ → $x < 6$

2) ▶ C
Concept(s) Tested: Algebra
Substituting $x = -3, 1, 3$ does not satisfy the equation:
$\sqrt{2x+3} + \sqrt{x+1} = 1$
But $x = -1$ satisfies the equation.

3) ▶ A
Concept(s) Tested: Algebra
Multiply $3m - n$ and 5 on both sides. It follows that:
$5m = 3m - n$ → $2m = -n$ → $\frac{n}{m} = -2$

4) ▶ C
Concept(s) Tested: Algebra
$(x + 3)^2 - (x - 3)^2 = x^2 + 6x + 9 - (x^2 - 6x + 9) = 12x$

5) ▶ D
Concept(s) Tested: Algebra
Substitute $a = 2$, $b = 1$, and $c = x$, then it follows
$2 \triangledown 1 \triangledown x = 2(x - 1) = 10$ → $x = 6$

6) ▶ C
Concept(s) Tested: Algebra
$S(T) = \frac{3(-55)}{5} + 331.4$
$S(T) = \frac{-165}{5} + 331.4$
$S(T) = -33 + 331.4$
$S(T) = 298.$

7) ▶ C
Concept(s) Tested: Functions and Graphs
The largest slope of $h(x)$ is 2 from $x \geq 2$.

8) ▶ A
Concept(s) Tested: Algebra
$(\sqrt{2} - \sqrt{3})^2 = 2 - 2\sqrt{2}\sqrt{3} + 3 = 5 - 2\sqrt{6}$

9) ▶ B
Concept(s) Tested: Factoring
First, factor $x^2 + bx - 16$ into the general form $(x + a)(x - c)$, using the factors of 16 for a and c, which are as follows:
$16 = 4 \times 4 = 2 \times 8 = 16 \times 1$
Trying these combinations, we find that $(x + 2)(x - 8) = x^2 - 6x - 16$, which gives us $b = -6$, or choice (B). The other factored forms do not expand to include any of the remaining answer choices.

10) ▶ A
Concept(s) Tested: Problem Solving, Algebra
Comparing 20 miles and 30 miles per hour,
$f(20) = 20 + \frac{20^2}{20} = 40$
$f(30) = 30 + \frac{30^2}{20} = 75$
Therefore, $f(30) - f(20) = 35$.

11) ▶ B
Concept(s) Tested: Algebra
Multiply the second equation by 2 to use the elimination method:
$2(5f + 6g = 15)$ → $10f + 12g = 30$.

Then subtract the first equation from the second:
$10f + 12g = 30$
$-8f + 12g = 27$
$\overline{2f = 3}$

Thus, $f = \frac{3}{2}$. Substitute this value into one of the original equations:

$$5\left(\frac{3}{2}\right) + 6g = 15$$

$$\frac{15}{2} + 6g = 15$$

$$6g = \frac{15}{2}$$

$$g = \frac{5}{4}$$

Therefore, $f + g = \frac{5}{4} + \frac{3}{2} = \frac{11}{4}$

12) ▶ B
Concept(s) Tested: Algebra

$$\frac{n}{x^2 - 36} = \frac{1}{x-6} + \frac{1}{x+6}$$

$$\frac{n}{x^2 - 36} = \frac{2x}{x^2 - 36}$$

Thus, $n = 2x$.

13) ▶ B
Concept(s) Tested: Geometry, Problem Solving
Let r be the radius of the base and h be the height of the cylinder.
We get the radius from the size of circumference of the base:
$2\pi r = 6\pi$ → $r = 3cm$
Using this, we calculate the height h:
$\pi(3)^2 h = 81\pi$ → $h = 9cm$

14) ▶ A
Concept(s) Tested: Problem Solving, Algebra
Note that Tyler's age is t years old. Let x be the elapsed years. Note that Tyler is three times as old as Isabella, so Isabella's age is $\frac{t}{3}$. Therefore, it holds that $t + x = 2(\frac{t}{3} + x)$. It results in $x = \frac{t}{3}$. So $\frac{t}{3}$ years later, Tyler's age will be twice Isabella's age.

15) ▶ B
Concept(s) Tested: Problem Solving
If a is the average price per concert ticket, x is the amount paid up front by each venue, and y is the average number of concert attendees, the band's earnings (T) can be expressed as: $T = 26(0.5ay + x)$
Based on the information provided in the question, the number of days, d, that the band spends on tour does NOT affect the band's earnings on tour. Note that the band plays 26 shows no matter how many days they spend on tour.

16) ▶ 40
Concept(s) Tested: Functions and Graphs
$f(5) = 5(5) - 1 = 24$

$f(-3) = 1 - 5(-3) = 16$
Adding both equation results in the following.
$f(5) + f(-3) = 24 + 16 = 40$

17) ▶ $\frac{8}{9}$ or .888 or .889
Concept(s) Tested: Algebra
Multiplying 7 and 9 on both sides, we get
$9x + 36 = 28$ → $x = \frac{(-8)}{9}$ → $|x| = \frac{8}{9}$

18) ▶ 1
Concept(s) Tested: Functions and Graphs
$(0, 2)$ and $(1, 3)$ satisfies $f(x) = ax^2 + bx + c$. After substituting these, we get $c = 2$ and $a + b + c = 3$. From these, we get $a + b = 1$

19) ▶ 54
Concept(s) Tested: Geometry
Let h be the height of the triangle. Note that the area of the triangle $A = \frac{1}{2}bh$ → $108 = \frac{1}{2}(24)h$
From this, we get $h = 9$. The line from the top of the triangle to the middle of the bottom side splits the triangle into two right triangles. From the Pythagoreans' theorem, we get $a^2 = h^2 + 12^2$, which results in $a = 15$. Therefore, the perimeter equals $2a + 24 = 54$.

20) ▶ 8
Concept(s) Tested: Functions and Graphs

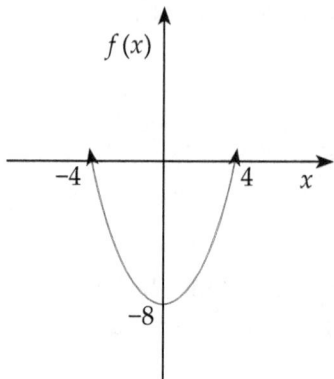

Note that x^2 is always positive, so to maximize absolute value set $x = 0$. This results in $f(x) = -8$ and $|f(x)| = 8$.

Calculator Portion

1) ▶ B
Concept(s) Tested: Data Analysis, Functions and Graphs
The percentage of the participants that preferred "A" is $\frac{140}{400} = 35\%$.

So (B) is not true, but the other choices are true.

2) ➤ C
Concept(s) Tested: Number Rules
Note that $x^2 - 9 > 0$, which implies that $x < -3, x > 3$.

3) ➤ A
Concept(s) Tested: Problem Solving; Ratios, Rates, and Percentages
If p is the retail price for the sweater, then $0.25p = \$45$ from the 25% discount. The money that Olivia paid for the sweater is as follows:
$0.75p = 3 \times (0.25p) = 3 \times \$45 = \$135$.

4) ➤ C
Concept(s) Tested: Ratios and Percentages
Note that the frequency on section 3 and 4 is $\dfrac{(10+11)}{50}$. This frequency applies the same to the 300 spins. Therefore, it follows that $300 \times \dfrac{21}{50} = 126$.

5) ➤ B
Concept(s) Tested: Functions and Graphs
Multiplying the first equation by 2 results in the second equation. So there is only one line.

6) ➤ B
Concept(s) Tested: Ratios and Percentages
Let x be the the cost of the SUV to the dealer. Then, $(1 + 25\%)x = 1.25x = \$39,000$. So $x = \$31,200$.

7) ➤ C
Concept(s) Tested: Problem Solving
Let x be the amount of gas used in 2014. Because Gerry spent the same amount of money both years, it follows that:
$200x = 250(x - 0.75)$ → $200x = 250x - 187.50$
→ $50x = 187.50$ → $x = \$3.75$
Thus, Gerry spent $200(\$3.75) = \$750$

8) ➤ C
Concept(s) Tested: Problem Solving, Functions and Graphs
The difference of car price from 1994 to 2002 is $\$19,126 - \$16,930 = \$2,196$.
So the slope of price, $a = \dfrac{2196}{2002 - 1994} = 274.5$.
From 2002 to 2008, the difference of years, $2008 - 2002 = 6$.
So the predicted average price for 2008, $y = \$19,126 + \$274.5 \times 6 = \$20,773$.

9) ➤ D
Concept(s) Tested: Factoring
Choice (A) can be quickly eliminated because it would not result in a positive value for b^3. Choice (B) would result in no negative values. Meanwhile: $a^3 - a^2b - ab^2 + b^3 = a^2(a - b) - b^2(a - b)$
$= (a - b)(a^2 - b^2) = (a - b)(a - b)(a + b) = (a - b)^2(a + b)$

10) ➤ D
Concept(s) Tested: Problem Solving
Note that the table contains only the most popular names from rank 1 to rank 5. We can infer that there are other names that are not contained in the table. Choice (A) is incorrect because the question only asks about *boys'* names, so girls' names are irrelevant. (B) is incorrect because the question refers only to boys born in a certain town, so boys' names in the entire U.S. are not relevant. Choice (C) is incorrect because the question asks only about boys' names in 1995, so names from other years are irrelevant.

11) ➤ A
Concept(s) Tested: Algebra
$|7 - 3x| > 2$ → $7 - 3x > 2$ or $7 - 3x < -2$
→ $x < \dfrac{5}{3}$ or $x > 3$

12) ➤ C
Concept(s) Tested: Algebra, Number Rules
$\sqrt[3]{n+8} = -0.5$ → $n + 8 = (-0.5)^3$ → $n = -8.125$.

13) ➤ A
Concept(s) Tested: Ratios and Percentages, Data Analysis
The rate of adults that received a return of less than $500 is 0.35. Therefore the number of adults that received a return of less than $500 for a group of 900 is $0.35 \times 900 = 315$.

14) ➤ A
Concept(s) Tested: Algebra, Factoring
$\dfrac{7 + 20x - 3x^2}{2x^2 - 11x - 21} = \dfrac{(x-7)(-3x-1)}{(x-7)(2x+3)} = -\dfrac{3x+1}{2x+3}$

15) ➤ B
Concept(s) Tested: Problem Solving
The shearing speed of Jim, Dolly, and Antonio is $\dfrac{30}{30}, \dfrac{30}{45}$, and $\dfrac{30}{90}$, respectively. Adding these speeds results in 2 sheep per minute. Therefore, the time to shear thirty sheep with this speed is $\dfrac{30}{2} = 15$ minutes.

16) ➤ C
Concept(s) Tested: Functions and Graphs
Note that shifting $f(x)$ down 4 units results in $f(x) - 4$ and shifting to the right 2 units results in $f(x - 2)$. Therefore, $h(x) = (x - 2)^3 - 4$.

17) ➤ C
Concept(s) Tested: Algebra, Problem Solving
Let p be the unit price of a pear, a be the unit price of an apple, and o be the unit price of an orange. Then, the following equations hold:
$p + 3a = 1.9$

$p + a + o = 1.62$
$2a + o = 1.7$
Subtracting the third equation from the second results in $p - a = -0.1$. Subtracting this equation from the first equation results in $a = \$0.5$

18) ▶ B
Concept(s) Tested: Problem Solving
If x is the number of days taken for Grace to paint the house, then Julia takes $x - 5$ days to paint the house. Note that it takes 6 days when they work together, so $\frac{1}{6} = \frac{1}{x-5} + \frac{1}{x}$.
Multiply $6x(x - 5)$ on both sides. It results in
$x^2 - 17x + 30 = (x - 15)(x - 2) = 0 \rightarrow x = 15$
days because $x - 5$ must be positive.

19) ▶ A
Concept(s) Tested: Functions and Graphs
Note that the slope of the line is almost −1 because the temperature drops almost 10 degrees as the wind speed increases by 10 miles per hour. Therefore, the equation in (A) approximates the line of best fit.

20) ▶ D
Concept(s) Tested: Algebra
Subtracting $\frac{2x}{3}$ on both sides results in $-4 \leq -1$.
Because $-4 \leq -1$ is a true statement, it holds for all real numbers x.

21) ▶ D
Concept(s) Tested: Functions and Graphs
Substituting (1, 12) and (3, 28) into the equation $y = x^2 + mx + n$ results in the following equations:
$m + n + 1 = 12$
$3m + n + 9 = 28$
Subtracting the first equation from the second equation results in $m = 4$.
Subsituting $m = 4$ into the first equation gives us $n = 7$ and $mn = 28$.

22) ▶ B
Concept(s) Tested: Problem Solving, Functions and Graphs
Note that the value of a car decreases as the age of a car increases, so (B) exhibits a negative correlation. Others exhibit positive correlations.

23) ▶ D
Concept(s) Tested: Number Rules
Note that denominator should not be 0 and $\sqrt{5-x} > 0$. Therefore, $x < 5$, and $x \neq 0$.

24) ▶ C
Concept(s) Tested: Geometry

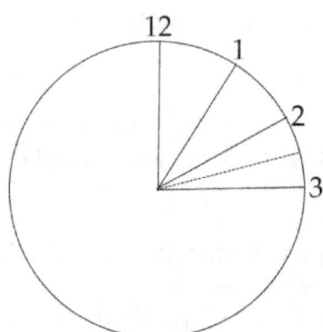

Note that one hour represents $\frac{1}{12}$ of the clock or $\left(\frac{1}{12}\right)(360) = 30°$. At 2:30, the hour hand has moved 2.5 times this distance or $(2.5)(30°) = 75°$.

25) ▶ C
Concept(s) Tested: Problem Solving
There are 2 ways between A and C, and there are also 2 ways between B and C. Therefore, the number of routes in a clockwise direction is 2×2 and that of the opposite direction is also 2×2. Therefore, total different number of routes is $2 \times 2 + 2 \times 2 = 8$.

26) ▶ D
Concept(s) Tested: Problem Solving, Algebra
One rotation of the wheel will cover the distance of one diameter. We know that $100x = d$ and we want to know what times $y = d$. Therefore, we must divide $100x$ by y.
Therefore, $r = \frac{100x}{y}$

27) ▶ A
Concept(s) Tested: Functions and Graphs
Substitute $x = 0$ to $5x + 4y = 12$. It results in $y = 3$. Therefore, the graph intersects the y-axis at (0, 3).

28) ▶ B
Concept(s) Tested: Data Analysis
Since the fertility chart above tells us the total number of babies born in 1950 (688,319), we can calculate the number of boys and girls born by the percentage chart given:

Babies born Female: 49.2%
688,319(.492) = 338,652.948

Babies born Male: 50.8%
688,319(.508) = 349,666.052

Now that we have the total number of each sex, we can add up the percentages associated with "Young."
 1.44%
+)1.29%
 2.7% of popularly named baby girls had "Young" in their name.

  1.68%
  1.54%
  1.25%
 +) 0.97%
 5.44% of popularly named baby boys had "Young" in their name.

Use these percentages to calculate the number of popularly named girls and boys with Young in their names, then add them up for the answer:

Girls: (.027)338,652.948 =   9,143.629596
Boys: (.0544)349,666.052 = +)19,021.8332288
         28,165.4628248 ~

28,165.5 ~ 28,166 popularly named babies with Young in their name.

29)  A
Concept(s) Tested: Data Analysis
Based on the chart, the TFR of women in 1980 is 2.82 babies per woman. Having determined the total number of baby girls born in 1950, we can add up the popular name percentages to calculate the number of baby girls in 1950 with popular names:
Percentages of popular names for baby girls in 1950:
 1.44% + 1.39% + 1.29% + 1.17% + 1.11% + 1.05% + 1.04% = 8.49% of baby girls born in 1950 had popular names in the chart above.
The number of baby girls in 1950 = 338,652.948 so (.0849)(338,652.948) ≈ 28,751.5548 of the girls born in 1950 were given the popular names above. Now we can multiply the TFR by the number of popularly named Korean girl babies:
(2.82)(28,751.5548) = about 81,079 babies will be born to the popularly named Korean girl newborns of 1950.

30) ▶ D
Concept(s) Tested: Data Analysis
The first conclusion cannot be drawn from the data, so it is incorrect. The range of TFR is equal to the highest value minus the lowest, and 6.4 − 1.122 ≠ 4. Therefore, I and II are both false, and (D) is the answer.

31) ▶ 75
Concept(s) Tested: Ratios and Percentages, Problem Solving
The quantity of antifreeze, in gallons, is
$\frac{1}{6} \times 3 + \frac{1}{2} \times 1 = 1$
and the quantity of fuel, in gallons, is
$\frac{5}{6} \times 3 + \frac{1}{2} \times 1 = 3$.

Therefore, fuel comprises three out of the four gallons of the solution, which is 75 percent.

32)  4.8 or $\frac{24}{5}$
Concept(s) Tested: Geometry
Let x be the length of DB. The length of AB is 8 by the Pythagorean theorem. The area of △ABC,
S(△ABC) = $\frac{6 \times 8}{2} = \frac{10x}{2}$ → $x = 4.8$.

33) ▶ 6
Concept(s) Tested: Algebra, Factoring
$(pq^{\frac{3}{2}})^2 = p^2 q^{\frac{3}{2} \times 2} = p^2 q^3 = 108$. Note that $108 = 54 \times 2 = 27 \times 4 = 3^3 2^2$ → $pq = 6$.

34) ▶ 5
Concept(s) Tested: Factoring, Algebra
$(3x + 2)(2x − 5) = 6x^2 − 11x − 10 = ax^2 + kx + n$
→ $a = 6, k = −11, n = −10$ → $a − n + k = 5$

35) ▶ 2.5 or $\frac{5}{2}$
Concept(s) Tested: Problem Solving, Algebra
The height $h = 40t − 16t^2 = 4t(10 − 4t) = 0$.
Note that $t = 0$ is the initial position. Therefore, the stone hits the ground at $t = 2.5$ seconds.

36) ▶ 60
Concept(s) Tested: Ratios and Percentages
Note that x is decreased by 25% and y is increased by 25%. Therefore, it follows that:
The new quotient $\left(\frac{1-0.25}{1+0.25}\right)\left(\frac{x}{y}\right) = \left(\frac{0.75}{1.25}\right)\left(\frac{x}{y}\right) = 0.6\frac{x}{y}$

37) ▶ 1.55
Concept(s) Tested: Ratios and Percentages, Problem Solving
Note that the number of new cases of this disease is 62 over a period of 3 years and the number of children in the population between 3 and 6 years of age is 4,000. Therefore,
IR = $\frac{62}{4000}$ = 0.0155 = 1.55%

38) ▶ 42
Concept(s) Tested: Problem Solving, Ratios and Percentages
Note that the incidence falls by 67% compared to the previous 3 years after the vaccine is introduced. Therefore, 62 × 0.67 = 41.54 fewer cases. The nearest whole number is 42 fewer cases.

SAT Practice Test 4: Answers & Explanations

Sample Essay Response

To change another's opinion on a divisive topic often seems impossible. Some studies have even substantiated this idea: people often double-down on their original opinion when presented with information that refutes it. After all, it is not easy to admit to being wrong. Yet in her essay on GMOs, Susanna Heckman uses many persuasive tools to do just that—to convince her readers that GMOs are not only beneficial, but necessary. The strength of Ms. Heckman's argument stems largely from its structure. She provides historical context for the use of GMOs; she addresses the concerns of the opposition; and she ends with a call to action, claiming that the future of agriculture relies on GMO-related research.

The first two paragraphs of Ms. Heckman's essay implicitly refute claims that all genetically modified organisms are "unnatural" by giving GMOs historical context. By informing the reader that humans have been selectively breeding (aka genetically modifying) crops for over 10,000 years, she dispels any notion that all GMOs "meddle with nature," as claimed by Greenpeace in paragraph 6. In paragraph 2, Ms. Heckman drives this point home by revealing that modern rice's progenitor is now considered a weed, and that modern agriculture and husbandry owe their existences to the modification of organisms to increase their nutritional value.

Having established that genetically modifying organisms for our benefit is nothing new, Ms. Heckman then acknowledges several common grievances against "modern" GMOs—that is, those produced in a lab rather than through generations of breeding. She appears to concede that the Flavr Savr tomato "seemed too impossibly unnatural to be healthy" (paragraph 4), and that "fishy-tasting strawberries" (paragraph 5) might be expected of fish-gene-spliced berries. However, even the language she uses to present these apprehensions reveals much about their validity: GMOs "seem unnatural" and "consumers mistakenly" expected fishy berries. While Ms. Heckman addresses these fears, she refuses to validate them. Rather than confirm these fears or immediately refute them, Ms. Heckman complicates the issue with a quote from Mr. W. Saletan, which describe genetic modification as "a process." With this quote, she reminds the reader that GMOs are neither good nor bad, yet in the following three paragraphs she exemplifies how the process can be used for good.

Once Ms. Heckman has established that GMOs have historical precedence, and that even modern, lab-based genetic modification is often used to desirable ends, she initiates a call to action, claiming that GMOs are not only beneficial, but necessary. However, Ms. Heckman does not state that all people must embrace GMOs immediately. Instead, she advocates for knowledge: "It is urgent," she claims, "that the global community… learn more about the science behind GMO foods" (paragraph 10). Ms. Heckman understands that blind fear of GMOs has created an issue and that blind acceptance of GMOs is not the solution—knowledge is. According to Ms. Heckman, "scientific consensus supports" GMOs, "farmers realize the financial benefits" of GMOs, and agronomist M.S. Swaminathan sees GMOs as the only "way of meeting global food needs." All that is left now is for the public to show the same acceptance.

Sample Response Score: 4/3/4

Reading: 4
The student demonstrates a thorough understanding of the source text and uses quotations throughout. The response does not misinterpret any of the author's claims.

Writing: 3
The response is well-structured and follows the author's claim closely. Word choice and sentence structure are varied; however, a few errors detract from the overall clarity and quality.

Analysis: 4
The student shows a thorough understanding of the author's central claim. The response clearly outlines Heckman's argument and closely analyzes each element of her assertion. The student's analysis is pertinent throughout.

SAT Practice Test 5: Answers & Explanations

Reading Test

1. C	6. C	11. B	16. D	21. D	26. A	31. C	36. D	41. A	46. D	51. D
2. B	7. D	12. C	17. B	22. B	27. B	32. B	37. A	42. D	47. A	52. A
3. B	8. D	13. D	18. C	23. C	28. C	33. B	38. D	43. D	48. B	
4. D	9. D	14. A	19. B	24. B	29. D	34. D	39. B	44. B	49. C	
5. A	10. B	15. C	20. B	25. D	30. C	35. A	40. C	45. C	50. B	

1) ➤ C
Concept(s) Tested: Summary
The narrative describes a freshman having bewildering experiences in his first days at college. He learns that older students bully first-year students and block them from the college's club house. Thus, choice (C) is correct; the passage consists of fictional "anecdotes" that introduce "a social hierarchy" as part of a story. Choices (A), (B), and (D) are incorrect because they each address college life in general rather than a specific fictional setting. Furthermore, choice (A) is incorrect because, while the passage does describe freshmen life at a (fictional) university, it does not provide a picture of sophomore university life there.

2) ➤ B
Concept(s) Tested: Analogy
Choice (B) is correct because the main character, Ken, was apparently celebrated (lines 5 – 8) in his hometown, and his experiences over the past summer had "given him a self-appreciation" (lines 9 – 10). Thus, the analogy of the big fish in the small pond fits. Now, he feels "lost in the shuffle of superior youths" (lines 15 – 16), or like a small fish in a big pond. Choice (A) does not fit because Ken is away from home, not returning. Choices (C) and (D) are incorrect because there is no indication that Ken seeks or relishes conflict, so comparisons with wrestlers and bullies would not work.

3) ➤ B
Concept(s) Tested: Words in Context
In the context (lines 18 – 21) we learn that Ken weighs 160 pounds and is "no stripling." Choice (B) ("weakling") is the best answer; "stripling" literally means "boy" or "young man," with the implication of slimness (as in a "strip" of cloth). It makes sense that Ken is treated like all the other freshmen even though he is "no weakling." The other choices do not work because they do not refer to weight and size.

4) ➤ D
Concept(s) Tested: Purpose
Lines 30 – 35 serve to reveal the character's growing humiliation as sophomores bully him over every detail of his appearance, to the point where it seems there is nothing right about him. The reader senses Ken's "feelings of inadequacy," and choice (D) is correct. Choice (A) is incorrect because although the narrator says that there is "something wrong" with Ken's clothes, the remark is disingenuously reporting what the sophomores have apparently implied. The text does not suggest that Ken lacks money for clothes. The topics suggested in choices (B) and (C) are not mentioned in the passage.

5) ➤ A
Concept(s) Tested: Words in Context
One of the many meanings of "mean" is "low in value or rank," as in "inferior," or choice (A). It would make sense that the character feels so "little and inferior" that he cannot retaliate against the bullies (lines 64 – 65). Choices (C) and (D) are incorrect because they would create a confusing sentence, as being "brazen" or "unkind" would not likely stop someone from retaliating against a wrong. Choice (B), "average," uses "mean" in its mathematical sense, which would not make sense in the sentence.

6) ➤ C
Concept(s) Tested: Summary
Lines 69 – 73 describe Ken's feelings toward the sophomores and seniors at the college after two weeks; he regards the sophomores with hatred ("loathing"), and he regards the seniors with awe ("deference"). Thus, choice (C) is correct. Ken does not feel brotherly affection for either group, making (A) incorrect; nor does he hate both groups, making (B) incorrect. Finally, choice (D) is incorrect because Ken does not regard the bullying sophomores with "indifference," as the narrator says that he hates them (line 69).

7) ➤ D
Concept(s) Tested: Citation
Choice (D) is correct because it encompasses the clearest support for the answer to the previous question. Lines 69 – 71 state Ken's feelings toward the older students. Meanwhile, choices (A) and (B) are incorrect because they do not mention anything about Ken's attitudes toward sophomores or seniors. Choice (C) does describe his feelings ("he passed from surprise to anger"), but it does not differentiate between sophomores and seniors, and therefore does not support the previous answer completely.

8) ➤ D
Concept(s) Tested: Summary
Lines 73 – 79 describe Ken's ability to identify other freshmen because for the first two weeks they either band together in noisy groups to run from sophomores, or they "sneak about alone." Thus, Ken identifies other freshmen by the size of their social groups, and choice (D) is correct. Choices (A), (B), and (C) would not fit because the passage does not mention the other freshmen's size, treatment of others, or clothing choices.

9) ➤ D
Concept(s) tested: Citation
Choice (D) is correct because in lines 73 – 79, the narrator describes Ken identifying freshmen by their

TEST 4: Answers & Explanations | 463

extreme social groupings, either banding together or being solitary. The other choices do not mention Ken identifying other freshmen, and so they cannot support the answer to the previous question.

10) ➤ B
Concept(s) Tested: Inference
The narrator's tone is purposely disingenuous as he describes Ken being "accidentally" pushed into the pool and finds out "the remarkable fact" that 15 other freshmen had been "accidentally" pushed in earlier. The mock sincerity implies that no one believed that the incidents were accidental, but rather that they were "intentional," and thus choice (B) is correct. There is no evidence to support the ideas that the students who pushed Ken in felt sorry (A), that Ken himself was pushed in 16 times (C), or that Ken pushed other freshmen into the tank (D), so these answer choices are all incorrect.

11) ➤ B
Concept(s) Tested: Summary
Lines 1 – 17 state that *Grand Theft Auto* is "one of the most successful video game series of all time" although "the *GTA* series has been accused of inspiring countless acts of real-world violence." Thus, it is popular but controversial, so choice (B) is the answer. Choices (A), (C), and (D) are not supported by the passage.

12) ➤ C
Concept(s) Tested: Words in Context
In lines 18 – 20, "ambivalent" is used to describe a love/hate attitude toward violent media. The word was coined from Latin words meaning "both" and "strength," and refers to feeling opposite ways with equal strength. Therefore, choice (C), "uncertain," comes closest in meaning, as consumers seem unable to decide whether to "devour" violent films and video games or "demonize" them (lines 21 – 23). Choices (A), (B), and (D) would not make sense in the sentence.

13) ➤ D
Concept(s) Tested: Purpose
In lines 30 – 39, the author agrees that some notorious murderers were regular players of violent video games. However, she points out that millions of other people also consume violent media and yet remain law-abiding. Thus, the information in line 36 serves to "undermine" the idea that consuming violent media causes people to commit violence, and choice (D) is correct. Choice (A) is incorrect because from the beginning the passage's focus is societal, not individual. Choice (B) is incorrect because the passage does not mention any specific group. Finally, (C) is not the best answer because the author has not exactly made an argument that can be reinforced; rather, she is raising a question.

14) ➤ A
Concept(s) Tested: Words in Context
The context for "inspires" in lines 48 – 50 is a description of a study that found no evidence of violent media causing real-world violence. The best answer is (A), "engenders," which means to "cause" something to exist. Choice (B) is incorrect because there is no indication in the passage that violent media promises incentives for committing real-world violence. Choice (C), "affects," is too general to be the best answer, and (D) refers to impacts on people; a person can be "galvanized" to commit violence, but violence itself cannot be "galvanized."

15) ➤ C
Concept(s) Tested: Summary
Choice (C) is correct because it summarizes the description of Ferguson's study in lines 60 – 64. Because the study outlined in lines 40 – 52 does not include factors such as "median household income, policing, [and] population density," we can conclude that Ferguson's study considers "social and economic factors," while the other study does not. Choice (A) is incorrect because Ferguson's study is more general, not more "specifically focused." Choice (B) is incorrect because neither study drew definitive conclusions regarding the influence of violent media. Choice (D) is incorrect because there is no indication that either study accounted for "unreported violent crimes."

16) ➤ D
Concept(s) Tested: Summary
In lines 73 – 78 a researcher proposes that public policy to reduce violence should not focus on media. He suggests that there are more urgent problems: poverty and mental health issues are offered as examples of "societal issues that impact violent crime rates" (lines 76 – 78), and choice (D) is correct. Choice (A) is not relevant to the text as there is no mention of paranoia. Choices (B) and (C) do not express the author's intended meaning about the examples.

17) ➤ B
Concept(s) Tested: Inference
The author suggests in lines 79 – 88 that people blame the media for violence because they want a simple solution, whereas people do not like to face issues such as poverty and mental health because they are "complex and sensitive" (line 87). Thus, the debate over media violence is a "distraction," and choice (B) is correct. (The idiomatic term "red herring" refers to fugitives dragging smoked fish across their trail to divert tracking dogs from finding them.) Choices (A), (C), and (D) are incorrect because they would not make sense referring to a "debate" (line 80).

18) ➤ C
Concept(s) Tested: Citation
Choice (C) is the answer because it summarizes Ferguson's conclusion that understanding the causes of societal violence requires looking beyond the influence of media. All other choices are incorrect because they do not summarize this same information as concisely or effectively.

19) ➤ B
Concept(s) Tested: Inference
The author of the passage says that, when it comes to the effects of violence in the media, "even the most rigorous studies remain riddled with ambiguities" (lines 50 – 52). Thus choice (B) is correct; we can infer that she would not accept unsupported claims that media violence inspires real-world violence. Choices (A), (C), and (D) cannot be supported by the text.

20) ➤ B
Concept(s) Tested: Citation
The author says that the effect of violence in media cannot be demonstrated easily because "correlation is not necessarily causation" (line 37); proving that two things occurring sequentially does not prove that the first thing caused the second. Choice (B) is consequently the best answer; it is the author's basic criticism of research on the effects of media

violence. Choices (A) and (D) do not provide support for the author's skepticism. Choice (C) is incorrect because it introduces a study, but does not provide information about the author's attitude.

21) **D**
Concept(s) Tested: Summary
Choice (D) is correct because paragraph 1 depicts a hypothetical situation in which a young boy unwittingly performs a simple science experiment. Choice (A) is incorrect because the author does not indicate that he is reflecting on anything. Choice (B) is incorrect because paragraph 1 does not contain any figures or statistics. Choice (C) is incorrect because the paragraph does not contain any questions.

22) **B**
Concept(s) Tested: Organization
The passage briefly follows the course of the discovery of electricity from ancient times to the author's time (1915). Therefore, choice (B) is the best answer because the passage is closest to being a "chronological-historical account." Choices (A), (C), and (D) are incorrect because the passage does not primarily focus on a study, on cause and effect, or on the author's personal experiences.

23) **C**
Concept(s) Tested: Purpose
Lines 15 – 22 describe how Thales, a philosopher in ancient Greece, wrote that amber can attract materials because it has a soul. The best answer is choice (C) because the author makes clear that he thinks this is a strange idea by adding, "whatever he meant by that" (line 21). We can conclude that he uses quotation marks around "soul" to indicate that the term is from Thales, not from the author, and that the author is skeptical of it. Choice (B) is not the best answer because putting quotation marks around a word does not indicate high regard. Choices (A) and (D) are incorrect because the passage is not focused on the ideas of Thales, so there is no reason that the author would want to emphasize or simplify the term.

24) **B**
Concept(s) Tested: Words in Context
In the preceding paragraphs, the author has focused on the electrical properties of certain substances when they are rubbed. In lines 23 – 29, the author describes the attitudes toward amber of some ancient peoples. He implies that because amber can draw materials toward it (with "attractive power"), they may have valued it more due to their "superstitious" beliefs. Thus, in the context the author clearly intends "attractive power" to mean "electrical properties," and choice (B) is correct. Choice (A) is incorrect because the author is claiming that ancient people did *not* see the "scientific value" of amber. Choices (C) and (D) are incorrect because they would not fit the context of the scientific passage.

25) **D**
Concept(s) Tested: Words in Context
"Slight" means small and slim; "to slight" means to treat something as small and unimportant. Choice (D) is correct because "to dismiss" can have the same meaning, and it makes sense to say that following Dr. Gilbert's discovery, electrical properties could no longer be *dismissed* "as a curious freak of nature" (lines 44 – 45). Choices (A) and (B) would not make sense in the sentence. Choice (C) is incorrect because it would state that people could no longer "deny" that electricity was trivial—the opposite of what the author means.

26) **A**
Concept(s) Tested: Inference
Choice (A) is correct because the author says that Dr. Gilbert's discovery "was the starting-point of the modern science of electricity" (line 40 – 41). He thus implies that Dr. Gilbert of Colchester was among "the first to formally investigate" electricity. Choices (B) and (D) are incorrect because the author indicates that electrical properties were not investigated before Dr. Gilbert (lines 30 – 32), so Dr. Gilbert could not have "built on" the work of others or been "inspired" by it. Choice (C) is incorrect because the author does not say that Dr. Gilbert disproved anything about electricity, but rather that he was the first to recognize it as a force contained in many materials (lines 37 – 40).

27) **B**
Concept(s) Tested: Citation
Choice (B) is correct because lines 40 – 41 indicate that Dr. Gilbert's work was "the starting point of the modern science of electricity," supporting the answer to the previous question: that Dr. Gilbert was among "the first to formally investigate electricity." Choice (A) is incorrect because it describes a hypothetical, informal investigation not connected to Dr. Gilbert. Choices (C) and (D) are incorrect because they address time periods after Dr. Gilbert's discovery, which would be irrelevant to the previous question.

28) **C**
Concept(s) Tested: Summary
In line 52, the author says that Otto von Guericke's invention was "improved by Sir Isaac Newton and others," making choice (C) correct. All other choices are incorrect because they are not supported by the text.

29) **D**
Concept(s) Tested: Summary
The final paragraph of the passage includes a description Charles du Fay's work. The reader must skim the paragraph for du Fay's findings: "when the rubber is of a different material to the thing rubbed … electricity is developed" (lines 72 – 74). Choice (D) is correct because it is a paraphrase of the preceding statement. Choices (A) and (C) misstate the findings and are thus incorrect. Choice (B) is incorrect because it describes the "properties of electrification" as "equal" in all substances, which would not describe du Fay's finding as presented in the passage.

30) **C**
Concept(s) Tested: Citation
Choice (C) is correct because it explains that "when the rubber is of a different material to the thing rubbed…electricity is developed." All other choices are incorrect because, although they mention some the electric properties of different materials, they do not summarize the discovery made by du Fay.

31) **C**
Concept(s) Tested: Graph Analysis
The chart is organized so that the most positively charged materials are farthest away from the most negatively charged materials; the farther away they are from each other, the greater the charge they could transfer between them if touched. Thus, the answer is (C), because gold and skin are nearly at opposite ends. They are the farthest apart compared to the other choices.

32) **B**
Concept(s) Tested: Graph Synthesis

TEST 5: Answers & Explanations | 465

Choice (B) is correct because from the chart we can see that sulfur is negatively charged, while skin is positively charged. We can infer that the machine described in the passage involved transfer of these opposite charges. Choice (A) is incorrect because electrical charges are not described as "canceling out" opposite charges. Choice (C) is not correct primarily because the chart does not claim to include all materials. Likewise, choice (D) is incorrect because it is beyond the scope of the chart.

33) ▶ B
Concept(s) Tested: Summary
Choice (B) is correct because, in lines 10 – 19, the author seems to agree with "moralists" that it would be preferable to have a fair distribution of wealth, but that considering the imperfect condition of society, providing luxury is "the only means" of achieving a more equal distribution. Choice (A) is incorrect because the author does not find decadence fascinating, nor does he indicate that its existence is inevitable. Choice (C) is incorrect; the author indicates a timelessness that does not suggest he finds luxury "outdated." Choice (D) is incorrect because the author makes no mention of political problems resulting from luxurious lifestyles.

34) ▶ D
Concept(s) Tested: Words in Context
The preceding sentences describe a system, or "process," in which some people earn money by serving land owners, so (D) is the correct choice. The remaining choices all define "operation," but fail to express the context-specific meaning as it is used in the passage.

35) ▶ A
Concept(s) Tested: Words in Context
The correct choice is (A) because it accurately expresses the idea that the provinces would lose their resources. Choices (B), (C), and (D) are incorrect because these words cannot be used to describe a province in this way.

36) ▶ D
Concept(s) Tested: Summary
The correct choice is (D) because the author discusses artisans making luxury goods to sell to landowners and landowners improving their farms so that they can buy more luxury goods. Choice (A) is incorrect because this selection does not mention neighboring countries. Choice (B) is incorrect because the author does not discuss the relationship between mechanics and artists, though both are mentioned in the paragraph. Choice (C) is incorrect because farmers are not directly mentioned in the passage.

37) ▶ A
Concept(s) Tested: Summary
(A) is the correct choice because the topic of the paragraph is luxury goods obtained by sailing in monsoons and traveling by camel, thus through "labor and risk." Choice (B) is incorrect because the author makes no mention of imported foods. Choice (C) is incorrect because the author explains that the trade was *extremely* profitable. Choice (D) is incorrect because the author makes no indication that trade improved political relations.

38) ▶ D
Concept(s) Tested: Citation
The correct choice is (D) because this selection clearly explains that trade with Arabia and India "provided valuable luxury goods" but was "time-consuming and dangerous." Choices (A) and (B) are incorrect because they describe aspects of the trade journey rather than indicate why such trade routes were unpopular. Choice (C) is incorrect because it describes the products acquired by trading, but makes no mention of the importance or unpopularity of these trade routes.

39) ▶ B
Concept(s) Tested: Words in Context
Choice (B) is correct. As used in the sentence, this phrase is a synonym for the luxury goods which have been the author's topic in the preceding paragraph. Choice (A) is incorrect because the author makes no mention of religious ceremonies in this paragraph. Choice (C) is incorrect because such objects are never introduced in the discussion. Choice (D) is incorrect because the author does not comment on the quality of Roman vs. non-Roman goods.

40) ▶ C
Concept(s) Tested: Purpose
The context reveals that the author refers to the "time of Pliny," and the "reign of Constantine" to give the reader reference points for a period when the proportion of silver increased, making (C) the correct choice. Choice (A) is incorrect because the author does not discuss the spending habits of either leader. Choice (B) is incorrect because the author does not indicate that either man acted to expand the trade of gold and silver. Choice (D) is incorrect because the author does not compare the two men in this way.

41) ▶ A
Concept(s) Tested: Summary
The correct choice is (A). The author describes the objects of trade as "female ornaments," and explains in lines 83 – 86 that Romans worried they were squandering their wealth on relatively useless goods. Choice (B) is incorrect because the author explains that Roman mines supplied gold stores faster than they were depleted. Choice (C) is incorrect because lines 82 – 83 imply that the Roman senate had to address widespread Roman discontent over the loss of societal wealth, not over the journeys themselves. Choice (D) is incorrect because the author does not discuss the Roman tax structure in this passage.

42) ▶ D
Concept(s) Tested: Citation
The correct choice is (D) because it clearly expresses the idea that Romans complained that Rome's wealth was being exchanged for useless objects. Choice (A) is incorrect because this excerpt does not address the issue of trade with India and Arabia. Choice (B) is incorrect because it does not give any discrete reason why such trade was unpopular. Choice (C) is incorrect because it describes only the goods acquired and fails to comment on the reasons Romans complained about overseas trade.

43) ▶ D
Concept(s) Tested: Purpose
The correct choice is (D) because the quotation about the storm reinforces the value of traditional knowledge. Choice (A) is incorrect because the view presented in the quotation does not contradict the author's view. Choice (B) is incorrect because the quotation does not prove that any of the information presented is true. Choice (C) is incorrect because the quotation does not serve to provide a characterization of the speaker.

44) ■▶ B
Concept(s) Tested: Inference, Summary
The correct choice is (B) because the U.N. secretary-general is quoted in the passage as saying, "'local knowledge...is especially important in an era when more and more disasters are climate- and weather-related'" (lines 33 – 38). In other words, "environmental changes are making traditional knowledge increasingly indispensable." Choice (A) is incorrect because the secretary-general never discusses combining local knowledge with modern technology. Choice (C) is incorrect because the secretary-general does not indicate that this is the case. Choice (D) is incorrect because the secretary-general does not comment on the ability of local knowledge to improve the health of surrounding ecosystems.

45) ■▶ C
Concept(s) Tested: Citation
The correct choice is (C) because this excerpt clearly relates the U.N. secretary-general's opinion of local knowledge and its impact on disaster reduction. Choice (A) is incorrect because this selection gives an example of how local knowledge helped save lives during a single disaster, but does not describe a general opinion. Choice (B) is incorrect because this excerpt does not clearly tie traditional knowledge to disaster risk reduction. Choice (D) is incorrect because it fails to discuss the relationship between local knowledge and resilience in the face of climate-related disasters.

46) ■▶ D
Concept(s) Tested: Words in Context
Choice (D) is correct because the author describes the steps in which *matupás* form, indicating that "sequential" is the best synonym to "successional" as it is being used in the passage. The remaining choices fail to fit the context in which the word is being used, so they are incorrect.

47) ■▶ A
Concept(s) Tested: Passage Organization
Choice (A) is correct. The passage is primarily concerned with introducing *matupás*, introducing the field of ethnoecology, and describing what the authors expected to find. Choice (B) is incorrect because the passage serves as an introduction to the research and does not reveal the conclusions reached by researchers. Choice (C) is incorrect because the authors briefly discuss fishing practices, but never encourage readers to adopt these habits. Choice (D) is incorrect because the passage is not focused on traditional customs and practices, and only briefly mentions these.

48) ■▶ B
Concept(s) Tested: Inference
The authors mention that "such knowledge...can be especially useful for understanding ecological processes that occur at temporal or spatial scales not easily observed by conventional scientific research" (lines 84 – 89). This implies that "traditional knowledge" has the advantage of accruing over many generations, shedding light on long-term or "protracted" natural processes, making (B) the correct answer choice. Choice (A) is incorrect because the authors never indicate that this may be so. Choice (C) is incorrect because the authors never mention altering landscapes in this way. Choice (D) is incorrect because the authors never compare the amount of information collected from the two different methods.

49) ■▶ C
Concept(s) Tested: Citation
Choice (C) is correct because this selection most clearly expresses the authors' claim that traditional knowledge may provide first-hand accounts of ecological processes taking place over great spans of time and space. Choice (A) is incorrect because this excerpt is focused on a specific feature of *matupás*, and does not mention local knowledge. Choice (B) is incorrect because it makes no generalizations about traditional knowledge, and only briefly mentions local people. Choice (D) is incorrect because it gives a specific example of how traditional knowledge might help researchers understand long-term ecological events, but fails to make clear the authors' general conclusions regarding such knowledge.

50) ■▶ B
Concept(s) Tested: Text Synthesis, Purpose
The correct choice is (B) because both passages discuss the importance of local knowledge and provide specific examples of ways in which traditional knowledge has been incorporated into the research and practices of international agencies (Passage 1) and individuals (Passage 2). Choice (A) is incorrect because only Passage 1 focuses on the role of local knowledge in meeting natural disasters. Choice (C) is incorrect because neither passage mentions updating local knowledge with modern scientific research. Choice (D) is incorrect because neither passage attempts to compile or categorize any information taken from local peoples.

51) ■▶ D
Concept(s) Tested: Text Synthesis, Inference
The correct choice is (D) because both passages focus on the benefits of learning from traditional societies. Choice (A) is incorrect because neither passage mentions interactions between traditional societies from different regions. Choice (B) is incorrect because the authors of both passages indicate that local knowledge can complement modern practices, but do not suggest abandoning current customs. Choice (C) is incorrect because the issue of government funding is not brought up in either passage.

52) ■▶ A
Concept(s) Tested: Text Synthesis
The correct choice is (A). Passage 1 discusses how local knowledge can be used to affect policy-making, while Passage 2 explains how traditional knowledge can be used to complement scientific understanding. Choice (B) is incorrect because neither passage focuses on methodologies for gathering information. Choice (C) is incorrect because both passages praise the benefits of local knowledge. Choice (D) is incorrect because neither passage focuses on specific or general local knowledge itself; rather, they comment on the value of traditional knowledge.

SAT Writing & Language Test 5 : Answers & Explanations

Writing & Language Test

1. A	5. B	9. C	13. D	17. B	21. A	25. D	29. C	33. A	37. B	41. B
2. C	6. D	10. C	14. B	18. B	22. D	26. D	30. C	34. B	38. D	42. B
3. A	7. D	11. B	15. C	19. A	23. B	27. B	31. A	35. C	39. C	43. D
4. D	8. B	12. A	16. C	20. C	24. A	28. B	32. A	36. A	40. B	44. A

1) ➤ A
Concept(s) Tested: Passage Development, Precise Diction
The paragraph contrasts two viewpoints about the Industrial Revolution. (A) is correct because it helps emphasize a positive viewpoint, with people "eagerly" taking advantage of "opportunities for acquiring wealth" through manufacturing. The image helps set up the later contrast with the "dark side" of the period as depicted by Charles Dickens.

2) ➤ C
Concept(s) Tested: In-Sentence Punctuation, Participial Phrases
Choice (C) is correct because it uses the word "including" before a partial list. Furthermore, the list beginning with "including" is correctly separated from the rest of the sentence by a comma. Choice (A) correctly uses a colon before the list but does not accurately list all 15 novels. (B) is incorrect because the information following the semicolon is a list, not an independent clause. (D) is incorrect because it fails to separate the non-essential information beginning with the phrase "such as" with punctuation.

3) ➤ A
Concept(s) Tested: Passage Development
The added sentence describes a story about "a young orphan who falls into the hands of murderous thieves," which would provide an example of the recurring motif of exploitation. Thus, (A) is correct, as the added sentence would provide focused support for the previous sentence about that motif.

4) ➤ D
Concept(s) Tested: Verb Tense
The passage is already in the simple-past tense. Therefore, a condition that existed at some point before that time should be in the past-perfect tense, as in (D).

5) ➤ B
Concept(s) Tested: In-Sentence Punctuation, Relative Clauses
As written in (A), the second sentence beginning with "where" cannot stand on its own. It does not express a complete idea because it is a relative clause. (B) is correct because it joins the sentences, separating the clause beginning with "where" from the main part of the sentence with a comma. (C) and (D) both inappropriately refer to the closest referent, "London," with "when," causing confusion. In addition, (D) incorrectly uses a semicolon, which can be used only to separate independent clauses or elements of a complex list.

6) ➤ D
Concept(s) Tested: Commonly Confused Words, In-Sentence Punctuation
The writer uses the correct forms of similar-sounding words in choice (D). They sold books belonging to them, requiring the possessive "their books"; they sold the books in London, requiring the use of the location pronoun "there."

7) ➤ D
Concept(s) Tested: Passage Development
Details about how the cousin was related to the family stray from the focus of the paragraph, which is on the sequence of events leading to Charles working in a factory. (A), (B), and (C) are incorrect because it is not necessary for the reader to understand more about the relationship in order to understand the events described.

8) ➤ B
Concept(s) Tested: Modifier Placement
The clearest sentence is (B), because it frames nonessential information within commas, where it will not get muddled up with the rest of the sentence. Choices (A) and (D) offer some confusion about whether the factory, the house, or the riverbank was "decaying and full of rats." Choice (C) is awkward, especially because prepositional phrases such as "on a riverbank" are rarely separated from the rest of a sentence by commas.

9) ➤ C
Concept(s) Tested: Syntax, Voice
Choice (C) is correct because it is the most direct, concise sentence. It follows a simple subject-verb-object pattern. The other choices have more complicated syntax, which is not necessary in this case for emphasis or style.

10) ➤ C
Concept(s) Tested: Precise Diction
The paragraph describes changing circumstances that allowed Charles to quit his job; since his mother "hated to see him give up his job," it is most precise to say that she "objected" to his quitting. Thus, (C) is the best choice

11) ➤ B
Concept(s) Tested: Passage Development
The first paragraph introduces the era in question and then makes the claim that "Charles Dickens…spent his literary career trying to illuminate the dark side of [people scrambling for wealth]." Thus, the best choice for restating that claim is (B) because it refers to his writing career and his main themes. Choices (A), (C), and (D) are interesting, but they stray from the focus of the passage.

12) ➤ A
Concept(s) Tested: Passage Development
The passage defines and describes atmospheric rivers throughout, making (A) (the only choice to mention atmospheric rivers) the best choice for the introductory paragraph.

13) ➤ D
Concept(s) Tested: In-Sentence Punctuation
Three clauses intersect at the underlined portion. (D) is correct because it provides the appropriate punctuation to avoid a run-on sentence. "When the system reaches land" is a dependent clause; it has a subject and verb, but it cannot stand on its own. When dependent clauses come before independent clauses, they are followed by a comma. Meanwhile, "it cools" is an independent

468 | KALLIS' Key to the SAT

clause, as is "the water vapor condenses to rain and snow." One way to separate independent clauses is with a comma plus a coordinating conjunction, such as "and."

14) ➡ B
Concept(s) Tested: Combining Sentences
Choice (A) is incorrect because it creates an illogical contrast between the two sentences. Only Choice (B) preserves and clarifies the meaning of the sentences while joining them in a logical manner. (B) clearly states that the large volume of water is the cause of the flooding and landslides. Choices (C) and (D) are incorrect because they change the facts.

15) ➡ C
Concept(s) Tested: Transition Words and Phrases
The paragraph begins with a general statement about the variability of rainfall from atmospheric rivers. The underlined section transitions into a specific discussion about the effects of that variability on California. Thus, the underlined portion should transition from the general to the specific, as is accomplished most precisely with "For example."

16) ➡ C
Concept(s) Tested: Participial Phrases, Sentence Boundaries
Here, an independent clause would need to be joined to the preceding clause with a comma and a coordinating conjunction, such as "and" or "so." Since no such conjunction is offered, the subject-verb combinations offered in choices (A), (B), and (D) create run-on sentences. The only correct choice is to make the underlined section the beginning of a phrase that begins with the participle "leaving." Participles act as modifiers rather than verbs, making (C) the correct choice.

17) ➡ B
Concept(s) Tested: Commonly Confused Words, Pronoun Use
Choice (B) is correct because "its" is the singular possessive adjective required in the sentence. "The state" is singular, and the sentence is about the water resources that it possesses.

18) ➡ B
Concept(s) Tested: Countable/Uncountable Nouns
According to the preceding sentence, "a handful" of atmospheric rivers exist at any given time. Choice (B) is correct because it effectively repeats the concept, describing the atmospheric rivers as "*few* in number." The words in choices (A) and (D) more precisely describe size than number. Choice (C) is incorrect because "little" refers to a small quantity of an uncountable noun, not to a countable noun.

19) ➡ A
Concept(s) Tested: Precise Diction
Only choice (A), "vulnerable", makes sense when describing places that are more at risk of experiencing "these weather patterns," namely severe storms. The word "liable" in choice (C) can have a somewhat similar meaning, but it does not fit the sentence because it must be followed by an infinitive, as in "liable *to receive* storms."

20) ➡ C
Concept(s) Tested: Passage Development, Style and Tone
The information about Alaska is related to the types of weather generated by a Pineapple Express, so the underlined portion should maintain this focus. Choice (C) mentions "snowfall in the Sierra Nevadas," maintaining the focus on weather conditions, so it is correct. Other choices fail to mention what types of weather result from a Pineapple Express, so they are not consistent in content with the information on Alaska.

21) ➡ A
Concept(s) Tested: In-Sentence Punctuation
The phrase beginning with "despite the importance…" is a prepositional phrase. In this context, "despite" is a preposition that helps explain logical relationships between ideas. When prepositional phrases of more than three or four words come at the beginning of sentences, they must be followed by a comma to indicate a slight natural pause to separate the preposition from the subject of the sentence. Semicolons, colons, and dashes, as in (B), (C), and (D), do not usually follow prepositional phrases.

22) ➡ D
Concept(s) Tested: Pronoun Use
Choice (D) is correct because the demonstrative adjective "these" indicates something near to the writer, and understood by the reader. In this case, "these phenomena" are the ones that have been examined in the passage, and thus near in an abstract sense. (A) and (C) are incorrect because they indicate something far from the writer, which would be unclear in this case; in addition, "that" refers to a singular noun, and "phenomena" is plural. (B) is incorrect because "them" is a pronoun, not an adjective, and would not make sense here.

23) ➡ B
Concept(s) Tested: Passage Development
The paragraph focuses on whether or not it is realistic to hope for a job in a beautiful, "far-flung place." Thus, (B) is the most effective introduction because it describes people who have "the dream of becoming closer to nature" but who think it is unrealistic (think about it "with a wistful sigh"). Choices (A), (C), and (D) do not introduce the main focus of either the paragraph or the passage.

24) ➡ A
Concept(s) Tested: Transition Words and Phrases
The paragraph is explaining the paradox that the Internet has made jobs both easier and more difficult to get. The phrase in (A), "at the same time," has a figurative meaning here: an additional fact needs to be considered alongside the first.

25) ➡ D
Concept(s) Tested: Concision, Syntax
Choice (D) is correct because it is simple and clear. (A) is not the best answer because, besides being wordy, it may cause confusion about where the "listing" took place. Was the opening listed on an island? Was it listed in the Great Barrier Reef? Meanwhile, (B) uses the vague term "someone," and (C) seems to indicate that the job, not the person holding the job, will take care of the island. Thus, (D) is the most precise in meaning.

26) ➡ D
Concept(s) Tested: Parallel Structure
The underlined word should be a gerund (an action word with an "-ing" ending that functions as a noun) because it is part of a two-item list and should have parallel structure. As such, the duties entailed *living* in a villa and *posting* blogs.

27) ➡ B
Concept(s) Tested: Style and Tone
Choice (B) is correct because an advertisement will usually promote a product using enthusiastic language, and "emphasized" is the only choice that implies enthusiasm. Choices (A) and (B) are incorrect because "bemoaned" and "undermined" have negative connotations; (D) is incorrect because "mention" is a neutral term, and we want a term that connotes enthusiasm.

28) ➡ B
Concept(s) Tested: Combining Sentences
The syntax in (B) is simple and concise, making it the best choice. (A) and (D) are incorrect because they have awkward structures. (C) is in the passive voice, which is often less desirable than the active voice as in (B).

29) ▶ C
Concept(s) Tested: Passage Development
The question asks for a link to the information that follows, which is about Southall getting stung by a dangerous jellyfish. Therefore, neither (A) nor (D) make sense. Choice (B), "ominously dangerous" is not correct because it would require an explanation; it would change the focus of the passage to explain how Southall could "relish the work" in an extremely threatening environment.

30) ▶ C
Concept(s) Tested: Verb Mood/Tense
The sentence is part of an example and is hypothetical. There is an implied "if" in the sentence. *If* a family bought an island, it *would need* someone to take care of it. Thus, the answer is (C).

31) ▶ A
Concept(s) Tested: Passage Development
Choice (A) is correct because "porpoises," "seals," and "natural beauty" are all part of what makes Muck an "extraordinary setting." All other choices are incorrect because they are not relevant to Muck as a *setting*, that is, a location with unique characteristics.

32) ▶ A
Concept(s) Tested: In-Sentence Punctuation
The underlined word comes at the end of a dependent clause beginning with "When." Dependent clauses that come before the main sentence must be separated by a comma. Therefore, (A) is correct.

33) ▶ A
Concept(s) Tested: Pronoun Use
The correct answer must be a pronoun that refers to the subject of the sentence, "the community." *Community* is a collective noun, meaning that it describes *one* group of people, and is therefore singular. Thus, the singular subject pronoun "it" is the correct choice. (B) is incorrect because "one" usually refers to "any one person," which would not make sense. (C) and (D) are incorrect because they are plural. In addition, (D) is not a subject pronoun.

34) ▶ B
Concept(s) Tested: Syntax, Voice
Choice (B) is the best answer because it is in the active voice (subject-verb, "the metaphor… conveys…"). The active voice is usually preferable because it is concise and promptly introduces the sentence's subject. Moreover, in this case choices (A), (C), and (D) have awkward structures that imply that the metaphor itself has said or suggested something.

35) ▶ A
Concept(s) Tested: Passage Development
The paragraph describes Oberg's speech as being "based on his own lifetime of experience." Choice (A) provides the best introduction as it mentions "personal insights." The other choices do not accurately describe the paragraph that follows.

36) ▶ A
Concept(s) Tested: Concision
The words "different," "varied," "an assortment," and "myriad" all have similar meanings in this case. Thus, using more than one would be redundant, and only (A) avoids that error.

37) ▶ B
Concept(s) Tested: Commonly Confused Words
The noun "advice" and the verb "to advise" have such similar spelling that they are often confused. In this case, "advice" is what Oberg offered, and (B) is correct. (C) is incorrect because "adverse" is an adjective. (D) is incorrect because it does not make sense to say that Oberg offered "adversity," or difficulty, along with "empathy" and "humility."

38) ▶ D
Concept(s) Tested: Sentence Boundaries
The first part of the sentence could make sense on its own: "Visitors may stay in hotels." The second part, "where staff members speak their language…" does not form a complete thought. It is therefore a dependent clause placed after an independent clause, and does not need to be separated by punctuation. Thus, (D) is correct.

39) ▶ C
Concept(s) Tested: Style and Tone
The underlined portion should maintain the same construction as the other items on the list. Only (C) retains the same structure and verb tense: *(noun) may be (adjective)*. In addition, choice (B) is incorrect because it uses the less formal second-person ("you").

40) ▶ B
Concept(s) Tested: Combining Sentences
The only syntax that retains the original meaning of the two sentences is (B). It clearly indicates that the native inhabitants are likely to ignore the discomforts, an act that frustrates the newcomers. Choice (A) incorrectly implies that one can only speculate about how the native inhabitants add to newcomers' frustration. Meanwhile, (C) and (D) imply that the native inhabitants are indifferent to the *newcomers* rather than to *the discomforts* that trouble the newcomers.

41) ▶ B
Concept(s) Tested: Passage Development
Social "cues" are unconscious signals people send each other when they interact. The examples listed in the passage are "facial expressions" and "hesitations," and the choice that fits most precisely with these is "gestures." Thus, (B) is correct. (A) is not the answer because "words" convey meaning explicitly, unlike the other cues in the list. Choices (C) and (D) would not make sense in the context.

42) ▶ B
Concept(s) Tested: Conventional Expressions
Only (B) uses the correct form of comparison. (A) is incorrect because the -er form of "less" is not used as an adverb to modify other adjectives such as "perfect," but rather modifies nouns as in "a lesser degree." (C) and (D) are incorrect because "least" and "most" are used only when comparing three or more things, and here only two cultures are being compared.

43) ▶ D
Concept(s) Tested: Verb Tense and Mood, Pronoun Use
Clues to the correct answer occur in the portion of the sentence that follows the underlined portion. We find that the noun must match a plural pronoun ("they"), and should maintain the present tense established in the previous sentence ("tends"). (D) meets these requirements. (B) is not correct because in a conditional sentence formed with "if," a condition in the past tense (ie. "stayed"), should have a consequence using "would" or "could" (ie. "would begin").

44) ▶ A
Concept(s) Tested: Passage Development
The topic sentence that begins the paragraph prescribes "communication" as the solution to culture shock. The sentence following the number 44 explains *how* learning the language eases culture shock. Thus, (A) is correct because the additional sentence introducing the concept of learning the host country's language would serve as an excellent transition between the general idea of communication and the more specific idea of gaining "a window" into the culture around them.

SAT Practice Test 5: Answers & Explanations

Math Test

No Calculator Portion

1. A	7. D	13. D	19. 2
2. B	8. B	14. D	20. 2
3. B	9. A	15. D	
4. A	10. C	16. 66	
5. D	11. B	17. 2	
6. A	12. D	18. 4	

Calculator Portion

1. C	7. C	13. D	19. D	25. C	31. 5	36. 1
2. C	8. B	14. A	20. C	26. D	32. 21	37. 6
3. D	9. D	15. B	21. B	27. D	33. 6	38. 1
4. B	10. C	16. D	22. C	28. B	34. 6	
5. C	11. B	17. D	23. A	29. A	35. 16	
6. D	12. D	18. C	24. A	30. C		

No Calculator Portion

1) A
Concept(s) Tested: Algebra
Adding both equations, $-5 < m < 10$ and $2 < n < 4$, results in $-5 + 2 < m + n < 10 + 4$, that is, $-3 < m + n < 14$.

2) B
Concept(s) Tested: Algebra
$f(3) = \dfrac{\sqrt{3 \times 3}}{b} = 3 \rightarrow b = 1$

3) B
Concept(s) Tested: Problem Solving, Algebra
Let h be the number of hours it takes to put c caps on b bottles. Thus:

$h = \dfrac{m}{60} \times \dfrac{b}{c} = \dfrac{mb}{60c}$

In the formula above $\dfrac{m}{60}$ describes the conversion of minutes to hours. The ratio $\dfrac{b}{c}$ is correct because the question tells us that the ratio of $b:c$ is 1:1, so (B) is correct.

4) A
Concept(s) Tested: Problem Solving, Algebra
Start by isolating the x-variable from the second equation and substituting this value into the first equation:

$x + 6y = 22 \rightarrow x = 22 - 6y$
$5(22 - 6y) + 4y = 32 \rightarrow 110 - 30y + 4y = 32 \rightarrow$
$-26y = -78 \rightarrow y = 3$

Plugging the value of y into either equation to find that $x = 4$

5) D
Concept(s) Tested: Functions and Graphs
$\dfrac{x^2}{x-4} = \dfrac{16}{x-4} \rightarrow x^2 = 16$, x cannot be 4 since it would result in a denominator of 0, so $x = -4$.

6) A
Concept(s) Tested: Functions and Graphs
The graph of any equation intersects the y-axis at $x = 0$. Substitute x for 0 in the equation. It results in $y = 3$. Therefore, (0, 3) is the intersection point between the graph and y-axis.

7) D
Concept(s) Tested: Algebra
$(5x + 4)(7x + 1)$
$= 35x^2 + 5x + 28x + 4$
$= 35x^2 + 33x + 4$

8) B
Concept(s) Tested: Algebra, Number Rules

$x + \sqrt{x - 4} = 4$

$(\sqrt{x - 4})^2 = (4 - x)^2$

$x - 4 = x^2 - 8x + 16$

$x^2 - 9x + 20 = 0$

$(x - 4)(x - 5) = 0$

$x = 4$ or 5. Plugging these values into the original equation reveals that only $x = 4$ satisfies the equation.

9) A
Concept(s) Tested: Algebra
Adding both equations $x^2 + y^2 = 25$ and $x^2 - y^2 = 7$ results in $x^2 = 16$ and $y^2 = 9$. Therefore, $y = 3$.

TEST 5: Answers & Explanations | 471

10) ▶ C
Concept(s) Tested: Functions and Graphs
Substituting $y = 2$ to the equation $y = 2x + 5$ results in $x = -\frac{3}{2}$. Therefore, the lines intersect at exactly one point.

11) ▶ B
Concept(s) Tested: Functions and Graphs, Algebra

$$\begin{array}{r} 2(3x - y + 5 = 0) \\ -) \; 3(2x + 3y - 4 = 0) \\ \hline -11y + 22 = 0 \\ \rightarrow y = 2 \end{array}$$

Substitute $y = 2$ to the equations. It results in $x = -1$. Therefore, $x = -1$, $y = 2$ is the solution.

12) ▶ D
Concept(s) Tested: Measures of Center and Spread
The median and mean do not increase if the added number is the smallest. Note that the added value is a new one, so the mode is the same.

13) ▶ D
Concept(s) Tested: Geometry
Let x be the length of AE and $x - 4$ be the length of ED. $\triangle CDE$ and $\triangle BAE$ are similar, so $\frac{3}{9} = \frac{x}{4-x}$.
Cross-multiply: $4 - x = 3x \rightarrow x = 1$.
To find the area of $\triangle AEC$, subtract the area of $\triangle EDC$ from $\triangle ADC$: $\frac{4 \times 9}{2} - \frac{3 \times 9}{2} = 4.5$

14) ▶ D
Concept(s) Tested: Functions and Graphs
Take the given equation and manipulate it to show the vertex form of the parabola.
$y = -x^2 + 4x + 5 \rightarrow -(x^2 - 4x + 4) + 4 + 5 \rightarrow$
$-(x - 2)^2 + 9 = y$
Given what we know about the vertex form, we now see that the parabola has a vertex at point (2, 9), so its line of symmetry is $x = 2$. From the line of symmetry, we can reflect our y-intercept (0, 5) from 2 units to the left of $x = 2$, to 2 units to the right of $x = 2 \rightarrow (4, 5)$.

15) ▶ D
Concept(s) Tested: Geometry, Problem Solving

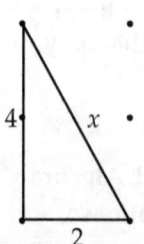

If the length of the longest vertical line segment equals 4, the length of the longest horizontal line segment should equal 2. If both were 4, the line would also pass through the center point. Therefore, based on the Pythagorean Theorem the length of the longest line segment equals $\sqrt{4^2 + 2^2} = \sqrt{20}$.

16) ▶ 66
Concept(s) Tested: Algebra
Adding both equations $6j - 5k = 11$ and $5j - 6k = -22$ results in $11j - 11k = -11$.
Therefore, $k = j + 1$.
Substituting this equation to the first equation, $6j - 5k$, results in $6j - 5(j + 1) = j - 5 = 11$.
Therefore, $j = 16$ and $k = j + 1$ results in $k = 17$ and It follows that $2j + 2k = 66$.

17) ▶ 2
Concept(s) Tested: Geometry

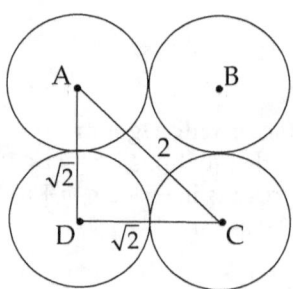

The length of AD equals $\sqrt{2}$ and the length of DC equals $\sqrt{2}$. By the Pythagorean theorem, the distance AC equals $\sqrt{2+2} = 2$.

18) ▶ 4
Concept(s) Tested: Algebra
Multiplying the three equations
$ab = \frac{1}{2}$, $bc = 4$, $ac = 8$ results in $(abc)^2 = 16$.
Therefore, $abc = 4$ because $abc > 0$.

19) ▶ 2
Concept(s) Tested: Algebra
Substituting $x = y + 5$ to the first equation
$x^2 - y^2 = 45$ results in $(y + 5)^2 - y^2 = 45 \rightarrow$
$y^2 + 5y + 5y + 25 - y^2 = 10y + 25 = 45$
$\rightarrow 10y = 20 \rightarrow y = 2$

20) ▶ 2
Concept(s) Tested: Algebra
From the information provided, we can conclude that $a = 16$, so $16 = x^2 + 4x + 4 \rightarrow$
$0 = x^2 + 4x - 12 \rightarrow 0 = (x - 2)(x + 6)$. Thus, $x = 2, -6$; x is positive, so x must equal 2.

Calculator Portion

1) **C**
   Concept(s) Tested: Problem Solving, Functions and Graphs
   The rent cost per video implies that the cost function has a slope 2.5. The cost to join the video club implies a y-axis intercept of 25.

2) **C**
   Concept(s) Tested: Algebra
   $3(2x + 5) - 4(x - 2) = 3(2x + 2) + 1$
   $2x + 23 = 6x + 7$
   $4x = 16.$
   $x = 4.$

3) **D**
   Concept(s) Tested: Functions and Graphs
   Note that each term in the sequence is 6 greater than the previous term.
   If a_n is the nth arithmetic sequence, then,
   $a_n = 6(n - 1) + 4$ for the positive integer n.
   Therefore, $a_{50} = 6(50 - 1) + 4 = 298$.

4) **B**
   Concept(s) Tested: Problem Solving, Functions and Graphs
   Company A charges $0.60 per foot of line painted, so $0.60x$ will be charged for painting x feet of line.

5) **C**
   Concept(s) Tested: Problem Solving, Functions and Graphs
   Company B charges a base price of $120, so (A) and (D) are not solutions. Note that the charging cost is linear, but graph (B) is not linear. Graph (C) represents the relation correctly. Therefore, (C) is the correct answer.

6) **D**
   Concept(s) Tested: Ratios and Percentages, Problem Solving
   $49,000 × (1 - 0.2) = $39,200

7) **C**
   Concept(s) Tested: Number Rules, Algebra
   $(5 + 6i)(3 - 2i) = 15 + (-10 + 18)i - 12i^2$
   $= 15 + 8i + 12 = 27 + 8i$

8) **B**
   Concept(s) Tested: Data Analysis
   The snowfall decreased steadily from 1960 to 1964. Therefore, (B) is correct answer.

9) **D**
   Concept(s) Tested: Number Rules, Algebra
   $$\frac{\sqrt{3}+1}{\sqrt{3}-1} = \frac{(\sqrt{3}+1)(\sqrt{3}+1)}{(\sqrt{3}-1)(\sqrt{3}+1)} = \frac{3+2\sqrt{3}+1}{3-1}$$
   $$= 2 + \sqrt{3}$$

10) **C**
    Concept(s) Tested: Problem Solving, Algebra
    To buy as many pens as possible, Jason should purchase as many of the least expensive pen, in this case the yellow pens from the second store (6 for $1). However, he must also purchase at least one dollar's worth of red pens, which are 4 for $1). Thus, if he spends the minimum of one dollar on 4 red pens, it leaves $9 for yellow pens from the second store:
    6 yellow pens × $9 = 54 yellow pens
    Thus, 54 yellow pens + 4 red pens costs $10, making (C) the correct choice.

11) **B**
    Concept(s) Tested: Number Rules
    $3^{x^2} = 9^8$
    $3^{x^2} = (3^2)^8$
    Because the bases are the same, we can solve for the exponents:
    $x^2 = 16$
    $x = -4, 4$

12) **D**
    Concept(s) Tested: Functions and Graphs
    $f(x) = g(x)$ implies $ax^2 = bx^4$. If $x = 0$, it always holds. Otherwise, $x^2 = \frac{a}{b} \rightarrow x = \pm\sqrt{\frac{a}{b}}$.
    Therefore, $f(x) = g(x)$ for a total of 3 values of x.

13) **D**
    Concept(s) Tested: Problem Solving, Algebra
    Let x, y, and z be the number of $1, $2, and $3 bills, respectively. Then $y = x + 11$, $z = x - 18$, and $x + y + z = 101$. Using these equations,
    $x + y + z = x + (x + 11) + (x - 18) = 3x - 7 = 101$.
    Therefore, $x = 36$.

14) **A**
    Concept(s) Tested: Problem Solving, Unit Conversion
    First, calculate the energy contained
    $770,000 \, l \times \frac{37.4 \text{ MJ}}{l} = 28,798,000$ MJ in the jet fuel:
    $1,200,000 \, l \times \frac{8.5 \text{ MJ}}{l} = 10,200,000$ MJ of kerosene
    and of hydrogen. Thus, Apollo 11 used 38,998,000 MJ of energy. Convert this to kcals:
    $38,998,000 \text{ MJ} \times \frac{1 kcal}{4184 J} \times \frac{10^6 J}{MJ} = 9,320,745,698 \, Kcal$
    Next, convert to grams of sugar:

TEST 5: Answers & Explanations | 473

$9{,}320{,}745{,}698 \text{ kcal} \times \dfrac{1 \text{ g sugar}}{4 \text{ kcal}} = 2{,}330{,}186{,}424 \text{ g sugar}$

Finally, convert to cups of sugar:

$2{,}330{,}186{,}424 \text{ g sugar} \times \dfrac{1 \text{ cup sugar}}{200 \text{ g sugar}} = 11{,}650{,}932$

Thus, it requires 11.7 million cups of sugar to travel to the moon.

15) ▶ B
Concept(s) Tested: Problem Solving
Let x, y, and z be the number of students that has tried one kind of candy bar, two kinds of candy bars, and three kinds of candy bars, respectively. Note that $x + y + z = 20$, $z = 3$, and $y = 5$. Therefore, $x = 12$.

16) ▶ D
Concept(s) Tested: Functions and Graphs
Note that $f(8, 3) = \dfrac{8}{4} - 3 = -1$.

(A) $f(12, 2) = 1$
(B) $f(16, 6) = -2$
(C) $f(2, 1) = -1.5$
(D) $f(-12, -2) = -1$

Therefore, (D) is the same with $f(8, 3)$.

17) ▶ D
Concept(s) Tested: Algebra
$2(x - 5)(x + 3) = -28 \rightarrow 2(x^2 - 2x - 15) = -28$.
Therefore, $2x^2 - 4x - 2 = 0$. Using the root formula, we get the following roots:

$x = \dfrac{-(-4) \pm \sqrt{(-4)^2 - 4(2)(-2)}}{2 \times 2} = 1 \pm \sqrt{2}$

18) ▶ C
Concept(s) Tested: Problem Solving, Algebra
$n \, \Phi \, -2 = n^{-(-2)} - 3(-2) = 70 \rightarrow n^2 = 64 \rightarrow n = \pm 8$

19) ▶ D
Concept(s) Tested: Data Analysis
Because the points of the graph are scattered with no discernable pattern, we can conclude that there is no relation between reading test scores and the number of fire drills.

20) ▶ C
Concept(s) Tested: Data Analysis
$\$35 \times 98{,}000 - \$55 \times 52{,}500 = \$542{,}500$

21) ▶ B
Concept(s) Tested: Data Analysis, Functions and Graphs
Note that the projected number of games sold decreases as the price of game X increases. Therefore, they are inversely proportional.

22) ▶ C
Concept(s) Tested: Problem Solving, Ratios and Percentages
Note that only 3 of the 20 cards are baseball cards. Therefore, the probability that it will be a baseball card equals 0.15

23) ▶ A
Concept(s) Tested: Geometry
$-\dfrac{5\pi}{12} \times \dfrac{180}{\pi} = -75°$

24) ▶ A
Concept(s) Tested: Number Rules

I. $(xy^2)^3 = x^3 y^6$
II. $\sqrt{-x^9} = -x^{\frac{9}{2}} \neq x^{-3}$
III. $(x^3 x^2)^2 = (x^5)^2 = x^{10} \neq x^{12}$

Therefore, only statement (I) is correct.

25) ▶ C
Concept(s) Tested: Ratios and Percentages, Problem Solving
The improvement ratio of Jade equals
$\dfrac{13-11}{13} = 15.4\%$, and that of David equals
$\dfrac{9-8}{9} = 11.1\%$. Therefore, (C) is the correct answer.

26) ▶ D
Concept(s) Tested: Functions and Graphs
Note that the minimum value of $f(x)$ equals
$f(3) = -\dfrac{2}{3}(3) + 11 = 9$. $f(x)$ increases as x increases for $x \geq 3$ and $f(x)$ increases as x decreases for $x \leq 3$. Therefore, the range of $f(x)$ is $y \geq 9$.

27) ▶ D
Concept(s) Tested: Ratios and Percentages, Data Analysis
Among 12 times, Emily was late 5 times. Therefore, the probability that Emily was late when she used route A equals $\dfrac{5}{12}$.

28) ▶ B
Concept(s) Tested: Functions and Graphs, Algebra
Note that when two lines are perpendicular, the product of their slopes is -1. Therefore, $(n + 2)(n - 4) = -1$. It results in $n^2 - 2n - 7 = 0$. By using the root equation, $n = 1 \pm 2\sqrt{2}$. Therefore, (B) $n = 1 + 2\sqrt{2} = 3.83$

29) ▶ A
Concept(s) Tested: Functions and Graphs
Note that x is shifted to the right-hand side. When $x = 35$, y is located at about 15 and when

$x = 45$, y is located at about 50. Therefore, the graph of the function is fit with the equation $y = 0.1(x - 23)^2 + 0.8$.

30) ▶ C
Concept(s) Tested: Functions and Graphs, Problem Solving
When the source is an infinite plane, $q = 0$. Therefore, PE = $-bx$, $b > 0$ implies that PE decreases linearly because the constant of proportionality between PE and x is negative.

31) ▶ 5
Concept(s) Tested: Problem Solving
Note that the elapsed time for A to cover 50 miles is $\dfrac{50 \text{ miles}}{100 \text{ miles per hour}} = \dfrac{1}{2}$ hour and the elapsed time for B to cover 50 miles is $\dfrac{50 \text{ miles}}{120 \text{ miles per hour}} = \dfrac{5}{12}$ hour. Therefore, the time difference between A and B equals $\dfrac{1}{2} - \dfrac{5}{12} = \dfrac{1}{12}$ hour = 5 minutes.

32) ▶ 21
Concept(s) Tested: Problem Solving
Let x be the total number of shots. By the end of the game, the proportion of hits to the total shots is $\dfrac{5}{2+5}$. Then $\dfrac{5x}{7}$ is the number of hits and $\dfrac{2x}{7}$ is the number of misses. Therefore, the following ratio should hold: $\dfrac{5x}{7} : \dfrac{2x}{7} - 3 = 5 : 1$.
Therefore, $\dfrac{5x}{7} = \dfrac{10x}{7} - 15 \rightarrow \dfrac{5x}{7} = 15 \rightarrow x = 21$.

33) ▶ 6
Concept(s) Tested: Problem Solving
Let x, y, and z be the ages of Andy, Maddie and Jack, respectively. Then $x = 2y$, $y = z + 4$. Therefore, $x + y + z = (2y) + y + (y - 4) = 4y - 4$. Note that $4y - 4 < 24$.
Therefore, it follows that $4y < 28 \rightarrow y < 7 \rightarrow y = 6$.

34) ▶ 6
Concept(s) Tested: Geometry, Problem Solving

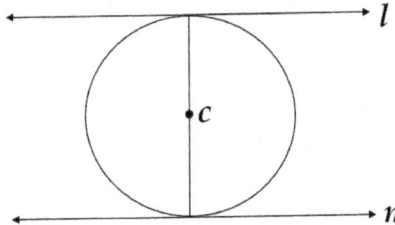

Note that the lines l and m are parallel because they never meet; both are tangent to the circle. This tells us that the distance between the two lines is the circle's diameter. Let r be the radius of the circle, then $\pi r^2 = 9\pi \rightarrow r = 3$. Therefore, the shortest distance between the two lines is $2r = 6$.

35) ▶ 16
Concept(s) Tested: Algebra, Problem Solving
$h(t) = -16t^2 + 32t$
$= -16(t^2 - 2t + 1 - 1)$
$= -16(t - 1)^2 + 16$
Note that in step 2 of the solution above, we completed the square by additon (+1 -1) to the equation. This does not change the overall equivalency of the equation, but it does allow us to facor the information inside the parentheses.

From this equation, the maximum height the projectile reaches equals 16 when $t = 1$.

36) ▶ 1
Concept(s) Tested: Geometry, Problem Solving
We are told that x is the angle in radians. Recall that the radius times the angle in radians equals the length of the arc.
Note that $r = 12$, and $6 < \overset{\frown}{PQ} < 18$. Therefore:
$6 < 12x < 18 \rightarrow 0.5 < x < 1.5$. Note that x is an integer. Therefore, $x = 1$.

37) ▶ 6
Concept(s) Tested: Functions and Graphs, Problem Solving
We are told that vertices A and B exist above or on the line $y = 1$. Therefore, $10 - x^2 \geq 1 \rightarrow -3 \leq x \leq 3$. Therefore, the interval length of the domain is 6.

38) ▶ 1
Concept(s) Tested: Functions and Graphs
Let P be the perimeter of the rectangle ABCD. Note that the length of CD is $2|x|$ and the length of AD is y.
Therefore, $P = 2y + 4|x| = 2(10 - x^2) + 4|x|$. This value is symmetric with respect to the y-axis. It is enough to find the maximum on $x \geq 0$. Therefore, it has the maximum value 22 when $x = 1$ as follows.
$P = 2(10 - x^2) + 4x \quad (0 \leq x \leq 3)$
$= -2x^2 + 4x + 20 \quad (0 \leq x \leq 3)$
$= -2(x - 1)^2 + 22 \quad (0 \leq x \leq 3)$

SAT Practice Test 5: Answers & Explanations

Sample Essay Response

Throughout his essay, Konrad Graf argues that the mission to colonize Mars needs to emphasize solutions to the reduced gravity on the red planet. To support this argument, Graf relies heavily on scientific facts and evidence from current space research. He appeals to the reader's emotion by focusing on data from mouse reproductive studies in space. Finally, Graf uses reasoning and logic to draw conclusions about the effects of low gravity (which have not been studied) from limited research conducted in zero gravity.

Early on, Graf emphasizes scientific facts that suggest long term habitation at zero gravity contributes to a number of health problems. He provides several examples of problems faced by astronauts, including muscle atrophy, decreased bone density, and circulatory disease. He emphasizes the limited usefulness of astronautical exercise routines in alleviating these symptoms. This strategy improves the effectiveness of Graf's argument by showing scientific support for his ideas.

Graf also highlights the reproductive consequences of life in space. Again, he uses scientific data to draw a conclusion about the health risks of colonizing Mars. Further, he uses the data to appeal to audience's emotions by focusing specifically on reproductive health and the potential consequences to a developing child or embryo. By questioning the reproductive capacity of a Martian colonization, Graf forces the audience to strongly consider the risks of leaving Earth.

While these strategies are effective for building his argument, the foundation of Graf's claim rests on logic: he extrapolates the effects of zero gravity to explain the consequences of low gravity on human life. Graf even admits that no research has been conducted at Mars gravity, and he emphasizes that scientists don't currently know what problems, if any, Martian colonists will face. This actually strengthens the overall argument by pointing out the need for research in a poorly studied subject in order to avoid the possible health risks addressed throughout.

Konrad Graf's argument is well structured and relies on scientific reasoning, appeals to emotion, and logical reasoning. The use of these strategies, as well as the author's disclosure of the limitation of his own logic, help support his claim. Indeed, Graf makes us fearful of the unknown and uses this fear to reiterate the need for caution and additional research.

Sample Response Score: 4/3/4

Reading: 4

The student demonstrates a thorough understanding of Graf's argument and the stylistic and rhetorical features he uses to make this argument. Although the student fails to include any quotations, his or her use of paraphrase and summary is excellent. Moreover, the essay does not indicate that the student misunderstood any feature of Graf's argument.

Analysis: 3

The student crafts a thorough and largely sound analysis of the author's argument. The student's breakdown of Graft's use of data and logic in paragraphs 2 and 3 is exceptional, while the argument about logic is compelling but not as well-substantiated as the student's other analyses.

Writing: 4

The student's essay is clear, comprehensive, and focused. The central claim in paragraph 1 succinctly outlines the student's analysis, and each body paragraph maintains a tight focus on one stylistic element. The conclusion restates and substantiates these claims, and the essay as a whole uses varied word choice and sentence structures to convey each idea.

SAT Practice Test 6: Answers & Explanations

Reading Test

1. B	6. C	11. D	16. A	21. C	26. B	31. C	36. D	41. C	46. A	51. B
2. C	7. C	12. A	17. B	22. D	27. D	32. B	37. D	42. D	47. A	52. A
3. D	8. A	13. D	18. A	23. D	28. D	33. A	38. B	43. C	48. C	
4. B	9. A	14. A	19. B	24. A	29. A	34. B	39. A	44. B	49. C	
5. D	10. D	15. B	20. A	25. C	30. B	35. A	40. D	45. C	50. D	

1) ▶ B
Concept(s) Tested: Purpose
Choice (B) is correct; the narrator "describes the hardships" experienced by himself and others since they ran out of "fresh provisions" (lines 6 – 7). Choice (A) is incorrect because, although the ship is described throughout the passage, these descriptions do not greatly contribute to the passage's primary purpose. Choice (C) is incorrect because, although the narrator does imply that the ship's captain is indifferent to their suffering (lines 47 – 49), the passage mostly describes the suffering itself. Choice (D) is incorrect because there is no indication that the narrator loves—or even likes—sailing.

2) ▶ C
Concept(s) Tested: Words in Context
Choice (C) is correct because a "billow" can refer to a mass of something pushed out by wind, which is similar in meaning to a "swell" of sea water. Choices (A) and (B) are incorrect because it is unclear how "gases" or "clouds" would toss a ship. Choice (D) is incorrect because the passage does not imply that the narrator is in the midst of a storm, so this choice lacks textual support.

3) ▶ D
Concept(s) Tested: Attitude and Tone
In lines 15 – 17, the narrator describes grass as "refreshing" and soil as "fragrant," so clearly the negative tone of choices (B) and (C) does not fit. The reader can infer from the context that the narrator is not able to enjoy grass or soil out at sea, making choice (A) illogical. Therefore (D), "wistful," best describes his attitude.

4) ▶ B
Concept(s) Tested: Purpose
In line 1, the narrator addresses himself to the "reader," so the rhetorical questions in lines 17 – 18 are meant to help the reader visualize the bleak surroundings and understand his distress and "desperation." Therefore, choice (B) is correct. Choice (A) is incorrect because there is no indication that the narrator is addressing anyone other than the reader in these lines. Choice (C) is incorrect because lines 17 – 18 contain a rhetorical question, not a conundrum. Choice (D) is incorrect; although the narrator does go on to describe the green paint on the inside of the ship in unflattering terms, that information does not explain the purpose of the rhetorical questions.

5) ▶ D
Concept(s) Tested: Attitude and Tone
The narrator fully understands and describes the reasons that the rooster is "moping," including bad food and lost companions; therefore, the narrator's attitude can be described as "sympathetic," and (D) is the correct choice. Choices (A) and (C) are incorrect because the narrator does not voice negative feelings or apathy toward the rooster. Choice (B) is incorrect because, although the narrator says that he wishes Pedro's "throat cut this very moment," he still sympathizes with the bird's plight and inevitable death.

6) ▶ C
Concept(s) Tested: Citation
The choice that most closely supports the claim that the narrator is "sympathetic" to the rooster is (C), where the narrator describes the rooster as "luckless" and those who wish him to be eaten as "cruel." Choice (B), which explains that Pedro will be eaten by the captain, is incorrect because it is a more neutral and less clearly sympathetic statement.

7) ▶ C
Concept(s) Tested: Summary
Choice (C) is correct because it provides an accurate summary of lines 47 – 49 ("They say...fresh meat"). Choice (A) is incorrect; although Jack says that "none of us can steer...[the ship] now" (lines 62 – 74), he is referring to the ship's seeming insistence on steering towards shore, which does not precisely support (A). Choice (B) is incorrect because there is no indication that the ship's crew is lost. Choice (D) is incorrect; the narrator indicates that they are "cruising after the sperm whale" (lines 2 – 3), but he does not imply that this is preventing them from going ashore.

8) ▶ A
Concept(s) Tested: Inference
Choice (A) is correct because in lines 63 – 71, Jack Lewis tells the captain that he cannot steer the ship (the "old lady") because "she" wants to go toward land, or in other words, that "she" can steer to wherever "she" wants to go. The other choices are incorrect because there is no textual support for them.

9) ▶ A
Concept(s) Tested: Words in Context
Choice (A) is correct; in lines 75 – 76, the narrator makes a sympathetic remark regarding the ship's appearance; thus, we can infer that the word "deplorable" here means that the ship's care has been deplorable, and she is "wretched" in the sense of being pitiable. The other choices are incorrect because they imply a moral failure or deficiency, and there is no indication in the passage that the narrator wishes to imply that the ship has morals or ethics.

10) ▶ D
Concept(s) Tested: Citation, Summary
Choice (D) is correct because in lines 56 – 57, the narrator

summarizes the feeling he expresses throughout the passage, that he wants to be on land. The other choices describe details and not an overall outlook.

11) ▶ D
Concept(s) Tested: Inference
The correct choice is (D). Franklin's long sentence explains that powerful people need trustworthy people ("honest instruments") to manage their businesses, but such trustworthy people are rare. Therefore, he predicts that employers will rely on and promote virtuous employees, leading to financial success. Choice (A) is incorrect because Franklin indicates that those who possess "probity and integrity" *are* virtuous. Choice (B) is incorrect because Franklin does not mention age requirements in paragraph 1. Choice (C) is incorrect because Franklin claims that "merchants, nobility, and princes" require virtuous employees, not that they are themselves virtuous.

12) ▶ A
Concept(s) Tested: Purpose
In paragraph 2 (lines 15 – 26), Franklin describes some helpful criticism he received about his arrogant manner, and how he decided to try to be humble. Thus, his purpose is reflected in choice (A) because he explains how he concluded that humility should be one of his personal goals. Choice (B) is incorrect because there is no indication that Franklin's views in paragraph 2 are "controversial." Choice (C) is incorrect because paragraph 2 reveals that Franklin respects the opinion of his "Quaker friend" (line 16). Choice (D) is incorrect because paragraph 2 introduces an obstacle (Franklin's arrogance), but the paragraph does not explain how Franklin overcame the obstacle.

13) ▶ D
Concept(s) Tested: Words in Context
Franklin says that he decided not to use words that "*imported* a fixed opinion," in the sense of words that "carried" the claim of certainty. Closest in meaning would be to say that he avoided using words "that *expressed* a fixed opinion," as provided in choice (D). The other choices all imply a conscious effort on the part of the words, which does not make sense.

14) ▶ A
Concept(s) Tested: Inference
The question is limited to Franklin's implications in paragraph 3 (lines 27 – 54). In this section of the passage, Franklin describes how he appeared humble by changing his way of speaking when contradicting someone. Choice (A) reflects the paragraph's implication that one reveals humility mainly by one's manner of speaking. Choices (B) and (D) are unsupported by the text, and choice (C) is disproven by lines 61– 68, where he describes how effective his attempts at humility were in eliciting positive responses.

15) ▶ B
Concept(s) Tested: Summary
In lines 50 – 51, Franklin mentions that one benefit of speaking humbly is that "I had less mortification when I was found to be in the wrong." Choice (B) is correct because it is a paraphrase of that statement. Choices (A) and (C) are unsupported by the text, and choice (D) is not the answer because, while Franklin says that he gained influence in society, he does not claim that people thought he was always right.

16) ▶ A
Concept(s) Tested: Citation
Choice (A) is correct because the answer to the previous question is a paraphrase of lines 48 – 51. The other choices are incorrect because, although they remark on the benefits of humility, they do not provide direct textual support for the answer to the previous question (that his humble manner made it less embarrassing to be wrong).

17) ▶ B
Concept(s) Tested: Words in Context
In lines 55 – 57, Franklin is describing how at first, he found responding to others with humility difficult, but later it became easier. That context allows us to infer that "violence to natural inclination" indicates a struggle to change one's ways; in other words, a *difficulty*.

18) ▶ A
Concept(s) Tested: Summary
In lines 69 – 77, Franklin humbly admits that he has not become completely humble, which serves to cancel out choice (B). He says that thinking he had overcome all arrogance would be arrogant. Thus, he points out an impossible (and humorous) contradiction, and (A) is the answer.

19) ▶ B
Concept(s) Tested: Summary
Much of the passage describes the changes Franklin experienced once he started using respectful ways of disagreeing with people. In other words, Franklin finds that he can act with humility even if he does not actually feel humble, for the two are distinct, making choice (B) the best answer. Choice (A) is incorrect because Franklin claims that there is "no one of our natural passions so hard to subdue as *pride*" (lines 69 – 70), so pride is hard to suppress, not "the most harmful…quality." Choices (C) and (D) are incorrect because they lack any textual support.

20) ▶ A
Concept(s) Tested: Citation
Choice (A) is correct because, in lines 27 – 29, Franklin uses himself to demonstrate his belief that one can appear humble without being so. Choice (D) at first appears like a possible answer because it discusses the difficulty of overcoming pride, but this idea alone does not specifically support the answer to the previous question.

21) ▶ C
Concept(s) Tested: Purpose
Lines 1 – 26 of the passage describe a corporation's advertising claim that turned out to be misleading. The claim is not the focus of the rest of the passage, but rather serves as an *example* of an *issue*—the need for the public to have more knowledge of statistics. Therefore, choice (C) is correct.

22) ▶ D
Concept(s) Tested: Inference
The passage begins by describing an instance of abuse of data and then lists types of data that "permeate our lives" (line 28). Choice (D) correctly identifies the implication that statistics affect many people, who would *benefit* by understanding them. The other choices all contain inaccurate interpretations of the passage. Note that (B) is incorrect because, although the author claims that "numbers permeate our lives," she does not claim that there is too much data for people to process.

23) ▶ D
Concept(s) Tested: Citation
Choice (D) is the answer because lines 75 – 77 state that improving the public's grasp of statistics ("incorporating more knowledge of statistics") helps

to "foster an educated citizenry," or in other words, an understanding of statistics "benefits many people."

24) ➤ A
Concept(s) Tested: Purpose
Lines 27 – 39 begin by referring to the toothpaste claim, and go on to describe how "numbers permeate our lives." Thus, the paragraph's purpose must be to broaden the discussion, as stated in choice (A). Choice (B) is incorrect because while the passage overall clearly assumes opposition to misleading or deceptive statistics, paragraph 4 does not directly *condemn* them. Choices (C) and (D) are incorrect because they are completely unsupported by the text.

25) ➤ C
Concept(s) Tested: Words in Context
Choice (C) is correct because line 55 – 58 make use of the term "status" in a literal sense, as a *position* from which one can ascend (or descend). Although the other choices are effective synonyms for "status," they are incorrect because they do not fit the context of the sentence.

26) ➤ B
Concept(s) Tested: Words in Context
Choice (B) is correct because the context of lines 69 – 71 indicates that figures "touted" by political candidates can also be "slammed," metaphorically hit and pushed down. The implication is one of opposites. Thus, to "tout" a statistic must mean to *extol* it (hold it up and praise it), the opposite of slamming.

27) ➤ D
Concept(s) Tested: Purpose
Choice (D) is correct. The quotation in lines 50 – 53 paraphrases the sentence that precedes it: the central argument of the passage, that knowledge of statistics helps people evaluate information. A direct quote from an authoritative source thus repeats and therefore "strengthens the passage's main argument."

28) ➤ D
Concept(s) Tested: Summary
The author describes the public as already "bombarded" (line 30) with numerical information, and suggests that young people need to study statistics to prepare for the future, which implies that the numerical data will increase. In the conclusion (line 75 – 79), the author directly states that society is "increasingly data-deluged." Thus, the answer is choice (D).

29) ➤ A
Concept(s) Tested: Graph Synthesis
Choice (A) is correct; based on lines 54 – 63, statistics, calculus, and precalculus are elective math courses, and according to the graph, approximately 5 percent of students completed statistics/probability in 2000, approximately 12 percent of students completed calculus in 2000, and under 30 percent completed precalculus in 2000. Thus, fewer than 50 percent of students completed any one of these courses in 2000. Choice (B) is incorrect because the graph shows completion rates, not failure rates. Choice (C) is incorrect because algebra, not calculus, has had the steadiest completion rate. Choice (D) is incorrect because the graph and the text do not indicate "expectations."

30) ➤ B
Concept(s) Tested: Graph Synthesis, Inference
Choice (B) is correct because the graph shows an increase in the proportion of people graduating from high school who had completed an elective math course such as statistics and calculus. Thus, we can infer that more high school students have been enrolling in elective math courses since 1990. Choice (C) is incorrect because of the word "always". Geometry was the most studied math course from 1990 – 2010, but the graph does not offer data outside this range.

31) ➤ C
Concept(s) Tested: Summary
While choices (A) and (B) are plausible, choice (C) most directly articulates Stanton's main argument in the passage: that women need to have equal opportunities. In lines 1 – 9, Stanton states that women must have opportunities to develop to their fullest potential.

32) ➤ B
Concept(s) Tested: Citation
The best textual support among the choices provided is (B), because it echoes the importance of the "complete development of every individual," in other words, equal opportunities to learn and develop to one's full potential.

33) ➤ A
Concept(s) Tested: Inference
In the passage, Stanton uses imagery of women needing to be self-sufficient, such as the analogy of knowing how to sail a ship in a storm (lines 22 – 27) as opposed to being sheltered from storms by men (lines 65 – 66). Therefore, we can infer that Stanton is mainly suggesting that men deprive women of opportunities to become self-sufficient, and choice (A) is correct. Choices (B), (C), and (D) lack textual support.

34) ➤ B
Concept(s) Tested: Words in context
Choice (B) is correct because in the context of lines 1 – 4, Stanton clearly means to use the term "forces" as in *capabilities* of mind and body, or in other words, *powers* of mind and body. The other choices do not make sense in the context of the sentence.

35) ➤ A
Concept(s) Tested: Purpose
Choice (A) is correct because each of the listed elements adds a domain that women influence or interact with (politics, religion, commerce), so we can infer that the list serves to "emphasize… women's involvement in society." Choices (B) and (C) are incorrect because the list states common spheres, not different roles for men and women in life. Choice (D) is incorrect because the list does not precisely compare men's and women's rights.

36) ➤ D
Concept(s) Tested: Words in Context
Choice (D) is correct because, in the context of lines 53 – 55, Stanton predicts defeat for a woman who has "no *resources* in herself"—a woman who is "uneducated" and "trained to dependence." Thus, she is referring to a woman who has no *capabilities*.

37) ➤ D
Concept(s) Tested: Summary
Lines 53 – 64 describe Stanton's argument that women who are "weak and ignorant" can wreck their own happiness, and that no one will stand by them when they do ("alone she bears her humiliation"). Thus, they are positioned for both failure and reproach, and choice (D) is correct.

38) ➤ B
Concept(s) Tested: Citation
The text that most closely supports the answer above is (B), because it points out the injustice in depriving a woman of knowledge and then rejecting her for her ignorant mistakes: "alone she bears the humiliation."

39) ➤ A
Concept(s) Tested: Inference

The clues to Stanton's outlook on life include her stance that women ultimately face all the "supreme moments of danger" that men do (lines 82 – 83). She also describes the "fierce storms of life" in lines 65 – 66. She thus implies that life is not easy for anyone, making choice (A) correct. Stanton may agree with statements (B), (C), and (D), but based on the information in the passage, they do not represent her "overall outlook on life" as well as (A) does.

40) ➡ D
Concept(s) Tested: Purpose
Stanton's rhetorical question in lines 89 – 92 emphasizes her main point about individuality. The answer to the question about who could, and who would dare, assume responsibility for another "soul" is meant to be obvious ("no one"), so that it is meant to underscore the futility and injustice of thinking otherwise. The question is meant to be profound, and thus (D) is correct.

41) ➡ C
Concept(s) Tested: Words in Context
In the context of lines 1 – 3, the effects of a group of diseases are described as "debilitating." The effects include pain, weakness, and diarrhea. Thus, "debilitating" must describe effects that are so damaging that they prevent one from having a normal quality of life; they are *impairing*, and (C) is correct.

42) ➡ D
Concept(s) Tested: Purpose
Paragraph 2 describes the effects of STHs on the lives of one billion people. Without paragraph 2, readers of Passage 1 would not necessarily grasp the significance of treating the diseases. The best answer is (D) because the author likely included the paragraph to raise concern, or to "emphasize the need" for improving the treatments.

43) ➡ C
Concept(s) Tested: Summary
Choice (C) is correct because lines 10 – 12 describe the study as a "reanalysis of data from other published studies" about sanitation and STHs. Although the "Millennium Development Goals" and "Ziegelbauer" are referenced in the passage, they are not the sources of information for the study described in the passage, eliminating choices (A) and (D). Choice (B) is incorrect because the passage does not mention interviews with study subjects.

44) ➡ B
Concept(s) Tested: Inference
Choice (B) is correct because lines 35 – 41 state that integrated control involved "education of at-risk communities" and "strong healthcare systems," which can be paraphrased as "educational and public initiatives." All other choices are incorrect because their assumptions are too extreme—the passage does not imply that integrated control will completely eliminate or replace any existing diseases or treatments.

45) ➡ C
Concept(s) Tested: Citation
Choice (C) is correct because it provides an effective paraphrase for the answer to the previous question. All other choices are incorrect because, although they directly or indirectly mention integrated control, they do not explain any of its requirements

46) ➡ A
Concept(s) Tested: Summary
Choice (A) is correct because lines 76 – 79 describe Afghanistan as unique among the countries with the highest TB rates in the sense that it "has been utterly decimated by over four decades of war and migration." Thus, choice (A) is correct. Choices (B) and (C) are circumstances that are not described as being unique to Afghanistan. Choice (D) is unsupported by the passage and therefore incorrect.

47) ➡ A
Concept(s) Tested: Inference
Choice (A) is correct because lines 89 – 91 state that the "causative pathogen" of TB "can remain in an asymptomatic form for a long time," which implies that those who have TB "can be unaware that they are infected." All other choices are incorrect because they lack textual support, or misinterpret information from the paragraph.

48) ➡ C
Concept(s) Tested: Citation
Choice (C) is correct because it paraphrases the correct answer to the previous question. An "asymptomatic" disease is one that does not show symptoms, so people with a disease in its asymptomatic form would "be unaware that they are infected." All other choices are incorrect because they do not relate to the answer to the previous question.

49) ➡ C
Concept(s) Tested: Inference
In lines 92 – 99, the author of Passage 2 says that TB pathogens become resistant to drugs because patients are hard to reach and "treatment programs are quite ineffective." This implies that structural changes in the approach could result in more follow-through for patients and more complete care. Thus, choice (C) is correct.

50) ➡ D
Concept(s) Tested: Text synthesis
Passage 1 describes the need for preventing as well as treating STH infections; Passage 2 describes the challenges of treating TB in Afghanistan. Therefore, both passages discuss general methods for treating these diseases, and choice (D) is correct. Choice (A) is incorrect because, although the World Health Organization is mentioned in Passage 2, it is not a focus of the passage. Choice (B) is incorrect because the passages do not mention "newly discovered" diseases. Choice (C) is incorrect because neither passage specifically mentions "American" programs.

51) ➡ B
Concept(s) Tested: Text Synthesis
While both passages suggest changes, neither author appears to be an opponent of current programs, eliminating choice (A). Rather, they each address the need for specific changes in response to the diseases: for building sanitation facilities (Passage 1) and faster diagnosis and shorter treatment regimens (Passage 2). Thus, the answer is (B).

52) ➡ A
Concept(s) Tested: Text Synthesis
Choice (A) is correct; Passage 1 mentions that one consequence of repeatedly treating STH infections is that there is the "possible of reduced efficacy and development of resistance" (lines 28 – 29). Meanwhile Passage 2 says that the bacteria that causes TB can "easily develop resistance to drugs if they are not administered appropriately" (lines 92 – 94).

SAT Writing & Language Test 6 : Answers & Explanations

Writing & Language Test

1. D	5. D	9. A	13. A	17. D	21. A	25. A	29. C	33. D	37. D	41. C
2. C	6. B	10. C	14. D	18. D	22. A	26. A	30. C	34. D	38. A	42. D
3. B	7. B	11. A	15. B	19. A	23. B	27. D	31. D	35. C	39. B	43. B
4. A	8. A	12. A	16. B	20. D	24. C	28. A	32. B	36. A	40. B	44. A

1) ➡ D
Concept(s) Tested: Passage Development
The original sentence focuses on the range of communication that actors can achieve through tone of voice. Only (D) offers evidence because it offers an example of actors communicating largely through tone. (A) is incorrect because rather than add a fact or example to support the first half of the sentence, it would add only the inconclusive statement that researchers have studied the phenomenon. (B) and (C) also provide no evidentiary support; (B) mentions actions rather than tone, and (C) veers into another topic.

2) ➡ C
Concept(s) Tested: Passage Organization
Sentences [3] and [4] provide an example for the process introduced in sentence [2] and elaborated upon in [5]. It would be logical to move sentence [5] to a spot just after it is introduced and just before it is illustrated with an example. Thus, (C) is correct.

3) ➡ B
Concept(s) Tested: Transition Words and Phrases
The paragraph mainly provides some historical background for information in the preceding paragraph. Only (B) provides a logical transition because "In some cases" signals that what follows is descriptive and particular; the writer does not claim to provide all the history of theatrical nonsense languages. Choices (A) and (D) are idioms more suited to a narrative, story-like paragraph, while (C) would more likely signal a concession in an argument.

4) ➡ A
Concept(s) Tested: Logical Comparison
The word "than" in the sentence indicates a comparison. Choice (A) is correct because it is logical to compare a village's dialect to "the one spoken" in another village. The other choices result in illogical comparisons between a dialect and people or places.

5) ➡ D
Concept(s) Tested: In-Sentence Punctuation
The sentence includes a descriptive phrase to define the term "the powerful." If it were removed, the sentence would still make sense; thus, the phrase is "non-essential." As a result, the phrase needs to be set apart by commas, dashes, or parentheses. (D) is correct because it places parentheses around the whole interrupting phrase "such as kings and nobles." (A) is not the answer because it creates a run-on sentence that ignores a natural pause. (B) and (C) are incorrect because their parentheses surround only part of the phrase.

6) ➡ B
Concept(s) Tested: Passage Development
Choice (B) is correct because it develops and explains the reason that nonsense words "came in handy" for troubadours who wanted to satirize individuals: they could not be accused of actually saying anything. The other choices fail to develop the main idea.

7) ➡ B
Concept(s) Tested: Precise Diction
The paragraph describes Dario Fo, who enthusiastically embraced an old theater technique in his plays. (A) is incorrect because "publicize" does not fit: the paragraph does not indicate that Fo's purpose was to announce or advertise the technique. (B) is a more precise description, because by using the technique to create good plays, Fo also succeeded in getting people to like it; he *popularized* it.

8) ➡ A
Concept(s) Tested: Passage Development
The correct answer is (A) because the sentence describing Fo's productive career would help the reader understand his winning the Nobel Prize for Literature. Thus, (A) helps set up a context for the sentence about the prize.

9) ➡ A
Concept(s) Tested: In-Sentence Punctuation, Sentence Boundaries
In the sentence, "with" indicates an accompanying action. It is correct to say that Fo won the prize, *with* the committee citing the reasons. Therefore, (A) is the best choice. (B) is not the answer because the phrase in question cannot stand on its own as a sentence. (C) is incorrect because it omits the relationship between the main idea and the long noun phrase starting with "the Nobel committee." (D) is incorrect because it misidentifies that relationship as one of cause and effect.

10) ➡ C
Concept(s) Tested: Syntax, Pronoun Use
Choices (A), (B), and (D) add "viewers" to the sentence, which creates another possible referent for "their." The sentence could create slight confusion: is it saying that viewers can focus on the Minions' antics? Or can they focus on their own antics? (C) is correct because its meaning is clear.

11) ➡ A
Concept(s) Tested: Conventional Expressions
"Not only" must be paired with "but" in a sentence. Together, the words make up a standard correlative conjunction: "**Not only** *x*, **but** (also) *y*." Choice (A) correctly preserves the structure, while (B), (C), and (D) fail to do so.

12) ➡ A
Concept(s) Tested: Combining Sentences
There are two possible ways to join independent clauses. Writers can add a semicolon, or they can add a comma and a coordinating conjunction (for, and, nor, but, or, yet, so). In this case, (A) correctly offers the latter: a comma and the coordinating conjunction "so."

13) ➡ A
Concept(s) Tested: Logical Comparison
The writer wants to compare *the growth* of two types of plants. Instead of repeating "the growth," the writer can use a pronoun. The pronoun must be demonstrative, meaning that it points to something specific in the sentence; (A) accomplishes this with "that." (B) uses

TEST 6: Answers & Explanations | 481

the personal pronoun "it," which does not make sense when paired with "of." (C) can be ruled out because the abstract idea of "growth" is a singular noun, while "those" is plural. Choice (D) is incorrect because it would result in comparing *growth* to *normal tobacco*, which is illogical.

14) **D**
Concept(s) Tested: Passage Development
The passage describes an investigation into the effects of nicotine in plants. The sentence in question describes the culmination of the experiment, namely how insects reacted to non-nicotine plants. Thus, (D) is correct.

15) **B**
Concept(s) Tested: Precise Diction, Commonly Confused Words
Here the writer is describing the rate or frequency with which insects ate mutated plants. Thus (B) is correct: the plants had "a much higher incidence of predation." Choice (C) offers "incidents," which would not make sense because an "incident" is an event itself, not its rate of occurrence. Choices (A) and (D) do not make sense in the context.

16) **B**
Concept(s) Tested: Verb Tense
Choice (B) is correct because the present tense is used for general truths. The writer wants to express what the researchers are suggesting based on the evidence: that nicotine (generally) *slows* the growth of insects. Choices (A), (C), and (D) are incorrect because they would imply a limited the time span rather than a general fact.

17) **D**
Concept(s) Tested: Precise Diction
The writer is describing an experiment in which moth larvae choose between eating ordinary tobacco plants and mutant tobacco plants. Evidently the larvae preferred the mutant plants but also ate the ordinary ones. Thus, *they did not feel a strong* distaste for the ordinary plants; they were not *averse* to them, and (D) is correct. The other choices would not make sense in the sentence.

18) **D**
Concept(s) Tested: Verb Tense, Participial Phrases
Choice (D) is correct because "using" begins a participial phrase. It looks like an action, but it is a participle describing the subject of the sentence—the researchers. (A) is incorrect because it would create a clause that could stand on its own; joining it to the previous clause would require the existing comma plus a conjunction such as "and." Choice (B) uses the present progressive, which does not make sense for an action taking place in the past. (C) is incorrect because there is no subject to which the verb "used" can apply.

19) **A**
Concept(s) Tested: Transition Words and Phrases
The paragraph is describing what happened when researchers replicated their laboratory experiment in the field. The results were the same: "Again, the mutated plants" were the larvae's food of choice, *and also as in the lab*, the ordinary tobacco plants attracted fewer larvae. Choice (A), "furthermore," is correct because it is closest in meaning to *and also*.

20) **D**
Concept(s) Tested: Concision
The writer does not need to include the adjectives "native" (choice A) or "indigenous" (choice B) to the sentence, since these descriptions would be redundant with the phrase "in its natural environment." Choice (C), "domestic," as in *not foreign*, has no clear meaning in the context. Therefore, the best answer is to delete the adjective altogether, as in (D).

21) **A**
Concept(s) Tested: In-Sentence Punctuation
The underlined section uses the term "secondary metabolites" and is interrupted with the statement that nicotine is an example. The example is not essential to the sentence, so it is appropriate to frame "such as nicotine" by parentheses, commas, or dashes. However, (B) is not correct because a comma should follow the underlined section to separate the main sentence from "which" and the clause that follows. The clause adds more information to define secondary metabolites, but it does not distinguish them from others (as in "the ones that…"). It is not essential for understanding the meaning of the sentence, so it should be separated by a comma.

22) **A**
Concept(s) Tested: Possession
The "field data" in the sentence is in the possession of the "group of researchers" introduced in paragraph 2. Thus, the plural possessive form is called for, and choice (A) is correct.

23) **B**
Concept(s) Tested: Passage Development
The main contrast described in the paragraph is between hard work that was once done by hand and is now done by machines. (B) most effectively sets up the contrast by referring to the "physical skills and stamina" demanded by jobs in the past. The other choices are vague and thus less effective for introducing a contrast.

24) **C**
Concept(s) Tested: Parallel Structure
The underlined section should consist of a structure that is parallel to the preceding items in the list: "robots performing surgery, vehicles driving themselves." Only (C) follows the same pattern: subject + verb + ing + object.

25) **A**
Concept(s) Tested: Passage Development
The paragraphs's central point is that while people fear that "nearly all jobs will become obsolete," in some contexts consumers may reject automation in favor of face-to-face, *personal* interaction. Thus, the focus of the grocery-store example is that consumers rejected it as too *impersonal*, and (A) is correct. The other choices refer to issues not mentioned in the passage.

26) **A**
Concept(s) Tested: Transition Words and Phrases
Choice (A) is the best choice because it is the most concise. Moreover, it serves as an excellent transition to a new paragraph because it refers to the sentence in paragraph 2 about people fearing that jobs will become obsolete. Thus, it contributes to the focus and coherence of the passage.

27) **D**
Concept(s) Tested: In-Sentence Punctuation
Only choice (D) correctly defines what kind of "mechanical devices" the writer means: those that "could do the work of many people." The information is essential to understanding the sentence, and thus should not be separated by a comma as in (A), or a dash as in (B). (C) is incorrect because the word "and" would make "hand tools" the subject of the clause— as in, "hand tools … could replace the work of many people," which does not make sense.

28) **A**
Concept(s) Tested: Passage Development
Choice (A) is correct because the sentence would support the extended example in the paragraph. It adds a mid-point between a time when nearly 100 percent of the workforce labored on farms and today, when only 2 percent do so. It also provides data to support the preceding statement about horse-drawn steel plows and mechanical devices replacing some farm labor. Choices (B) and (C) incorrectly assume that the focus of the paragraph is on 19th century agriculture itself.

(D) is incorrect because the reason for mentioning the year 1870 is apparent; it was a time when agriculture employed 50 percent of the workforce.

29) ▶ C
Concept(s) Tested: Dangling Modifiers
Choice (C) is the answer because the writer must indicate *who* is "looking at all the evidence." Choices (A), (B), and (D) do not offer a subject. They leave "After looking at all the evidence" as a dangling modifier, one with nothing to modify. (C) provides the pronoun "one," as in "any person," and an appropriate verb, "can conclude." Thus, the sentence becomes logical with (C).

30) ▶ C
Concept(s) Tested: Possession, Commonly Confused Words
The sentence refers to people who assist with administrative work; typing "is only one of many specialized skills required" of them. Thus, the plural noun "assistants" is the correct answer, as provided by (C). (A) and (D) are incorrect because "assistance" and "assists" refer to *the act* of assisting, and it would not make sense to say that "skills were required of the act of assisting." (B) is incorrect because the noun is not possessive.

31) ▶ D
Concept(s) Tested: Concision, Syntax
The best answer is (D) because it is the clearest and most concise. The other choices contain redundancies by mentioning both agriculture and farms/farmers. In choice (B), the meaning of "agriculturally" is unclear.

32) ▶ B
Concept(s) Tested: Style and Tone
The tone of choice (B) is consistent with that of the formal and neutral tone of the passage. Choices (A) and (D) are somewhat colloquial and do not quite fit the style and tone of the passage. Choice (C) does not fit the tone either, as it sounds too "official" and formal.

33) ▶ D
Concept(s) Tested: Passage Organization
Paragraph 4 interrupts an extended example involving agriculture, so (A) is not the best choice. Paragraphs 1 and 2 introduce the topic of automation in the workplace more broadly, so (B) and (C) are also poor choices. The best choice is (D), placing paragraph 4 at the end of the passage, because it has a concluding statement based on "all the evidence." Like many concluding paragraphs, paragraph 4 also refers back to the introduction by pointing to an occupation that changed due to automation but did not disappear.

34) ▶ D
Concept(s) Tested: Verb Tense/Syntax
Only (D) expresses a sensible timeframe for the introductory sentence: some protocols *have shifted* before this moment, and as the second sentence describes, there is a "new routine." Choices (A) and (C) indicate that the protocols shift constantly, which is not supported by the rest of the paragraph or passage. Meanwhile, (B) is incorrect because it would turn the verb "shifted" into a description, "shifted protocols," depriving the sentence of a verb.

35) ▶ C
Concept(s) Tested: Noun Agreement
The underlined section must describe the plural noun "interrupters." (C) is correct because it contains a plural noun, so it is consistent. The only other choice that is plural is (B), but (B) includes an apostrophe, and there is no possessive meaning.

36) ▶ A
Concept(s) Tested: Combining Sentences
Choice (A) has the clearest syntax out of all the choices. The clause "The interrupter does not share information with law enforcement" explains the second clause beginning with "the patient," so a comma and the word "so" make sense. The structure of the other choices is awkward and creates some confusion about the relationship between the two ideas.

37) ▶ D
Concept(s) Tested: Parallel Structure
The underlined section is part of a list that includes restarting education and getting a job. The writer must maintain parallel structure, and the third item on the list should be structured as the first two, in this case as gerund + object. Choice (D) accomplishes this goal.

38) ▶ A
Concept(s) Tested: Precise Diction
Paragraph 1 introduces the topic of a "new routine" in some hospitals; in paragraph 3, the underlined portion describes the larger public health approach. Choice (A), "novel," echoes paragraph 1 and makes the most sense in a passage describing a change. Choice (B), "unfamiliar," would be a possible fit, but it is not quite as precise, because the approach may be already familiar to some people.

39) ▶ B
Concept(s) Tested: Passage Development
Contagion means the spreading of a disease or harmful influence through close contact. In this case, the best answer is (B) because it fits most closely with the focus on contagion: being in contact with violence results in acting violently. While (A), (C), and (D) may be true, they do not explain the concept.

40) ▶ B
Concept(s) Tested: Passage Development
The question specifically asks for a link to the preceding paragraph. That paragraph describes a possible "epidemiological response," the idea that violence can be treated as a contagious disease that is transmitted. Thus, (B) is the best choice because it refers to *epidemiology*, the study of the health of whole populations, especially transmittable diseases.

41) ▶ C
Concept(s) Tested: Passage Organization
Choice (C) is correct because the added sentence serves as an introduction to sentence [4]. It explains that CeaseFire tried to change the mindset of the entire community by, as described in sentence [4], holding vigils and protests. Sentence [5] elaborates on the reasoning behind the actions.

42) ▶ D
Concept(s) Tested: Dangling Modifier
Choice (D) is correct because it avoids confusing readers. Choices (A) and (C) create dangling modifiers; in other words, they sound as if it is the "hospitals and local governments" that are attracting notice, rather than the results of the program. Choice (B) is confusing because it offers the pronoun "they" before indicating who "they" are.

43) ▶ B
Concept(s) Tested: Pronoun Use, Verb Tense
Choice (B) is correct because the sentence indicates that the doctor founded one organization, which should be referred to with the singular pronoun "it." Moreover, the sentences that follow in the paragraph indicate that the programs are ongoing, which means that the answer should be in the present tense.

44) ▶ A
Concept(s) Tested: Passage Development
The passage illustrates and explains the proposition of Dr. Gary Slutkin, which is that violence is contagious in the community and that an epidemiological approach can be effective in reducing it. Only choice (A) restates this proposition. The other sentences may make sense, but the question specifically asks for a restatement of the proposition.

SAT Practice Test 6: Answers & Explanations
Math Test

 No-Calculator Portion

1. C	7. C	13. D	18. 2013
2. A	8. B	14. C	19. 27
3. D	9. B	15. B	20. 3
4. D	10. B	16. 45	
5. C	11. D	17. $\frac{1}{5}$ or 0.2	
6. C	12. D		

 Calculator Portion

1. B	7. D	13. B	19. D	25. D	31. $\frac{18}{5}$	36. 5
2. B	8. D	14. C	20. D	26. D		37. 4
3. B	9. D	15. D	21. B	27. D	32. 9	38. 20
4. B	10. C	16. C	22. B	28. D	33. 30	
5. B	11. C	17. B	23. B	29. B	34. 0.6	
6. A	12. C	18. B	24. A	30. C	35. 10	

No-Calculator Portion

1) ➤ C
Concept(s) Tested: Algebra
Multiply $100(x + 3)$ on both sides.
It results in $400 = 4 \times 100(x + 3) = 4(100x + 300)$
→ $400 = 400x + 1{,}200$ → $-800 = 400x$
Therefore, $x = -2$.

2) ➤ A
Concept(s) Tested: Problem Solving, Functions
$$c = 80W \times \frac{1\,KW}{1000\,W} \times \frac{2\,hours}{day} \times 200\,days \times \frac{\$0.18}{KWh}$$
$$= \frac{80}{1000} \times 400 \times 0.18$$

3) ➤ D
Concept(s) Tested: Problem Solving, Algebra
From $7 - 8(x - 2) = ax + 5$, it follows that $(a + 8)x = 18$. Therefore, both values $a = 7$ and $a = 8$ results in an equation with exactly one solution.

4) ➤ D
Concept(s) Tested: Functions and Graphs
Note that the multiplication of the equation $2x + 2y = 6$ by -7 is equal to the multiplication of the equation $-7x - 7y = -21$ by 2. That is, both equations are the same line.

5) ➤ C
Concept(s) Tested: Problem Solving, Ratios and Percentages
$(1 - 0.1)(1 - 0.15)D = 0.765D$

6) ➤ C
Concept(s) Tested: Algebra
Double the second equation, and then subtract it

from the first:
$4r + 3s = 7$
$-)\ 4r + 2s = 2$
$\qquad s = 5, r = -2$
$2(-2) + 2(5) = t - 4$ → $t = -4 + 10 + 4 = 10$

7) ➤ C
Concept(s) Tested: Geometry

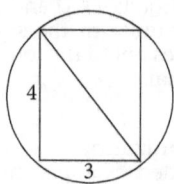

By the Pythagorean theorem, the length of the diagonal line is 5, which is the diameter of the circle. The radius is then 2.5. The circumference is $2\pi r$, or 5π.

8) ➤ B
Concept(s) Tested: Problem Solving
Steven can prepare 4 drinks per minute, Ashley can prepare 2 drinks per minute, and Ethan can prepare $\frac{4}{3}$ drinks per minute. So they can prepare $4 + 2 + \frac{4}{3} = \frac{22}{3}$ drinks per minute together. Therefore, they can prepare 20 drinks in the following minutes: $20 \times \frac{3}{22}$, that is, 2 minutes and 44 seconds.

9) ➤ B
Concept(s) Tested: Problem Solving, Algebra
Let x be the number of members playing both badminton and tennis. Then, the total number of members $17 + 19 - x + 2 = 30$. Therefore, $x = 8$.

10) ➤ B
Concept(s) Tested: Problem Solving, Algebra
Let x be the number of people who got on at the first stop. At each stop, half of the remaining

passengers depart. Thus, $\frac{x}{2^{n-1}}$ people get off at the nth stop. Therefore, $\frac{x}{2^{7-1}} = 1 \rightarrow x = 64$.

11) ➤ D
Concept(s) Tested: Functions and Graphs
Note that the slope is $\frac{3}{4}$ because the percentage increased at a constant rate of about 3 percentage points every 4 years. Let y be the ratio of seats in national parliaments held by women. Note that $y = 19.5\%$ when $t = 2,000$. Therefore, the following equation models the situation best:
$y = 19.5 + \frac{3}{4}(t - 2000) = 28$

12) ➤ D
Concept(s) Tested: Functions and Graphs
Convert the equation to vertex form.
$f(x) = x^2 + x + 4 = \left(x + \frac{1}{2}\right)^2 + \frac{15}{4}$.
Therefore, the minimum value of $f(x)$ is $\frac{15}{4}$.

13) ➤ D
Concept(s) Tested: Number Rules
$\frac{1}{6+i} = \frac{6-i}{(6+i)(6-i)} = \frac{6-i}{36+1} = \frac{6-i}{37}$

14) ➤ C
Concept(s) Tested: Functions and Graphs
The must be a real number and therefore cannot have a negative square root. Thus:
$9 - x^2 \geq 0 \rightarrow -3 \leq x \leq 3$

15) ➤ B
Concept(s) Tested: Algebra
Multiply $(x - 2)(x - 3)$ on both sides.
It results in $x(x - 3) + x = 4x - 8 \rightarrow x^2 - 6x + 8 = 0$.
Therefore, $(x - 2)(x - 4) = 0$. Note that $x \neq 2$, $x \neq 3$ because $x - 2$ and $x - 3$ are denominators. Therefore, the solution is only $x = 4$.

16) ➤ 45
Concept(s) Tested: Geometry, Trigonometry
If y is the length of the bottom line of the triangle, then the area of the right triangle is $\frac{10y}{2} = 50$. It results in $y = 10$. Note that we have an isoceles right triangle, so both angles must be equal to each other and to 45°.

17) ➤ $\frac{1}{5}$ or 0.2
Concept(s) Tested: Algebra
$3^{5-x} = 81^{x+1}$
$3^{5-x} = (3^4)^{x+1}$
$3^{5-x} = 3^{4x+4}$

$5 - x = 4x + 4 \rightarrow x = 0.2$

18) ➤ 2013
Concept(s) Tested: Functions and Graphs
Note that the population p has its maximum value when $t = 8.25$, because that is when nothing will be subtracted from 132. If t represents the number of years after January 1st, 2005, p's maximum value is 8.25 years after January 1st, 2005, which is 2013.

19) ➤ 27
Concept(s) Tested: Algebra
Substitute $k = 2$ into the equation $k + 3 = \sqrt{a-k}$. It results in $5 = \sqrt{a-2}$. Squaring both sides results in $25 = a - 2$. Therefore, $a = 27$.

20) ➤ 3
Concept(s) Tested: Geometry, Functions and Graphs
Let AD = x and CD = y. Note that AD = 2, and that $2x + 2y = 10$.
Note that $y = p$ when $x = 1$. The perimeter of rectangle ABCD equals $4 + 2p = 10$, so $p = 3$.

Calculator Portion

1) ➤ B
Concept(s) Tested: Problem Solving
Let y be the air temperature and x be the height in feet. It follows that $y = \frac{-5}{1500}x + 68$. Therefore, $y = -62$ results in $68 = \frac{5}{1500}x - 62$.

2) ➤ B
Concept(s) Tested: Ratios and Percentages
The number of remaining pieces equals $p - 2$.
Therefore, the percentage of pie that is left equals $\frac{100(p-2)}{p}\%$

3) ➤ B
Concept(s) Tested: Problem Solving
First, determine how many students have black hair (x): $x - 21 = 109 \rightarrow x = 130$.
Then, calculate how many students have neither black nor brown hair: $282 - 109 - 130 = 43$.
Finally, determine what percent of 282 is 43: $\frac{43}{282}$ equals approximately 15 percent, making (B) correct.

4) ➤ B
Concept(s) Tested: Geometry
The perimeter of $\triangle$OPN is $6 + 3\sqrt{2}$. The perimeter of $\triangle$OQN is the same when Q = (1, -3). Other points

have different length of perimeters.

5) **B**
Concept(s) Tested: Problem Solving
When we put the equation in vertex form, as in (B), we can see the maximum; (B) displays that $P(x)$ becomes maximum when $x = 10,000$.

6) **A**
Concept(s) Tested: Algebra
$$\frac{qx}{p-x} = 1 \rightarrow qx = p - x \rightarrow x = \frac{p}{q+1}$$

7) **D**
Concept(s) Tested: Problem Solving, Algebra, Geometry
Let x be the length of a side of the original square:
$(x + 2)^2 = x^2 + 80 \rightarrow x^2 + 4x + 4 = x^2 + 80$
$4x = 76$, so $x = 19$.

8) **D**
Concept(s) Tested: Problem Solving, Functions and Graphs
Note that the slope of the cost line is 0.1 and it costs $2 per month. Therefore, the total cost in dollars is equal to $0.1m + 2$.

9) **D**
Concept(s) Tested: Problem Solving, Functions and Graphs, Data Analysis
To find the line of best fit, first calculate the average rate of change among the given coordinates; calculate the slope (m) for each pair of consecutive points, then take the average of these slopes:

$$\frac{2 - 1.2}{2 - 1} = 0.8$$

$$\frac{2.8 - 2}{3 - 2} = 0.8$$

$$\frac{3.95 - 2.8}{4 - 3} = 1.15$$

$$\frac{4.6 - 3.95}{5 - 4} = 0.65$$

The average of these slopes is
$$\frac{0.8 + 0.8 + 1.15 + 0.65}{4} = 0.85$$

Next, plug slope (0.85) and any given (x, y) coordinate into $y = mx + b$ to find the y-intercept (b):
$1.2 = 0.85(1) + b \rightarrow 0.35 = b$
Thus, $y = 0.85x + 0.35$ is an acceptable line of best fit for the coordinates in the table.

10) **C**
Concept(s) Tested: Algebra
Isolate x from the second equation and substitute in the first: $x + 8y = 4 \rightarrow x = 4 - 8y$
$4(4 - 8y) - y = 3y + 7 \rightarrow 16 - 33y = 3y + 7 \rightarrow$
$-36y = -9 \rightarrow y = \frac{1}{4}$

$x = 4 - 8(\frac{1}{4}) = 4 - 2 = 2$ Therefore, $xy = \frac{1}{2}$.

11) **C**
Concept(s) Tested: Data Analysis, Measures of Center and Spread
The median value is the middle number in a sequence, or the 50th percentile. In this case, there are a total of 50 values, with the middle value being the 25.5th value, or $100.

12) **C**
Concept(s) Tested: Data Analysis, Measures of Center and Spread
Note that there are 50 employees. The 25th and 26th employees in the order of amount paid in bonuses are located in $100. Therefore $m = 100$. The most frequently paid bonuses is also 100. That is $p = 100$. Note that $n = 101$.
Therefore, $m = p < n$.

13) **B**
Concept(s) Tested: Algebra
$4|9 + 3x| - 39 \leq -3 \rightarrow |9 + 3x| \leq 9$
$\rightarrow -9 \leq 9 + 3x \leq 9 \rightarrow -18 \leq 3x \leq 0$
$\rightarrow -6 \leq x \leq 0$

14) **C**
Concept(s) Tested: Data Analysis
Note that the two months with the lowest number of sales for Paige's Bookstore are July and August.

15) **D**
Concept(s) Tested: Algebra
$a_3 = \frac{2 \times 3 + 3}{1} = 9$,

$a_4 = \frac{2 \times 9 + 3}{3} = 7$,

$a_5 = \frac{2 \times 7 + 3}{9} = \frac{17}{9}$

16) **C**
Concept(s) Tested: Data Analysis, Ratios and Percentages
The ratio of the number of foreign locations to the number of the United States locations are as follows:

A: $\frac{4,200}{1,500} = 2.8$, B: $\frac{3,500}{1,400} = 2.5$

C: $\frac{4,400}{1,250} = 3.52$, D: $\frac{1,900}{1,050} = 1.8$

Therefore, the company with the greatest ratio is (C).

17) **B**
Concept(s) Tested: Problem Solving, Algebra
Let x and y be the length of the side of the square

486 | KALLIS' Key to the SAT

and the equilateral triangle, respectively. Then $4x + 3y = 47$ and $x + y = 15$. From both equations, it follows that $x = 2$, $y = 13$.

18) ▶ B
Concept(s) Tested: Data Analysis
Note that the number of apples sold in the month of June is 60 and the number of apples sold in the months of February and March combined is $25 + 30 = 55$. The difference between the two numbers 60 and 55 is 5.

19) ▶ D
Concept(s) Tested: Data Analysis, Geometry, Problem Solving
Note that the total number of apples sales is 240 and the number of apples sales in the month of January is 40, which is $\frac{1}{6}$ of the total number of apples sales. Therefore, if it is illustrated by a circle graph, the central angle of the sector that represents the month of January is $\frac{1}{6} \times 360° = 60°$.

20) ▶ D
Concept(s) Tested: Algebra
Note that $a^b = 1$ when $a = 1$ or $b = 0$. Therefore, the equation is 1 when:
$x^2 - 6x + 9 = 1$ or $x^2 - 8x + 12 = 0$
$x^2 - 6x + 9 = 1$ implies $x = 2$ or $x = 4$.
$x^2 - 8x + 12 = 0$ implies $x = 2$ and $x = 6$. It means that $x = 2, 4, 6$ satisfy the equation. Therefore, 3 distinct real values exist.

21) ▶ B
Concept(s) Tested: Number Rules
Note that $a - b$ has its maximum when a is in maximum and b is in minimum, and $a - b$ has its minimum when a is in minimum and b is in maximum.
Therefore, $(30 - 70) < a - b < (40 - 50)$, so, $-40 < a - b < -10$.

22) ▶ B
Concept(s) Tested: Algebra
$w^3 = 9w$ → $w^2 = 9$ → $w = 3$ because w is a positive integer. Therefore, $w^5 = 243$.

23) ▶ B
Concept(s) Tested: Algebra
$E = mc^2$ → $c^2 = \frac{E}{m}$ → $c = \sqrt{\frac{E}{m}}$ →
$c = \frac{\sqrt{E}}{\sqrt{m}} \left(\frac{\sqrt{m}}{\sqrt{m}} \right)$ → $c = \frac{\sqrt{Em}}{m}$

24) ▶ A
Concept(s) Tested: Number Rules

$\frac{5 - \frac{1}{a}}{a^{-1}} = a(5 - \frac{1}{a}) = 5a - 1$

25) ▶ D
Concept(s) Tested: Problem Solving, Functions and Graphs
To find how many tickets must be sold for the film to earn double its budget, set $E(n)$ equal to double the film's budget, and solve the function for n:
$E(n) = 2(110,000,000) = 8.25n - 110,000,000$ →
$330,000,000 = 8.25n$ → $n = 40,000,000$
Thus, choice (D) is correct.

26) ▶ D
Concept(s) Tested: Problem Solving, Data Analysis, Functions and Graphs
Note that $\frac{34}{24} = 1.4$, or a 40% increase. This rate holds true for the remainder of the points on the chart. Choices (A) and (C) are incorrect because the chart shows growth every 2 years, so speculating on yearly growth would not be accurate based on the chart information. Choice (B) is incorrect because the growth over any 2-year period is always greater than 13%.

27) ▶ D
Concept(s) Tested: Problem Solving
Note that $g(x) = -\{(x - 2)^3 + 6\}$.
Therefore $g(-1) = -(-27 + 6) = 21$.

28) ▶ D
Concept(s) Tested: Geometry

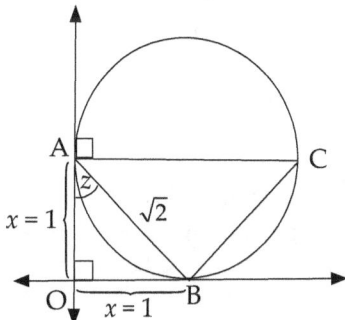

Set angles BCA and OAB equal to z degrees.
Notice that angle OBA must be equal to z degrees if $\overline{AO} = \overline{OB} = x = 1$. Notice also that triangle AOB has equal and opposite legs, making $z = 45$ degrees. Since the y-axis is tangent to the circle at point A, we see $90° - \angle OAB = 45° = \angle BAC$. Since angles BAC and BCA each equal 45 degrees, triangle ABC is a 45-45-90 triangle. Thus, I is false and III is true. If we extend the lines BC and AB below the x-axis, we create equal vertical angles: $y_1 = \angle OBA = z = 45°$ and $y_2 = \angle ABC$. Since angle ABC is 90 degrees, and z is 45 degrees, we find that $y_3 = 180° - 90° - 45° = 45°$. Since $y_3 = \angle BCA$, line AC is parallel to the

x-axis, and II and III are true, Therefore, (D) is the answer.

29) ▶ B
Concept(s) Tested: Trigonometry

$$\sin 2x = \cos\left(\frac{\pi}{2} - 2x\right) = \cos x \rightarrow \frac{\pi}{2} = 3x \rightarrow x = \frac{\pi}{6}$$

30) ▶ C
Concept(s) Tested: Geometry

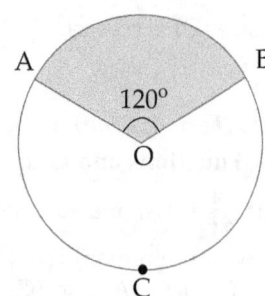

Note that the angle of AOB (120°) is $\frac{2}{3}\pi$ in radians. Let r be the radius of the circle. Then, the length of arc AB, $l = r\theta \rightarrow 12\pi = r\frac{2\pi}{3}$. It results in $r = 18$. Therefore, the area of the sector AOB $= \frac{rl}{2} = \frac{18 \times 12\pi}{2} = 108\pi$.

31) ▶ $\frac{18}{5}$ or 3.6
Concept(s) Tested: Algebra

$f(k) = g(k)$ means $\frac{3}{2}k - 2 = \frac{2}{3}k + 1$. Therefore, it follows that $\frac{5}{6}k = 3 \rightarrow k = \frac{18}{5}$.

32) ▶ 9
Concept(s) Tested: Problem Solving
Let c be the number of hours Andrew spends commuting, and w be the number of hours Andrew spends working. Based on the information in the question, we can create the following equations:
$42 + c = w$ and $c + w = 60$
Substituting $42 + c$ for w in the second equation gives $c + c + 42 = 60 \rightarrow 2c = 18 \rightarrow c = 9$.

33) ▶ 30
Concept(s) Tested: Geometry, Algebra
The length of the perimeter is equal to
$x + (x + 7) + (x + 8) = 3x + 15 = 30$.
It follows that $x = 5$.
Therefore, the area of the triangle is
$\frac{x(x+7)}{2} = \frac{5(5+7)}{2} = 30$

34) ▶ 0.6 or $\frac{3}{5}$
Concept(s) Tested: Measures of Center and Spread
The average score
$$M = \frac{74 + 76 + 80 + 81 + 92}{5} = 80.6 \text{ and the median}$$
score is $m = 80$.
Therefore, the difference $M - m = 0.6$.

35) ▶ 10
Concept(s) Tested: Problem Solving, Ratios and Percentages
Let S be the original salary. Then, the charity increase equals $0.15(1.1S - S) = 0.1 \times 0.15S$. Therefore, the percentage of increase for the charity donations equals:
$$\frac{0.1 \times 0.15S}{0.15S} \times 100\% = 10\%$$

36) ▶ 5
Concept(s) Tested: Geometry
Let x be the length of the radius of the smaller circle. Then $\pi(6)^2 : \pi x^2 = 4 : 1 \rightarrow x = 3$. Let E be the middle point of the line BC. Then $\triangle$CDE is a right triangle. Therefore, from the Pythagorean theorem, the length of DC equals
$\sqrt{4^2 + (6 - 3)^2} = \sqrt{25} = 5$

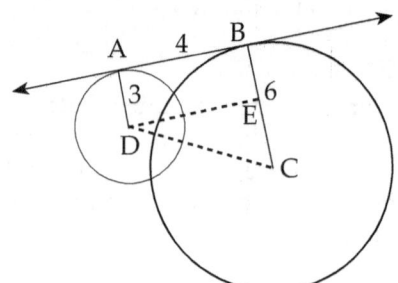

37) ▶ 4
Concept(s) Tested: Data Analysis
Note that the quantity of the radioactive element is $A(0) = 320g$ in the beginning, 4 years later we get $A(4) = 160g$, and 8 years later we get $A(8) = 80g$. This implies that the quantity of the radioactive element decays half per 4 years.

38) ▶ 20
Concept(s) Tested: Data Analysis, Algebra
Note that the quantity of the radioactive element decays half per 4 years and $A(8) = 80g$. This implies that $A(8) = 2A(12) = 4A(16) = 80g$. Therefore, $A(16) = 20g$.

SAT Practice Test 6: Answers & Explanations

Sample Essay Response

As automation becomes more commonplace, business leader Bill Gates offered a solution to the fear of massive unemployment: governments could impose a tax on robots and use the money generated to retrain displaced workers. Dean Baker argues that this strategy is counterproductive and would further stymie economic growth, leading to greater unemployment. In his essay, Baker uses facts and examples to support his claim, then offers alternatives to Gates' proposed tax.

To start, Baker uses simple facts and definitions to convince his audience that a tax on robots is really a tax on productivity growth. By defining Gates' proposed tax in such a way, Baker easily demonstrates its pitfalls. Again, Baker uses facts to prove that productivity growth is currently very slow, which logically counters the notion that growth is too fast implicit in Gates' proposal.

As he continues his argument, Dean demonstrates that increased productivity growth actually reduces unemployment. He uses two historical examples of times when productivity growth was relatively high and points out how wages increased consistently and unemployment was low. He also claims that "the conventional view of economists is that productivity growth is too slow" (paragraph 7). Word choice here convinces the reader that Baker's is an informed opinion, and helps to prove his point.

Having proven that a tax on robots would further slow weak productivity growth, Baker offers an alternative solution. Here, he uses logic and reasoning to show how lowering interest rates and increasing demand can lead to an increase in wages and a decrease in unemployment. He shows us that an increase in productivity growth creates an overall boost in the economy. This alternative solution further challenges Gates' notion that taxing robots will strengthen the economy.

Though Baker's solution is purportedly good for the economy, he acknowledges shortcomings, and admits that workers will always be displaced in a dynamic economy. He offers an additional solution to this problem, which offers employers incentives to retrain obsolete workers. By considering the ramifications of his claims, Baker strengthens his own argument and further convinces the reader that Gates' solution is not sound.

Sample Response Score: 4/3/4

Reading: 4

The student demonstrates a strong understanding of the concepts presented in the passage. The student concisely identifies the basis for Baker's argument—a statement made by Bill Gates—and succinctly explains how Baker crafts his response to Gates' claim. The essay contains both summaries of Baker's arguments and a quotation to build an analysis.

Analysis: 3

The student constructs an insightful analysis of the source material, identifying both logical and persuasive elements used by Baker. Each element analyzed by the student is relevant to Baker's central argument. The essay would be improved by the inclusion of additional elaboration or examples from the text, especially in paragraph 2, but the overall analysis is thorough and cohesive.

Writing: 4

The student crafts a tightly focused essay that introduces a clear central claim at the end of paragraph 1, and which supports this claim with well-structured, articulate, and logical support. The essay is free of grammatical errors and contains a variety of sentence structures.

References

- "File:Beta-carotene.png." *Wikimedia Commons*, the free media repository. 1 May 2015. https://commons.wikimedia.org/w/index.php?title=File:Beta-carotene.png&oldid=159392468

- "File:PSM V46 D168 Mesial view of the human brain.jpg." *Wikimedia Commons*, the free media repository, 18 Apr 2015. https://commons.wikimedia.org/w/index.php?title=File:PSM_V46_D168_Mesial_view_of_the_human_brain.jpg&oldid=157467177

- "OCD at School/How OCD Affects Studies and Grades." *Anxiety and Depression Association of America (ADAA)*, accessed in 2016. https://adaa.org/understanding-anxiety/obsessive-compulsive-disorder/ocd-at-school

- Aronoff, Kate, "Crisis, opportunity and climate austerity in drought-stricken California." *Waging Nonviolence Blog*. Waging Nonviolence, 17 April 2015. https://wagingnonviolence.org/2015/04/crisis-opportunity-climate-austerity-drought-stricken-california/

- Baker, Dean, "Bill Gates Is Clueless on the Economy." *CEPR Publications*. Center for Economic and Policy Research, 27 February 2017. http://cepr.net/publications/op-eds-columns/bill-gates-is-clueless-on-the-economy

- Bates, Mary, "Bats and Wind Turbines." *PLoS Blogs Network*. PLoS Blogs, 8 July 2016. http://blogs.plos.org/blog/2016/07/09/bats-and-wind-turbines/

- Bates, Mary, "Why Sloths Live in the Slow Lane." *PLoS Ecology Community*. PLoS Blogs, 25 July 2016. http://blogs.plos.org/ecology/2016/07/25/why-sloths-live-life-in-the-slow-lane/

- Buffie, Nicholas, "Women Earn Less than Men in 302 of 311 Occupations." *CEPR Blog*. Center for Economic and Policy Research (CEPR), 5 October 2015. http://cepr.net/blogs/cepr-blog/women-earn-less-than-men-in-302-of-311-occupations

- Brown, Maggie, "Sanitation is Key in Controlling Worm Diseases." *Speaking of Medicine*. PLoS Blogs, 27 January 2012. http://blogs.plos.org/speakingofmedicine/2012/01/27/sanitation-is-key-in-controlling-worm-diseases/

- Dr. Razai, Mohammad, "Ending Tuberculosis in Afghanistan: working together towards a common goal." *Speaking of Medicine*. PLoS Blogs, 27 June 2016. http://blogs.plos.org/speakingofmedicine/2016/06/27/ending-tuberculosis-in-afghanistan-working-together-towards-a-common-goal/

- Chou, Felicia, "NASA's Kepler Mission Discovers Bigger, Older Cousin to Earth." *National Aeronautics and Space Administration*. NASA, 23 July 2015. https://www.nasa.gov/press-release/nasa-kepler-mission-discovers-bigger-older-cousin-to-earth

- de Freitas, Carolina; Shepard, Jr, Glenn; and Piedade, Maria, "The Floating Forest: Traditional Knowledge and Use of Matupá Vegetation Islands by Riverine Peoples of the Central Amazon." *PLoS ONE*. PLoS Blogs, 2 April 2015. http://journals.plos.org/plosone/article?id=10.1371/journal.pone.0122542

- Gibson, Sarah, "Happy Fins: Plesiosaurs Flapped like Penguins." *PLoS Paleo Community*. PLoS Blogs, 18 December 2015. http://blogs.plos.org/paleocomm/2015/12/18/happy-fins-plesiosaurs-flapped-like-penguins/

- Graf, Konrad S., "SpaceX can get there, but biology a probable Mars residence limiter." *Konrad S. Graf Blog*, 29 September 2016. http://www.konradsgraf.com/blog1/2016/9/29/spacex-can-get-there-but-biology-likely-a-critical-mars-residence-limiter

- Kim, Yoo Jung, "Why Statistics Should Be A Mandatory Part of High School Education." *Sci-Ed. PLoS Blogs*, 18 August 2016. http://blogs.plos.org/scied/2016/08/18/why-statistics-should-be-mandatory/

- Knoll, Stefanie, "Waging war on poverty: Historical trends using the Supplemental Poverty Measure." *Journalist's Resource*, 24 January 2014. https://journalistsresource.org/studies/economics/inequality/supplemental-poverty-measure-historical-trends

- Kukaswadia, Atif, "Science is political and we ignore that at our peril." *Public Health Perspectives*. PLoS Blogs, 25 April 2017. http://blogs.plos.org/publichealth/2017/04/25/science-is-political-and-we-ignore-that-at-our-peril/

- Maylie, Devon, "Violent media and real-world behavior: Historical data and recent trends." *Journalist's Resource*, 18 February 2015. https://journalistsresource.org/studies/society/culture/violent-media-real-world-behavior-historical-data-recent-trends

- NIMH, "Obsessive Compulsive Disorder: When Unwanted Thoughts Take Over." *National Institute of Mental Health (NIMH)*. U.S. Department of Health and Human Services, accessed in 2016. https://www.nimh.nih.gov/health/publications/obsessive-compulsive-disorder-when-unwanted-thoughts-take-over/index.shtml

- Olney-Hamel, Marianne, "Pumas, Wolves, and Eagles, Oh My! Early Captive Carnivore Remains Found in Ancient Mexican Ruins." *PLoS One Community Blogs*. PLoS Blogs, 16 December 2015. http://blogs.plos.org/everyone/2015/12/16/pumas-wolves-and-eagles-oh-my-early-captive-carnivore-remains-found-in-ancient-mexican-ruins/

- Plous, Scott, "The Psychology of Prejudice: An Overview." *Understanding Prejudice*. Social Psychology Network, accessed in 2016. http://www.understandingprejudice.org/apa/english/page2.htm

- SPLC, "Extremist Files/Anti-Muslim Hate Groups." *Southern Poverty Law Center*, accessed in 2016. https://www.splcenter.org/fighting-hate/extremist-files/group/act-america

- United Nations (UN) News Centre, "Knowledge Saves Lives, UN Stresses on International Day for Disaster Reduction," *United Nations News*, 13 October 2015. http://www.un.org/apps/news/story.asp?NewsID=52254#.WacrsMiGOUk

- U.S. Department of the Interior, "Ghosts of the Prairie: The Reintroduction of the Black-footed Ferret." *U.S. Department of the Interior Blog*, accessed in 2016. https://www.doi.gov/blog/ghosts-prairie-reintroduction-black-footed-ferret

- U.S. Department of the Interior, "15 Facts About Our National Mammal: the American Bison." *U.S. Department of the Interior Blog*, accessed in 2016. https://www.doi.gov/blog/15-facts-about-our-national-mammal-american-bison

- Wikipedia contributors. "Origin of birds." *Wikipedia, The Free Encyclopedia*. Wikipedia, The Free Encyclopedia, 28 August 2017. https://en.wikipedia.org/wiki/Origin_of_birds

- Yurkiewicz, Shara, "Time of death." *This may hurt a bit….* PLoS Blogs, 19 July 2015. http://blogs.plos.org/thismayhurtabit/2015/07/19/time-of-death/

Try our other SAT practice books !

Kallis offers extensive guidance and practice for students who want to boost their scores on the SAT, beginning with our SAT Pattern Strategy book. It is packed with clear explanations, efficient strategies, and step-by-step practice materials.

ISBN-13: 978-1535296120 - 2nd Edition
ISBN-13: 978-1727853469 - 3rd Edition

Try our other SAT practice books !

For a focus on the Writing and Language section, see our SAT Writing & Language Pattern book. It is packed with clear explanations, efficient strategies, and brand new practice materials.

ISBN-13: 978-1535296120